CRIMES AND VICTIMS

FRANK SMYTH

Abbeydale Press

This paperback edition printed in 2008

Copyright © Bookmart 1992

Revised and updated in 2007

ISBN 978-1-86147-222-9

3 5 7 9 10 8 6 4 2

Published by Abbeydale Press
An imprint of Bookmart Limited
Registered Number 2372865
Blaby Road, Wigston
Leicester LE18 4SE

Every effort has been made to contact the copyright holders for the pictures.
In some cases they have been untraceable, for which we offer our apologies.
Thanks to the following libraries and picture agencies which supplied pictures:

Associated Press, APWorldwide, AGIP, Black Museum, Cavendish Press, Corbis, Culver Pictures,
Jack Hickes Photography, Fairfax Ltd, Getty Images Editorial, Illustrated London News,
Hulton-Deutsch Collection, Mary Evans Photo Library, Mirrorpix, News Ltd of Australia,
Popperfotos, Press Assocation, Rex Features, Frank Spooner Pictures,
Syndication International, Suddeutscher Verlag, Topham, UPI/Bettmann

The Authors
Frank Smyth is the consultant editor of *Crimes and Victims* and also wrote the chapters *Crimes of Horror*
and *Crimes of Passion*. He began his career as a crime reporter in Yorkshire,
and has since written numerous books on all aspects of crime, including
Detectives in Fact and Fiction, I'm Jack: The Police Hunt for Jack the Ripper and
Cause of Death: A History of Forensic Science.

J. Anderson Black wrote the chapters *Murder Most Foul* and *Organized Crime.*
He is a fine arts graduate from Edinburgh University.
He has been a professional writer for more than twenty-five years,
and his published work covers a wide range of topics from art to crime,
as well as three novels and several screenplays for feature films.

Production by Omnipress Limited, UK

Printed in Thailand

Contents

CRIMES AND VICTIMS

THE RANGE of human folly, delusion and evil seems to be endless. Just when we think we have read or heard of some atrocity or outrage that marks the limit, along comes another, even more appalling. Sometimes it seems that we live in a world that must surely collapse under the weight of its own corruption and violence. Passions appear to rage unchecked, vices breed like disease, people have no control over their most primitive instincts. Yet the world goes on, despite the litany of horror and scandal that follows it like a shadow.

It is that shadow, and the terrible damage it inflicts, that is the subject of this book. We investigate that many-headed creature called crime, telling in vivid detail the stories of the atrocities, deceptions and heartbreaks it has left in its wake.

From acts of murder, gang-land intimidation, financial corruption, drug-dealing and much more a picture of terror and degradation looms out from these pages. From serial killers to men and women driven insane by thwarted love, and from mobsters gripped in fantasies of megalomania to businessmen seduced by dreams of wealth beyond comprehension, we see the crimes and we count the cost.

For the grim truth is that there is no such thing as a victimless crime. Criminals and victims are locked together in the most gruesome of relationships, like two sides of a coin. And while the guilty may pay the price for their misdeeds, it is all too often the forgotten victims who are the real story. They are the innocent ones who lose their money, their welfare or even their lives, yet they sink back into obscurity while the criminals live on forever in the Hall of Infamy to shock and haunt the imagination.

MURDER
MOST
FOUL

**Dr CRIPPEN
Hen-pecked Killer**

Dr Crippen is notorious as the first murderer to be arrested with the help of Marconi's newly invented wireless telegraphy. This quiet little patent-medicine salesman was hanged in 1910 for poisoning a wife who had treated him shamefully

Early in 1900 a slight, modest gentleman enquired about an flat in Shore Street, Bloomsbury. He had a high-domed, bald head, a large sandy moustache, and greyish eyes which bulged behind a pair of gold-rimmed spectacles. With him, and seeming to loom over him, was his wife, a florid, full-figured woman in garish silks.

The oddly assorted pair were American, they explained. They had just arrived on the boat from New York, she to make a name on the music-hall stage, he to manage a patent medicine firm. Their names were Dr Hawley Harvey and Mrs Cora Crippen, and they were to become almost synonymous with twentieth-century murder.

THE MEDICAL MAN

Hawley Crippen was born in 1862, the son of a dry goods merchant in Coldwater, Michigan, who had ambitions for his son to be a doctor. In 1879, when he was just seventeen, the young Crippen embarked on his medical training.

In subsequent years he was to be reviled as an out-and-out quack, or defended as a highly qualified medic who was simply unlicensed to practise in England. The truth lies somewhere in between.

He received a general scientific

Above: *Mrs Cora Crippen, an extravagant woman who totally dominated her husband.*

Opposite: *Dr Hawley Harvey Crippen, the mild-mannered purveyor of patent medicines who was driven to murder.*

Left: *39 Hilldrop Crescent, Kentish Town, the Crippen family home where the murder was committed.*

WASP PREJUDICE AGAINST
CENTRAL EUROPEAN
CATHOLIC IMMIGRANTS DID
NOTHING TO DIMINISH
CRIPPEN'S ARDOUR FOR
HIS YOUNG WIFE.

background at the California University, Michigan, and then went on to study medicine at the Hospital College in Cleveland, Ohio. Probably, though not certainly, he left without a degree.

In 1883 he sailed for England and spent some time attending lectures at Guy's and St Thomas's hospitals in London, before returning to New York and enrolling at the Opthalmic Hospital there, gaining a diploma in 1885.

While in Santiago in 1887 he met and married a woman named Charlotte Bell, and the following year their son, Otto Hawley Crippen, was born. This boy was to spend his life in Los Angeles.

The Crippens moved to Salt Lake City, where, in 1890, Charlotte died. Hawley drifted back to New York. Two years later he met a striking young woman of seventeen who called herself Cora Turner and was the mistress of a rich stove manufacturer.

Crippen fell in love with her, and for her part she seemed to like the idea of being a doctor's wife. In 1893 he married her and took her with him to St Louis, where he was working as consultant physician to an optician. There he learned that his wife's real name was Kunigunde Mackamotzki. She was the daughter of a Russian Polish father and a German mother.

Despite the strong prejudice then current among 'White Anglo-Saxon Protestants' against mid-European Catholics, the revelation did little to affect Crippen's passion for Cora.

For her part, Cora was growing dissatisfied with Crippen's earnings as an orthodox doctor, pointing out that there was much more money to be made in the world of 'patent' medicines. One of the best-selling of these was 'Professor Munyon's Pills for Piles'. In 1897, Crippen joined the firm in New York and parted company with the mainstream of medicine for ever.

When Munyon's opened an office in Shaftesbury Avenue, London, Crippen was appointed first manager. The summer of 1900 saw him and Cora taking the lease on the flat in Shore Street, Bloomsbury.

AMBITIONS

Bloomsbury was at the heart of the London music hall world. Cora lost no time in introducing herself into the pubs and restaurants in which the music-hall artistes met, and even hired herself an agent, 'billing' herself under the stage name of Belle Ellmore.

She looked the part. Cora was pretty enough, with dark eyes and raven hair. Her looks, together with her American accent, described as 'twangy', and the stagey clothes she affected reeked of the American vaudeville theatre of which she claimed to have been a part.

The trouble was that Belle Ellmore could not sing – at least she could not project her voice to reach the far corners

Left: *Cora Crippen had a passion for the music hall and a taste for garish fashion.*

WOULD-BE MUSIC-HALL ARTISTE CORA WAS BOOED FROM THE STAGE — PARTLY FOR STRIKE-BREAKING AND PARTLY FOR BEING DREADFUL

Below: *Cora hired herself out as an artiste's agent under her stage name of Belle Ellmore.*

of a theatre. Once, during a music-hall strike, she obtained work at the Euston Palace. But she was hissed and booed from the stage, partly for being a 'blackleg', and partly for being dreadful. After that distressing experience, Cora's active theatrical days were over.

Despite this she remained friendly with such artistes as Marie Lloyd. She also became a member and later honorary treasurer of the Music Hall Ladies' Guild, a charitable organization. And she took to wearing expensive jewellery, which she bullied Hawley Crippen into buying.

In 1901, urged on by Cora to 'better' himself, he took an appointment as consultant to a dubious firm of ear specialists named the Drouet Institute. Its bookkeeper-secretary was a seventeen-year-old named Ethel Neave who shared with Cora a dissatisfaction with her surname and called herself LeNeve. Two years after Crippen joined, the Institute was bankrupted after a charge of negligence was levelled against it – the charge did not involve Crippen. By this time he had fallen in love with Ethel.

Under any name, Ethel LeNeve does not seem to have been particularly prepossessing. Despite her pretty face she was a mousey child with a slight limp who suffered from chronic catarrh.

But, like Cora, she had a strong dominant trait which seemed to appeal to Crippen. And there is no doubt that she loved the by-now infatuated doctor as much as he loved her.

She followed him, as secretary, to the Sovereign Remedy Company, which failed, then to the Aural Company, which also failed, and then back to Professor Munyon's, where he took up his old post as manager.

Later, she became secretary to a dental practice which Crippen set up as an extra source of income at Albion House, New Oxford Street, with a dental surgeon named Dr Rylance.

HEN-PECKED HUSBAND

In 1905, the Crippens left Shore Street and moved north to a leased semi-detached villa at 39 Hilldrop Crescent, off the Camden Road in Kentish Town. By this time Crippen was making money,

ONCE THE LODGERS WENT, THE CRIPPENS LIVED IN THE KITCHEN SURROUNDED BY THE UNTOUCHED FILTH OF EVERYDAY EXISTENCE

Below: *Ethel LeNeve, Dr Crippen's lover, thinly disguised as a boy for their flight to America.*

most of which was spent on entertaining Cora's friends and on buying Cora's dresses and jewellery. However, by now the couple slept in separate bedrooms and were polite to each other only in company. Cora openly had men friends, and occasionally took them to bed in the afternoons when Crippen was at work.

When her interest in the new house waned a little, Cora took in four lodgers. She had an antipathy towards 'living in' domestic servants, so she buckled down to the task of being a landlady herself, with the help of a daily cleaner.

Crippen was ordered up at six in the morning to clean the lodgers' boots, lay and light the fires, and prepare the breakfast – all before he set off for his office at 7.30.

Incredibly, the doctor continued to pay all the household bills, while the lodgers' rents went into Cora's dress and jewellery account.

In December 1906 Crippen came home to find Cora in bed with one of the lodgers, a German. The following day he told Ethel, and for the first time in their four-year relationship she consented to go to bed with him. Their affair was consummated in a cheap hotel one afternoon on Ethel's day off.

Soon after this, Cora tired of the game of being a landlady and dismissed the lodgers. Instead she entertained her friends on two or three evenings a week. For the rest of the time, she and her husband virtually lived in the kitchen. Both of them gave up housework, and cleaning was done only spasmodically.

Over the next four years Crippen continued to live at Hilldrop Crescent, though life with Cora became more and more intolerable. There was no longer any pretence at amiability. Cora mocked him in front of her friends and Hawley Crippen bore it all stoically, buoyed up by his love for Ethel LeNeve.

Cora was by now aware of the affair. At one point Ethel became pregnant and decided to have the baby, thus forcing matters to a crisis. But she miscarried.

Cora's response was to speculate, to a group of her music-hall friends and in her husband's hearing, as to which of Ethel's many lovers was responsible for the child. It may have been at that moment that Hawley Harvey Crippen's patience came abruptly to an end.

THE WORM TURNS

On 1 January 1910 he went to the firm of Lewis and Burrows, wholesale chemists, and ordered seventeen grains of the vegetable drug hydrobromide of hyoscine. It was, he said, on behalf of Munyon's – though the American company did not manufacture in Britain. On 19 January he took possession of the drug, which he had seen used to calm violent patients in mental hospitals. It was also an anaphrodisiac – it killed sexual ardour.

On 31 January the Crippens entertained a couple named Martinetti, theatrical friends of Cora's, to dinner.

During the course of the evening Cora picked a quarrel with her husband because he had not shown Mr Martinetti to the lavatory. It was an odd grudge, even for Cora. But, according to Crippen's later evidence, she took it as a 'last straw' and threatened to leave him.

It is doubtful whether Crippen would have worried overmuch if his wife had simply walked out of his life. But she had access, through their joint account, to his savings, and she would also have taken her valuable jewellery and have had a legal right to their joint property. She had threatened before to leave and take 'her' money – though in fact, apart from the abortive night treading the boards of the Euston Palace, she had never earned a penny in her life.

At 1.30 on the morning of 1 February the Martinettis bade Cora and Hawley goodbye. Cora Crippen was never seen alive again. That afternoon, Crippen called on the Martinettis, as he often did, and remarked that Cora was well.

On 2 February, Crippen pawned for £80 a gold ring and a pair of earrings belonging to his wife. The same evening Ethel LeNeve came to Hilldrop Crescent for the first time and stayed overnight.

The same day a letter arrived at the Music Hall Ladies' Guild office, apparently from their treasurer, Belle Ellmore. It said that she was leaving immediately for America to nurse a sick relative and was therefore tendering her resignation.

On 9 February Crippen pawned more jewellery, this time for £115. At his trial Crippen was to point out indignantly that he had every right to dispose of his wife's

Above: **The** SS Negantic *is towed into port with Crippen and LeNeve on board. They were initially arrested aboard the* SS Montrose.

Below: **Police accompany Dr Crippen and Ethel LeNeve down the gangway of the** SS Negantic *after his arrest in 1910.*

jewellery in any way he thought fit, since he had bought it.

On 20 February Crippen carried openness to potentially dangerous lengths when he escorted Ethel LeNeve to the Music Hall Ladies' Guild ball. She was decked out in some of Belle Ellmore's finest jewels – a fact not lost on the Martinettis, among other guests present.

Ostensibly Ethel was still simply Crippen's secretary, standing in for his absent wife at a social occasion. But on 12 March caution was thrown to the winds. Ethel moved in permanently to 39 Hilldrop Crescent.

FAKED DEATH, SUSPICIOUS FRIENDS

On 20 March, with Easter approaching, Crippen wrote to the Martinettis to say that he had heard from his wife and that she was seriously ill with pleuro-pneumonia. He was thinking, he said, of going to the United States to look after her. Contemporary writers have suggested that this may have been his original plan – to go to America and then quietly disappear. But something stopped him, and that something was probably Ethel LeNeve.

At this stage, it seems unlikely that Ethel knew that Cora was dead. But she knew that she was finally with the man

she loved and she was not going to let him leave her, even for a short while.

On 23 March, instead of going to America, Crippen and Ethel took a cross-Channel ferry to Dieppe, where they stayed during Easter week.

But from Victoria station he sent the Martinettis a telegram: 'BELLE DIED YESTERDAY AT SIX O'CLOCK. PLEASE PHONE ANNIE. SHALL BE AWAY A WEEK – PETER.' 'Peter' was a nickname for Crippen used by Belle Ellmore's theatrical friends.

When he returned, Crippen was inundated with enquiries from his wife's friends. Where exactly had she died? Where could they send a wreath? Crippen told them that he was having her cremated in America. When her ashes were shipped back 'we can have a little ceremony then'.

Lil Hawthorne, the well-known music hall comedy singer who had been one of Belle Ellmore's closest friends, was not satisfied. She checked with shipping lines but could find no record of either a Cora Crippen or a Belle Ellmore embarking for the States around the first week in February. Lil and her agent husband, John Nash, had to go to New York on business in March, and their enquiries there also drew a blank.

On his return to London, Nash confronted Crippen. Under questioning, Crippen broke down and sobbed pathetically. Nash, knowing of the doctor's kindly nature and tolerance of what even her friends had to acknowledge as his wife's often outrageous treatment of him, was almost convinced of the truth of Crippen's story.

And yet if Crippen was so distressed, why was his mistress living openly with him? Eventually Nash went to Scotland Yard and, on 30 June, poured out the whole tale.

INTERVIEWED BY THE YARD

A week later, on 8 July, Detective Chief Inspector Walter Dew, accompanied by Detective Sergeant Mitchell, went to call on Crippen at Albion House. Dew was one of the Yard's most experienced detectives. He was impressed, by Dr Crippen's demeanour.

Above: *Crippen arrives at the police station after his arrest in a taxi.*

Below: *Superintendent Frost, head of the Crippen investigation, discusses evidence with his colleagues.*

Asked about his wife's disappearance and alleged death, Crippen immediately confessed that the whole story was untrue. In fact, he said, Belle Ellmore alias Cora Crippen had run off to Chicago with an old prize-fighter lover of hers. Crippen had been so ashamed, and so worried about damaging his medical career with a scandal, that he had invented the story of her fatal illness.

Dew spent all day with Crippen, sitting in the waiting room between Crippen's periodic surgery calls to dental patients.

In the evening, Crippen took the two policemen to Hilldrop Crescent and showed them over the house, from attic to basement. All seemed perfectly normal.

'Of course,' said Dew, 'I shall have to find Mrs Crippen to clear the matter up.'

'Yes,' agreed the doctor, 'I will do everything I can. Can you suggest anything? Would an advertisement be any good?' Dew thought an advertisement in the Chicago papers an excellent idea, and helped Crippen draft one before finally saying goodnight.

In fact, Dew later admitted, the advertisement was unnecessary. He was convinced by that time that Crippen was telling the truth at last, and that the flighty Belle Ellmore had run off.

The investigation was to all intents and purposes finished. However, Crippen had no means of knowing this.

THE FATAL MISTAKE

Despite numerous theories, no one has ever given a satisfactory reason why Crippen, whose nerve had so far held, should suddenly at this point make the mistake of flight. But flee he did.

After carefully putting his affairs in order Crippen and LeNeve took the boat to Rotterdam on the night of 9 July. From there they made their way to Antwerp, where they embarked on the SS *Montrose,* bound for Quebec, under the names of Mr and Master Robinson.

Ethel had had her hair cropped short and was wearing cut-down men's clothes, probably Crippen's, and they kept under cover as much as possible before the ship sailed on 20 July.

Even now, the fleeing lovers might have got away but for a fluke. Chief Inspector Dew had forgotten some minor point during his questioning of Crippen. It was not important and there was no urgency. But on Monday 11 July, finding himself in the vicinity of Albion House, he decided to drop in and check it out. There he was told that Crippen had left.

Suddenly alarm bells were beginning to ring, and Dew dashed up to Hilldrop Crescent. All seemed to be in order, but he carried out a thorough search, checking the garden for recent signs of digging and testing the bricks in the empty basement coal cellar with his foot.

All was solid and normal. But Dew was certain that somewhere in this ordinary little house and its garden lay

---

THE TENACIOUS DEW WAS CONVINCED THAT THIS ORDINARY SUBURBAN HOUSE AND GARDEN CONTAINED THE ANSWER TO CORA'S DISAPPEARANCE

---

the solution to Cora's disappearance.

On the following day he returned with extra men. Again they searched, digging and probing. Again nothing. On Wednesday the 13th they were there again, but towards evening it began to look as if Dew's instinct was wrong. Then, standing in the brick-floored cellar, he probed one of the cracks with a poker and found that the brick was loose. He prised it out, and found loosely packed soil underneath. This time he got a spade, removed the rest of the bricks, and dug. Eight inches down he found what he described at the trial as 'a mass of flesh' wrapped in a striped pyjama top.

On preliminary examination by Dr

Right: *August 1910 – crowds gathered outside Bow Street Court as Crippen stood before magistrates.*

Below: *The trial of Dr Crippen and Ethel LeNeve at the Old Bailey in October 1910 attracted huge public interest.*

Above: *Dr Crippen in the dock at the Old Bailey during his trial for the murder of his wife.*

THE 'MASS OF FLESH' IN THE CELLAR PROVED TO BE A BODY THAT HAD BEEN FILLETED, WITH SURGICAL PRECISION, JUST LIKE A FISH

IN COURT, THE DISPUTED PIECE OF HUMAN FLESH WAS EXHIBITED TO JUDGE, JURY AND COUNSEL ON A SOUP PLATE

Marshall, the police surgeon, it proved to be a human torso from which the neck and head, arms and legs had been severed. The vagina and uterus had been excised, and the trunk had been neatly filleted – all the bones had been removed – with considerable surgical skill.

On 15 July, Marshall and Dr Augustus J. Pepper, a Home Office pathologist based at St Mary's Hospital, Paddington, removed the remains for further examination. The following day a warrant was issued for the arrest of Crippen and LeNeve.

On 20 July, the westward-bound SS *Montrose* steamed out of Antwerp. Sharing a cabin were a Mr John Robinson and his son, who between them had only one small valise as luggage. The ship's master, Captain Henry Kendal, thought them an odd couple, and kept an eye on them.

Among other things he noticed that 'Mr Robinson' was reading a copy of Edgar Wallace's *Four Just Men*, a famous murder yarn of the time. But he also noticed that the 'son' wore an ill-fitting hat and trousers, which were held together with safety pins at the back, and that the couple held hands in a manner most unusual for a father and son. When he saw a picture of Crippen in a copy of the *Daily Mail* which had been brought aboard just before the *Montrose* sailed, Captain Kendal despatched a wireless message which began: 'Have strong suspicion that Crippen London cellar murderer and accomplice are among saloon passengers....'

The message went out on 22 July, and the following day Dew and Mitchell embarked on the SS *Negantic* at Liverpool just before she sailed. On 31 July, Dew boarded the *Montrose* as she lay at anchor off Father Point, Quebec, and arrested the pair.

Crippen's first words were: 'I am not sorry. The anxiety has been too much.' He was the first murderer to be arrested by wireless telegraphy, for which Marconi had received the Nobel Prize the previous year.

Back in London Dr Pepper, assisted by his colleagues Dr William Willcox and Dr Bernard Spilsbury, had conducted a thorough examination of the remains from the cellar. They contained at least five grains of hyoscine which, as Willcox the toxicologist was to point out, was derived from henbane. When used as a sedative, one-fortieth of a grain had been known to produce 'severe symptoms'.

The defence were to claim that these remains were not those of Belle Ellmore-Cora Crippen, but of some previous murder, coincidentally committed in the house before the arrival of the Crippens. Even this credulity-stretching defence was scotched when pubic hairs on the torso were matched for colouring with Cora's head hair, and Bernard Spilsbury showed that a mark on the skin was not a fold, as alleged by the defence, but the scar of an ovariotomy such as Cora was known to have undergone. At the trial, the piece of flesh and skin showing the scar was handed about, to the judge, jury, defence and defendant Crippen, on a soup plate.

Finally, Crippen was caught out in a direct lie when he claimed that the pyjamas in which the body was wrapped were not his. They were proved to have been bought by him in 1909.

Left: *Ethel LeNeve leaves Bow Street Magistrates Court.*

Below: *Ethel LeNeve, Crippen's lover, was a mousey young woman with a limp and chronic catarrh.*

The trial had begun at the Old Bailey on 18 October before the Lord Chief Justice, Lord Alverstone, and the jury took twenty-seven minutes to reach their verdict. Crippen was sentenced to hang, while Ethel LeNeve, tried separately, went free.

Crippen's only concern, after his arrest, had been for the welfare of his mistress. He told Dew: 'She has been my only comfort for the last three years.' In jail at Pentonville his courtesy and pleasant nature almost endeared him to his warders. When he asked the Governor that a photograph and two letters from Ethel LeNeve be buried with him, the Governor readily complied.

Crippen was hanged on 23 November 1910. To this day the graveyard within the walls of Pentonville prison in which he and other executed prisoners were buried is known to staff and inmates as 'Crippen's Patch'.

Exactly when he killed his wife, and how he disposed of the body, remains a mystery. It was most probable that he poisoned her on either the night of 31 January or the following morning. He then cut her up in the bath, and dropped the missing head and limbs overboard in a suitcase during his subsequent trip to Dieppe.

The other abiding mystery is exactly why, after tolerating his apparently intolerable wife for so long, he suddenly decided to kill her. Many theories have been produced over the years, but none have resolved the mystery satisfactorily.

After her acquittal, Ethel LeNeve emigrated to Canada until the fuss died down, and then quietly returned to England in 1916. She took a job as bookkeeper for a company in Trafalgar Square, and married a man who was said to look remarkably like Crippen. They lived in East Croydon.

In 1954, novelist Ursula Bloom published a book entitled *The Woman Who Loved Crippen*. Afterwards, she was approached by an elderly lady who revealed herself to be Ethel. She told Miss Bloom that she had never ceased to love her little doctor. Ethel LeNeve died in 1967, aged eighty-four.

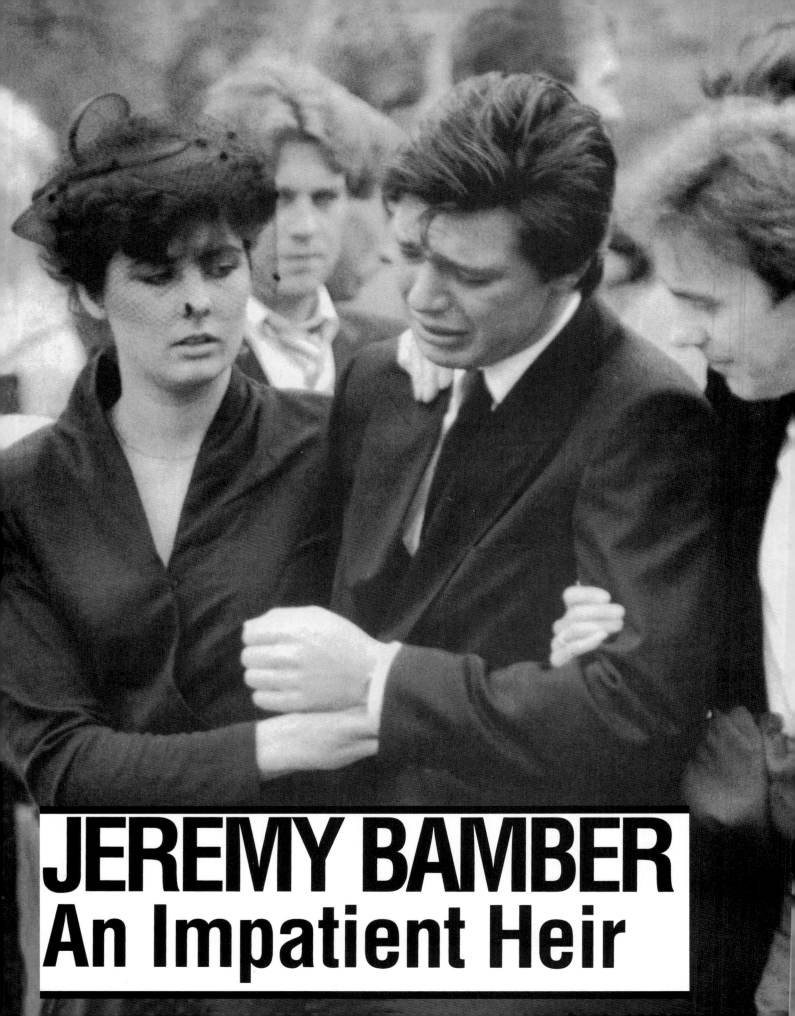

JEREMY BAMBER
An Impatient Heir

The horrific mass killing seemed to be the work of a deranged family member who had then committed suicide. Eventually the real murderer was nailed – but no thanks to the police who jumped to conclusions and destroyed vital evidence

At 3.26 in the morning of 7 August 1985, the duty officer at Chelmsford police station in Essex received a phone call from a young man calling himself Jeremy Bamber. The caller sounded agitated.

He explained to the policeman that he was calling from his home at Goldhanger and that he had just received a frantic call from his father who lived in the nearby village of Tolleshunt D'Arcy. According to Bamber, his father had shouted: 'Come over. Your sister's gone crazy and she's got a gun....'

Bamber had then heard a shot and the line had gone dead. He had tried to call back, but the telephone was off the hook. What should he do?

The duty sergeant told Bamber to go to his father's farm and wait for the police.

Above: *Sheila 'Bambi' Caffell was a pretty young woman but was dogged by psychological problems.*

Opposite: *Jeremy Bamber is consoled by his girlfriend, Julie Mugford, after the funeral of his family.*

Left: *White House Farm at Tolleshunt D'Arcy where the Bamber family were slaughtered.*

Under no circumstances should he enter the building. Within minutes Detective Inspector Bill Miller had assembled an armed squad of forty men which included Special Firearms Unit marksmen.

The police reached White House Farm shortly after 4a.m. There were lights in some of the windows but everything seemed peaceful. Marksmen took up their positions and covered every door and window in the elegant Georgian farmhouse. There was still no sign of life.

Minutes later, Jeremy Bamber arrived at the farm. He was hurried over to Inspector Miller who wanted to know what they were dealing with. Was there

normally a gun in the house?

Yes, Jeremy explained. His father, Nevill Bamber, was a keen shot and kept a rifle, a high velocity semi-automatic .22 Anchutz, which he used for rabbiting.

What about his sister? From the start, Jeremy made it clear that there was no love lost between them. He stressed that they were not really brother and sister, but that they had both been adopted.

'My sister is a nutter,' Jeremy explained. 'She could go mad at any time...She's gone mad before.'

WAITING GAME

The police kept their vigil for a while longer and then made a series of appeals over a loud hailer. There was no response.

Above: *Sheila 'Bambi' Caffell with her adoptive mother, June Bamber, and her two sons, Nicholas and Daniel. All of them died at White House Farm.*

Above right: *Colin Caffell, Sheila's estranged husband, with their two children.*

'MY SISTER IS A NUTTER,' JEREMY BAMBER EXPLAINED. 'SHE'S GONE MAD BEFORE.'

The basic brief in circumstances like these is for police to minimize the risk of loss of life. Since there was a possibility that members of the family were being held hostage, they opted to wait it out.

Bamber, meanwhile, provided police with a detailed picture of the house and family. His adoptive parents, Nevill and June Bamber, both sixty-one, lived there and farmed the surrounding 400 acres. His adoptive sister, twenty-seven-year-old Sheila Caffell, nicknamed 'Bambi', had been staying with them since March with her six-year-old twins, Daniel and Nicholas. Bambi, Jeremy explained, had a long history of depression and had recently come out of mental hospital after a 'nervous breakdown'.

As dawn broke there was still no sign of life in the farmhouse, and the police decided to move in. A squad of ten armed officers inched their way towards the kitchen door. One of the assault team then smashed down the door and the others moved quickly into the building.

But there was no sign of violence – in fact no sign of life at all.

SCENES OF CARNAGE

As the police reached the sitting room, however, they were confronted with a glimpse of the carnage which was to come. The room was a shambles, and lying near the telephone was the body of Nevill Bamber. He had been shot six times in the head, once in the shoulder and once in the arm. He had also been brutally beaten about the head and face.

Other officers moved upstairs. In one of the bedrooms they found the bodies of the twins, Daniel and Nicholas. Both had died from multiple gunshot wounds. They had obviously been murdered while they slept; Daniel was still sucking his thumb.

The master bedroom was the scene of more horror. June Bamber was sprawled in her nightdress on the floor beside the door, a Bible lying open by her side. She had been shot seven times, once directly between the eyes.

And by the window was the body of Sheila 'Bambi' Caffell. She was lying on her back in her nightdress. She had one gunshot wound in the throat and another in her jaw. Across her lap was lying a .22 Anchutz rifle, its butt splintered and its magazine empty.

BERSERK

The forensic team, led by Detective Inspector Ronald Cook, moved into the house together with police surgeon Dr Ian Craig. Craig examined each of the five bodies in turn.

Nevill Bamber had multiple wounds to the head and had probably been beaten unconscious before he was shot. Upstairs, the children and June Bamber were quite obviously victims of a surprise attack.

That left Bambi. Dr Craig examined her two wounds. The shot to her throat had severed her jugular vein. The other had passed through her chin and entered her brain. This would have killed her instantly. Bambi had one impact bruise to her cheek but was otherwise unmarked. Her long fingernails had survived the night of violence unscathed.

Dr Craig went downstairs and joined Detective Inspectors Cook and Miller. There was no sign of a break-in and the

THE SIX-YEAR-OLD TWINS HAD BEEN SHOT WHILE THEY SLEPT — ONE OF THEM WAS STILL SUCKING HIS THUMB

Below: *Whitehouse Farm, a monument to upper-middle class respectability, and scene of one of the worst mass murders of recent times.*

three men agreed that the most obvious scenario was that Sheila Caffell had gone beserk, murdered her entire family and then turned the gun on herself.

They expressed this opinion to Detective Chief Inspector Tom 'Taff' Jones when he arrived at the farm later that morning. Jones was apparently happy to accept their conclusions.

Having 'solved' the case to their own satisfaction, Cook and his forensic team apparently decided that a detailed examination of the house and its contents was surplus to requirements – a decision which would later attract violent criticism from both the press and the judiciary.

The police did remove the rifle and some other items of evidence, but officers failed to wear gloves, and no fingerprints were ever taken of the dead family members, or of Jeremy Bamber, for elimination purposes. The only rooms that were searched were the sitting room and the two bedrooms where the bodies had been found.

Then, in an act of misplaced kindness to Jeremy Bamber, the police destroyed the very evidence they had already failed to examine properly. They washed bloodstains from the walls. Then they removed bedding and carpets from the living room and bedrooms and burned them on a bonfire.

Jeremy Bamber remained outside while his family's bodies were removed from the scene. He remained calm and subdued. The only person he wanted to see was his girlfriend, Julie Mugford. A police officer was despatched to collect her from her home in Colchester.

When Julie was told of the massacre, she looked grim but made no comment. She was driven to White House Farm and she and Jeremy Bamber held each other as they watched evidence being carried from the house and destroyed.

As police moved the focus of their enquiries to neighbours and friends, everything they heard seemed to confirm what they already suspected. The wealthy and eminently respectable Bamber family had died tragically at the hands of a deranged family member.

The suggestion that Bambi might have been involved with drugs was raised by several of the Bambers' neighbours. The

Above: *Police fingerprint Jeremy Bamber's Citroën estate car outside his home at Goldhanger, Essex.*

Below: *A police officer holds up the .22 Anchutz rifle and silencer used in the Bamber murders.*

press were quick to accept salacious village gossip as fact, and this case had everything the tabloids could ask for – a glamorous, drug-crazed heiress had apparently murdered her own children and her adoptive parents.

THE SCEPTICS TAKE ACTION

The police and press had effectively convicted Bambi of murder. Not everyone felt comfortable with that idea, however.

Nevill Bamber's nephew, David Boutflour, had been very fond of his adoptive cousin. He was horrified by the allegations being made against her.

Boutflour said the very idea that Bambi could have carried out the killings was preposterous. He knew from police reports that twenty-five shots had been fired. This would have meant reloading twice in a situation of mayhem, an operation which would have required skill and co-ordination. 'Sheila,' said Boutflour, 'couldn't put baked beans on toast without knocking them over.'

Boutflour's protests fell on deaf ears so he decided it was up to him to obtain evidence which would exonerate Bambi and, he hoped, identify the real killer.

On Sunday, 11 August, while a service for the Bambers was being held at St Nicholas's Church in Tolleshunt D'Arcy, David and his sister, Mrs Christine Eaton, went to White House Farm. They worked their way methodically through the house, looking for possible clues.

Much of the evidence had already been removed or destroyed, but the amateur sleuths found two vital clues. At the back of the gun cabinet David Boutflour discovered a .22 silencer with some specks of blood on it. Christine noticed scratches on the kitchen window-ledge which suggested that the window had been closed and locked from the outside.

Boutflour immediately informed the police of their findings. Detectives were polite but unimpressed, and it was two days before they even bothered to go out to the farm to collect the silencer.

More doubt was cast on the murder-suicide theory two days later by the Home Office pathologist. He reported to detectives involved in the case that, in his opinion, their scenario was absurd.

Firstly it required slender, 5ft 7in Sheila Caffell to bludgeon 6ft 4in Nevill Bamber unconscious. And the 'suicide' shots didn't add up either. The first shot,

Above: *Jeremy Bamber is every inch the grief-stricken son as he follows his father's coffin.*

'SHEILA,' SAID DAVID BOUTFLOUR, 'COULDN'T PUT BAKED BEANS ON TOAST WITHOUT KNOCKING THEM OVER'

THE HOME OFFICE PATHOLOGIST FOUND SEVERAL REASONS WHY SHEILA COULD NOT HAVE FIRED THE GUN, BUT THE POLICE IGNORED HIM

WITH BAMBER AWAY IN FRANCE, JULIE MUGFORD WENT TO THE POLICE AND TOLD A VERY DIFFERENT STORY

Below: Jeremy Bamber handcuffed to a prison officer as he leaves court in a police van.

through her jugular vein, would have rendered her incapable of firing the second into her brain. In addition, the second shot had been fired with a silencer, and there was no sign of a silencer near Bambi's body. And if the rifle had been fitted with a six-inch silencer, the weapon would have been so long that Bambi would not have been able to reach the trigger while the muzzle was pressed under her chin. She could not possibly have fired that shot.

Despite these glaring inconsistencies, detectives ignored the pathologist's findings. No mention was made of them at the coroner's inquest, which was held at Chelmsford on 14 August.

The bodies of Nevill and June Bamber were released to Jeremy Bamber. Two days later friends and relatives of the Bambers returned to St Nicholas's church for the funeral service. Then the coffins were driven to Colchester for cremation.

THE TRUTH FILTERS OUT

On 8 September, three weeks after his family's funeral, Jeremy Bamber was arrested – not for murder, but for an unrelated burglary which dated back some six months. He was charged with stealing £980 from a caravan park which he co-owned with his late parents.

The following day, Bamber appeared at Chelmsford court and was refused bail. This was extremely unusual for a first offender accused of a non-violent crime, and it suggests that the police were starting to look at the White House killings in a new light. Jeremy was held in gaol for five days before being released in his own recognizance.

Jeremy left immediately for a holiday on the French Riviera. Surprisingly, he went with a friend, Brett Collins, rather than his girlfriend. This would prove Bamber's most expensive mistake.

A few days after Jeremy left for France, Julie Mugford went to see the Essex police. She told them she was certain that Jeremy had killed his family.

According to Julie, Jeremy had been planning the murders for months. She explained that Jeremy loathed his parents and he resented the fact that he had not been given his inheritance while he was young enough to enjoy it.

Julie said that on the night of the massacre Jeremy had telephoned her and said: 'It's got to be tonight or never.' Julie said she had told him not to be stupid, but that he had hung up. At three the following morning, Jeremy had rung again and said: 'Everything is going well.'

At first, detectives were inclined to believe that they were listening to the bitter rantings of a spurned woman. After all, hadn't Jeremy just taken off to France without her? But, as her story unfolded, they were reminded of the pathologist's findings and the evidence submitted by David Boutflour and Christine Eaton. It was becoming increasingly obvious that they had made a terrible mistake.

On 30 September, police were waiting at Dover ferry terminal when Jeremy Bamber returned from his holiday. He was arrested and charged with murdering Nevill and June Bamber, together with Sheila, Daniel and Nicholas Caffell.

GREED AND EXTRAVAGANCE

On Tuesday, 2 October 1986, more than a year after the massacre at White House Farm, the trial of Jeremy Bamber opened at Chelmsford Crown Court. Bamber had secured one of the country's best criminal solicitors, Sir David Napley, and he in turn had briefed Geoffrey Rivlin QC to conduct the defence. Bamber pleaded not guilty to five charges of murder.

The prosecution, led by Anthony Arlidge QC, opened by describing the massacre in graphic detail. He said that he would prove beyond all reasonable doubt that the perpetrator of the five killings was Jeremy Bamber. His motive, Arlidge claimed, was greed. Bamber knew that if all his family died, he would inherit almost half a million pounds.

The prosecution produced a plethora of evidence and expert witnesses. It all indicated that Sheila Caffell could not have committed the murders, and suggested that Jeremy Bamber might well have done so. The evidence against Bamber was, at best, circumstantial. Mr Arlidge chastised the police for their handling of the case, saying that if they had done their job properly his own job would have been made simpler.

On the morning of 9 October, Arlidge put his star witness on the stand. Julie Mugford wept as she told the jury of the months during which Jeremy Bamber's

Left: *Jeremy Bamber is remanded in custody at Maldon Magistrates' Court.*

IF BAMBER'S WHOLE FAMILY DIED, EXPLAINED THE PROSECUTING COUNSEL, HE WOULD STAND TO INHERIT £500,000

Below: *May 1986 – Jeremy Bamber arrives at Maldon Magistrates' Court for the committal proceedings.*

fantasies of killing his family had threatened to become a horrifying reality. Her answers during cross-examination were precise and consistent, and bore an unmistakeable ring of truth.

On 16 October, Rivlin opened the defence. He set out to prove that Sheila Caffell was a more likely murderer than he was. His argument came unstuck, however, when he was unable to discredit evidence submitted by the ballistics expert and the Home Office pathologist.

The following day, Rivlin put Jeremy Bamber on the witness stand. Bamber denied the killings and claimed to have had a loving relationship with his family. Under cross-examination, however, Bamber displayed a petulant, arrogant streak which did nothing to help his case.

Arlidge went to town on Bamber's character, portraying him as a greedy, vain and idle young man. None of this was very flattering, but it didn't prove that Jeremy Bamber had killed his family. In the final analysis, it all came down to who the jury chose to believe – Jeremy Bamber or Julie Mugford.

In the afternoon of 27 October, the jury retired to consider their verdict. Two days later they returned a verdict of 'guilty' on all five counts by a majority of 10–2.

Sentencing Bamber to five concurrent life sentences, the judge recommended that he should not be released for at least twenty-five years.

REIGN OF TERROR
The Boston Strangler

In 1963 a serial killer stalked the streets of Boston. His female victims were first sexually assaulted, then strangled and left lying in obscene postures. And this demented psychopath left no clues ...

Just before seven o'clock on the evening of 14 June 1962 Juris Slesers, a twenty-five-year-old research engineer, climbed the stairs to his mother's third-floor apartment at 77 Gainsborough Street in Boston. He had arranged to drive her to a memorial service at the Latvian Lutheran church in nearby Roxbury.

Mrs Slesers, a petite fifty-five-year-old divorcee, had fled Soviet-occupied Latvia with her son some twenty years earlier and settled in Boston, where she worked as a seamstress. For the past three months, since Juris had moved out, she had lived alone in this tiny apartment.

Juris knocked on the door and waited. There was no answer. He knocked again, pressed his ear to the metal door and listened. There was no sound from within.

He presumed his mother had popped out to do some shopping and went downstairs. He sat on the front steps and waited. Three-quarters of an hour passed and Juris was becoming concerned. He went back upstairs, hammered on the door and shouted his mother's name. There was still no response.

He put his shoulder to the door, backed

Opposite: Albert de Salvo. Was he indeed the Boston Strangler?

Below: Massachusetts State Troopers search for the Strangler.

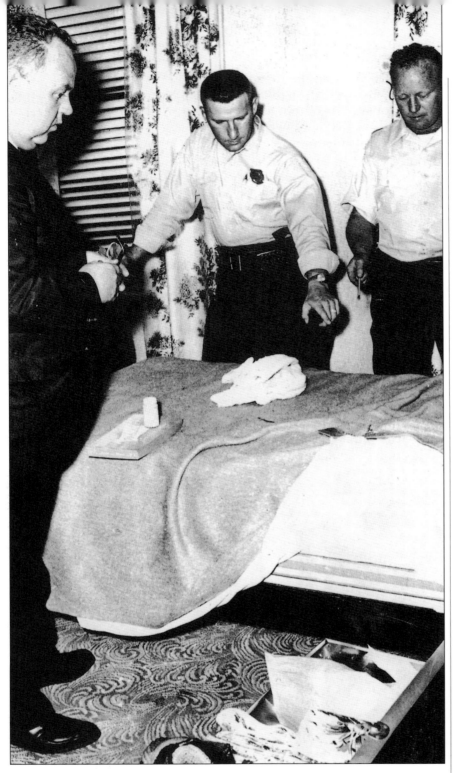

hallway and headed for the bathroom.

Anna Slesers was lying just outside the bathroom door. She was wearing her blue taffeta housecoat which was spread wide apart at the front, leaving her effectively nude. She lay with her left leg stretched straight out and her right flung at right-angles with the knee bent so that she was grossly exposed. The cord of her housecoat was knotted tightly round her neck and then fastened under her chin in the fashion of a crude bow. She was quite obviously dead.

The police, led by Special Officer James Mellon, arrived on the scene within minutes of receiving Juris Slesers's call.

Despite the fact that there was little sign of disturbance, it was immediately obvious to Officer Mellon that he was dealing with homicide. Mrs Slesers had been sexually assaulted and then strangled.

His initial suspicion was that someone had broken into the apartment with the intention of committing a robbery, had found Mrs Slesers in a state of undress – she looked younger than her years – and was seized by an uncontrollable sexual urge. He had raped Mrs Slesers and then strangled her to prevent her from identifying him.

The police conducted a thorough investigation. House-to-house enquiries were carried out. Relatives and friends were interviewed. A few possible candidates for the crime were picked up and questioned.

But the officers made no headway and, gruesome though the crime was, it soon became just another statistic. Boston averaged more than a murder a week at that time and, with a total lack of clues, the police accepted that their chances of ever finding the man responsible for Anna Slesers's death were very slim.

up and then rammed it with all his strength. The door sprang open.

JUST ANOTHER STATISTIC

Inside the apartment it was quite dark, and Juris tripped over a chair which had unaccountably been left in the middle of the narrow hallway. He looked into the living room and the bedroom, both of which were oddly untidy. There was no sign of his mother. He returned to the

Above: *The police search for clues in Helen Blake's apartment.*

THE FIFTY-FIVE-YEAR-OLD WOMAN HAD BEEN RAPED AND THEN STRANGLED WITH HER HOUSECOAT CORD

SEXUAL PSYCHOPATH

At five o'clock on 30 June, two weeks after the murder at Gainsborough Street, Nina Nichols, a sixty-eight-year-old retired physiotherapist, returned home to 1940 Commonwealth Avenue in Boston. She had just spent a pleasant few days in the country staying with friends.

As soon as she got into her apartment Mrs Nichols called her sister, Marguerite Steadman, to say that she was back safely and that she would be over for dinner at six o'clock as planned. The sisters chatted for a while but then Nina Nichols cut their conversation short, saying: 'Excuse me, Marguerite, there's my buzzer. I'll call you right back.'

Mrs Nichols didn't call her sister back, nor did she arrive for dinner at six o'clock. By seven, her sister was becoming concerned and asked her husband, attorney Chester Steadman, to telephone and make sure everything was all right. There was no reply to his call.

Another half an hour passed, and the Steadmans were becoming really alarmed. Maybe she had been been taken ill? Chester Steadman called the janitor of the building, Thomas Bruce. Would he go up to Mrs Nichols's apartment and see if she was still there?

Bruce went upstairs, knocked on the door and, when there was no reply, opened it with his pass-key. He never set foot inside. What he saw from the doorway was enough.

The apartment had obviously been burgled. Drawers had been pulled out, and clothes strewn all over the floor.

But there was worse, much worse. Directly ahead of him, Bruce could see into the bedroom. And on the floor, legs spread wide apart, was the nude body of Nina Nichols. Around her neck, tied so tightly that they cut into her flesh, were a pair of stockings. They were knotted under her chin in a clumsy bow.

Police Lieutenant Edward Sherry was soon at the scene with medical examiner Dr Michael Luongo. The similarities to the Slesers murder were immediately obvious to both men.

Nina Nichols had been sexually molested and then strangled. Both women had been left in a grossly exposed state. And then there were the tell-tale bows in the ligatures. There had been no sign of forceable entry to either apartment. Both had been ransacked but apparently nothing had been stolen in either case, despite the fact that high-value, easily disposable items like jewellery and cameras had been lying around. And there was no reason to

Above: *District Attorney John Burke and homicide officers search the scene where the body of Carrol Anne Donovan, one of the Boston Strangler's victims, was discovered.*

'EXCUSE ME, MARGUERITE,' SAID NINA NICHOLS, 'THERE'S MY BUZZER. I'LL CALL YOU RIGHT BACK.' BUT SHE NEVER DID

---

believe that the intruder had been interrupted on either occasion.

The police came to the conclusion that the murderer had never intended to commit a robbery – he had merely wanted to give the impression of committing a robbery. So what were they dealing with? Two murders did not constitute a serial, but Sherry and his colleagues had a gut feeling that there was a sexual psychopath at large in Boston.

They did not have to wait long before their fears were confirmed. On 2 July, two days later, police received a call from the neighbours of Helen Blake, a sixty-five-year-old retired nurse.

Helen had not been seen for a couple of days. Her friends had been concerned and borrowed a pass-key from the building supervisor. They had opened the door of her apartment, seen signs of a burglary and been afraid to go in.

The police entered the apartment and found Helen Blake lying face down on her bed. She was naked except for a

Below: *Mary Sullivan, 19, was found strangled on 5 January 1964 in her Beacon Hill apartment.*

pyjama top, which had been pushed up to her shoulders. She had been sexually assaulted and strangled with a pair of stockings. A brassiere was also tied around her neck, and fastened under her chin in a bow. The medical examiner estimated that she had been dead for about three days.

Police Commissioner McNamara was winding up a conference on the murders of Anna Slesers and Nina Nichols when Lieutenant Donovan told him that Helen Blake's body had been found. As Donovan gave him the details, McNamara expressed the feelings of the whole police department. 'Oh God,' he said. 'We've got a madman loose!'

What McNamara could not know was that these three murders were just the beginning and that, over the next year and a half, a total of eleven women would be strangled and sexually assaulted in Boston. The city would become a town paralysed by terror.

As the public screamed for a solution to the atrocities, the police mounted the greatest man-hunt known in modern crime, using every known detection technique, both natural and supernatural. They would use computers, clairvoyants and psychometrists, psychiatrists with hypnotic drugs and truth serums, psychologists, experts on anthropology, graphology and forensic medicine, as they found themselves confronted by a man whose brutality and insanity were matched by enormous cunning. He appeared to be able to gain access to locked apartments, molest and kill women, and never leave a single clue.

EXHAUSTIVE ENQUIRIES

The day after the discovery of Helen Blake's body, Commissioner McNamara cancelled all police leave. All his detectives were reassigned to homicide. There was a round-up of all known sex offenders. And anyone between eighteen and forty who had been released from a mental institution in the previous two years was investigated.

The police held a press conference during which they appealed to women, particularly women living alone, to keep their doors and windows locked, to admit no strangers, and to report any prowlers, obscene phone calls and letters.

Over the next few weeks the police were deluged with telephone calls and letters conveying tips, suspicions and alarms, both genuine and spurious. Lieutenants Sherry and Donovan, Special Officer Mellon and Detective Phil DiNatale, together with scores of other detectives, spent long hours and weekends covering leads and tracing and picking up possible suspects. The police held identity parades and administered lie-detector tests on scores of men. None of them was the strangler.

By mid-August there had been no more killings, and McNamara was beginning to hope that the strangler had sated his hideous cravings. Then, on 21 August, they found Ida Irga.

A seventy-five-year-old widow, Mrs

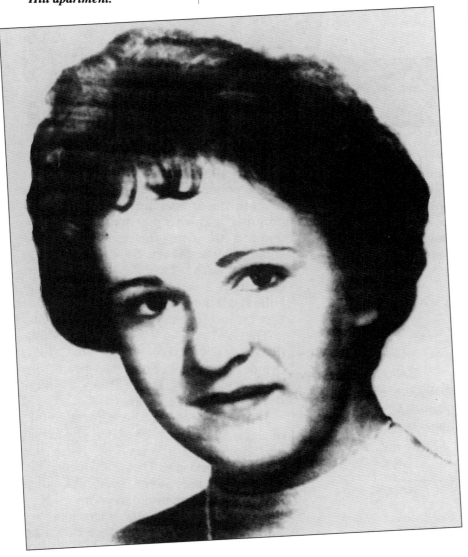

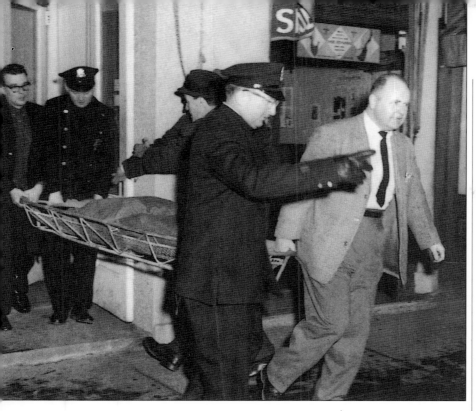

Above: *Police remove the body of Mary Sullivan from her apartment.*

Irga had been dead for two days. She had been strangled by human hands, but a pillow case had also been tied round her neck in a bow. Like the other victims, she had been sexually molested and, in her case, the murderer had added an appalling refinement to his attack. He had placed two chairs widely apart and tied one ankle to each in an obscene parody of a gynaecological examination. Again, the apartment had been ransacked yet no property had been removed.

Ten days later, the strangler struck again. His victim was Jane Sullivan, a sixty-seven-year-old nurse. She was found in the bathroom of her apartment; she had been dead for more than a week.

Her body was half kneeling in the tub, her face and arms submerged in six inches of water so that her buttocks were exposed. She had been strangled with two of her own stockings and placed in the bath after death.

UNBRIDLED HYSTERIA

Three months passed without a strangling but, far from relaxing, the people of Boston built themselves up to a state of unbridled hysteria. Every prowler, every flasher, every obscene phone caller was automatically presumed to be the strangler. A housewife in Brockton dropped dead of a heart attack when she found herself confronted with a stranger

THE FOURTH BODY WAS LEFT LYING IN A POSITION THAT OBSCENELY PARODIED THAT OF A GYNAECOLOGICAL EXAMINATION

ONE HOUSEWIFE DIED OF HEART FAILURE WHEN SHE OPENED THE DOOR TO A STRANGER. HE WAS ONLY SELLING ENCYCLOPAEDIAS

on her doorstep. He turned out to be selling encyclopaedias.

The police, with the help of a host of experts, had built up a complex psychological profile of the strangler. He was, they decided, between eighteen and forty years old, white, highly intelligent but psychopathic. He might well be homosexual or bi-sexual. He probably suffered from schizophrenia. He hated women, particularly older women, and had probably been brought up by a domineering mother. To his actual identity, however, they still had no clue.

When the next killing occurred, on 5 December 1962, even their psychological profile proved at least partially inaccurate. The latest victim, Sophie Clark, could not have been more different from the established strangler 'type'. She was an attractive black student of twenty who shared a flat with two other women. And Patricia Bisset, who was found strangled and sexually assaulted on New Year's Eve, was twenty-three and white.

It was now obvious that the strangler struck at random and no woman in Boston, young or old, black or white, living alone or living with others, was safe from him.

FURTHER GROTESQUE ATTACKS

On Wednesday, 8 May 1963, thirty-three-year-old Oliver Chamberlin called round to see his fiancée, Beverly Samans, a graduate student at Boston University. There was no answer when Chamberlin rang the bell of Beverly's apartment, so he let himself in with his own key.

He saw her at once. She was sprawled on a sofa bed in the living room, naked, her legs spread wide apart. Her wrists were tied behind her back with sequin-studded silk scarves. A bloodstained stocking and two handkerchiefs were knotted around her neck.

Beverly, however, had not died of strangulation. She had been stabbed twenty-two times in the throat and left breast. There was no doubt, however, that this was the work of the strangler, whose body count had now risen to eight.

Three months passed before the strangler struck again. Number nine was a vivacious fifty-eight-year-old divorcee called Evelyn Corbin. Strangled, assaulted and grossly exposed, she was found by a neighbour. Again the police found no clues, save a doughnut on the fire escape outside Mrs Corbin's apartment.

Friday 22 November 1963 is a day that no American will ever forget. President Kennedy was gunned down in Dallas, Texas. The following day, the entire nation was reeling from the blow, but for the strangler it was business as usual. This time his victim was a shy twenty-three-year-old, Joann Graff. He strangled her with her own black leotard and left her nude body on a day bed in her apartment.

Christmas came, and the people of Boston did their level best not to let the strangler ruin the holiday season. Indeed he did not strike over that period. But shortly after New Year Pamela Parker and Patricia Delmore returned from work to find their nineteen-year-old flatmate, Mary Sullivan, brutally murdered. It was the most grotesque and macabre killing so far.

Mary's body – in the words of the police report – was 'on the bed in a propped position, buttocks on pillow, back against headboard, head on right shoulder, knees up, eyes closed, viscous liquid dripping from mouth to right breast, breasts and lower extremities exposed, broomstick handle inserted in vagina...' Knotted round her neck were a stocking and a silk scarf tied together in a huge, comic bow. A bright greetings card which read 'Happy New Year!' was propped against her left foot.

The public outrage was intense, and two weeks later the Attorney General, Edward W. Brooke Jnr, announced that the Attorney General's Office of the Commonwealth of Massachusetts was taking over the investigation.

NO LONGER TOLERABLE

The strangler task force worked tirelessly throughout 1964. There were no further stranglings, but the police force's determination to identify and convict the man responsible was undiminished. But, by the autumn of 1964, the authorities were no nearer catching the strangler. It

Top: *Newsmen and photographers gather outside the apartment of Strangler victim Mary Sullivan.*

Above: *Police officers look for clues on the roof of Mary Sullivan's apartment.*

THE ONLY CLUE LEFT BY THE STRANGLER AT THE SCENE OF HIS NINTH MURDER WAS A DOUGHNUT DROPPED ON THE FIRE ESCAPE

was now nine months since he had struck and there was a feeling that the killer might have moved from the area, committed suicide or merely quit.

Then, on 27 October, the police in Cambridge, Massachusetts received a complaint from a young housewife. It was destined to open a whole new avenue of enquiry.

She told detectives that she was dozing in bed, after seeing her teacher husband off to work, when a man appeared at the bedroom door. He was about thirty, of medium build, wearing green slacks and large sunglasses.

The man had come slowly towards her and said: 'Don't worry, I'm a detective.' The young woman had yelled at him to get out, but the man had leaped forward, pinned her to the bed and held a knife to her throat. 'Not a sound,' he had commanded, 'or I'll kill you.'

The intruder had gagged his victim with her underwear, then tied her ankles and wrists to the bedposts so that she was spread-eagled. He had proceeded to kiss and fondle her body. Suddenly he had stopped, got to his feet and loosened her bonds slightly.

'You be quiet for ten minutes,' he said. 'I'm sorry,' he added and then fled from the apartment.

After she had finished giving her statement to detectives, the young woman spent several hours with a police artist trying to establish a likeness of her attacker. Between them they did a good job. One of the detectives recognized the face immediately. 'That,' he said, 'looks like the Measuring Man.'

THE MEASURING MAN

This was a character well known to the Boston police. He had been convicted and gaoled in 1960 for breaking and entering and indecently assaulting young women. He had gained his nickname because he had a habit of posing as an artist's agent, calling on young women and taking their measurements for supposed employment as models. The Measuring Man's real name was Albert H. De Salvo.

Thirty-three-year-old maintenance man De Salvo was picked up and brought to the police headquarters at Cambridge. He denied assaulting the young woman, but she identified him immediately. De Salvo was charged and taken into custody. As a matter of routine, the Cambridge police teletyped De Salvo's picture to neighbouring states. The response was astounding.

Messages poured in from New Hampshire, Rhode Island and Connecticut to say that De Salvo had been identified by scores of women as being the man who had sexually assaulted them. In some areas he was known as the Green Man because of his penchant for green trousers.

De Salvo denied everything and refused to answer any questions until he had spoken to his German-born wife, Irmgard. She was duly delivered to him and detectives watched them as they whispered together.

The police got the impression that Irmgard knew her husband had been 'up to something with women'. She confirmed their suspicions by saying aloud: 'Al, tell them everything. Don't hold anything back.'

De Salvo heeded his wife's advice and told detectives: 'I have committed more than four hundred breaks [breaking and entering], all in this area, and there's a couple of rapes you don't know about.'

As the investigation widened,

Below: *Police Commissioner McNamara with the special tactical squad he formed to catch the Boston Strangler.*

detectives soon realized that De Salvo was not exaggerating. They estimated that in the past two years he had committed sexual assaults on more than three hundred women.

De Salvo was shipped to Boston State Hospital for observation while he awaited trial for the Green Man offences. Doctors found him to be 'overtly schizophrenic and potentially suicidal', and on 4 February 1965 Judge Edward A. Pecce ordered him to be committed to a hospital for the criminally insane 'until further orders of the court'.

Al De Salvo should really have been caught up in the 'strangler dragnet' three years earlier. But, because of an administrative anomaly, he had been listed on the computer as a breaking-and-entering man rather than as a sex offender. So he had been overlooked when Boston police were conducting routine questioning early in the case. Now they wanted to know if he was involved.

But De Salvo was horrified at the suggestion that he might be connected with the killings. 'No, no' he wept, 'I've

done some terrible things with women – but I've never killed anyone.' Detectives were initially inclined to believe him. De Salvo didn't fit their profile of the Strangler, and he simply wasn't smart enough to have got away with it.

In hospital, De Salvo befriended a convicted killer named George Nassar. Soon he was using him as a confidant.

He did not come straight out and say he was the strangler, but his hints were sufficiently pointed for Nassar to get a distinct impression that he might be. A $110,000 reward had been offered to anyone giving information which led to the capture and conviction of the strangler, and Nassar saw this as a perfect chance to make a fast buck. He informed his attorney, F. Lee Bailey.

Bailey went to see De Salvo and recorded his confession to all eleven Boston stranglings, plus another two killings which the police had not previously connected with the strangler. Bailey turned a copy of his tape over to the police and the Attorney General's Office.

At first everyone was sceptical about

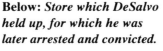

Below: *Store which DeSalvo held up, for which he was later arrested and convicted.*

De Salvo being the strangler. Not only did he not fit their profile, he had also gained a reputation as a braggart.

But when he was questioned at length, he started to disclose facts about the killings that only the strangler could have known – facts that had been deliberately kept secret to catch out the 'confessors'. De Salvo drew diagrams of the various apartments where the killings had taken place, and under hypno-analysis described the actual stranglings in gruesome detail.

Finally, the authorities were forced to accept that he might indeed be the Boston Strangler.

NO CASE

It was now the spring of 1965. The man-hunt, now in its third year, was wound down, and the investigation team was reduced to two men. Assistant Attorney General John Bottomley spent the next seven months interviewing De Salvo, talking him through each crime in minute detail. De Salvo proved to have an incredible memory and his descriptions of the various murders left Bottomley in absolutely no doubt that Albert De Salvo and the Boston Strangler were one and the same person.

Bottomley had his confession, but he had no one to corroborate it. De Salvo's victims could not testify against him and there were no eye-witnesses to identify him, and in America no one can be convicted solely by their own uncorroborated testimony. After all that effort, the state still had no case.

De Salvo had committed other crimes, however, for which the police had ample evidence. On the last day of June 1966 Albert De Salvo attended a hearing at Middlesex County Courthouse in East Cambridge, which was designed to determine whether he was mentally fit to stand trial for the Green Man offences.

It was his first public appearance since he had been committed to the institution at Bridgewater on 4 February 1965. Everyone in the court knew that De Salvo was probably the Boston Strangler, yet that case was not allowed to be mentioned.

Dr Mezer and Dr Tartakoff appeared as expert witnesses for the prosecution. They said that in their opinion Albert De Salvo was suffering from a committable mental illness, but was quite capable of standing trial.

Dr Robey, however, who had originally committed De Salvo to Bridgewater, disagreed completely: 'He is suffering from schizophrenic reaction, chronic undifferentiated type with very extensive signs of sexual deviation...My opinion is that I cannot – repeat – cannot consider him competent to stand trial....' Dr Robey added that, in his opinion, De Salvo would react to cross-examination by getting 'in such a state that he would not be making sense'.

Ten days later Judge Cahill accepted the prosecution argument and found Albert De Salvo competent to stand trail. The following year De Salvo was tried and convicted of armed robbery, breaking and entering, theft, assault and sexual crimes against four women, all of whom were lucky enough to live to identify their attacker. He was sentenced to life imprisonment.

While Albert De Salvo was never to stand trial as the Boston Strangler, the system had made sure he would never be free again. As it turned out, the length of his sentence was academic. On 26 November 1973, Albert De Salvo was found dead in his cell in Walpole State Prison. He had been stabbed sixteen times. The identity of his killer has never been established.

Above: *Women of all ages crowd into the Middlesex Superior Courtroom, hoping to catch a glimpse of the Strangler.*

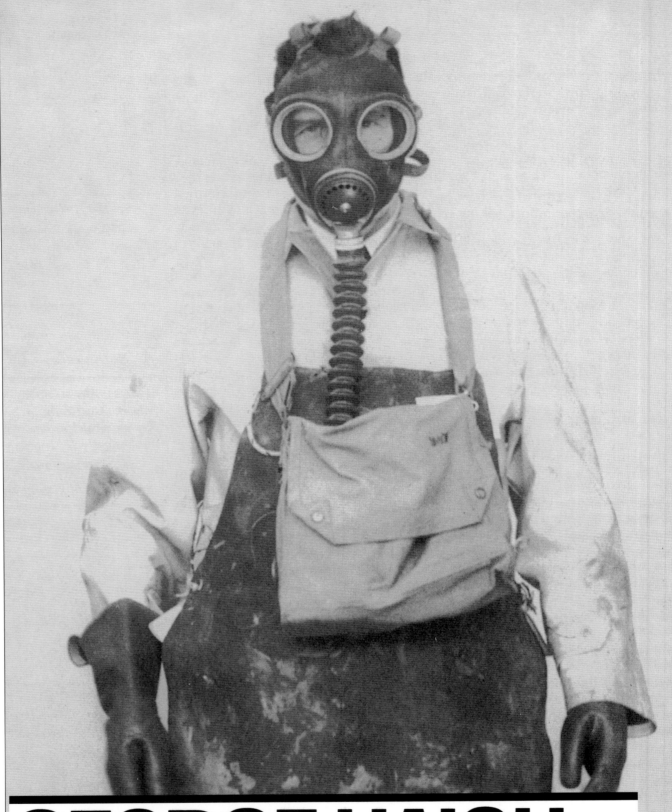

GEORGE HAIGH
Acid-Bath Murders

The dapper thirty-nine-year-old charmed the ladies of a London hotel – until one of them disappeared. The suspicions of her best friend led to the conviction of one of the most shocking murderers of the century. Not content with robbing his victims, he also did sickening things to their bodies

Mr John George Haigh was something of an odd-man-out at the Onslow Gardens Hotel in South Kensington. In 1949 this genteel establishment in a fashionable part of London was the haunt almost exclusively of elderly, well-heeled, upper-class ladies.

Not that Mr Haigh's presence was in any way resented by the other permanent residents of the hotel. On the contrary, for the most part they found the dapper thirty-nine-year-old engineer handsome, charming and meticulously well-mannered.

One of his particular fans was Mrs Helen Olivia Robarts Durant-Deacon, a well-preserved, buxom sixty-nine-year-old widow. She was quite smitten with 'young Haigh' and confided in him freely.

Mrs Durant-Deacon's husband, a colonel in the Gloucester Regiment, had died some years earlier and left her a legacy of £40,000. It was enough to allow her to live in some comfort for the rest of her life. But, as she explained to Haigh, she wasn't the sort of person to sit around doing nothing.

She was thinking of starting a business, designing and manufacturing artificial fingernails. She had already made some paper prototypes, but she knew absolutely nothing about the technical side of things. Perhaps Mr Haigh, as an engineer, could give her some pointers?

Above: *The .38 revolver used by Haigh to kill Mrs Durant-Deacon.*

Left: *.38 bullets found by the police at the scene of the crime.*

Opposite: *George Haigh took elaborate precautions while handling the acids he used to dissolve his victims' bodies.*

Below: *Mrs Durant-Deacon's handbag was one of many clues found by police at Haigh's workshop.*

APPOINTMENT WITH DEATH

In reality, Mrs Durant-Deacon's idea was a commercial non-starter in ration-bound post-war England. But Haigh feigned enthusiasm. Of course he would be delighted to help. Perhaps she would like to come out to his factory in Essex some time, and they could look at some possible materials from which the nails could be made.

At about 3p.m. on Friday, 18 February 1949, Haigh picked up Mrs Durant-Deacon and drove her down to a factory in Crawley, Sussex. He did not, as he had claimed, own the factory, but he did know the owner, and had the use of a storeroom for his 'experimental work'.

The grimy brick shed was cluttered with bottles, vats and drums. It was not what Mrs Durant-Deacon had expected, but Haigh reassured her. Experimental laboratories were always chaotic.

Mrs Durant-Deacon took his word for it and reached for her handbag, which held her designs. As she turned away from Haigh, he pulled a .38 Enfield revolver from his jacket pocket. He calmly shot her through the nape of the neck, killing her instantly.

Haigh then kneeled by his victim's body and made an incision in her neck with a knife. He collected a glassful of her still coursing blood and drank it.

Having quenched this gross thirst, Haigh gathered Mrs Durant-Deacon's valuables – a Persian lamb coat, rings, a necklace, earrings and a gold crucifix – and stowed them in his car.

Now it was time to get rid of the body. The very clutter which had offended Mrs Durant-Deacon was, in fact, the paraphernalia of her destruction. There were vats of sulphuric acid, a specially lined metal drum, rubber gloves and a rubber apron, a gas mask and a stirrup pump. Haigh needed all these things to dissolve his victim's body. He knew precisely what to do. He'd done it before.

He laid the forty-five gallon drum on its side and pushed Mrs Durant-Deacon's head and shoulders inside. Then he righted the drum so that the whole body slumped down to the bottom. He donned his rubber apron and gloves, his wellington boots and gas mask and

LEAVING THE BODY TO DISSOLVE IN A DRUM FILLED WITH SULPHURIC ACID, HAIGH DROVE TO A RESTAURANT TO EAT SOME POACHED EGGS

Below: *Haigh's apron found in the Crawley workshop.*

proceeded to pour concentrated sulphuric acid into the drum.

Using the stirrup pump, Haigh adjusted the level of acid to cover the entire body. Once satisfied, all he had to do was wait for the flesh and bone to dissolve. He knew this would take at least two days. So, tired and hungry after his exertions, he drove to Ye Olde Ancient Priors restaurant in Crawley for a little supper, before driving back to London.

NAGGING SUSPICIONS

At breakfast the following morning several residents of the Onslow Court Hotel remarked on Mrs Durant-Deacon's

Above: *The gas mask worn by George Haigh to protect himself from acid fumes.*

Left: *Haigh wore these rubber gloves as he manhandled Mrs Durant-Deacon into her acid bath.*

absence. Her closest friend at the hotel, Mrs Constance Lane, was particularly concerned and started to make some discreet enquiries. The chambermaid told Mrs Lane that Mrs Durant-Deacon's bed had not been slept in.

Later that morning Mrs Lane was approached by John Haigh who solicitously enquired about Mrs Durant-Deacon's whereabouts. He said that he had had an appointment with her the previous day, and that Mrs Durant-Deacon had failed to show up.

Below: *The barrel used by Haigh to dissolve his victim's body.*

Mrs Lane already knew about the trip to Crawley. She had seen her friend just as she was about to leave the hotel. She couldn't understand how Mrs Durant-Deacon could have 'failed to show up'. Mrs Lane had never liked Haigh. He was too oily for her taste, and his involvement with Mrs Durant-Deacon had always made her uneasy. Now she had a creeping feeling that something awful had happened to her friend.

Mrs Lane toyed with the idea of going to the police. But she was afraid that there might be some perfectly good reason for Mrs Durant-Deacon's absence and was anxious not to embarrass her friend – or to make a fool of herself. She decided to wait.

The following morning there was still no sign of Mrs Durant-Deacon. Mrs Lane was at breakfast, pondering her next move, when she was again approached by Haigh, expressing concern. Mrs Lane was suddenly galvanized into action. She told Haigh that she was going down to the police station, and that she would like him to go with her. Haigh had little choice but to agree, so he drove her to Chelsea Police Station.

The report Haigh made to the police was plausible enough. He had arranged to meet Mrs Durant-Deacon outside the Army and Navy Stores in Victoria Street at 2.30p.m. on 18 February. He had waited there until 3.30. Mrs Durant-Deacon had never materialized, and he had driven down to his workshop in Crawley alone.

He was, of course, extremely concerned about Mrs Durant-Deacon's welfare, and would do anything he could to help them locate her. The police thanked Haigh for his cooperation and said that they would be in touch if they thought of anything else.

Haigh drove Mrs Lane back to the Onslow Court and hoped against hope that that was the last he would hear of the matter. It wasn't. Four days later, on Thursday, 24 February, Woman Police Sergeant Alexandra Lambourne went to the hotel to gather additional background information on Mrs Durant-Deacon. She

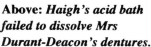

Above: *Haigh's acid bath failed to dissolve Mrs Durant-Deacon's dentures.*

Above left: *Home office pathologist Keith Simpson immediately identified three round 'pebbles' as Mrs Durant-Deacon's gallstones.*

Below: *George Haigh's diary was scrutinized by police.*

interviewed Haigh at some length.

Like Mrs Lane, she was immediately repelled by his superficial charm and his unctuous concern for the well-being of the missing widow. She was an experienced police officer and was convinced that Haigh was lying.

WPS Lambourne had no evidence to support her gut feeling, but she felt strongly enough about it to mention it in her report to her divisional Detective Inspector, Shelley Symes. 'Apart from the fact I do not like the man Haigh and his mannerisms,' she wrote, 'I have a sense that he is "wrong", and there may be a case behind the whole business.'

Symes had sufficient respect for Sergeant Lambourne's judgement to ask the Criminal Record Division at Scotland Yard to run a check on Haigh. Within a matter of hours, they came back to him with a file which showed that John George Haigh had been jailed three times, twice for obtaining money by fraud and once for theft. Further enquiries in London and Sussex showed that he owed substantial sums of money – to the Onslow Court Hotel, among others.

On Saturday, 26 February, Sergeant Pat Heslin of the West Sussex Constabulary, accompanied by Police Sergeant Appleton, went to see Mr Edward Jones, owner of Hurtslea Products, a small engineering company located on Leopold Street in Crawley. Jones told the police that he had known John George Haigh

for some years. Over the past few months he had let him use a store-house at the back of the factory for a nominal rent. Haigh had been using the premises for 'experimental work', but had never said precisely what that entailed.

The police were anxious to look round the shed, but Jones told them that Haigh had the only set of keys. So Heslin picked up a steel bar and prised the padlock off the door. At first glance, the whitewashed interior looked ordinary enough. There was the usual clutter – paint pots, old bits of wood, a couple of work benches, vats of chemicals, protective clothing.

Then something caught the sergeant's eye. On one of the workbenches there was a small hatbox and an expensive leather briefcase. They simply didn't belong.

Heslin looked through the case. He found a variety of papers and documents, including ration books and clothing coupons. The contents of the hatbox were even odder. It contained several passports, driving licences, diaries, a cheque book and a marriage certificate, none of which bore the name of Haigh. At the bottom of the box was the most alarming find of all, a .38 Enfield revolver and a small white envelope containing eight bullets.

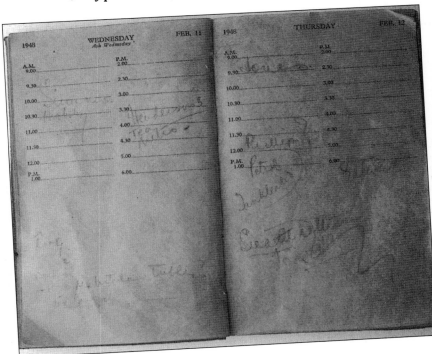

Above: The basement flat in Kensington where Haigh is believed to have killed Dr and Mrs Archibald Henderson.

The following evening, 27 February, Haigh was invited back to Chelsea Police Station to answer further questions. He appeared totally unconcerned as he was led into an office and given a cup of tea. He had dozed off by the time Detective Inspector Shelley Symes, Inspector Albert Webb, and Superintendent Barratt arrived to interview him at 7.30.

They came at him well-armed with evidence. Not only did they have the obviously stolen documents from the Crawley workshop, they had also traced Mrs Durant-Deacon's jewellery to a dealer in Horsham, Sussex. His description of the seller matched John George Haigh precisely. As did that of a dry-cleaner to whom he had taken Mrs Durant-Deacon's Persian lamb coat.

THE AWFUL TRUTH EMERGES

Confronted with this, Haigh was barely ruffled. Puffing on a cigarette, he said, 'I can see you know what you're talking about. I admit the coat belonged to Mrs Durant-Deacon and that I sold her jewellery.'

'How did you come by the property?' asked Symes, 'And where is Mrs Durant-Deacon?'

Haigh thought for a while before replying. 'It's a long story,' he confided. 'It's one of blackmail and I shall have to implicate many others.'

Below: Police search a cellar in Gloucester Road for clues in the Haigh murders.

Just then the telephone rang, and Symes and Barratt were summoned from the room. Left alone with Inspector Webb, the most junior of his interrogators, Haigh changed his tack. 'Tell me frankly,' he asked. 'What are the chances of anyone being released from Broadmoor?'

Webb's immediate reaction to Haigh's extraordinary question was to caution him and advise him of his rights. Haigh dismissed the warning with a wave of the hand. 'If I told you the truth,' he continued, 'You would not believe it. It is too fantastic for belief. I will tell you all about it....

'Mrs Durant-Deacon no longer exists. She has disappeared completely and no trace of her can ever be found. I have destroyed her with acid. You will find sludge that remains at Leopold Road. Every trace has gone. How can you prove a murder if there is no body?' Haigh added, obviously pleased with himself.

Webb's first reaction was to disbelieve Haigh's confession. It was simply too fantastic, too grotesque. Haigh was obviously setting himself up for an insanity plea. After all, he had already mentioned Broadmoor.

When Symes and Barratt returned to the interview room, Webb asked Haigh to repeat what he had said. Haigh did so. Symes cautioned him again, but there was no stopping Haigh now. He talked for two-and-a-half hours. And Inspector Symes wrote it all down.

He described the events of Friday, 18 February, in meticulous detail. He told how he had shot Mrs Durant-Deacon, how he had drunk her blood, put her in the acid bath, and then gone to the Ancient Priors for tea and poached eggs. He explained how, on Monday, he had disposed of her jewellery for £110. Then he had returned to Crawley and emptied the sludge – Mrs Durant-Deacon's decomposed body – out of the drum with a bucket, and poured it on to some wasteground at the back of the shed.

The police said nothing as Haigh told his terrible story of murder and theft, vampirism and genteel cups of tea. When he had finished the story of Mrs Durant-Deacon's death, Haigh moved back in time. By the early hours of 1 March he had confessed to five additional murders.

The first, he claimed, had been committed on 9 September 1944. The victim had been an old acquaintance, William McSwan. He had killed him at a basement flat in Gloucester Road. A year later, he had lured William's parents, Donald and Amy McSwan, to the same flat. There he had beaten them to death.

He had forged Donald's signature to gain power of attorney over the McSwans' estate. While selling one of their properties in February 1948, he had met Dr Archibald Henderson and his wife Rosalie. He had killed them in a storeroom in Giles Yard.

In each case, he had acquired money or other property belonging to his victims by skilful forgery and deception. Years after he had disposed of their remains, he had written forged personal and business letters, 'successfully staving off enquiries from relatives, friends and associates.'

Haigh added that he had destroyed all the bodies by his acid bath method – after drinking a glass of their blood.

The arrest of John George Haigh caused an immediate public sensation. His remand at Horsham magistrates court drew huge crowds – predominantly of jeering women.

BUT WHERE IS THE PROOF?

On 4 March, after being transferred from the Chelsea police cells to Lewes Prison, Haigh sprang more surprises. He asked to see Inspector Webb, with whom he clearly felt some sort of affinity. He confided in the young detective that he had committed three murders which he hadn't mentioned in his earlier statement – a woman and a young man in West London, and a girl in Eastbourne. This brought his total to nine.

The police, however, were having their time cut out establishing a case against Haigh for the murder of Mrs Durant-Deacon. Even though he had admitted to the crime, to be certain of a conviction, the prosecution needed proof that the woman was, in fact, dead, and that Haigh really had killed her.

The Home Office pathologist, Dr Keith Simpson, first carried out routine blood tests at the workshop in Crawley. He

Above: *Rosalie Henderson – she died at Haigh's hands along with her husband Archibald.*

The pathologist searched for the human 'sludge' on wasteground near Haigh's laboratory of death

---

established that blood stains found there were of the same group as Mrs Durant-Deacon. He then turned his attention to the wasteland where Haigh claimed to have deposited the 'sludge' from his acid bath. Soon he found a stone 'the size of a cherry'. It was a gallstone.

Simpson soon found more human remains, including fragments of a left foot. He managed to reconstruct it and cast it in plaster. The cast fitted one of Mrs Durant-Deacon's shoes perfectly.

He discovered other, non-human remains – the handle of a handbag, a lipstick container, a hairpin and a notebook. All of these could be traced back to the victim. His most sensational find, however – the clincher – was a set of dentures which were positively identified as having belonged to the missing woman.

In Lewes Prison, Haigh was well aware of the forensic evidence being amassed against him, but he still remained optimistic. He was certain that he could escape the gallows by convincing a jury that he was insane. And on being told that the eminent barrister Sir Maxwell Fyfe was to represent him, Haigh was delighted. He wrote: 'I'm very glad to see we have got old Maxy. He's no fool.'

THE MIND OF A KILLER

The trial of John George Haigh for the murder of Mrs Durant-Deacon – that was the only charge ever brought against him – opened at Lewes Assizes on 18 July 1949 and lasted less than two days.

There was no real question as to whether Haigh had killed Mrs Durant-Deacon. The case rested on whether or not he was sane. The defence called Dr Henry Yellowlees, a consultant psychiatrist at St Thomas's Hospital, as an expert witness.

Dr Yellowlees was no doubt an able man in his field, but he was a rotten witness. He was a pompous windbag. 'In the case of pure paranoia,' Yellowlees explained, 'it really amounts, as it develops and gets a greater hold, to practically self-worship, and that is commonly expressed by the conviction in the mind of the patient that he is in some

summoned the black cap and condemned him to death. Haigh was taken to Wandsworth Prison to await execution.

While there was no expression of pity for him from the press, there was a great deal of editorial speculation. How was it, they wondered, that an intelligent boy from a good home – his parents were members of the Plymouth Brethren – could grow into a monster like Haigh?

Haigh himself went some way to answering them. He wrote from prison: 'Although my parents were kind and loving, I had none of the joys, or the companionship, which small children usually have. From my earliest years, my recollection is of my father saying "Do not" or "Thou shalt not". Any form of sport or light entertainment was frowned upon and regarded as not edifying. There was only condemnation and prohibition....

'It is true to say that I was nurtured on Bible stories but mostly concerned with sacrifice. If by some mischance I did, or said, anything which my father regarded as improper, he would say: "Do not grieve the Lord by behaving so." '

On 24 July, five days after his trial ended, Haigh's mother sent him a fortieth birthday card, but he rejected any suggestion that she visit him in prison.

mystic way under the control of a guiding spirit which means infinitely more to him and is of infinitely greater authority than any human laws or rules of society.'

Dr Yellowlees rambled on in this vein for some considerable time. He was frequently interrupted by both Sir Travers Humphry, the judge, and Sir Hartley Shawcross, counsel for the prosecution, neither of whom had the faintest idea what he was talking about.

As for the jury, he had lost them after the first few sentences. It took them only fifteen minutes to return a verdict of Guilty on John George Haigh. Sir Travers Humphry was equally speedy as he

Top and above: *George Haigh leaves Horsham Court with his police escort. Haigh is besieged by photographers as he leaves court.*

Right: *Dr Keith Simpson, the Home Office pathologist, was the greatest forensic scientist of his day.*

As the day of his execution approached, Haigh's apparently limitless poise began to crumble. He started to suffer from depression and complained of recurrent nightmares about blood.

Despite his depression, Haigh maintained his sense of theatre. He bequeathed his favourite suit and tie to Madame Tussauds, ensuring himself a place in the Chamber of Horrors. He even requested his model should show at least one inch of shirt cuff.

Then Haigh became concerned about the hanging itself. He contacted the prison governor, Major A.C.N. Benke, and requested to rehearse his own execution. 'My weight is deceptive,' Haigh insisted, 'I have a light springy step and I would not like there to be a hitch.'

The governor turned down his request, assuring him that the executioner was highly experienced and that there would be no hitches.

On 9 August, the eve of his execution, Haigh wrote a letter to his parents. It began: 'My dearest Mum and Dad, Thank you for your very touching letter which I received this morning and which will, I suppose, be your last....'

He went on to say that he had found parts of his upbringing very restrictive: 'There was much that was lovely.... We cannot change the inscrutible predictions of the eternal.... I, that is my spirit, shall remain earthbound for some time: my mission is not yet fulfilled....'

Haigh did not go on to explain what he thought his mission was, nor expressed any remorse for his terrible crimes. In the end, the ultimate mystery of Haigh's life – what was going on inside his mind? – would go to the grave with him.

At 9a.m. on 10 August, John George Haigh was executed. His depression had left him and he was his old self, all swank and swagger, as he faced the gallows. He was buried the same day inside the prison walls, as is the custom in cases of execution.

Below: 10 August 1949. A crowd gathers outside Wandsworth Prison as John George Haigh is executed.

SNYDER & GRAY
Momsie and Loverboy

The mousey little underwear salesman wanted a passionate woman to dominate him. The blonde good-time girl was after a man whom she could control utterly. It seemed the perfect match – but after sex came murder

They were an odd couple. He was a submissive traveller in ladies' underwear; she was a domineering good-time girl. Dubbed 'Putty Man' and 'Granite Woman', they fulfilled a need in each other and, while their relationship was always faintly ludicrous, it was also to prove ultimately deadly.

ATTRACTION OF OPPOSITES

Judd Gray and Ruth Snyder first met in June 1925 at Henry's, a small Scandinavian restaurant in New York City. It was a blind lunch date set up by two of Ruth's friends, Karin Kaufman and Harry Folsom.

Judd and Ruth hit it off from the start. It was an attraction of opposites. She was an attractive twenty-eight-year-old blonde, an extrovert who enjoyed drinking, dancing and sex. He was thirty-one, slight, shy and myopic. He too had a thirst for excitement which he had never had either the courage or the opportunity to slake. In Ruth he saw the chance for a passionate affair, an escape from the drudgery of his bourgeois life.

Judd and Ruth spent their first three hours together in the restaurant booth swapping personal and marital histories. She explained that she was married with a seven-year-old daughter, Lorraine, and lived in the suburb of Queens with her husband, Albert, who was much older than she. Art editor with *Motor Boating* magazine, he was a great outdoors man and spent most of his time and money on boating and fishing.

In fact, he was away on one of his trips as they spoke. She didn't care for the outdoor life. She preferred dining in good restaurants and dancing – not that Albert cared. In all, she painted her marriage in fairly grim terms with herself as the grass widow to a selfish and insensitive man.

What she neglected to mention to Judd Gray was that he was merely the latest in a long string of 'men friends' whom she had cultivated to compensate herself for her marital dissatisfaction.

Judd responded by saying that he too was married with a daughter and lived in East Orange, New Jersey. He described his wife Isabel as a good mother and a

Opposite: *'Granite Woman', Ruth Snyder was a good-time girl who liked to dominate the men in her life.*

Below: *Judd Gray, 'Putty Man', was an ineffectual underwear salesman who lusted after excitement. He found it in Ruth Snyder.*

Above: *The Snyder house in East Orange, New Jersey.*

Opposite: *In her younger years, Ruth Snyder cut a glamorous figure.*

meticulous housekeeper, but made it plain that she did not provide the excitement he wanted from life.

The one bright spot in his otherwise dull existence was his job. As a travelling salesman for the Bien Jolie Corset Company, he spent much of his time on the road. The company's headquarters were in New York and so he came to the city on a regular basis. Would Ruth like to meet him again? Yes, she would.

By the time Ruth and Judd parted company on the sidewalk outside Henry's it was after 4p.m., and both of them had found what they had been searching for: Judd, a passionate affair in which he could be led and dominated; Ruth, a man she could control utterly.

CONSUMMATION ON THE OFFICE FLOOR

Despite this obvious mutual attraction, it was almost two months before the couple met again for their first real date. On 4

August, Judd called Ruth and asked if she would care to join him for dinner at 'their place' – Henry's Swedish restaurant. After the meal Judd, fortified with copious quantities of rye whiskey, invited Ruth back to the Bien Jolie offices on Fifth Avenue. 'I have to collect a case of samples,' he explained lamely.

Once inside the empty office, Judd made his move. 'You really ought to try one of the new glamour corsets,' he suggested. 'I'll fit it for you if you like.'

Ruth took off her coat. 'Okay,' she said. 'You can do that. And from now on you can call me Momsie.'

And so, on the floor of the Bien Jolie Corset Company, Ruth Snyder and Judd Gray consummated their affair, an affair which was to burn with increasing ardour for almost two years. Soon after their first tryst, Judd and Ruth started to meet regularly, spending nights – or parts of nights – together in Manhattan hotel bedrooms. While Judd needed no excuse to be away from home, Ruth would tell

Albert that she was visiting girlfriends. Despite the fact that the meetings became increasingly frequent, Albert suspected nothing – or perhaps he didn't care.

As the relationship developed, its true nature became more apparent. Ruth became increasingly dominant and Judd became correspondingly more besotted. He would sink to his knees and caress her feet and ankles. 'You are my queen, my Momsie!' he would simper, gazing up into her imperious face. 'And you are my baby, my Bud, my Lover Boy,' she would reassure him.

By the end of 1925 the couple had abandoned the last vestiges of discretion and Judd started to visit Ruth at home. Ruth took little Lorraine on her visits to New York, leaving her in the care of the hotel concierge while she went upstairs to spend a few hours with her Lover Boy.

From their first meeting, Ruth had made it clear that her marriage was not happy. As time passed she amplified this point with frequent references to Albert's cruelty, claiming that he beat and humiliated her. When she spoke of these things, she always made a point of saying how wonderful things would be if only she and Judd were both free and could be together all the time.

'ACCIDENTS'

Ruth did not come right out and say that she wished her husband was dead, but she was soon sowing the seeds of the idea in her lover's mind. Just before Christmas 1925, Ruth told Judd about a series of strange 'accidents' which had befallen her husband in recent months.

On one occasion, while he had been changing a tyre, the jack had slipped and the car had almost crushed him to death. A few days later, he had been in the garage stretched under the car with the engine running. Ruth, the ever-dutiful wife, had brought him a glass of whiskey and, not thinking, had closed the garage door after her. A few minutes later Albert had felt very dizzy, and he had just managed to escape from the garage before being asphyxiated by exhaust fumes.

Albert might have seen nothing ominous about these incidents, but Judd

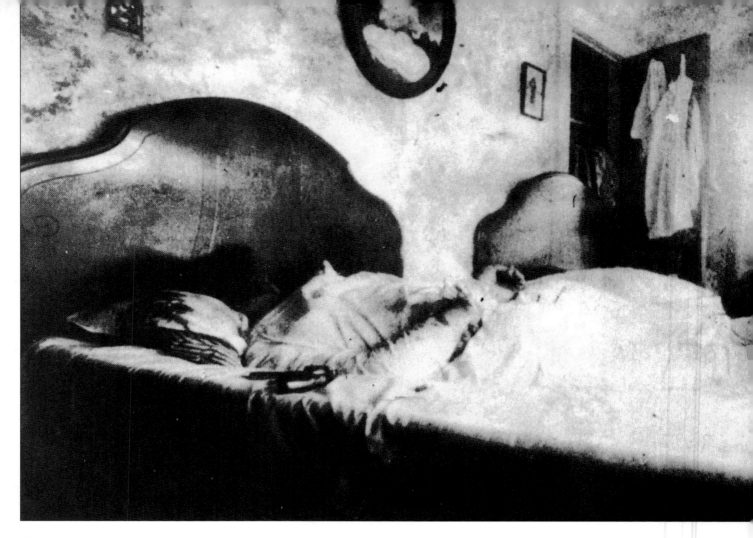

Gray certainly did. 'What are you trying to do?' he asked, horrified. 'Kill the poor guy?'

Ruth pouted: 'Momsie can't do it alone. She needs help. Lover Boy will have to help her.' They had both been drinking heavily and Judd wrote off this first suggestion of murder as alcoholic bravado.

The next time the couple met, however, Judd realized that she was deadly serious. 'We'll be okay for money,' Ruth said. 'I've just tricked Albert into taking out some hefty insurance. He thinks it's for $1000, but it's really for $96,000 with a double indemnity clause.'

Judd made light of the idea and changed the subject, but Ruth was not about to be dissuaded. Over the next few months she gradually chiseled away at Judd's resistance.

In December she told him that Albert had bought a gun and was threatening to kill her. She appealed to Judd directly to help her kill Albert. When he refused, she said she would do it by herself.

Above: *Beaten, smothered, gagged and bound, Albert Snyder lies dead on his own bed.*

TIRED OF HER LOVER'S NON-COMPLIANCE IN HER MURDER PLANS, RUTH ORDERED HIM TO BUY SOME CHLOROFORM AND PICTURE WIRE

THREATS AND BULLYING

Finally Ruth tired of trying to persuade and cajole her lover into action. It was time, she decided, to capitalize on her dominant position in the relationship and to give a few outright orders.

In February 1927 the couple spent the night together in the Waldolf-Astoria Hotel. Ruth instructed Judd to purchase some chloroform, a sash weight and a length of picture wire. These, she explained, were to be their murder weapons: 'That way,' she explained gleefully, 'we have three means of killing him. One of them must surely work.'

But again Judd baulked at the idea of becoming involved in murder. Ruth flew into a rage and threatened him: 'If you don't do as I say, then that's the end of us in bed. You can find yourself another Momsie to sleep with – only nobody else would have you but me!'

Cowed by the prospect of losing Ruth and returning to his old, dull life, Judd reluctantly agreed to help. Two days later, while passing through Kingston in

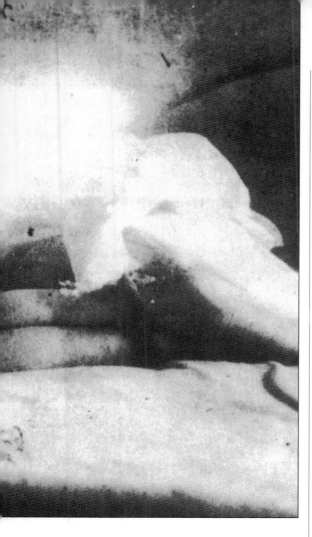

New York State, he bought a bottle of chloroform in a drug store. He then walked a few doors further along the street to a hardware store and bought a foot-long, lead sash weight and a coil of picture wire.

The next day, Judd returned to New York City and met Ruth at Henry's Restaurant. There he handed over a parcel containing his purchases. Despite the fact that Ruth had brought her daughter with her she was anxious to get on with things, and so the couple discussed the murder of Lorraine's father by exchanging notes scribbled on table napkins. By the time they got up from the table, a date for the killing had been set – Saturday, 19 March.

THE PLAN TAKES SHAPE

On Friday the 18th, Judd Gray registered at the Hotel Onondaga in Syracuse, New York State. In the lobby he bumped into an old friend, Haddon Gray (no relation). Judd saw this as a piece of good fortune and decided to use him as an alibi for the following night.

He told Haddon that he had an assignation with a lady in New York. Would he cover for him? He asked Haddon to 'muss up' his bedclothes and to hang a 'Do Not Disturb' sign on the bedroom door. Haddon readily agreed to this 'manly' conspiracy.

Having thus established his alibi – and, in the process, established the premeditation of his crime – Judd set off by train for New York City.

He arrived at Grand Central Station at 10.20p.m. on the evening of 19 March. After stopping briefly at the Pullman window to purchase a return ticket to Syracuse on the morning train, he walked out on to 42nd Street.

It was raining, but Judd chose to walk the four miles to Queens rather than risk being recognised by a cab driver. He made frequent stops along the way to drink from his hip flask, and he was already quite drunk when he reached his destination.

Judd reached the Snyders' three-storey, clapboard house shortly after midnight. He knew that Ruth and her family would be out at a party until very late, and he let himself into the house by a side door, using a key that Ruth had hidden for him. He went upstairs and into the spare bedroom. Keeping on his buckskin gloves, he removed his hat and coat and hung them in the wardrobe. Then he felt under the pillow and retrieved the sash weight, chloroform, picture wire and a bottle of whiskey which had been left there by Ruth. He laid these props on the bed along with various other items which he had brought with him – a handkerchief, some cheesecloth and an Italian newspaper he had found on the train.

Judd opened the whiskey, took a long slug and settled down to wait.

At about 2am, Judd was woken from his drunken sleep by the sound of the Snyders' car pulling up outside. He heard the front door open, and then footsteps on the stairs. He recognized the voices of Ruth and Lorraine. Ruth slipped into the room where Judd was hiding.

She kissed him and whispered: 'Have you found the sash weight?' Judd nodded. 'Good,' she said. 'Keep quiet and I'll be right back.'

JUDD'S ALIBI HAD ANOTHER, LESS DESIRABLE EFFECT: IT ESTABLISHED THAT THE MURDER OF RUTH'S HUSBAND WAS PREMEDITATED

She returned a few minutes later in her negligee. 'He's just brushing his teeth.' she said, and slipped away again. And so the farce continued for half an hour with Ruth toing and froing, updating Judd on the status in the master bedroom.

'He's getting undressed now.... He's in bed but he's still awake.... I think he's dropped off, but we'd better leave him to settle for a while....'

It was almost 3a.m. before Ruth decided the time was right and joined Judd in the bedroom. He was sitting on the floor and, having almost finished the bottle of whiskey, was very drunk.

'You are going through with it tonight, aren't you?' Ruth asked him.

'I don't know whether I can or not. I'll try.' he replied. Ruth helped him to his feet. 'Now,' she said.

Judd removed his buckskin gloves and pulled on a pair of rubber housegloves in their place. He picked up the sash weight with one hand and with the other took Ruth's arm. And so the odd couple picked their way along the darkened corridor towards the master bedroom.

Ruth led Judd over to the bed where Albert was sleeping. Judd lifted the sash weight above his head and brought it down with all the force he could muster. The blow should have smashed Albert's skull but Judd's aim was off. The weight only glanced the side of Albert's head and crashed into the wooden bedhead.

Albert sat bolt upright and started lashing out at his unseen assailant. Judd hit him again, harder this time, but Albert continued to struggle. Judd dropped the weight and climbed on to the bed, trying to smother his victim with the bedclothes. Albert managed to get his hands round Judd's throat and started to throttle him. Judd screamed at Ruth: 'Momsie, Momsie, for God's sake help me!'

Ruth picked up the sash weight and smashed it into her husband's skull, time and time again. Once Albert stopped struggling, Judd climbed off the bed and watched Ruth put the finishing touches to the job. She tied Albert's hands and feet with a towel and a tie and stuffed his mouth and nostrils with cotton rags soaked in chloroform. Then, just for good measure, she garotted him with the length of picture wire.

'HE'S CLEANING HIS TEETH...
HE'S GETTING
UNDRESSED... HE'S IN BED
BUT HE'S STILL AWAKE...'

'MOMSIE, MOMSIE, FOR
GOD'S SAKE HELP ME!'
CRIED THE INCOMPETENT
WOULD-BE MURDERER AS
HIS VICTIM STARTED TO
THROTTLE HIM

Below: *Ruth Snyder and her defence team. Their argument failed to convince the jury.*

There was blood everywhere, and Ruth and Judd spent the next half-hour cleaning themselves up. Ruth changed nightdresses and Judd borrowed one of Albert's shirts to replace his own, which was ripped and bloodstained.

Ruth then reminded Judd that they had agreed to ransack the house to make it look like a robbery. They overturned furniture in the living room and scattered the contents of various drawers around the floor. Ruth took all the money out of Albert's wallet and gave it to Judd, and then offered him her jewellery. He refused, and suggested she hide it under the mattress.

In an equally futile attempt to destroy the evidence, Ruth went down to the cellar. There she burned the bloodstained shirt and nightdress in the furnace, and hid the sash weight in a tool box.

Satisfied that everything was just so, Ruth gave Judd another bottle of whiskey for the journey, and told him to knock her out, so that it would look as if she too had been a victim of a robbery.

Judd could not bring himself to do this, but tied her hands and feet and gagged her with a piece of cheesecloth. He left her on the spare bed, with the Italian newspaper – his idea of a false clue – by her side.

As he left, he looked back at Ruth and

was momentarily overcome with disgust and guilt. 'It may be two months,' he said, 'it may be a year, and it may be never before you see me again.'

CLUMSY LIES, SCATTERED CLUES

The murder of Albert Snyder must have been a noisy affair, but little Lorraine Snyder apparently slept through the whole thing. She was woken at 7.45 by a knocking at her bedroom door. She opened the door and found her mother, bound and gagged, lying on the floor in the hallway.

Lorraine undid the cheesecloth gag, and her mother told her to run and get help. Minutes later, the child returned with Louis and Harriet Mulhauser, their friends and neighbours.

'It was dreadful, just dreadful!' Ruth screeched at the Mulhausers. 'I was attacked by a prowler.... He tied me up.... He must have been after my jewels.... Is Albert all right?' Louis Mulhauser crossed the hall and went into the master bedroom. Seconds later, he returned with the awful news. Albert had been battered to death.

Ruth Snyder repeated her version of events twice more that morning, elaborating a little with each successive version. 'He was a big, rough-looking

Above: *Huge crowds gathered outside the court hoping to gain access to the Snyder-Gray trial.*

'IT MAY BE TWO MONTHS, IT MAY BE A YEAR, AND IT MAY BE NEVER BEFORE YOU SEE ME AGAIN'

SHE HAD POWER OVER ME. SHE TOLD ME WHAT TO DO AND I JUST DID IT

guy of about thirty-five with a black moustache,' she told Dr Harry Hansen. 'He was a foreigner, I guess. Some kind of Eyetalian.'

Dr Hansen was not convinced by her story, and nor were the police when they arrived. Police Commissioner George V. McLaughlin, heading the investigation, had investigated enough robberies to know the real thing when he saw it. And this definitely was not the real thing.

It had all the hallmarks of an inside job, carried out with the help of an accomplice, probably a man.

A clue to that man's identity came when one of the detectives found a tiepin with the initials JG on the floor of the master bedroom. Then another detective found Ruth's address book which contained the names of twenty-eight of her men friends; the most recent entry was one Judd Gray. Then they found a cancelled cheque made out to Gray by Ruth Snyder in the amount of $200.

By this time, other detectives had discovered the bloodstained sash weight in the cellar and Ruth's jewellery stuffed under the mattress in the spare bedroom. They also found insurance policies taken out on Albert Snyder's life to a total of $96,000.

After twelve hours of questioning, Ruth caved in and admitted that she had been present at her husband's murder, but she denied playing any part in the actual killing. That was all Judd's doing. She was shipped off to the Jamaica Precinct police station and charged.

Acting on information from Ruth Snyder, police arrested a snivelling and terrified Judd Gray at the Onondaga Hotel later that evening. They brought him back to New York City by train.

By the time they arrived, Judd too had confessed to being a party to the murder, but he did not cover up for Ruth. 'I would never have killed Snyder, but for her,' he wept as he completed his statement. 'She had power over me. She told me what to do and I just did it.'

GOOD NEWS FOR THE TABLOIDS

From then on, the case against Snyder and Gray proceeded with all the implacability of the law. Their trial opened on 18 April at the Queens County Courthouse and lasted eighteen days.

The central issue at stake for the jury was not whether the defendants were guilty of killing Albert Snyder. They had both confessed to being present and playing a part in the murder. What had to be decided was whether the crime was premeditated, and whether or not it had been executed for financial gain. Both these factors would have a bearing on the eventual sentencing.

The two defence teams tried to push the blame on to each other's clients to a point where the case became not so much the State v Snyder & Gray as one of Ruth Snyder v Gray. This did nothing for the cases of the two defendants.

On 9 May, Snyder and Gray were duly found guilty of murder in the first degree and sentenced to die in the electric chair at Sing Sing prison in upstate New York.

CHANGED CHARACTERS

Immediately after sentencing, both teams of defence lawyers filed appeals. Ruth's appeal was heard on 27 May, Judd's on

---

> FROM THE CONDEMNED CELL RUTH TOLD A REPORTER: 'I ALWAYS WANTED AN ELECTRIC HEATER, BUT MY HUSBAND WAS ALWAYS TOO STINGY TO BUY ME ONE'

> 'I NEVER SAW ANYTHING MORE TERRIBLE,' SAID RUTH'S LAWYER. 'I CANNOT DESCRIBE HER AGONY, HER MISERY, HER TERROR'

Below: *Ruth Snyder being followed by jail matron, Mrs Irene Wolf.*

---

10 June. On 23 November both appeals were rejected and Snyder's original sentence was upheld.

With all legal means for clemency now closed to her, Ruth started writing her autobiography, My Own True Story – So Help Me God! which was syndicated by the Hearst newspaper chain.

She also promoted herself in the media by granting audiences to press men from her condemned cell. She even managed moments of black humour. Talking of her forthcoming execution, she told reporter Jack Lait: 'I always wanted an electric heater, but my husband was always too stingy to buy me one.'

While awaiting execution, Ruth had a regular flow of fan mail. It included 164 proposals of marriage, mainly from men desperate to take Judd Gray's place as her slave.

For all her bravado, however, the 'Granite Woman', as the press had dubbed her, was terrified of dying. Screams could be heard coming from her Sing Sing cell at night.

Judd Gray, in contrast, appeared totally resigned to his fate. He spent much of his time writing letters to his family and friends. When he was not busy with his correspondence, he studied the Bible and discussed religious matters with the prison chaplain.

The execution was set for 11 p.m. on 12 January 1928. At 7.30 p.m., Ruth Snyder was moved to her death cell, 30 feet from the execution chamber.

Shortly before the evening meal she was visited by her lawyer, Edgar Hazleton. Her condition was pitiful, he recalled. 'She was too far gone to know what she was doing. I never saw anything more terrible. I cannot describe her agony, her misery, her terror.'

A little later Samuel Miller, Judd Gray's attorney, visited him in his death cell, a few feet away from that of his erstwhile lover. Miller painted a very different picture of his client to that of Hazleton. 'He is absolutely resigned and courageous,' Miller said. 'He indulges no self-pity. He realizes the enormity of his act.'

A few minutes before 11 p.m. twenty-four witnesses, most of them reporters, were shown into the death chamber.

Among those who took their seats opposite the electric chair was a young photographer, Thomas Howard. Cameras were strictly forbidden in the chamber, but Howard had managed to smuggle in a tiny one strapped to his ankle.

At precisely 11 p.m. Ruth Snyder, her head shaved, was led from her cell by two female warders. As she was strapped to the chair, she wept: 'Father, forgive them, for they know not what they do.' Seconds later the state executioner, Robert Elliot, threw the switch and a massive surge of electricity shot through Ruth's body. At precisely that moment, Thomas Howard released the shutter of his hidden camera, recording the death of Ruth Snyder on film and

guaranteeing for himself a place in journalistic folklore.

At 11.10, after Ruth Snyder's body had been removed to the nearby autopsy room, Judd Gray was brought into the death chamber. He stood between two warders, calm and composed. A priest stood by him as he was strapped into the chair, and they recited the Beatitudes together. Gray continued to pray as the electrodes were fitted and a mask was pulled over his face.

Ten minutes later, Judd Gray was reunited with Ruth Snyder for the first and last time since the fateful night of Albert Snyder's murder. This time they lay side-by-side on a slab in the Sing Sing prison morgue.

Above: *Ruth Snyder at the moment of her death in the electric chair: taken by a camera smuggled into the death chamber strapped to the photographer's leg.*

GRAY CONTINUED TO PRAY EVEN AS THE ELECTRODES WERE FITTED AND A MASK WAS PULLED OVER HIS FACE

HAROLD SHIPMAN
Doctor Death

Until recently Britain's worst serial killer was Victorian serial poisoner, Mary Ann Cotton, who murdered an estimated 21 people in the 1870s. Now that dubious distinction is claimed by Dr. Harold Shipman.

D r Shipman ran a one-man practice in Hyde in the north of England. Most of Harold Shipman's patients were elderly women, living alone and vulnerable. They adored their doctor, Harold 'Fred' Shipman, and even when their contemporaries began dying in unusually high numbers, patients remained loyal to the murderous M.D. It seemed that as long as he spared them, his victims loved their doctor – to death.

A KILLER'S CHILDHOOD

Harold Frederick Shipman was born into a working class family on June 14, 1946 and was known as Fred or Freddy. His childhood, however, was far from normal. He always kept a distance between himself and his contemporaries – mainly due to the influence of his mother, Vera. The reason for this distance was to become clear in later years.

It was Vera who decided who Harold could play with, and when. For some reason she wanted to distinguish him from the other boys – he was the one who always wore a tie when the others were allowed to dress more casually. His sister Pauline was seven years older, his brother Clive, four years his junior, but in his mother's eyes, Harold

'VERA WAS FRIENDLY ENOUGH, BUT SHE REALLY DID SEE HER FAMILY AS SUPERIOR TO THE REST OF US. NOT ONLY THAT, YOU COULD TELL HAROLD (FREDDY) WAS HER FAVOURITE — THE ONE SHE SAW AS THE MOST PROMISING OF HER THREE CHILDREN.'

was the one she held the most hope for.

Shipman was comparatively bright in his early school years, but rather mediocre when he reached upper school level. Nonetheless, he was a plodder determined to succeed, even down to re-sitting his entrance examinations for medical school.

Funnily enough, he had every opportunity to be part of the group – he was an accomplished athlete on the football field and the running track. In spite of this, his belief in his superiority appears to have prevented him from forming any meaningful friendships.

There was something else that isolated him from the group – his beloved mother had terminal lung cancer. As her condition deteriorated, Harold willingly played a major supportive role.

WATCHING VERA DIE

Shipman's behaviour in his mother's final months closely paralleled that of Shipman the serial killer. Every day after classes, he would hurry home, make Vera a cup of tea and chat with

Above: *Dr Shipman's surgery in Hyde, Greater Manchester*

her. She found great solace in his company and always eagerly awaited his return. This is probably where Shipman learned the endearing bedside manner he would later adopt in his practice as a family physician. Towards the end, Vera experienced severe pain, but, because pumps to self-administer painkillers did not exist at that time, Vera's sole relief from the agony of cancer came with the family physician.

No doubt young Harold watched in fascination as his mother's distress miraculously subsided whenever the family doctor injected her with morphine. Ms. Shipman grew thinner and frailer day by day, until on June 21, 1963, the cancer claimed her life. Harold felt a tremendous sense of loss following his mother's death. After all, she was the one who made him feel special, different from the rest. Her passing also left him with an indelible image – the patient with a cup of tea nearby, finding sweet relief in morphine.

This must have made a great impact on the 17-year-old, as it was a scene he would recreate hundreds of times in the future once he became a doctor – with no regard for human life or feeling.

HAROLD THE STUDENT

Two years after his mother died, Harold Shipman was finally admitted to Leeds University medical school. Getting in had been a struggle – he'd had to re-write the exams he'd failed first time around. His grades, however, were sufficient enough for him to collect a degree and serve his mandatory hospital internship.

It is surprising to learn that so many of his teachers and fellow students can barely remember Shipman. Those who do remember claim that he looked down on them and seemed bemused by the way most young men behaved. 'It was as if he tolerated us. If someone told a joke he would smile patiently, but Fred never wanted to join in. It

seems funny, because I later heard he'd been a good athlete, so you'd have thought he'd be more of a team player.' He was simply remembered as a loner. The one place his personality changed, however, was the football field. Here, he unleashed his aggression and his dedication to win was intense.

Shipman finally found companionship in a girl, Primrose, who was three years his junior. He married her when he was only nineteen years old.

Above: *Primrose, Shipman's wife.*

Primrose's background was similar to Fred's, whereby her mother restricted her friendships and controlled her activities. Being rather a plain girl, Primrose was delighted to have finally found a boyfriend. Shipman married her when she was only seventeen and 5 months pregnant.

By 1974 he was a father of two and had joined a medical practice in the Yorkshire town of Todmorden. At this stage in his life Fred seemed to undergo a transformation. He became an outgoing, respected member of the community in the eyes of his fellow medics and patients.

But the staff in the medical offices where he worked saw a different side of the young practitioner. He had a way of getting things done his way – even with the more experienced doctors in the practice.

ADDICTION

His career in Tod-morden came to a sudden halt when he started having blackouts. His part-ners were devas-tated when he gave them the reason – epilepsy. He used this faulty diagnosis as a cover-up. The truth soon came to the surface, when the practice recep-tionist Marjorie Walker came across some disturbing en-tries in a druggist's controlled narcotics ledger. These records showed how Ship-man had been pre-scribing large and frequent amounts of pethidine in the names of several of his patients, when in fact the pethidine had found its way into the doctor's very own veins.

Not only that, he'd also written numerous prescriptions for the drug on behalf of the practice. Although this was not unusual because drugs were kept for emergencies, the prescribed amounts were excessive.

Following the discovery of Ship-man's over-prescribing, an investi-gation by the practice uncovered the fact that many patients on the prescription list had neither required nor received the drug.

When confronted in a staff meeting, Shipman's way of dealing with the problem was to provide an insight into his true personality. Realizing his

SHIPMAN WAS CHALLENGED IN A STAFF MEETING. THEY PUT BEFORE HIM EVIDENCE THAT HE HAD BEEN PRESCRIBING PETHIDINE TO PATIENTS, THAT THEY'D NEVER RECEIVED THE PETHIDINE, AND IN FACT THE PETHIDINE HAD FOUND ITS WAY INTO HIS VERY OWN VEINS.

career was on the line, he first begged for a second chance.

When this request was denied, he became furious and stormed out, threw his medical bag to the ground and threatened to resign. The partners were dumbfounded by this violent – and seem-ingly uncharac-teristic – behaviour.

Soon afterwards, his wife Primrose stormed into the room where his peers were discus-sing the best way to dismiss him. Rude-ly, she informed the people at the meet-ing that her husband would never resign, proclaiming, 'You'll have to force him out!'

And this was exactly what they had to do. They forced him out of the practice and into a drug rehabilitation centre in 1975.

Two years later, his many convic-tions for drug offences, prescription fraud and forgery cost him a surprisingly low fine – just over £600. Shipman's conviction for forgery is worth noting, because he was to use this skill later when faking signatures on a patently counterfeit will – that of his last victim, Katherine Grundy.

BACK TO WORK

Today, it is unlikely Harold Shipman would be allowed to handle drugs unsupervised, given his previous track record. However, within two years, he was back in business as a general practitioner in the Donneybrook Medical Centre in Hyde in the north of England. How readily he was accepted demonstrates his absolute self-confidence – and his ability to convince his peers of his sincerity. Again, he played the role of a dedicated, hardworking and community-minded doctor. He gained his patients' absolute trust and earned his colleagues' respect, but perhaps he was not watched carefully enough. In Hyde, Harold Shipman was home free – and free to kill!

A DIARY OF DEATH

Because of the nature of the Shipman case, it may never be possible to document every murder he committed, but it is estimated that he is responsible for the deaths of at least 236 patients over a 24-year period.

KATHLEEN GRUNDY, 81 (RIGHT)

A former mayoress of Hyde and the last victim, Mrs Grundy died on June 24 1998. She was found fully clothed on a settee at home. Dr Shipman killed her with a heroin overdose on a visit to take a blood sample. He has also been found guilty of forging her will and two letters to secure her £386,000 estate, as well as altering his medical records to suggest that the widow was addicted to morphine.

JEAN LILLEY, 58

Mrs Lilley was visited by Dr Shipman on the morning of her death on April 25, 1997. A neighbour became increasingly concerned about the length of time that the GP had been with Mrs Lilley, who was suffering from a cold. She found her friend's body within moments of the doctor leaving her home. An ambulance crew later said Mrs Lilley had been dead for some time, killed by a lethal dose of morphine. She was the only one of the 15 victims to have been married at the time of her death. Shipman contacted her husband by mobile phone to tell him his wife had died.

MARIE WEST, 81

On March 6, 1995, Harold Shipman injected Mrs West, his first victim, with a fatal dose of diamorphine (the medical term for heroine), unaware that her friend was in the next room. Shipman first told Mrs West's son that she had died of a massive stroke, then said it was a heart attack. Mrs West ran a clothes shop in Hyde, a suburb of Manchester, where all the victims came from.

IRENE TURNER, 67

Mrs Turner was found dead fully clothed on her bed by her neighbour, after Dr Shipman had called at Mrs Turner's house on July 11, 1996. Earlier, he had asked the neighbour if she could help pack Mrs Turner's belongings for hospital, but told her to wait for a few minutes before going over. Morphine was later found in Mrs Turner's body.

KATHLEEN WAGSTAFF, 81

Shipman confused Mrs Wagstaff with another patient, Anne Royal, whose daughter was married to Kathleen's son Peter, and called on the wrong person on December 9 1997 to announce she had died. Harold Shipman visited Angela Wagstaff at her workplace to tell her her mother had died, but the dead woman was in fact her mother-in-law Kathleen. After injecting Mrs Wagstaff with morphine, Shipman put her death down to heart disease.

BIANKA POMFRET, 49 (RIGHT)

Mrs Pomfret, a German divorcee, was found dead at her home by her son William on the same day she had been visited by Shipman, on December 10, 1997. Excessive morphine levels were found in her body, but the GP claimed Mrs Pomfret had complained to him of chest pains on the day of her death. He fabricated a false medical history to cover his tracks after killing her.

LIZZIE ADAMS, 77

Mrs Adams, a retired sewing machinist, died at home on February 28 1997. Dr Shipman stated that she had died of pneumonia and pretended to call for an ambulance, although no such call was made.

NORAH NUTTALL, 65

Mrs Nuttall, a widow, died on January 26 1998 after visiting Shipman's surgery for cough medicine. The GP later visited Mrs Nuttall at her home, where her son Anthony found his mother slumped in a chair.

MAUREEN WARD, 57

Mrs Ward, a former college lecturer, died on February 18 1998. Although she had been suffering from cancer, she was not ill at the time of her death. Dr Shipman claimed she died of a brain tumour.

WINIFRED MELLOR, 73

Mrs Mellor, a widow who had been Dr Shipman's patient for 18 years, was found dead on May 11 1998 in a chair at home with her left sleeve rolled up to suggest a heroin habit, following an earlier visit by Dr Shipman. He killed her with a fatal injection of morphine, and then returned to his surgery to create a false medical history to support a cause of death from coronary thrombosis.

JOAN MELIA, 73

Shipman murdered the divorcee on a visit to her home in Hyde on June 12 1998. She was found dead by a neighbour in her living room, having earlier visited Dr Shipman at his surgery about a chest infection. Shipman issued a death certificate stating she had died from pneumonia and emphysema. Her body, later exhumed, was found to contain morphine. The GP also claimed to have phoned for an ambulance, but didn't.

IVY LOMAS, 63

Dr Shipman killed Mrs Lomas at his surgery on May 29 1997 in Market Street, Hyde. He then saw three more patients before telling his receptionist that he had failed to resuscitate her. Morphine was later found in her body. She was such a regular there that Shipman told a police sergeant who was called after her death he thought her a nuisance. He joked that part of the seating area should be reserved for her and a plaque put up.

MURIEL GRIMSHAW, 76

Mrs Grimshaw was found dead at her home on July 14 1997. Shipman, who was called to examine her, said there was no need for a postmortem. Morphine was later found in her body.

MARIE QUINN, 67

Dr Shipman injected Mrs Quinn with morphine at her home on November 24 1997. Shipman claimed she had contacted him complaining of feeling unwell before her death. But her telephone bills showed no such call was made.

PAMELA HILLIER, 68

Shipman gave Mrs Hillier's family a confusing account of how she had died, on Feb 9 1998, saying she had high blood pressure, but that it wasn't high enough to give him major concern, although she had died from high blood pressure. He had in fact given her a lethal dose of morphine.

ANGELA WOODRUFF

In this macabre and still unfinished story, Shipman's former patients are grateful indeed he was finally stopped. The feeling that they could have been next will always haunt them, and there is little doubt that some owe their lives to a determined and intelligent woman named Angela Woodruff.

This lady's dogged determination to solve a mystery helped ensure that, on Monday, January 31, 2000, the jury at Preston Crown Court found Shipman guilty of murdering 15 of his patients and forging the will of Angela's beloved mother, Katherine Grundy.

Following her mother's burial Ms. Woodruff returned to her home, where she received a troubling phone call from solicitors. They claimed to have a copy of Ms. Grundy's will.

A solicitor herself, Angela's own firm had always handled her mother's affairs, in fact her firm held the original document lodged in 1986. The moment she saw the badly typed, poorly worded paper, Angela Woodruff knew it was a fake. It left £386,000 to Dr Shipman.

It was at this time that Angela went to her local police. Her investigation results ultimately reached Detective Superintendent Bernard Postles. His own investigation convinced him Angela Woodruff's conclusions were accurate.

THE TRIAL BEGINS

To get solid proof of Kathleen Grundy's murder, a post mortem was required which, in turn, required an exhumation order from the coroner. By the time the trial had begun, Det. Supt Postles' team would be uncomfortably familiar with the process. Of the fifteen killed, nine were buried and six cremated. Katherine Grundy's was the first grave opened. Her body was the first of the ongoing post mortems. Her tissue and hair samples were sent to different labs for analysis, and the wait for results began.

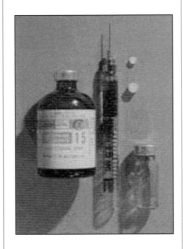

IT WAS DISCOVERED THAT THE MORPHINE LEVELS IN THE DEAD WOMAN'S BODY WOULD UNDOUBTEDLY HAVE BEEN THE CAUSE OF DEATH.

At the same time, police raided the doctor's home and offices. It was timed so that Shipman had no chance of learning a body had been exhumed for a post mortem. Police had to be certain no evidence could be destroyed or concealed before their search. When the police arrived, Shipman showed no surprise; his approach was one of arrogance and contempt as the search warrant was read out.

One item crucial to police investigations was the typewriter used to type the bogus will. Shipman produced an old Brother manual portable, telling an improbable tale of how Ms Grundy sometimes borrowed it. This unbelievable story was to go against Shipman – especially when forensic scientists confirmed it was the machine used to type the counterfeit will and other such fraudulent documents.

The search of his house also yielded medical records, some mysterious jewellery and a surprise. The Shipman home was littered with filthy clothes, old newspapers and, for a doctor's home, it was nothing short of unsanitary. But an even bigger surprise was due.

When toxicologist Julie Evans filed her report on the cause of Ms Grundy's death, Det. Supt Postles was astounded. It was discovered that the morphine level in the dead woman's body would undoubtedly have been the cause of death. Not only that, her death would have occurred within three hours of having received the fatal overdose.

Shipman would claim later that the stylish and conservative old lady was a junkie. Even today psychologists speculate on the possibility that he wanted to be caught. Otherwise, why would he hand them the typewriter and use a drug so easily traced back to him? Others believe he saw himself as invincible, believing that, as a doctor, his word would never be questioned.

The detective realized the case went far beyond one death, and the scope of the investigation was broadened immediately.

THE VERDICT AND SENTENCE

The outcome of all the tests carried out was consistent. In case after case, it was proved that the victims had not died from old age or natural disease. Typically, morphine toxicity was the cause of death.

It took the judge, Mr. Justice Forbes, two weeks to meticulously dissect the evidence heard by the jury. He urged caution, noting that no witness had actually seen Shipman kill, and he also urged the jurors to use common sense in arriving at their verdict.

At 4:43 pm on Monday January 31, 2000, the foreman declared all the jury's verdicts were unanimous – they found Shipman GUILTY on 15 counts of murder and one of forgery.

THE SHIPMAN LETTERS WERE WRITTEN BETWEEN SEPTEMBER 1998 WHEN HE WAS FIRST ON REMAND, AND JANUARY 2000 WHEN HE KNEW HIS TRIAL DEFENCE WAS DOOMED – THESE INTIMATE LETTERS ARE THE ONLY INSIGHT TO THE TRUE THOUGHTS OF DOCTOR DEATH.

Judge Justice Forbes presided in Shipman's trial .

The disgraced doctor stood motionless showing no sign of emotion as he heard the jurors' verdicts read. Wearing black, Shipman's wife, Primrose, also remained impassive. Her boys – one beside her and the other seated behind – looked down and seemed to visibly shrink on hearing the results.

In the public gallery, some gasped as Shipman's previous forgeries were described. The defence counsel asked that sentence be passed immediately.

The judge passed fifteen life sentences for the murders and a four-year sentence for forgery.

Then the Judge broke with the tradition that usually involves writing to the Home Secretary about his recommendations on length of the sentence:

'In the ordinary way, I would not do this in open court, but in your case I am satisfied justice demands that I make my views known at the conclusion of this trial . . . My recommendation will be that you spend the remainder of your days in prison.'

Fifteen murders, a mere fraction of the suspected death toll, had been dealt with and the fifty-seven day trial was over. But there was one last life for Shipman to take.

At 6.20 a.m. on Tuesday January 13, 2004, Harold Shipman was found hanging from the window bars in his cell in Wakefield Prison by a ligature made of bed sheets. Staff at the prison tried to revive him but he was pronounced dead at 8.10 a.m.

As Shipman died before his 60th birthday, his widow, Primrose, will receive a pension of £10,000 per year, and a tax-free lump sum reported to be in excess of £100,000. Had he died after 60, the pension would have been halved, with no additional sum. This, it is believed, is the reason for his suicide.

Within hours of his suicide, the word "justice" had been graffitied 12 times across his former Hyde surgery.

TED BUNDY
The Charmer

Serial killer Ted Bundy terrorized young women throughout various American states and claimed the lives of many young women in vicious sexual assaults and killings. Ted Bundy is estimated to have murdered between 35 to 50 young women in almost a dozen states.

As a youth, Ted was terribly shy and was often teased and bullied in his junior high school. Despite this he was able to maintain a high grade average that would continue throughout high school and later into college. Ted was more popular in high school than he was in junior high. Although he was very shy, Ted was thought of as being well dressed and exceptionally well mannered . He was not known to have dated anyone during this period, it seemed his interests lay elsewhere such as in skiing and politics. In fact, it was in high school that Ted's interest in politics began to bloom.

Ted graduated from high school in 1965 and won a scholarship to the University of Puget Sound. In 1966 he transferred to the University of Washington, where he began his intensive studies in Chinese. He worked his way through the university by taking on low-level jobs such as a bus boy and shoe clerk. It was in the spring of 1967, when he began a relationship, that would change his life forever.

Stephanie Brooks was everything

TED WAS A MAN WITH A MISSION AND MOST IMPORTANTLY HE WANTED TO IMPRESS STEPHANIE. HE RE-ENROLLED AT THE UNIVERSITY OF WASHINGTON AND STUDIED PSYCHOLOGY, A SUBJECT IN WHICH HE EXCELLED. BUNDY BECAME AN HONOURS STUDENT AND WAS WELL LIKED BY HIS PROFESSORS AT THE UNIVERSITY.

Ted had ever dreamed of in a woman. She was a beautiful and highly sophisticated woman from a wealthy Californian family. Although they had many differences, they both loved to ski and it was during their many ski trips together that they began to fall in love. Stephanie was Ted's first love and they spent a lot of time together. However, Stephanie was not as infatuated with Ted as he was with her. She believed that he had no real direction or future goals and it appeared she wanted someone who would fit in with her lifestyle. Ted tried too hard to impress her, even if that meant lying, something that she didn't like at all.

In 1968, after graduating from the University of Washington, Stephanie broke off relations with Ted. Ted never recovered from the break-up. Nothing, including school, seemed to hold any interest for him and he eventually dropped out, dumb-founded and depressed over the break-up. Ted was totally obsessed with Stephanie and he couldn't get her out of his mind. It was an obsession that would span his lifetime and lead to a series of events that would shock the world.

A TIME OF CHANGE

Ted re-enrolled at the University of Washington, to study psychology. It was at this time that he met Meg Anders, a woman with whom he would be involved with for almost five years. Meg worked as a secretary and was a somewhat shy and quiet woman. She was a divorcee who seemed to have found the perfect father figure for her daughter in Ted Bundy. Meg was deeply in love with Ted from the start and wanted to one day marry him. She was totally unaware of the infatuation that he still held for Stephanie. Ted, however, was not yet ready for marriage because he felt there was still too much for him to accomplish.

Outwardly, Ted's life seemed to be changing for the better. He was more confident with high hopes for his future. Ted began sending out applications for various law schools, while at the same time he became active in politics. He worked on a campaign to re-elect a Washington governor, a position that allowed Ted to form bonds with politically powerful people in the Republican Party. Ted also did some voluntary work at a crisis clinic on a work-study programme. He was pleased with the path his life was taking at this time, everything seemed to be going in the right direction. He was even commended by the Seattle police for saving the life of a three-year-old boy who was drowning in a lake.

In 1973, during a business trip to California for the Washington Republican Party, Ted met up with his old flame Stephanie Brooks for a night out. Stephanie was amazed at the transformation in Ted. He was much more confident and mature. They met several times, unknown to Meg. During Ted's business trips he romantically courted Stephanie and she once again fell in love with him.

Ted raised the subject of marriage many times during that autumn and winter. But suddenly it all changed. Where once Ted lavished affection upon Stephanie, he was suddenly cold and despondent. It seemed as if Ted had lost all interest in her over the period of just a few weeks. Stephanie was undoubtedly confused as to the sudden change in Ted. In February 1974, with no warning or explanation Ted ended all contact with Stephanie. His plan of revenge worked. He rejected Stephanie as she had once rejected him. Stephanie was never to see or hear from Ted again.

A TIME OF TERROR

On December 6, 1973, a young couple stumbled across the remains of a 15-year-old girl in McKenny Park, Washington. Kathy Devine was last seen by friends on November 25, hitch-hiking to Oregon, trying to run away from home. Shortly after she began her journey Kathy met her death. She had been strangled, sodomized and her throat cut. A month after the discovery of the Devine girl came the attack of Joni Lenz, which was soon followed by an even more gruesome attack.

Left: *Lynda Ann Healy*

Lynda Ann Healy didn't show up for work or for dinner on January 31, 1974. Healy's parents immediately called the police and soon after their arrival, they discovered a mass of blood drenching Lynda Ann's mattress. They also found a nightdress close to the bed with blood on the collar.

During that spring and summer, seven more women students suddenly and inexplicably vanished within the states of Utah, Oregon and Washington. There were striking similarities among many of the cases – all the girls were white, thin, single and wearing slacks, had long hair parted in the middle, and they all disappeared in the evening. Police interviews of college students revealed that they had seen a strange man wearing a cast on either his arm or leg. Others reported a strange man in the campus car park who had a cast and asked for assistance with his car. A man wearing a cast was also spotted in the same area where two of the girls mysteriously disappeared.

Finally, in August of 1974 in Lake Sammamish State Park, Washington State, the remains of some of the

SHE WAS NOT ASLEEP, AS HER ROOMMATES HAD THOUGHT WHEN THEY APPROACHED THE BED OF JONI LENZ ON THE AFTERNOON OF JANUARY 4, 1974. THEY FOUND HER LYING IN A POOL OF BLOOD THAT WAS SEEPING FROM HER HEAD AND FACE.

missing girls were found and two were later identified. It was remarkable that police were able to identify two of the bodies considering what was left. The girls identified were Janice Ott and Denise Naslund who disappeared on the same day, July 14th.

The similarities between the Washington State and Oregon murders caught the attention of local police in Utah, who were frantically searching for the man responsible for these awful crimes. The evidence was slowly mounting and Utah police consulted with Oregon and Washington State investigators. Almost all agreed that it was highly likely that the same man who committed the crimes in Oregon and Washington State had been responsible for the killings in Utah.

When Lynn Banks, a close friend of Meg Anders, saw the account of Melissa Smith's murder in the paper and the composite picture in the paper of the could-be-killer, she knew Ted Bundy must be the man. Meg also had to agree that the sketch of the killer did resemble Ted, yet she couldn't believe the man she loved and lived with could do such horrible things. Hesitantly, she contacted the police on the advice of her friend. Meg was one of five people to have turned in Ted Bundy's name to police. Her report, along with the others, was filed away and forgotten until a few years later. Police were so inundated with tips that when they came to Ted Bundy, an apparently respectable man, they set him aside to investigate other more likely suspects.

It wasn't until November 8, 1974, that police investigators were to get the break in the case for which they had been waiting.

CAROL DARONCH

One rainy night in November 1974, Carol DaRonch was window-shopping in Salt Lake City, Utah when she was approached by a man in his twenties who said he was a policeman. He asked her if she had left her car in the car park and asked for her registration number.

The plain-clothes policeman said a man had been arrested for trying to break into her car and asked if she could come and see if anything had been stolen. But she became suspicious as they walked to the car park because he did not seem to know the way.

The 17-year-old then asked him for proof of his identity and he produced his wallet and showed her what appeared to be a police badge. When they got to the car – and found nothing stolen – he asked her to accompany him to police headquarters to make a statement. He led the way to his own car, an old Volkswagen Beetle, and she

Above: *Ted Bundy drove around in a Volkswagen Beetle and used such ruses as feigning a broken arm to seek help from women. He would then lead his victims into his car and to their death.*

became suspicious again and asked for his name. The man said he was Officer Roseland of the Murray Police Department. He was so convincing that she got into the Beetle and they drove off.

A LUCKY ESCAPE

She began to panic when she smelt alcohol on his breath and realised he was driving in the opposite direction to the police station. When he stopped briefly in a side street, she reached for the door handle and tried to get out. But he was too quick for her and he snapped a handcuff on one wrist but was unable to secure the other one.

She continued to struggle and he pulled out a gun and threatened to shoot her. Then Carol's instincts took over – she pulled the door open, clambered out and began to run. The man began chasing her, but he stopped when a car turned into the street. He got back in his VW and sped off.

Carol had been lucky, but Bundy was determined to claim a victim. Later that night he abducted and murdered 17-year-old Debbie Kent. And she would not be the last of his victims . . .

Bundy's first victim was Lynda Healy, 21, a psychology student at the University of Washington in Seattle, who was abducted from her basement flat.

Five more young women vanished from the Seattle area in the spring and summer of 1974, but the case did not merit national newspaper headlines until July, when two girls disappeared from Lake Sammamish State Park on the same day.

SEATTLE

It had been a sunny day and the park, 12 miles from downtown Seattle, had been crowded with people walking their dogs, sailing boats and enjoying picnics. Several women reported having seen a man, calling himself Ted, with an arm in a sling. He had been asking for help with his boat. Doris Grayling had accompanied him to his

ONE OF THE MOST FEARED SERIAL KILLERS IN AMERICAN HISTORY, TED BUNDY WAS KNOWN IN SOME CIRCLES AS 'THE CHARMER' DUE TO HIS POLITE AND WELL-SPOKEN MANNER.

BUNDY NEARLY ESCAPED DEATH BY THE CHAIR WHEN IT WAS DISCOVERED THAT HE WAS A MANIC-DEPRESSIVE, BUT IN THE END, NOT EVEN THAT COULD SAVE HIM FROM EXECUTION.

brown VW, but then became suspicious and left.

Two other women, however, Janice Ott, 23, and Denise Naslund, 19, must have fallen for Bundy's trick, and they were never seen alive again. The double murder struck terror into women in Seattle but Bundy, having finished his psychology degree, was about to leave the city and move to Salt Lake City to study law.

It wouldn't be long before Bundy continued his murder spree. In October, he claimed his first Utah victim. Three more killings followed that first murder and another happened in the ski resort of Snowmass in neighbouring Colorado.

DISCOVERED BY CHANCE

In the early hours of August 16, 1975, Bundy was stopped while driving without lights in a Salt Lake City suburb. Bundy's evasive answers fuelled the suspicions of Utah Highway Patrolman Bob Hayward, who soon discovered a balaclava, a stocking mask, an iron bar and a pair of handcuffs on the floor of the car.

Bundy was arrested but he remained cool under pressure and explained away the items, saying he needed the balaclava and mask for skiing and had found the handcuffs in a rubbish bin. A search of Bundy's flat uncovered a brochure from a hotel in Snowmass.

Bundy denied having been to Colorado but by now the police were beginning to see through his harmless, self-confident exterior. Bundy was ordered to attend an identity parade and was picked out by Carol DaRonch and two other witnesses. It seemed that Ted Bundy had been caught.

He was convicted of the aggravated kidnapping of Carol DaRonch and was jailed for 15 years. In June 1977 he jumped out of the window of a court building and escaped, only to be recaptured eight days later. The authorities in Colorado were confident they could put him on trial for the murder of Caryn Campbell, the girl who was killed in Snowmass at the height of the skiing season.

But in December 1977 Bundy escaped again – this time by cutting a hole in the ceiling of his cell with a hacksaw blade and this time he would not be caught so easily.

BUNDY ON THE RUN

Bundy fled east and by mid-January was in sunny Florida, 1,500 miles from chilly Colorado. By now he had adopted a new identity. Bundy was no longer the dapper, mild-mannered Republican, he had become an unkempt fugitive from justice, whose murderous urges were out of control.

On January 15 he broke into a sorority house on a university campus in Tallahassee, Florida. He strangled 21-year-old art history student Margaret Brown and beat to death Lisa Levy, 20, after assaulting her. Two other girls who lived in the house had also been beaten with a wooden club but they survived.

A month later Bundy claimed what would be his final victim, 12-year-old Kim Leach. She was abducted from a high school gym, sexually assaulted and strangled. Bundy's days as a free man were, however, numbered.

RECAPTURED

Bundy was finally arrested in the early hours of February 15, 1978, as he drove a stolen car, an orange VW, towards Pensacola, and in June 1979, he went on trial for the sorority house murders. Bundy protested his innocence and conducted his own defence.

The evidence for the prosecution - including evidence from a dentist that his teeth matched bite marks found on Lisa Levy – was overwhelming and the jury found him guilty, sentencing him to death.

Bundy spent the next ten years on Florida's Death Row, using legal tactics to delay his execution and offering confessions to his crimes in exchange for a

reprieve. After years of living in denial – insisting his innocence – Bundy finally confessed to the murders of 28 women. However, many believe the number of deaths to be much higher.

No one will ever really know how many women fell victim to Ted Bundy; it would be a number he would take to his grave. After countless appeals, Ted was finally executed on January 24, 1989.

Above: *Theodore R. Bundy (right) is taken from a Pensacola jail by Pensacola police Captain Raymond Harper, following his arrest on February 15, 1978 for driving a stolen car.*

DONALD NEILSON
The Black Panther

For three years police pursued a man who committed sixteen robberies and four murders and terrorized a large part of England. But the real Donald Neilson was very far from the hooded 'Black Panther' image of popular imagination

O n the evening of 13 January 1975, seventeen-year-old Lesley Whittle was at home alone and went to bed early. She lived with her widowed mother, but on this particular night Mrs Dorothy Whittle was out for the evening. When she did return to her comfortable home in the village of Highley, Shropshire at 1.30a.m., Mrs Whittle made a point of checking her daughter's bedroom. Lesley was sound asleep.

HOODED FIGURE CLAD IN BLACK

Shortly after Mrs Whittle herself retired to bed, a man forced the lock on the garage door. He was dressed from head to foot in black and was wearing a hood. Working silently and in total darkness, the intruder cut the telephone line and then moved into the house. Passing through the living room, he climbed the stairs and made his way directly to Lesley's room.

Lesley Whittle was woken by a hand shaking her roughly. She looked up to see the black-clad figure standing over her, pointing a sawn-off shotgun in her face. Lesley lay transfixed as the intruder taped her mouth, and indicated that she should get out of bed. He led Lesley downstairs and outside to a waiting car, a green Morris 1300. He laid her on the back seat, bound her wrists and ankles and placed tape over her eyes.

The intruder then removed his hood, got into the driving seat and set off on a sixty-mile trip to his hiding place. He drove down the M6 motorway, turned off at Junction 16 and drove to Bathpool Park, near Kidsgrove. He parked the car alongside the access shaft of the town's drainage system, removed the manhole cover and forced Lesley to climb 65 feet down a rusty ladder.

When they reached a tiny platform, on which he had installed a foam rubber mattress, the kidnapper removed Lesley's dressing gown, placed a wire noose around her neck and clamped it to the wall. Below, the access shaft fell away. If Lesley were to slip she would hang.

The kidnapper then made his next move in an elaborate plan to extort money from his victim's family. He

Above: *Lesley Whittle's disappearance prompted a nation-wide hunt.*

Opposite: *The Black Panther. A model dressed in the outfit adopted by Donald Neilson.*

uncovered Lesley's eyes, proffered a memo machine, and instructed her to read two messages which he had written on a pad.

Lesley did not know her kidnapper. She had never laid eyes on him before in her life. His name was Donald Neilson.

The name would have meant nothing to her. It would have meant little to the police either, even though they had been chasing him for more than three years, during which time he had been responsible for armed robberies and the murder of three sub-postmasters. Yet they only knew him by a nickname.

No one knew it yet, but Lesley Whittle had been kidnapped by the 'Black Panther'.

HOAXES AND MISTAKES

On the morning of 14 January, Mrs Dorothy Whittle woke to find her daughter missing. She was more puzzled than alarmed. Lesley had been safely tucked up in her bed at 1.30. Nothing bad could have happened to her since then. Mrs Whittle checked round the house and then tried to telephone her son, Ronald.

The phone, of course, had been cut. But, assuming it was merely out of order, Dorothy Whittle drove to her son's house at the other end of the village.

Neither Ronald nor his wife Gaynor had seen Lesley that morning. Mrs Whittle was now becoming uneasy.

Gaynor drove back home with Mrs Whittle, and the two women checked the house more carefully in the hope of finding a note. They found a note all right, but it wasn't from Lesley.

In a cardboard box, resting on a flower vase in the lounge, they discovered a long roll of Dymo tape. There were three messages carefully typed into the coloured plastic. The messages were ransom demands.

The first read: 'No police £50,000 ransom to be ready to deliver wait for phone call at Swan shopping centre telephone box 6 p.m. to 1 a.m. if no call return following evening when you answer give your name only and listen you must follow instructions without argument from the time you answer you are on a time limit if police or tricks death.'

Above: *The access shaft to the sewer system at Bathpool Park where Neilson held, and finally murdered, Lesley Whittle.*

Despite the warning in the note, Mrs Whittle did not hesitate to call the police. Within an hour the case was being led by the head of West Mercia CID, Detective Chief Superintendent Bob Booth.

He was in no doubt that this was a professional kidnapping. Lesley was a logical target. Two years earlier she had been the beneficiary of a large and highly publicized inheritance.

Booth advised the Whittle family that their best chance of getting Lesley back alive was to comply fully with the kidnapper's demands.

While Ronald Whittle, who owned a successful coach company, was raising the money, Booth had his own elaborate arrangements to make. He installed taps on the phones at Mrs Whittle's home and the phone box at Kidderminster.

After midday, Booth and his detectives were joined by a team of kidnap specialists from Scotland Yard.

Shortly after 5p.m. Ronald Whittle, armed with a white suitcase full of money, installed himself in the phone box at Kidderminster, and waited.

The police, who were watching Whittle from a discreet distance, hoped to have the whole episode dealt with that night, but it was not to be. A freelance journalist had somehow got wind of the operation and started making a nuisance of himself.

Rather than alerting the kidnapper to the fact that the police were indeed involved, Booth decided to abort the mission.

The following evening, Ronald Whittle returned to the phone box with the money. Shortly after 8 p.m., the police called him out again. They had received a call from a man claiming to be the kidnapper and had been given delivery instructions for the ransom money. The call, however, proved to be a hoax.

Meanwhile, another drama was unfolding. Donald Neilson left his hideout in the drains of Bathpool Park and did a dummy run of the route he had mapped out for the ransom carrier. He travelled to Dudley in Worcestershire, stopping at various telephone boxes to conceal more Dymo tape instructions.

In Dudley itself, he decided to check over the final drop-off point, the Freightliner depot. He was browsing around when he was challenged by the night supervisor, Gerald Smith.

Neilson shot Smith six times. He then ran from the scene, abandoning his stolen Morris car.

When local police investigated the shooting, they failed to check the car. This was a tragic oversight, because the boot of the car was a positive treasure trove of clues.

Amazingly, Gerald Smith survived the shooting – though he died fourteen months later as a result of his wounds – and was able to give the police a description of his assailant. What he told them left police in no doubt that he was the victim of the 'Black Panther'.

At 11.45 p.m. on the night of 16 January, the third day of the kidnap,

Leonard Rudd, transport manager of Whittle's Coaches, received a telephone call. On the other end of the line was Lesley Whittle's recorded voice instructing the courier to take the ransom money to a phone box at Kidsgrove.

Ronald Whittle was extensively briefed by Detective Chief Superintendent Lovejoy of Scotland Yard.

Whittle reached the Kidsgrove telephone box shortly after 3 a.m., and waited there for half an hour before discovering another Dymo message. It read: 'Go up road to Acres Nook sign. Go up Boathouse Road turn right into public footpath deadend go into entry service area. Drive past wall and flash headlights looking for torchlight run to torch instructions on torch. Go home wait for telephone.'

Below: *The boot of Neilson's Morris car yielded a host of clues for police.*

Ronald Whittle got back into his car and followed the directions. After a few minutes he arrived at Bathpool Park. He flashed his headlights and waited for the torch signal. It never came.

Donald Neilson had been watching as Ronald Whittle arrived, and was immediately suspicious. He could smell police.

Certain that he would never now get his hands on the ransom money, he flew into a rage. As soon as Whittle had left he climbed back down the drainage access shaft, pushed Lesley Whittle off her precarious platform and left her to hang by her neck until she died.

By dawn, he was on the train north to his home in Bradford.

VITAL NEW EVIDENCE

Most of Booth's and Lovejoy's efforts now centred around the village of Highly, where the abduction had taken place. Everyone in the village and the surrounding area was interviewed. But this revealed absolutely nothing.

And then, on 23 January, a week after the last abortive attempt to deliver the ransom money, a police constable patrolling the Freightliner depot at Dudley became interested in a green Morris 1300. He noticed it had been parked in the same spot for several days.

The car was towed into the police station and searched. The boot revealed startling new evidence. There were a tape recorder containing a tape of Lesley Whittle's voice, a gun, torches and a foam mattress. A ballistic examination of the gun confirmed that it had been used in the 'Black Panther' raids.

As the days passed, Detective Chief Superintendent Booth felt sure that Bathpool Park was probably the most important location they had encountered in their investigation, and he was determined to search it thoroughly. To this end, he planned an elaborate ruse.

On the evening of 5 March, Booth appeared on a television news programme with Ronald Whittle and the two men acted out a pre-rehearsed confrontation. Whittle described how he had gone to Bathpool Park on the night of 16 January. Booth, pretending this was

Above: *A press conference given by the police during the hunt for the 'Black Panther'.*

the first he had heard of the abortive rendezvous, flew into a rage and stormed out of the studio. The effect was to make Booth look extremely foolish. In fact, the deception gave him the excuse he had been looking for to search the park.

At dawn the following day, the police moved into Bathpool Park. At first their search yielded nothing. But then, two schoolboys came forward with a torch they had found there a few weeks earlier. Wrapped around the handle was a strip of Dymo tape which read: 'Drop suitcase into hole.'

On the next day, Friday, 7 March, Police Constable Paul Allen removed the manhole cover of the drainage system and climbed slowly down. He had descended about twenty feet when he paused and shone his torch downwards.

He was confronted with the grisly spectacle of Lesley Whittle's naked body, hanging from its wire noose.

UNITED AGAINST THE PANTHER

Up to this point, different teams of police had been working on 'Black Panther' murders in Accrington, Harrogate and Langley, as well as the team investigating the kidnap of Lesley Whittle. There had been close cooperation between the forces, but now it was decided to form a single 'Black Panther' task force under Scotland Yard's murder squad.

The murder squad took over Kidsgrove police station, and 800 officers were drafted in to interview every one of the town's 22,000 population.

In an attempt to solicit help from the public, a local actor was dressed in black and drove the green Morris along the route thought to have been taken by the Panther. The reconstruction was shown on national television and attracted more than a thousand phone calls. Scores of names were submitted but the name Donald Neilson was not among them.

Nine months passed, and the murder squad were no nearer identifying the 'Black Panther'.

On Thursday, 11 December, Donald Neilson finally obliged them. It was 11 p.m. and Constables Stuart McKenzie and Tony White were sitting in their Panda car in Mansfield Woodhouse, Nottingham, when they caught sight of a man with a hold-all loitering outside the Four Ways public house.

McKenzie did a U-turn and pulled up alongside Neilson. White got out of the car and asked him what his name was, and what he was doing. Neilson smiled, gave them a name and a local address, and said he was on his way home from work. Still suspicious, White asked him to write down his particulars.

Suddenly Neilson produced a sawn-off shotgun from under his coat. He forced White into the back seat of the Panda car and got into the front passenger seat himself. He instructed McKenzie to drive to Blidworth, a village six miles away.

As they drove, White in the back noticed the shotgun waver away from his partner's side. He lunged forward and grabbed the barrel of the gun. McKenzie slammed on the brakes; the shotgun went off, blowing a hole in the roof of the car.

The Panda screeched to a halt outside a fish and chip shop, which was still open. As the two constables wrestled with Neilson, two customers, Keith Wood and

Above: *Police sniffer dogs search for clues in the murder of Lesley Whittle.*

AS WHITE GRABBED THE GUN BARREL HIS PARTNER SLAMMED ON THE BRAKES - THE SHOTGUN BLEW A HOLE IN THE CAR ROOF

*Above: **The diminutive figure of Donald Neilson, head covered, is led away from the committal proceedings.***

THE JURY WATCHED IN OPEN-MOUTHED HORROR AS THE DEFENDANT RELATED HIS GHASTLY CRIMES IN MATTER-OF-FACT DETAIL

Roy Morris, rushed over to help.

Despite his diminutive stature, Neilson fought ferociously and it took all four of them to subdue him. A few minutes later, other police cars arrived on the scene. Donald Neilson was driven the 70 miles to Kidsgrove police station.

Neilson was questioned for twelve hours before he finally admitted to the abduction of Lesley Whittle.

The burning question for the police was, just who was this man Donald Neilson? For a man who had terrorized an entire region, he did not cut a very impressive figure – forty years old, 5 ft 4 ins tall, and slightly built.

Yet, over the previous ten years, he had committed more than four hundred robberies – sixteen on sub-post offices – and had killed four people. All this, and he had never so much as been questioned by police.

The secret of his 'success', the police were to discover, was discipline and meticulous planning, qualities he had developed courtesy of Her Majesty's armed forces. In 1955–7 Neilson had spent his National Service in the King's Own Yorkshire Light Infantry, where he rose to the rank of lance corporal and served in Kenya, Aden and Cyprus.

At the time of his arrest, Neilson lived a quiet life with his wife Irene and their fifteen-year-old daughter Kathryn at their terraced house on the outskirts of Bradford. He made a modest living as a jobbing carpenter and, according to his neighbours, had no enemies and few friends.

WHEN LIFE MEANS LIFE

The trial of Donald Neilson began on 14 August 1976 at Oxford Crown Court. In addition to the murder of Lesley Whittle, Neilson stood charged with the murder of three sub-postmasters – Donald Skepper of Harrogate, Derek Askin of Accrington and Sidney Gray-land of Langley – all of whom had been shot to death in 1974. He was defended by Gilbert Gray QC and entered a plea of Not Guilty to all four charges.

Neilson's behaviour in court was nothing short of extraordinary. He maintained his military posture throughout the trial, standing smartly to attention and answering questions with a brisk 'Yes, sir,' or 'No, sir'.

Neilson seemed to have the idea that by being calm, precise and matter-of-fact he could persuade the court that he was the victim of a ghastly misunderstanding. At no time did he show one iota of sadness or remorse.

When it came to the murder of the three sub-postmasters, Neilson again tried to portray himself as the victim of misfortune. On all three occasions, he claimed, the gun he was carrying had gone off accidentally.

All in all, it was one of the most feeble defences ever presented to a British criminal court, and the jury wasted no time in returning a verdict of Guilty on all charges.

Sentencing Donald Neilson to life imprisonment, Mr Justice Mars-Jones would not set a minimum number of years. 'In your case,' he said, 'life must mean life. If you are ever released from prison it should only be on account of great age or infirmity.'

CRIMES
OF
HORROR

PETER SUTCLIFFE
The Yorkshire Ripper

In the 1970s Yorkshire women were terrorized by a serial killer who, like the notorious Jack the Ripper, inflicted hideous mutilations on his victims. Was Peter Sutcliffe a paranoid schizophrenic, or just 'a wilfully evil bastard'?

L ate on the afternoon of 22 May 1981, a dark-haired, bearded, scruffy little man rose to his feet in the dock beneath the dome of Number One Court at the Old Bailey to hear judgement passed upon him.

Found guilty of murdering thirteen women, and attempting to murder seven others, thirty-five-year-old Peter William Sutcliffe, 'The Yorkshire Ripper', was sentenced to life imprisonment with a recommendation that he should serve at least thirty years.

AN ORDINARY MURDER

The Ripper murders began in 1975 in the rundown Chapeltown area of Leeds. A milkman spotted a frosted bundle of what appeared to be rags on the white-rimmed grass. He went and peered at it. It was a woman's body.

She lay on her back, her dyed blonde hair dark and spiky with dried blood. Her jacket and blouse had been torn open and her bra pulled up, revealing breasts and abdomen, and her trousers were round her knees, though her pants were still in position. Her torso had been stabbed and slashed fourteen times, after her death from two crushing hammer blows to the back of the skull.

The dead woman's name was Wilma McCann. She was twenty-eight years old, and what the police classed as a 'good time girl'. Because Mrs McCann's purse was missing, West Yorkshire Metropolitan Police treated the case as murder in the pursuance of robbery. Despite the brutality of the attack there seemed no other motive. Yet, when another murder was committed just over two and half months later, the similarities convinced the police that they were dealing with a double murderer.

ANOTHER GOOD TIME GIRL

Emily Jackson, like Wilma McCann, came to Chapeltown only once or twice a week to sell herself on a casual basis.

Her body was discovered in the early

> THE MILKMAN THOUGHT THE PILE OF RAGS WAS AN ABANDONED GUY FAWKES FIGURE – WHEN HE LOOKED, HE SAW IT WAS A WOMAN'S BODY

morning of 21 January 1976. She had also been killed from behind by two blows from a heavy hammer. Her breasts were exposed and her trousers pulled down, though again her pants were in place. On her right thigh was stamped the impression of a heavily ribbed wellington boot. The only solid clue the police had so far was that the perpetrator took size seven in shoes.

SERIAL KILLER ON THE LOOSE

No progress was made on either case, and a year passed by. Then, on 5 February, 1977, the killer struck again. Another 'good-time girl', twenty-eight-year-old Irene Richardson, was discovered by a jogger on Soldiers' Field, not far from Chapeltown. She was lying on her face and had died from three hammer blows to the back of her skull. Her killer had stripped her from the waist downwards. Her neck and chest had been subjected to a frenzied knife attack. The pattern of wounds now left no doubt that the police were dealing with a serial killer.

This alarmed the street-girl population, and their numbers in Chapeltown declined. Not so, however, in the red light district of Bradford, some ten miles away, where 'Tina' Atkinson lived and worked. On Sunday, 24 April, Tina's friends called for her at her flat, but got no answer. She had been out boozing the night before, and the door was ajar so they went in. Tina lay naked on her bed, the back of her head crushed by four hammer blows. Seven knife wounds had lacerated her stomach, and her side had been slashed open.

Any doubts about the killer's identity were dispelled by a clue found imprinted on the bottom bedsheet. It was the mark of a size seven wellington boot, identical with the imprint found on Emily Jackson's thigh.

The police believed that the killer was specifically targeting prostitutes and so began touring the red light districts, questioning street girls about any regulars who might have acted suspiciously. But, it soon became clear

Above: *Police examine the scene where Emily Jackson was murdered.*

IT WAS WOUNDED MALE PRIDE THAT HAD LED SUTCLIFFE TO CARRY OUT HIS FIRST 'REVENGE' ATTACK ON A PROSTITUTE

Below: *Assistant Chief Constable George Oldfield and Superintendent Richard Holland at a 'Ripper' press conference.*

that the Yorkshire Ripper regarded any woman out alone at night as fair game.

THE RIPPER SPREADS HIS NET

On Sunday, 26 June 1977, a sixteen-year-old girl named Jayne MacDonald was found slumped and dead in a street on the fringes of Chapeltown. She had sustained at least three hammer blows to the head. She had been stabbed once in the back and several times through the chest. But she was no prostitute or good-time girl. A fortnight later, a Bradford housewife, Maureen Long, was struck down near her home but

miraculously survived.

The police stepped up their enquiries. Three hundred and four officers were assigned to the case. And to hear them, veteran detective George Oldfield, Assistant Chief Constable (Crime), came out from behind his desk at administrative HQ in Wakefield.

The next time the Ripper struck he changed his location and killing pattern, but left a vital clue.

On 1 October 1977, Jean Bernadette Jordan, was picked up near her home in Moss Side, Manchester and driven by her murderer to the Southern Cemetery two miles away. She demanded £5 in advance and was paid with a crisp new note, which she stored in her purse.

As she climbed from the Ripper's car on to allotment land adjoining the large cemetery, Mrs Jordan was knocked to the ground with a hammer blow and beaten eleven times more. Then she was pulled into a clump of bushes.

Disturbed by a car, the killer then fled.

The £5 note had been given to Sutcliffe in his wage packet two days before the attack. He realized that it might be a valuable clue, so eight days later returned to the scene. He searched in vain for the handbag, then attacked

Below: *Police search the alley where the body of Barbara Leach was discovered.*

Bottom: *Police search for clues in their hunt for the Yorkshire Ripper.*

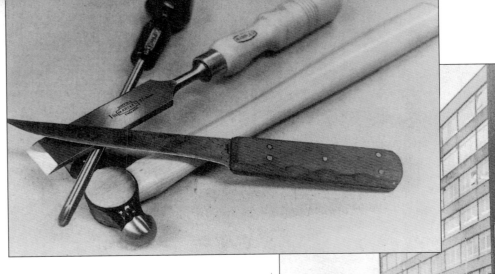

the decaying body with a shard of glass.

Two days after the second attack, Mrs Jordan's remains were discovered along with the missing handbag which had fallen among the bushes. The £5 note, serial number AW51 121565, was traced to the wage packets of the road haulage firm T. and W. H. Clark. One of their drivers was Peter Sutcliffe, who had worked there since October 1976.

LIVING VICTIMS

Detectives visited Sutcliffe at his home. He seemed a steady, quiet man, and the officers left, satisfied that he was not the Ripper.

But had they had time and reason to do so, they would have discovered from old Bradford City Police files that Peter Sutcliffe had once been questioned by police regarding an attack back in August 1969. This first attack was not quite motiveless. Earlier that summer he had suspected his girlfriend Sonia of seeing another man. To 'get even', he had approached a Bradford prostitute, but had been unable to maintain an erection. The woman had laughed at him, taken his £10, and got her pimp to chase him away.

In August he had seen her in the St Paul's red light district, crept after her, and hit her violently on the back of the head with a stone in a sock. The woman had noted the number of his van, and Sutcliffe had been traced. But because he had no record, he had been let off with a caution.

Since then he had left five women damaged but alive. Each of these living

*Above left: **Peter Sutcliffe's murder weapons could have been bought at any local hardware store.***

*Above: **The bus stop at Leeds' Arndale Shopping Centre where Jacqueline Hill was accosted and murdered by the Yorkshire Ripper.***

victims had tried to describe their attacker. One described him as thirtyish, about 5 ft 10 ins tall, and bearded. Another had described him accurately as having a black, crinkly beard.

On the evening of 21 January 1978, a twenty-two-year-old 'career' prostitute named Yvonne Pearson was seen in Bradford, climbing into a car driven by a man described as having a dark beard and black, piercing eyes - it was Sutcliffe. He took her to waste ground in Arthington Street, killed her with a club hammer and jumped on her chest until her ribs cracked. He then piled an old abandoned horsehair sofa on top of her. About a month later, when the body remained undiscovered, Sutcliffe returned and placed a current copy of *The Daily Mirror* under one of her mouldering arms. Between this killing and the newspaper incident he had also paid a visit to Huddersfield.

On the snowy night of Tuesday, 31 January 1978, Sutcliffe picked up Helen Rytka. They went into a timber yard under railway arches near the centre of the town and, uncharacteristically, Sutcliffe managed to have intercourse with her before killing her in his usual fashion.

Immediately after this murder, the police were optimistic. Helen's abduction had taken place in the early evening on a busy street. But despite tracing a hundred passers by, and with all but three cars and one man eliminated, there was no real result.

The police were convinced that the Ripper lived in the locality of Leeds or Bradford, but they little realized that, by the end of 1978, they had interviewed him no fewer than four times. Apart from two visits concerning the £5 note clue, they had called at his home because routine checks had turned up Sutcliffe's car registration in red light areas. They also called to check on tyre tracks to compare them with some found near the scene of Irene Richardson's murder.

But they did not check two vital clues they knew about the Ripper against

Sutcliffe. The Ripper was a B secretor – a rare blood type. And he took size seven boots – very small for a man.

On the night of 16 May 1978, two months after Yvonne Pearson's body was found, Sutcliffe killed Vera Millward, a forty-one-year-old prostitute. He then waited eleven months before he killed again. His next victim was nineteen-year-old Josephine Whittaker, a clerk in the Halifax Building Society headquarters. She was attacked and killed with sickeningly familiar ferocity.

TAUNTS AND HOAXES

Between Josephine's death and September of the same year there was another lull. This time it was filled by a brutal hoax which almost certainly cost

Above: *Peter and Sonia Sutcliffe's house in Garden Lane, Heston, Bradford.*

Obsessed with the 'Sunderland connection', the police disregarded one officer's deep suspicions of Sutcliffe

---

Left: *Police dig up Peter Sutcliffe's garden shortly after his arrest on suspicion of being the Yorkshire Ripper.*

three women their lives.

Since March 1978 George Oldfield had received two letters supposedly from the Ripper. Shortly before the Whittaker murder a third letter came, mentioning Vera Millward's death. All three letters were postmarked from Sunderland. On the third, traces of engineering oil, similar to traces found on Josephine Whittaker's body, were discovered. This seemed to confirm that the letters were written by the Ripper.

When, on 18 June 1979, a tape recording addressed in the same handwriting as the letters was received, West Yorkshire police were convinced that this was their man. The tape, a taunting message to Oldfield, was in a broad Geordie accent. Therefore, the West Yorkshire police became convinced that anyone without a

Geordie accent could be eliminated from their enquiry. This, of course, put Sutcliffe temporarily in the clear.

In July Sutcliffe was visited by Detective Constable Laptew, who had noticed that his car had been spotted in one red light area on thirty-six separate occasions. Laptew was deeply suspicious of Sutcliffe but he went unheeded by his superiors who were convinced their killer was a Geordie. As a result, Sutcliffe went on to kill three more times.

On 1 September 1979 Sutcliffe ambushed and killed a social sciences student named Barbara Leach.

On 18 August 1980 his victim was forty-seven-year-old civil servant Margaret Walls. Because she had been bludgeoned and strangled, but not mutilated further, the Ripper Squad were reluctant to add her to their list of

Below: *There was tight security as a crowd assembled to watch the arrival of Peter Sutcliffe at Dewsbury Magistrates' Court.*

Left: *Police help Sonia Sutcliffe as she enters Dewsbury Court for her husband's hearing.*

SUTCLIFFE CLAIMED THAT A VOICE IN A GRAVEYARD HAD ORDERED HIM TO GO OUT AND KILL PROSTITUTES

Below: *Peter Sutcliffe after being attacked in prison.*

victims. But there was no question of the authenticity of his thirteenth and final slaying.

Twenty-year-old Jacqueline Hill, a language student at Leeds University, was walking home when she was dragged by Sutcliffe on to waste land and savaged with a hammer, a knife and a screwdriver. This brutal death caused a backlash of frustration among the public and police.

The Home Office set up a 'super squad' of four outside detectives and a forensic scientist. The idea was that this team should review the evidence. They did make some progress, but eventually, it was by chance that Peter Sutcliffe was caught. On 2 January 1981, two police officers were cruising along Melbourne Avenue, Sheffield – a haunt of prostitutes – when they saw a girl getting into a Rover V8 3500. They stopped the driver, a short, bearded man, who gave his name as Peter Williams. It was discovered that his number plates were false and had been stolen from that town.

The bushes in Melbourne Avenue were searched, and officers found a ball-pen hammer and a knife, which eventually were to be matched to the Ripper's crimes. Then Sutcliffe finally confessed to the Dewsbury police. 'I'm glad it's all over. I would have killed that girl if I hadn't been caught.'

What made him do it? Some experts argued that he was a paranoid schizophrenic who had little control over the delusions and impulses that haunted him, while one of the Home Office pathologists who worked on the case echoed the thoughts of the general public: 'He was quite simply a wilfully evil bastard.'

While awaiting trial in Armley gaol, Leeds, Sutcliffe was overheard by a warder planning with his wife Sonia that he would fake 'madness' and 'be out in ten years'. As it was, his plot failed. He was sent to Parkhurst maximum security prison on the Isle of Wight.

Peter Sutcliffe's mental condition did begin to deteriorate, and in March 1984

IAN HUNTLEY
Child Killer

The mother of Holly Wells could not have known that when she took the picture of her 10 year-old daughter with best friend Jessica Chapman at just after 5 p.m. on Sunday, August 4 2002, in their beloved Manchester United football shirts, it would be a photo which would dominate front pages of both national and international newspapers for weeks to come – used first in the search for two missing girls and then in the hunt for their murderer.

The truth of exactly what horror befell Jessica Chapman and Holly Wells after leaving Holly's house on that fateful day may never be completely revealed.

'TEENAGERS SCREAMING'

There were just two confirmed sightings of the girls before they simply vanished. The first, at 6.17pm, was CCTV footage, which showed them walking happily together across the car park of the Ross Peers sports centre in Soham. The second, and last, sighting was at 6.30p.m. when they were seen walking along Sand Street by somebody who knew them. A jogger claims to have heard what he believed to be 'teenagers screaming' between 10 and 11p.m. in the Warren Hill area near to Newmarket, but did not report it to the police until two days later.

The alarm was raised at 7.30 p.m. by Holly's parents when they realised that the girls were not upstairs playing, as they had originally thought. Consequently, at the break of dawn the following morning, police and volunteers began the search for the girls in Soham, and by midday, following the broadcast of a national appeal, the search was on not only in

Above: The last ever photograph of Holly Wells and Jessica Chapman alive. After the photograph was taken, they changed into trousers and set off on a walk from which they were never to return

Soham but across the country. By the end of the day, the girls' parents had attended a press conference in which they appealed for information regarding their daughters' safety and whereabouts. The police search continued into the night.

NATIONWIDE SEARCH

The girls' disappearance triggered one of the biggest police searches in British history. Hundreds of local people, friends and neighbours had joined the police in the search for the girls, and amongst the volunteers was 29 year-old Ian Huntley, the caretaker at Soham Village College, which occupied the same site as the primary school that the girls attended. He not only helped in the search, but also informed the police that he too had seen the girls on the day they went missing. He told them how the girls had come to his door, 'happy' and 'giggly', and he had watched them walk away and continue down the road. He spoke to the media and even sought out Holly Wells's father, 'Kev' as he called him, to offer his condolences.

On Tuesday August 6, the football star David Beckham joined the parents and families of the girls in appealing for Holly and Jessica to come home, and a reconstruction of the girls' last confirmed movements was filmed on Saturday August 10.

The news that everyone had been dreading came a week later, on August 17. Two naked and decomposing bodies had been found in a ditch in Lakenheath, Suffolk, approximately 10 miles from the village of Soham where the girls lived. The nation's worst fears were confirmed when the police announced that these were indeed the bodies of Holly and Jessica. The following week, the burnt remains of the clothing that the girls had been wearing when they disappeared was discovered by police in a bin in the Soham Village College.

THE CARING CARETAKER

It had very quickly become clear to the police that Ian Huntley, the Soham caretaker who had been so helpful with their enquires and who had been happy to talk to the media, was one of the last people to see the girls alive. They arrested him on the day the bodies of the two girls were found, and three days later he was charged with both of their murders. His girlfriend, Maxine Carr, a temporary teaching assistant in Holly and Jessica's class, was also arrested, although charged not in connection

Above: Reward posters for Holly Wells and Jessica Chapman are shown outside St. Andrew's Church in Soham, Cambridgeshire

Below: Parents of murdered Soham schoolgirls Holly Wells and Jessica Chapman, Kevin and Nicola Wells and Leslie and Sharon Chapman hold a press conference

Above: A cordoned off search area in Warren Hill, Suffolk. The area was investigated when a jogger claimed to have heard 'teenagers screaming' there on the night of the girls' disappearance

with the murder of the girls, but for lying to the police and perverting the course of justice in providing a false alibi for Huntley's whereabouts on the day of the murder. Both denied the charges against them.

'PANICKED AND FROZE'

The court-case which lasted over a year, made headline news nationally and worldwide, and in it, Huntley did finally admit that the girls had died in his house. However, he denied murder. Rather, he claimed that the deaths of both girls were the result of a tragic sequence of events. He claims to have been outside his house washing his dog when the girls passed by, and he noticed that Holly was suffering with a nose bleed. He therefore invited the girls into his house and took them up to his bathroom, where he intended to curb the flow of blood from Holly's nose.

Left: The burnt remains of one of the red Manchester United shirts belonging to the two murdered ten year old girls which were found along with traces of Huntley's hair in the school grounds where he worked

'ONE DIED AS A RESULT OF MY INABILITY TO ACT AND THE OTHER DIED AS A DIRECT RESULT OF MY ACTIONS'

Holly sat on the edge of the bath while he dampened a tissue to hold to her face. However, as he approached her with the tissue, he stumbled and bumped into her, causing her to fall backwards into the bath, already filled with approx 45cm of water. She banged her head as she fell which caused Jessica to begin screaming at Huntley accusing him of pushing her friend. To stop Jessica screaming, Huntley placed his hand over her mouth, where it remained until he realised that instead of simply calming the second little girl, her body was now limp and no longer supporting itself. As he let go of Jessica, her body slumped to the floor. He turned to the bath, where Holly's lifeless body lay. He checked her pulse, no longer beating, and then put his face close to Jessica's, where there was no longer breath. He said he 'panicked and froze' when he realised what had happened, unable even to attempt to revive them. His next memory of the events was being sat on the carpet in his bathroom, next to a pile of his own vomit. He knew he should call the police, he said, but also knew that they would never believe that such a tragedy had occurred when he failed to believe it himself.

He pleaded guilty to manslaughter only, but went on to concede all the other given facts of the case – that he had bundled the bodies of Holly and Jessica into his car, bending their legs to make them fit, cut the clothing from them - their red Manchester United shirts, trousers, underwear, the bra which Holly's mother had bought for her only the day before - and left the corpses to burn in a remote ditch

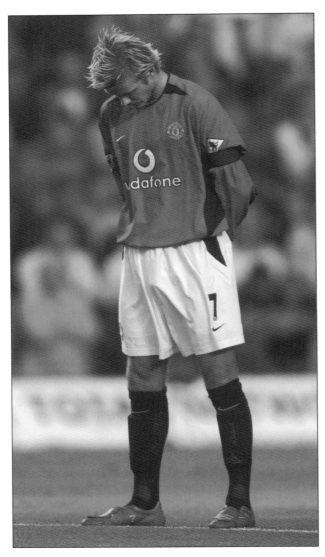

Above: Holly and Jessica's football hero, David Beckham, looks to the ground during the minute silence during the Barclaycard Premiership match between Chelsea and Manchester United in London on August 23, 2002, a tribute to the two murdered school children

Right: Flowers laid down in memory of Jessica and Holly

where the nettles grew thickly. He had then taken the girls' clothing and deposited it in a bin at Soham Village College.

Prosecutor Richard Latham supported this with forensic evidence that hairs, proven to be Huntley's, were found amongst the charred remains of the clothes in the bin, and that his fingerprints were present on the bin liner. He also presented evidence regarding Huntley's car. All four tyres on the car had been replaced the day following Jessica and Holly's disappearance. Latham claimed that this was to prevent his car being traced in any way to the girls' bodies.

Latham went on further to claim that Huntley's primary motive had been sexual. He asserts that the girls were lured into Huntley's house, possibly in the belief that Maxine Carr

was inside, and that when his advances towards one or the other had been rejected, both girls had had to die. 'They had to die in his own selfish self-interest. Each were potential witnesses - he was quite merciless.'

Huntley's version of events, that the death of the two girls had simply been the result of a tragic accident, was believed neither by the public, nor the jury who found him guilty on two counts of murder, the most serious of all the charges he could have faced, and when trial judge Justice Moses sentenced him to two life imprisonments a hushed 'yes' echoed around the courtroom. Moses told Huntley that he was '...the only person who knows how you murdered them.', and said that he displayed 'no regret' after the murders, even increasing the pain of the families by continuing to lie and deceive the police and investigators.

CATALOGUE OF OFFENCES

Information regarding Huntley's past had to be kept private during the trial in order not to influence the court, but on the conclusion of his case, a dark and disturbing catalogue of offences against children and teenagers was made public. It

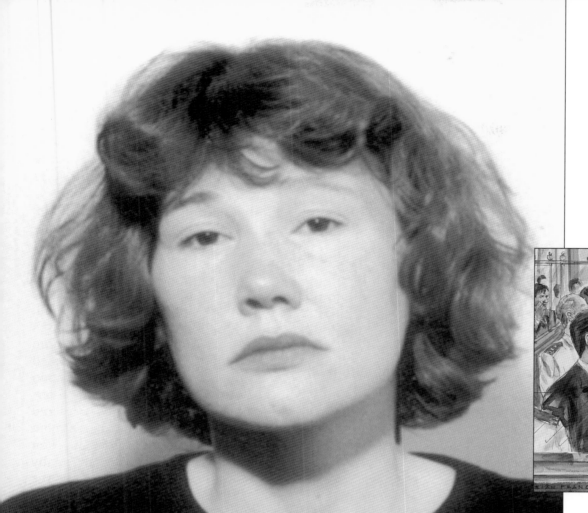

"I'M NOT GOING TO BE BLAMED FOR WHAT THAT THING IN THE BOX HAS DONE TO ME OR THOSE CHILDREN."

emerged that between the years of 1995 to 1999, Huntley was investigated by police no less than 10 times following accusations of rape, underage sex, assault on children and adults, and burglary.

Current regulations state that anybody applying to work with or around children has to undergo local police checks to ensure their suitability. Huntley's past went undetected by two police forces, Cambridgeshire and Humberside. Humberside, where the alleged offences had been reported, defended themselves by saying that the data protection act declares it unlawful to hold data concerning allegations which did not lead to a conviction. They have faced criticism from other police forces who believe this to be too strict an enforcement of the act. Perhaps aware of these regulations anyway, Huntley had changed his name when applying for the job in

Soham to Ian Nixon - his mother's maiden name.

Much is still not known about what actually happened inside Huntley's house. It is reported that Huntley and Carr had cleaned the house of every DNA trace of the girls. There were no hairs, blood or saliva and not a single fingerprint. The clean-up operation had centred around the dining room, although what happened to the girls in that room has never emerged.

'LOVELY GIRLS'

Maxine Carr, although not present on the day of the girls' deaths, was living with Huntley in the house where the girls died. On that fateful Sunday, she was in fact visiting her parents in Grimsby, although told police that she had been at home with Huntley all day in order to protect him. On August 20, she was charged with lying to the police. She appeared in

Above: Court drawing by artist Sian Frances. Ian Huntley and Maxine Carr stand to hear the verdict being read out December 17, 2003 in London

Above left: Police photograph of Maxine Carr following her arrest in August 2002. She was found guilty of conspiring to pervert the course of justice, but cleared of helping an offender

court on charges of assisting an offender and perverting the course of justice. In response to the first charge, she claimed that she had no knowledge of what had actually transpired in the house, and had only lied to protect Huntley, believing him to be innocent. She was found not guilty. She was therefore, found guilty of the second, less serious, charge of perverting the course of justice and received a sentence of three and a half years imprisonment. By the time the trial had concluded though, she had already served 16 months in prison, almost half of her sentence, and was later released on probation on May 10, 2004. During the trial she spoke of Holly and Jessica as 'lovely girls', and referred to Huntley as 'that thing', saying that she would not take the blame for his actions, and had been feeling guilty for long enough believing that she could have prevented Holly and Jessica's deaths had she been in the house on the Sunday. The judge proclaimed her imminent release to be a sentence in itself, and that she would lead a terrible existence, forever looking over her shoulder.

For her involvement with Ian Huntley, Carr is now a hate figure and considered to be at such a risk from the public that she is to be issued with a new identity. Threats have already been made on her life, some claiming

Above: Queen's Council for the prosecution Richard Latham arrives at the Old Bailey on December 12, 2003 in London

HOW DID IT FEEL TO CARRY JESSICA'S DEAD BODY DOWN THE STAIRS?" HUNTLEY DID NOT REPLY. "WELL?" "NOT GOOD," SAID HUNTLEY IN A LOW VOICE

that she would be dead within a week of her release from prison. Consequently, on her release from Foxton Hall Prison in Derbyshire, Maxine Carr was moved to a secret location pending her official release.

As a result of speculation by British newspapers on whether Carr would be given plastic surgery, or sent to live abroad, an injunction was granted by London's High Court preventing any photographs of Carr, or details of her whereabouts, treatment or new life, being published. Her movements may be protected by the courts for the rest of her life. This was granted for reasons of her health and safety, and also to enable the Probation Service to supervise her and ensure that she settles back into society and doesn't re-offend.

However, documents containing full details of her release and new identity were stolen from the car of a Home Office official parked in Hampstead Heath just days before her release date. In spite of this, the Home Office confirmed that her release had

Right: Parents of Holly Wells and Jessica Chapman arrive for the first day of the murder trial. They sat together in the courtroom, remaining silent. They were commended for their strength and dignity throughout the proceedings.

not been compromised and would go ahead as planned. They stated that there was nothing in the stolen documents which could give away her new location and identity.

Ian Huntley is no safer in prison than Maxine Carr is out of it. Knocked unconscious by another inmate who is now considered a 'hero' by fellow prisoners, Huntley has reportedly become the target of a deadly 'race' between two prison gangs to murder him. Bets have been placed on which will succeed, and prison guards are on 'extra high alert' for his safety. Rumours have leaked to the prison authorities that plans are first to disfigure Huntley by throwing boiling water on him, and then to kill him. An unnamed source described Huntley as a 'scared rabbit' in prison. He had previously been rushed to hospital in a 'life-threatening condition' having taken an overdose in an attempt to take his own life.

HUNTLEY'S HOUSE OF HORROR

The house, 5 College Close, owned by the local education authority, is due to be pulled down, along with the hangar at the Soham Village College in which the burned clothing was discovered. Until recently, for legal reasons, the house could not be touched, but lawyers for Huntley have given their consent to demolition, stating that no further evidence from the house would need to be used in any appeal. Plans for the sites are to be discussed with the relatives of Jessica and Holly.

Above: Candles are lit in remembrance of Holly Wells and Jessica Chapman inside St Andrew's Church August 18, 2002 in Soham, Cambridgeshire

YOUR RIGHT TO GROW, TO MATURE AND PLAY
SO CRUELLY DENIED IN A SINISTER WAY
ATTENTIVE AND CARING, A PARENT'S DELIGHT.
BUT SO YOUNG AT HEART, NEEDING COMFORT AT NIGHT.

- First verse of a poem written and read by Kevin Wells, in a service to celebrate the girls' lives at Ely Cathedral

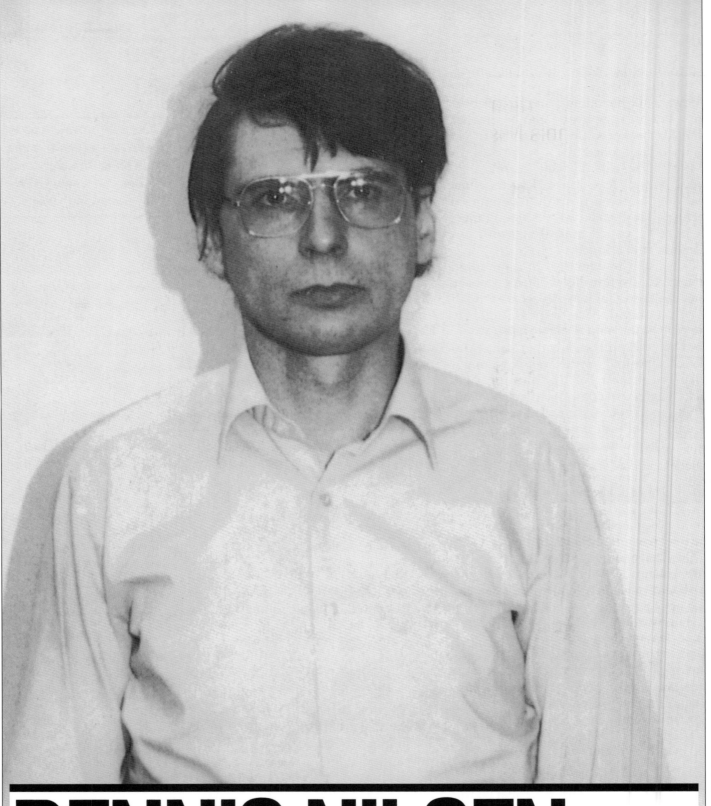

DENNIS NILSEN
A Quiet Civil Servant

Was it fear of desertion that caused Dennis Nilsen to become a mass murderer in the most gruesome of circumstances? And was he merely evil, or was he himself one of life's victims – a schizophrenic?

At 6.25 on the morning of 8 February 1983, Michael Cattran parked his Dyno-Rod van outside 23 Cranley Gardens in the north London suburb of Muswell Hill. It was a routine call. Jim Allcock, one of the residents of No. 23, had phoned to say that the drains had

Above: *A police constable stands guard at the back of 23 Cranley Gardens, Muswell Hill, where Dennis Nilsen rented an attic flat.*

Opposite: *Dennis Nilsen, the quiet civil servant who became Britain's most prolific mass murderer.*

AT THE BOTTOM OF THE STINKING SHAFT WAS A GLUTINOUS, GREYISH-WHITE SUBSTANCE

been blocked for five days. After a quick examination of the interior plumbing, Cattran decided the problem lay outside the house itself. He walked round to the side of the house and removed the manhole cover.

The smell was nauseating as Cattran climbed down the 12-foot inspection shaft. At the bottom he found a glutinous greyish-white mass.

Cattran told Jim Allcock that it was nothing serious and that he would be back shortly to straighten things out. When he called his boss, however, he voiced his real suspicions. The matter which was clogging the drains at 23 Cranley Gardens was, in his opinion, human flesh.

Cattran and his boss returned to Muswell Hill the following morning. To Cattran's surprise, the glutinous mass had vanished. He knew that, even though it had been raining the previous day, the drains could not possibly have cleared themselves. Cattran reached deep into the drainpipe and pulled out several pieces of meat and a number of bones.

Cattran explained the mystery of the missing sludge to Jim Allcock and another tenant, Fiona Bridges. They told

Left: *The front of 23 Cranley Gardens.*

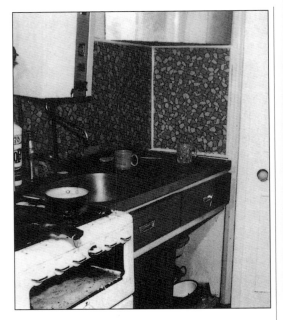

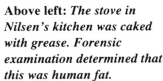

him they had heard someone moving the manhole cover in the early hours of the morning. They thought it might be Mr Nilsen who lived above them in the attic flat. Cattran and his boss decided it was time to call the police.

Detective Chief Inspector Peter Jay arrived on the scene shortly after 11a.m. and collected the meat and bones for forensic examination. At Charing Cross Hospital, it took pathologist Professor David Bowen only minutes to confirm that the meat was indeed human flesh and that the bones were from a man's hand.

THE TENANT OF THE ATTIC FLAT

Police attention immediately focused on the occupier of the attic flat, Dennis Andrew Nilsen, an executive officer at

Above left: *The stove in Nilsen's kitchen was caked with grease. Forensic examination determined that this was human fat.*

Above: *Black plastic bags in Nilsen's wardrobe contained the remains of two bodies.*

Right: *Two bodies had been dissected in Nilsen's bath, and the remains of Stephen Sinclair had been hidden under it.*

Below: *A cooking pot used by Nilsen to simmer the head of one of his victims.*

the Kentish Town Jobcentre, who lived alone with his dog, Beep. The other tenants had seen him leave for work that morning at his usual time of 8.30.

Peter Jay, together with Detective Inspector McCusker and Detective Constable Butler, waited outside 23 Cranley Gardens for Nilsen to return.

When he walked up to the front door at 5.40, Peter Jay intercepted him. Nilsen, a polite, quietly spoken man in his late thirties, seemed surprised but not alarmed when Jay introduced himself and his colleagues as police officers.

The four men went inside the house and climbed the stairs to Nilsen's tiny flat. Once inside, Jay told Nilsen about the human flesh which had been found in the drain outside. Nilsen feigned horror, but Jay was not remotely convinced. 'Stop messing about,' he said. 'Where's the rest of the body?'

Nilsen didn't even bother to protest his innocence. 'In two plastic bags in the wardrobe. I'll show you,' he said, unlocking the doors. The awful stench from the cupboard confirmed that Nilsen was telling the truth.

He arrested Nilsen, charged him with murder and shipped him off to Hornsey Police Station.

En route, Inspector McCusker asked Nilsen if there was anything he wanted to say. Nilsen replied, 'It's a long story. It goes back a long time. I'll tell you everything. I want to get it off my chest.'

'Are we talking about one body or two?' McCusker asked Nilsen.

'Fifteen or sixteen,' Nilsen replied calmly. 'Since 1978.... Three at Cranley Gardens and about thirteen at my previous address, 195 Melrose Avenue in Cricklewood.'

CONTENTS OF A WARDROBE

Detective Chief Inspector Jay returned to 23 Cranley Gardens with Detective Chief Superintendent Chambers and the pathologist, Professor Bowen. They removed the two stinking black plastic bags from Nilsen's wardrobe and took them to Hornsey mortuary.

When Bowen opened the first he found it contained four smaller shopping bags. In the first of these was the left-hand side of a man's chest with the arm attached. The second contained the right-hand side of a chest. The third held a torso, and the fourth an assortment of human offal.

In the other black bag, Bowen found two human heads and another torso with the arms attached but missing the hands. One of the heads had most of the flesh boiled away.

Nilsen told the police that one of the heads belonged to a young drug addict called Stephen Sinclair. The second he knew only as 'John the Guardsman'. He could put no name to a third victim whose remains were later found in a tea chest at his flat.

Nilsen seemed willing, even anxious, to help the police. On 11 February, three days after his arrest, he accompanied Peter Jay to the ground-floor flat at 195 Melrose Avenue which he had occupied from 1976 to 1981.

'ARE WE TALKING ABOUT ONE BODY OR TWO?' ENQUIRED THE POLICEMAN. 'FIFTEEN OR SIXTEEN,' WAS THE CALM REPLY

Below: *Nilsen's obsession with death was already evident during his days in the National Service.*

He told Jay that he had cut up the bodies and burnt them on a series of huge bonfires in the back garden. He even pointed out where the fires had been and where they should look for human remains.

Using this information, forensic teams started the laborious task of sifting through the earth for evidence. A day later they had found enough human ash and bone fragments to establish that at least eight people had been cremated in the garden.

Despite his willingness to cooperate with the police, Nilsen was unable to identify many of his early victims. None of them had ever been more than casual acquaintances. They had been, for the most part, young, homeless homosexuals – social misfits, drug addicts or alcoholics, men who could simply disappear without anyone knowing or caring. However, based on dates and

physical descriptions given by Nilsen, and comparing them with missing persons' records, the police were eventually able to identify six victims with reasonable certainty.

The question now for the police and Nilsen's lawyer was not if Nilsen was a mass murderer, but rather why he had killed more than a dozen young men. On this point, Nilsen could not help. 'I am hoping you will tell me that,' he said.

FOUR YEARS OF CARNAGE

Nilsen was questioned for the next few weeks, during which time he gave a meticulous account of his four years of carnage. It was a story so monstrous and grotesque that it made even case-hardened police interrogators physically ill to listen to it.

It had all started on New Year's Eve 1978. Nilsen had met a young Irish boy in a pub in the West End and taken him back to his flat in Melrose Avenue. After seeing in the New Year, the two men had gone to bed together. They were both stupefied with drink, and no sex took place between them.

In the morning, according to Nilsen, he woke to find the young Irishman still asleep beside him. He was suddenly overcome with terror that the boy would want to leave as soon as he too awoke. Nilsen desperately wanted him to stay, and could only think of one way to ensure that he did so.

Nilsen picked up a tie from the floor, straddled the boy's chest, placed the tie around his neck and pulled. The boy woke and a mighty struggle ensued before he finally passed out.

But he was not dead yet. So Nilsen went to the kitchen, filled a bucket with water and held the boy's head under the water until he drowned.

Nilsen then bathed the boy's body, dressed it in clean underwear and socks, took it back to bed with him and masturbated. For the next week, Nilsen went off to work as usual. He returned each evening to his dead companion who would be sitting in an armchair, waiting for him.

After eight days, Nilsen prised up some floor boards and hid the corpse. It

Above: *After a brief stint with the police, Nilsen, aged 28, spent three months working as a security guard.*

Below: *In the winter of 1975, Nilsen moved into a ground floor flat at 195 Melrose Avenue. It was here that he committed a dozen murders.*

remained there for seven months before Nilsen dissected it and burnt it on a bonfire in his back garden.

On the evening of 3 December 1979, almost a year later, Dennis Nilsen was cruising the gay bars of Soho when he met a twenty-six-year-old Canadian tourist, Kenneth Ockendon. Ockendon, who was staying at a cheap hotel in King's Cross, was due to fly home the following day.

Nilsen persuaded him to accompany him back to Melrose Avenue for a meal. He could stay the night if he wanted, and pick up his things from the hotel the following morning.

By the early hours of the morning the two men were in Nilsen's sitting room, both much the worse for drink. Nilsen was watching Ockendon as he listened to music through a set of headphones.

His feelings of imminent desertion were similar to those he had experienced a year earlier.

So Nilsen walked behind Ockendon's chair, grabbed the flex of the headphones and strangled him with it. Again he

built an enormous bonfire which was constructed in part from human remains wrapped in carpet. He crowned the fire with an old car tyre to disguise the smell of burning flesh.

At the end of 1981, Nilsen was planning to move. By this time he had accumulated a further five bodies and, shortly before he left, he had another massive fire.

No. 23 Cranley Gardens, Nilsen's new home, presented some real problems for a mass murderer of his ilk. It was an attic flat with no floorboards and no garden – in fact nowhere decent to hide a body at all. But this didn't stop him.

Within weeks of his move to Muswell Hill, Nilsen strangled John Howlett with an upholstery strap and then drowned him. Graham Allen was the next to die. Nilsen couldn't actually recall killing him, but thought he had strangled him with a tie while he was eating an omelette.

On 26 January Nilsen met his last victim. Stephen Sinclair, a drug addict and petty criminal, was wandering the streets of Soho looking for a hand-out. Nilsen offered to buy him a hamburger and then persuaded him to go back to Cranley Gardens with him.

Two weeks later, Michael Cattran of Dyno-Rod found what was left of Stephen in the drain outside 23 Cranley Gardens.

NO EMOTION, NO REMORSE

On 24 October 1983, Dennis Andrew Nilsen stood before Mr Justice Croom-Johnson at No. 1 Court in the Old Bailey. He was charged with six murders and two attempted murders.

There was no doubt that Nilsen had committed the offences. What the court had to evaluate was Nilsen's mental state at the time when he committed them.

If Nilsen had pleaded Guilty, as he originally intended, he would have saved the jury a considerable ordeal. Instead, they were forced to spend two weeks listening to detailed evidence of Nilsen's gruesome acts.

Detective Chief Superintendent Chambers spent almost an entire day reading out a transcript of Nilsen's

washed the body, dressed it in clean underwear, placed it next to him in bed and went to sleep.

Ockendon's corpse remained his constant companion for the next two weeks. Nilsen spent the evenings watching television with the body in an armchair next to him. When he was ready for bed, he would wrap it in a curtain and place it under the floorboards for the night.

Unlike the Irish boy, Ockendon's disappearance caused a considerable stir. Several of the tabloids carried his picture and Nilsen felt sure that his days were numbered. But the police didn't come. And over the next eighteen months eleven more young men were destined to die at Melrose Avenue.

By the end of 1980, Nilsen had accumulated six bodies. Three were stowed under the floorboards, while the others were cut up, stuffed in suitcases and stored in a garden shed.

At the beginning of December, Nilsen

Above: Police remove human remains from Nilsen's flat at Melrose Avenue.

EVERY EVENING NILSEN WOULD WATCH TELEVISION WITH OCKENDON'S BODY IN AN ARMCHAIR NEXT TO HIM

WITH NO FLOORBOARDS AND NO GARDEN, HOW WAS NILSEN GOING TO DISPOSE OF HIS VICTIMS AT HIS NEW ADDRESS?

confession. The graphic descriptions of decapitations and dissections, of the boiling and mincing of human flesh, and of necrophilia, sickened and enraged the jury. Nilsen, for his part, sat through the evidence without betraying a single vestige of emotion.

The prosecution called three witnesses to give evidence that Nilsen had attempted to kill them. Paul Nobbs, a university student, told how he had been rescued by Nilsen from the unwanted attentions of another man.

Nilsen had taken him back to Cranley Gardens and had shown him genuine kindness. He had not tried to ply him with drink or force him to have sex. He had even suggested that he call his mother so that she would not be worried. Nobbs had gone to bed alone but had woken in the early hours of the morning with a splitting headache. He had looked in the mirror and had seen that his eyes were completely bloodshot and that there was a bruise around his neck.

Nilsen had feigned concern, saying that Nobbs looked awful and should go straight to a doctor.

At the casualty department of the hospital he went to, Nobbs was told that he had been partially strangled. He had realized that Nilsen must have been his attacker, but had been reluctant to report the incident to the police because he felt sure that he would not be believed.

The defence made much of Nobbs's testimony. It demonstrated that Nilsen could behave perfectly normally one minute and then be possessed of murderous impulses the next, without provocation or reason. It proved, they said, that Nilsen was clearly insane.

If Nobbs's story was difficult to credit, Karl Strotter's encounter with Nilsen was nothing short of fantastic. Strotter had met Nilsen in a pub in Camden Town. He was depressed after the break-up of a relationship and, like Nobbs, he described Nilsen's behaviour towards him as sympathetic and undemanding.

They had gone back to Cranley Gardens together and Nilsen had put him to bed in a sleeping bag. Strotter described what happened next: 'I woke up feeling something round my neck. My head was hurting and I couldn't breathe

*Above: **Having confessed his crimes, Nilsen is remanded at Highgate Magistrates' Court in north London.***

NOBBS WOKE UP WITH BLOODSHOT EYES AND A SPLITTING HEADACHE. DOCTORS TOLD HIM SOMEONE HAD TRIED TO STRANGLE HIM

---

properly and I wondered what it was.

'I felt his hand pulling at the zip at the back of my neck. He was saying in a sort of whispered shouting voice, "Stay still. Stay still." I thought perhaps he was trying to help me out of the sleeping bag because I thought I had got caught up in the zip, which he had warned me about. Then I passed out.

'...the pressure was increasing. My head was hurting and I couldn't breathe. I remember vaguely hearing water running. I remember vaguely being carried and then felt very cold. I knew I was in the water and he was trying to drown me. He kept pushing me into the water....I just thought I was dying. I thought: "You are drowning. This is what it feels like to die." I felt very relaxed and I passed out. I couldn't fight any more.'

Strotter said he was amazed to awake lying on a sofa with Nilsen massaging him. Nilsen had then helped him to the underground station and wished him luck.

This apparent detachment from reality was echoed in Detective Chief Inspector Jay's evidence as he described Nilsen's behaviour during his interrogation. He was, Jay said, relaxed, cooperative and matter-of-fact. He did not, however, show any remorse. It was as though he was talking about someone else.

Both the prosecution and defence trotted out their 'expert witnesses', a mandatory feature of insanity pleas. Two equally well-qualified psychiatrists proceeded to give directly conflicting evaluations of the mental condition of the accused, thus effectively cancelling one another out in the eyes of the jury.

The judge spent four hours summing up, addressing himself in particular to the question of Nilsen's personality. 'A mind can be evil without being abnormal,' he advised the jury. 'There must be no excuses for Nilsen if he has moral defects. A nasty nature is not arrested or retarded development of the mind.'

The implication of what Mr Croom-Johnson was saying was obvious. Dennis Nilsen was, in his opinion, evil rather than insane, and the jury should therefore find him guilty of murder.

The jury retired on the morning of Thursday, 3 November 1983. Despite the clear guidance given by the judge, they returned the following morning to say that they were unable to reach a

Above: *Two that got away: Douglas Stewart (left); Karl Stotter (right). Both testified at the trial that they had been victims of attacks by Dennis Nilsen. Their evidence was vital for the prosecution as it argued that Nilsen was not technically insane.*

Below: *Nilsen's face bears the scar from an attack by a fellow prisoner.*

consensus about Nilsen's state of mind at the time of the various murders.

Mr Croom-Johnson said that he would accept a majority verdict. At 4.25 that afternoon the jury returned to court with a verdict of Guilty on all six counts of murder, by a majority of ten to two.

The judge condemned Dennis Andrew Nilsen to life imprisonment, with the recommendation that he should serve no less than twenty-five years.

Nilsen spent the first nine months of his sentence in Parkhurst Prison on the Isle of Wight.

In the summer of 1984 Nilsen was transferred to Wakefield Prison. He remains there to this day, sharing his cell with a budgerigar called Hamish.

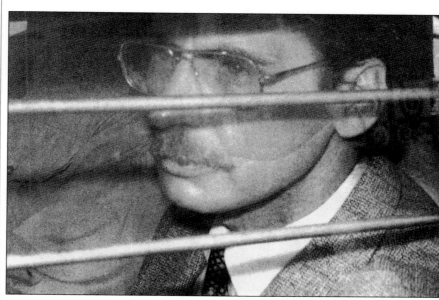

25
Cromwell
St

THE WESTS
House of Horrors

On 24 February 1994, police began to dig up the garden at 25 Cromwell Street to look for Heather West, daughter of Rosemary and Frederick West. On 13 December 1994, Frederick West was charged with twelve murders. Rose also received life imprisonment on each of the ten counts of murder.

Young women would go and stay at 25 Cromwell Street, either as nannies, lodgers or friends, but very few of them made it out of the West house alive. It was slowly becoming a House of Horrors.

FRED'S CHILDHOOD

Frederick West was born in 1941 to Walter and Daisy West, who lived in Much Marcle, a village about 120 miles west of London. After Fred, Daisy had another six children during the following ten years.

As Fred grew older, he developed a close relationship with his mother, doing everything she asked. Fred also had a good relationship with his father whom he admired as a role model.

While being a scruffy looking boy, Fred inherited some of his mother's features, a rather large mouth with a gap between his big teeth, resembling the looks of a gypsy.

At school, Fred was always in trouble for which he was frequently caned. His mother, Daisy, would then go to the school and yell at the teacher, which made Fred the victim of many jokes.

BEING A MAMMA'S BOY MADE FRED THE VICTIM OF MANY JOKES AT SCHOOL

Opposite: *Police guarding 25 Cromwell Street as evidence is being removed.*

Right: *Fred and Rosemary West, the happy couple.*

HE WAS EXTREMELY AGGRESSIVE TO THE OPPOSITE SEX AND WOULD PURSUE ANY GIRL THAT TOOK HIS FANCY

At the age of fifteen and virtually illiterate, Fred left school and went to work as a farm hand. By the time he was sixteen, he had become very aggressive to the opposite sex and persued any girl that took his fancy.

Fred, recognised as a notorious liar, claimed that his father had sex with his daughters using the excuse 'I made you so I'm entitled to have you'. Then at seventeen, he was seriously injured in a motorcycle accident. After a week in a coma, a broken leg and having a metal plate inserted into his head, Fred was left with one leg shorter than the other. This head injury may have resulted in

Fred being prone to sudden fits of rage and the loss of control over his emotions.

After this accident Fred met a pretty 16-year-old called Catherine Bernadette Costello. Nicknamed Rena, she had always been in trouble with the police since early childhood and was an accomplished and experienced thief. They quickly became lovers. The affair ended months later as she returned to Scotland. Then, after plunging his hand up a young woman's skirt while on a fire escape at a local youth group, Fred

Left: *Rosemary as a child.*

fell, banged his head and lost consciousness. It may be that he suffered brain damage due to his two head injuries and this could have been the cause of a lasting impact on Fred's behaviour.

After being fined for theft in 1961, Fred was accused of getting a 13-year-old girl pregnant. He couldn't understand that he had done anything wrong, as this girl was a friend of the family, it caused a scandal and he was told to find somewhere else to live. Working on construction sites, it wasn't long before he was caught stealing and having sex with young girls.

At the age of 20, although he got off without a prison sentence, Fred had become a convicted child molester and petty thief; a complete disgrace to his family.

ROSE'S CHILDHOOD

Daisy Letts was hospitalized in 1953, due to her deepening depression, and trying to cope with a violent husband, three daughters and son, she had electroshock therapy. Shortly after this treatment she gave birth to Rosemary. Rosemary Letts was born in Devon in November 1953. Her mother suffered from severe depression and her father, Bill Letts, was a schizophrenic. Bill

'DOZY ROSIE' — AS SHE WAS CALLED, WAS NOT VERY INTELLIGENT ALTHOUGH SHE WAS SMART ENOUGH TO BECOME HER FATHER'S PET, ALWAYS DOING WHATEVER HE WISHED IMMEDIATELY.

was a violent and dominant man, demanding obedience from both his wife and children and enjoyed looking for reasons to beat them. The family was short of money because Bill was not an ideal employee and only maintained a series of unskilled and low paid jobs.

Rose had developed a habit of rocking herself in her cot and as she became older, she would swing her head for hours until she reached semiconciousness. Being quite pretty, if a little chubby, she was called 'Dozy Rosie', although she was smart enough to become her father's pet. But at school, due to cruel jokes and teasing, Rose was recognised as an ill-tempered, aggressive loner.

In her teens she walked around naked after baths, fondled her brother and became sexually precocious. As boys were not interested in her she focused her attentions on the older men of the village.

During 1968 Rose was raped by an older man who had taken advantage of her innocent ways. Then at the beginning of 1969 Daisy, her mother, took 15-year-old Rose and moved in temporarily with one of her other daughters to escape from Bill. At this time Rose began to spend a lot of time out with men. Later that year, Rose moved back home with her father.

As Rose Letts was not a very smart nor good tempered girl she became unfocused towards any productive goal except finding a lover older than herself.

THE FIRST VICTIM

In 1962 Fred was allowed to move back home in Much Marcle. Rena Costello returned from Scotland in the summer and they met up immediately, continuing their relationship. Although Rena was pregnant by an Asian bus driver, she and Fred secretly married and moved to Scotland. Charmaine was born March 1963. They both wrote to Fred's parents, stating that their baby had died at birth, therefore they had adopted a child of mixed race.

Fred's interest for normal sex was small, although he had a voracious appetite for oral sex, bondage and sodomy. As an icecream man, his apparent politeness and sincerity attracted teenagers around his van. This led to many sexual encounters. With his growing number of infidelities, Rena and Charmaine were pushed out of his mind.

FRED AND ROSE

Rena gave birth to Fred's child in 1964, and they named her Anne Marie. During their turbulent marriage, the West's embarked on a friendship with Anna McFall. Then Fred, Rena and their two children, as well as Anna, moved to Gloucester where Fred found work in a slaughterhouse. This is probably where Fred developed a morbid obsession with blood, corpses and dismemberment.

As the marriage fell apart, Rena returned to Scotland alone. When she returned to Gloucester in July 1966, she found Fred living in a trailer with Anna McFall. Due to pressure from Anna to marry her, Fred responded by killing her and her unborn child sometime in July 1967. He slowly and methodically dismembered her and the foetus, cutting off her fingers and toes, and buring her body somewhere near the trailer park.

Rena then moved back in with Fred, earning money as a prostitute, while he began, openly, to fondle Charmaine.

Then in February 1968, due to his mother dying, Fred started a series of petty thefts, which caused him to change his job frequently. In November 1968, while on one of these many jobs,

Left: *Anne Marie daughter of Fred and Rena Costello.*

AT THE AGE OF JUST 16, ROSE LEFT HOME TO LOOK AFTER CHARMAINE, ANNA MARIE AND FRED, WHO WAS CONSTANTLY IN TROUBLE WITH THE POLICE.

Fred met Rose Letts, his future wife.

Although Rose's father did not approve of Fred, she carried on seeing him until she found herself pregnant with his baby. At the age of 16, Rose left home to take care of Charmaine, Anna Marie and Fred.

CHARMAINE

Rose gave birth in 1970 to Heather. While Fred was in jail, Rose was left at home with the all the children whom she treated quite badly. Then one day during the summer of 1971, Charmaine went missing. Although this happened while Fred was in prison, he probably helped to bury her body under the kitchen floor of their home in Midland Road, removing her fingers, toes and kneecaps, only to be discovered 20 years later. It was only a matter of time before Rena came looking for Charmaine. When she found Fred, he got her drunk, then strangled, dismembered her body and buried her as he had done with Anna, cutting off her fingers and toes.

Fred and Rose married in Gloucester registry office in 1972, then Rose gave birth to a daughter, Mae West. As the family increased in size, they moved to 25 Cromwell Street, where Rose also had room for her prostitution business.

As the cellar was soundproof, they used it as a 'torture chamber'. Anne Marie, their 8-year-old daughter was the first victim, her mother held her down and her father raped her. The pain was so bad that she could not attend school.

CAROLINE OWENS

The couple hired a nanny, 17-year-old Caroline Owens. They abducted, raped and threatened her but she got away and reported this to the police. There was a hearing. At this time Fred was thirty-one and Rose only nineteen, and they were found not guilty.

> HE WOULD DISMEMBER THE BODY, CUTTING OFF THE FINGERS, TOES AND KNEECAPS — THEN PUT THE REMAINS INTO BAGS READY FOR BURIAL.

Below: *Leading into the cellar at 25 Cromwell Street.*

LYNDA GOUGH

Lynda Gough, a friend who helped take care of the children, became the next victim. She was dismembered and buried in a pit in the garage, having had her fingers, toes and kneecaps removed.

A terrible pattern was beginning to develop.

CAROL ANN COOPER

In August 1973, Stephen, their first son was born. Fred and Rose abducted 15-year-old Carol in November, abusing her sexually until they strangulated or suffocated her. They dismembered and buried her body at the growing graveyard of 25 Cromwell street.

LUCY PARTINGTON AND THE REST

The cellar was enlarged and the garage was transformed into an extension of the main house, all done by Fred at strange hours of the day. On December 27, 1973, Lucy Partington went to visit her disabled friend but had the misfortune to bump into Rose and Fred. She was tortured for a week and then murdered, dismembered and buried under one of Fred's many construction projects at 25 Cromwell Street.

During the period from April 1974 to April 1975 another three women became victims like Carol and Lucy. They were Therese Siegenthaler 21, Shirley Hubbard, 15 and Juanita Mott, 18. The Wests buried these bodies under the cellar floor. Juanita had been gagged by a ligature made from a pair of white nylon socks, two pairs of tights and a bra, then tied up with plastic covered rope, the type used for a washing line. Tied up so tightly so that she could hardly move, she was probably suspended from the beams in the cellar. As for Shirley Hubbard, her body was wrapped entirely with tape, a plastic tube had been inserted up her nose, allowing her to breathe.

Fred continued to get into trouble with the police with thefts and stolen

> NOT ONLY DID HE KILL HIS MISTRESS AND THEIR UNBORN CHILD, HE SLOWLY AND METHODICALLY DISMEMBERED HER CORPSE AND BURIED HER ALONG WITH HER FOETUS.

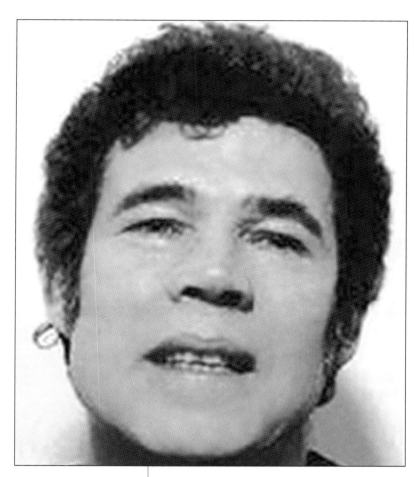

Above: *Fred West – the last photograph before his death.*

> FRED'S INTEREST IN 'NORMAL SEX' WAS MINIMAL. HE WANTED ORAL SEX, BONDAGE AND SODOMY — AT ALL HOURS OF THE DAY AND NIGHT.

goods, which he needed to maintain his home improvement projects.

The Wests took in lodgers. One of these, Shirley Robinson, 18, a former prostitute, developed a relationship with them and later became pregnant with Fred's child. Rose had also became pregnant, but by one of her black clients. Rose became uncomfortable with this situation and wanted Shirley to leave. Seven months later, Tara was born to Rose in December 1977, Shirley and her unborn baby became the next victims and were buried in the garden of Cromwell Street. Yet another baby girl, Louise, was born to the Wests in November 1978, making a total of six. Fred's daughter, Anna Marie also became pregnant by Fred, although this was terminated.

After Rose's father died in May 1979, the Wests raped, tortured and murdered their next victim, Alison

Chambers who was only 17. She was also buried in the garden at Cromwell Street. The rest of the children in the West household were aware of strange happenings. They knew that their mother was a prostitute and that Anna Marie was continually raped by her father. Anna moved in with her boyfriend, so Fred made advances towards his other daughters, Heather and Mae. Heather was beaten for trying to resist her father's advances. Rose gave birth to Barry, Fred's second son in June 1980, followed by Rosemary junior, who was not Fred's, in April 1982. She also had Lucyanna in July 1983, who was half-black like Tara and Rose junior. With all these children to contend with, Rose became extremely bad tempered.

After Heather broke the silence and

Above: *The house in Northam, Devon where Rose West lived as a child.*

WHEN HE CUT OFF HER HEAD, IT MADE A SOUND, 'A HORRIBLE NOISE... LIKE SCRUNCHING — VERY UNPLEASANT.' BUT ONCE HER HEAD WAS OFF, HE STARTED ON HER LEGS, TWISTING HER FOOT UNTIL ONE ALMIGHTY CRACK.

told her girlfriend of the abuse from her father, she too was murdered This happened after an argument with her father got out of control. Fred grabbed her round the neck, she went blue and stopped breathing. After trying to revive her, he dragged her to the bath and ran cold water over her. After taking all her clothes off and drying her, he tried to fit her in the rubbish bin. But as she did not fit, strangled her with tights just to make sure she was dead, and then cut her up into smaller pieces. Stephen, Fred's son, helped his father dig a hole in the back garden for Heather's dismembered body.

Katherine Halliday began to participate in the West's prostitution business, although this did not last long as she became very alarmed at their collection of suits, whips and chains and left abruptly.

Due to one of Fred's young rape victims talking, Detective Constable Savage, who had experience in dealing with Rena, was assigned to his case. On 6 August, 1992, Police arrived at Cromwell Street with a warrant to look for child abuse and pornography. Fred was arrested. While the Police had enough evidence to bring child abuse charges against Fred, Detective Constable Savage was curious as to the disappearance of Charmaine, Rena and Heather.

The West's children were put into care and with Fred in prison, Rose attempted suicide but failed. After rumours emerged that Heather was apparently buried under the patio, the house and garden were searched. Fred confessed to killing his daughter when human bones, other than Heather's, were found in the garden. The police began to dig the garden and it became only a matter of time before they found the first remains of a young woman, dismembered and decapitated.

Fred then told the police of the girls in the cellar, admitting to murder but not rape. In the cellar, nine sets of bones were discovered, although the police could not identify them and Fred was no help as he couldn't remember the victims.

Rena, Anna McFall and Charmaine's bodies were found, although Mary Bastholm was not.

At the joint hearing, Fred tried to console Rose, but she brushed him off, telling the police that he made her sick.

GUILTY

Fred was charged with twelve murders on December 13, 1994. After being devastated by Rose's rejection, Fred hung himself with his bedsheet on New Year's day at Winson Green Prison, Birmingham.

On October 3, 1995, Rose went to trial linking her to the murders and sadistic sexual assaults on young women. Among the witnesses were Caroline Owens, whom they had hired as a nannie in 1972, along with Anna Marie. The defence, led by Richard

---

AFTER BRUSHING OFF FRED, HE WROTE A LETTER SAYING THAT SHE WOULD ALWAYS BE HIS MRS WEST, THEY WOULD ALWAYS BE IN LOVE.

Below:
Rosemary West

Ferguson QC, tried to show that Rose was unaware of what Fred was up to, and that the evidence of sexual assault was not the same as evidence of murder. But after taking the stand, the jury were left believing that she ill-treated her children and was completely dishonest.

The most dramatic evidence was given by Janet Leach, who witnessed Fred's police interviews. During these interviews, Fred had said how he had involved Rose with the murders and that Rose had murdered Charmaine and Shirley Robinson on her own. After this testimony, Janet Leach collapsed and was admitted to hospital.

It did not take the jury long to find Rose guilty of murdering Charmaine, Heather, Shirley Robinson and the other bodies all buried at Cromwell Street. With ten counts of murder, the judge sentenced Rose to life imprisonment.

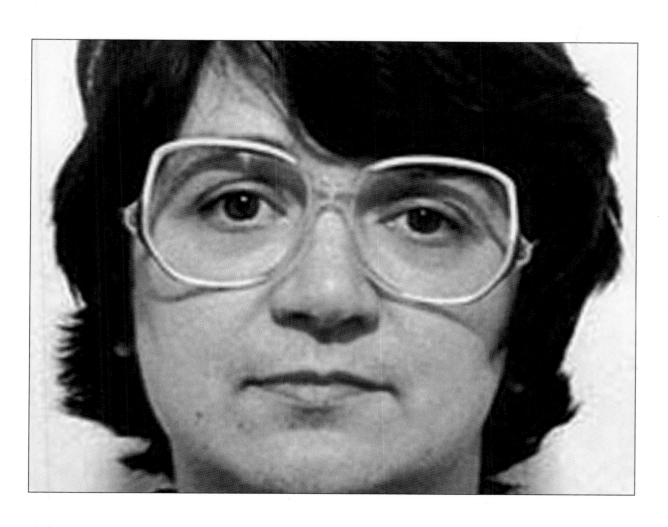

BRADY & HINDLEY
The Moors Murderers

Ian Brady and Myra Hindley were both obsessed with Nazi paraphernalia, pornography and sadism. Most of their victims were children whom they sexually molested before killing. These sadistic love birds would document their murderous deeds. As well as recording the screams of one of their victim's torturous end, they kept an extensive collection of photographs of the victims.

Above: *Myra Hindley*

Opposite: *Police searching Saddleworth Moor, north east of Manchester.*

Ian Brady and Myra Hindley met while woking for a chemical company in Hyde, Greater Manchester. Hindley fell in love with Brady as soon as she laid eyes on him, thinking that he was quite an intellectual as he sat reading *Mein Kampf* in German in the lunch room. Therefore Hindley was thrilled when he asked her out. They went to see a movie about the Nuremburg war crimes tribunal, and when they returned home to her grandmother's house, Brady introduced her to sex. Soon they became inseparable.

MYRA'S CHILDHOOD

Being the first child of Nellie (Hettie) and Bob Hindley, Myra was born in Gorton in the industrial district of Manchester on July 23 1942. She was raised by her mother alone, as her father served in a parachute regiment, and lived with Myra's grandmother, Ellen Maybury. This worked out well because when Myra's mother went to work, her grandmother was able to look after her.

When Myra's father, Bob, returned from the army, they bought a house just round the corner from Myra's grandmother. Bob spent most of his time in the pub when he wasn't working, as he had trouble re-adjusting to civillian life.

The Hindley's second child, Maureen, was born in August 1946. As

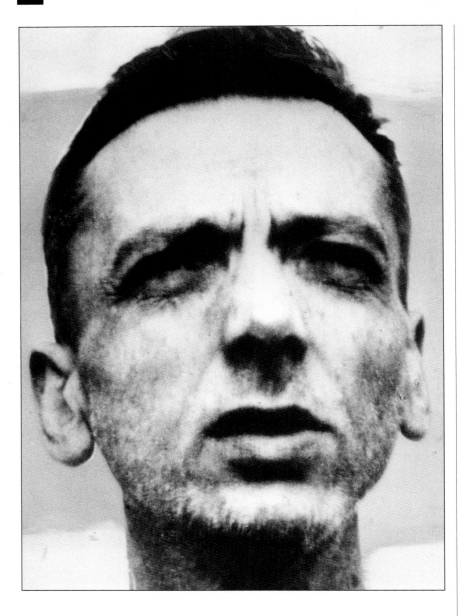

Above: *Ian Brady*

HE WAS DIFFERENT
FROM ANY OF THE BOYS
SHE HAD KNOWN.

---

all her subjects her attendance was still very bad. She seemed talented at creative writing and poetry and loved sports and athletics. Myra was not considered particularly attractive and was given the nickname 'Square Arse'. She was also teased because of the shape of her nose.

During her teens, Myra became a popular babysitter, being very capable and demonstrating a genuine love of children.

Then at 15, Myra befriended a timid and fragile 13-year-old called Michael Higgins. She protected and looked after him, treating him as if he were her younger brother. She was convinced that they would be life long friends. Unfortunately he drowned in a resevoir, often used by local children as a swimming hole. This devastated Myra, made worse by her sense of guilt as she had turned down his offer of going swimming with him that day. She had been convinced that she could have saved him as she considered herself to be a very strong swimmer.

Fluctuating between depression and hysteria, Myra became inconsolable over the following weeks. She dressed in black, lit a candle in church every night for Michael and converted to his religion of Roman Catholicism. With an IQ of 107, she did not complete her O levels and left school shortly after Michael's death.

Junior clerk at an electrical engineering firm at Lawrence Scott and Electrometers, was to be her first job. Myra behaved much like any other teenager, going to dances and cafés, listening to Rock and Roll and flirting with boys. At this time, her appearance becoming more important to her, she began to wear make-up and bleach her hair in an attempt to look older.

She got engaged to Ronnie Sinclair, a local boy, on her 17th birthday. Although this apparent contentment with ordinary life did not last long, as she began to question the lifestyle to which she was supposed to conform. Myra called off the engagement.

both parents found this to be too much of a strain, Myra was sent to live with her grandmother. Although this meant that Myra never developed a relationship with her father, instead she enjoyed the devoted attention from her grandmother.

At the age of five, Myra started school at Peacock Street Primary School. Although regarded as a sensible and mature girl her attendance at school was poor. This led to her inability to gain the necessary grades required to attend the local grammar school. Instead, she went to Ryder Brow Secondary Modern. Although she was constantly in the 'A' stream in

Looking for more excitement, she applied for entrance forms to the Navy and Army, although she never actually sent them in. Another idea was to become a nannie in America. In the end she went in search of a job in London. It was two years before something new and exciting occurred. Then in January 1961 she met Ian Brady.

IAN'S CHILDHOOD

He was born Ian Stewart on January 2, 1938 in Gorbals, an area of one of the roughest slums in Glasgow. Being the illegitimate son of a single, Scottish waitress, he never knew his father except that, as his mother later told him, he was a journalist for a Glasgow newspaper and had died a few months before Ian's birth. Signing her name as Mrs. Stewart due to disapproval from society, his mother, Margaret (Peggy) Stewart was a tearoom waitress in a hotel.

Unable to afford a babysitter, his mother would often leave baby Ian at home on his own. Realising that this could not continue, she advertised for a permanent babysitter to provide the necessary attention and care that she was unable to give.

At the age of four months Ian was unofficially adopted by Mary and John Sloane, who also had another four children. Margaret would visit him every Sunday and bring gifts, but never telling him that she was his real mother. As the years went on, the visits occurred less often.

Although the Sloanes tried to provide a loving environment, Ian always felt as though he didn't belong and therefore showed no response to their attentions. He became difficult, angry and lonely resulting in him banging his head on the floor due to his temper tantrums on many occasions.

He attended Camden street Primary School and was thought to be a bright child by his teachers. But his classmates saw him as an outsider, as he was different and secretive. He was also called a 'sissy' because he didn't play sport like the others.

> FAMILY, FRIENDS AND COLLEAGUES NOTICED A BIG CHANGE IN HER. AT WORK, MYRA BECAME SURLY, OVERBEARING, AGGRESSIVE AND BEGAN TO WEAR 'KINKY' CLOTHES.

When Ian was nine, he was taken for his first outing away from the Gorbals to the moors of Loch Lomond. The Sloanes had a nap after the picnic lunch. When they awoke they saw Ian about 500 yards away, standing at the top of a steep slope. They could not gain his attention as he stood there for an hour. When two of the Sloane boys finally climbed the hill to fetch him, he told them to go home without him as he wanted to be alone. But afterwards, on the bus ride home, and for the first time, he became very talkative. Being on the hillside alone seemed to fill him with a sense of strength and power as well as being a profound experience, one that would influence his future life.

Ian was accepted into Shawlands Academy at the age of eleven, a school for children with above-average intelligence. But Ian was lazy and naughty. It was not long before he started getting into trouble with the police. Also at this time his obsession with the Nazis began. He read books on the Second World War and insisted on playing German war games with his

Right: *Pauline Reade, the frst victim of Brady and Hindley's gruesome murders.*

friends.

By the time Ian reached twelve years old his mother's visits ceased. She had married Patrick Brady and moved to Manchester to be with her husband.

During the ages of thirteen to sixteen, Ian was charged with burglary and housebreaking. The court then decided that he was to be sent to live with his mother in Manchester. After meeting his stepfather for the first time, he began to use his surname of Brady which he kept permanently.

His stepfather found him a job as a porter at the local market, but Ian Brady still harboured feelings that he did not belong and looked for direction in his reading. These were books such as Dostoyevsky's *Crime and Punishment*, and sadistic titles such as the *Kiss of the Whip* and *The Torture Chamber*, which he found exciting.

Returning back to crime, Brady's next job was in a brewery. Then, arrested for aiding and abetting, he was sent to Borstal for two years. He was now 17, but as places were full, the first three months were spent in Strangeways prison in Manchester. Here he very quickly learnt to toughen up. He was soon moved to Hatfield Borstal in Yorkshire, where among other things, he ran gambling books. He also became frequently drunk while brewing his own alcohol. It wasn't long before he was sent to a much tougher Borstal in Hull Prison where he made a great effort to learn more of the criminal way of life.

In November 1957, Brady was released and after several months found work as a labourer, while studying bookkeeping. His family noticed that he had become more brooding and silent than ever before. Brady was offered the position of stock clerk with Millwards Merchandising in 1959. It was about a year later when a new secretary arrived.

THE FATAL ATTRACTION

Every night Hindley would write in her

AS THE WEEKS WENT PAST, IAN WOULD PLAY RECORDS OF HITLER'S MARCHING SONGS FOR MYRA, AND ENCOURAGED HER TO READ SOME OF HIS FAVOURITE BOOKS — *MEIN KAMPF*, *CRIME AND PUNISHMENT* AND *DE SADE'S* WORKS.

Below: *16 Wardle Brook Avenue, the council house in East Manchester where Brady and Hindley lived*

---

diary of the feeling of longing that she held for Brady. They started to date and went to see *The Nuremberg Trials*. During the following weeks Hindley was happy to listen to records of Hitler's marching songs, and was encouraged to read books on crime and punishment. Having waited so long for someone like Brady, but due to her inexperience, she was unable to distinguish between what was healthy and dangerous.

Brady became Hindley's first lover and she was totally besotted, always wanting to please him. This even extended to dressing for him in the Germanic style with long boots, mini skirts and bleached hair. Brady would take pornographic pictures of her, including photographs of the two of them having sex. As Brady became increasingly outrageous and paranoid, Hindley's personality became fused with Brady's and she stopped attending church, believed as Brady had told her, that rape and murder were not wrong, and that murder was the 'supreme pleasure'.

Hindley's family noticed a big change in her personality, she had become aggressive, overbearing, secretive, hated babies, children and people and began to wear 'kinky' clothing.

Brady planned a bank robbery at the beginning of 1963, and although this was not followed through, Hindley's

blind acceptance and her willingness to go along with him seemed to cement their relationship. She took driving lessons (as Brady needed a getaway driver), joined Cheadle Rifle Club and bought two guns.

THE VICTIMS

Sixteen-year-old Pauline Reade became Hindley's and Brady's first victim on the night of July 12, 1963. Pauline had been on her way to a dance at the Railway Worker's Social Club. Enticed away by Hindley, she was never to be seen alive again.

Four months later, 12- year-old John Kilbride disappeared on November 23 from Ashton-under-Lyne.

On Tuesday June 16, 1964, 12-year-old Keith Bennett was next. As he set off to his grandmother's house which he did every Tuesday, he never arrived and was never seen alive again.

Brady and Hindley moved in with Hindley's grandmother in September of 1964. This was when Brady was first introduced to Myra's sister and her 17-year-old husband, David Smith. Brady was keen to impress Smith with his stories of criminal knowledge and theft.

The most horrifying murder was that of Lesley Anne Downey. She disappeared without trace on December 26, 1964. Lesley Anne had been gagged, stripped and sexually assaulted. She was then strangled and buried in a shallow grave up on Saddleworth Moor in Lancashire. While Lesley Anne had been tortured, Brady had photographed and recorded it all. On the tape recording, Lesley Anne can clearly be heard begging them to let her go home to her mother as she was brutally abused. The cries of the child fell on deaf ears and photographs were taken, of Lesley Anne tied down on the bed.

It was on October 7, 1965, that Brady offered Smith a practical demonstration of a murder. Edward Evans, the next victim, was a 17-year-old

> WHILE DAVID SMITH WATCHED, BRADY STOOD OVER EVANS HOLDING A HATCHET, STRUCK HIM THIRTEEN TIMES, COVERED HIS HEAD WITH A SHEET AND CONSTANTLY PULLED TIGHTER A PIECE OF ELECTRICAL WIRE THAT HE HAD WRAPPED ROUND HIS VICTIM'S NECK, CHANTING "YOU F...ING DIRTY BASTARD".

> IN TWO SUITCASES FILLED WITH PORNAGRAPHIC AND SADISTIC PARAPHENALIA, NINE SEMI-PORNOGRAPHIC PHOTOGRAPHS OF LESLEY ANNE DOWNEY WERE FOUND. THESE SHOWED THE GIRL NAKED, BOUND AND GAGGED IN A VARIETY OF POSES IN MYRA HINDLEY'S BEDROOM.

homosexual. Smith watched as Brady stood over Evans with a hatchet and struck him 13 times with it. As the young man let out a quiet groan, Brady hit him once more with the hatchet. As Evans lay on the ground making gurgling noises, Brady covered his head with a sheet and then wrapped a piece of electrical wire around his head. As Brady pulled the wire tighter and tighter, he kept repeatedly chanting 'You f...ing dirty bastard'. When Evan's finally stopped making any noise, Brady turned to Hindley and said, "That's it, it's the messiest yet."

CONVICTED OF MURDER

Smith was horrified and contacted the police the following morning, directing them to Brady's address. Brady and Hindley were discovered collecting a fresh corpse from the bedroom, along with a blood-covered hatchet. Brady's library of pornography, perversion and sadism were also found.

Also, a young 12-year-old girl, who had only lived doors away from Brady and Hindley, was able to recall several trips she had made with the couple to Saddleworth Moor, northeast of Manchester. After this bit of information, the authorities launched a search which uncovered the body of Lesley Anne Downey. A search of Brady's flat uncovered two left luggage tickets for Manchester Central Station. Once retrieved, the police found contained in them, nude photographs of Lesley Anne along with recordings of her torturous end and seemingly innocent snapshots of Saddleworth Moor. After another visit to the moor by the police, they discovered the body of John Kilbride.

While in custody, Brady seemed proud of his crimes, as police opened their files on eight missing persons lost over the previous four years.

Hindley and Brady were brought to trial on April 27, 1966, held at Chester Assizes. The jurors were stunned by the Downey recording as Brady described it as nothing more than 'unusual'. Throughout the trial, Brady and Hindley appeared cold and heartless as they continually attempted to blame David Smith for all the murders. Accused of the murders of Edward Evans, Lesley Anne Downey and John Kilbride, Hindley and Brady pleaded 'not guilty' to the charges brought against them. The couple had luckily escaped the death penalty by just a couple of months as 'The Murder (Abolition of the Death Penalty) Act of 1965' had just come into effect a few weeks before their arrest.

Both were convicted of the murders of Edward Evans and Lesley Anne Downey; Brady was also convicted of murdering John Kilbride, while Myra was convicted as an accessory.

Brady was sentenced to concurrent life terms on each count. Hindley received two life terms plus seven years in the Kilbride case.

Brady was transferred from prison to a maximum security hospital in November 1985, here he confessed to the Reade–Bennet murders during an interview with tabloid reporters. The

> BOTH PLEADING
> 'NOT GUILTY'
> THROUGHOUT THE TRIAL,
> BRADY AND HINDLEY
> MADE CONTINUAL
> ATTEMPTS TO BLAME
> DAVID SMITH FOR THE
> MURDERS.

Below: *Police retrieving the buried body of Lesley Anne Downey, from Saddleworth Moor on 10 October 1965.*

remains of Pauline Reade were discovered on June 30, 1987. Pathologists took a month to decide how she had met her death. It was confirmed that the girl had been sexually assaulted and her throat slashed from behind. Police reopened files on 55-yearold Veronica Bondi in Manchester, and a 38-year-old prostitute, Edith Gleave from Stockport.

Myra Hindley, became a born-again Christian asking repeatedly to be let out as she had been a model prisoner. Successive Home Office ministers denied her the chance at Parole. After unconfirmed media reports that Hindley was suffering with advanced lung cancer, she eventually died in prison, at the age of 60, due to respiratory failure. Her funeral and cremation were attended only by prison officials with her final burial place remaining unmarked.

Ian Brady remains alive in the high security Ashworth Hospital on Merseyside. After failing several attempts to legally starve himself to death, he remains on continual hunger strike being force fed through a plastic tube.

CRIMES
OF
PASSION

RUTH ELLIS
Spurned in Love

On a summer's day in 1955 a woman walked out of the condemned cell in Holloway prison to await the hangman's noose. Having shot to death a lover who had treated her appallingly, Ruth Ellis became the last woman in Britain to be executed.

For most of the year, the north London suburb of Hampstead keeps to itself on the edge of its leafy and spacious Heath. But at Easter the area's tranquillity is jovially disrupted. Outsiders flock in, as they have done for 150 years, to enjoy the fun of the fair. Lights and music flicker and boom across the green slopes, and the balmy spring air is scented with the pungent odour of fried onions from the fast food stalls.

On the evening of Easter Sunday, 10 April 1955, everything was running true to form. Downhill from the fairground, the Magdala pub in South Hill Park was packed and boisterous. Just after nine o'clock two young men parked their grey green Vauxhall Vanguard van and crossed the road to push into the saloon bar.

AS THE TWO MEN LEFT THE PUB A SMARTLY DRESSED BLONDE EMERGED FROM THE SHADOWS WITH A SMITH AND WESSON IN HER HAND

Below: *Ruth Ellis with her mother, father and sister Elizabeth.*

Twenty-six-year-old David Blakely and his friend Clive Gunnell had been to the fair, and were now after a quick drink before buying beer to take out to a nearby party.

As they re-emerged, neither of them noticed the slender blonde standing with her back to the wall of the pub. She was twenty-nine, her name was Ruth Ellis, and she had had a stormy relationship with Blakely which had lasted for two years. That evening, her pale, pretty face was grim behind her horn-rimmed spectacles as she called out: 'David!'

Blakely had been intent on avoiding Ruth all day. Now he ignored her. 'David!' she said again, sharply. Clive Gunnell looked up and saw that she was holding a .38 Smith and Wesson service revolver which was levelled at his friend.

David Blakely turned from the door of his van, opened his mouth, and then dropped his car keys and the bottle of beer he was holding as the first bullet slammed into his white shirt. A second bullet knocked Blakely on to his back.

'Clive!' Blakley's voice was a gurgled choke.

'Get out of the way, Clive,' said Ruth, deadly calm. She pulled the trigger again. Blakely, crawling on his stomach by now, was slammed into the tarmac. She

Leonard Crawford at Hampstead's Haverstock Hill police station, David Blakely was being declared dead on arrival at nearby New End Hospital.

When cautioned by DCS Crawford, Ruth Ellis was detached and composed. 'I am guilty,' she said. 'I am rather confused.' Then, little by little, she began to spill out her story...

positioned herself beside him, and then she fired twice more, sending fragments flying from the back of his jacket.

David Blakely lay prone and still. Ruth unfocussed from what she had done, looked Gunnell blankly in the eye, raised the pistol to her own temple, and pulled the trigger. Amazingly, the 'four-inch Smith', renowned for its reliability, did nothing.

She lowered the gun to her side and almost absent-mindedly tried the trigger again. The sixth and last bullet splintered the pavement, whined off up the road and clipped the hand of a passer-by, Mrs Gladys Kensington Yule.

Ellis and Gunnell stood facing each other. The whole bloody little drama had lasted less than ninety seconds, but those six shots were to reverberate for an unconscionable time in criminal history.

Someone had already called for the police and an ambulance when Ellis herself seemed to come out of a trance to tell a young man nearby: 'Fetch the police.'

'I am the police,' said Alan Thompson, an off-duty Hampstead officer who had been drinking in the pub. He took the pistol from her hand – inadvertently smudging latent prints, as it later proved – and led her off to await the squad car.

By the time it delivered Ruth into the hands of Detective Chief Superintendent

Above: *Ruth had a brief and not very successful stab at modelling.*

Right: *David Blakely, Ruth Ellis's lover and eventual victim.*

'FETCH THE POLICE,' SAID ELLIS TO A BYSTANDER. 'I AM THE POLICE,' REPLIED THE OFF-DUTY OFFICER AS HE TOOK THE GUN FROM HER

FROM FACTORY WORKER TO CLUB HOSTESS

It had begun a quarter of a century previously in Rhyl, North Wales, where Ruth was born the daughter of dance band musician Arthur Neilson and his wife Bertha on 9 October 1926. When Ruth was fifteen the family moved to Southwark in south London, and the girl found work in the local Oxo factory. She was ordered to take a year off work after contracting rheumatic fever. As part of her convalescence she took up dancing.

By 1943 she was working as a dance hall photographer's assistant when she met a Canadian soldier named Clare, and in September 1944, she bore him a son, christened Andria. Unfortunately Clare proved to have a wife back home, and Ruth, her mother Bertha and her older married sister Muriel were left to care for the boy.

In 1945, with the war in Europe ending and Ruth in her nineteenth year, she found another kind of career when she met Morris Conley.

Conley was a property racketeer, pimp and gangster who was to be dubbed 'Britain's biggest vice boss' by the press. But he did not attempt to draw Ruth into prostitution. Astutely, he spotted her greater potential as a club hostess.

At that time Britain's licensing laws were stringent. Pubs were permitted to open for only nine hours or less a day.

To beat the drinks ban, afternoon and late-night drinking clubs were set up, often in seedy basements and garret rooms. Usually there were rooms off the main bar where the prostitutes who were an integral part of such places could entertain their clients.

Conley owned a number of these dives in Soho, Bayswater and Kensington. Most were sleazy, but a few, like his Court Club in Duke Street near Marble Arch, catered for the raffish 'officer classes' with money to spend. He set Ruth up as hostess at the Court, and her rather tinsel good looks and natural wit were soon drawing in a fast set of hard-spending drinkers.

Ruth herself was soon earning up to £20 a week – about ten times the national average. For a time, she and her infant son lived well.

SHORT-LIVED RESPECTABILITY

Despite her lifestyle, Ruth Neilson's maternal instincts, though erratic, were strong. She yearned for respectability not only for herself but for Andria. When she met George Johnston Ellis, a forty-one-year-old-dentist with a practice in Surrey, she thought she had it within her grasp.

Ellis was a bore and a drunk, but Ruth pursued him, moved in with him and finally, in November 1950, married him.

In October 1951 the couple had a daughter, Georgina, though by then the marriage was over. Ruth now had two young children to support. After recovering from Georgina's birth, she went back to London. Morris Conley was delighted to see her, and in October 1953 he made her manageress of his Little Club in Brompton Road, Knightsbridge.

A NEW JOB AND NEW ADMIRERS

She was paid £15 per week plus commission, with a £10 per week entertainment allowance, and a rent-free two-bedroom flat above the club rooms. Even if the job lacked respectability, it

> A SINGLE MOTHER AT SEVENTEEN, RUTH TURNED TO NUDE MODELLING TO SUPPORT HERSELF AND HER CHILD

Below: *For a while, David Blakely had the money to race cars but lacked the talent to do it particularly well.*

was security of a sort. But among her first customers were two men destined to be fatal to her very existence.

Desmond Cussen was a rich and well-established businessman, with a large car and an elegant bachelor flat in Devonshire Place, near Baker Street. Aged thirty-two, he had had several minor affairs, but when he set eyes on Ruth Ellis it was love at first sight.

For her part she was fond of him – with his money and status he fitted her needs very nicely. But within hours of their first meeting a complication in the shape of a handsome young drone named David Blakely was to enter the picture.

The first time Blakely came to the Little Club he was drunk and abusive. Ruth had him thrown out, commenting: 'I hope never to see that little shit again.'

But Blakely came back to apologise, and Ruth let him buy her a drink. Within a month, Blakely had moved into Ruth's flat above the club.

David Blakely was twenty-four when he first entered Ruth Ellis's life. He had been born on 17 June 1929 in Sheffield, the fourth child of a Scottish doctor. In 1940 his parents divorced, and David's mother married a well-to-do racing driver named Humphrey Cook, who imbued his stepson with a love of his sport.

Blakely's real father had left him £7,000 – then a considerable sum. Between about 1951 and his death David was to spend all of that and more on his dream, a prototype racing car that he called the Emperor. The Emperor was probably his only real love, though Ruth Ellis learned this too late.

So Blakely moved into Ruth's rooms above the Little Club, and they began a turbulent affair. Blakely had a fiancée, Linda Dawson, the daughter of a rich Halifax millowner, whom he tried to string along for a while, but he lost her as his life became more and more centred on Ruth.

Ruth Ellis's first judgement of Blakely had in fact been the correct one. Most of his acquaintances thought him a 'little shit' and he proved it by living off his new mistress, cadging drinks from her club and openly flirting with her female customers.

The pair had violent rows, but Ruth

BLAKELY'S PROTOTYPE RACING CAR, AFFECTIONATELY KNOWN AS THE EMPEROR, WAS PROBABLY HIS ONLY REAL LOVE

Below: *Ruth had a passion for night life.*

tolerated Blakely's behaviour until it started driving customers away. She had a confrontation with Morris Conley about it and, favourite or no, she was fired.

Meanwhile, Desmond Cussen had proved a faithful friend to Ruth, constantly by her side whenever she felt the need of a shoulder to cry on. When Conley threw her out of her job and her flat, it was he who took her into his own apartment along with Andria – Georgina had by then been adopted. Cussen and Ellis slept together, but her benefactor was by no means possessive. He allowed her to go on seeing Blakely, and even connived at the pair sleeping in his flat.

A CYCLE OF BETRAYAL, VIOLENCE AND RECONCILIATION

In August 1954 Blakely finally broke off his engagement with Linda Dawson. Ruth thought, wrongly, that this was for her benefit. Blakely took her to Buckinghamshire and his family, but she was treated there as a London tart. And she discovered that he was in any case sleeping with other women.

One of these was Carole Findlater, wife of Anthony 'Ant' Findlater, a skilled amateur mechanic who worked on Blakely's Emperor. He and Clive Gunnell, another skilled mechanic, were almost as keen as Blakely on the expensive racing car.

After every betrayal there followed

gin-soaked acrimony, violence and finally reconciliation. But it was a punishing cycle which must have damaged Cussen almost as much as the two principals.

In any case, in January 1955 he paid for a one-bedroom service flat at 44 Egerton Gardens, Kensington. Ruth – and by tacit agreement Blakely – could now have privacy, of a sort, for their rows.

That spring, Ruth discovered she was pregnant. Her divorce from George Ellis was almost final, and Blakely was free, but when she brought up the subject of marriage his response was to beat her so badly that she miscarried. The usual boozy, tearful remorse followed, with Blakely sending a bunch of red carnations and a note of apology.

On Good Friday, 7 April, they spent what was to be their last night together. Over breakfast Blakely gave her a signed photograph proclaiming his love, and finally proposed to her. They parted with Ruth blissfully happy, and with Blakely promising to take her to drinks with the Findlaters that evening. But he failed to keep his promise.

Instead, he went alone to meet the Findlaters at the Magdala. He told them that Ruth had him trapped, that he wanted to leave her, but that he feared the consequences. And he had a sympathetic audience. Both Ant and Carole thought Ellis a grasping, vulgar woman, totally unsuitable for their friend. They suggested that Blakely stay with them for the Easter holiday.

The following morning was Easter

Above left: *The .38 Smith and Wesson revolver with which Ruth Ellis committed murder.*

Above: *Ruth Ellis with long-time friend Desmond Cussen.*

WHEN RUTH TOLD BLAKELY SHE WAS PREGNANT HE BEAT HER UP SO BADLY THAT SHE SUFFERED A MISCARRIAGE

Saturday, and the fair on Hampstead Heath was in full swing. Blakely, the Findlaters, Clive Gunnell and other friends spent a jovial day.

Ruth Ellis spent a distracted one. On the previous evening, she had insisted that Cussen drive her to Hampstead in search of Blakely, but she was turned away from the Findlaters' house in Tanza Road, just up from the Magdala.

Now she returned, banging vainly on the Findlaters' front door and ringing them from a telephone box nearby – only to have them hang up on her. In the afternoon she began to kick Blakely's Vanguard van, screaming at the top of her voice, and the police were called to send her away.

Finally, on Sunday evening, she took a taxi to Tanza Road, spotted Blakely and Gunnell getting into the van, and followed them to the Magdala. She had a revolver in her bag....

ARREST AND TRIAL

That, in essence, was the story Ruth Ellis told DCS Crawford. She remembered little, she said, about Sunday afternoon, other than that 'I intended to find David, and shoot him.'

And therein lay the whole case, as far as the police were concerned. Ruth Ellis had cold-bloodedly gunned down her lover in front of a pub full of witnesses, and then admitted to the crime. But where had she got the gun? Unfortunately PC Thompson, in taking the weapon from her, had accidentally

Above: *Ruth and Desmond enjoy an evening out with friends.*

wiped all prints from it.

However, Ruth said that she had had the gun and ammunition for three years. It had been left with her as a pledge against a bar bill by one of her customers. The police were satisfied with her story.

So Ellis was charged with murder and removed to Holloway women's prison to await trial.

On 11 May 1955 she was arraigned at the Central Criminal Court of the Old Bailey before Mr Justice Barrie. The defence team was a distinguished and formidable one: Melford Stevenson QC, Sebag Shaw and Peter Rawlinson. Melford Stevenson asked for, and was granted, an adjournment of forty days in order to look for a precedent which would allow his client to plead guilty to manslaughter provoked by jealousy.

Unfortunately, no precedent could be found. Accordingly, when the trial proper began on 20 June, Ruth was advised to plead not guilty in the hope that her story would sway the jury to pity. But Stevenson had reckoned without Ruth's vanity.

Throughout her stay in Holloway, her main concern seems to have been that mousy roots were beginning to show through her platinum hair, and the day before her trial the Governor, Dr Charity Taylor, allowed her to bleach it. The result was that when she appeared in court she cut an impossibly glamorous figure in her smart black suit. Her lawyers were convinced that her dazzling

appearance alienated half the jury before the evidence was heard.

As it was, the trial lasted barely two days. On 21 June the jury took just twenty-three minutes to return a verdict of guilty, and made no recommendation for mercy. Ruth Ellis was sentenced to death by hanging.

PUBLIC OUTRAGE

Back in Holloway she refused her solicitor, Victor Mishcon, permission to appeal on her behalf, though he wrote in vain to the Home Secretary begging for mercy. Instead she asked her brother, Granville, to smuggle in poison so that she could kill herself. He refused.

Granville Neilson, in fact, rightly mistrusted Ruth's story of how she had come by the fatal gun, and spent his time in a frantic search for its real owner.

Meanwhile the general public – women in particular – launched an outcry against the sentence. Letters were written to MPs and petitions were launched.

It was all to no avail. As the clock began to strike nine on the morning of 13

Right: *Mr and Mrs Neilson, Ruth Ellis's parents, leave their home in Hemel Hempstead to visit Ruth on the eve of her execution.*

July 1955, Ruth drank a last glass of brandy and walked steadfastly to the Holloway gallows.

There is no retrospective doubt that Ellis's death was a turning point in the anti-hanging campaign, though another decade was to pass before the rope was abolished competely.

THE MISSING DETAILS EMERGE

It took even longer for what seems to have been the real truth to emerge. On the night before her death, Ruth summoned Victor Mishcon to the condemned cell and dictated her account of what she said really happened on that fateful Easter Sunday.

Desmond Cussen, she said, had given her the gun. The pair had been drinking Pernod in Cussen's flat while Ruth poured out her misery. Cussen drove her and the boy Andria out to Epping Forest, where he had shown her how to load the weapon and had given her tips on aiming and firing.

Later that afternoon, after having more to drink, she had taken the loaded pistol and demanded that Cussen – not a taxi, as she had stated – drive her to the Findlaters' house in Tanza Road. From there she had made her way to the Magdala.

If this was true, what were Cussen's motives? He was certainly besotted with Ruth, lavishing money, presents and offers of marriage upon her. He had never refused her slightest whim. Perhaps he was simply going along blindly, as usual, with her wishes.

Or, as has been suggested, did he simply give her the gun, knowing that in her mood of jealous, drink-fuelled rage she would kill his rival Blakely. In which case, was he also convinced that she would be acquitted?

Desmond Cussens visited Ruth Ellis every day during her remand in Holloway prison, bringing her flowers, chocolates and other presents. But as soon as the guilty verdict was pronounced he broke all contact with her. He died twenty years after his troubled lover, in Australia, without apparently ever having told his side of the story.

Below: *Huge crowds gathered outside Holloway Prison on the morning of Ruth Ellis's execution.*

SAM SHEPPARD
A Travesty of Justice

A well-respected citizen is arrested for the brutal murder of his pregnant wife. Vital forensic evidence is ignored and the trial is a travesty of justice. In this, as in so many murder cases, there are no winners, only losers

Saturday, 3 July 1954 – the eve of Independence Day – was a busy one for Dr Sam Sheppard, though his wife, four-and-a-half-months pregnant Marilyn, took things rather more easily. Dr Sheppard was on call at his father's Bay View Hospital in Bay Village, Cleveland, Ohio and split his day between work and socializing with their close neighbours, Don and Nancy Ahern.

THE FATAL EVENING

The Aherns' two young sons and seven-year-old Chip Sheppard ate first, while their parents sat on the porch overlooking the lake and sipped drinks. Later the Ahern boys were sent home and Chip went to bed, after which the four adults spent a relaxed evening.

By midnight Marilyn and Sam were drowsing. The Aherns decided to go home to bed. Before leaving, Nancy Ahern locked the lakeside door of the house for Marilyn. Then she and her husband went out by the main door on to the road. Marilyn had gone upstairs to the bedroom, Sam was snoring on the sofa.

At 5.45a.m. John Spencer Houk, a businessman friend of Sheppard's who

Above: The Sheppards' clapboard house in Bay Village, Cleveland, Ohio.

Opposite: Dr Sam Sheppard on his way to court.

Below: A detailed diagram of the Sheppard house shows the scene of the crime.

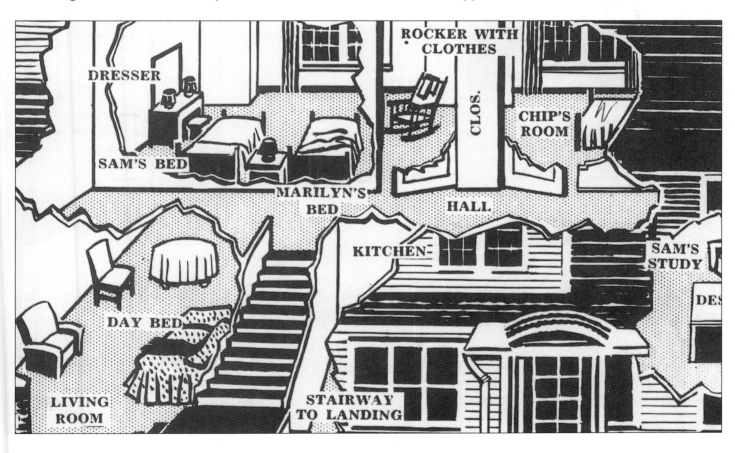

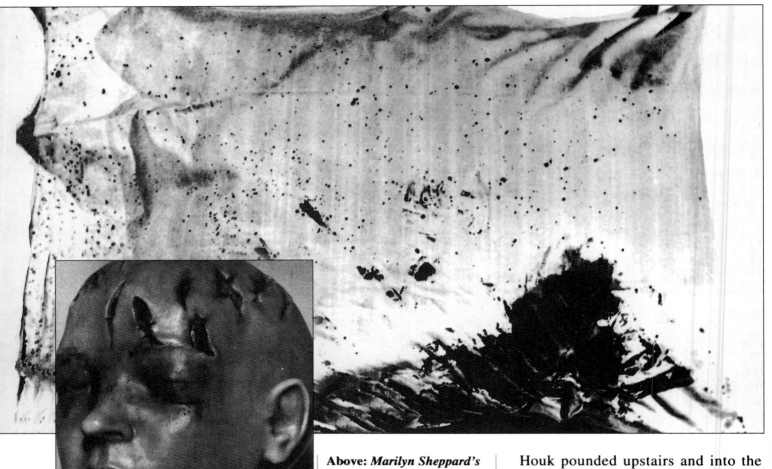

Above: *Marilyn Sheppard's blood-spattered pillow.*

Left: *A model shows the horrific wounds inflicted on Marilyn Sheppard's skull.*

was also mayor of Bay Village, was awakened by the shrilling noise of his bedside telephone. Sleepily he picked it up and heard the voice of Sam Sheppard: 'For God's sake, Spen, come quick! I think they've killed Marilyn!'

SCENES OF VIOLENCE

Houk's house was just 100 yards from that of the Sheppards. He and his wife arrived at 5.55 to a scene of chaos. The roadside door was open and Sheppard's medical bag lay inside, its contents scattered around. A desk drawer hung open, and the immediate impression was of a burglary. Sam Sheppard sat, stripped to the waist, in his den. His trousers were wet and his face was bruised. His neck was contorted with agony.

IT WAS A COSY, RELAXED, EVE-OF-INDEPENDENCE-DAY SUPPER WITH A COUPLE OF CLOSE NEIGHBOURS

Houk pounded upstairs and into the Sheppards' bedroom. Marilyn lay on her back, her legs protruding from the bottom of the bed. Her face, hair and pillow were plastered with blood from over thirty deep head wounds.

Three minutes after sunrise Patrolman Fred Drenham arrived. He was closely followed by Richard Sheppard, one of Sam's elder brothers, and his wife, and by the other brother Stephen and the local Chief of Police, John Eaton. At 6.30a.m., as police began their systematic work at the murder scene, Sam was driven by Stephen and John Eaton to Bay View Hospital for a check-up. Nurses who tended Sam were later to testify that his lips were badly cut and swollen, and his front teeth were loose.

By 9a.m. Sam had been fitted with a neck brace and was heavily sedated. He was, however, able to answer questions from the coroner of Cuyahoga County, Dr Samuel Gerber, who had already made a brief visit to the house. At 11a.m., Detectives Robert Schottke and Patrick Gareau of Cleveland Police took over the questioning.

The two detectives had already noted that there had been no signs of forced entry into the Sheppard house, and the only fingerprint was a thumb-mark which subsequently turned out to be Chip's. Sam's corduroy jacket, which the Aherns had seen him wearing the night before, was neatly folded and lying on the sofa. No bloodstained weapon had been found, and, despite the confusion, the detectives were pretty sure that the motive had not been burglary.

They were not happy that Sheppard had been taken to his family-run hospital, and they were certainly not happy with his uncorroborated story. As Schottke was to tell him: 'The evidence points very strongly at you. I don't know what my partner thinks, but I think you killed your wife.'

By that evening the murder was headline news, not merely because of its bloody drama but because it involved the Sheppards, one of Ohio's most prominent and controversial medical families.

PROMINENT MEDICAL FAMILY

Samuel Holmes Shepherd was born in Cleveland on 29 December 1923, the youngest of Dr Richard and Ethel Sheppard's three boys. Richard Sheppard was a general surgeon who was beginning to gain a reputation as an osteopath, at a time when this holistic form of medicine was little known in the United States.

Academically Sam was not particularly bright, but he had an ability for hard work which got him through his exams. In 1943, as an alternative to military service, he began to study medicine at the Western Reserve University in Cleveland, at Hanover College, Indiana, and finally at the Osteopathic School of Physicians and Surgeons in Los Angeles.

In the meantime he had met and fallen in love with Marilyn Reese, and in November 1945, when she was nineteen, the couple were married at the First Hollywood Methodist Church in Los Angeles.

In 1948 Sam graduated as a doctor of medicine, and he and his wife intended to stay in California. Sam's father, however, had that same year founded the Bay View Hospital back in Cleveland, and Sam,

'I DON'T KNOW WHAT MY PARTNER THINKS, BUT I THINK YOU KILLED YOUR WIFE'

Below: *Newsmen pack the courtroom during the trial.*

with his two brothers, was pressured into joining the family 'firm'.

Within months, business was booming. By 1954 Bay View was one of the most prestigious hospitals in the state.

Now, despite their suspicions, the police were reluctant to arrest one of the Dr Sheppards of Bay View. As his attorney, William Corrigan, told him: 'The only way to convict yourself, Sam, is by opening your mouth.'

PRESS CAMPAIGN

There was one man, however, who was unimpressed by Sheppard's status in the community. He was Louis Benson Seltzer, editor of the *Cleveland Press*, and well known for his hard-hitting campaigns against crooked politicians and 'soft' police departments.

On 21 July, seventeen days after the killing, the *Cleveland Press* ran a splash headline: 'Why No Inquest? Do It Now, Dr Gerber.'

Dr Gerber, the fifty-seven-year-old coroner for Cuyahoga County, had felt Seltzer's righteous wrath before. The next day he called an inquest. Gerber refused witnesses the right to counsel, and when William Corrigan protested he had him thrown out to tumultuous cheers.

Above: *Police search Dr Sheppard's medical bag after the murder.*

Sheppard was knocked out from behind. When he regained his senses he saw on the floor his own police surgeon's badge – he was unpaid police surgeon for the Bay Valley force – which he normally kept in his wallet. He took Marilyn's pulse 'and felt that she was gone'.

After checking that his son Chip was still asleep and safe, Sheppard had heard a noise, ran downstairs and saw 'a form rapidly progressing somewhere'. Sheppard had chased the figure down from the porch to the lake, where he had grappled with a large man with bushy hair. The man had caught his neck in an armlock, and he had passed out.

When he came to he had woken up on his face by the water's edge. His T-shirt was missing, though he could not recollect what had happened to it.

Also missing from his wrist was his gold watch, which was later found, spattered with Marilyn's blood, in a duffle bag in the Sheppards' boat-house by the lake. This watch was to be the centre of vigorous controversy later. Sheppard had then staggered back to the house.

TRIED FOR FIRST DEGREE MURDER

The trial of Sam Sheppard on the charge of first degree murder began in the Court of Common Pleas, Cleveland, on Monday 18 October 1954. But because of delay in jury selection – many admitted that they had firm ideas on the case – it did not properly get under way until 4 November. The judge was Edward Blythin, and Sheppard pleaded Not Guilty.

The main thrust of the case against Sheppard was indicated by prosecuting counsel John Mahon in his opening address: 'The state will prove that Sheppard and Miss X talked together about divorce and marriage. No one was in that house that morning on 4 July attempting to commit a burglary. No evidence has been found that any burglar or marauder was there.'

The Aherns were called early in the trial. Don said that he had never seen the placid Sam Sheppard lose his temper, though Nancy introduced a hesitant note when she said that, though she was sure

Sam Sheppard waived his right not to give evidence, and was questioned for eight hours by Gerber. Among other things, Sheppard denied having committed adultery with a mystery woman in California named only as 'Miss X'. Finally, on 30 July, he was arrested, even before Gerber recorded his verdict that Marilyn had been murdered.

Sheppard's statement at the time of his arrest was essentially the same as he had made shortly after the crime was committed. He said that he had been awakened, as he lay on the sofa, by his wife's screams from upstairs. He refused to guess what time it might have been.

'I charged into our room and saw a form with a light garment,' he said. 'It was grappling with something or someone....'

He and this person had wrestled, until

Marilyn was very much in love with her husband, she had never been sure of Sam's feelings towards Marilyn.

Dr Samuel Gerber, the coroner, caused a sensation when he spoke of a 'blood signature' on the yellow pillowcase under Marilyn's battered head. 'In this bloodstain I could make out the impression of a surgical instrument,' he said. The instrument, he suggested, 'had two blades, each about three inches long, with serrated edges'.

No weapon of any kind had been found at the house, but, said Gerber, 'the impression could only have been made by an instrument similar to the type of surgical instrument I had in mind'. Curiously, he was not asked to specify just what the mysterious instrument was.

On 1 December came another sensation, when Miss X entered the witness box. She identified herself as Susan Hayes, a twenty-four-year-old laboratory technician who had worked at the Bay View Hospital and met Sam there in 1951.

They had begun their affair in California, after she had left Bay View to work in Los Angeles in 1954. She admitted that they had slept together, as well as making love in cars. 'He said that he loved his wife very much but not as a wife, and was thinking of getting a divorce,' she testified.

This evidence meant that Sam was not only a perjurer – he had denied adultery at the inquest – but guilty of the then criminal offence, under Ohio law, of adultery.

On the stand, Sam now admitted lying at the inquest, saying that he had done so to protect Susan Hayes rather than himself. In any case, he went on, he had never truly been in love with her, and had never discussed divorce with either her or his wife. He admitted that he had committed adultery with women other than Susan Hayes, but refused to name them.

Summing up for the prosecution, Thomas Parrino, an assistant prosecutor, said: 'If the defendant would lie under oath to protect a lady, how many lies would he utter to protect his own life?'

Corrigan's defence was, on the face of it, poor. He made no mention of one or

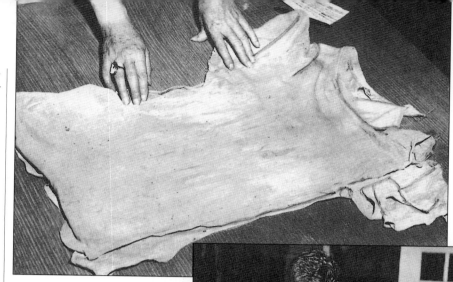

Above and right: *Police examine evidence during the investigation of the case.*

THE CORONER CAUSED A SENSATION WHEN HE SPOKE OF A 'BLOOD SIGNATURE' ON THE PILLOWCASE UNDER MARILYN'S BATTERED HEAD

IF THE DEFENDANT WOULD LIE UNDER OATH TO PROTECT A LADY, HOW MANY LIES WOULD HE UTTER TO PROTECT HIS OWN LIFE?

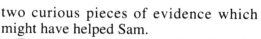

two curious pieces of evidence which might have helped Sam.

Tooth chippings had been found on the bedroom floor which belonged neither to Sam nor to Marilyn. There was firm evidence that Marilyn had bitten her attacker savagely, though Sheppard bore no bite marks. There was the business of the mysterious surgical instrument. And there were wool threads, found under Marilyn's nails, which matched no clothing in the house – not hers, not Sam's, not Chip's. Above all, there was the blood-spattered watch.

Instead, Corrigan took up the prosecution's sex theme and made a negative mess of it. 'Is sex the only thing in a marriage?' he asked. 'Sheppard wandered from the path of rectitude. That didn't prove he didn't love his wife, his home, or his family.'

After a briefing from Judge Blythin on the laws governing circumstantial evidence, and the difference between first and second degree murder, the jury retired. They returned on Tuesday, 21 December after over four days' deliberation. Their decision was that Sam Sheppard was guilty of second degree murder, and Judge Blythin sentenced him to life imprisonment.

After what must have been a melancholy Christmas for the Sheppard family, William Corrigan retrieved the keys of Sam's house from the police and handed them over to Dr Paul Leland Kirk. One of the country's leading forensic scientists, he had undertaken to do independent tests.

EXHAUSTIVE FORENSIC WORK

Dr Kirk began work in the Sheppards' house in January 1955, and after studying the results in his California headquarters produced a 10,000-word report three and a half months later.

Among the detailed facts examined in the report the most important was Dr Kirk's emphatic assertion that a fourth person, other than Sam, Marilyn or Chip, had been in the house on the night of the murder. Blood on the wardrobe door demonstrably did not match that of any of the Sheppards. And teeth fragments on the carpet showed that Marilyn had bitten her attacker very deeply, though, as had been shown at the trial, Sheppard bore no such scars.

Dr Kirk was able to show that whoever delivered the death blows to Marilyn would have been covered in her flying blood, but the only stain on Sam's clothing was a spot on the knee of his trousers – gained, he claimed, when he had knelt to take his wife's pulse.

Furthermore, bloodstains on the walls showed that the killer had struck with his left hand, while Sam was right-handed. The blows had undoubtedly been made with a blunt instrument such as a piece of piping, which made nonsense of the coroner's 'surgical instrument' theory.

'No actual proof of a technical nature

was ever offered indicating the guilt of the defendant,' he concluded.

Despite what seemed to be Kirk's irrefutable report, Judge Blythin refused, on 10 May 1955, to grant a retrial. Six weeks later the Ohio Court of Appeals praised 'the originality and imagination' of Dr Kirk, but nevertheless turned down an appeal for a new trial.

The following summer, on 31 May 1956, the Ohio Supreme Court upheld Sheppard's conviction by five votes to two. Hope was raised, however, by the two dissenting judges, who expressed the view that there had been little real evidence to prove Sheppard guilty, and that Judge Blythin had accepted gossip as evidence.

But on 19 December the highest judicial body in the land, the United States Supreme Court, refused to review the case on technical grounds. Again, however, doubts were expressed about the conduct of the Ohio judiciary.

A CONVICT'S CONFESSION

Sheppard's hopes were raised once more six months later, when, in June 1957 a convict named Donald Wedler, who was serving a ten-year sentence for a Florida hold-up, confessed to the murder. He claimed that he had been in Cleveland, Ohio on the day of Marilyn's killing, and after taking heroin had stolen a car and driven around looking for a house to burgle.

He had found a suitable one, a large white house on a lake front, had broken in, crept past a man asleep on a settee and gone upstairs.

A woman in an upstairs bedroom had awakened as he was preparing to rifle her dressing table, and he had beaten her repeatedly with an iron pipe. Then, as he fled downstairs, he had encountered a man, whom he had struck down with the pipe, before flinging the impromptu weapon into the lake and driving away.

The coroner was quick to point out discrepancies in the story. Sheppard had said that he was struck down from behind in the bedroom, not on the stairs, and Wedler had made no mention of a struggle in the garden by the lake. Nor was Wedler a burly man with the 'bushy' hair mentioned by Sheppard – he was slight, though he did have unruly, curly hair.

What interested Sheppard's lawyers most was the fact that a lie-detector expert who tested Wedler was quite certain that he was telling the truth, 'or what he believed to be the truth'.

Unfortunately, there were many imponderables about the Wedler story. As a heroin user, he might have been telling the truth and have confused the details, but equally he might have invented the whole thing after reading newspaper accounts of the case, and convinced his

Below: *Susan Hayes. It was revealed that she was Sam Sheppard's mistress.*

drug-addled mind that he was the murderer.

In the end, it was the plethora of newspaper speculation surrounding the original event which led to a successful appeal – but only after Sheppard had served ten years in jail. In 1961 William Corrigan died, and in his place Stephen Sheppard hired a smart, fast-talking young attorney from Boston named F. Lee Bailey.

RETRIAL AT LAST

In April 1963, after a series of legal moves, Bailey lodged a petition with the US District Court, a federal rather than state body, that the case be reopened. This time he was successful. After almost a year's deliberation, Judge Carl Weinman delivered his verdict on 15 July 1964. The original trial, he said, had been a 'mockery of justice'. He ordered Sheppard to be released pending a retrial.

Lawyer F. Lee Bailey immediately swept into the attack. Quoting the exhaustive inquiry undertaken by Dr Kirk, he compared it with the muddled and pathetic attempts of the Cleveland Police, whose search for clues, he forced them to admit, had been perfunctory to a degree. Their check for fingerprints had been particularly casual. They had not even tried to get prints from the bloodstained watch found in the duffle bag, and had also ignored a key-ring and chain which accompanied it.

Bailey produced a photograph of the watch, which had blood speckles across the face such as could have been caused had Sheppard been wearing it when he battered his wife to death. But, as Bailey pointed out, there were also speckles of blood on the back of the watch and the inside of the wristband, which certainly could not have got there if he really had been wearing it under such conditions.

On 6 June, 1966, the United States Supreme Court overturned Sheppard's conviction, and he walked free.

UNANSWERED QUESTIONS

There were, of course, still questions which remained unanswered. One was the old Sherlock Holmesian puzzle of the

Above: *Sam Sheppard outside Ohio Supreme Court.*

'THE ANSWER TO THE SHEPPARD CASE RIDDLE,' WROTE A PRIVATE DETECTIVE, 'LIES IN BAY VILLAGE'

---

dog that did nothing in the night.

For if an unknown intruder had indeed broken in, why had the family dog Koko not barked a warning? Although neither police nor defendants thought fit to bring their suspicions into the open, privately they admitted that, if Sam did not kill his wife Marilyn, then it was someone who knew her, and the house, well.

As Harold Bretnall, a New York private detective hired by the Sheppard family, wrote in a report dated 1955: 'The answer to the Sheppard case riddle lies in Bay Village.' At the first trial, the jury had heard part of a statement made by Sam to detectives, in which he had said that Marilyn had 'spurned lovers – potential lovers...three that I know of and I am pretty sure more'.

Although not named at the trial, the men had, it was claimed, been identified to the investigating officers. Bretnall also claimed that a pair of Marilyn's bedroom slippers bore evidence that she had left the house during the night of 4 July 1954 while she was wearing them. 'Marilyn Sheppard was murdered by someone who was a frequent visitor to the Sheppard home,' wrote Bretnall.

The blood-speckled watch, too, posed unanswered questions. For if it had been splashed with Marilyn's blood, it must surely have been lying on the bedside table when she was killed – when it should have been downstairs on her husband's wrist. Did he come to bed, leaving his corduroy jacket downstairs, place his watch on the bedside table and batter his wife to death?

Or did he come to bed, take off his watch, hear an intruder, put on his trousers to investigate, get himself laid out – and then inexplicably lie to the police about his movements?

FURTHER TRAGEDY

One thing was sure: Marilyn's death and Sam Sheppard's ruined career were not the only tragedies involved in the drama. Sam's mother Edith was deeply shocked by the event, and took an overdose of sleeping pills during the first trial. She recovered at the family hospital.

But on 17 January 1955, soon after her youngest son was convicted of murder, she shot herself. Eleven days later Sam's father, Dr Richard Sheppard, died at the age of sixty-five of a bleeding gastric ulcer. Almost exactly eight years after Mrs Sheppard's suicide, Marilyn's father, Thomas Reese, also shot himself.

Soon after his release, Sam married Ariane Tebbenjohanne, who had supported his cause. In December 1967, after a vigorous fight to regain his medical licence, it was granted, and Sheppard joined the staff of the Youngstown Osteopathic Hospital, Ohio. His appointment lasted a year, until a malpractice claim was made against the hospital. The insurance company refused to pay out until Sam resigned.

On the day of his resignation, 3 December 1968, Sheppard was sued for divorce by Ariane. She claimed that she had suffered mental and physical cruelty at the hands of 'that maniac'.

Sheppard had authorized a ghost-written autobiography entitled *Endure and Conquer*, but most of the proceeds went to pay F. Lee Bailey's legal fees. While fighting once more to re-establish his medical career, he took up wrestling. In October 1969 he married his manager's daughter, a twenty-year-old named Colleen Strickland.

For a while his wrestling career and the third marriage seemed to prosper, but Sheppard was consuming heavier and heavier amounts of vodka. On 5 April 1970 he died of liver failure.

ORGANIZED CRIME

THE KRAY TWINS
A Lethal Double-Act

From playground bullies via the boxing ring, East End twins Reggie and Ronnie Kray went on to build a gangland empire the like of which London had never seen before. 'The Firm' allowed no liberties to be taken, and was feared by all

On 24 October 1933 twin boys were born to Mrs Violet Kray of 178 Vallance Road, Bethnal Green. She named them Reginald and Ronald.

The twins grew up in London's East End, surrounded by street traders, boxers and petty criminals. Fighting was a way of life for children in Bethnal Green. But Reggie and Ronnie seemed to derive enormous pleasure out of terrifying and hurting other human beings.

BOXERS

At fourteen they found another, more acceptable outlet for their violent tendencies – boxing.

Both lads showed real promise as amateurs, but demonstrated a completely different approach to the sport, a difference which was reflected in their personalities as men. Reggie was a skilful

Above: *'I gotta horse!' Ronnie Kray, with minder, poses briefly as a racehorse owner.*

Opposite: *At 18 years of age, Reggie and Ronnie Kray were successful young boxers with two years of professional experience behind them. Their styles were very different, however: Reggie was a skilled fighter, but Ronnie won his matches by vicious slugging.*

Left: *The twins were adored by their mother Vi, for whom they could do no wrong. But their career in boxing soon came to an end when they were put on probation for beating up a police constable.*

Above: *To the end of her life Vi kept her faith in her sons. They are seen together here with the twins' grandfather, who had also been a professional boxer, outside her modest East End house in Vallance Road.*

IN BOXING AS IN LIFE, RONNIE WAS A HARD AND FEARLESS SLUGGER

and resourceful boxer, whereas Ronnie was a slugger, totally fearless and vicious. The net result of these contrasting styles, however, was the same. They both won every fight.

At sixteen the twins turned professional and maintained their unbeaten record until their careers were brought to an abrupt halt. They both got into a street fight during which they beat up a police constable.

They were let off with a probationary sentence. But fight managers dislike boxers with a reputation for violence outside the ring, since any serious conviction usually costs a fighter his licence.

The next watershed in the Krays' young lives came in March 1952, when they were called up to do their National Service. They had no intention of spending two years in the Royal Fusiliers and made that immediately and absolutely clear. The boys absconded and were back at Vallance Road for tea after a mere six hours of army service.

They were arrested, escaped, arrested again and escaped again. They continued their running battle with the army for more than a year before the Royal Fusiliers gave up on them. After spending nine months in a military prison at Shepton Mallet they were given a dishonourable discharge.

MANAGEMENT PROSPECTS

When they were released in 1953, the twins went straight back to the East End.

While they considered their career prospects, the twins established semi-residence in the Regal Billiard Hall in the Mile End Road. It was a seedy, down-at-heel place which had become a popular hang-out for small-time criminals.

Around the time the Krays arrived at the Regal, there was a sudden outbreak of violence and vandalism. The twins never seemed to be directly involved, but there were fights every night, and there were anonymous threats to burn the place down.

ASPIRATION 'UP WEST'

By 1955, the Firm was the established power through Hackney and Mile End to Walthamstow. And they were starting to make real money.

But the twins had their sights set on bigger things. Reggie wanted the 'good life', the wealth that West End crime offered, and Ronnie craved the kudos that came with being a big-time gangland boss.

Ronnie spent most of his time planning elaborate deals and alliances which would establish the Firm 'up West', but none of them ever quite worked out. The Krays were too wild and too dangerous for the established West End gangs to deal with. They closed ranks and shut the twins out.

This frustrated Ronnie, and the more frustrated he became, the more violent his thinking became. He grew increasingly paranoid and psychotic, toting his guns in public and threatening to 'do' people all the time.

Ronnie finally had his chance to use his gun for real when a young docker tried to cheat one of the Firm's associates. The docker gave Ronnie some lip, and Ronnie promptly shot him in the leg.

Everyone in the East End, including

The manager eventually left and the twins approached the owners with an offer. They would pay the owners £5 a week to take the hall over. The owners accepted, the Krays became managers, and the violence and vandalism stopped as abruptly as it had started.

Reggie, who proved an astute businessman, set about renovating and redecorating the Regal, and before long it was becoming a successful commercial concern.

It also continued to serve as a meeting point for local criminals, but now the Krays offered them a genuine service. There were lock-up cubicles under the seats for thieves' tools, and stolen goods could be stashed round the back. The Krays received a cut of every job planned or executed from their premises.

The billiard hall was now making good money, and the Krays were supplementing this with extortion. Clubs, billiard halls, unlicensed gambling dens and illicit bookmakers from Bethnal Green and Mile End were soon paying a 'pension' to 'the Firm', as the Kray gang was now known.

Despite their growing reputation, however, the Krays still had no real power. Each section of the East End had its own 'guv'nor', and the twins hadn't yet achieved 'guv'nor' status.

However, their activities were causing some displeasure with these established gang bosses. There were a number of bloody showdowns and, despite being outnumbered and outgunned by their rivals, the twins always seemed to come out on top.

Above: *From the Regal Billiard Hall in London's Mile End Road, the Kray twins soon moved on to bigger and better enterprises. At a charity evening in the Kentucky Club, they line up for a photograph with brother Charles (behind Ronnie, right).*

Right: *The psychopathic Ronnie was a practising homosexual, but Reggie did not resemble his twin brother in this respect. Here he escorts long-standing girl-friend Frances Shea in Vallance Road.*

the police, knew that the Firm were responsible for the shooting, and after a few hours they picked up a man they believed to be Ronnie Kray and put him into an identification parade.

'Yes, but I'm not Ronald Kray,' said the man in the line-up. 'I'm Reggie Kray. I can prove it – and, what's more, I can prove I wasn't anywhere near where this bloke says he was shot.' The police, angry and embarrassed, had no option but to free Reggie with an apology.

OUT FOR REVENGE

The police, who do not like to be bested, now had it in for the Krays. Their chance to nail one of them came the following year, in 1956.

Terry Martin, a street trader from Stepney, had been taking 'extreme liberties', and Ronnie decided that he needed 'teaching a lesson'. He dragged Martin out of the Britannia pub in Watney Street, slashed him twice on the head with a bayonet, stabbed him in the shoulder and then kicked him unconscious.

Ronnie was being driven home in his new black Buick when police picked him up. They found a crowbar and a bayonet in the car and when they asked how he got blood on his shirt, Ronnie shrugged. 'I 'ad a nose bleed, di'n' I?'

Ronnie was found guilty of grievous

Above: *Reggie eventually married Frances Shea. He looks on as best man Ronnie kisses the bride.*

DESPITE THE BAYONET FOUND IN HIS CAR, RONNIE CASUALLY TOLD THE POLICE HIS BLOODSTAINED SHIRT WAS CAUSED BY A NOSE BLEED

---

bodily harm and sentenced to three years' imprisonment.

It was the first time since they were born that the twins had been separated for more than a few days at a time, and most East End pundits said it would be the end of the Firm.

They were wrong. Reggie, freed from his brother's manic influence, not only continued to run the gang's illegal activities but also embarked on several legitimate enterprises. He rented an empty shop in Bow Road with his older brother Charles and converted it into a drinking club, the Double R – in honour of himself and his absent brother.

The club was a huge success, not only

Left: *Bride and groom and best man pose for the camera at the wedding reception.*

Right: *All for one and one for all: the twins and brother Charles affirm their family ties.*

with local villains but also with certain members of the entertainment and sporting fraternities who considered it was chic to rub shoulders with the criminal element.

INSANITY

In prison, Ronnie Kray soon showed signs of severe mental illness. He became paranoid and depressed and complained of 'hearing voices'. He couldn't sleep, and wouldn't eat because he was convinced that he was being poisoned.

He was transferred to the psychiatric wing of Winchester Prison for observation. There he was put on sedatives and showed some signs of improvement until the morning he received news that his favourite auntie, Rose, had died of cancer.

By that evening Ronnie was totally incoherent and had to be strapped into a straitjacket for his own protection. The following day, doctors at Winchester certified Ronald Kray as legally insane.

Ronnie was transferred to Long Grove Hospital near Epsom where he received the very best psychiatric treatment. He was diagnosed as a paranoid schizophrenic.

Doctors treated his illness with a new wonder drug called Stematol. Within days Ronnie was stabilized and was showing marked signs of improvement.

But he was still technically insane which meant that, despite the fact that he had only a year of his sentence to serve, the authorities could detain him indefinitely.

Alarmed by this prospect, Reggie Kray decided something had to be done to rectify the situation. He drove up to Long Grove, switched clothes with his brother and took his place in the hospital while Ronnie walked to freedom.

On the run, Ronnie was taken to see a top Harley Street psychiatrist who, not knowing his patient's true identity, pronounced him sane.

But Ronald Kray was most certainly not sane. Without close medical supervision, his condition deteriorated rapidly. Even Reggie was eventually forced to face the fact that his brother needed professional help. So he did the

Above: *Although Reggie was cleverer and more responsible than his brother, he was constantly influenced by Ronnie, dressing like him and following him in his pose as a big-time gangster.*

RONNIE KRAY, IN COMMON WITH HIS HERO AL CAPONE AND THE BOSTON STRANGLER, WAS A PARANOID SCHIZOPHRENIC

unthinkable. He called the police.

Ronnie was returned not to hospital, but to jail to complete his sentence. He was no longer technically insane, so the ploy had worked. He was released in the spring of 1959.

CLEVER BUSINESS MOVES

During Ronnie's absence, Reggie and Charles Kray had proved extremely shrewd. They had moved away from street violence and consolidated their section of the East End by negotiation, albeit with underlying menace. They had also formed a loose partnership with one of the big-time West End bosses, Billy Hill. Hill had recently gone into semi-retirement but retained extensive interests in the West End, particularly illicit gambling, and he had needed someone to look after the show.

In the mid-fifties, gambling fever had hit London. Illegal casinos had become a major industry which was almost completely controlled by the underworld. Even high-society 'chemin de fer' parties at their secret Belgravia and Mayfair addresses were paying a 'fee' to the Mob to ensure that their sport continued uninterrupted.

Hill had introduced Reggie and Charles Kray to several of these parties where they acted as minders. It was a good source of income and, more important, it gave them contacts and a presence in the West End.

Parliament was on the verge of legalizing gambling, a move which was intended to legitimize the industry and to remove the criminal element from it. Reggie Kray, however, reckoned it would be just like Las Vegas – a licence to print money.

The casinos would have to be run by someone, and who better than the men who already knew the ropes, men like Reggie Kray? All he had to do was keep his nose clean and grab the opportunity when it came along. The only problem was Ronnie. He was now back on the scene, paranoid and hostile, toting guns and talking about 'doing' people.

Ironically, it was Ronnie's thuggery that eventually got the Krays their first solid stake in the West End. He had been putting pressure on racketeer landlord Peter Rachman to pay protection.

Rachman was too clever to let himself get on that particular treadmill, but knew he would have to do something to get Ronnie off his back. So he negotiated a deal which gave the Krays an interest in Esmerelda's Barn, a newly licensed casino in Belgravia's Wilton Place.

In addition to this, the Krays established themselves as 'security consultants' to other casinos in Mayfair, Chelsea and Knightsbridge, some thirty in all, each paying £150 a week for the benefit of the Firm's expertise.

By 1962, the American Mafia had started to buy stakes in some of the smarter casinos and the Krays established themselves as the Mob's London minders.

Despite Ronnie's ongoing lunacy, Reggie continued with his efforts to smarten up the Krays' image. He opened a new, plusher club in the East End, and became actively involved in a whole range of charitable works – old folks' homes, cancer appeals and boys' clubs.

By this time a certain policeman, Detective Inspector Leonard 'Nipper' Read was starting to take an unhealthy interest in the Kray twins and their Firm.

Below and bottom: *As the twins' influence grew 'up West', so did their ambition to rub shoulders with showbiz personalities such as film star Judy Garland or actress Barbara Windsor.*

LAUNDRYMEN TO THE MOB

By 1965, business was booming for the twins. They had their casinos and clubs and their protection racket, and they were involved in large-scale fraud.

Then, in April, they were approached by one of their American Mafia contacts, Angelo Bruno, to launder $55,000 worth of stolen bearer bonds. They were part of a $2 million consignment of bonds that the Mafia was holding in New York. If the Krays did well, they could act as the exclusive Mafia fence in London.

The whole idea appealed to the Firm – particularly to Ronnie, whose dream of being a big-time Mob boss seemed finally to be becoming a reality. The Firm bought the first shipment of bonds at a quarter of their face value and found, with the help of a crooked merchant banker, Alan Cooper, no trouble in disposing of them. Things had never looked better.

ORGY OF VIOLENCE

But soon people started 'taking liberties' again, and Ronnie couldn't stand for that. The target of his displeasure on this occasion was one George Cornell, an enforcer for the rival Richardson gang.

On 9 March 1966, Ronnie slipped his 9mm Mauser automatic into his shoulder holster, collected henchman Ian Barrie, and told 'Scotch' Jack Dickson to drive them down to one of Cornell's hangouts, a pub called the Blind Begger.

When they arrived, Cornell was sitting perched on a stool at the far end of the bar, drinking a beer with a couple of friends.

'Well, look who's here!' said Cornell, smiling. But his smile soon evaporated as Barrie fired two warning shots into the ceiling. Ronnie Kray never spoke. He raised his Mauser and shot Cornell through the head. The massive 9mm shell exploded his skull and he died instantly.

When the police arrived at the Blind Begger, nobody had seen anything. The identity of George Cornell's killer,

Above: *An unlikely pairing. The homosexual Ronnie in conversation with Christine Keeler, central character in the sex-and-security scandal involving War Minister John Profumo and Russian spy Ivanov in 1963.*

IN THE EARLY SIXTIES THE KRAYS MADE THEIR FIRST CONTACTS WITH THE US MAFIA - WHICH WOULD PROVE VERY USEFUL LATER

JACK 'THE HAT' MCVITIE HAD DONE MUCH TO IRK THE TWINS, BUT HIS ONE SUICIDAL ERROR WAS TO CALL RONNIE A 'FAT POOF'

---

however, was the worst-kept secret in the East End. And among those who were fully aware of his identity was Detective Inspector 'Nipper' Read.

Rather than lying low after the murder of Cornell, Ronnie seemed to have his taste for violence heightened and he embarked on an orgy of maiming and killing.

All reason seemed to leave the twins at this point in time. Perhaps their most bizarre escapade involved Frank 'Mad Axe Man' Mitchell.

Mitchell, an old friend of Ronnie's, was serving a thirty-two-year sentence in Dartmoor for robbery with violence.

On 12 December 1966 they had him snatched from a working party on the moor. A massive manhunt ensued and the Krays hid Mitchell in a friend's flat in Barking. But it wasn't long before the twins regretted taking Mitchell on. His incessant, child-like demands on them became intolerable. He, too, would have to be taught a lesson.

On Christmas Eve, Reggie Kray told Mitchell that he was going to be moved down to a safe house for the holiday. At 8.30 p.m., he was bundled into the back of a van which sped off down Barking Road. Frank Mitchell was never seen again.

THE KILLING OF JACK 'THE HAT'

The Firm was falling apart at the seams, but desertion from the ranks was rare. Deemed a 'diabolical liberty', it was dealt with appropriately.

One exception was Jack 'The Hat' McVitie, a strong-arm man who had worked with the Krays at various times over the years. He was definitely a liberty-taker. He had taken money from Reggie for a contract killing and then bungled it. He had threatened the twins behind their back. And, worst of all, he had described Ronnie as a 'fat poof'.

The twins agreed that McVitie must be punished. At Ronnie's insistence, Reggie would be the one to mete out that punishment.

McVitie was lured to a basement flat in Stoke Newington with the promise of a lively party. Arriving at the flat just before midnight, he demanded: 'Where's all the birds and all the booze?'

As Ronnie Kray got up to greet him from the sofa, Reggie stepped out from behind the door, aimed a .32 automatic at McVitie's head and pulled the trigger.

The gun jammed and Reggie threw himself at his hapless victim. Ronnie watched the ensuing struggle, egging his brother on with hysterical screams. McVitie broke free and dived through a window, but Reggie caught his legs and dragged him back into the room and plunged a carving knife into his face, chest and stomach. He slid on to the floor and died in an ocean of his own blood.

Like Mitchell and the others, McVitie's body was spirited away and never found. But again the East End underworld and the police, notably Detective Inspector 'Nipper' Read, were well aware of what had happened and who was responsible.

GUNNING FOR THE TWINS

'Nipper' Read was a textbook detective. Hard-working, methodical and totally dedicated, he was a five-foot-seven terrier who had his teeth into the Krays and wasn't about to let go.

After the McVitie murder Read was assigned a team of fourteen detectives and set up an undercover operation in an anonymous block of government offices south of the Thames. Their sole task was to build a case against the Kray twins.

Read knew that any attempt to convict the Krays of a specific crime was doomed to failure. They were too powerful and too well organized. They could intimidate witnesses and threaten jurors. They had the money to retain top lawyers and pay others to take the blame or provide them with an alibi.

Above: *After the murder of George Cornell the Kray twins were held for questioning by the police for 36 hours, before returning to Vallance Road to give an informal press conference.*

> 'I HATE THE SIGHT OF BLOOD,' SAID ONE MAN WHO REFUSED TO TESTIFY AGAINST THE KRAYS. 'PARTICULARLY MY OWN'

Left: *Reggie leaves the Central Criminal Court (the 'Old Bailey') in 1965, after successfully evading charges of extortion with menaces.*

No – if Read was to get them, he would have to persuade one or more of their past victims to testify against them.

Read made a list of thirty people whom the Krays had maimed or robbed over the past decade. Then he and his team went about the laborious process of questioning them all.

As well as making countless enquiries in London, detectives travelled to Scotland, Canada, Belgium, Spain and the United States.

They were met with a wall of silence. The reason for people's reticence was not hard to understand. In the words of one potential witness whom the Krays had maimed and ruined, but was reluctant to talk: 'I hate the sight of blood, particularly my own.'

Evidence might have been slow in materializing, but 'Nipper' Read and his team did start to accumulate information, first from Leslie Payne, the Krays' erstwhile business manager, and later from Alan Cooper, the merchant banker who had fenced the Mafia's bearer bonds.

The police were gradually building up a complete picture of the Firm's activities. But they still didn't have any hard evidence which they could take in front of a jury.

Six months passed and the investigation had stalled. Read, however, felt confident that, if the Krays and their associates were all safely behind bars, reluctant witnesses would summon up the

courage to come forward.

He would have to arrest and charge the Krays before he had finished preparing his case. It was a massive gamble, but Read was rapidly running out of options.

At 6a.m. on 9 May 1968, sixty police officers descended on twenty-four separate addresses across London. 'Nipper' Read had his revolver drawn as his men broke down the door of Braithwaite House, where the twins each had a flat.

He needn't have worried. Both men were sound asleep, Reggie with a girl from Walthamstow, Ronnie with a fair-haired teenage boy from Bethnal Green.

FIGHT TO THE FINISH

The twins were charged with murder, extortion and sundry other offences, and were remanded in Brixton Jail.

Read had only a few weeks before the preliminary hearings in which to persuade witnesses to talk and thereby clinch his case. His job wasn't made any easier by the fact that two of the firm, Ronnie Hart and Ian Barrie were still on the loose.

Because the twins were still on remand and technically innocent, they were allowed as many visitors as they wanted. It was therefore easy for them to pass messages to their fugitive henchmen, who in turn could continue to intimidate witnesses.

Above: *The picture of innocence, Ronnie and Reggie sip tea while answering journalists' questions after their 36-hour detention.*

So Read went all out to get the two men. Hart was the first to be caught. The police found him hiding in a caravan with his girlfriend. He gave them no trouble and confessed to everything.

Three days later they picked up Barrie in Mile End. He was drunk, broke and frightened. He, too, told the police everything they wanted to know.

With the threat of a Kray reprisal force removed, the whole situation changed. Conmen, club owners and racketeers suddenly got their memories back. When the trial opened on 6 July, long-forgotten victims, accomplices saving their own skins, and eye-witnesses all trooped through the witness box.

The death blow for the Krays came, however, with the appearance of the barmaid from the Blind Beggar. Previously she had been too frightened to identify Ronnie after the shooting of George Cornell. Now she said she was absolutely certain that it had been Ronnie Kray who had fired the fatal shot.

The defence made a brave attempt at discrediting the witnesses, but the barmaid's story stuck, and the Krays were effectively finished.

The twins were arrogant and defiant throughout the long trial, but even they must have realized that the verdict was a foregone conclusion. They were found guilty of the murders of Cornell and McVitie and sentenced to life imprisonment, '...which,' Mr Justice Melford Stevenson said, 'I recommend should not be less than thirty years.' If his wishes were respected, the Kray twins would be sixty-four before they were released.

It would be easy to write off Reggie and Ronnie Kray as a couple of vicious East End thugs. They certainly were that, but they were much more besides. They were professionals of violence who operated on a scale previously unknown in Britain.

The odds against their rise to power were enormous. They were both mentally unstable and had no education or finesse. Yet they came closer to building a crime empire on the lines of Al Capone than any other criminal organization that London has ever known. They were truly dangerous men on the grand scale.

AL CAPONE
Public Enemy No. One

Neither a Mafioso nor even a Sicilian, by the age of twenty-six Al Capone had connived and murdered his way to become the biggest gangland boss in the most lawless city in America. But what was the truth and how much was legend?

For most people the very mention of organized crime conjures up a whole range of vivid images – the roaring twenties, Chicago, bootleg whiskey, speakeasies and, of course, Al Capone.

It is not that Chicago, or even America, ever had a monopoly on organized crime, it is merely the very public nature of its criminals which is so evocative. Gangsters with colourful nicknames like 'Pretty Boy' Floyd, 'Legs' Diamond, 'Machine Gun' Jack McGurn and Al 'Scarface' Capone, captured the public imagination and became a part of criminal folklore.

THE YOUNG BROOKLYN IMMIGRANT

Contrary to popular myth, Al Capone was never a member of the Mafia. He wasn't even a Sicilian. He hated Sicilians and spent most of his active years at loggerheads with various branches of the Mob. Capone was a gangster pure and simple, a racketeer whose only loyalty was to himself and his immediate family.

Born in Brooklyn in 1899, Alphonse was the fourth son of Gabriele and Teresa Capone, a Neapolitan couple who had emigrated from Italy some six years earlier. As a teenager, Al ran with the

Opposite: From a flashy teenage thug, Capone rapidly grew into a portly, conservatively-dressed figure who could have been taken for a successful middle-aged businessman.

Below: Capone's career as a big-time mobster lasted a mere six years, but in that time he acquired all the trappings and habits of a rich man.

murderous Five Points gang which was led by fellow-Italian and partner-to-be John Torrio.

He had his first brush with the Mafia when he was fifteen. The Black Hand, a Mafia murder squad, had been extorting money from his father. Capone hunted down the two men responsible and shot them dead. Torrio was impressed by the young man's nerve and ruthless efficiency. Six years later, in 1919, when Torrio was in the process of building his bootlegging empire in Chicago, he remembered the name of Al Capone.

Torrio had been in Chicago for about five years when the Volsted Act was passed and America went dry. The country developed an immediate and insatiable thirst which organized crime was ready and willing to slake. In Chicago, drinkers were supplied by one of a dozen big gangs, each with its own clearly defined territory.

Torrio's gang controlled the South Side of the city and soon teamed up with the Irish Druggan-Lake gang who supplied the inner West Side. The North Side of Chicago was the territory of Dion O'Banion, a florist and failed safe-cracker, who had a flower shop opposite the Holy Name Cathedral.

O'Banion could have made a legitimate income by supplying floral tributes to the victims of gangland slayings. Instead he teamed up with two Polish Catholics, George 'Bugs' Moran and Hymie Weiss. Together, these three were the biggest challenge to Torrio's pre-eminence in the city.

The other important gang were the Gennas who controlled the West Side. These six brothers from Marsala in Sicily were the most ruthless of all the Chicago gangsters; they didn't only kill for gain and self-protection – they killed for fun.

In the first year of Prohibition, there was comparatively little trouble between the rival gangs. There was more than enough business for everyone, and most of the gangsters' energy was devoted to maintaining supply to meet the enormous demand.

By 1920, however, things were getting better organized and some of the smaller gangs were looking to expand their territories. The O'Donnell gang from the

Above: *Chicago was no place to bring up his children, said Capone, and in 1928, after an unsuccessful attempt to settle in California, he purchased a magnificent house on Palm Island, Miami.*

IMPRESSED BY THE TEENAGE CAPONE'S STYLE, WHEN GANG LEADER TORRIO STARTED BOOTLEGGING HE TOOK HIM ON AS A PARTNER

South Side started hijacking Torrio's beer trucks and smashing up his speakeasies. Torrio retaliated by killing several of O'Donnell's drivers. Elsewhere in the city, other gangs were at each others' throats.

Torrio could see the way things were going and decided that, if he was to fulfil his ambition and have overall control of Chicago, he would need to import some extra muscle. So he called up Al Capone, now twenty-one and a lieutenant in the Five Points gang, and made him an offer he couldn't refuse: 25 per cent of existing turnover and 50 per cent of all new business.

In the early days of the partnership Capone did the killing for both himself and Torrio. One of his first victims was a small-time crook called Joe Howard. Howard had ideas above his station and one night hijacked two of Torrio's booze trucks. The following evening, Joe was having a drink in his neighbourhood bar. Capone walked in with a broad grin on his face. It was happy hour.

preferred to sit back and pick his moment.

In late October 1924, the O'Banion gang hijacked a large shipment of the Gennas' Canadian whiskey. They swore revenge. 'To hell with them Sicilians,' O'Banion said to reporters. A war was in the offing and this was just the situation Torrio and Capone had been waiting for.

WAR BREAKS OUT IN CHICAGO

On 4 November O'Banion was in the back room of his florist's when he heard someone come into the shop. He went out to welcome three customers.

Six shots rang out, the last of which exploded into O'Banion's left cheek. He sprawled back into his flower display as his assassins made good their escape. When the police arrived at the shop, Dion O'Banion was dead.

Torrio, Capone and the Genna brothers were all questioned by the police, but all had satisfactory explanations as to their whereabouts at the time of the killing. The street outside O'Banion's shop had been crowded, yet no one had seen anything. Faced with the customary wall of silence, the coroner was forced to bring in a finding of 'unlawful killing at the hands of a person or persons unknown'.

The tradition of lavish funerals for American gangsters started with O'Banion. His body lay 'in state' at the undertaker's for three days. A contemporary report describes the scene: 'Silver angels stood at the head and feet with their heads bowed in the light of ten candles that burned in solid golden candlesticks they held in their hands. Beneath the casket, on a marble slab that supports its glory, is the inscription: "Suffer the little children to come unto me." And over it all the perfume of flowers.'

At the funeral, mounted police kept order as the cortege of gangsters rolled slowly through the streets of Chicago, followed by twenty-six trucks of flowers, valued at more than $50,000. Among the floral tributes was a basket of red roses with a card which read, 'From Al'.

Both Capone and Torrio solemnly attended the funeral, but no one was

'Hi, Al,' Joe said, sticking out his hand. Capone fired six shots into his body at point-blank range, and Howard fell to the bar-room floor with a smile of welcome still on his face. The police immediately put out an arrest warrant on Capone, but had to release him when all the eye-witnesses developed amnesia.

By the end of 1923, Capone had gained control of the middle-class Chicago suburb of Cicero and made it his personal headquarters. By a combination of bribery and intimidation, he had the entire administration in his pocket – mayor, town clerk and town attorney. So backed, he was free to do whatever he liked. His illegal casinos and brothels and bars were open day and night.

By this time Torrio and Capone were each making in excess of $100,000 a week, but they were still a long way from gaining absolute control of the city. The O'Banion gang and the Gennas still controlled the North and West sides. Capone was in favour of all-out war to eliminate the competition; Torrio

---

CAPONE WALKED INTO THE BAR AND FIRED SIX SHOTS INTO HOWARD AT CLOSE RANGE. IT WAS HAPPY HOUR

BENEATH GANGLAND CHIEF O'BANION'S FUNERAL CASKET WAS THE INSCRIPTION: 'SUFFER THE LITTLE CHILDREN TO COME UNTO ME'

---

fooled – least of all Hymie Weiss, O'Banion's most trusted lieutenant and the new boss of his organization. Weiss was a cold-blooded killer who had devised a method of assassination in which the victim was seated in the front passenger seat of the car with his killer directly behind him. He was then shot in the back of the head. After such a murder, Weiss would calmly say that his victim had been 'taken for a ride'. And so the expression became part of modern parlance.

Weiss, who was genuinely heartbroken by O'Banion's death – observers described him as crying like a baby, swore to get his revenge. Days later Capone's car was machine-gunned. Al escaped unhurt, but two weeks later John Torrio was gunned down in front of his wife by another O'Banion man, Bugs Moran.

Torrio recovered from his wounds, but only weeks later he was jailed for nine months for operating a brewery. Badly shaken by Moran's attack, he had steel screens fitted to the windows of his cell and hired three extra deputy sheriffs to stand sentry.

On his release in October 1925, he announced that he was leaving Chicago, which he described as being 'too violent'. The fact is, at the age of forty-eight, Johnnie Torrio had lost his nerve. This was a game for young men, and the young man on the spot was Al Capone.

THE KING IS DEAD – LONG LIVE THE KING!

So, at the age of 26, Al Capone inherited the entire Torrio empire. His promotion to unrivalled boss of Chicago was helped by the demise of the six Genna brothers. Angelo, Mike and Antonio were killed in separate gun battles within the space of six weeks. The three surviving brothers fled to their home town of Marsala in Sicily. While there is no evidence to connect Capone with the killings, he made no secret of his pleasure at the Gennas' departure.

The Sicilians might have been out of the way, but Hymie Weiss wasn't finished yet. His second attempt on Capone's life was anything but subtle,

Above and right:
14 February 1929. At 10.30 a.m., while Al established an alibi in Miami, six members of Bugs Moran's gang were shot down in a Chicago garage by Capone's men disguised as policemen.

and highlighted the level of lawlessness that existed in Chicago in 1925. In broad daylight, eight carloads of gunmen made an assault on Capone's Cicero headquarters, the Hawthorne Inn, firing more than a thousand rounds into the building in a matter of seconds.

Again Capone escaped unscathed and, with customary largesse, paid $10,000 out of his own pocket to save the sight of a woman who had been injured in the cross-fire. Capone had overlooked the first attempt on his life by the North Side

gang, considering it legitimate revenge for the killing of their boss Dion O'Banion. Now he had had enough.

On 11 October 1926, Weiss was machine-gunned to death on the steps of Holy Name Cathedral.

Now only Bugs Moran was left alive to challenge Capone's absolute control of Chicago. And Moran could wait. Ten days after the execution of Weiss, Capone chaired a meeting of Chicago gang bosses to negotiate a peaceful division of Cook County: 'We're a bunch of saps to be killing each other,' he postulated.

For a while after that the peace held and there were no gangland slayings. Everyone was making a fortune, and none more than Al Capone. His turnover was truly astonishing. In Cook County he controlled ten thousand speakeasies, each purchasing an average of six barrels of beer a week costing a total of $3.5 million. In addition they were each buying two cases of liquor at $90, making another $1.8 million. (Beer was costing Capone about $5 a barrel to make, and liquor about $20 a case.) Added to all this, Capone had his other rackets – gambling and vice – which contributed to a grand total of about $6.5 million per week.

He had huge overheads, of course, not least of which was his illicit payroll. Everyone was on the take in Chicago, from humble patrolmen to the city's mayor 'Big Bill' Thompson, whose 1927 re-election campaign Capone financed to the tune of $260,000. It is estimated that his annual graft bill to the police, judges and politicians came to more than $30 million.

Capone was no longer the flashy, loud-mouthed thug that arrived in Chicago in 1919. He was now an immaculately tailored, even conservative figure, sporting hand-made silk shirts and solitaire diamond tie-pins. Despite the fact that he was still only twenty-six, he gave the impression of being a successful, middle-aged businessman.

Capone's public image was important to him, and he was given to ostentatious displays of generosity. He paid for church roofs to be restored; he gave $10,000 to Pennsylvania's striking miners and,

during the Depression, he opened a string of soup kitchens and contributed more than $2 million of his own money to help down-and-outs.

Everyone in Chicago knew that Al Capone was a bootlegger, and most of them didn't care. To the vast majority of ordinary people Prohibition was a nonsense anyway, so bootlegging wasn't a real crime. He had become a success story, a working-class hero.

THE ST VALENTINE'S DAY MASSACRE

By 1928 Al Capone felt secure enough about his hold on Chicago to spend time away from the city. He was a devoted family man, who wanted his dependants to benefit from his vast wealth. Chicago was no place to bring up children, he said, and so he set about looking for a suitable second home away from the turmoil of the big city.

He quite liked the look of California, but California didn't like the look of him and summarily booted him out. Next he tried Florida and, despite the violent objections of honest citizens, managed to procure a magnificent house on Palm Island, Miami.

Capone spent Christmas and the New Year of 1929 in his new home. He had a lot to be thankful for. He was not yet thirty, had amassed a vast fortune and was the undisputed boss of America's

Above: *When Herbert Hoover was elected President of the United States in 1929, he named Capone as his prime target in an attack on lawlessness. The mobster was finally indicted on a charge of income tax evasion. Here seated with his lawyers, he looks confident of a successful outcome to the hearing.*

second city. Unfortunately for Capone, one man didn't quite see it like that.

Bugs Moran had neither forgotten nor forgiven the murder of his two associates Dion O'Banion and Hymie Weiss. He decided to take advantage of Capone's absence to make him pay. With his North Side gang Moran regularly hijacked Capone's liquor shipments and then started to move in on some of his other legitimate businesses, notably dog racing and dry cleaning.

Capone may have been in Florida, but his finger was very much on the pulse. He heard all about Moran's activities and decided that they had to stop. Over the telephone he instructed Jake Guzik, his most trusted aide in Chicago, to 'take care' of Moran. The time and method of execution were discussed in minute detail, and on 14 February 1929 Capone made a point of keeping an appointment in Miami with a city official. He wanted a watertight alibi for that particular Valentine's Day.

At 10.30 a.m., as Al Capone was trying to explain to the Miami official where he had got the money to buy his Palm Island home, six of Moran's men were waiting for a truckload of hijacked whiskey in a garage on Chicago's North Clark Street. They were Frank and Peter Gusenberg, Moran's top executioners; James Clark, a Sioux Indian and Moran's brother-in-law; Al Weinshank, his accountant; Adam Heyer, his business manager; and Johnny May, a burglar and safe cracker. There was also a seventh man, whose presence has never been satisfactorily explained – an optician called Dr Richard Schwimmer. Moran himself should have been there, but had been delayed.

Shortly after 10.30 Mrs Max Landesman of 2124 North Clark Street heard shots from the garage next door. She looked out of the window and saw a man leaving the garage and getting into a large touring car. From the flat below, Miss Josephine Morin saw two men, apparently under arrest, come out of the garage with their hands up. They were followed by two uniformed police officers. All four of them got into a black Cadillac and drove off.

Mrs Landesman hurried over to the

garage, pushed open the door and saw seven men sprawled on the floor, blood streaming from their bodies. Minutes later Sergeant Tom Loftus arrived on the scene with a dozen other officers. Only one of the victims, Frank Gusenberg, was conscious, and Loftus tried to persuade him to say who had done the shootings. Gusenberg declined to comment and was shipped to hospital along with the other six victims, all of whom were pronounced dead on arrival.

Loftus maintained a vigil at Gusenberg's bedside but, true to the gangster's code of honour, he died three hours later without revealing anything.

Moran had arrived on Clark Street fifteen minutes late, and, seeing the police cars outside the garage, assumed that there had been a raid, and promptly left. Later, when he heard about the massacre, he said: 'Only Capone kills like that!'

The police were of the same opinion. So they picked up Capone's top killer, 'Machine Gun' Jack McGurn. McGurn claimed to have been with his girlfriend at the time of the killings. He was indicted for perjury, but married his girl so that the police could not force her to testify against him. Other Capone men were questioned, but soon released for lack of evidence.

In the end, no one was ever charged in connection with the St Valentine's Day massacre. But no one was in any doubt that it was carried out on the direct orders of Al Capone from the safety of his Florida retreat.

Even though Moran had survived, Capone returned to Chicago confident that he had finally crushed any opposition to his authority. Instead he found that two of his own lieutenants, John Scalise and Albert Anselmi, had been conspiring to take over the Outfit. Al invited them, along with other gang members, to a meeting at a restaurant in Hammond, Indiana. Capone was his usual jovial self until halfway through the meal, at which point he rounded on the two conspirators: 'I understand you want my job,' he said. 'Well, here it is!' and promptly clubbed them both to death with a baseball bat. It was a salutary lesson to the assembled diners.

Early in his career, Capone was known for his surgical use of violence. It was never used gratuitously – only as a tool to protect himself and to promote his business interests. This was no longer the case. Anyone who incurred his displeasure – policemen, politicians, journalists – could expect to be summarily dispatched.

'GET CAPONE!'

In March 1929, Herbert Hoover was inaugurated President of the United States. He came to office primed with a promise to tackle lawlessness in America, and he named Al Capone as his primary target.

By May of that year, Capone was feeling the heat. There were rumours of a massive contract out on his life. Some said it had been taken out by Bugs Moran, others that it was the families of Scalise and Anselmi. Whatever the truth, Capone decided it would be wise to get out of circulation for a while and, rather than going to Florida, he contrived to have himself arrested for a minor firearms offence in Philadelphia. He was expecting to get a jail sentence of thirty days, but in the event he was sent to prison for a year. Capone was initially horrified, but he soon adapted to the situation. His status was such that he was able to continue running his Chicago

WHEN BUGS MORAN HEARD ABOUT THE MASSACRE WHICH HE HAD SO NARROWLY ESCAPED, HE EXCLAIMED: 'ONLY CAPONE KILLS LIKE THAT!'

FACED WITH A 'COLONELS' REVOLT', CAPONE INVITED THE MISCREANTS TO DINNER AND THEN CLUBBED THEM TO DEATH WITH A BASEBALL BAT

Below: *Matters are not going so well in the hearing in Chicago Federal Court in October 1931, and Capone looks grimly concerned as his financial affairs are brought out into the light.*

Right: *The style of elaborate gangster funerals in Chicago was set by that of Dion O'Banion.*

HUNTED BY EVERY LAW AND ORDER AGENCY IN THE UNITED STATES, AL CAPONE WAS DUBBED PUBLIC ENEMY NUMBER ONE

empire from his prison cell with the minimum of inconvenience.

While Capone was in prison, the new administration in Washington were devising ways to keep him there for ever. President Hoover discussed a variety of approaches with his various agencies – the Prohibition Bureau, the Justice Department's Federal Bureau of Investigation (FBI) and the Treasury Department. Their brief was simple. Get Al Capone any way you can.

The Justice Department set about destroying Capone's booze empire by brute force. In the space of six months they raided and wrecked thirty of his breweries and seized fifty of his heavy trucks. But this was no more than an annoyance for Capone.

In Washington it was the Treasury that really took the Capone challenge on board. Their Special Intelligence Unit sent top investigator Frank Wilson to Chicago to look at Al Capone's books.

Wilson had already enjoyed spectacular success jailing gangsters who had escaped conviction for years. Among his victims were Frank Nitti, Capone's deputy; Jack Guzik, his accountant; and Capone's brother, Ralph. They had received prison terms of between eighteen months and five years. But Al Capone himself would prove tougher for Wilson than his associates.

Capone had never filed a tax return in his life. This was not a crime, so long as he did not earn more than $5000 in any given year. It was Frank Wilson's job to prove that he had. Considering Capone's lavish lifestyle, this might appear to have been a simple matter. It wasn't. Capone had no bank accounts in his own name and all his assets were listed to third parties.

Wilson and his team started a detailed probe into Capone's personal spending. They found that in the three-year period 1926-29 he had purchased more than $25,000 worth of furniture for his homes in Chicago and Florida. He had spent $7000 on suits and $40,000 on telephone calls. In all the Treasury men unearthed $165,000 worth of taxable spending. They could have gone to court with that, and they would probably have secured a conviction, which would have jailed

Capone for about three years. But that wasn't good enough. Wilson had been told to go for broke.

After months sniffing around Chicago, Wilson managed to persuade some of Capone's casino employees to turn state's evidence. Now he had Al where they wanted him. He was charged with failing to pay tax on $1 million in the years from 1925 to 1929 and, while this was a fraction of Capone's true income, it could still mean thirty years in a federal prison.

Capone's attorneys initially struck a deal with the prosecution – if Capone pleaded guilty, he would receive a sentence of not more than two and a half years. Judge Wilkerson, however, was outraged by this and threw it out. Capone withdrew his plea and elected to go to trial.

His associates immediately set about bribing or threatening members of the jury, but this was discovered and, at the very last minute, a new jury was sworn in. They heard stories of Capone's extravagant lifestyle – a lifestyle he could not possibly have supported on the $450 a month he claimed to earn – and on 24 October they returned a verdict of guilty on all charges. He was sentenced to eleven years and fined $50,000, the most severe sentence ever imposed for a tax offence.

Capone was sent to Cook County jail pending an appeal and when that failed, in May 1932, he was shipped to Atlanta Federal Penitentiary. A year later he became one of the first convicts to take up residence at Alcatraz in San Francisco Bay. He emerged from there in 1939 a physical and mental wreck. He was still only thirty-eight years old.

Capone had been diagnosed as suffering from syphilis shortly after his imprisonment in 1931. The disease had now reached its tertiary stage, and his brain was being eaten up. After his release he returned to his home on Palm Island, Florida where he lived for another seven years, increasingly mad, surrounded by his adoring family.

In 1947 he suffered a fatal brain haemorrhage. He was forty-eight years old. His body was shipped back to Chicago and buried in an elaborate mausoleum in Mount Olivet cemetery.

ON HIS RELEASE FROM ALCATRAZ CAPONE WAS SUFFERING FROM ADVANCED SYPHILIS WHICH WAS SLOWLY DESTROYING HIS BRAIN

Above left: *The trial concluded, Capone is led away from Chicago Federal Court on 24 October 1931 to begin his eleven-year sentence.*

Left: *Guarded by a US Marshall, Al Capone puts a brave face on his defeat as he is taken by train to Atlanta Federal Penitentiary.*

CARELESS THIEVES
Great Train Robbery

It was called the 'robbery of the century', yet when thieves audaciously robbed a mail train of £2.5 million they were unbelievably careless in concealing the evidence. The law was draconian, but the public secretly admired them

Shortly after 2a.m. on Thursday, 8 August 1963, the Glasgow to London mail train was nearing the end of its journey. As it passed through Leighton Buzzard in Bedfordshire, half an hour should have seen it safely into Euston. It wasn't to be, however.

A few miles further down the line, the driver, forty-eight-year-old Jack Mills, spotted an amber signal. He slowed the big diesel and prepared to stop. A mile on, at Sears Crossing, he was faced with a red light and pulled to a halt.

Mills sent his fireman, David Whitby, down the line to phone ahead for information. Within a matter of seconds, however, Mills found himself confronted by a gang of masked men clambering into his cab.

He tried to fight them off but was coshed into submission, as the biggest and most audacious robbery in history began. Half an hour later the train had been divided, moved and relieved of 128 mail sacks containing more than £2.5 million in used banknotes.

Left: *Train robber Ronald Biggs may have been a fugitive in Brazil, but he was seldom out of the public eye. In 1980 he appeared in the film* Honeymoon *as a swimmer who rescued German actress Dolly Dollar from drowning.*

Opposite: *Ronnie Biggs, one of the instigators of the 'robbery of the century'.*

Below: *Post Office workers lean out from the robbed train as the police start their search for clues.*

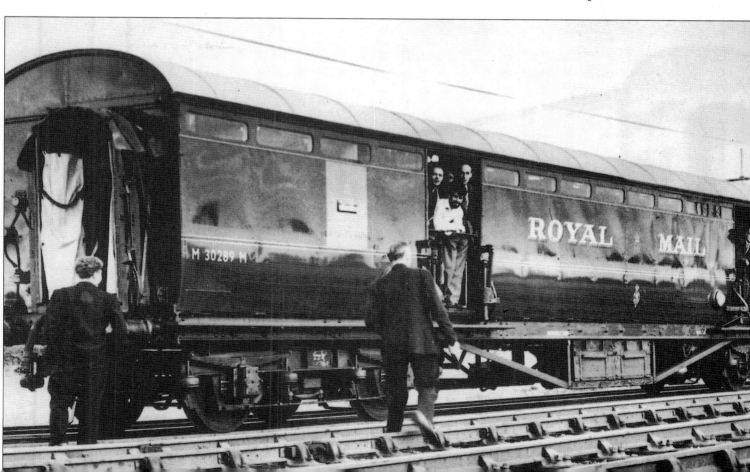

Above: *Forensic experts inspect the Royal Mail van from which the 128 mail sacks were taken.*

THE LOCAL POLICE SOON REALIZED THAT THIS CRIME WAS TOO MAJOR FOR THEIR OWN RESOURCES, AND CALLED IN SCOTLAND YARD

FEW CLUES TO START WITH

By the time Detective Superintendent Malcolm Fewtrell, head of the Buckinghamshire CID, arrived the robbers and their spoils were long gone. Fewtrell, a seasoned professional, started routine investigative procedures, gathering physical evidence and interviewing the eighty-odd people who had been on the train.

But no one, not even Mills, Whitby or the post office sorters from whose HVP (high-value packages) coach the mail sacks had been taken, could give Fewtrell anything to go on.

It was soon obvious to Fewtrell that he was not dealing with any ordinary crime. This robbery was the work of a highly organized team, and the investigation would be on a scale far beyond the meagre resouces of his force. After consulting with his Chief Constable, he elected to 'call the Yard' – to ask for the assistance of the Metropolitan CID.

Later that day, Fewtrell attended a meeting at the headquarters of the Post Office. Present were Post Office officials including their own senior investigator, Frank Cook, and George Hatherill, deputy chief of the CID at Scotland Yard, together with a team of detectives.

Cook told the police that, in his estimation, the haul from the robbery might well be in excess of £3 million. The police for their part could give little comfort to the Post Office. All they could say for certain was that approximately fifteen men had been involved in the robbery, and that the fireman, David Whitby, had noticed an army lorry parked on the Bridego Bridge where the robbery took place.

Hatherill agreed to send two of his

Right: *Five days after the robbery, police discovered the deserted Leatherslade farmhouse where the gang had hidden out and divided their loot.*

most able detectives – Gerald McArthur and Jack Prichard – down to Buckinghamshire to assist the local police with their enquiries. The two men returned to Aylesbury with Fewtrell that night.

The three detectives had to try and put themselves in the robbers' shoes. What would they do immediately after the robbery? A total of 128 mail sacks would not be easy to hide or transport for long distances without attracting attention.

The police decided that the robbers would hole up somewhere near the scene of the crime and distribute the money at their leisure, partly because one of the robbers had ordered the men in the HVP coach not to move for 'half an hour'. This suggested that the gang had a safe haven within half an hour's drive from the scene of the crime.

It was a guess, but they decided to back it with all their resources. Every policeman from Buckinghamshire and neighbouring forces was mobilized in a search of barges, houses and barns in a thirty-mile radius of Bridego Bridge.

So far the police were spot on. The perpetrators of the Great Train Robbery were holed up some twenty miles from Bridego Bridge at Leatherslade Farm. They had purchased it through a nominee, some weeks earlier, specifically for this purpose.

The robbery itself had gone like clockwork. The only minor hitch had been Mills, the train driver, who had offered token resistance. The haul, something over £2.5 million, had been less than they had expected. But even after they had paid their German backers a million for financing the robbery, each member of the seventeen-strong gang had received £90,000, a huge sum of money in 1963. All in all, no one was complaining.

TWO GANGS WITH COMBINED TALENTS

The robbery, which had been almost a year in the planning, was the work of not one but two London-based gangs or 'firms'. The first firm, the men who conceived the idea and did most of the ground work, consisted of Buster Edwards, Gordon Goody, Charlie Wilson,

Bruce Reynolds, John Daly, Jimmy White, Ronnie Biggs and Jimmy Hussey.

They were a loose-knit team of thieves who had worked together over the years on numerous occasions with a varied degree of success.

In January 1963, Buster Edwards and Gordon Goody were approached by a friend, Brian Field, a crooked solicitor's clerk who had worked for them in the past. He claimed to have information for them about a huge shipment of cash which was theirs for the taking.

Field introduced them to an Irishman (whose name is still unknown) who told them about the high-value-package coach which made up part of the overnight mail train from Glasgow to London. It was on this coach that the banks sent all their

Above: *Roy James, known as 'the Weasel', was arrested in December after a chase over the roof of this house in a mews in St John's Wood, north London.*

EVEN AFTER PAYING THEIR GERMAN BACKERS, THERE WAS A SMALL FORTUNE LEFT FOR DIVISION AMONG THE GANG

Above: *In the summer of 1965, after serving little more than a year of his sentence, Ronald Biggs escaped from Wandsworth prison. More than 150 armed police surrounded Winterfold House in Surrey when told he was hiding out there, but a six-hour search revealed no trace of him.*

surplus cash down to London.

Normally the coach would carry about sixty bags, the Irishman told them, but if they timed their raid to follow a bank holiday they might find upwards of two hundred, each holding about £25,000, a total haul in excess of £5 million.

Edwards and Goody were incredulous. But they assured the Irishman that if such a robbery was possible, they had the team to pull it off. They arranged a meeting with Bruce Reynolds and Charlie Wilson.

All four of them were torn between euphoria and scepticism. Before they went any further, they had to check that their informant was himself well informed.

So they staked out Euston station and saw for themselves HVP sacks being off-loaded from the night mail train. There was no doubt that the prize was there.

The only way the job could be done, they decided, was to stop the train on the track, separate the engine and the HVP coach from the main body of the train, and ransack it at their leisure. The trouble was, how do you stop a train at a predetermined spot?

Buster Edwards had a solution to the problem of stopping the train. He had heard of a south London firm, headed by one Thomas Wisbey, which had been robbing trains on the London to Brighton line for a couple of years. They had a expert who knew how to tamper with th signalling system.

Buster approached the rival gang bos and, after a period of intense hagglin terms were agreed. Wisbey would le them have his man, Roger Cordrey, a long as Wisbey himself and his partne Bob Welsh were included in the robber as full partners.

And so the team to rob the mail trai started to take shape, and the preparation began: researching a suitable location fc the ambush, buying a hide-ou instructing various members of the gan in their specific tasks, and rehearsing th ambush in the most minute detail.

And now it had all paid off. The Grea Train Robbers were sitting i Leatherslade Farm with more than £2 million in used notes.

That team of faces, already known the police, would soon be known to th world at large. The first piece of ba news for the robbers came over the radi in the form of a public appeal by th police. They were asking for informatio on strange goings-on in remo dwellings, and they wanted to kno about movements of army vehicles.

This presented the robbers with tw problems. They had originally planned stay at Leatherslade Farm until th

Left: *Charlie Wilson escaped from Winson Green prison in August 1964. In January 1967 he was recaptured in Montreal, Canada, and was brought back to Britain by Detective Chief Superintendent Butler.*

Below: *For more than five years Bruce Reynolds was a wanted man. Eventually, in November 1968, police found him in this rented house in Torquay.*

Fewtrell and McArthur dashed to the farm. After a cursory glance they ordered that the whole area be cordoned off in readiness for the forensic team.

In London, Butler and his team had compiled a list of possible suspects to be pulled in for questioning. The bulk of the gang's names appeared on that list.

Roger Cordrey, the signals expert, was the first to be picked up. The local police found him in Bournemouth along with £141,000 in used notes, money which he found extremely difficult to explain.

The next break for the police came on Friday, 16 August. A man called John Ahern was taking a stroll in the woods near Dorking in Surrey when he came upon a briefcase, a holdall and a camelskin bag containing no less than £100,900. More important, a receipt was found made out by a German restaurant in the name of Herr and Frau Field.

Sunday night and then disperse the money using the army truck and two army Land Rovers. This was now clearly out of the question.

For the first time they were in a state of disarray and, from this point on, it was effectively every man for himself. They cleared up the farm as best they could, burning clothes and mailsacks, but in their haste to get away they were forced to leave the job half done. The various members of the gang returned to their homes and jobs in London, unaware they had left a plethora of clues for their pursuers.

THE INVESTIGATION TAKES OFF

Once the scale of the robbery was appreciated, Scotland Yard decided to beef up its support for the investigation. They brought in Chief Superintendent Tommy Butler to head up the London end. Butler would prove the downfall of many of the Train Robbers.

The first mention of Leatherslade Farm came from a cowman called John Maris on Monday, 12 August. In outbuildings the police found an army lorry and the two Land Rovers. Once inside the farm proper, half-burnt mailsacks and money wrappers left them in no doubt that they had found the hide-out.

Fewtrell and McArthur knew that one Brian Field, a solicitor's clerk, had acted for several of their suspects, including Buster Edwards and Gordon Goody. They also knew that the company for which Field worked had acted in the purchase of Leatherslade Farm. They went to his home and questioned him but did not arrest him – yet.

The following day, more money – £30,440 – was found in an old caravan in the Dorking Woods by Surrey Police. Fingerprints in the caravan matched those on file for Jimmy White. At Leatherslade Farm fingerprint experts were also doing well. They had identified the prints of Charlie Wilson and Bruce Reynolds. Wilson was picked up within a few hours, but Reynolds had gone to ground.

On Thursday, 22 August local police arrested Gordon Goody in Leicester where he was having dinner with a girlfriend. They questioned him and then released him for lack of evidence.

Ronnie Biggs was next. He was pulled in on 4 September, and three days later they brought in Jim Hussey for questioning. Thomas Wisbey was questioned, released and then rearrested.

PLAYING A WAITING GAME

By the middle of September the police were fairly certain they had a complete picture of who had robbed the mail train, but Tommy Butler was in no particular hurry to find them. He reckoned that, by playing the waiting game, he stood a better chance of catching them with some of the money.

However, Butler did decide it was time to pull in Brian Field. He charged him with conspiring to rob a mail train and for being an accessory after the fact.

Police efforts were now on two fronts. The Flying Squad were trying to track down Buster Edwards, Bruce Reynolds, John Daly, Roy James and Jimmy White. The forensic team, for their part, were building up a case against them and the men already in custody, trying to tie them to the scene of the crime. It was thanks to this work that they felt confident enough to rearrest Gordon Goody on 3 October.

Over the next few weeks, Butler and his men arrested Bob Welsh and John Daly. They ran Roy James to ground in the St John's Wood area of London and, after a spectacular rooftop chase, took him into custody and charged him.

By the end of the year, nine of the sixteen men who had been at Bridego Bridge were in jail awaiting trial. Bruce Reynolds, Buster Edwards and Jimmy White were still on the run, while the other four had been overlooked or released for lack of evidence.

With no prospect of an early arrest of the three fugitives, the authorities decided to press ahead with the trial of the others.

SHOW TRIAL

The trial began on 20 January 1964. All the accused pleaded not guilty to all charges except for Roger Cordrey. He pleaded guilty to robbery and was

Above: Ronald Biggs hid out in Australia, where he worked as a carpenter, until a new spate of publicity forced him to flee to Brazil. Here police search his baggage, left behind in a Melbourne motel.

> ROY JAMES WAS FINALLY ARRESTED AFTER A SPECTACULAR ROOFTOP CHASE IN LONDON

Right: Chief Superintendent John Slipper and Inspector Peter Jones return to Gatwick Airport in February 1974, foiled in their attempt to repatriate Ronald Biggs.

removed from the dock to await sentence, while the trial of the others continued.

Only Mr W. Raeburn QC, counsel for John Daly, was successful in persuading Mr Justice Davies that his client had no case to answer. Daly walked from the court a free man.

The jury returned with a verdict of guilty on all the accused.

On Wednesday, 15 April the convicted prisoners were brought to court to be sentenced. Mr Justice Edmund Davies called first for Roger John Cordrey. The judge told him that he would take into consideration Cordrey's plea of guilty and the fact that his share of the stolen money had been recovered, and would reduce his sentence accordingly. 'In respect of the four counts you must go to prison for concurrent terms of twenty years.' There was a moment's stunned silence from the court, and then a gasp. Journalists and barristers alike were astounded by the severity of the sentence. If this was Mr Justice Davies's idea of leniency, what would the others get?

One by one the guilty men faced the bench: Ronnie Biggs, thirty years; Thomas Wisbey, thirty years; Bob Welsh, Jim Hussey and Roy James, thirty years; Brian Field, twenty-five years. The convicted men were whisked off to various prisons around the country, where the true horror of their situation sank in. Even with full remission, most of them would not be released for at least twenty years.

EXPATRIATES

To the gang members still on the loose, news of the sentences was no less shattering. Any idea they may have had about turning themselves in, hoping to make a deal, evaporated. Bruce Reynolds sneaked out of the country in August 1964, Buster Edwards spent a short time in Germany having plastic surgery before leaving for Mexico City in March 1965.

In the same month that Reynolds fled to France, Charlie Wilson was sprung from Winson Green prison in Birmingham. He too was smuggled out of the country and headed for the South of France. Less than a year later, Ronnie Biggs escaped from Wandsworth and flew to Australia via

Above: *Ronnie Biggs with Miss Brazil.*

Paris. By 1967 Edwards, Wilson and Reynolds had all been rearrested.

Ronnie Biggs was now the only member of the gang still at liberty. In 1969 he fled from Australia to South America, finally settling in Rio. Confident that he was finally safe – Brazil had no extradition treaty with the United Kingdom – Biggs went about making himself into an international superstar. Despite attempts to rearrest – and even to kidnap – him, he remains there to this

BRINK'S-MAT
Robbers Strike Gold

It was almost by chance that the trio of vicious armed robbers realized they had struck gold. Their getaway van drove off groaning under the weight of three tons of bullion. Yet the biggest haul in criminal history proved harder to track down than a needle in a haystack.

At 6.25 on the morning of Saturday, November 26, 1983, a group of men were gathered outside Unit 7, a warehouse on the Heathrow International Trading Estate in Hounslow, London.

Despite its unprepossessing appearance, Unit 7 is one of the world's biggest safes. It is used by Brink's-Mat, Britain's leading security company, to store hugely valuable cargoes of precious metals, currency, bonds, jewels, fine art and other high-risk consignments en-route for Heathrow International Airport.

The ground floor of the building is a huge vault containing three safes. Above this are the manager's office, a radio room, a common room and a locker room for the thirty or so guards who usually work from the building.

At precisely 6.30 Michael Scouse, the senior duty guard and 'keyman', unlocked the unit, leaving the rest of the crew outside. He switched off the alarm system, then returned to the main door. He allowed the other men to enter and locked the door again from the inside.

Scouse reset the alarms and went up to the office. He was joined by Robin Risley, the crew leader for the day. Risley knew the men had been brought in specially for a bullion run. Scouse looked through his bills of lading. 'It's gold. Three tons. Gatwick airport for the Far East via Cathay Pacific Airways. It's got to be there by 8 a.m.'

Risley walked over to the common room, where the rest of the crew were warming themselves up with cups of tea. They were discussing the run when the doorbell rang. It had to be Tony Black, late as usual. The guards heard Scouse go down the stairs to let him in. Seconds later, Black walked into the common room. The 31-one-year-old guard looked pale and drawn as he glanced around the room. He muttered that he needed to go to the toilet, and then went back downstairs.

A couple of minutes later, the guards heard footsteps returning. They paid no attention until a voice bellowed out, 'Get on the floor or you're fucking dead!'

A figure appeared in the doorway of the common roof. He was about 5ft 8in, dressed in a black blazer and black trousers. His face was covered with a canary-yellow balaclava and he brandished a 9mm Browning automatic.

The guards, immobilized by fear, failed to react quickly enough for the intruder's satisfaction. Without a word, he pistol-whipped one of them, sending him crashing to the floor. The other guards quickly dropped to the floor.

Above: *The police arrive at Unit 7 of the Brink's-Mat warehouse on the morning of November 26, 1983.*

Opposite: *Even when the thieves were in prison, the police still had to track down the loot, like these bars of bullion found in Kenneth Noye's garage.*

THE SECURITY TEAM HAD BEEN BROUGHT IN SPECIALLY FOR A BULLION RUN TO GATWICK AIRPORT

'Lie still and keep quiet,' the intruder said in a Cockney accent. As he spoke, two other masked men rushed into the room. Soon the gang had handcuffed all four guards. They also taped their legs together and placed cotton bags, secured with drawstrings, over their heads.

In the radio room, Michael Scouse was suffering a similar ordeal. After letting in the late arrival, Tony Black, Scouse had returned to the radio room. Seconds later he had found himself confronted by two masked men brandishing handguns.

'Are you Scouse?' a voice asked. Scouse nodded and a knife sliced through the front of his jeans. Petrol was poured down his front and over his genitals.

'You'd better do as I say, or I'll put a match to the petrol and a bullet through your head. You have two numbers . . . What are they?'

With a gun pressed under his chin, Scouse was in no mood for heroics. He shouted the numbers: '94-45-57-85'.

That combination opened the vault door. But there were several other lines of defence which needed to be neutralized before the intruders could reach their treasure.

They were fully conversant with the sophisticated arrangement of silent alarms, combinations and time locks. And they knew exactly what authority Scouse had as shift supervisor. There was no way to bluff them, so Scouse had no option but to lead them through the maze of defences.

As the robbers stepped into the vault, their attention was immediately focused on the three safes at the far end of the room. They totally ignored the stacks of small boxes, bound with metal straps, which littered the floor. They didn't know, and Scouse wasn't about to tell them, that these were the real treasure. Each of these inconspicuous little boxes contained a gold ingot. Together they were worth more than £25 million.

Scouse explained to the gang leader that he couldn't open the safes alone. He had the keys, but only Robin Risley knew that day's combination. Risley was dragged down to the vault and was told to enter the relevant numbers.

Risley was in a panic. The safe numbers had just been changed and he had barely committed them to memory. As he fumbled with the dials, the intruders became increasingly impatient. As

Risley continued to struggle with the locks and pleaded with the Cockney, another member of the gang asked Scouse what was in the boxes. Scouse, realizing that it was the only chance to save Risley and probably himself, told him that they contained bullion.

The man ripped open one of the boxes and saw that Scouse was telling the truth. Immediately the gang lost interest in Risley and the safes, and turned their attention to shifting the

Below: *John Palmer, a jeweller in Bath, was acquitted at the Old Bailey in 1987 on charges of handling gold from the Brink's-Mat robbery, and was presented with a congratulatory 'All Gold' Easter egg by the press.*

three tons of gold into the loading bay.

The gang leader asked Scouse how the shutter doors to the loading bay opened. Scouse replied that that was Tony Black's job. The leader went back upstairs. 'Which one of you is Black?' he asked. Black, who was lying in a pool of petrol on the office floor, identified himself and was frog-marched into the radio room at knifepoint. He opened the shutter doors by remote control, and a van drove into the warehouse.

Fifteen minutes later the same van drove out again, suspension groaning under the weight of £26 million worth of gold, the biggest haul in criminal history.

Within minutes of Michael Scouse freeing himself and raising the alarm, the Flying Squad were at the scene of the robbery. The investigation was headed by Commander Frank Cater.

From the outset, Cater had no doubt that this was an inside job. The most obvious suspects were the guards. They had all been taken to the casualty department of Ashford Hospital. The pistol-whipped Peter Bentley was treated for head wounds, and Scouse and Risley were suffering from petrol burns. The other men were unhurt.

By 10 a.m., all six men were being grilled by Cater and his team at Hounslow police station.

PRIME SUSPECT

The most obvious suspects, because of their special knowledge and responsibilities, were Scouse and Risley. But, as the morning wore on and more information about the six men came into the incident room, another name caught Cater's eye.

Anthony John Black stuck out like a sore thumb. He did not have a criminal record himself, but his common-law brother-in-law, Brian Robinson, was well known to the police.

Despite the fact that he was sure that Black was the man he was after, Commander Cater elected to send him home along with the other guards. At 8 a.m.

on Sunday, 4 December, more than a week after the raid, detectives arrived simultaneously at the homes of all six guards and invited them down to Hounslow police station for further questioning. Five of the guards were asked to go over their statements again. It was all routine.

Tony Black, however, was given the full treatment. His interrogation, led by Detective Inspector Tony Brightwell, lasted more than six hours as they went over his statement again and again in minute detail.

Then Detective Sergeant Alan Branch dropped his bombshell. He looked Black straight in the eye and asked, 'What does your brother-in-law think about the robbery?'

The fact that the police knew about his connection with Brian Robinson obviously shook Black, but he was not ready to fold yet. The game of cat and mouse lasted until 3 p.m. the following day. The police piled more and more pressure on the prisoner and he was obviously getting ready to crack.

'Can I have a cup of tea?' Black asked.

Detective Sergeant Nicholas Benwell left the interview room and returned with a plastic cup from the vending machine. Black took a sip and looked up.

'Where do I start?' he asked.

MOLE TURNS GRASS

When Tony Black decided to talk, he talked with a vengeance. It took Sergeant Benwell more than eight hours to take down his statement. He explained how he had been approached by his sister's common-law husband, Brian Robinson, to provide inside information about shipments, security arrangements, the layout of the warehouse and details of personnel and procedures. Black admitted that on the day of the robbery, he had let the gang into the warehouse.

According to Black, Robinson had two accomplices. One was a man in his

> **BLACK WAS ALLOWED HOME, NOT REALIZING THAT THE POLICE WERE CONVINCED HE HAD BEEN IN ON THE ROBBERY**

> **THE SECURITY GUARD HAD PROVIDED THE ROBBERS WITH PHOTOGRAPHS, KEYS AND DETAILED INFORMATION**

Below: *John Palmer's house outside Bath. Armed police raided the house on the morning after the death of DC Fordham, but found Palmer and his wife had left for a holiday in the Canary Islands.*

early thirties called Mick. The other was a giant of a man who went by the name of Tony.

Shortly after Black finished his statement, Detective Sergeant Branch came into the interview room with two files containing mugshots of known associates of Brian Robinson. Black leafed through the photographs and did not hesitate in identifying two of them – Tony White and Mick McAvoy.

Having broken every rule in the criminal code book, Tony Black was taken back to his cell.

At 6.30 the following morning, Tuesday December 6, the Flying Squad picked up Robinson, McAvoy and White. The three men were taken to separate police stations well away from Hounslow. Robinson was polite but firm in his denial of any wrongdoing, and provided the police with a detailed alibi for the day of the robbery. White was aggressive and blunt. McAvoy would say nothing without his lawyer being present.

Under normal circumstances, Frank Cater knew that breaking the three men down would take time. He decided to take a short cut. He showed them Tony Black's statement. White was the first

to capitulate. He admitted being a party to the robbery and wanted to explore the possibility of doing a deal. At the end of the interview, however, White refused to sign his statement and he would later withdraw his admission of guilt at his trial.

Brian Robinson realized that, in the light of Black's testimony, his position was hopeless. He admitted that he had helped set up the robbery but denied being involved in the execution of the crime itself.

McAvoy stuck to his tactic of silence until he too had read Black's statement, at which point he folded completely.

There would be no deal for McAvoy or White, but there certainly was for Tony Black. On February 17, 1984, Black – the 'Golden Mole' – stood trial at the Old Bailey. In less than an hour he was arraigned, tried and sentenced to six years' imprisonment. This meant that, with full remission and parole, he would serve no more than two years.

Black's next appearance in court was at the Old Bailey in October 1984 – not as the accused but as the chief prosecution witness in the trials of Brian

Above: *The makeshift smelting shack found in the grounds of John Palmer's house. Inside, police discovered a foundry crucible and lifting gear, and in the house itself they came across two ingots of gold, still warm.*

Robinson, Mick McAvoy and Tony White. Black's testimony lasted almost three days and was frequently interrupted by catcalls and abuse from the public gallery. Nobody, it seems, likes a grass.

Since identity parades and forensic evidence had proved inconclusive, the prosecution's case rested almost totally on Black's evidence. In the cases of Brian Robinson and Mick McAvoy, this proved insufficient to convince the jury of their guilt. But Tony White, who claimed the police had tricked and coerced him into his confession, was found not guilty.

The Judge warned Robinson and McAvoy that he had no choice but to impose a heavy sentence of 25 years' imprisonment.

ONGOING INVESTIGATION

For the police, the matter did not end with the conviction of Black, Robinson and McAvoy. There was still the small matter of £26 million in gold bullion to be accounted for.

The police used their vast network of criminal intelligence to narrow down the field in their hunt for the Brink's-Mat haul. They came up with a list of names, known associates of Robinson and White. This list included Kenneth Noye, a Kent businessman and property dealer with a considerable criminal pedigree.

After months of investigation, Cater became convinced that Noye was the main link in an elaborate chain through which the Brink's-Mat bullion was being channelled. It went from Noye to his friend Brian Reader and on to Garth Chappell, John Palmer and Scadlynn Ltd, a bullion dealer in Bristol.

The police's main problem was that if they moved in on any member of that chain, the others would be alerted and go to ground. In the short term it was decided to keep the key players under surveillance. Detective Chief Superintendent Brian Boyce, who had taken over the Brink's-Mat case, was sure that at least part of the bullion was being stored at Hollywood Cottage, Noye's Kent mansion.

THE WAITING GAME GOES TRAGICALLY WRONG

By January 1985 Boyce was getting ready to move in. The round-the-clock observation on Hollywood Cottage was intensified. On the evening of Thursday January 10, Detective Constables John Fordham and Neil Murphy of the elite C11 surveillance team were sent into the grounds of the house for close observation. Seconds later, three Rottweilers leapt out of the dark.

Murphy made a dash for the perimeter fence. Once safely in the road, he waited for his partner. Detective Constable Fordham never materialized.

Almost half an hour elapsed before Detective Constables David Manning and John Childs went into the grounds of Hollywood Cottage to look for their missing colleague. Almost immediately they saw Fordham lying on his back, with the Rottweilers pulling at his clothes. Standing over the fallen policeman was Kenneth Noye, pointing a shotgun at him.

Manning whipped out his warrant card and shouted, 'I am a police officer.' He walked over to where Fordham was lying and immediately saw blood oozing from his chest and stomach. 'He's done me,' Fordham gasped. 'He's stabbed me.'

Noye was dragged off, and charged with malicious wounding, a charge which had to be changed to murder a few hours later. With the tragic loss of Detective Constable Fordham, the nature of the police operation became public and Boyce had to move quickly.

Within an hour of the stabbing, police raided the home of Brian Reader and discovered almost £70,000 in new £50 notes along with several lumps of yellow-coloured metal. They took these away, together with notebooks, diaries and address books – anything which would help establish Reader's

ONCE IN POSSESSION OF THE GOLD, CHAPPELL WOULD RESMELT IT, MIXING IT WITH COPPER TO HIDE ITS PURITY. SCADLYNN WOULD THEN SELL IT ON THE OPEN MARKET AS SCRAP.

connection with other members of the bullion chain.

The search of Hollywood Cottage and its grounds did provide ample evidence that Kenneth Noye was involved in the Brink's-Mat robbery. In a shallow gully beside the garage wall, they found eleven gold bars, weighing some 13kg and worth something in excess of £100,000.

Nearly 50 officers sealed off the village of Litton, home of Garth Chappell. Inside Chappell's home they discovered a briefcase containing £12,500 in £50 notes. Armed police raided John Palmer's house. Palmer was not there. Three guests at the house informed police that Mr and Mrs Palmer had left the day before with their children for a three-week holiday in the Canary Islands. In the grounds of the house, police found a makeshift smelter. In the house itself they discovered two gold ingots, still warm, along with a selection of firearms, and a large quantity of cash.

It took months for the detectives to piece everything together. As they had suspected, the gold had been passed from Noye to Reader and from him to Chappell. Chappell had paid Reader for each shipment in £50 notes, and Reader had paid Noye.

Once in possession of the gold, Chappell would resmelt it, mixing it with copper to hide its purity. Scadlynn would then sell it on the open market as scrap. In the space of six months, Chappell had managed to dispose of about half of the Brink's-Mat haul – some £13 million worth of gold.

Noye was jailed for thirteen years and fined £250,000. Chappell received ten years and a £200,000 fine. Reader was sentenced to ten years, and John Palmer, who returned from Spain voluntarily, was found not guilty.

CRIMES
OF
TERROR

SEPTEMBER 11
World Trade Center

On September 11, 2001, terrorists unleashed a shocking air assault on America's military and financial powers by hijacking four commercial jets and then crashing them into the World Trade Center in New York, the Pentagon and the Pennsylvania countryside.

It was the most dramatic attack on American soil since Pearl Harbor and caused the most incredible scenes of chaos and carnage. With the estimated death toll at over 5,300, this was definitely one of the most devastating terrorist operations in American history.

HIJACKED PLANES

The terrorists hijacked four California-bound planes from three airports on the Eastern Seaboard. The planes were loaded with the maximum amount of fuel, which suggested a well-financed and well-co-ordinated plan. The planes were identified as American Airlines flight #11 and United Airlines flight #175 both flying from Boston, Massachusetts to Los Angeles, California. There were a total of 157 people on board the two planes.

At 8.45 a.m. the first hijacked passenger jet, Flight #11, crashes into the north tower of the 110-storey World Trade Center, tearing a gaping hole in the building and setting it on fire.

As if this wasn't horrifying enough, at precisely 9.03 a.m. the second hijacked airliner, Flight #175, crashes

Above: *The second plane hits the south tower of the World Trade Center.*

THE WORLD TRADE CENTER'S NORTH TOWER COLLAPSES FROM THE TOP DOWN AS IF IT WERE BEING PEELED APART, RELEASING A TREMENDOUS CLOUD OF DEBRIS AND SMOKE.

into the south tower of the World Trade Center and explodes – both buildings are now burning. They had ripped a blazing path through the Defence Department, bringing the domestic air traffic system to a halt and plunging the whole nation into an unparalleled state of panic.

Immediately the Federal Aviation Administration shut down all New York City area airports, halting all flight operations for the first time in US history. The Port Authority of New York and New Jersey ordered that all bridges and tunnels in the New York area were to be closed.

President Bush put US military forces, both at home and abroad, on their highest state of alert, and navy

Above: *Firefighters attempting to put out the blaze at The Pentagon.*

In a grim address to the nation, President Bush condemned the attacks as a failed attempt to frighten the United States and promised a relentless hunt to find those responsible. 'We will make no distinction,' he said, 'between the terrorists who committed these acts and those who harbour them.' Bush also promised that America would continue to function 'without interruption'.

Below: *The collapse of the south tower at the World Trade Center.*

warships were deployed along both coasts for air defence.

The horrors of the attack, however, were not yet over. At 9:43 a.m. American Airlines Flight #77 out of Dulles International Airport, ripped through the newly renovated walls of the Pentagon – perhaps the world's most secure office building.

Evacuation of The Pentagon and the White House began immediately.

At 10:05 a.m. the south tower of the World Trade Center collapses, plummeting into the streets below. A massive cloud of dust and debris forms and slowly drifts away from the building. At the same time as the collapse of the tower, a fourth jet, Flight #93, is reported to have crashed 80 miles southeast of Pittsburgh, shortly after it was hijacked and turned in the direction of Washington.

None of the 266 people aboard the four planes survived. There were even more horrific casualties in the World Trade Center and the Pentagon, which together provided office space for more than 70,000 people.

The spectacular collapse of the historic twin towers and another not so famous skyscraper during the rescue operations caused even more bloodshed. At least 300 New York firefighters and 85 police officers lost their lives.

GROUND ZERO

The site of destruction became known as 'Ground Zero'. The extent of the devastation, even the limited view of it that could be seen from outside the perimeter, was a horrifying sign of just how evil mankind can be. However, you could also see many signs of the good side of humanity, in the numerous outpourings of love and support for the victims and their families that surrounded the site. You could see the tributes everywhere – in the yard of a describe the place as clean, the cleanup of the World Trade Center site is now complete. What was just a pile of jagged, knotted steel and concrete, is now a hole, a neatly squared-off, rectangular cavity of 16 acres.

One prominent reminder of the scale of the disaster that engulfed New York on that fatal day was the remains of 'The Sphere' which stood in the fountain. This was once the centrepiece of World Trade Center plaza.

The search for bodies has now officially been called off.

Above: *Recovering the body of the firefighter's chaplain from the Ground Zero site.*

church near the site, and along the fence surrounding the area. There were signs, posters, greeting cards, dolls, stuffed animals, flowers and numerous other messages and items indicating that people all over the world cared about the people who died in this tragedy. It seemed to show the sheer determination of the people to stand up against the terrorists.

Though it may never feel right to

THE GRIM AND EXHAUSTING TASK OF CARTING AWAY THE RUINS OF THE WORLD TRADE CENTER TOOK MONTHS AND A BILLION DOLLARS — AND FINISHED UNDER BUDGET AND AHEAD OF SCHEDULE.

WHO IS RESPONSIBLE?

Although no one claimed responsibility for the attacks on September 11, federal officials said they suspect the involvement of Islamic extremists with links to fugitive terrorist Osama bin Laden. Bin Laden has been implicated in the 1998 bombings of two US embassies in Africa and several other attacks. There is also a lot of evidence implicating bin Laden's militant network in the attack. Politicians from both parties predicted a major and immediate escalation in America's worldwide war against terrorism.

Following the cataclysmic events of September 11, the US authorities were quick to name Osama bin Laden as their prime suspect. The reasons for their suspicions were many, and the evidence collected during the ensuing investigation seemed to support their theory.

Although the evidence seemed compelling, at least two people weren't convinced. Milt Beardon, a former CIA agent who spent time in Afghanistan advising the mujahedeen during their fight against the Soviets, told ABC's Sunday programme that the attacks may have been the work of Shi'ite Muslims because the hijackers on the aircraft that crashed outside Philadelphia were described as wearing 'red head bands,' an adornment known to date back to the formation of the Shi'ite sect. While Pakistani journalist, Hamid Mir, also doubts that bin Laden was behind the September 11 attacks, saying the terrorist leader did not have the resources to pull it off.

Despite these doubts, another piece of information provided a chilling insight into what was to come. While recording a segment for the CBS *60 Minutes* programme, the show's producer George Creel, was travelling in a car with Khaled Kodja, a known bin Laden associate, when Kodja told him:

> 'America is a very vulnerable country, you are a very open country. I tell you, your White House is your most vulnerable target. It would be very simple to just get it. It is not difficult. It takes only one or two lives to have it, it's not difficult. We have people like this.'

Although the world intelligence community has been aware of bin Laden and his al-Qaeda network for some time, no one was able to predict where and when he would strike next. The organization is not only more sophisticated than past terrorist groups, but it is controlled and financed by a man who has dedicated most of his adult life to fighting a jihad against anyone he sees as an 'enemy of Islam', particularly America.

FROM A LARGE FAMILY

Osama bin Laden (Usamah bin Muhammad bin Awad bin Ladin) was born in 1957 or 1958 in Riyadh, Saudi Arabia. He was the seventh son in a family of 52 children.

His father, Sheik Mohammed Awad bin Laden, was a poor, uneducated

> 'MY PRIME SUSPECT IS OSAMA BIN LADEN BECAUSE HE WAS INDICATING HE WAS GOING TO DO THIS, HE WAS CALLING FOR THE KILLING OF AMERICANS JUST RECENTLY AND HE HAD THE CAPABILITY, SO WHY WOULDN'T WE SUSPECT HIM — WE'D HAVE TO BE CRAZY.'
>
> Professor Bard O'Neil from the National War College in Washington

Above: *Osama bin Laden*

labourer from Hadramout in South Yemen who worked as a porter in Jeddah. In 1930, the elder bin Laden started his own construction business, which became so successful that his family grew to be known as 'the wealthiest non-royal family in the kingdom.'

Bin Laden tops the FBI's most wanted terrorist list and, until recently, has been living in exile under the protection of Afghanistan's Taliban regime. Since the collapse of the Taliban regime, he has been in hiding. Though his current whereabouts are unknown, most reports indicate that, if alive, bin Laden is probably in Afghanistan.

Although the September 11 attacks shocked the world with their audacity and far-reaching repercussions, one positive factor remains. A large percentage of the world's population was united in a collective resolve to never let it happen again. Perhaps, at least in this case, some good will come out of it and the thousands of victims will not have died in vain.

THE BIGGEST AL-QAEDA CATCH

The arrest and interrogation of Khalid Sheikh Mohammed is the biggest catch yet in the global hunt for al-Qaeda suspects. Western security sources say they have no doubts that Khalid played a major role as al-Qaeda's operational commander in the September 11 attacks.

Kuwaiti-born Mohammed was one of three al-Qaeda suspects detained in the city of Rawalpindi near the Pakistani capital Islamabad as part of Pakistan's support for US President George W. Bush's war on terror.

Nobody but a few Pakistani intelligence agents had heard of Khalid until a 1,200lb bomb of fertilizer, petrol and hydrogen exploded in the underground car part of the World Trade Center in New York on February 26, 1993. This attack, which killed six people and injured more than 1,000, was Khalid's spectacular debut in international terrorism.

Chilling details have begun to emerge regarding Khalid's alleged activities since September 11. He is reported to have commanded Richard Reid, the shoe-bomber now serving life in an American prison for attempting to blow up a US aircraft over the Atlantic. Jose Padilla, who was arrested in Chicago last June on suspicion of planning a 'dirty bomb' attack, is said to have been another one of his protégés. Attacks on an Israeli aircraft, bombings on the USS Cole in Yemen and a hotel in Kenya last October were planned by him, according to reports. He has also played an important role inspiring and fostering ties with Asian terrorist groups, particularly those responsible for the Bali bombings.

Witnesses in Pakistan are also reported to have confessed that Khalid personally killed Daniel Pearl, the Wall Street Journal reporter who was kidnapped in Karachi last year.

Some of America's most senior politicians are already saying that the normal rules governing the torture of terror suspects, should be set aside because Sheikh Mohammed is the repository of so much important information.

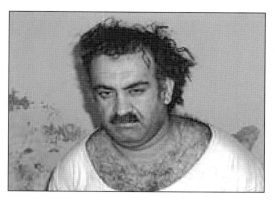

Left: *Khalid Sheikh Mohammed following his arrest.*

Sheikh Mohammed has already disclosed the names and descriptions of about a dozen key al-Qaeda operatives believed to be plotting terrorist attacks on American and other Western interests. He has also filled in important gaps in what U.S. intelligence knows about al-Qaeda's practices.

WAR ON TERRORISM

Following September 11, America justifiably declared a 'War on Terror' against all terrorists and the countries which harboured them. They also vowed to hunt down those in possession of weapons of mass destruction. Intelligence in this field led them directly to Iraq.

After many months of threats and a long military build-up, the United States finally attacked Iraq on Thursday, March 20, 2003. The war faced strong opposition from France, Germany, Russia, China and the great majority of UN member states as well as world public opinion. The combined military ground force of the US and the UK was around 300,000, and they encountered stiff Iraqi resistance.

THE REASONS BEHIND THE WAR

Iraq posed as a threat mainly because of the Iraqi regime's own actions. It had a history of aggression and also a continual drive towards an arsenal of terror. One of the conditions for ending the Persian Gulf War (1990–1991), was that the Iraqi regime was required to destroy all its weapons of mass destruction, to cease production of such weapons, and finally to stop all support for terrorist groups. However, the Iraqi regime continued to violate all of these obligations. It was still considered to possess and produce chemical and biological weapons, and was thought to be also seeking nuclear weapons. It was known to give shelter and support

"THE FUNDAMENTAL PROBLEM WITH IRAQ REMAINS THE NATURE OF THE REGIME ITSELF. SADDAM HUSSEIN IS A HOMICIDAL DICTATOR WHO IS ADDICTED TO WEAPONS OF MASS DESTRUCTION"
President George Bush

to terrorists, and practised terror against its own people.

After the attack on September 11, America started to feel vulnerable. They resolved to fight the war against terrorism, to confront every threat, from whatever source, that could bring sudden terror and suffering to their country.

It is a known fact that Iraq and the al Qaeda terrorist network share a common enemy – the United States of America. Iraqi and al Qaeda connections are known to go back more than a decade, and some of the al Qaeda leaders who fled Afghanistan went to Iraq. Not only has Iraq willingly harboured these terrorists, it is also known they also trained al Qaeda members in bomb-making, poisons and deadly gases.

The United States knew that on any given day Iraq could provide a biological or chemical weapon to a terrorist group or individual terrorist, leaving America open to attack.

Below: *The statue of Saddam Hussein, in Paradise Square, is set on fire amidst cheers from the Iraqi civilians. This enabled it to be brought crashing down as the world watched on (left).*

THE TYRANT

While there are many dangers in the world, it was thought that the threat from Iraq was the strongest due to the fact that their weapons of mass destruction were controlled by a murderous tyrant who had already used chemical weapons to kills thousands of people – Saddam Hussein. This same tyrant had tried to dominate the Middle East, had invaded and brutally occupied a small neighbour, had struck other nations without any prior warning and had led a burtal regime of terror and suffering against his own people. He was also known to hold an unrelenting hostility towards the United States. Saddam Hussein was considered to be a homicidal dictator who was addicted to weapons of mass destruction.

THE ATTACK

The attack on Iraq began at around 5.30 a.m. on March 20, 2003 when the United States launched 'Operation Iraqi Freedom'. The attack was an attempt to target Saddam Hussein and other Iraqi leaders, using air strikes and ground troops which entered the country by crossing southern Iraq from Kuwait. The following day the major phase of the war began with heavy aerial attacks on Baghdad and other cities. There was also fighting in the north of the country, with some reports that it involved US Special Forces. During the day, a number of oil wells – seven, according to the British

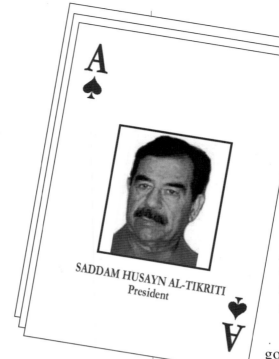

SADDAM HUSAYN AL-TIKRITI
President

Left: *In the aftermath of the war, with many members of the Iraqi regime still evading capture, the US issued a set of playing cards, depicting the faces of those that the coalition forces still had to 'pursue, capture and kill'. Saddam Hussein was the ace of spades.*

government – were reported to be on fire. According to the British government, two of the fires were extinguished by special firefighting troops. The Iraqi government denied that oil wells had been set on fire, saying that it had set fire to oil-filled trenches as a defensive measure against airstrikes.

By March 23 USA and British forces succeeded in taking the airport outside of Basra, and were in battle with Iraqi forces for control of the city itself. On April 9 Baghdad fell to US forces. Some Iraqis cheered in the streets after American infantrymen seized deserted Ba'ath Party ministries and pulled down a huge iron statue of Saddam Hussein, ending his brutal 24-year rule of Iraq.

The looting and unrest, especially in major cities Baghdad and Basra became a very serious issue. In Baghdad, with the notable exception of the Oil Ministry, which was guarded by American troops, the majority of government and public buildings were totally plundered. On April 13, Tikrit, the home town of Saddam Hussein, and the last town not under control of the coalition, was taken by American marines.

> THE GUNFIRE GREW LOUDER, UNTIL CLUSTERS OF BULLETS SWARMED INTO THE AIR AMID GRENADE BURSTS. IN THE MAIN STREET OF BAGHDAD, CARS CRASHED INTO ONE ANOTHER IN THE ENSUING CHAOS.

Left: *The Iraqi people celebrate the capture of their ousted dictator.*

With the fall of the Tikrit region, the coalition partners declared the war effectively over on April 15.

CAPTURE OF SADDAM HUSSEIN

On Saturday, December 13, 2003, US troops converged on a two-room mud hut squatting between two houses on a Tigris farm near the village of Ad-Dawr. One room, which appeared to serve as a bedroom, was in disarray with clothes strewn about the place. Inside the hut, dirt and a rug covered the entryway to a subterranean hideaway. The US troops had finally caught up with the man who had eluded them for many months. Saddam Hussein's last hiding place was a miserable 8-foot hole dug in the mud. Although Saddam was armed with a pistol, he showed no resistance during his capture. The former dictator of Iraq appeared tired and disoriented when he was pulled from his hiding place, which was found to contain arms and around $750,000 in cash. The US proudly declared 'We got him', and paraded the once proud man, now unkempt and with a scraggy beard, around in front of a world audience.

While world leaders and many Iraqis welcomed his capture, there were angry protests throughout the Iraqi area known as the Sunni Triangle. Saddam was handed over to the Iraqi authorities on June 30, 2004, and his trial opened in Baghdad on October 19, 2005.

Saddam Hussein was defiant throughout, pleading not guilty and challenging the legality of the proceedings. Saddam was found guilty and sentenced to death together with his co-defendants Barzan al-Tikriti, Saddam's half-brother and former head of Iraq's intelligence service, and Awad Hamed al-Bandar, former Revolutionary Court chief judge.

All three men were executed on December 30, 2006, 56 days after the death sentence was passed. Iraq's fallen dictator finally had to face the same fate he was accused of inflicting on his own people during his ruthless reign.

Above: *Fear and terror still reign in Iraq even after Saddam's capture. Here, a car burns at the entrance to one of the police stations in Basra, southern Iraq, hit by an explosion only hours after 3 car bombs had already killed 60 people and wounded a further 100.*

Below: *Saddam Hussein after his capture.*

THE TERROR CONTINUES
Bali and Madrid

In spite of the West's efforts to counter terrorism, the attacks continue . . .

BALI

The Indonesian island of Bali was rocked by two explosions on October 12, 2002. It was the worst incident ever to occur on this normally peaceful island, and the repercussions had a major impact on the lives of the people of Bali. At 11.05 p.m. October 12, an electronically triggered bomb ripped through Paddy's Bar, forcing the injured out into the street. About ten to fifteen seconds later, a second much more powerful car bomb concealed in a white Mitsubishi van, exploded in front of the Sari Club. Windows throughout the town were blown out. Scenes of horror and panic inside and outside the bars followed, with many acts of individual heroism. The final death toll was 202, the majority of them holidaymakers in their 20s and 30s who were in the two bars. Hundreds more people suffered horrific burns and other injuries. The largest group among those killed were holidaymakers from Australia. The Bali bombing is sometimes called 'Australia's September 11' because of the large number of its citizens killed in the attack.

The organisation claiming responsibility for the bombing was Jemaah Islamiyah, an Islamist group linked to the al Qaeda network. On April 30, 2003, the first charges relating to the Bali bombings were made against Amrozi bin Haji Nurhasyim, known as Amrozi, for allegedly buying the explosives and the van used in the bombings. On August 8 he was found guilty and sentenced to death by shooting.

Left: *Searching Bali rubble.* Below: *Madrid train explosion.*

MADRID

At the height of Madrid's morning rush hour, on Thursday, March 11, 2004, ten terrorist bombs tore through trains and stations all along the commuter line. It killed more than 191 people and wounded over 2,000 and was timed to take place before the weekend's general elections.

Panicked commuters abandoned their bags and their shoes as they trampled each other to escape the train terminal at Atocha. Some people, in their panic, fled into dark, dangerous tunnels at the station, which was a bustling hub for subway, commuter and long-distance trains, just south of Madrid's famous Prado Museum.

The explosives that were used in the blasts were a type of dynamite that was normally used by the ETA Basque separatist group. However, only eleven days after the atrocity in the Spanish capital, ties started to emerge between a key suspect in the bombing and Islamic militants elsewhere in Europe and North Africa. It pointed towards a widening web of organizations that may have direct links to al Qaeda.

The suspected ringleader of the Madrid bombings, Serhane ben Abdelmajid Fakhet, blew himself up along with four other suspects, during a police raid. Spain has provisionally charged fifteen suspects in connection with the blasts, six of whom have been charged with multiple counts of murder, and nine accused of collaborating with, or belonging to, a terrorist organization.

TIMOTHY McVEIGH
The Oklahoma Bomber

It was April 19,1995 – a perfect, sun-drenched spring morning in Oklahoma. A yellow Ryder Rental truck carefully made its way through the streets of downtown Oklahoma City. Just after 9 am, the truck pulled into a parking area outside the Alfred P. Murrah building and the driver stepped down from the trucks cab and casually walked away. A few minutes later, at 9.02, all hell broke loose as the trucks deadly 4000-pound cargo blasted the government building with enough force to shatter one third of the seven-story structure to bits

Above: *Timothy McVeigh as a child*

GLASS, CONCRETE, AND STEEL RAINED DOWN. INDISCRIMINATELY MIXED IN THE SMOULDERING RUBBLE WERE ADULTS AND CHILDREN —ALIVE AND DEAD.

Timothy McVeigh was born on April 23, 1968 in Pendleton, New York, and grew up in a rural community. He was the middle one of three children, and the only boy.

His father worked at a nearby General Motors manufacturing plant and his mother worked for a travel agency. His parents marriage was rather stormy and they separated for a third and final time in 1984.

Timothy's school classmates remember him as small, thin and quiet. He became involved in the normal school functions – football, track, extra-curricular activities – but usually dropped out shortly after joining them. He was shy, did not have a girlfriend, and in reality was somewhat of a loner.

McVeigh graduated from high school in June, 1986 and in the autumn, entered a two-year business college course. He attended for only a short time, during which time McVeigh lived at home with his father, and worked at a Burger King and drove dilapidated, old cars.

In 1987 he got a pistol permit from Niagara County and a job in Buffalo as a guard on an armoured car. A co-worker recalls that McVeigh owned numerous firearms and had a survivalist philosophy – a tendency to stockpile weapons and food in preparation for what he believed to be the imminent breakdown of society. In 1988 McVeigh and a friend bought 10 acres of rural land and used it as a shooting range.

JOINING THE ARMY

McVeigh enlisted in the Army in Buffalo in May 1988, and went through basic training at Fort Benning, Georgia. After basic training, his unit was transferred to Fort Riley, Kansas, and became part of the Army's 1st Infantry Division.

McVeigh had finally found his calling. The Army was everything he wanted in life, and more. When he joined, he was no leader, but an eager follower. There was discipline, a sense of order, and all the training a man could want in survivalist techniques. Most of all, there was an endless supply of weapons, and instruction on how to use and maintain them.

McVeigh became a gunner on a Bradley Fighting Vehicle. He was promoted to corporal, sergeant, then platoon leader. Fellow soldiers recalled that McVeigh was very interested in military stuff, kept his own personal collection of firearms and constantly cleaned and maintained them. Other soldiers went into town to look for entertainment or companionship but McVeigh stayed on base and cleaned his guns. During his time in the Army, he also read and recommended to others *The Turner Diaries* – a racist, anti-Semitic novel about a soldier in an underground army. A former roommate said that McVeigh would panic at the prospect of the government taking away peoples' guns, but that he was not a racist and was basically indifferent to racial matters.

While at Fort Riley, McVeigh re-enlisted in the Army. He aspired to be a member of the Special Forces and in 1990 was accepted into a three-week school to assess his potential for joining that elite unit. He had barely begun to prepare himself physically for Special Forces training when, in January 1991, the 1st Infantry Division was sent to participate in the Persian Gulf War. As a gunnery sergeant, McVeigh was in action during late February, 1991. Pursuing his desire of joining the Special Forces, he left the Persian Gulf early and went to Fort Bragg, North Carolina, where he took a battery of IQ, personality and aptitude tests to qualify for Special Forces. However, his participation in the Persian Gulf War had left him no time to prepare himself physically for the demands of Special Forces training. McVeigh was unable to endure a 90-minute march with a 45-pound pack, and he withdrew from the programme after two days.

This disappointing experience left him facing years of active service due to his re-enlistment at Fort Riley. The Army was downsizing however, and after 3½

ONE OF MCVEIGH'S FAVOURITE FILMS WAS THE 1984 PATRICK SWAYZE EPIC 'RED DAWN'. IT FOLLOWS A GROUP OF SMALL TOWN TEENS' CONVERSION TO GUERILLA FIGHTERS WHEN A FOREIGN ARMY INVADES AMERICA.

Left: *Sgt. Timothy James McVeigh*

years of service, McVeigh took the offer of an early discharge and got out of the military in the autumn of 1991.

OUT OF THE SERVICE

By January 1992, at the age of 24, McVeigh was back where he had started, living with his father in Pendleton, New York, driving an old car and working as a security guard.

In January 1993 McVeigh left Pendleton, and began to travel, moving himself and his belongings about in a

Left: *Timothy McVeigh, top centre, with his platoon, Fort Benning, Georgia, 1988.*

series of battered old cars. He lived in cheap motels and caravan parks, but also stayed with two Army buddies, Michael Fortier in Kingman, Arizona, and Terry Nichols in Decker, Michigan from time to time.

McVeigh travelled to Waco, Texas during the March-April 1993 standoff between the Branch Davidians and federal agents, and was said to have been angry about what he saw. He sold firearms at a gun show in Arizona and was heard to remark on one weapon's ability to shoot down an ATF helicopter.

Although both Arizona and Michigan are host to militant anti-tax, anti-government, survivalist and racist groups, there is no evidence that McVeigh ever belonged to any extremist groups. He advertised to sell a weapon in what is described as a virulently anti-Semitic publication. After renting a Ryder truck that has been linked to the Oklahoma City bombing, McVeigh telephoned a religious community that preached white supremacy, but no one there can remember knowing him or talking to him. His only known affiliations are as a registered Republican in his New York days, and as a member of the National Rifle Association while he was in the Army.

CHANGES IN THE GUN LAW

On September 13, 1994, the gun shows that McVeigh attended had become sombre occasions. New laws had been passed to stop the manufacture of many types of weaponry, including a range of semi-automatic rifles and handguns. Gun traders and buyers alike were outraged to learn the government was controlling their 'right to bear arms'.

To McVeigh, it also meant his livelihood had become endangered. He had been buying weapons under his own name and charging a brokerage fee to other buyers – those who didn't want their names on government forms.

Paranoia rose on rumours that owners would be subject to surprise

HOMEGROWN TERRORISM HAD ARRIVED WITH A VENGEANCE, AND THE TERRORIST WAS THE KID NEXT DOOR — AND HE WAS CRUISING AWAY FROM THE CARNAGE — DOWN INTERSTATE 35.

searches of their homes and businesses. McVeigh decided that action could no longer be postponed. From the Nichols home in Marion, Kansas, he wrote to Fortier. He insisted that the time had come for action, and he wanted Fortier to join him and Terry Nichols in their protest. Imitating *The Turner Diaries*, they planned to blow up a federal building. McVeigh cautioned Fortier against telling his wife Lori – but this was an instruction Fortier ignored. Furthermore, Fortier said he would never be part of the plan.

Undeterred, McVeigh and Nichols took advice from various bomb-building manuals. They followed the recipe and stockpiled their materials – bought under the alias 'Mike Havens' – in rented storage sheds. The recipe also called for other ingredients like blasting caps and liquid nitro methane, which they stole – but that's not the only thing they stole.

To pay for their despicable enterprise, Nichols robbed gun collector Roger Moore at gunpoint. Moore claimed the thief had taken a variety of guns, gold, silver and jewels – about sixty thousand dollars' worth. Nichols also stole Moore's van to transport the loot. When police made a list of visitors to the ranch, McVeigh's name was on it.

Earlier, McVeigh and Nichols travelled to the Fortier's Kingman home and stashed the stolen explosives in a nearby storage shed McVeigh had rented. When Fortier saw the explosives, McVeigh explained his plan. He stayed with the Fortiers, and while there, he designed his bomb. He showed Lori – using soup cans – how the drums he planned on using, could be arranged for maximum impact.

McVeigh wanted a rocket fuel called anhydrous hydrazine for his bomb. He phoned around the country to find some, but its expense made it impossible for him to obtain. So he settled on a satisfactory equivalent – nitro methane. In the course of trying to locate volatile fuels, McVeigh had phoned from the Fortiers, knowing full well his calls could be traced to the Fortier's telephone number – and the calling card he bought under the alias, Darel Bridges.

In mid-October 1994, McVeigh's plans were suddenly complicated, when he received news that his grandfather had died. He headed home to Pendleton, New York. There, he helped sort out his grandfather's estate and further poisoned his younger sister against the government.

While McVeigh was in Pendleton, he was unable to reach Terry Nichols. The co-conspirator had gone to the Philippines to see his current wife and baby daughter. But before he left, he visited his son and first wife Lana Padilla. He left her a few items including a sealed package, telling her it was to be opened only in the event of him never returning, but she opened it anyway. Included in its contents was a letter detailing the location of a plastic bag he'd hidden in Padilla's home. It contained a letter to McVeigh telling him he was now on his own – along with twenty thousand dollars. There was also a combination to Nichols' storage locker. When she opened the shed, she found some of the spoils of the Moore robbery.

In mid-December 1994, McVeigh and the Fortiers met in McVeigh's room at the Mojave Motel in Kingman, Arizona. There, he had Lori giftwrap boxes containing blasting caps in Christmas paper. He then promised Fortier a cache of weapons from the Moore robbery if he would accompany McVeigh back to Kansas. On the way, McVeigh drove through Oklahoma City to show Fortier the building he intended to bomb, and the route he would take to walk away from the building before the blast. They parted.

The getaway car would be his 1977 yellow Marquis since his other car had been damaged in an accident. The plan was for Nichols to follow the car in his truck and, after McVeigh parked it away from the bombsite, they would drive back to Kansas. The night before the bombing, they left the Marquis

TERRY NICHOLS WAS BITTER, SEEING MCVEIGH AS HAVING BULLIED HIM INTO PARTICIPATING IN THE BOMB PLOT. SENTENCED FOR LIFE FOR HIS PART IN THE BOMBING, HE HAS – SO FAR – ESCAPED THE DEATH PENALTY. OKLAHOMA WANTED TO TRY HIM ON STATE MURDER CHARGES, BUT HIS LAWYERS ARGUED HE CAN'T BE CHARGED TWICE FOR THE SAME CRIME.

Below: *An FBI agent comforts a weeping man whose loved one is still trapped in the rubble of the bombed Murrah building.*

after McVeigh removed the licence plate and left a note on it saying it needed a battery. Then, they drove away and Nichols dropped him off at his motel.

The next afternoon, McVeigh picked up the Ryder truck and parked it at the Dreamland Motel for the night. The following morning he drove it to the Herington storage unit. When Nichols finally arrived – late – they piled the bomb components in the truck and drove to Geary Lake to mix the bomb. When they had finished, Nichols went home and McVeigh stayed with the lethal Ryder vehicle.

He parked in a gravel parking lot for the night and waited for the dawn – and the drive to his target. He was dressed for the mission in his favourite T-shirt. On the front was a picture of Abraham Lincoln with the motto *sic semper tyrannis*, the words Booth shouted before he shot Lincoln. The translation: 'Thus ever to tyrants'.

On the back of the T-shirt was a tree

with blood dripping from the branches. It read, 'The tree of liberty must be refreshed from time to time with the blood of patriots and tyrants'.

Like his role model in *The Turner Diaries*, he headed for a federal building where he was convinced ATF agents were working. There, the people of Oklahoma City would pay a terrible price for McVeigh's compulsive and irrational paranoia.

Around 9:03 a.m., just after parents dropped their children off at day care at the Murrah Federal Building in downtown Oklahoma City, the unthinkable happened. A massive bomb inside the rental truck exploded, blowing half of the nine-storey building into oblivion.

A stunned nation watched as the bodies of men, women and children were pulled from the rubble for nearly two weeks. When the smoke cleared and the exhausted rescue workers packed up and left, 168 people were dead, including 19 children and hundreds more wounded.

THE ARREST

McVeigh was finally arrested on the basis of a traffic violation and the charge of carrying a weapon. McVeigh's yellow Mercury was left on the side of the highway and was not impounded.

Between April 19, 1995, and April 21, 1995, federal law enforcement officials traced a Vehicle Identification Number appearing upon the axle of the truck believed to have carried the bomb to a Ryder rental truck dealership in Junction City, Kansas. The FBI prepared a composite drawing of 'unidentified subject #1' based upon descriptions provided by witnesses at the Ryder rental dealership. By showing the composite drawing to employees at various motels in Junction City, Kansas, the FBI determined that the drawing resembled a man named Timothy McVeigh that had been a guest at the Dreamland Motel in Junction City from April 14-18, 1995. On checking their records it then came

> '*I* EXPLAIN HEREIN WHY I BOMBED THE MURRAH FEDERAL BUILDING IN OKLAHOMA CITY. I EXPLAIN THIS NOT FOR PUBLICITY, NOR SEEKING TO WIN AN ARGUMENT OF RIGHT OR WRONG. I EXPLAIN SO THAT THE RECORD IS CLEAR AS TO MY THINKING AND MOTIVATION IN BOMBING A GOVERNMENT INSTALLATION.' (LETTER WRITTEN BY MCVEIGH)

to light that a man named Timothy McVeigh was in custody in the Noble County Jail in Perry, Oklahoma, facing state misdemeanor charges.

THE SENTENCE

It was a trial fraught with pitfalls and tough decisions for U.S. District Judge Richard P. Matsch, who maintained strict control in his Denver courtroom. McVeigh was deemed responsible for the blast that killed 168 people – the worst terrorist attack ever on American soil until September 11, 2001.

Timothy McVeigh was found guilty of bombing the Oklahoma City federal building on April 19, 1995. During a separate phase of the trial, jurors condemned the 29-year-old Gulf War veteran to die by lethal injection.

Convicted Oklahoma City bomber Timothy McVeigh was put to death by lethal injectionon at 7.14 a.m. on Monday, June 11. He is the first federal prisoner to be executed in 38 years.

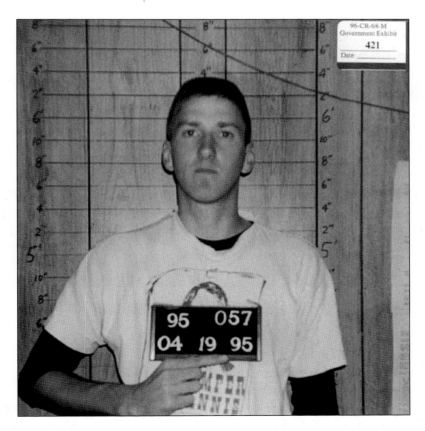

Prisoner number 95 057 04 19 95.

ILICH RAMIREZ SANCHEZ
Carlos the Jackal

'Carlos' is one of the best known 'revolutionary terrorists' known in the history of modern insurgent movements. He reportedly has worked for Mohamar Qaddaffi of Libya, Saddam Hussien of Iraq, President Assad of Syria, Fidel Castro of Cuba, George Habash and the Popular Front for the Liberation of Palestine (PFLP), the Italian Red Brigade, Columbia's M-19 Movement, the Baader-Meinholf Gang, and any number of other 'Communist and Socialist' employers.

Left: *Carlos at the age of sixteen*

Carlos was born in Caracas, Venezuela, on October 12, 1949. His mother, Elba Maria Sánchez had planned to give him a Christian name in keeping with her strong Catholic beliefs. José Altagracia Ramírez Navas, the boy's father, however, had other ideas. As a devout Marxist, he insisted that his first son should be named after his hero, Vladimir Ilich Ulyanov or Lenin, as he was better known. Stubbornly ignoring his wife's protests, José registered his son as Ilich Ramírez Sánchez.

Ironically, in his youth, José had entered a Catholic seminary with the intention of becoming a priest. However, after completing only three years of study, he declared himself an atheist and returned home to the town of Michelena in Tachira. Determined that Ilich would not waste his life pursuing Christian ideals, José taught his son the Marxist beliefs.

Carlos, a 1969 graduate of Moscow's Patrice Lamumba University, had been tied to 'Communist revolutionary movements' since the age of fourteen, when he became a member of the Communist party in Venezuela. His father, a wealthy Venezuelan Communist party leader, was dedicated to Leninist/Marxist theory and practice. In his teens, Carlos was allegedly given guerrilla training in Cuba, and by the age of twenty, had moved to Jordan and was being trained in weapons and explosive usage by hard-core members of the PFLP commando. Soon after, he began what has turned out to be an infamous career as an international 'pay for hire' terrorist.

HIS RESUME IS ALMOST UNPARALLELED IN THE EXPLOITS OF TERRORISTS OF THE LAST THREE DECADES. ACCORDING TO ANTI-TERRORIST ANALYSTS, THE ONLY INTERNATIONAL TERRORIST OF GREATER REPUTE IS PROBABLY ABU NIDAL (SABRI BANNA).

THE POPULAR FRONT

In July 1970 Ilich travelled to the Middle East. His first stop was Beirut where he arrived unannounced at the office of Bassam Abu-Sharif, the unofficial 'recruiting officer' for the Popular Front. Abu-Sharif was impressed with the passion of Ilich's convictions and made arrangements for him to start his training. According to subsequent investigations, it was at that first meeting that Ilich was given the name that, in the years to come, would strike terror throughout the world. From that day forward, Ilich was known only as 'Carlos'

Within weeks of the meeting, Carlos went to a Palestinian training camp in the hills north of Amman, Jordan to begin training in the handling of weapons and explosives. Carlos longed for real action and, in the final week of his training, he got his wish. Israeli jets bombed an adjoining camp and killed a member of Yasser Arafat's personal guard. Keen to move on to 'more exciting' pursuits, Carlos contacted Abou Semir, a senior member of the Popular Front, and was sent to an advanced commando training camp.

BLACK SEPTEMBER

On September 6, 1970, the Popular Front, acting on the instructions of Dr Wadi Haddad, carried out one of the most memorable hijackings in history. They began with the simultaneous diversion to Jordan of a Swissair DC-8 and a TWA Boeing 707, which was followed six days later by the hijacking

EDWARD HEATH'S GOVERNMENT IN LONDON HAD ALREADY CONCLUDED THAT RESCUING THE HOSTAGES WAS NOT FEASIBLE, AND BEHIND THE SCENES BRITAIN BEGAN TO NEGOTIATE WITH THE HIJACKERS, THROUGH BOTH OFFICIAL AND ITS OWN SECRET CHANNELS.

of a BOAC VC-10. The aircraft were forced to land at Dawson Field, 30 miles from Amman, which was quickly renamed Revolutionary Airport. Meanwhile another Popular Front hijack team, which had failed to board an El Al plane, managed to hijack a Pan Am Boeing 747 to Cairo and blow it up, while the media recorded the incident for a gasping world audience. The resulting conflict was dubbed 'Black September' and was to become Carlos's first taste of real warfare.

THE PLAYBOY

Carlos was appointed as the Popular Front's representative in London. His task was to ingratiate himself into British society and draw up a list of 'high profile' targets that would either be murdered or kidnapped. Carlos was sent to another training camp to learn the 'finer points' of terrorism and by February 1971, Carlos was considered ready for his appointment. He travelled to London to be reunited with his family. With his mother's help, he quickly slipped back into the 'cocktail-party set' and developed his playboy habits.

He attended the University of London to study economics and later took Russian language courses at Central London Polytechnic, all part of his carefully planned façade. His Popular Front contact in London was Mohamed Bouria, an Algerian who, as one of Haddad's most loyal followers, was responsible for European operations. In search of targets, Carlos read English newspapers selecting any prominent citizens who were either Jewish or had Israeli sympathies. Once he had created his list, he went to great pains to learn as much about his targets as he could, including home addresses, telephone numbers, nicknames and as many personal details as he could glean. His list of names included famous film identities, entertainers politicians and prominent business figures.

Above: *The Popular Front demanded the release of Fedayeen (members of the Palestinian movement) imprisoned in Germany, Switzerland and Israel.*

By December 1971, he had compiled a detailed list containing hundreds of names. It was during this time that his early career as an undercover terrorist was almost terminated. Acting on a tip-off, members of Scotland Yard's Special Branch raided the house in Walpole Street, Chelsea, where he lived with his mother, but after searching the house, found nothing of an incriminating nature. They were led to believe that Carlos was linked to a cache of illegal weapons that had been seized in a previous raid at the house of one of his friends. Incredibly, a fake Italian passport bearing a picture of Carlos was found in the raid but the police considered it unimportant. Apart from being placed under surveillance for several days after the raid, the police left him alone. The family later moved to a new apartment in Kensington.

During February 1972, while Carlos languished in London, one of Haddad's teams was hijacking a Lufthansa airliner to Aden. One of the 172 passengers taken hostage was Joseph Kennedy, son of the late Robert Kennedy. Following a short period of negotiations, Kennedy and the other hostages were released safely after the West German government paid a $5,000,000 ransom. The following May, Haddad sent three members of the Japanese Red Army to carry out a brutal attack at Tel Aviv's Lod airport. After arriving at the airport, the three men retrieved automatic weapons and grenades from their luggage and opened fire on the crowd. By the time the firing had stopped, 23 travellers were dead and another 76 were wounded.

MARIA TOBON

Maria Nydia Romero de Tobon was an attractive, 37-year-old Colombian divorcee who moved to London following her divorce to resume her University studies. She was not only attracted to Carlos's Latin American charm and impeccable manners, but

IN THIS MURKY WORLD WHERE ESPIONAGE, TERRORISM AND INTERNATIONAL POLITICS MEET, LITTLE IS EVER KNOWN FOR CERTAIN.

Below: *The first floor flat at Phillimore Court, Kensington, which was occupied by Ilich Ramirez Sanchez during his period in London.*

also became enamoured by his passion for politics. Nydia, whose grandfather had founded the Colombian Liberal Party, was a revolutionary at heart and was won over by Carlos and the fervour he showed for his cause. Some months later, Carlos successfully recruited Nydia and enlisted her aid in securing a string of safe houses for visiting envoys.

At one point she posed as the wife of Antonio Dagues-Bouvier, the Ecuadorian guerrilla who had supposedly trained Carlos in Cuba, and rented three apartments in central London. Her other duties included transporting documents and funds. Carlos would later tell investigators that he and Dagues-Bouvier had, at that time, carried out several 'missions' against selected targets. No record has ever been found of any such events having taken place. The general belief is that

Carlos's time in London was largely one of inactivity, while in other parts of the world; Haddad had selected others to play his deadly games.

TERRORIST ACTIVITIES

It is thought that by early 1972, Carlos was fighting and learning combat tactics in a guerrilla war against King Hussein, in Jordan. It is also possible that 'The Jackal' had begun acting as an intelligence agent or informer for the KGB.

By 1973, however, his terrorist activities had begun in earnest. He has publicly admitted to his 1973 assassination attempt on a British Millionaire named Joseph Edward Sieff, who was a well-known Jewish businessman and owner of the Marks and Spencer stores in London. Within the next two years, he was involved in the takeover of the French Embassy at the Hague, the killing of two French Intelligence agents for which he has been recently captured, and a 1976 takeover/ kidnapping of OPEC oil ministers in Vienna, Austria. Later in 1976, he was involved in a Skyjacking, that led to the now famous Entebbe raid by Israeli commandos.

In the late seventies and early eighties, Carlos was blamed for any number of skyjackings, bombings and machine gun/grenade attacks on British, French and Israeli targets. He became a master of disguises and was known to have obtained any number of false identities, complete with passports and credit cards. Adding to his reputation as a 'terrorist master-mind' was the fact that, even if no real evidence could be produced to link him to an atrocity, it was often blamed on him, out of convenience or ineptitude. Carlos was described as 'a ruthless terrorist who operates with cold-blooded, surgical precision', according to Ahmed Zaki Yamani. Acclaimed by some as a 'professional killer' with 'cool, deliberate actions', he has also been described by others as a 'bumbling psychotic who shoots people in the face, and is

Above: *Joseph Edward Sieff, 68, was one of the most successful and influential Jewish businessmen in London, and was Carlos's first victim.*

extremely lucky'. Whatever way you look at it, Carlos seemed to revel in the limelight of his deadly performance.

In 1982 and 1983, Carlos was suspected of several bombings in Paris, France, resulting in deaths of at least 13 people and the wounding of 150 more. In the mid-1980s, it is believed that he may have also participated in the planning and execution of several operations against Israel, operating out of Syria and Lebanon. He is also reported to have consulted with Col. Mohammar Qaddaffi and even Saddam Hussein, during their conflicts with the United States.

CARLOS THE PRISONER

Nothing was heard of Carlos during the late 1980s and there were even reports of his death. Unconfirmed reports have placed him in Mexico, Columbia, Damascus and Syria during recent years. However, on Friday, December 12, 1997, Carlos was led into a courtroom in the Palais de Justice and placed in the dock. Over the next eight days, Carlos tried every tactic he could think of to counter the prosecutions case against him. On December 23, 1997, after three hours and 48 minutes of deliberation, the jury returned with their verdict, guilty on all counts, the sentence – life imprisonment. Ironically, the death sentence that Carlos should have received for his crimes had been abolished years earlier by President Francois Mitterrand, the same man who had ordered his agents to find Carlos and kill him.

To this day Carlos is held in the maximum-security wing of Le Sante prison. He is allowed few visitors and spends his time reading, writing and watching television.

One thing is certain, the man who began life as Ilich Ramirez Sanchez and named himself Carlos the Jackal, is now known by a less flamboyant title. In Le Sante he is known simply as 'Detainee 872686/X' and probably will be for the rest of his life.

Acknowledgements

This book would not have been possible were it not for the help and support given by all the staff at Chapel Break First School. I cannot thank them enough for their patience and endless understanding. I feel privileged to have worked with such amazing children and their families, and without their wonderful questions and ideas this book would be significantly thinner.

My special thanks go to our wonderful and inspirational headteacher, Jane Rolph, my wonderful teaching assistant and spiritual guru Marian Ross, and of course my partner in crime, Maria Cornish. Her support, enthusiasm, expertise and friendship has kept me focused and motivated since the day we met. Thanks to her and her class as well for trialling *Dojen the Wanderer* and to Cathy Al-Bay, Ann Blackwell, Angela Moore and Glenys Shorter who let me loose on their classes to trial the other books in the pack. Thanks also to Jane Calderwood, Chapel Break's gifted and talented co-ordinator, for her involvement.

I am hugely grateful to Karin Murris, Joanna Haynes and Roger Sutcliffe for their fantastic training and for sparking my enthusiasm.

Thank you also to Steve Bowkett who was the reason I embarked on this whole project. I am very grateful for his expert contributions as a storyteller and master of meditation; as well as the three story books, his sections on poetry, story connections and relaxation techniques add another dimension to the pack, for which I am hugely thankful.

Special thanks must also go to my editor, Debbie Pullinger, for making it all make sense.

Lastly, my never-ending thanks go to Charlie, Lauren, Harry and Lois for putting up with my absences, and to our two sets of wonderful parents who have filled those absences. You have all ensured I never forget the meaning of life!

The author and publisher gratefully acknowledge the following for permission to reproduce material: Wapping First School and Colby Primary School, for the Ofsted reports (pages 23 and 24); Cathy Al-Bay for the Year 1 class case study (page 46); all the children and their families for the drawings whose drawings appear throughout this book.

Contents

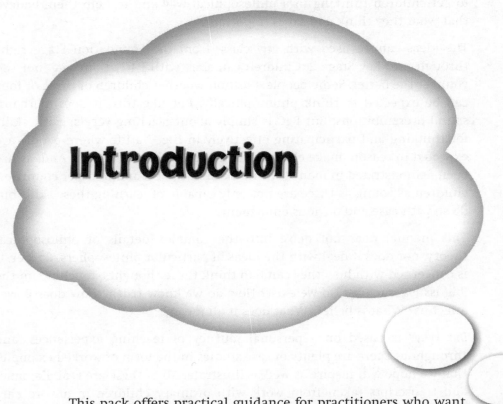

Introduction

This pack offers practical guidance for practitioners who want to give their pupils a voice in their own education. It is for those teachers who want to release children's potential for imaginative and creative thinking. You do not have to be a 'superteacher' to do P4C – Philosophy for Children. You only have to be prepared to value what the children have to say, to respect the questions they ask and to provide them with the opportunities to develop their thinking. We firmly believe that if you are interested enough to read this book, you will certainly be able to do P4C.

The skills young children develop in philosophy have far-reaching effects on their attitudes to learning, their behaviour and their thinking processes. The benefits to the children, as well as the impact on the school community and beyond, can be surprising – and you will almost certainly feel the effects on a personal level as well. As you spend time learning to really listen to the children you teach, you will probably find that their ideas and questions challenge your own thinking, forcing you to reconsider your own views and reflect upon your own development and practice in a truly philosophical way. Through P4C we have an opportunity to journey with the children to a re-examination of all the things we wondered about in our own childhood – before mundane problems became the main focus. If in doubt, try it! Doing P4C with children is challenging, but great fun.

The aims of *But Why?*

The aim of this pack is to help practitioners get started with P4C. Above all, it offers a very practical guide to conducting P4C sessions and introducing philosophy into your school. It will help you to develop the skills you need as a P4C facilitator as well as providing a rich source of ideas to get children thinking in a philosophical way and to help them believe that what they think and say is important.

The ideas can be used with any class, from the Foundation Stage right through into Key Stage 2. Children can start with P4C at any age, but the younger the better. Some people question whether children of three or four can be expected to think philosophically. Put like this, it does, perhaps, sound overambitious. But P4C is simply about teaching very specific skills for thinking and participating effectively in life – a life where people are expected to reason, make choices and act upon their decisions. And, as has been demonstrated in many settings both in the UK and in other countries, children as young as three are not only capable of learning these skills but do so with ease and obvious enjoyment.

This manual does not delve into the complex details of philosophical theory, nor does it deal with the ideas of particular philosophers. Rather, it is concerned with how they came to think those thoughts, touching on the 'big issues' such as: Do we exist? How do we know truth? How does power affect us? What is belief? What does it all mean?

But Why? is based on a personal journey of teaching experiences, and throughout there are plenty of case studies in the form of worked examples that we hope will inspire as well as illustrate. All of these are real dialogues and transcripts taken from work with ordinary children in an ordinary school. But it is from educational foundations where philosophical thinking is nurtured that these children have become extraordinary.

The pack contents

The *But Why?* pack comprises:

- This teacher's manual
- A mini Philosophy Bear
- Four picture books for use with children:

    Philosophy Bear and the Big Sky

    Pinocchio

    If I Were a Spider

    Dojen the Wanderer

Philosophy Bear and the Big Sky is designed to introduce philosophical thinking and language to children and their parents, while the three other books can be used in the classroom as stimulus for philosophical enquiry.

Part 1 of the manual gives a very brief introduction to philosophy and the development of P4C. It explains why P4C is such a valuable tool in education and how practising philosophy with children will enable us as teachers to open our own minds, address our ideas and challenge our assumptions.

Part 2 explains in detail how to run a P4C session in the classroom. It will show you how to structure a philosophy lesson and guides you through the strategies that will lead to fruitful thinking. Worked examples of dialogue illustrate the development of questions and ideas using different types of stimulus material.

Part 3 puts P4C into the wider context, showing how philosophy can be integrated into the curriculum and the life of the school, and introduced into the home and community.

Part 4 comprises a stock of tried-and-tested strategies, techniques, games and activities that will help you create a classroom climate conducive to thinking, develop creativity, encourage philosophical thought and foster enthusiasm for philosophy as an enjoyable and inspirational way to learn.

Part 5 focuses on using Philosophy Bear and the picture books in support of the strategies covered in Parts 2 and 3. It is recommended that you acquaint yourself with the ideas and methods covered in Parts 2 and 3 before beginning to use the resources with children.

Using Philosophy Bear

Philosophy Bear is simply a tool for engaging children in philosophy in much the same way as any puppet, toy or other prop can be used to engage their learning in other educational areas. Having used Philosophy Bear for several years, I have found that he can be an invaluable aid to doing P4C. The character of Philosophy Bear is essentially rather like that of a questioning child – someone whose thoughts wander freely, who ponders the 'big ideas' and who is always asking questions. Thus, he is ideally suited to the role of a facilitator who encourages talking and questioning, and who helps the children gain confidence and understanding about the skills they are developing. In Part 3 there are suggestions for various ways in which he can be used, but there are no hard and fast rules: you can include him as much or as little as you wish – and be as creative as you like!

Using the picture books

Philosophy for Children is especially powerful when it is done through the use of stories and poems. These often embody a wide variety of issues, implied or stated questions and multiple viewpoints in a very accessible yet condensed form. Stories follow an ancient narrative structure that is deeply wired into the brain: the whole story creates a broad perspective that satisfies the need to see the Big Picture, while the linear–sequential nature of a narrative allows the events that make up the tale to be understood logically and consciously. In other words, the structure of stories and poems supports the meaning-making that we do in order to understand the world, to survive and flourish in it. Both types of narrative, of course, appeal at least as much to the emotions as to the intellect. We 're-member' them, which is to say that as we recall the content of a story or poem we bring back into the members (the body) the feelings we experienced originally. Some become body memories that can stay with us for a lifetime.

Many different kinds of stories, poems (and also other types of stimuli such as artefacts or music) can be used as stimulus material in a P4C session, and in Part 2 there are detailed suggestions for using different types of stimuli. The story and poem books in this pack are therefore provided simply as a starting point. Along with accompanying notes and worked examples in Part 5 of this manual, each one is offered as the basis of a fruitful P4C session – providing you with extra support as you and your children gain confidence in doing philosophy.

Each book has been purposefully written to raise particular issues and to encourage the philosophical exploration of those issues. It is important, however, that any books used in P4C are enjoyable and fun in themselves: being memorable as 'narrative events', but also providing a rich source for the active engagement of children's imaginations. For this reason, the *But Why?* resources have also been extensively trialled with children.

Philosophy Bear and the Big Sky is different to the other three books in that it is not intended to be used as a conventional P4C stimulus. Rather, it is designed as an introduction to the idea of philosophical questioning and as a specific tool for opening up communication on the subject at home and at school. The book introduces the idea of philosophy, and can help practitioners, parents and children begin to consider the thinking and questioning skills involved in philosophical thought.

Pinocchio, *If I Were a Spider* and *Dojen the Wanderer* are each provided as a stimulus for a P4C session. The books are not intended to be used one after the other, but over the course of the children's increasing experience and development of philosophical skills. *Pinocchio* and *If I Were a Spider* will be appropriate for young children and for classes starting out with P4C, while *Dojen* is a more overtly philosophical text that will appeal to slightly older children and is more appropriate for those who have had some experience.

It is important to note that young children's progress in philosophy is dependent on skills, not age. It comes with both the experience of the children and the skills of the facilitator. Progress in philosophy can be gauged by the development of philosophical skills such as children's ability to ask open-ended questions, to move into secondary questioning, to make links and connections and tie them into philosophical concepts, to listen and to build on ideas, and to organize their thinking and communication. Progress can also be measured by their levels of participation. Joanna Haynes (2001) describes participation as intellectual, emotional and social. She believes that children make progress when the teacher is able to support development in all three areas by focusing on specific skills (such as listening) and addressing those aspects with the group (for example, by teaching listening skills overtly through stilling techniques, relaxation and meditation). Progress is dependent on all three aspects being worked interdependently.

We hope that *But Why?* will breathe life into the notion of a return to a more creative curriculum, where children are taught not just knowledge but the skills necessary to use it wisely and to create a life that they are able to reflect upon, decide about and live to the full.

Part 1

Introducing P4C

What is philosophy?

Philosophy often gets a bad press for being inaccessible to anyone outside the world of academia. To be a philosopher does not mean you have to have numerous academic degrees or a thorough understanding of what ancient or modern-day philosophers have spoken about. Philosophy simply is a method of thinking, reasoning and making sense of arguments and counter-arguments. We are all philosophers at heart.

We all philosophize at various times in our lives, and perhaps more so as we are growing up. We want to know about our existence, our relationships, and our place within society and the wider world. Adults and children alike have an innate desire to investigate and make sense of the world. We ask questions about the things that happen to us – what? how? and why? Philosophy is about asking those important questions and trying to justify our answers. It is concerned with questions and theories that are relevant not only to our present life, but also to our past and our future. Often these questions are seemingly unanswerable, but it is important that we don't just give up. Sadly, many children do. Such children have often been brought up in environments where questions are not answered, and ideas are dismissed, misunderstood or ignored. As teachers we are frequently frustrated that children are unable to think as creatively as we would like. But if that is what we are faced with – then it is what we can do about it that should be the focus of our attention. We need practical, usable and exciting ways of getting children to unlock their curiosity. Teaching philosophical skills provides children with the tools for genuine enquiry.

Philosophy can become addictive; a child who is encouraged to think about

Lovers of wisdom read on ...

their own ideas and those of others will want to find out more and will take nothing for granted. Being able to think philosophically is a highly transferable skill. It enables us to make informed and reasoned choices when making everyday decisions.

Philosophy is closely related to the beliefs we hold. It is our developing beliefs that help shape who we are and how we live our lives. If we never question these beliefs, we are in danger of leading narrow and shallow lives. We might never learn to reflect on what we really think, but instead follow the prevailing norms and fall victim to false ideologies. We might never learn to be courageous in standing up for ourselves or others. We might never learn to find inspired new ways of solving old problems. When we introduce philosophy into children's education, we are aiming to enable them to think deeply about their lives and the world around them. We want them to develop greater understanding of how their thoughts, ideas and personal beliefs equate to those of their community and of wider society.

The basic premise of Philosophy for Children (P4C) is that through exploring interesting, enjoyable and imaginative concrete stimuli, such as stories and poems, children learn the skills necessary to develop their thinking towards the big issues that relate directly to their past, their present and their future. The discovery of new thoughts and questions about things that really matter will inevitably have a significant impact on their lives.

Philosophical concepts

As a facilitator in a P4C session, it is helpful if you have some knowledge and understanding of the philosophical concepts that you want children to think about. The following themes often arise:

- love
- revenge
- power
- consciousness
- religion
- friendship
- death
- anger
- truth
- hate
- justice
- reality
- freedom
- authority
- morality
- identity
- belief

These concepts might arise from such questions as:

- Why are we born?
- Should children be punished?
- How do we know what is real?
- Can life ever be fair?
- Should we always do as we are told?

- Would I still be me if I swapped brains with my friend?
- Was there ever a first thing?
- Is it ever right to hurt someone?
- Why is it OK to eat meat, but not our pets?
- How do we know that life is not a dream?
- Will I still be the same person when I am old?

A skilled facilitator will endeavour to highlight the philosophical elements of the children's statements or questions, and help them expand their thinking into those areas. Part 2 goes into greater detail about these concepts and gives some guidelines for facilitating discussion.

A brief history of P4C

In the 1970s, Matthew Lipman and Ann Sharp produced a curriculum called Philosophy for Children, based on the belief that children can and should be encouraged to philosophize. They were influenced by the Socratic method of systematic questioning and dialogue: starting from the point of assuming that one knows nothing, an argument is built up through step-by-step reasoning and agreement, with any inconsistency being challenged.

Through the Lipman and Sharp programme, children were encouraged to talk and listen to each other within a 'community of enquiry' that was facilitated, not controlled, by the teacher. Lipman wrote a series of philosophical texts to use with children. These texts explored, among other things, the big issues of morality, power, love, religion and the nature of our existence. He also founded the Institute for the Advancement of Philosophy for Children, based at Montclair State University in America, and in 1992 his work in New Jersey was the subject of a BBC television documentary, *Socrates for Six Year Olds*.

Lipman's programme was beginning to attract a great deal of interest, and Dutch philosopher, counsellor and educator Karin Murris went to train with him. She developed his methods further by using picture books, which meant that philosophy could be accessed by much younger children and without the added costs of expensive and difficult-to-find resources. It is now estimated that more than 50 countries worldwide employ the methods of Philosophy for Children. It is being used increasingly throughout the UK in schools, including special schools; in the business sector; and in prison services. The Society for the Advancement of Philosophical Enquiry and Reflection in Education (SAPERE) works tirelessly to promote P4C in the UK, not only in the classroom but also in the wider community.

The P4C stimulus

Central to P4C is the use of the stimulus. All kinds of stimuli can be used – and it is good to use a variety – but perhaps the richest opportunities lie in the use of stories. It might be imagined that to do philosophy with children you need a philosophical text. Stories that are not overtly philosophical are more subtle, and it is quite true that it takes time to get children to ask deeper questions. Is this making the process needlessly difficult? We think not. If P4C is about questions in life, then everything in life can be seen as having potential as a stimulus. In short, how can it be philosophy for all, if it is only done with specialist texts? Through P4C, children learn to ask questions and to think deeply about the things that are in front of their eyes What P4C might lose in intellectual credibility (as claimed by the purists), it gains in power as a lifelong learning tool – and this is where its strengths lie.

But Why? – a skills-based approach

The work presented in this manual has developed from the highly respected and valuable work of Karin Murris, Roger Sutcliffe and Joanna Haynes, under whom Sara Stanley trained. Taking the P4C structure, we have extended philosophy through the Early Years curriculum and into the homes of children. In our development of the programme, we have focused particularly on building the skills that very young children need in order to become better thinkers. In this respect, philosophy is treated in the same way as a subject such as literacy: just as children are given the opportunity to acquire literacy skills – such as identifying phonemes and digraphs – as a foundation for reading and writing, they are also given the chance to acquire thinking skills as a first step in doing philosophy. The evidence from our work with the programme suggests that this more overtly skills-based method of introducing P4C to young children equips them with deeper understanding of their thinking processes enabling them to progress at a more advanced rate. We have also concentrated on finding practical ways to embed philosophy within a whole-school setting.

The *But Why?* pack therefore offers not simply a translation of the theory, but a tried-and-tested approach to the practicalities – and this, we hope, will encourage many more colleagues to introduce P4C into their schools.

Why do philosophy in school?

> The unexamined life is not worth living.
>
> SOCRATES

Children are naturally nosy. They enter school with a wealth (and we use the word deliberately) of unanswered questions. What we want for our children is the rediscovery and validation of their innate curiosity. However, in today's educational climate – when objectives are highly prescribed and time is at a premium, when 'facts' must be delivered and content covered, and when targets of attainment seem to be the *raison d'être* of a child's schooling – it is easy to overlook children's interests, ideas, concerns and fears regarding the world in which they find themselves. As professional educators we must remember that it is a world of which we already have great experience, but it is also a quite different world from the one *we* passed through as children. It is therefore surely worth bearing in mind the words of the poet Matsuo Bassho: 'Do not follow in the footsteps of the wise. Seek what they sought.'

As teachers are increasingly held accountable for raising standards in all areas of learning, we find that we are expected to justify any subject not included in the national curriculum. In this context, philosophy might look like something of a 'luxury item', but the experience of schools who have tried P4C would suggest that this is far from the case. In fact, doing philosophy has far-reaching benefits for many curriculum subjects, for the life of the school and for the lives of children both in the short and long term.

The following summary of benefits is by no means exhaustive, but it does indicate some important reasons for incorporating philosophy into the curriculum.

Creating a climate for learning

Philosophy is an effective tool in 'de-stressing' the classroom. The formation and evolution of a 'community of enquiry' takes away the emotional and intellectual fear of many children for whom answering questions is a high-threat occupation. The community welcomes all children's opinions, emphasizing that the process is more important than the product (the 'right answer'). In such an environment there are no right or wrong answers: children know that nobody will judge them or force them to join the dialogue unless they wish to. The dialogue supports young learners as they formulate their ideas and those of others, as they begin to make connections, and as they see and explore unsuspected possibilities and question their way towards understanding. Philosophical enquiry is a process that encourages a sharing of views to reach a balanced, personal perspective, using a variety of tools from the thinking toolbox.

Increasing motivation

Motivation to learn is enhanced through the use of philosophy. Children from as young as four have an innate desire to compete with others and themselves, so building ideas with someone else leads to increased use of higher-order thinking skills and problem-solving capabilities.

Encouraging creativity and imagination

The systematic questioning and reflective dialogue inherent in philosophy tap into children's natural spirit of enquiry through reasoning, problem solving, imagination, creativity, and social and emotional development. These processes move children away from simply supplying the answers they think teachers want to hear. Critical discussion will help children connect thoughts and ideas – and a critical thinker is a challenger. The combination of systematic questioning and positive debate cultivate confidence to 'go outside the box' into the most productive areas of exploration.

Thus, children are more likely to be more self-confident, sensitive, able to empathize and able to use greater initiative and imagination. In P4C, the stimuli are used as aids to develop the imagination and to encourage movement away from hard facts. (For more on creativity, see page 18.)

Developing communication skills

Philosophical dialogue provides a rich source of ideas and language for articulation, listening and turn-taking. Children learn the language of debate and gain valuable practice in making connections between statements, as well as between their own thoughts and the thinking of others. They also make connections to other curriculum areas. The National Literacy Strategy alone provides all the justification teachers could ever need to fit philosophy into their literacy sessions.

Fostering healthy scepticism as a method of acquiring knowledge

Philosophy equips children to challenge assumptions and have a point of view. To do this requires reasoning and reflection, higher-order thinking skills and awareness of the scientific method of discovery. Philosophical discussion within a community of enquiry fosters open-mindedness: a healthy 'show me' attitude that leads young learners away from gullibility and from cynicism (a particularly limiting form of what has been called 'a hardening of the categories').

Encouraging justification of beliefs through analysing and hypothesizing

Through philosophy, children learn the art of self-correction in light of reasoned counter-arguments, reflective thought and the presentation of evidence. They also become more able to analyse the behaviours of other people. Giving children the opportunity to explain their ideas clearly encourages them to have a point of view, to really understand what they believe and why. This can be classed as true lifelong learning.

Learning moral citizenship

When they learn to reflect on issues of morality and propriety, and to challenge when they disagree or are uncertain, children are thinking about real issues that directly affect their lives. A philosophical, questioning nature also leads to a greater responsibility for actions in general. Through philosophy, children learn responsibility (response-ability) for actions and views, as well as gaining an understanding of the relationship between such responsibility and accountability. The difference between argument and quarrelling is also highlighted. Within the community of enquiry, relationships can form based on empathy and compassion. Children come to appreciate the rules for equality and their joint ownership of dialogue as co-enquirers.

> The same principles which at first lead to scepticism, pursued to a certain point bring men back to common sense.
>
> GEORGE BERKELEY

> In questions of science, the authority of a thousand is not worth the humble reasoning of a single man.
>
> GALILEO (attrib.)

> I strive not to laugh at human actions, not to weep at them, not to hate them, but to understand them.
>
> BARUCH SPINOZA

Developing confidence, self-esteem and emotional identification

The importance of self-esteem for learning has been increasingly acknowledged in recent years. Building and maintaining self-esteem is one of the strands of Alistair Smith's Accelerated Learning programme, where the BASIS model (Smith and Call, 1999) is used to describe the elements of positive self-esteem and self-belief. The benefits of doing philosophy can be mapped on to the BASIS model, as illustrated by the children's quotations below.

- **Belonging** *"When we do philosophy I feel that we are part of a real group, like the class is a family. We do argue but we like each other as well."* Amy, aged 7

- **Aspirations** *"Philosophy makes me clever. I feel like I can do anything in my life."* James, aged 6

- **Safety** *"We do argue, but you know that you can still be best friends after."* Nikita, aged 7

- **Identity** *"We learn all about who we are inside. We all think different thoughts, that's because we all have different brains, I think."* Kelsey, aged 5

- **Success** *"It's really hard sometimes to think about whether you agree or disagree with your friends, but I feel really good when I work it all out."* Ryan, aged 6

Philosophy encourages self-review and reflection on beliefs and ideas, both of which lead to a greater sense of self-awareness. This in turn validates for children the authority of their own experiences, such that they are more likely to develop a questioning nature as a form of protection from potential abusers. This self-awareness also helps children understand their relationships with peers, parents, teachers and other adults.

The community of enquiry is a place where self-belief can grow and flourish in an environment of curiosity and active interest. This can be both an interest in the subject as well as in the ideas of others and their relevance to one's own experiences and thoughts. The feedback that children receive from their peers, teachers and parents when discussing philosophical ideas enables them to feel respected and valued. They are motivated to continue to build on their platform of ideas with an appreciation of the fact that their communications are worth listening to.

Building healthy relationships based on mutual respect

Through philosophical dialogue, children can develop ideas about democracy, equality and respect – even where there is disagreement. This fosters healthy relationships with peers. The community of enquiry enforces the principle that every child has a right to be heard and that their ideas are worthy of discussion. When their views are respected, then children are more likely to reciprocate this respect. The children are

> **Freedom is not something that anybody can be given; freedom is something that people take and people are as free as they want to be.**
>
> ALBERT CAMUS

> **I disapprove of what you say, but I will defend to the death your right to say it.**
>
> VOLTAIRE

encouraged to make reference to the ideas and statements of others: the use of the children's names makes them feel that they have been listened to, whether they are agreed with or not. Opinions are opinions – but within the supportive community of enquiry, children are guided towards strengthening and justifying their opinions through logic, reason and recourse to evidence.

Philosophy, creativity and intelligence

The basis of creativity is curiosity – and children are innately curious: they bring a 'natural nosiness' with them into the world. This imperative to find out more underpins the raft of intelligences (in Howard Gardner's sense of the word) that act as the bases of understanding on which meaning is built. We might usefully define 'intelligence' as the capacity to handle information. This capacity can be developed by first allowing children to be nosy by noticing things and by asking questions. Then they need to be made aware of the fact that we *can* notice things going on, both in the world and inside our own heads. Once children begin to develop an awareness of the way their minds work, they can start to reflect on those mental processes. Such 'thinking about the thinking we do' – known as *metacognition* – is widely recognized as accelerating the effectiveness of a child's learning strategies.

A first step in metacognition is to recognize the different ways of being nosy: to differentiate between closed (or convergent) questions and open (or divergent) ones. Once children understand that they can ask 'little pointed' questions to elicit specific information, and 'big wide' questions that open up a world of speculation and possibilities, they have access to a powerful tool for further exploring the world.

This platform of curiosity (which Steve Bowkett calls 'the creative attitude') naturally gives rise to creative thinking – which involves seeing the world from multiple perspectives, making new connections, becoming increasingly aware of insights and intuitions, and being flexible in applying strategies to verify one's ideas, beliefs and paradigms (networks of belief). Creative thinking in turn percolates up through a range of domains of human knowledge and understanding. Again, this is what Gardner meant by the natural intelligences (talents or potentials) with which we are born. Thus, if I am curious and playful about the way in which numbers work and the way they form patterns that relate to the 'real world' (whatever that might mean!), then this act of systematic nosiness boosts my *numerical intelligence*. Similarly, by noticing and exploring the way words link up to form meanings that cause pictures and sounds to form in my head, and if I notice how words can affect my own and other people's feelings and behaviours, then my *linguistic intelligence* will develop most effectively. (The point should be made here that the notion of numerical and linguistic intelligences is more powerful and more profound than the idea of numeracy and literacy: these, it seems to us, are just facets of a much richer jewel.)

Philosophical enquiry spans and draws upon all of the natural intelligences because it encourages nosiness about ideas, theories and beliefs – in other words, the basic attributes of human consciousness. The tasks and activities with which we engage children in this field lead them more swiftly towards the fixed goal of being independent and effective thinkers.

Philosophy and the national curriculum

The revised national curriculum requires that schools address a number of cross-curricular skills in thinking. They must also ensure that children are given opportunities to learn about beliefs and values. Great emphasis is placed on the development of children's spiritual, moral, social and cultural responsibilities:

> *The school curriculum should pass on enduring values, develop pupils' integrity and autonomy and help them to be responsible and caring citizens capable of contributing to the development of a just society.*

A school that provides a curriculum where children's thinking is steered towards consideration of life's wonders and puzzlements encourages children to grow into citizens who will question life creatively and critically and who have the ability to reflect on right and wrong.

Among the key skills listed in the national curriculum, one of the most prominent is communication. This area is always one of concern, especially for those who teach in the Foundation Stage, and the government have recently highlighted their anxieties about the lack of communication skills in young children on entry into the school system. An ideal way to improve the quality of both thinking and communication skills in school is to introduce the discipline of philosophy into the curriculum. This view was endorsed by the Rt Hon. Charles Clarke in the House of Commons in 1999:

> *I declare my interest in the subject. My mother's degree was in philosophy – she was tutored by Wittgenstein at university. She has been a constant pressure on me to raise the value and worth of philosophy in our education system – not only now, but for a long time. When I was involved in educational policy some 15 years ago, I remember her sending me newspaper cuttings detailing how philosophy had been brought into classes in primary schools in the Bronx in New York – precisely the kind of alienated area that my Hon. Friend mentioned – because it developed the skills of thinking and articulacy which could counter the alienation that otherwise existed.*

> *I am not quite sure whether I was the product of a Socratic midwife. However, I assure my Hon. Friend that I am wholly committed to the general approach that he set out so clearly today.*

> *The Government attach great importance to teaching pupils to think flexibly and to make reasoned judgments. We consider those skills to be a vital part of young people's education and preparation for life, and for lifelong learning. To emphasize the quality of thinking skills is a critical means of raising standards in schools; it is a key element in our overall drive to raise educational standards.*

What children and parents say about P4C

The perceptions of children and their parents reveal much about the benefits of doing philosophy.

What children say

Roxanne: Philosophy is good for your brain. It's a hard subject and those subjects that are hard make you cleverer.

Josh: We get together with ideas and carry things on – joining together is fun. I know it's hard, but it means when you get to high school you'll be cleverer.

Jade: It's challenging thinking of the questions.

Nikita: It's kind of hard to make the links, but when you get to the point it becomes easier.

Roxanne: I reckon philosophy isn't hard enough. I think as we get cleverer we have to make it harder for ourselves. (1)

Leo: Links are the hard part though; it's the questions that are easy.

Jasmin: In the time we are doing it, we forget what we're supposed to be doing and time goes so fast and so quickly, and we don't realize how much we've talked – where does the time go?

Roxanne: I think we should talk about our philosophy more, like outside at playtime with other people, that way we get more and more ideas. (4)

Robert: You get to listen to a story first, which relaxes you. (5)

Josh: It makes me feel good when I do philosophy. Basically it means I don't have to hold something in my hand – I just don't need to fidget like I do in other lessons. (6)

Jade: It's so interesting to hear what others think that are different thoughts to yours.

Chelsea: You can get to think about fun things and interesting stuff. (2)

Nikita: I disagree with you a bit because fun is different. It's like fun is stuff you do on the playground or when you have a party. (3)

Jade: The best bit is revisiting ideas that you've thought of before, and it means you can think of more stuff next time. (7)

Robert: It's definitely a lesson we look forward to because it belongs to us. I think more kids should be allowed to learn what they want in school, not what teachers tell us.

This short dialogue taken from an interview with a group of seven year olds, reproduced here in its entirety and without any further annotation or explanation, shows how passionately these children feel about the subject of philosophy.

The fact that the children feel it is a 'hard' subject is evident, but there is no sign of the reluctance or worry that children often express about some other academic subjects. This is perhaps all the more striking given that most of these children were not academically high achievers.

What is interesting is that these children evidently *feel* themselves to be academic and clever: they understand that it is difficult to think and talk philosophically, and they use the word 'challenging' to describe the processes of thinking up questions and making links. Roxanne even goes as far as saying that it is not hard enough! (1) Here she both recognizes and highlights a very important skill; she shows awareness of the process of self-evaluation and expresses a desire to expand her own thinking and that of others. In this remark, she has encapsulated all that we believe is so valuable in teaching philosophy to children.

Another interesting point that arises from this exchange is that the children perceive philosophy as fun. There is certainly the element of 'time flies when you're having fun', but Chelsea's comment (2) seems to indicate, more specifically, an intellectual enjoyment of the subject, something which is clearly seen by Nikita (3) as different to the physical fun found in play. The overall impression gained from listening to this group of children is that the whole process of joining together in this way is enjoyable both socially and academically. Roxanne (4) ties together the two ideas about fun in her statement that philosophy should be extended into the playground. Thus, philosophy might be seen as crossing the boundaries between social, physical and intellectual play.

Robert (5) and Josh (6) both touch on finding an aspect of relaxation in philosophy. Clearly some children find it easier to relax when the fear of failure is diminished; others find the process of meditation and enjoying a story relaxing in itself. We were pleasantly surprised to hear this come up in the interview because it has been demonstrated that being in a physically relaxed state is conducive to thinking. The fact that the children feel relaxed also indicates that they see the actual process of thinking and contemplating as an end in itself, rather than a means to an end where they feel pressurized to produce a concrete result.

Jasmine (7) sums up the group's enthusiasm for what she sees as the ever-expanding process of finding out, renewal and growth of new ideas. It is this element of intellectual enjoyment that seems to excite the children most, and it is also one of the most exciting things for a teacher to witness. It is at this point when the children get together and begin to take over ownership of the dialogue, that the power of their thoughts and ideas shows a freedom and energy comparable to any of the greatest eureka moments!

What parents say

In a questionnaire we asked parents of children participating in philosophy to tell us what they thought about the work and how it had affected their children. Below are some representative comments from the overwhelmingly positive response.

1   Has philosophy helped open up communication at home? If so, in what way?

By getting together and answering questions.

We are able to discuss things on an equal level, which doesn't happen with day-to-day problems.

It has helped W to discuss issues with older siblings from a more dominant position.

better now life

2 Do you enjoy participating in the homework? If so why?

Yes, but some of the issues were hard to deal with as it was very relevant to our family situation. (single parent)

Yes, my son often talks about things I didn't know he knew.

Yes, it leads to discussion with one parent or the other. We live separately.

It is time we are able to spend together, one-to-one, and I look forward to it.

Yes I do. It is nice to know what she is thinking about.

Yes, it is interesting to see how my child thinks, and a lot of the time I see things differently from her. It now makes me question things more.

3 Has your thinking been challenged by your child or through your child's homework? Can you give any examples?

Yes, he said he would forgive in school situations, instead of retaliating.

R has asked me questions that I can't answer.

My thinking has definitely been challenged, especially by the debates in the Philosophy Bear diary on the wolf and the humans.

Another perspective is sometimes offered, for example, single-parent issues from a child's point of view.

Yes, particularly the topic of anger. My child said he only got angry and shouted when I did the same to him. I'd never thought of that.

4 How do you think philosophy will help your child's learning?

Infinitely. In every area of his life.

Developing communication skills early will improve my child's confidence in dealing with potential conflict situations when she is older.

By opening up her mind to different viewpoints. She will have a greater base of knowledge to draw from.

She will know a lot more about the future just by asking 'Why?'.

I think it will encourage him to look beyond the surface of things. Also, as there are no right or wrong answers, it builds confidence.

Philosophy encourages my child to think about how others feel and to show understanding.

5   Have you any other comments to make about philosophy?

My child enjoys philosophy and I get lots of 'Why Mum?' – which is good.

I thought it would be too difficult for a six year old, but I have been pleasantly surprised how much she enjoys it and how much she is getting from the philosophy club. I'm really pleased she wanted to join.

I like the way that it encourages children to question the topics raised. It leads to debates, but ultimately no one is right or wrong – it is just opinion.

You have got to have courage to take on sensitive issues or ones that may upset either of you.

It has made me think of things in a different way. Not taking the things I already know for granted. I now question how and why things happen a lot more.

Philosophy has got the whole family into the habit of investigating topics. It has made us talk about many things that we probably wouldn't even have given a second thought to.

Doing philosophy has helped our son to listen to others and not be too critical, but to understand that we are not all the same; that we are all entitled to our own opinions.

Please carry on. My other son (14) is very jealous of his brother's opportunities here. He would love to study it (and does with us at home, of course) but feels it should be part of everyone's school curriculum. He said this today as he is choosing his GCSE options.

Ofsted and P4C

Ofsted looks favourably on ways to promote creativity and imagination alongside good practice in basic skills. It has acknowledged the benefits of philosophy for children's learning across the curriculum, as evidenced in the following extracts from Ofsted reports.

The inclusion of philosophy contributes to and directly impacts on:

Pupils' moral and social development

- *positive attitudes to themselves and others: respecting others*
- *telling right from wrong in a reflective and mature manner*
- *speaking with confidence*
- *listening to each other and with concentration*
- *responding to questions*

- *taking an active part in discussions*
- *offering confidently their own personal feelings and opinions in an atmosphere of trust and respect*

Pupils' capacity to become independent learners

- *discussing ideas*
- *questioning each other's ideas and opinions*
- *taking active part in discussions when opportunities are presented*
- *using appropriate vocabulary to engage listeners*

Wapping First School Ofsted Inspection Report (1997)

The school places considerable emphasis on nurturing high quality personal and social skills and this has a very positive effect on pupil standards of achievement and their attitude to learning. A particular strength is the teaching of philosophy and thinking skills. In these lessons pupils learn to listen, consider and respond in a mature way to the ideas of others. This work is taken to a high level and clearly has a very positive impact on children's work across the curriculum, giving them confidence to speak and discuss ideas to a high level. For example, in one excellent lesson, older pupils discussed themes about imagination and the thoughts they have following the reading of a poem about the ideas existing in the boy's head. Each individual pupil had specific targets to do with the amount of time they had joined in and responded to others. This work is developing a mature, self-confident and deep-thinking group of pupils.

Initiatives such as Philosophy for Children ... have forged a solid foundation on which the clear improvements of standards have been created.

Through philosophy lessons, pupils are encouraged to think about what is within them that enables them to make choices and subjects such as creation and the existence of life after death are discussed with openness and sensitivity.

Colby Primary School Ofsted Inspection Report (2001)

Part 2

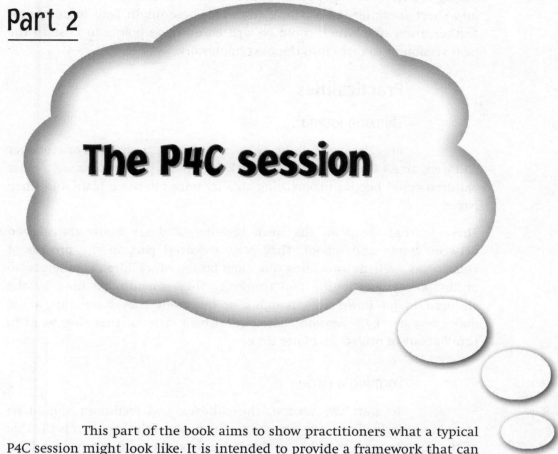

The P4C session

This part of the book aims to show practitioners what a typical P4C session might look like. It is intended to provide a framework that can be used and adapted for any stimulus and any theme, and within which teachers can feel prepared to have a go. Suggestions for an introductory session using Philosophy Bear are given in the next part of the book (page 78), but it is recommended that you read through this part first to gain an understanding of the general principles.

Fitting philosophy into the timetable

Ideally the P4C session should be treated as part of the school's creative curriculum, so the first step is deciding where you will fit it into your timetable. It is advisable to have it weekly, and on the same day, at the same time. A good plan is to use one of the literacy-hour sessions – the first session of a day usually works best as the children are bright and fresh at this time.

The session should be a minimum of an hour, but there are no hard and fast rules. Sometimes a session might be shorter because the dialogue just isn't working, for whatever reason, and you decide to leave it for that day. Or it might be longer because the dialogue is slow to pick up at first but gets going eventually, or because the children are so enthused they wish to return to it after a break. Allow yourself the flexibility to deal with both scenarios. As well as this timetabled hour, many teachers find that extra philosophical thinking and activity can be slotted into other parts of the school day. For example, as homework diaries are returned at various times during the week, it might be possible to fit discussions based on homework into short speaking-and-listening sessions. These might lead to points for further discussion which could be written down as points to raise in the next session or to carry into the next homework.

Practicalities

Thinking journals

Provide each child with a thinking journal. For younger children, an A4 landscape exercise book with plain paper works well; older children could be given something smaller with alternate plain and lined pages.

These journals keep all the work together, and are easily transported between home and school. They play a central part in the process of enquiry as well as providing documentation of children's progress in philosophical questioning and thinking. They can also be used by the children to jot down any thoughts or questions they have during the dialogue part of the session that they wish to raise, or that they want to think about in private at a later time.

Forming a circle

To start the session, the children and facilitator should be seated in a circle. This circle symbolizes the unity of the group. It is the role of the class to work together to think deeply and considerately within an enquiring and caring community – the *community of enquiry*. When the children are seated in this way, it enables them all to see each other and to direct their comments anywhere within the circle.

Depending on the size of your class and the space available, you may wish to experiment with different ways of sitting. Children could form their circle sitting on the carpet, or bring chairs or stools to the circle, or move their desks into a circle formation. If chairs are put in a circle, they can provide a useful surface for drawing or writing when the children kneel in front of them.

Group size

An ideal number for a community of enquiry is between 12 and 24. It is possible to run a successful group with up to 30 children, but there are particular difficulties with larger groups, such as ensuring all children get a chance to speak and allowing enough time to collect in questions. Some solutions to these problems are suggested in the sections covering the different elements of the session. Conversely, working with too small a group could mean that the children are more self-conscious or are unable to offer a sufficiently wide range of ideas to build on effectively.

Setting the rules

Before introducing P4C to a class, it is important to lay down some ground rules. These are negotiated by the children and facilitator, and should be displayed in the classroom. In the early stages it is useful to go over them before the beginning of every session.

A set of rules might look something like this.

Community rules

Remember …

- to look at the person who is talking so they know we are listening
- to share our thoughts with the whole class, not just the person next to us
- to wait until there is no one else speaking if we want to say something
- to give reasons why we think something
- to respect everybody's ideas
- to keep our bodies calm and still
- to keep listening and thinking
- to talk in a clear voice so that everybody can hear
- not to get upset if someone disagrees with us – we all have our own ideas
- that our brain does not think exactly the same things as our friend's.

The P4C session structure

A P4C session will normally involve the following elements.

Session element	Approximate timing	Activity	Resources
Presenting the stimulus	10 mins	Facilitator presents a stimulus to the whole class	• Stimulus material
Thinking time	5–15 mins (depending on children's literacy skills and experience in philosophy)	Children have some time to think, draw, write and produce questions. This includes both periods of quiet and time to talk to peers and the facilitator	• Thinking journals and pencils
Collecting questions	10 mins	Questions are collected in and written up by adult scribe on a large sheet of paper	• Large sheets of paper • Black marker pen
Analysing and selecting questions	10 mins	Children make connections between questions	• Coloured marker pens • Tape or digital audio recorder (optional)
Dialogue	20–30 mins	Children build their argument through reasoning, explaining, agreeing and disagreeing. The facilitator will use questioning to bring out the philosophical dimension but tries not to *steer* the discussion	Tape or digital audio recorder (optional)
Closure and evaluation	5 mins	The facilitator uses a range of strategies to close the session, e.g. summing up, finding the next question, asking for comments	Journals and pencils
Facilitator evaluation	*After the session*	*The facilitator's own evaluation of the session*	*Facilitator's own journal*

Do note that the timings given in the table are only approximations. You will find that some sessions involve the children spending more time connecting the questions. In others you may find that after transition to dialogue you return to analysis of the questions, then move back and forth several times between the two. In some sessions you may wish to start from the point you reached the previous week, in which case it will be possible to vote on a question straightaway, the analysis having been done in the previous session. Such a session would clearly have a greater proportion of the time spent in dialogue.

As long as you stick to the principle of having the children leading the discussion and working together as a community to try and uncover the philosophical, you will be able, in due course, to experiment, to vary the sessions and to develop your own style that works for you and the children.

We will now consider each element of the P4C session in turn.

Introduction

It is a good idea to begin the sessions with a relaxation exercise or thinking game; see Part 4 for lots of ideas. You might then do a quick review of the previous session, including a discussion about any homework set. You may also want to set targets for skills to concentrate on in the current session (see page 68).

Presenting the stimulus

Having ensured the children are settled in their circle, you can present the stimulus. You may wish to involve Philosophy Bear in this presentation, especially when you or the class are just starting out with P4C (see pages 77–82).

Many different types of stimuli can be used for P4C, for example:

- picture books
- short stories
- poems
- comics

- television and popular culture
- newspaper articles
- artefacts
- music

The stimulus needs to get you and the children wondering. There are no hard and fast rules about what can and cannot be used, but the best stimuli will:

- **be sufficiently open-ended** – allowing children to ask questions that cannot be answered by the text or illustrations.

- **have a high level of ambiguity** – encouraging children to produce questions of greater range and depth.

- **not present a single theme or moral** – rather, they will contain strong elements of puzzlement and allow the children to engage their emotions. They will provoke some reaction from the children that can be explored. Ideas and theories can then be tested out among the peer group with the children feeling safe in the knowledge that there are no absolute right or wrong answers.

- **excite and engage the children's imaginations** – the discussion will flow more easily about a question raised from a stimulus that the children are able to relate to. It will provoke a curious and engaged response because the quest for truth will be based on deeper thinking about issues that are relevant and important to their own lives, culture, experience and dreams. They will be more able to put themselves in a position of empathy.

A stimulus can be chosen to fit in with a current topic or scheme, but you should always be prepared to journey in a different direction to the one you might have expected. Ultimately, it is the children's enquiry and it is they who set the direction of the dialogue. As a skilled facilitator you will aim to develop their thinking towards the philosophical, but it should be around the ideas they are interested in discussing – not the ones you favour!

Picture books

When you are starting out with P4C, the easiest way of inviting questions is to use a picture book. The format of the picture book is one already very familiar to young children, and they have both the text and illustrations on which to base their questions. There is a wealth of good quality picture books on the market which are suitable for enquiry (see page 163 for suggestions).

Simply read the story, allowing the children plenty of time to absorb both text and illustrations. Teachers used to using large-format books for literacy may be concerned that the illustrations and details are too small for the children to see clearly. Here are a few possible ways round this problem.

- Break up the circle formation for the presentation of the story or book, encouraging children to move into a position where they can see clearly.

- Provide several copies of the book and allow the children to sit in small groups to look at the pages as you read.

- While the children remain in the circle, you walk around, showing each illustration to the group.

- Photocopy or scan and print out some of the illustrations, enlarging them so they can be displayed on the whiteboard while you read the text.

- Photocopy or scan and print out any complex or detailed illustrations for the children to look at individually, in pairs or in small groups.

As the children become more familiar with P4C sessions, you can try exploring philosophical issues through a variety of other stimuli as suggested below.

Poetry

Poetry is often fun. Rhyme, rhythm, unusual word combinations and crazy takes on life make the experience of reading, listening to and exploring poetry very enjoyable. Much poetry is condensed: there are rich meanings enfolded in relatively few well-chosen lines. Many poems also have a degree of ambiguity and uncertainty, and there may be no 'right answer', but a number of answers. All these features make poetry a fertile seedbed for philosophical enquiry; for unpacking the treasures wrapped up inside what is written. See page 164 for suggestions for poetry to use as a stimulus.

Comics

Many ideas can be found in children's comics and magazines. They often deal with topical issues and present problems that are relevant to young children's lives and experiences. For example, Barbie comics could raise issues such as gender stereotyping, the development of identity and acceptable behaviours in girls. Friendships and appearances are heavily emphasized in these publications and both sexes can find plenty to talk about and plenty of concepts to explore.

Using a comic – issues of gender difference

CASE STUDY

A Reception class given a comic as a stimulus came up with the following questions:

> Why do girls play with Barbies?
> Why do girls have long hair?
> Why don't girls play with cars?
> Why do girls like wearing dresses?
> Why does Barbie always smile?

The analysis of these questions led these four and five year olds into lengthy discussion about the differences they perceived between girls and boys.

Erica:	You have to give girls dolls and boys Action Men.
Ruby:	I agree, boys must like Action Men.
Liam:	No, that's not right, I play with Barbies.
Danielle:	Yes, and I chose an Action Man from McDonald's.
Hayden:	I think it's up to us to tell our mums what we want and to tell Father Christmas.
Jordan:	And it's up to us what clothes we wear too.
Lewis:	No, I think its your mum, because she sees which clothes you wear. If you wear the wrong ones, your mum will change them.
George:	Yes, boys can't wear white tights.
Lewis:	I agree, because someone might say you look stupid because tights are for girls.
George:	If a boy wore pink things he wouldn't like it, and he would rip it up. I decided I liked blue when I was a baby.
Liam:	I like pink but I wouldn't wear it.
Jordan:	But boys can't wear pink, they have to wear blue.
Megan:	I disagree. Some boys do like pink. My brother likes pink and I like blue. We share our toys.

→

CASE STUDY

Bryony:	Some toys boys and girls can play with. Like playstations. But I don't play fighting on the playstation.
Danielle:	Girls do fight, though.
George:	Not all boys fight. I don't.
Jordan:	Yes, my sister fights me.
Megan:	Girls do all the work. Boys watch TV.
George:	I help my mum, so boys can help.
Bryony:	If I wore an army suit, people would call me stupid – except people who loved me very much.
Reece:	You can't get girl army suits.
Megan:	You can. I've seen girls in army suits when I was with my dad.
George:	And girls can play football. Bryony plays football.
Bryony:	Yes I play football, and my dad likes my Barbie doll.
Callum:	Men play football as well.
Jordan:	Ladies don't, they play horsies.

Television and popular culture

Popular culture is an ideal way of entering a philosophical dialogue. The genre of children's television deals with the excitement, tedium, wonder and mystery of the child's world. The sort of television that interests children is often dismissed or undervalued as a source of discussion. No child talks as well as the child in the role of the expert, and the majority of young children have television as their specialist subject. Short video clips, comics or magazines, books, posters and postcards relating to television programmes can all be used as stimuli.

The Simpsons is especially appealing to children of primary age and beyond. There are endless themes to explore and a variety of media in which to explore them. The stories contain issues of peer pressure, sexual politics, stereotyping of race and gender, religion, morality, reality, the family, friendships and education – to list a few. The satire of *The Simpsons* raises numerous opportunities for children to access traditional philosophical issues in a meaningful way. As Matt Groening studied philosophy at university, perhaps it is not surprising that his creations should contain material ideal for enabling children to think about philosophical questions.

The Simpsons – a rich source of philosophical themes

CASE STUDY

A five-minute extract from the episode, 'The Telltale Head', elicited the following questions from a mixed-age group of children (Reception to Year 3).

- Why did the older boy be horrible to the little kid?
- Why do older kids play tricks on the others?
- Is it right to do nasty things?
- Why would Bart be naughty when he knew it was wrong?
- Why did Bart copy the big boy at the movies?
- Why do people copy other people?
- Why do people make statues?
- Why can't we all be famous?
- Why did they pretend to be his friend?
- Why didn't Bart know he was doing everything wrong?
- Why didn't the boys pay for their ticket?
- Why do people steal?

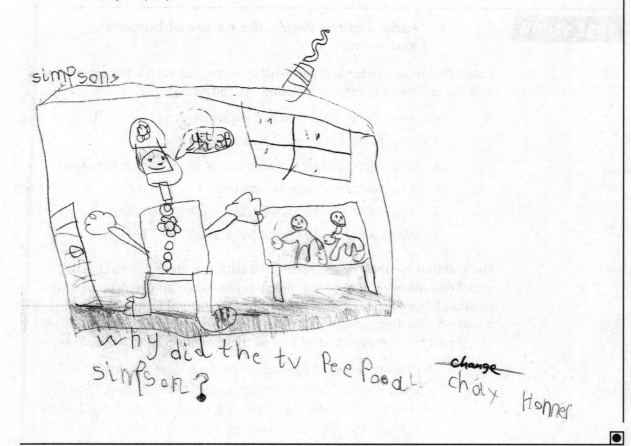

Music

Music is integral to our lives to the point where it is often taken for granted. Children often listen to music and respond to it emotionally without understanding where these emotions have come from. Through using music in philosophy, their responses can be examined and explored. Music is not only about aesthetics; it is also about placing ourselves within a range of emotions. Listening to music can trigger many psychological and physiological responses; it can, for example, put us in a physical state of relaxation where contemplation becomes easier. We may become more 'tuned in' to the feelings or thoughts that emerge from our musical interpretations, and better able to discuss them. Like books, poetry and television, music can also tell complex stories about the human condition.

Younger children can simply listen to music. If the music has lyrics then these could be printed out for older children to read as they listen. (Many song lyrics can be found on web pages via the internet.) Using music as a stimulus can lead to consideration of such questions as:

- Why does music often produce pictures in our minds?
- Where do these pictures in our heads come from?
- Why do we have emotional responses to music?
- How can music alter our mind?

See page 165 for some suggestions for music to use as a stimulus.

CASE STUDY

Peter and the Wolf – the nature of humans and animals

I used Prokofiev's *Peter and the Wolf* as a stimulus with a Reception class, and the children's questions included the following:

- Why were the duck and bird always arguing?
- Why did the cat want to chase the duck?
- Why did the bird try to save the duck when he didn't like him?
- Why didn't Peter do as he was told?
- Why didn't Grandfather let Peter do what he wanted?
- Why are wolves always bad and scary?

The children were especially fascinated with the idea of wolves, and the initial discussion resulting from the stimulus led to an exploration of the nature of humans and wolves that lasted for several follow-up sessions. We discussed whether humans or wolves were the nastier, and the question was posed for homework after one of these sessions. One child wrote:

> People are better than wolves because wolves don't eat food like people do. Wolves scratch people and they don't have nice thoughts, they only have bad ones. People are good because they know how to behave themselves. Wolves are wild animals and they have to be nasty to people, they don't understand people.

His mum disagreed:

> I disagree because wolves aren't nasty. Their desire to hunt and kill other creatures is just natural. They do this for food just as people pop to the shops! Not all people are nasty either, but as we are supposed to be civilized and intelligent, we should be aware of what behaviour hurts others. But read any newspaper and it's plain to see that many people behave far worse than any animal – even wolves.

Another child believed people are nastier:

> People are nastier because they shoot wolves. Wolves are nice but people might think they are horrible and that's why they shoot them.

Her mother agreed:

> People are nastier because they can be murderers and thieves and they cause war and conflict.

Some parents (and children) thought that there was little difference:

> Wolves, like people, will do anything to protect and feed their young. The only difference is that people have more dangerous weapons.

One parent wrote:

> This question triggered many questions and a lot of discussion about how to identify nasty people – do they look any different to a 'nice' person? Did the wolf eat grandma because he was bad or because he was hungry? Was he spiteful or was he desperate?

> A person has a choice. We do not need to be nasty. A wolf is acting on instinct. It is not a deliberate act of spite or vengeance. Are humans wrong to kill an animal for food? Can this be perceived as being nasty? I suspect the animal might have strong thoughts, or would that just be fear?

The daughter said:

> In my picture the nice wolf is smiling, the nasty one is not. People who smile can be nasty though.

Pictures

There are many different types of pictures suitable for use in a philosophical enquiry. Works of art, photos, and adverts from magazines or newspapers can all work well. Again, choose something intriguing or mysterious. The advantage of a picture is that you can often photocopy or scan and print it out to allow better viewing. The children will bring their own interpretations of a picture to the discussion, and no two children will have exactly the same one – although obviously there will be some common ground.

CASE STUDY

The Adoration of the Kings and *Christ Mocked* – God, heaven and death

A Year 3 class examined two pictures: Jan Gossaert's *The Adoration of the Kings,* depicting the birth of Jesus, and Hieronymus Bosch's *Christ Mocked (The Crowning with Thorns)*, depicting his death. The children were invited to ask questions about one or both of the pictures. They came up with:

- Why do people care and love?
- Why do people kill each other?
- Why do people have to die?
- If God made the earth, who made God?
- Did God make the world?
- Why do people believe so strongly in their religion?
- Why don't they break Jesus' legs and arms instead of killing him?
- If heaven or graveyards or graves or planets or hell wasn't here, where will we be when we are dead?
- Why did Jesus have to die when he did nothing wrong for no reason?
- Why couldn't he die when he was much older than in the picture?
- Why did Jesus die when he was older, not a baby?

At this point the children were keen to start discussing some of the issues raised.

Will: I have an answer for that. When he grew up he said, 'Look at me! I'm a sort of God,' and so the Romans didn't like him. When he was a baby he did not say he came from God.

Daisy: Some of the people were jealous of him and did not like him.

Perry: I know how to answer Chelsea's question. The other King [Herod] wanted to be King – he was not killed because he was protected.

Georgia: When they didn't find Jesus or his mum or dad, they killed every baby boy. So they went and hid in a cave and that's when the spider's web covered them. They stayed very quiet and tried to hold their breath.

Josh: But how come Jesus could heal people just by touching them?

Daisy: Because the Lord told Mary that she was going to have a very special baby. He had special powers.

The facilitator then asked the group what themes were running through the discussion. The children's responses revolved around:

- How the earth was made.
- Why people believe or don't believe in God.
- Why people die and kill each other.
- Whether people have powers to heal.

Further discussion followed:

Will: It's the spit that heals – spit has the thing in it that heals cuts.

Josh: I said to Robert that he did not look bothered that he was going to get killed.

Daisy: He wasn't, because in the Bible it says that he went to the forest to pray to God and angels were with him. He knew something was going to happen, but it would be good when it did.

Facilitator: Do you think it was good to kill him?

Will: Well, he would have lasted longer.

Roxanne: Sometimes it's OK to do bad things.

Facilitator: What do you feel about Daisy saying Jesus knew it was okay? Would you feel happier about dying if you knew you were going to heaven?

Perry: Heaven is just clouds.

Will: No, it's a graveyard.

Jasmin: Some people say that if you have a bad life you can come back to life again, but some people don't believe that.

Lily: My sister says when you die you go to an animal – or if you're a boy you go to a girl.

Will: Some people believe in reincarnation.

Josh: People say that Jesus is still alive and is everywhere but you can't see him.

Daisy: He is invisible – you can't touch him 'cos you don't know where he is.

Sam: How do you know?

Facilitator: What is the next question that comes out of this, do you think?

Roxanne: Why did Jesus believe he was God's son?

Will: Is heaven and hell true?

Jacob: What is God?

Artefacts

As the children become more confident and competent at asking questions and sharing dialogue, they will welcome alternative types of stimuli. Here are some ideas for artefacts to use, together with possible issues for discussion.

- A small coloured glass bottle with a 'Drink me' label (whether size matters, trust, curiosity, power)

- A selection of fossils and model dinosaurs (knowledge and belief, creation, extinction of species)

- A mask (identity, deception, appearance, personality, dualism)

- An interesting sculpture (interpretation of art, representation, the abstract)

- A wooden puppet (properties of life)

- A toy chicken and an egg (evolution, genetics)

- A wand or selection of magic tricks (belief, deception, cause and effect)

- A 'magic' mirror (reality, identity, wish-fulfilment, fate)

- A toy person in a cage (freedom, power, justice, crime and punishment)

- A piece of wood (life, growth, change)

- An apple cut in half, showing the pips (creation, life, ecology and the environment)

- A baby doll wrapped in a blanket (love, identity, gender, fate, genetics)

- A wrapped present (love, materialism, celebration)

Thinking time

After the stimulus has been shared, invite the children to spend some time thinking about anything that puzzles or interests them. First ask them to talk quietly in pairs or small groups about the stimulus, encouraging them to tell each other their thoughts. If the stimulus is a story or a poem, for example, encourage them to discuss the parts they found strange or interesting. After a few minutes, ask all the children to sit silently – closing their eyes if they wish – and spend a short time reflecting on their thoughts. When they feel ready they may begin to draw their ideas and form their questions in their thinking journals.

The questions children ask do not have to be directly concerned with the stimulus, but could be about something they have connected with it. It is very important that children are encouraged to draw pictures that illustrate their thinking, and from which they can draw their ideas and questions. This is especially important for younger children or those with communication difficulties. Most children find it much easier to talk about the stimulus through their drawing.

As the children illustrate their thoughts, you and any teaching assistants can move among the group. Some children may need the added reassurance and support of an adult with whom to share their ideas; the circle arrangement will make it easier to see which children this applies to. Talk quietly with these children and ask questions about what parts of the stimulus they found interesting and about any likes or dislikes. Gain clarification from the child about the question or statements they offer. This can serve as a form of rehearsal for shy or reticent speakers, enabling them to feel more confident when presenting their question later in the session. Having listened to children who are less likely to contribute to the dialogue later also means that you can bring in their ideas at relevant points in the discussion, confirming with that child you have the details right, for example:

> 'When I was talking with ... she said something really interesting about ... Am I right?'

> 'Can you tell us why you think that?'

A reticent child may well feel more able to speak in front of others when they have received the go-ahead and are assured that their idea is considered important. Another way of encouraging these children is to draw others into the quiet discussions during thinking time. In the smaller group setting, the shy child may be less wary of airing their ideas. During the dialogue session you can then call upon more confident members of those small groups to mention the ideas of others in their group, for example:

> 'When we were talking about this in thinking time (child) said they thought ... '

This form of peer-group recognition can also be a very strong starting point for encouraging a less-confident speaker to participate in the session.

Another useful way to encourage children to think and talk before they formulate and present their question is to ask them to move around the class and compare their pictures with each other. In talking about what their picture represents, children will find others who are interested in the same theme or idea as they are. On finding others with a common interest, children can then group together and negotiate a question.

Younger or less-literate children can also be asked during the thinking and drawing time if they wish to have their questions written in their journal. For these children, and for any who find it difficult to contribute to the session, having their question already written down means they can show their book while the facilitator reads their question out. It can also take away the fear of not being able to think up a question on the spot. It is important, however, that these children understand they do not have to present this same question in the discussion that follows. It could be that they wish to change it, or to form a second question that has arisen either from another child's question or from one of their own – something that often happens as the children gain confidence. More experienced pupils are encouraged to think of as many questions as they can, and also to make their questions more philosophical by taking the questions away from the context of the book. For example, 'Why did Arthur become angry?' might become 'Why do people get angry?'

The class may need up to 15 minutes for thinking time. Children who finish quickly should be encouraged to illustrate another thought or question, or talk quietly in pairs about each other's work. Remind them that this is still a thinking time, so even when they have finished they must respect others in the group who are trying to think and work. Enforce community rules, and ask children to ensure they are talking to others about their thoughts and ideas only.

The children may also use this time to revisit the stimulus; they may wish to check details of the story or ask for further clarification.

Collecting questions

When children learn to ask questions in philosophy, they are asking questions to which they really do not know the answers. They are often asking questions to which the facilitator has no answer either, and this can be very empowering for them. When children ask 'but why?', instead of having the frustration of being told 'just because' or 'I don't know', they are encouraged to try and work it out together within the community of enquiry. It is the quest for the answers that reveals so much, and children enjoy the adventure of the journey. The questions they ask are based on hearing and voicing opinions rather than facts, and it is this that enables them, with time, to learn to trust their own judgements and value their opinions and those of others.

In thinking time, children will have recorded their thoughts and questions in their thinking journals. In this next stage, the task is to collect all the questions in and record them for everyone to see. It is important to note that to begin with, and especially if it is a group of very young children, some individuals may not know how to formulate a question and instead offer a statement. This is fine; statements can be collected and recorded in the same way as questions. The children very quickly learn what is expected of them through good modelling from their peers. Very often, children who have made only statements in their journals, on hearing their peers present questions, are able to turn their own statements into questions without any adult support.

Each child's questions or statements must be written in the child's exact words with their name or initials next to it. Doing this on a large piece of paper makes it into a permanent record for children to see up on the wall and reinforces ownership of the discussion. The sheet can be kept as a useful assessment record.

It is important that children identify what they want to find out and that they are helped to frame their thinking in words that are as clear as possible to others. When you collect the questions, ensure that each child has a chance to explain what they are trying to ask and why. Collecting all the questions can be quite time-consuming, but there are various ways of managing the process and speeding it up.

Ways to collect in the questions

- Ask the children to volunteer their questions one at a time while you write them on the paper. Asking children to choose which colour pen they would like for their name can help keep them focused on the task.

- Use a question hot spot. The 'hot spot' could be represented by a circle of red paper on the floor. Children are allowed to come and stand on the hot spot to present their question. Tell them that they can only approach the spot if it is vacant; this serves to reinforce the turn-taking ethos of the community of enquiry. Another advantage of a well-managed hot spot is that other members of the class can be encouraged to join the questioner on the spot if they feel they have the same question. You must, however, ensure that the wording of the question is exactly the same. Children may not yet have learned that having just one different word in a question could change its meaning completely, for example, 'Why do people fight each other?' is a completely different question to 'How do people fight each other?'

- More literate children can start to write their own questions on the big sheet during thinking time. Alternatively, they could record their questions on sticky notes and attach those to the paper.

- Teaching assistants could write up questions from journals onto the big sheet during thinking time.

- Use shared questions. This method cuts down the number of questions collected in and helps the children see connections between questions. Ask the children to move around the class to find others with a similar question or picture to their own. When they have done this, they can talk to each other about the meanings of their questions or pictures, and negotiate between themselves a new question that sums up all the questions in their small group. When this question is presented and recorded on the big sheet, the facilitator puts by it the names or initials of everyone in that small group.

- Use paired questions. Ask the children to work in pairs to discuss their thoughts on the stimulus and then formulate a question.

Analysing and selecting questions

Once the questions have been collected and recorded, they need to be sorted and classified. In the early days of a community of

enquiry, the children have to learn what sort of questions can form the basis of a philosophical discussion. This involves looking at the list as a class and deciding what type of questions you have. One way to assist this process is to use symbols to show the different types of questions. The main categories of question are described below with suggested symbols and some real examples raised by children during sessions on fairy tales.

✔ Closed questions with a clear answer

Closed questions that have a clear and non-negotiable answer could be marked with a tick to show that you know the answer and would therefore be unable to discuss the issue in a meaningful or purposeful way. The tick also signals to the children that their questions are not wrong, simply not ones on which people will have a range of opinions that can be discussed. Examples:

- Did the girl eat her tea?
- Did the bear eat his porridge up?
- How many beds were there?
- Did the witch have a cat?

Factual questions

Factual questions could be ones where the answer is contained in the stimulus itself, or they could be ones that the children could research or ask someone to explain – as, for example, with questions about scientific or historical facts. The answer will invariably be factual. These questions could be marked with a book symbol. Examples:

- How did Rapunzel's hair grow so long?
- How did the wolf get down the chimney?
- How old were the pigs when they left home?

- Why did the illustrator draw trees as people?
- Why did the stone sink?
- What was the cat's name?
- Why can't wolves talk?

 Open-ended questions

Open-ended questions are those for which various points of view or opinion can be presented and discussed. These questions are useful for working with in the enquiry and have the potential to lead on to philosophical discussion. These could be marked with a smiley-face symbol. Examples:

- Were the beans really magic?
- Should the pigs' mother have sent them to live by themselves?
- Why are stepmothers always horrible?
- Why was Jack scared of the giant?
- Was Pinocchio real?
- Why didn't the stepsisters like Cinderella?
- How did Beauty fall in love with the Beast?
- Why did Goldilocks steal the porridge?

 Philosophical questions

A philosophical question is one which explicitly raises awareness of a profound concept about which there is potential for enquiry. As the children become more familiar with the ideas used in philosophy sessions, they will be able to ask increasingly philosophical questions. The symbol used here could be a smiley face with a question mark above the head. Examples:

- What is love?
- What is a conscience?
- Where does evil come from?
- Is it wrong to steal?
- What is truth?
- Where do our dreams come from?

Sorting the questions can sometimes be difficult as there is some overlap between the categories, and what category a question falls into may not always be clear-cut. The poor construction of some questions can sometimes mask some excellent philosophical thinking; conversely, some apparently excellent questions may not be asking what you think they are asking. For example, the child who asks 'What is life?' may actually have little understanding of the profundity of that question. Philosophy is about challenging assumptions, and as facilitators we should not assume we can understand the child's thinking.

Many of the children's questions may not be obviously philosophical in content, but the role of the facilitator is to spot whether there is any potential in a question and to ask the child about the thinking behind it. The following questions asked by some Year 3 children would not be categorized as philosophical questions, but nevertheless point to philosophical issues and yielded some excellent discussion.

Stimulus	Question	Concepts discussed
Painting: *Self-portrait*, 1889, Van Gogh	Why did he paint pictures of himself?	identity, thought, knowledge, power
Story: *Zoo* by Anthony Browne	Why were the boys always fighting?	love, family, difference, communication
Story: *Zoo* by Anthony Browne	Why was the orang-utan in the corner?	animal rights, freedom, power
Story: *Voices in the Park* by Anthony Browne	Why did mum say 'sit' to the boy?	childhood, equality, power, authority
Story: *How to Live Forever* by Colin Thompson	Can people live forever?	faith, death, religion, God
Painting: *Crucifixion with donor Jacopo di Bartolomeo* by Giovanni de Paolo	Why did they kill Jesus?	death, power, fear, authority, love
Story: *Where the Wild Things Are* by Maurice Sendak	How did the room grow into a forest?	truth, reality, dreaming, imagination, emotions, relationships.
Story: *Dulcie Dando Football Player* by Sue Stops and Debi Gliori	Why did they have an all boys team?	equality, power, community, feminism, authority
Story: *Pinocchio* by Carlo Collodi	Why did he lie?	truth, morality, conscience, love, consequence

Making links and connections between questions

Up to this point in the session, especially when your community of enquiry is just starting out with P4C, you will have been concentrating on getting the children to develop questioning skills, for example, by classifying and by encouraging open-ended questions. As children become more experienced, we aim to encourage them to think about asking questions that can be discussed in a philosophical way. As the children become more familiar with philosophy and start to form better questions with greater understanding, they will be able to work with the questions at a deeper level of thinking. In addition to explaining the meaning behind their question, they should now be encouraged to think about how their question fits in with those of others, and whether this line of questioning will lead to discussion about things that are important to them.

When the questions have been collected in, they need to be analysed and clarified. It is through this process that the questions can be fully understood and the children's thinking stimulated. Many practitioners feel daunted when the questions have been collected in, and wonder where they go from there. Making the children think about where they can see connections between questions not only cuts down the number of questions by identifying those that are actually asking the same thing, but also facilitates clearer thinking about the issues the questions are presenting.

The easiest approach is first to ask the children if they notice any *links* between questions. For example, these questions were elicited by the *Pinocchio* story:

- Why did Pinocchio tell a lie?
- Why did Pinocchio tell a big lie?
- Why did Pinocchio's nose grow big when he told a lie?
- Was Pinocchio a real person or was he just a piece of wood?
- Why was Pinocchio wood first?
- Why did Pinocchio listen to the cat and the fox?
- Why did the cat and the fox trick Pinocchio?
- Why didn't Pinocchio listen to the cricket? Could he hear him?

Children might spot that the first three questions are linked because they all have the word 'lie'. A further link might be found with the seventh question, which mentions tricking – something similar to lying.

The next step is to work out the *connection* between the questions that they have linked. So, in this case, they could say that the questions are linked because they talk about people who lied; the connection could be that these questions are all asking:

- Why do people lie?

Reread the questions and ask the children to volunteer any links they can see between questions. Use prompts such as:

> 'Which questions are asking the same thing?'
>
> 'What are those questions actually about?'
>
> 'What is the bigger question?'

It may be helpful to draw coloured lines between the questions to illustrate the connections, and to write the bigger issues or secondary questions along these link lines. For example, questions arising from using Anthony Browne's *Piggybook* as a stimulus were linked as follows.

> **Why did the mother leave home?**
>
> *Mum had to do all the work.*
>
> **Why did the boys treat the mother so badly?**

The connection between the questions offered by the children in this case was that both questions were about mum having to do all the work. The secondary question raised was:

- Why do some men think they are better than women?

During the course of the dialogue, this issue was developed to the point where it led to a homework question of:

- Are men and women able to do the same jobs?

The lines between questions can be drawn in different colours, with each colour representing a concept or theme that the children have used to categorize the questions. This makes the clarification process much easier for the children, and it enables you to ask questions such as: 'What are the *red* questions drawing our thinking towards?' Children will then be able to see better where concepts interlink or where new connections can be made.

At the end of this process, you will have a connections map along the lines of the example opposite.

CASE STUDY　　　　　**Making connections**

After using Anthony Browne's *The Tunnel* as a stimulus, a Year 1 class was having difficulty finding connections between the questions they had gathered. Seeing that the children were struggling, the class teacher asked the children to list all the themes they could see in the story. The children offered the following:

- opposites
- looking after people
- being friends
- family
- being scared
- being kind
- getting on with people
- losing someone
- things that make you cry
- your age affects your thoughts

The children were then asked to keep these themes in mind while they reconsidered and reread the questions. They were then asked to decide which questions related to which themes. This made the children more aware of the links between the questions, and they were then able to discuss which questions were linked and where the potential for philosophical discussion lay.

Connections map

The questions came from a Reception class who had watched a video of *The Adventures of Pinocchio* as a stimulus.

Why did Pinocchio follow the boys? (Katie)

Why did the teacher tell Pinocchio off?
(Kelsie, Kaomi, Maya)

Why did his nose grow big? (Joe, Joanna, Georgia)

Why did Pinocchio run away? (Maria, Ashley)

Why was he alive? (Nikita)

Why did he hit the boy? (Kelsie)

Why did the puppet master nick the puppet?
(Dylan)

Why did the man want all the puppets? (Harry)

Why did Pinocchio want to go to school? (Sam)

Why did Pinocchio tell lies? (Liam)

Why did wood dust come out of his nose when he sneezed?
(Cameron)

<u>Links to philosophical questions</u>

→ Did Pinocchio know he was doing something wrong?
(Do we know or do we learn what is 'wrong'?)

--→ Why was the puppet master nasty?
(Why are some people nasty?)

·····→ Can wood be alive?
(What does 'alive' mean?) (Is 'alive' the same as 'real'?)

→ Why did Pinocchio want to be a real boy?
(What is a 'real' person?) (How do we know what is 'real'?)

Making questions philosophical

It is through the process of searching for the links and connections between the questions that the facilitator models an important aspect of the aim of philosophical enquiry. In this process, we are uncovering the important issues that lie behind the questions children have asked – and it is these that the community will work on together.

At a later stage, when the children are familiar with this way of connecting and thinking in themes, you will find that they form much more philosophical questions from the start of the session. As a facilitator, you are aiming to develop the children's abilities to apply philosophical questions to the stimulus. It can help if you explain to the children that it is easier to make a philosophical question by imagining that they are putting a question to someone who has never read the book or seen the stimulus before, for example:

Why did Pinocchio tell lies	could become →	Why do people lie?
Why did Arthur get so angry?	could become →	Why do people get angry?
Why didn't the boys let Darcie play football?	could become →	Why do people treat boys and girls differently?

Understanding philosophical concepts in P4C

As a facilitator in a P4C session it is not necessary to be trained in philosophy, but it is helpful to know about the sorts of questions to which philosophers have sought and still seek answers. It can be very beneficial to read about some of the various arguments put forward by philosophers, and to question assumptions and construct counter-arguments for yourself. But be warned: you may find that philosophical thinking becomes addictive – for you, as well as for the children you share the sessions with! See page 166 for a list of books that offer an accessible introduction for those wishing to think about the 'bigger issues' of life.

The following lists are provided as a sort of quick guide to some major philosophical themes and the 'big questions' associated with them. Being aware of these themes and questions can help you to identify them when they occur in children's questions. They can then be introduced into a session, as appropriate, to facilitate dialogue and develop children's further thinking. They will, of course, need to be offered in terms that are suitable for the age group.

The lists are by no means exhaustive. There are many other 'big questions' associated with these and with other themes – and you will doubtless find many coming from the children themselves as they become more confident.

Philosophical themes and questions

What is love?

- Do we choose who we love?
- Do we have to love our family?
- How do you know if you love someone?
- Can you love and hate the same person?
- Where does love come from?
- Does love always make us happy?
- Can you love someone unconditionally?
- Do you have to be loved to know how to love?
- Can you control how much you love?
- Can you love too much?
- Can you lead a fulfilled life without love?
- Is it better to have a short life with lots of love or a long life with no love?
- Do you love with your heart or your head?
- Is loving someone the same as loving something?
- Is love physical or mental?

What is knowledge?

- How much knowledge are we born with?
- Do we know anything at all when we are born?
- How do you gain knowledge?
- Is knowledge belief or truth?
- If we believe something, does that mean we know it?
- Do we only know something if we know it is true?
- How do you show that you have knowledge?
- Can we ever really know anything?
- Can you have knowledge without understanding?
- Are memory and knowledge different things?
- If you lost your memory, would you still have knowledge?
- How do you test knowledge?
- How do you judge whose knowledge is best?
- Are there such things as good knowledge and bad knowledge?
- Can knowledge change you?
- If you are knowledgeable, are you a better person?

What is real?

- How do we know if something is real?
- Can you trust your senses to tell you what is real?
- If you say something is real because you can see it, is it still real if you close your eyes?

Philosophical themes and questions continued

- Is something real if you have never seen it?
- Are dreams real?
- How do you know you're not dreaming right now?
- Does reality matter?
- What is the difference between real and make-believe?
- Do we all have the same experiences of reality?
- Is what I think is real the same as what you think is real?
- How do you know you are real?
- What can you trust to know something is real?

What is identity?

- Have we always been the person we are?
- Do we learn how to be who we are or is it inside us already?
- Where were we before we were born?
- Do we exist when we are dead?
- Will we be the same person when we are old?
- Can anything change who we are?
- If we swapped bodies with someone else, would that change who we were?
- If we swapped brains with someone else, would that change who we were?
- Why are twins different?
- Can there ever be anyone who is exactly like you?
- Can you be a girl in a boy's body?
- What is the difference between boys and girls?
- Do we have to learn to be a boy or a girl?
- How do we know we are real?
- If we made an exact replica of our brain and put it into another person, would they be the same as us?
- Can we ever really change who we are?
- Is your mind separate from your body?
- What is the thing that makes you you?

What is anger?

- Are there different sorts of anger?
- Is anger just a feeling?
- Does anger come from our mind, body or brain?
- Is anger always bad?
- Do some people get more angry than others?
- Are some people born less angry than others?
- Are we born with anger or do we learn it?

Philosophical themes and questions

- Would it be good if nobody could get angry?
- Why do we get angry?
- Are animals capable of anger?
- If we had no contact with other humans, would we ever get angry?
- What would happen if we could not express anger?

What is free will?

- Who controls what you do?
- Are you ever free to do what you want?
- If we had no free will, would we be like robots?
- Does free will allow people to make bad choices?
- Do you still have free will in prison?
- Do children have less free will than adults?
- Do we live in a free country?
- Should we have laws?
- Does having free will make us different from animals?
- Do animals have free will or instinct?
- Do babies have free will?
- Do we choose to be born?
- What is it that makes us make choices?

What is right and wrong?

- Are we born knowing what is right and wrong?
- What is the difference between right and wrong?
- Do we choose to be good or bad?
- Do we have a conscience?
- Where does our conscience come from?
- How do we know what is right and wrong?
- Should people be punished?
- Are everybody's ideas of right and wrong the same?
- Who says what is right or wrong?
- Is it ever OK to break the law?
- Is it ever right to kill anything?
- Does doing the right thing make you truly happy?
- Does doing the wrong thing make you a bad person?
- Is there such a thing as pure evil or pure good?
- Is there ever such a thing as an unselfish act?

What is God?

- If there is a god, where did he come from?
- Why do we think God is a male?

Philosophical themes and questions

- Where is God?
- How can God have so many powers?
- Can God control our lives?
- What is God?
- Would the world exist without God?
- Would people exist without God?
- Why do people believe in God?
- Can we ever prove God exists?
- Can there be more than one god?
- If God is good, why do bad things happen?
- Do we have to have evidence to believe that God exists?
- Can God be responsible for miracles?

What is the mind?

- Is our mind the same as our brain?
- What is the mind?
- Is everybody's mind different?
- Do we need a body and a mind to live?
- What does 'mind over matter' mean?
- Can our mind exist outside our body?
- Does our mind control our life?
- Does our mind tell us what to do or do we tell our mind what to think?
- Can two minds ever be alike?
- What are thoughts?
- Do we feel colour?
- How can you see when your eyes are closed?
- What is intelligence?

What is power?

- Is everybody born equal?
- Why are some people more powerful than others?
- Why do we need leaders?
- What makes someone a leader?
- Does a country need a king or queen?
- Should leaders get more money?
- Should everybody get paid the same money?
- What makes someone more important?
- Should adults be more powerful than children?
- Does money give you power?
- Does being clever give you more power?
- Can one person be more powerful than a hundred people?

Voting on a question

When you have classified the questions, the next phase is the transition into discussion. When you are starting out with a new community of enquiry, it can be useful to vote on a question for discussion. As you and the children become more confident, you could vote on a concept that has arisen from making links and connections, or you may find that the voting process is unnecessary as the children become used to entering a dialogue from the clarification of questions. Voting on a question can be done in several ways:

- **Uni-vote**. First explain to the children that they are allowed to vote on the questions that have been classified as open-ended. The children each choose one question and raise their hand when that question is read out. They must then sit on their hands so they cannot vote again. The facilitator records the number of votes for each question and the one with most votes becomes the dialogue subject.

- **Multi-voting**. The children vote as many times as they wish. All votes are counted for each question.

- **Blind voting**. The children vote for one or more questions, but with eyes closed.

- **Corner voting**. Four questions are chosen. The facilitator either chooses the areas children seem most interested in or works with them to decide which four they think are the most interesting. The facilitator writes the questions on separate sheets of paper and places one in each corner of the room, making it clear where each question is. Each child then decides which question they want to vote for and moves to the appropriate corner.

- **Ballot voting**. The questions are numbered. The children secretly write down one number on a slip of paper and post their votes in a ballot box or bag.

The dialogue

Starting the dialogue

You should ensure that children observe the community rules during the dialogue; you may want to give a reminder about them at the beginning of this phase.

With a new community of enquiry, it is unlikely that dialogue will happen spontaneously. It is more likely to feel like a separate part of the session, with dialogue beginning after a question has been decided on, probably by voting. When the children are more familiar with the way the sessions work, you may well find that the dialogue starts naturally from the questioning and connecting process. It could be that the children start talking about a particular question, or that they can see strong links between the questions and want to start talking immediately about their views on the underlying issue or concept. In this case, do not stop the

children from talking simply so you can finish collecting the remaining questions or making further links! You can always return to these if the dialogue leads nowhere.

If a dialogue has not started spontaneously and you have selected a question by voting, a good way of getting the dialogue going is to ask the owner of that question what they were trying to find out, and why. Other children will then probably need to be encouraged to join in. You could ask whether anyone agrees or disagrees with that statement, and why. Alternatively, you could ask children to stand up if they agree with that child's thinking. You can then ask any of the children standing to expand on their ideas. Likewise, the children sitting down could say why they are not standing. Is it because they disagree, or because they are unsure? If you then remember which children are on which side of the camp, you can use this to bring them into the dialogue. This 'stand up, sit down' method is also useful if a dialogue runs dry: it reminds the children that they are responsible for the dialogue and need to make decisions about the issues raised in order to have a worthwhile discussion. It keeps attention focused on the dialogue and serves as a reminder of where the thinking has moved to for those whose concentration may have lapsed.

The role of the facilitator in a dialogue

The facilitator's job is to ensure that a dialogue is not just a speaking and listening exercise or a conversation between children. Allowing a conversation or discussion to simply follow its course will not make it a true enquiry. Enquiry comes from the desire to push for deeper understanding.

Karin Murris and Joanna Haynes (2000) describe the roles of the facilitator as listener, guide, guardian and co-enquirer. If these roles are modelled well, then the children will in time be able to take them on for themselves within the community of enquiry. Our ultimate aim as facilitators is to allow the children to question and to think for themselves. The facilitator should encourage and support the children in their interaction with each other and eventually keep their own involvement to a minimum. This can be achieved relatively quickly when the children understand the importance of the skills involved in enquiry: when they understand how to listen, clarify, expand on and search together for deeper understanding.

It is important to hold back from correcting children's statements, however tempting it may be. The key thing about the process of dialogue is that children are allowed to develop thinking strategies for complex questions. These are vital skills that they will be able to apply throughout their education.

As the facilitator you will, initially, have to lead the children in a philosophical direction, using questioning skills to push for depth of thinking. Here are some useful questions to help in this process.

- Can you give me an example of that?
- Has that ever happened to you?
- Is that always true?
- Why do you believe that?
- What do you mean by ... ?
- Can you say that in a different way?
- Is it ever right/OK to ... ?
- What is the difference between (a) and (b)?
- Is there a difference between (a) and (b)?
- Where is that happening?
- What is doing the thinking/feeling?
- Does anyone agree or disagree with ... ? Why?
- Does anyone have a different idea?
- How is that connected to ... ?
- Whose thoughts are you making links with?
- What evidence have you got to back that up?
- How could we find that out?
- Can you summarize what you have said?
- What other reasons would make us believe that?
- Could it ever be possible that ... ?
- Is that exactly what you meant?
- Would there be any circumstances that would make you give a different view?
- What might change your mind?

Teaching assistants

Teaching assistants can be especially valuable during the P4C session. As well as working with children during thinking time, they can join in with the dialogue sessions. If they have been closely involved with children in thinking time, they will be in a position to read children's questions for them during the collecting process and also draw less confident children into the discussion. This can be done tactfully by saying things like, 'I remember (child's name) had a really good question that might have been connected to that. Can you remember your question? Shall I read it for you?'

During the dialogue, teaching assistants are valued as members of the community of enquiry, and their contributions treated in the same way as all the other contributions. This makes the valuable point that adults also try to work through questions and ideas, and that they have opinions, not just answers. Children will see the relationship and interaction between the adults as a role model for respect and co-operation. Seeing that philosophical thinking is something adults do as well, will encourage children to continue into their own adulthood.

Developing skills

With increased age, maturity and philosophical experience, the children will become more skilled in the processes of P4C. They will develop secondary questions and eventually ask philosophical questions directly from the stimulus. Increased dialogue skills will be evident in their ability to recognize the big issues. They will often pick up on previous themes and return repeatedly to ideas they have explored before in an attempt to gain deeper understanding.

They will also become more adept at recognizing changing views and handing over the facilitation of the dialogue to the community. This community spirit becomes stronger as the children work together over the weeks. They begin to see and understand the thinking processes of others and take increased ownership of their sessions, becoming less reliant on facilitator support as confidence increases. They will challenge assumptions as they begin to understand that philosophy is not blindly believing what others say, but questioning things for themselves and thinking hard about a measured response. It means they will recognize with increased clarity their own uncertainties – and see these as a challenge.

Developing secondary questions

This session was a follow-up to the previous week's work, where the children were asked to raise questions from posters of wolves. The posters depicted wolves in a variety of situations, for example there were pictures of wolves with babies, howling sharp-toothed wolves, fluffy, cute-looking wolves, wolves hunting in packs, and wolves looking like domestic pet dogs. The objective for the session was to develop a high-quality dialogue where the children could see how ideas build upon each other and realize that thinking about questions leads to more questions.

At the start, Philosophy Bear asked the children to be on the lookout for times when he could write down where one question had led to another question. He also wanted to count how many important questions we could write down from the dialogue.

The starting question, which had arisen from the homework diaries, was:

- Does a wolf know that it is nasty?

Philosophy Bear introduced the session by saying how interested he was in this question because although bears are often seen as cuddly, most bears are in fact very dangerous. Philosophy Bear wrote the question at the top of a large sheet of paper and asked the children to help him think about this issue and see what other questions this could lead to. This led to an initial dialogue:

Danielle:	Creatures don't know things 'cos they can't talk or hear.
Lewis:	A wolf needs someone to help him know that he is doing something wrong.
Cameron:	Wolves don't know that they are nasty.
Danielle:	But they must know it's wrong to eat a person.
Facilitator:	Are you saying that wolves understand right and wrong?
Ryan:	Yes, they do know it's wrong.
Facilitator:	I think we can ask a new question here: Does a wolf have a conscience?
Dylan:	Yes, because they have wolf consciences. Their conscience lets them be bad because their life is bad.

Lewis:	They have to learn to be bad.
Facilitator:	Is what we are asking here about whether people or animals are born bad, or is badness something we learn?
Danielle:	Well, I think everyone is born good.
Facilitator:	Can you explain a bit more why you think that?
Danielle:	If people were not born good, their mummies wouldn't love them and they would have a bad life then.
Facilitator:	Do you need to be loved to be good, do you think?
Bryony:	Well, wolves have a bad life because God made them like that and their mummy wolves still like them.
Cameron:	No, the God that made them like that is a God Wolf.
Dylan:	But maybe wolves are born to be good but they grow up to be bad.
Facilitator:	Do animals, in this case wolves, have rules? If so who makes them?
Liam:	Wolves don't have rules because they don't make them, and they don't know what we say.
Dylan:	They do have a different conscience from us. They have a different brain to us.
Harry:	I think animals don't have a conscience 'cos they don't talk.
George:	Animals must have consciences because babies can't talk but they have a conscience.
Liam:	My brother is only three and he goes up to the toilet, but he doesn't know it's wrong if he wees on the stairs.
Dylan:	Yes, babies have consciences but they are little consciences, and little consciences can't talk.
Bryony:	If you are only nought, you don't have a conscience. The conscience only comes when you are one. When babies are older they get a conscience.
Liam:	Animals don't talk 'cos they don't have two buttons in their bodies. One is red and one is an angry button and it says 'No, no, no!'
Ryan:	Wolves do have a conscience because they eat animals and they know it's wrong.
George:	Animals like to say wolves can kill other animals.
Megan:	No, that's the wolf's conscience that says that.
Danielle:	Animals have a different conscience to people because they kill people.
George:	Yes, I agree. They are bad 'cos they kill and hurt other animals.
Dylan:	Wolves' consciences are bad. The conscience tells the wolf to do bad things and that's because they have something nasty in them.
Liam:	Animals like crocodiles, rhinos, leopards all kill animals. And they are different to zebras and giraffes – they are nice animals.
Megan:	Yes, they are nice 'cos they don't have anything nasty in them.
Facilitator:	What is it that makes us nasty? Why are some animals or people nice and some nasty?
Ryan:	Some people have nasty things in them too.
Danielle:	People are the same as animals. Nice people and nasty people.

Harrison: I think animals have rules because they know what they are doing.

Liam: I agree with Harrison. Animals make up the rules – some animals have rules and some don't.

Lewis: But animals don't know what people are saying.

Danielle: People make up the rules for animals.

Lewis: I've changed my mind – I think they do have rules. They make their own rules – what they can do – themselves.

Liam: They do have rules, but they don't really know the rules they are supposed to do and they do have a conscience.

Bryony: But some animals don't.

Ryan: I'm not sure. I think they don't understand their rules.

Dylan: I think wolves' consciences are bad. They say all bad things to them and the brain is what is thinking about making up the rules, and then the wolves fight.

At the end of the session I asked the children if they could tell Philosophy Bear any extra questions our dialogue had led to. These were recorded on the paper. Then I asked them if they could think of any other questions that might follow on from these ideas. They were still at the stage where they needed modelling of this skill, but one child asked:

- Are babies like animals if they can only make howling?

This was the question sent home for homework.

This session was successful in modelling the creation of secondary questions through the process of pushing for greater depth. The children participating in this session had been practising P4C for one term only, and already they were beginning to understand how their questioning led on. I pointed out to them that several children had used the language 'agree' and 'disagree' and one child had even changed his mind at one point. We had a final stand-up vote to see how many children now believed wolves have rules. It was roughly the same as before, but several children had changed their minds.

CASE STUDY

Challenging own assumptions and changing views

With a class who had been doing philosophy for almost a year, I wanted the children to recognize inconsistency of argument both in themselves and others, and to be able to recognize when and why they might have changed their minds.

The stimulus used for the session was a toy chicken and an egg (hard-boiled!). I asked the children to draw in their thinking journals a picture of what they thought would have come first.

The chicken came out of the egg.

The egg came from an old mummy chicken

After thinking time, I asked them to draw next to their picture where they thought that thing came from. In almost all cases, of course, the final picture was of both objects. A bit of string was laid down the middle of the carpet area, and those who had drawn a chicken first were asked to sit together on one side of it and those who drew an egg first to sit on the other. The initials of children on each side were recorded on the board. I then explained the objectives for the lesson and told the children that if anyone at any time felt they had changed their mind and could say why, they would be allowed to cross the line. I also reminded them that even though there would probably be lots of movement in this session, they were still expected to keep to the rules of the community and not disturb the dialogue more than necessary.

I then asked anyone on the chicken side to volunteer the reason for their choice. (The children were encouraged to dialogue in the normal way building on or questioning each other's arguments while still remaining in the circle.)

Tayma: The egg came from the chicken.

Ben: They had to find a chicken and then he laid the egg.

Samuel: The mummy laid the egg in the nest.

Matthew: We don't know how we got the egg in the first place without the bird.

Damian: You need a chicken to lay the egg, otherwise there will be no more chickens – they will just die.

Ben:	The chicken was from a baby. There is just an egg.
Facilitator:	Does something new always come from nothing?
Tayma:	Well, all chickens have to be in eggs or they won't grow up.
Adrianna:	I think the egg came first because chickens lay the eggs first.
Facilitator:	What about if there were no chickens. Where would the eggs come from then?
Katie:	They would come from a mummy chicken.
Kaomi:	But there are no mummy chickens, are there, miss?
Letitia:	Well, nanny chicken has a baby and that grows into a new mummy chicken.
Tayma:	The nanny chicken was born in an egg before there was ever a family. I don't really know now, 'cos where do eggs come from?
Kaomi:	From the shops.
Liam:	They don't make eggs though – they get made by birds.
Benji:	And ducks and birds have eggs.

At this point I asked if anyone wanted to move across the line – and there was mass upheaval with children from both sides moving back and forth. I explained that this was an age-old problem for philosophers and that they were going to move this dialogue on to a different question, thinking about the nature of creation and how our world began.

Facilitator:	How did the first person come to be on earth?
Tayma:	God made them. I read it in my Jesus and God story. God came from the sky.
Liam:	I think the clouds made them.
Ben:	Before God there was no shop, no school, no trees or grass or houses.
Letitia:	I agree, it was all brown and rubbish.
Sean:	Before the world was made, it was all just brown rocks all over the place.
Reece:	When God came, all the rocks disappeared.
Samuel:	God came from a spaceship and he lives in the sky.
Reece:	Yes, and his family all go there.
Tayma:	I disagree. There were no spaceships at that time. We know that.
Liam:	But we don't know 'cos we were not there.
Matthew:	But Jesus was there before us.
Samuel:	He came from another country.
Tayma:	I disagree, because there was no other country if there was no world.
Matthew:	Well, God lived in Jerusalem when he said the wine is my blood. He died at Christmas … no, Easter.
Reece:	And we will die when we get one hundred.
Sean:	Like the Queen Mother.
Adrianna:	And my Grandad.
Sean:	And Jesus looks after us.

CASE STUDY

Tayma:	Jesus was a baby before all of us.
Ben:	We didn't see him, but the Queen Mother and the evil king and Mary did.
Liam:	But Jesus had a mum. Everybody has a mum, even when you are a grown-up. Well God is dead now we pray to him, and if we believe in him, we say 'Amen'.
Matthew:	He's in the sky.
Letitia:	No, he's in the ground.
Sean:	God is in the sky – people go to heaven.
Tayma:	Just his spirit and the body is in the ground.
Reece:	But where does the skin go?
Tayma:	That goes up to heaven.

At the end of the session we discussed how important it is to change our minds sometimes – and why. We discussed where and why the children had changed their minds, and I highlighted examples of different thinking within the session. I also asked the children to think of other times they may have changed their minds, and concluded the session by mentioning that things might never change in our world if people were not brave enough to say what they think and acknowledge changes in their thinking.

CASE STUDY

Handing over facilitation of the dialogue to the community of enquiry

This Reception-year lesson began with thinking about something we take for granted, especially in the noisy environment of a busy school at nine o'clock in the morning. I asked the children to sit in silence as a group for 5 minutes and listen to all the voices they could hear outside the classroom. As well as trying to identify who the voice belonged to, they had to see if they could identify its tone and purpose, and its location. After 5 minutes was up, the children contributed their findings to the large sheet of paper. Contributions included the following:

Voice	Tone	Purpose	Location
Teacher (Mrs Moore)	Happy and funny	Singing the register	Next-door classroom
Parent	Cross/angry	Telling child to hurry up	In cloakroom
Year 2 child	Excited/ silly	Talking to friend	In courtyard
Teaching assistant	Nice	Helping find a reading book	In corridor

I then asked them to bear in mind the different ways people talk to each other while I read the story.

The stimulus used was Anthony Browne's *Voices in the Park*. This multi-layered story about a trip to the park is told in the voices of the four interlinking characters and is based on their differing perspectives of the experience and its relevance to their individual lives.

After listening to the story, the children were given some thinking time. They could draw or write about anything in the text or illustrations that puzzled them or made them curious to find out more. Their questions were listed, and any statements turned into questions. These included:

- Why did the lady shout to the boy?
- Why did they climb a tree?
- Why was there a gorilla on top of the roof?
- Why did the pictures come alive?
- Why did the boy do the same as the girl?
- Why did mum say 'Come home'?
- Why did the little boy stay at home on his own?
- Why did the streetlight turn into a flower?
- Why did mum say 'sit' to the boy, not the dog?
- Why were there fruit trees with big fruit?
- Why did the dog swim in the fountain?
- Why did the girl slide so fast?
- Why did Charles pick a flower for Smudge?
- Why did the boy play with the girl?
- Why did the girl put the flower in a cup?

There was a mix of question types: not all were open-ended, but all were equally accepted and valued. We used coloured chalks to put the questions into categories:

- **green** for strange and curious events
- **blue** for children's relationships
- **red** for adult relationships.

The children voted for a category, and then with eyes closed voted for a question within that category. The question chosen to discuss in this instance was:

- Why did the mum say 'sit' to the boy, not the dog?

The children's dialogue was written up in the form of a simple mind map on large paper, but this time with a smaller pen. This dialogue started off with an offering from the pupil who gave the original question.

CASE STUDY

Dylan:	Well, I asked the question because if she [the mum] was a little girl she wouldn't want her mum to be nasty to her.
Danielle:	It's like in school. It's hurting someone's feelings. If I had a dog I would say 'sit', but my mum would say, 'Come here, please.'
Lewis:	We have to say 'please' to dogs as well.
Liam:	I disagree. We don't need to say 'please' to dogs, because they will sit if you just say 'sit'.
Lewis:	But dogs have feelings too, because they can talk.
Jade:	They can't talk because they are not people.
Lewis:	They *can* talk – they say 'woof, woof, woof'.
Megan:	When dogs bark, it means they need their water or food or something.
George:	Animals are talking because I know what monkeys are saying. Everyone talks, even animals.
Reece:	Animals talk because they used to be people.
Liam:	No, that's not real. Animals can't be real people.
Jade:	They can, because animals come from pet shops.
Liam:	They didn't go in there on their own. Someone has to make them.
George:	No, I disagree. Animals come out of the ground, not pet shops.
Megan:	No, they come from God.
Hayden:	But when they come down from God and they land, they run away.
Liam:	Umm, maybe God did make them.

This statement produced a stalemate in the conversation. As can often happen, the children seemed content to solve this problem with an easy answer: it's either God or magic. In this situation, I tell them that they need to think as philosophers: they need to look beyond the easy answer and work together to really justify their answers and question each other's thinking. In this session, we looked back over the elements of their previous conversation that I said I found intriguing, and considered whether we could push these statements even further. The points highlighted for philosophical dialogue were:

- Do animals have feelings?
- Do they deserve to be treated equally?
- Do you have to be able to talk to communicate with others?

I then asked if anyone wanted to ask one of these questions to the group. It is often useful to hand over the leadership of the dialogue in this way. This strategy enables the children to begin to learn to facilitate their own dialogues and, over time, become less reliant on teacher interjections. It also helps to refocus the pupils and reinforce the fact that it is their session.

The challenge was taken up by Reece.

Reece:	Are animals all equal to people then?
Megan:	Well, if you are nasty to the boy he will be upset, and if you are nasty to the dog he won't be.

Liam:	What about if she was nasty to the dog? The dog would feel cross as well.
Megan:	We have to be nice to everybody.
Danielle:	Children are more important than dogs.
Hayden:	I agree, because you need to feed dogs, but children can feed themselves. But babies can't get their own food.
Danielle:	But dogs are a responsibility, so you have to look after them most.
Liam:	You have to look after children as well.
Reece:	But babies need lots of help to get dressed and eat. They can't do anything.
Liam:	Everything's important here. The whole world is, except for burglars who steal things. They don't have to be treated nicely.
Facilitator:	Do you think we should be nasty to people who are nasty to us?
Lewis:	Yes, we should, because they steal.
Danielle:	It doesn't matter if we are nasty back, but we mustn't do it first.
Lewis:	If they steal your stuff, you should steal their stuff.
Ruby:	But your mum would tell you off.
Reece:	And you could go to prison as well.
Liam:	Only big kids get arrested.
Lewis:	But little kids can, because I've seen a child arrested for stealing. When I went to the supermarket I saw someone nick something because he had no money.
Hayden:	You can't nick stuff from shops – they have security guards.
Liam:	No, they are policemen because they have handcuffs.

At this point, I asked whether they felt it was ever OK to take something from a shop. I introduced a scenario where they had a mum ill at home with no money, and everyone in the house was very, very hungry.

Danielle:	If you've got no money, then you should ask and they might make it free.
Liam:	But what if the police or manager was looking at you?
Jade:	It would be OK because my mum forgot her purse once so we had no money, but they let us have the food because we asked really, really politely.

The lesson had lasted 75 minutes. It was wrapped up by reading through some of the interesting points that had been raised. I then pointed out that there was actually a link between the original question asked and their final statements: both were asking about right and wrong and how we treat people.

Reflecting on the lesson, I noted that the children were, after almost a year of weekly philosophy sessions, returning to familiar themes time and time again. One of the dominant themes is that of punishment and revenge. Several discussions have centred on the village supermarket, and it is noticeable that the class are able to bring themselves together to talk about a shared common experience.

Facilitating difficult areas

Although the facilitator's aim is for the children to assume increasing responsibility for the quality of their dialogues, there may occasionally be problems within the dialogue when adult support or intervention is needed. Again, however, the aim is that eventually the children will be able to sort problems out for themselves within the community of enquiry. This is achieved with experience and good modelling,

Difficult topics

Death and war are two areas in which there is a possibility that children may become upset. As facilitators we know that these issues must be covered with sensitivity. It may be that children are quite happy to discuss these things, but philosophy in the classroom is not therapy, and as their teachers we will know how far to take discussion on these issues, should they arise. However, it is unreasonable to expect that children would not be upset at certain times. When children feel passionately about things that matter to them, we should not disregard their feelings. We owe them the knowledge that we care about their thoughts. After all, we do not want our children to be completely anaesthetized by the horrors of the world; neither, though, do we want to pursue things beyond the level of comfort. It needs to be OK for both facilitator and children to be able to say, 'I don't feel comfortable talking about this in this way.' As a facilitator, you can move the direction of the dialogue if you feel it necessary, but you will also find that the children will do this themselves. If they are not comfortable, they will turn the discussion elsewhere or simply stop talking.

Difficult personal situations

When children are talking about their lives and what affects them, it can become quite personal and they may start to reveal things that are inappropriate for public discussion. In such cases, it is wise to be overt and explain that this is a personal issue and that others, including you, might feel uncomfortable with it in this particular setting. (This does not mean, of course, that you are closing doors for that child to talk to you or other adults privately if you feel it is necessary.)

Difficult behaviour

You might find that you have children who dominate the dialogue or contribute endless personal anecdotes at length. In both these situations you need to develop the child's thinking through gentle questioning, and make them accountable for what they say. You might use some of the facilitator questions (page 55) yourself – or encourage the community to ask them – in order to help the child move to a more abstract level of thinking.

If you have children who misbehave during the dialogue, it may be necessary to give a warning or even exclude them for a short while. The aim, however, should be for philosophy to be all-inclusive. It is often the case that those with behavioural problems or special needs find success in philosophy because they are able to reason well. It also allows opportunities for their peers to see them succeed, which in turn enhances their confidence and self-esteem. Within the community of enquiry, the high levels of responsibility together with clearly defined boundaries provide a feeling of safety for all children.

Closure and evaluation

To finish the session, there needs to be some closure and some evaluation. As a group, decide where the dialogue has ended up. What issues have been discussed? Where has there been uncertainty? What could be the focus for further discussion? Which of the questions could be chosen, or new question negotiated, to take for homework? Older and more experienced children should be given a few minutes to quietly reflect on the session beforehand (see below).

Evaluation with the children

As well as considering the content of the dialogue, the children can also be encouraged to reflect on how they worked together as a community of enquiry and, specifically, what skills they used. Here are some methods for doings this.

Community of enquiry building blocks

A way of assessing the skills used in the enquiry is to build a 'wall of skills', using a set of cards made to look like bricks or building blocks. Over the course of the sessions, these 'blocks' are introduced as the building blocks of philosophical enquiry.

The blocks are made from A4 card and then laminated. Each building block shows one skill as follows:

(In today's session we aim to)

- Follow the listening rules
- Follow the talking rules
- Illustrate our thoughts and questions
- Share our thinking homework
- Look for open-ended questions
- Look for links between questions
- Work together to sort out any problems within the group
- Give reasons for our ideas
- Make connections to previous dialogues
- Follow on from the person before
- Make connections with other people's ideas
- Recognize a change of mind
- Relax our minds and bodies
- Look beyond the expected answer to the emotion
- Ask others to clarify meaning
- Recognize inconsistencies in arguments

These are the core enquiry skills and the most useful ones to focus on, although the list can be adapted or added to as appropriate to the group.

At the start of each P4C session, spend a few minutes reviewing progress as a class in the previous session and decide on a community target of skills for that day's session, choosing from the enquiry building blocks. This review can be based on the previous week's wall, looking at its strengths and weaknesses, for example: 'Last week we didn't use the turn-taking building block in building the wall. Maybe we can aim to build with that one today.' It is important to make the objectives for the session clear to the children and involve them in the process. This ensures that these aims become the responsibility of the whole community of enquiry.

At the end of the session, make time to consider whether the target was reached, or if any other new skills have been used, either by individuals or by the whole community. Quickly go through the blocks and decide together whether enough people used the skill described on each card to allow it to go into the wall. You can then lay the cards out on the floor or stick them on the whiteboard. The blocks should be laid out like bricks in a wall to represent the fact that the skills are interlinked. Well-used bricks can go on the bottom to form a strong base, with bricks representing more recently added and less secure skills at the top. Remember, of course, that the aim is to encourage children and to make them feel skilled, so unless they have completely failed in the use of a particular skill, you might say, 'Well, we'll put it in the wall, but it's a bit wobbly!' The ultimate aim is to build a solid wall using all the blocks, however long it might take. Emphasize that it is the strength of the wall that matters, not how quickly it is built. By the end of each term, and ultimately the year, you can decide which blocks have been used most effectively and determine how strong the wall has become.

After the session, it is useful to sketch that week's wall on the back of the large sheet of questions so it can be referred to the following week. It is also helpful and informative to jot down names of those who made good questions or took an active and important part in the session. This can encourage more reluctant members of the class to participate, in order to get a special mention at the end.

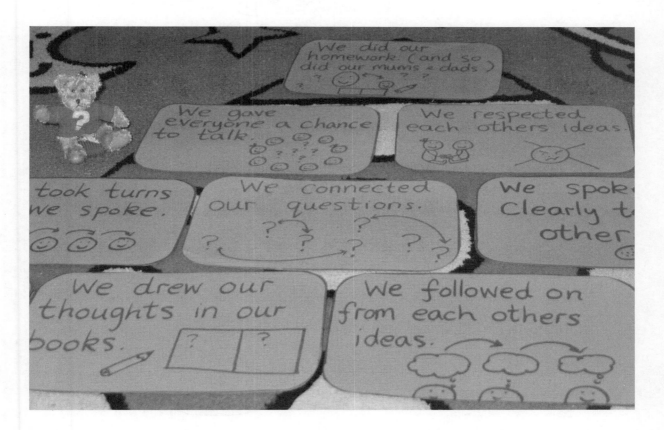

The building blocks can be kept pegged on a string around the carpet area for use in P4C sessions; they can also be useful to refer to in other types of carpet session.

The Talkometer

Lots of people spoke

12th March

Not many people spoke

Draw a vertical line in a space on the front or back of the question sheet and write 'not many people spoke' at the bottom of the line and 'lots of people spoke' at the top. At the end of the session decide as a class where to put the indicator line. Alternatively, you could also make a large-scale talkometer along the lines of the one shown above and put it on display in the philosophy display area of the classroom. You could then date the indicator line and see whether it has moved up or down the scale since the last session. The ultimate aim and challenge is to get the indicator to hit the top of the scale.

Silent reflection

A method that can be used with older and more experienced children (probably Year 3 and up) is to allow them silent reflection time at the end of the session. During this time, they jot down any thoughts or feelings they have about the session, for example anything they feel is unresolved, or indeed anything that has been clarified for them. They might record a moment of interest from the dialogue, a further question they might want to ask, something about their role in the session or their own reaction to the class as a community. These thoughts can remain private or be shared with the class, depending on each child's personal preference.

Class journal

Another method of review suitable for older children is to keep a class journal as a record of their feelings about the work. At the end of a session, children comment on their thoughts and feelings using the building block skills as a way of focusing on achievements made by the community. The children are encouraged to mention and praise their peers by name for building on ideas, making connections and joining in dialogue. These comments about the session are written down by the class teacher and the book is made available in the philosophy display area for children, parents and others to read.

Facilitator's self-evaluation

It is really helpful to keep a journal. A facilitator's journal becomes a record of the progress made in thinking – yours as well as the children's. It clarifies your personal journey as a facilitator. Useful things to record could be:

Key points of the session

- Where did it start?
- What paths of enquiry were followed?
- Where did it finish?
- How will you follow it up?
- Homework question (if any)
- Ideas for next session

The community of enquiry

- What was the quality of the questions asked by the children?
- Did the children see links and connections between questions?
- Which parts of the enquiry went well, and why?
- Which parts did not go well, and why?

- Were there any comments or responses that surprised you?
- Did the children follow trains of thought and build on ideas?
- How were the behaviour and relationships within the class as a community?
- Which children participated?
- Which children struggled and which succeeded?
- Were the children excited by the session?

Your role as facilitator

- Did you model without dominating?
- Did you ask children to clarify their thinking?
- Did you allow children to think for themselves?
- Did you allow children enough time to express their ideas?
- Did you push for deeper thinking into the philosophical?
- Did you pick up potential for philosophical discussion?
- Did you encourage children to work together?
- Were you able to bring children into the dialogue?

Recording the sessions

Whenever you can, try and record the session. You might prefer to use an audio cassette recorder – doing this means I can listen to the session on the drive home! Alternatively you could use a digital voice recorder which enables you to transfer speech onto computer files. This is another way of keeping a record of sessions and takes up much less space than large pieces of paper.

Listening to the enquiry can be very revealing. Often, the speed and tenacity of a session means you cannot attend to everything – least of all to yourself. By recording and listening, you can reflect upon and review your role as a facilitator.

The first time I listened to myself as a facilitator, I was horrified to hear how many times I slipped into 'teacher mode' and interrupted a child's thinking. I had also left ideas unclarified, and this meant that children were finding it hard to develop the dialogue because of a lack of common understanding. Listening back on a session offers opportunities to develop the way you participate in the enquiry. You can see where dialogue took off in new directions. You can pick up on moments where you asked a question that enabled the children to move forward in their thinking. You might also find times where you asked the wrong question – one that stopped the dialogue dead. With the advantage of hindsight you can ask yourself:

- What could I have said?
- Where could I have pushed for clarification?
- Where could I have modelled a secondary question?

- Where could I have kept quiet or pushed for deeper thinking?
- Where could I have directed ideas back to previous questions or ideas?

Recording the sessions may be useful for the children too. I put the cassette recorder in the children's listening corner for them to listen to. They love to hear each other talk and it gives them time to reflect on what others have said. Very often it is the least vocal participants who really enjoy listening to these recorded dialogues.

Transcribing dialogue

Another way to assess and evaluate sessions is by writing down the dialogue on large sheets (A0) of paper. You could ask a teaching assistant to do this if you prefer to concentrate on listening to the dialogue yourself. As the children become more adept at talking, their thoughts become more complex and it becomes much harder to write down their ideas. When they reach this stage it is easier to just jot down key points.

With Reception children, I find that my writing as they talk gives them encouragement. Sitting on the floor with them and also giving much less eye contact helps them to understand that they are not directing all their ideas to me but to the community itself.

These sheets of writing are themselves a valuable way to assess the session. They show the quality of questions, and if you record notable comments from individuals it becomes easy to track each child's progress. Ideally the sheets should be displayed for children and parents to see; if you have a philosophy display area (see page 99), this would be an ideal place.

Tips and reminders

Doing philosophy with young children inevitably takes time and patience. As in other areas of learning, skills and confidence need to be developed – by both children and facilitator. The list below provides an at-a-glance reminder of some of the key ideas and strategies, along with a few additional tips.

Preparation and stimulus

- Think about your lesson objective. It may not necessarily be to achieve sustained, high-quality dialogue. The community may profitably focus on meeting other valuable targets.
- Choose a really good stimulus. Are the children going to be excited by it? Does it hook into their experiences?
- Think beforehand about the sort of questions and issues that may arise from the stimulus. Make sure you are prepared.

Questions

- Allow enough time for children to draw their thoughts and ideas.
- List their questions or statements and initial them.

- Highlight links and connections between the questions. What are they asking?

- Categorize them and decide together which are quality questions.

- Take the questions away from the book: can they make secondary questions? What are the big issues?

- When a child finds it hard to formulate a question, they can offer a statement. You could then model ways of putting that statement into question form. Offer choices and ask the child which best portrays their thinking. Other children could be encouraged to help by offering questions that mirror the statement, always ensuring the child keeps ownership of their question and its meaning.

- It is important that the children are seeing the connections between questions. This will have to be modelled to begin with. Show the connections on the list with arrows or make separate groups for types of questions.

- Feel free to go with whichever questions draw the children's interest. Alternatively, vote to select from the questions or concepts discovered through making connections.

Dialogue

- Don't worry about the quality of the dialogue to begin with. It may be more useful to concentrate on improving the quality of questions that children ask. Can the children see for themselves which questions are 'good quality'? Do they already know the answer? Can they find the answer through research? Or is it a question that would be good for philosophical enquiry: will there be many opinions or points of view? This process of evaluation will need to be modelled.

- Children need to understand the importance of good listening. (A session on how it feels when people listen / don't listen to us in circle time could be a good preparation.)

- A long-term aim should be to enable the children to push for each other's reasons for thinking as well as their own. You want them to learn to reflect and to research their enquiries, to be analytical and to challenge their own thinking as well as that of others, within the safety of a community of enquiry.

- Encourage children to use the language of debate – for example 'agree' and 'disagree', 'undecided', 'change of mind' – and to back up every statement with an explanation of their thinking.

- Ensure the children understand the importance of turn-taking. To begin with, use 'hands up' or some other bodily signal to indicate wishing to speak. Practise or refer back to the stand up / sit down game (see page 120) to reinforce the importance of not interrupting. You will find that with good facilitation, the children will eventually facilitate and organize their turn-taking within the session, as they do in other subjects and at other learning times.

- If children get hooked on a particular subject and are going nowhere with it, don't be afraid to tell them that they have to move on.
- Always push for clarification.
- Ask questions to push for depth.
- Don't be afraid to pull children into the dialogue or tell dominant children to participate fairly.

What if the dialogue runs dry?

- Rephrase the last comment made: maybe they didn't understand it.
- Ask whether anyone thinks *nearly* the same thing. They might agree but have a slightly different perception of it.
- Ask a question from the list of facilitator questions.
- If dialogue is slow or non-productive, break it up with thinking activities about the questions they are trying to explore, or start afresh with a new question.
- Ask the children to stand up if they agree (or disagree or are not sure) with the previous statement or idea.
- Play a quick Corners game (see page 132), using a statement from where the thinking has stalled, to promote deeper thinking and dialogue.
- Refer back to another question from the list with a similar concept.
- Hand over responsibility to the children. It is *their* enquiry. Ask them where they think they need to go from here.
- If the children are finding the dialogue too hard, break it up with a game using the concepts in the dialogue (see pages 132–139).
- Play devil's advocate! Promote disagreement.
- If dialogue is really not getting anywhere, revisit the topic again in another session, using a different stimulus but covering the same concepts.

Ending and recording

- Close the session by asking: 'Where are we with our thinking?' 'Where do we go from here?'
- Evaluate the session with the children. Also keep your own diary for your thoughts about the session.
- Whenever possible, record the session with an audio cassette recorder, digital voice recorder or video camera.

- Ask teaching assistants to help by recording what the children say.

- Put your record of their ideas on display. Value their ideas. You will also be able to see the evidence of their progress.

- Encourage children to talk to friends and family about their pictures, ideas and questions.

Useful pointers for the facilitator

- Remember that it will take time for you and the children to feel completely at ease with the sessions.

- Remember that the children will feed off your curiosity and enthusiasm as well as off each other's.

- Your role is facilitator, not chairman. You do not need to give them any answers.

- It is OK to interject at times. You are aiming to pull away from the stimulus towards the more philosophical concepts.

- Have confidence in yourself, but remember that it is not easy and it will take time.

- Don't be afraid to stop if you or the children are uncomfortable with any issues raised. If issues concerned with child protection, deeply personal family issues or unacceptable comments are offered, tell the child this is not the place to air them but let them know that you can speak privately later.

- Finally, don't be afraid to talk to others about success and frustrations.

Part 3

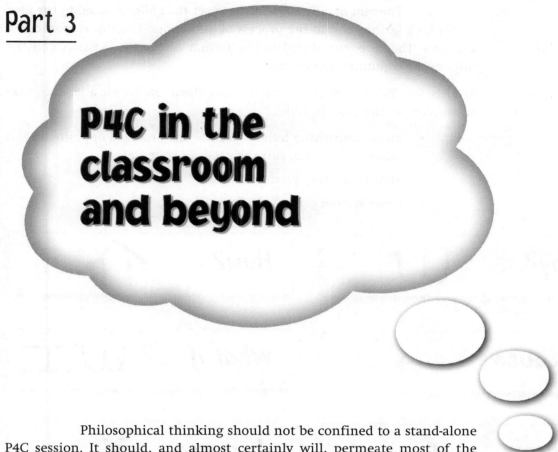

P4C in the classroom and beyond

Philosophical thinking should not be confined to a stand-alone P4C session. It should, and almost certainly will, permeate most of the curriculum. This section aims to show how you can get the most from philosophy by taking it beyond the confines of the P4C session, beginning with the classroom.

Introducing P4C with Philosophy Bear

When you are starting out with P4C, Philosophy Bear can be used to capture children's interest and as a tool to develop their philosophical skills. I have used Philosophy Bear for several years to engage children in philosophy in the same way puppets, props and toys can be used to engage their learning in other educational subjects. He can be a facilitator and a participator in the sessions, a tool to encourage talking and questioning, and a means of introducing the stimulus. He can help both children and parents understand how philosophy works and be used as a home–school link. Below are suggestions for ways to do this, but there are no hard and fast rules – be as creative as you like!

Philosophy Bear can be used right at the outset to introduce children to the idea of doing philosophy. This outline of an introductory lesson can be adapted to the needs of your class.

An introductory session with Philosophy Bear

The aim of a first session is to get the children used to the idea of thinking lessons and to the process of asking questions in response to a stimulus. They are introduced to the format of the P4C session and the rules of the community of enquiry.

Arrange for Phil Bear to be delivered to the classroom inside a labelled case or bag. Also in the case, include:

- an accompanying letter – use the one provided opposite, or make your own to suit the needs of your class
- an introductory picture stimulus
- some symbol cards.

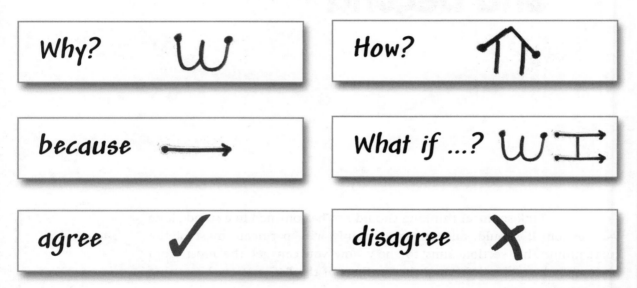

Having read the letter, you might begin by looking at the postscript and discuss what it means to be wise. From this, you can introduce the idea of philosophy as a way of thinking.

Philosophy Bear can be used to explain that, in philosophy sessions, we have rules of thinking and listening which are negotiated by the whole class. The first rule is to sit in a circle so that everyone is part of the group and everybody can be seen. You might talk about your community rules (see page 27) at this point, or you might introduce a select few and then develop them in another session.

Philosophy Bear can be used to explain to children that asking questions is an extremely important part of thinking and wondering. You can then talk about how to ask a question in a philosophy session. It is useful at this stage to spend some time practising asking a question. Phil Bear can show the introductory picture stimulus and invite the children to ask questions about it using the word or symbol on the card he holds up. The symbols mean that they can be used with pre-literate children, but you should ensure they understand that the tick and the cross do not represent right and wrong.

Dear Children,

My name is Philosophy Bear and I have heard about the thinking you do in your school. I was wondering whether you would let me join your class, as I love to think.

I am always wondering about the world I live in. I am always thinking about questions such as: Why do I exist? What made the world? Why do people love each other or hate each other? The great thing about this sort of thinking is that I can never be wrong, because these sorts of questions have no right or wrong answers.

I have been told I ask too many questions, but I think it is very important to ask questions and listen to other people's ideas. It helps me understand my thoughts and how they affect my life.

Please would you let me join in your thinking lessons? Maybe I could take it in turns to come home with you. I would love to meet your families and listen to all your ideas.

Love from

Philosophy Bear

P.S. I expect you are wondering about my name. Philosophy is a very old word and it means 'love of wisdom'.

Using symbol cards and an introductory stimulus

In the following extract from a first lesson with a Reception class, the stimulus was a copy of the painting *Exhibition of a Rhinoceros at Venice* by Pietro Longhi (found in Quentin Blake's *Tell Me a Picture*). The picture was used first to extract some *why* and *how* questions. (*What if* questions are usually introduced when children have got the hang of the two simpler question forms.)

Philosophy Bear held up the Why? symbol card and invited the children to ask that question about something they could see in the painting. They came up with:

- Why are those men wearing black hats?
- Why is the pig sad?
- Why has that girl got a black circle on her face?
- Why has the man got a stick?

Phil Bear then showed the How? symbol card and asked for some more questions. Responses included:

- How did the pig get in the house?
- How did the pig get all wrinkly skin?

The children found it much harder to ask *how* questions and many offered statements instead, such as:

- The man has got a pointy thing in his hand.
- The lady has got a bird in her basket.
- Those men have got white masks on their faces.

When a child offered a statement, Philosophy Bear asked which symbol card they would like to put with their statement to change it into a question. For the three statements above, we ended up with:

- Why has the man got a pointy thing in his hand?
- Why has the lady got a bird in her basket?
- Why have the men got masks on their faces?

All the questions and statements were recorded on a large piece of paper with the children's names.

Philosophy Bear then introduced the Because ... symbol card and asked children to think of some answers to the questions we had collected. To begin, Philosophy Bear chose a question from the list we had compiled:

- Why has the man got a stick?

Ellie, the owner of the question, was asked to tell Philosophy Bear why she wondered that. She replied:

- I think it's because he wants to get a fish.

Her reply prompted discussion:

Lois: I think he's not going to catch a fish because it hasn't got a sharp pointy thing. It's for getting things up and down a tall tower like water and stuff.

Elliot: That bit of string might be a fishing string, because they are going to fix a sharp thing on it.

At this point, I explained that Philosophy Bear thought it was probably a whip, and asked if anyone knew what it would be used for.

Euan: People in a cage with lions use that because they use it to hit the lion.

Facilitator: Philosophy Bear wonders why would they hit the animal.

Euan: Because it would keep him back.

Elliot: Yes, it would scare him away.

Alex: Because it makes him roar.

Facilitator: Philosophy Bear wonders how would that make you feel, being hit with a stick.

Lois: It would make you sad, because you'd want your mum and dad and not be in a cage and if you were hit by a stick it would hurt.

Euan: It wouldn't hurt me because I'd pull it off them.

Facilitator: Philosophy Bear wonders what the man in the picture is going to do with his stick.

Amy: He would hit the black thing. [the rhinoceros]

Alex: Because he doesn't like him.

Facilitator: Is it OK to hit the animal?

Euan: It's a bad thing because you might hurt it if you hit it really hard.

Facilitator: Is it always bad to hit an animal then?

Euan: You might hit a big lion with a stick because it might eat you.

Phil Bear asked what they thought the animal might be. Most children agreed it was a pig, although we had suggestions of a cow, a hippo and an elephant!

Philosophy Bear was asked what the painting was called and he gave the title, informing us that the animal was in fact a rhinoceros. This prompted one child to ask why it didn't have a horn. Philosophy Bear pointed out that she had in fact asked a really good question. He explained it had been cut off and asked if that would make the animal sad. The children began to talk about whether the man with the stick had cut off his horn and how it must have hurt. The children were asked to vote on their response to the following statement:

- It is OK to hurt animals?

I asked the children to decide if they agreed with that statement: if they thought, 'Yes, it is OK to hurt animals', they should stand up when Phil Bear held up the Agree symbol card; and if they thought, 'No, it is not OK to hurt animals', to stand up when he held up the Disagree symbol card.

I also stressed to the children that it was important they should each think for themselves, not just copy their friends or the person next to them,

CASE STUDY

because Philosophy Bear would be interested to hear about *their* ideas. In this lesson, all the children stood up when Phil Bear held up the Disagree symbol card. And when he showed them the Because ... symbol card and asked them to say why they had made this decision, most could give an answer based on the idea that you should always be nice to animals. Phil Bear then asked the question:

- Would you be nice to a big scary tiger who wanted to eat you for his dinner?

The children were asked to stand up if they would be nice to the tiger. The majority remained seated. I then asked some sitting children to explain why they wouldn't be kind and what they would do to the tiger. One child said:

> I would get my big gun and shoot the tiger in the belly.

And when asked why:

> Because he was going to eat me, so I can shoot tigers.

The discussion was developed by using Phil Bear as facilitator. He then asked the children to think about a homework question to give their parents. They were asked to vote on four options:

1. If people are allowed to kill tigers, then can tigers be allowed to kill people?
2. Why do we kill cows to eat but not our pets?
3. Is it ever right to hurt an animal?
4. Would we kill a fierce mummy tiger that was looking after her baby?

The children voted for question 3.

A brief summary of the day's session and the question for homework were posted on the philosophy notice board. Ideas to help the discussion at home were also provided, for example a list of situations which might involve an animal being hurt:

- medical science
- to prevent suffering
- in self-defence
- harmful insects
- hunting and sport
- for food.

Once Philosophy Bear has been introduced to the class, he can be given a home in the independent philosophy area (see page 99).

Using *Philosophy Bear and the Big Sky*

Included in the *But Why?* pack is the picture book, *Philosophy Bear and the Big Sky*. This book is designed to introduce children, and also parents, to the idea of doing philosophy. It provides teachers with a platform on which to discuss what a philosophical person (or, in this case, bear) thinks about, and what sorts of questions they ask. It can be used to explore the difference between the sort of questions that have clear answers and those that open the door onto puzzling ideas and that tend to prompt further questions.

The simple story revolves around the notion of 'big ideas', encouraging the reader to believe that everyone is capable of 'thinking big'. Philosophy Bear himself looks to the sky for inspiration and – in the same way that the looking at a huge expanse of ocean can make us feel small and insignificant – he finds it makes him wonder what his place in the world is. With young children, and to an extent older children with limited experience of higher-order thinking, scientific questions are the first questions they ask. But questions about the universe and stars naturally lead on to questions such as: Where did it all come from? Is there a God? Why was the world created? and Why am I here?

Philosophy Bear is a symbol of our questioning nature; a bear who shares his puzzlement with his friends in a safe and secure environment but who will stop for tea and stories! The story introduces two main characters who humanize and personify what we feel to be very useful qualities in philosophical enquiry. Phil Bear himself thinks the big thoughts and asks those huge open questions in search of basic purposes and reasons. Pinkerton the very curious cat, meanwhile, becomes absorbed by the details and her playfulness is endless. These characters complement one another and highlight the value of wondering. The story says to us that it's OK to be confused by what is uncertain or ambiguous, that it's fine not to know the right answer right now. More implicit in the story is the notion that not every aspect of existence may be answerable in clear, logical, measurable terms. As the theological philosopher Alan Watts suggested, life is a mystery to be enjoyed and experienced, not just a puzzle to be solved.

> **Two things fill the mind with ever increasing wonder and awe ... the starry heavens above me and the moral law within me.**
>
> IMMANUEL KANT

Using the story with children

In conjunction with the mini-bear, the book can be used in an early P4C session and also as a home–school link (for further details on this, see page 86).

After reading the book with the children, use the story as a starting point for a discussion about the nature of questions. You could ask the group:

- Can you answer any of the questions asked by Pinkerton or Philosophy Bear?
- What are the most interesting questions Philosophy Bear asks?
- Can we answer every question in the world?
- Can you think of a question you know the answer to? Will it always be the same answer every time? Will everybody have the same answer?

- Can you ask a question that has lots of different answers?
- Why is it important to ask questions?
- What is a question?

You can also encourage the children to express their ideas about things they wonder about.

Record and display the children's responses to this discussion to make a display about philosophical questioning. The children's big questions for Philosophy Bear can be written up on a philosophy display board. You could also encourage visitors (other pupils, members of staff and the school community, visitors from outside school) to add their big questions to the list.

The following dialogues around the story are taken from Philosophy Bear's diary (see page 88).

Lois was wondering why we have stories. She thinks stories might be true sometimes. If you think people may have made it up, like if there's talking animals, then you know it's not true. Animals don't talk like chattering, they have their own voices, like horses neigh. In films animals can talk because it's just made up. Animals talk about their feelings, but in real life they have feelings but don't talk.

Lois' dad wonders the same thing as Philosophy Bear. Does a leaf know it is part of a tree? Lois thinks that it does, because trees have feelings and can be sad if they get cut down. A leaf would feel sad when it fell off the tree, it would feel like it's going to fall and be dead.

Euan wonders about the stars. He thinks that falling stars are the best because you can make wishes. Little stars can grant your wishes because once he wished for a dog and then he got one 'cos the wishing star sent it. Euan's mum wonders why she doesn't get the things she wishes for. Euan says maybe it's the wrong star – you have to find the right ones first.

The story book can also be sent home with children – perhaps in a travelling case along with notebook, pencils and Philosophy Bear. You could include an explanatory letter to parents such as the one opposite.

Dear Parents,

This week Philosophy Bear would like to show you a book written all about him and his big thoughts! Please read the book with your child and take some time to talk about the sorts of important things that they wonder about. You could also talk about some of the things Philosophy Bear wonders about in the book.

Please record your own ideas and those of your child in their own words. Please also encourage your child to think of a big question to ask Philosophy Bear. Big questions are ones that have no absolute right or wrong answers. Big questions are important because they encourage us to think about things with an open mind and work out what we think.

Please return the case and contents tomorrow.

Thank you.

Working with parents

Introducing philosophy to parents

If Philosophy for Children is to have a lasting effect on children's lives, the thinking must extend beyond the weekly timetabled sessions. This is why parental involvement is so valuable.

You can, of course, do philosophy in the classroom without involving the home: how much to involve parents is a decision that individual schools and teachers have to make. You might already have a high degree of involvement with your parents through other school activities, or you may feel it would not work for your school at all.

Whether and how frequently you wish to send out philosophy homework is, again, very much an individual decision for the teacher and for the school. If you feel there would be strong support for it, then it could be set weekly; equally it could be set only when you feel it would be beneficial or when it ties in with another topic.

On the other hand, you may prefer to inform parents about what the children are doing without asking for the homework commitment. You could start off with a 'Thought of the week' notice board and gauge the level of interest before gradually introducing philosophy to parents in other ways (see pages 96–97).

Whether or not you decide to involve parents in homework activity, it is worth considering how you can communicate to them what you are doing with philosophy in school, as well as its uses as a learning tool and its value within their child's education. As with many areas of the school curriculum, it is important that parents understand how the subject is taught, and why. In the case of philosophy, links with national curriculum requirements for thinking, communication and PSHE can be demonstrated (see page 19).

Philosophy does have something of a reputation as an inaccessible academic subject, and may be regarded with suspicion by some parents. Similarly, they may find it hard to see philosophy as something relevant to very young children; this is another reason why it is important to share the structures and benefits with them. In the long term, gaining the support of the parents has a significant impact on the children's philosophical development, but do not be surprised if this support does not happen overnight. In my experience, it takes a few years to build up both the teachers' confidence and parents' knowledge and understanding of P4C and its role in the life of the school

Using Philosophy Bear as a home–school link

One way of helping parents to understand what you are doing in philosophy is to use Philosophy Bear as a home–school link, which can be done in the following way. Philosophy Bear 'visits' each child's family in turn, being sent home in a small bag or case. Include in the case: Philosophy Bear's diary (see page 88), a pencil case and a letter to the parents. Copy and use the letter provided here or produce your own to suit the needs of your school situation.

Dear Parents,

Your child has brought home Philosophy Bear. Like all children, this bear is always wondering and asking questions to find out about life and the world he lives in. Because Philosophy Bear discusses his ideas, he is learning a very important skill – the ability to reason. By doing this, he is developing a sense of who he is and his place in the world. This in turn helps him become more motivated to learn.

Philosophy Bear has a diary that he would like to share with you and your child. Inside the diary is a question or thought that he would like to hear your views on. Please read Philosophy Bear's question or thought to your child and talk together about what you both think and why. Then write down your child's thoughts **in your child's own words.** Your child may also draw a picture to illustrate their ideas.

Please give us your thoughts as well. Don't forget that there are no right or wrong answers! But do remember to give us the reasons for your points of view.

As well as visiting each member of our class at home, Philosophy Bear will join us in our regular philosophy lessons. He hopes that the children will learn to talk to each other on equal terms, and become more tolerant and thoughtful critical thinkers.

Please help Phil Bear to return this letter and all the equipment to his case and send him back to school the next day, where he will share his diary with the class.

Thank you very much for your support.

Philosophy Bear's diary

Philosophy Bear's diary is a way of developing ideas that come out of the philosophy sessions. At the end of the session, the children and/or the facilitator select a question to go in Philosophy Bear's diary. You could say, 'What question do you think Phil Bear would like to ask your mums and dads?' The question could be taken from the big sheet of questions, or it could be something mentioned during the dialogue. If they can't think of a question, you could 'ask' the bear and have him 'tell' you one. The question is then written down at the top of a page in the diary. A vertical line is drawn down the middle of the rest of the page, with 'Child thinks ...' on one side and 'Adult thinks ...' the other:

> **Philosophy Bear wonders what you think about ... (question)**
>
> | Child thinks ... because ... | Adult thinks ... because .... |
> |---|---|

The diary is then sent home to several families in turn. The parents are encouraged to read back through other people's ideas about the question and to build on the ideas by adding their own thoughts.

Ideally, you should find a slot to look briefly at the returned diary each day. I usually read the family responses just after registration and we might chat about them for a few minutes. Or it could be done in a 5-minute slot after lunch or playtime. A daily 5–10-minute diary session helps to keep the ideas fresh in everyone's minds. It also helps children to understand that the enquiry is an ongoing process because there are always new thoughts and ideas to add to our thinking on a subject.

The diary might also be used at the beginning of the weekly P4C session, especially if it fits in with the stimulus you are planning to use that week. Alternatively, you might use it instead of a conventional stimulus to develop their thinking in that session.

Using Philosophy Bear's diary 1

CASE STUDY

From a Reception class topic on *The Three Little Pigs*, parents and children used Philosophy Bear's diary to develop ideas around the concept of conscience.

Philosophy Bear wonders whether animals have a conscience like humans? What do you think and why?

Child thinks ... because ...

A wolf has got a conscience but he doesn't know when he is being naughty. If a dog poos on the grass he doesn't know this is wrong but he wouldn't hurt his puppies on purpose so he must know that is wrong.

Cousin N thinks ... Animals do not have a conscience because they only kill to eat, feed their young and to defend themselves against predators. However, they don't seem to have a conscience, apart from the fact that they usually kill the weak, sick or old.

Adult thinks ... because ...

Auntie M thinks ...
A conscience is something that has been developed by society to keep us humans behaving within given parameters.

Mum thinks ... A conscience must be something that is a basic animal instinct, as animals ordinarily don't kill indiscriminately. Also, within certain groups of animals there is an accepted code by which animals behave.

CASE STUDY

PB has read what this family thinks. Do you agree or disagree with any of these ideas? If so why or why not?

Child thinks ... because ...

Animals don't mean to be nasty but some are. Animals know what's right and wrong. Animals feel bad when they are naughty so they do have a conscience. But they have a different conscience to us.

Adult thinks ... because ...

Mum and Dad think ... We disagree with Auntie M. We don't think that society developed the notion of conscience. Auntie M is referring to the moral code which society dictates we live our lives by. Humans have different conscience levels. For example, criminals that live beyond the moral code of society tend not to have much of a conscience. They feel little or no guilt for the crimes they commit. It's difficult to say whether animals do have a conscience or not. Some animals have to kill for food. This is essential for their survival. This may seem quite barbaric to us humans, leading us to assume they have no conscience. But because killing is natural to them they have nothing to feel guilty about. Some animals live in social groups and they have their own code of conduct. But it is impossible to say how they feel if they break the rules that are set. Do they ever feel sorry?

→

This has really made PB think. Does every living thing have a conscience?

Child thinks ... because ...	Adult thinks ... because ...
It is not an animal's fault when they are nasty. It is their conscience telling them to be nasty. Their conscience tells them they need food to eat so it makes them hunt and kill. It is easier for a human to control their conscience.	Dad thinks ... I have to disagree with Auntie M as well. I do agree with the parents on the previous page. It is very hard to know whether animals have a conscience as it is in the nature of animals to harm or kill for food or survival. But that is an animal instinct that they are taught from a young age by their parents. I am also sure that some criminals deep down do have a conscience but sometimes due to depravity they feel they have to carry out these crimes, and due to the intoxicating substances that a lot of criminals are addicted to – it's not their real mind committing these offences. So, again, it's difficult to say whether they have a conscience. Where most of us with an easy mind do have a conscience, when it comes to regret or remorse we try to stick to the code of conduct.

CASE STUDY

Phil Bear wonders whether animals ever feel sorry or sad about killing. Do you think animals have emotions? If so what and when?

Child thinks... because ...

I don't think animals feel sorry because they don't talk. But they sometimes feel sad because they get hurt when they fight. Sometimes they feel lonely as they don't always have others to play with.

Adult thinks... because ...

Mum thinks... I don't think an animal would be sorry as they don't learn what the word sorry means like we humans do. I do think though that every living thing has emotions. They must feel sad sometimes and anger when things don't go right for them (e.g. when they can't get the food they work hard to get). They feel pain when they are hurt or ill or when humans hurt them. Some animals which are hunted must hate humans, but probably not in the way we hate. It's probably more a scared hate.

This example of continuous dialogue illustrates how parents talked through their thoughts and listened to the ideas of their children. Writing both sets of ideas in the book showed the children that their ideas were given equal value.

Using Philosophy Bear's diary 2

From using Tony Ross' *I Want to Be* as a stimulus, the class enquiry had developed into a dialogue about life and death and had just begun to explore the concept of identity. We decided to build on this area in Philosophy Bear's diary.

Do we have to grow up?

Child thinks ... because ...	Adult thinks ... because ...
Maria agrees that we have to grow up because we have to have birthdays and because we have those hurty things that make you taller (growing pains).	Mum thinks that it is good to grow up because then you can choose to have a job you like or travel or get married or have children ... all sorts of nice things. Dad disagrees and says that he doesn't think you have to grow up. It is only a belief when people like your parents tell you what your life will be like, such as marriage, jobs, buying a house.

When we shared these ideas with the class briefly the next day, we talked about whether we only grow up because people expect us to behave differently as we get older. The class discussion helped Philosophy Bear formulate a new question:

- If people were not expected to be responsible and work or be parents, would we behave like children all our lives?

CASE STUDY

In Billy's family, as in many of the other families, not everyone agreed on this:

Child thinks ... because ...	Adult thinks ... because ...
Billy thinks that you had to grow up, even bears, although his baby bear Fred didn't want to grow up and get big and hairy and watch football all day!	Billy's dad thinks that all men never really grow up – they are like Peter Pan. Billy's mum thinks that everyone would treat life like a party if no one had to be responsible.

The next day's discussion about the diary focused on whether Billy's bear would have to behave differently just because he had grown big and hairy? Would he still feel young on the inside?

Over the course of a week since first exploring the stimuli, we had built on ideas about the concept of growth and identity.

Using Philosophy Bear's diary validates parents' interest in their children's thinking and the questions they ask. It can also be a valuable tool for opening up communication within the home generally: you may well find that many children are discussing the ideas at home with their parents – whether they have taken the bear home or not.

Parents and children begin to understand that philosophy is not just about discussing, but also about listening and sharing, making meaning, and exploring experiences of and ideas about life. As educators, our aim and our hope is that it will open up communication at home about things that really matter.

Using the thinking journals

When you feel ready, you may wish to start sharing the children's thinking journals with parents by sending them home. It is a good idea to prepare for this by sending a short letter home, explaining when you will send books home and when they should be returned. Parental responses to the homework are usually very supportive and they often appreciate the fact that their opinions are valued.

If you decide to send journals home, you might consider sticking an explanatory information sheet into the book – inside the front cover is a good place. The sheet can remind parents what you are doing in philosophy and what benefits it brings. Opposite is the letter that I use. You may wish to copy or adapt it to your particular situation. In my school, each teacher writes their own version of the letter, because we all have slightly different personal perspectives on its value for learning.

What do we do in philosophy?

We are shown a stimulus. It could be a story, a poem or piece of music. We might also use a photo or other picture, or an object to look at.

We draw a picture in our journal to explain what we think or what we want to find out.

We then have some thinking time alone or in small groups to discuss our pictures or anything about the stimulus that has made us curious.

We ask interesting questions about the stimulus and the teacher records them on a large piece of paper.

We look for connections and links between the questions.

We decide which question we want to discuss in our session. To do this, we might vote on the ones that most interest us.

We discuss our thoughts and ideas about issues that arise from the questions. This is called a dialogue.

We take a question that has arisen from the session and write it in our journal to talk about with an adult at home. Any members of the family are invited to share their ideas as well.

Please take some time to think and talk together at home about the homework question. Please write down what your child thinks using their exact words, and then write what the adults or other family members think too. Please return this journal to school for the following week.

Thank you for your support.

What is your child learning?

Philosophy taps into your child's curiosity through reasoning, problem solving, imagination and creativity.

It develops their communication skills enabling them to articulate, listen and take turns.

It teaches them the language of debate and how to make connections between statements.

It helps them become more critical thinkers and question their own ideas as well as those of others in a non-threatening situation.

It develops good relationships with their peers as they learn to work together to build on each other's ideas and thoughts.

It teaches moral citizenship. They learn to take responsibility for their actions and views.

It helps build self-confidence and self-esteem.

Because there are no definite right and wrong answers, philosophy will challenge their thinking and they will want to share their thoughts with you and find out your opinions as well.

The more a philosopher questions, the more they will want to find out.

CASE STUDY

Sending thinking journals home

The following homework questions were pasted into a journal for a Reception class.

Homework (Ellie asked this question for us to think about this week)

> What is 'fake' anyway?

Points to consider:

> How do we know if something is real?
>
> What things are fake? How do we know?
>
> Are things on TV real?
>
> How do we know if something is real or not?
>
> Can we always trust our senses or believe what we are told?
>
> Do we really have to see something to know if it is real?

Child thinks... because...   **Adult thinks ... because....**

Homework

> If you swapped bodies with someone else, would you still be you?

Points to consider

> Would people treat you differently and would that make you different?
>
> What is it that makes you you?
>
> Is it your brain or your body that makes you you?
>
> Is your brain separate to your body?
>
> Would you feel or behave the same if your body changed?

Child thinks... because...   **Adult thinks ... because....**

More on communicating P4C

As stated earlier, it is a good idea, where possible, to involve parents fully and to gain their support for your work in P4C. At the very least they should be made aware of how and why the school is doing philosophy, and there are many ways to build this knowledge and understanding.

Intake meetings for new parents are a good opportunity to communicate the part philosophy will play in their child's education. You could set up a small display showing examples of children's work and resources, and giving information about why and how you do philosophy in school. Home visits or visits to the classroom for new children are also ideal opportunities to share information and examples of philosophical work that you do – in just the same way that you share your methods of teaching reading, writing and numeracy.

For the first few weeks you could display the children's questions and comments from the P4C sessions somewhere the parents will see them.

Here are some further ideas for communicating ideas about P4C to parents.

Parents' philosophy board

Use a large notice board or whiteboard placed outside the classroom at the beginning or end of the day. The board can be used to display the homework question and any related points to consider. It could also display the sheet of children's questions and any dialogue you have written up.

At the end of school on the day after the philosophy session, it is useful to put out a copy of the stimulus for parents to look at.

Parents' question board

This could be a notice board in the cloakroom or a board that you take outside. Display an explanation and instructions for its use, and ensure parents know that they do not have to put their names on any contributions. The idea is that they should feel free to write up any questions that they have wondered about or questions that have come from the children at home. These questions could then be used in the classroom as the basis for discussion. Alternatively, parents could be encouraged to respond to each other's ideas. It may be a good idea for you to model the use of this board by writing up your own questions or 'thoughts of the week' along with some responses from others – or encourage others to write their own responses.

Invite parents to a session

You may like to invite a small number of parents (probably three or four at a time) to join a philosophy session. Clearly it is better to do this in the latter part of the year, when you and the children are comfortable with the structure of the session. The children will be able to explain the format and the rules for the session and will enjoy listening to parents' opinions and sharing their ideas. Alternatively, you may wish to arrange for someone to video a session, and then invite parents in to watch it with the children.

Include philosophy in the home–school reporting system

Mention each child's contribution to philosophy in school reports under literacy or PSHE. Take time to discuss their thinking skills at parents' evenings and draw attention to work the child has done. It is fitting that philosophy is presented as being important to the child both socially and academically, and this will encourage parents to value it at home.

Parent enquiries (for the experienced facilitator)

If you have a high level of interest and support from parents in the school, and you feel confident about facilitating enquiry, you may decide that you would like to offer opportunities for interested parents to experience a dialogue with other parents, with you acting as facilitator. You might, for example, offer a session using a high-quality picture book.

Hold a book evening

You could invite parents and children to come in after school and look at the picture books that you use for philosophical enquiry. You may also be able to invite a book shop to bring copies of these books for parents to buy.

How to deal with parental concerns

You may very occasionally come across parental concerns about the type of issues that come up in your philosophical enquiry. It might be, for example, that they feel it is inappropriate to discuss death, especially if they have suffered bereavement in the family. Or some parents may think that discussing crime or monsters may frighten the child unnecessarily. There could also be concerns for families with strong religious views. Of course, each will be an individual case, and the best way to deal with the situation is to invite the parent(s) in to discuss their concern. In most cases, the parents will be reassured just to know that you and they are working in a partnership.

Children may well be scared of monsters or robbers, but the parents need to be reassured that the issues have been raised by the children themselves. P4C is not about teachers indoctrinating children with their views, but allowing them the opportunities to develop their thinking as part of a community of enquiry and with the support of their families at home.

It is often the case that the things that frighten us most are the things we don't understand, and these are the very things we want and need to discuss. By the age of four, children have already been exposed to many things beyond their comprehension through television or events in the everyday world. They think to themselves about these things, but philosophy gives them an opportunity to listen to other people's ideas, to speak aloud about them and to challenge their own thinking – all of which help to allay fears.

One of the things we have to remember is that in today's society, more than ever before, children are bombarded with information that adults decide they must have. Marketing, for example, is geared towards telling people what they should think. So it is especially important that our children are not brought up to believe passively all they see or hear.

Integrating philosophy into the classroom

One of the benefits of practising philosophical enquiry in the classroom is that this quality of thinking begins to infiltrate the whole curriculum. Children who are used to questioning and working through problems are more likely to succeed and persevere when faced with scientific, literal and mathematical problems. Children also bring their skills of enquiry to topic work, and classroom learning becomes more interesting when it is fuelled by curiosity and a journey towards a greater understanding of everything we encounter.

We have found that children who do philosophy value questioning to the point where they make philosophical comment on problems within the classroom and playground. Issues that arise from books, topic work and the school council often get the response: 'That's a good question for philosophy!'

Children quickly understand that the thinking they are learning to do in philosophy is the sort of thinking that makes them cleverer children. They appreciate that because they do philosophy they are good thinkers. And as in other subjects, to get better at something they need lots of opportunities to practise, both within the classroom community and through small-group and individual play. Here are some ideas for providing children with further opportunities to practise their philosophical thinking skills through experiential learning.

The independent philosophy area
(Philosophy Bear's thinking cave)

You might like to set up your classroom with a philosophy corner. This could be an area on the carpet, made to look like a small den or cave. Inside have a table and some cushions, leaving enough room to fit two children. Philosophy Bear can sit on the table with a stimulus (an object, a picture or a book). Try to link the stimulus to the concepts you are discussing in the philosophy sessions and change it weekly. Also on the table, place a notice (which has previously been read to the children) saying something along the lines of the one below.

> *Philosophy Bear is sitting and wondering about the thing on his table. Can you guess what questions he wants to ask?*
>
> *Find a friend and see if you can ask each other some puzzling questions. Tell Philosophy Bear your thoughts.*

The symbol cards (see page 78) could also be displayed to act as reminders of things the children can say.

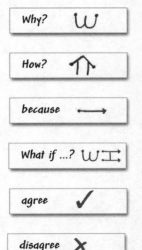

Provide a notebook and pencil for children to write about and draw their thinking. They could also be given the option of using a tape recorder to record their own or each other's questions or thoughts if they wish. Encourage the children to seek out an adult to scribe or translate their ideas. In this way a written dialogue will be created.

Display

Setting aside an area of display board for a philosophy display can be very worthwhile as it makes information accessible to parents and other visitors to the classroom, as well as to the children. This can be used to display any or all of the following:

- the sheet of children's questions from the P4C session, and any recorded dialogue (the most recent week's work pinned up over the previous week's)

- a copy of the stimulus used

- examples of children's work

- that week's homework, with points to consider

- a write-up of what other people thought about the homework question (anonymous quotes from parents, brothers and sisters, or other family members)

- a tape recorder with a cassette of the latest dialogue, and headphones

- a notice board where incidental thoughts or questions that children have brought up could be noted for later discussion

- a box next to the display board – children are encouraged to write letters or questions to Philosophy Bear and post them into the box.

Because this display area reflects what is happening in the sessions, the content is changed weekly.

It is also very easy to incorporate a philosophical theme into larger display areas, for example showing work done on fairy tales or books with a philosophical slant. Questions and thoughts that have arisen during philosophy sessions that are related to thematic displays can be pinned around the border, hung in front, or incorporated into the display itself.

Thematic philosophy

As the class becomes more confident, you may decide that you wish to extend your work with philosophy. One way of doing this is to take a theme or concept, and develop it over several sessions. As a community of enquiry, you can see where you want to take the discussion and dialogue next; you as the facilitator can then find a stimulus on the same theme that will offer further opportunities for enquiry. Working in this way helps to keep interest in both the thematic curriculum content and the philosophical content fresh and interesting to the children and the teacher.

The theme you follow could be connected with a concept, and this could be something quite abstract and/or complex, for example 'power and revenge'. Alternatively, you could choose to link in with a curriculum area, for example 'rocks and minerals'. There are philosophical aspects to most curriculum areas.

Both types of thematic study lend themselves well to making a class book. The book could contain a weekly write-up of the themed work, including:

- details of the stimulus used
- the questions asked
- key points of the dialogue
- the homework question
- children's responses to homework
- adult responses to homework
- illustrations from thinking diaries.

As the work is written up and assembled, it becomes a memorable and more permanent record of the sessions. It can be viewed by parents and visitors, and the children themselves can look through and comment on their work.

Making a class book

CASE STUDY

This is an extract from a class book put together over the five weeks with a class of Reception children. The work was based on the pack resource book *Pinocchio*.

Week 1

Stimulus: *Pinocchio*
We read the whole book and looked at the pictures. Then we reread the beginning of the story.

Concepts covered:
What is real? what is imagination?

Are voices in our head real?

CASE STUDY

These are some of the things we thought about:

- What is real? If we were deaf or had no ears, could we still hear voices?
- What is imagination? Where does imagination come from?
- Where do voices in our head come from?

How could the Wood talk?

"maybe there was a mouse inside "

Lois.

What do we think?

Voices in our head are real. They tell us what to do and are our friends because they live in our heads.

Voices in our heads come from our mouths.

But everyone has a good voice and a naughty voice in their head. The good voice tells you the right thing to do and the bad voice tells you to do naughty things, like 'play with matches'. On the Tweenies, Jake went into the garden and his good voice said, 'Don't light a match'; his bad voice said, 'Do light a match'. He did the right thing and told a grown-up.

I don't think voices are real because people think there are monsters in their heads and monsters are not real. The voices in our heads come from other people.

What do our mums and dads think?

Voices in our heads are our subconscious.

Voices are our brains telling us what to do. We could hear voices if we were deaf because our brains would still be working.

We can only know if something is real if we can see it, so maybe that's true if we hear it?

I think voices are our conscience. Some people actually believe that voices talk to them – are these people very perceptive or mentally unstable?

The voices are a way of putting things into perspective. If we were born deaf, then we probably wouldn't hear these words or voices as we hear and remember words. Whether we choose to act on these words or voices or ignore them is a matter of choice.

Voices are quiet thoughts. Our emotions and senses intensify and at the time seem real enough.

Sometimes people who are ill hear voices telling them to do things that are dangerous or bad. They may well hear the voices, so in that sense they are 'real', but it doesn't mean people really are telling them what to do.

A philosophy club

A philosophy club provides opportunities for interested children to develop philosophical thinking further. The club can provide the opportunity to work in a smaller group than in class (probably about 12 to 18 members) and within a mixed-age group. (Ours is drawn from Reception to Year 5, with children who have moved up to middle school being invited back as well.) The advantage of the mixed-age group is that the younger children can have access to a wide range of experiences and ideas from their peers, rather than from the adult facilitator alone. It also offers a more relaxed and informal setting because the children have a collective disposition towards the subject and have chosen to join the club for their own enjoyment. The following guidelines for running a philosophy club are based on my experience of what has worked in my own school. The club runs for an hour and a half after school, once a week, and the children each have a philosophy diary which they use just for the club.

> For all knowledge and wonder (which is the seed of knowledge) is an impression of pleasure in itself.
>
> FRANCIS BACON

Start with drinks and biscuits. During this drinking, eating and chatting time, the children have a chance to look through their diaries and share with the group any of their thoughts, ideas or comments from adults. This also provides a chance to refresh everyone's memories of the last session and where it was agreed to take the present session.

As in classroom philosophy, encourage the children to draw up a set of common rules for the club sessions. These can be written up in their philosophy diaries.

Do not hurt anyone's feelings.

Look at the person talking.

Do not interrupt – wait for them to finish talking.

Don't talk over the top of anyone else.

Try to be fair and let everyone speak.

Never shout or get cross with anyone.

Keep your body still and calm.

Rules agreed by Philosophy Club at Chapel Break School

Because the group is smaller in size, it can provide an opportunity to try out new games (see Part 4) and activities. Here are some that have proved successful.

- **Role play**. Re-enact a Socratic dialogue, dressed as ancient Greek philosophers.

- **Drama starter**. Use drama as a starting point for discussions. Anthony Browne's *Piggybook* proved especially fruitful. The children were asked to write letters in role as either Mrs Piggot, Mr Piggot or the boys. The letters were read out and used as a stimulus.

- **Philosophy buddies**. Each child chooses someone else from philosophy club to share their ideas with. They write in each other's journals and respond to each other in writing or annotated pictures. Some children might even choose to correspond by posting the journal back and forth to a friend in another school or another part of the country, or to grandparents, cousins or a separated parent. These journals are treated as private, and it should be the child's choice as to whether they share any correspondence with the club. The principle is that thoughts and ideas about philosophy and how it fits into their lives are given high status.

- **Web discussion**. Find and join in with some philosophical message boards on the web. We use the children's discussion board on childrenthinking and the Philosopher's Tea Party (details on page 165).

- **A philosophy club book**. Compile a record of the club sessions and include questions and thoughts about themes or favourite stories.

- **Posters**. In pairs or individually, make posters to put up around the school with philosophical questions and illustrations.

- **Philosophy murals**. Provide a large roll of paper and present the stimulus in the normal way. Children then record any thoughts and questions in writing and pictures on the roll of paper to produce a mural of ideas and questions.

- **Display board.** Work together to produce a display board based on a stimulus or on a philosophical theme. Alternatively, create a What is philosophy? display. Make sure the board is credited as the philosophy club's work.

- **Leaflets.** Make leaflets for parents and visitors about the philosophy club. As well as giving basic information about when and where, explain what the club is, what you do and what you get from it.

Philosophy club – dialogue from a homework question

CASE STUDY

In a philosophy club, dialogues may often arise directly from reviewing homework. For example, after a session on *Zoo* by Anthony Browne, one child had written in her homework diary:

- If humans evolved from monkeys, why do we still have monkeys?

During our informal chat time, it became clear that this should be the topic for the dialogue. In fact, the children were so eager to start this discussion that the biscuits were left half eaten!

Here is some of the dialogue that ensued.

Tayma: I think the answer is that human monkeys are different from animal monkeys.

Josh: Monkeys come from cells.

Dylan: But where do cells come from?

Jacob: Species in the sea come from a shell, but how did it get there?

Roxanne: Well, people came from heaven because God is up there. Maybe God made us exist.

Nikita: But who exactly invented God?

Mark: Mary and Joseph of course.

Tayma: Well, where did they come from?

Mark: God – well – they must have come from heaven.

Kyle: Who are God's mum and dad then?

Maria: God isn't from Mary and Joseph – Jesus is.

Kyle: But God made the planets.

Ryan: How?

Roxanne: With salt and water.

Nikita: But where did God come from?

Roxanne: It's all like in a cycle, round and round. We have to work out where the beginning is. First salt and water and clouds make the person.

Josh: Maybe one girl was Eve and one was Adam. They were the first ones made.

Jacob: But God was the first one made. Something in the sky has a mind and that was God, and then he made himself into a human and he made Adam and Eve and they had babies, and that's where the life cycle began.

Jasmin: I disagree. I think that Adam and Eve used to live on another planet far, far away, that was really beautiful, until they bit into a poisoned apple and then they had to come to this planet and they died.

Tayma: We don't know for sure that they are even dead.

Jasmin: They are, because a few weeks after that a terrible storm came, and she died, and Adam died for no reason, because loneliness makes you die, you know.

Josh: But it comes from the Bible.

Nikita: How do we know the Bible is real?

Josh: It's about who you trust, isn't it?

Daisy: There are different gods for different countries.

Mark: Yes, and God is our god.

Leo: He isn't real – Jesus is real, but God isn't.

Kyle: But Jesus is God's son, so why do people say they are the same person?

Jasmin: But Joseph is Jesus' dad, so maybe God is Joseph's dad.

Daisy: I think we are all getting confused here, There are lots of gods. Jesus is our second god, but only God is our real god.

God can fly.

At this point the children themselves admitted their confusion and turned to me for help. I wanted them to think more carefully about what they meant when they used the terms 'God' or 'magic' to explain a cause for an event they didn't understand. I gave a simplified and brief explanation of the two arguments of creationism and Darwinism. We then found a piece of material and we worked together to dress our first philosopher up in a Greek-style toga. The role-play dialogue began with the assumption that we were looking for an alternative explanation for the creation of our world. The philosophers had to think of their reasons and justify their ideas to the assembled crowd.

→

Roxanne: I think that God didn't make us. Probably salt and water from heaven made us. They dissolve in the clouds and make humans. We are made from salt and water and clouds because we are protected.

Jasmin: I don't understand why you are saying God isn't real. Why are you saying that?

Roxanne: He can't be real because who exactly made God? People are made from salt and water because salt and water are very useful to lots of people. It's useful for cuts and ulcers. You can make things from salt and water, but it's a bit like glue and you can stick and you can build a castle with sand and water, but not when it is dry sand. You can shape it with your hands when it is wet.

Leo: But our bones aren't sand and water though. How are we made from clouds? Because I can touch myself and I don't go right through me, do I?

Jasmin: And where did our skin come from? Because that's not cloud either.

Roxanne: But our skin gets wet when we run about and get sweaty, and sweat is made from the clouds inside and under our skin.

Jasmin: Oh yes! And our body has other liquid in, like when we go to the toilet and stuff, I see what you are saying, Roxanne!

In the course of this dialogue Jasmin had turned her thinking around and begun to further develop Roxanne's argument. I seized the opportunity to discuss the progress they were making as philosophers and the advantages of listening to each other's ideas with open minds.

The rewards of working with philosophy come when you realize how prepared the children are to lead their own enquiries and facilitate such discourse themselves; to step away from what they think the adults want to hear and be confident in their ideas and reasons.

Philosophy resources

Finally, it is worthwhile having a box (or several) in which to collect resources for use in philosophy. These could include useful books, pictures and other stimuli as well as reference books and articles you find on P4C. If these boxes are kept in the staffroom, then all staff will be able to find a good stimulus quickly without having to search the library or book shelves. It is also helpful to keep a notebook to record any new ideas for stimuli that you have used, or books that you have seen and would like to order for use in philosophy.

Why do they have these bad thing's on the New's

Frankie Massingham

Part 4

Practical ideas to support philosophical thinking

Relaxation and philosophy

Relaxation is an important part of preparing a class for philosophical enquiry. Although the philosophy sessions are best suited to early morning slots, we have to remember that many young children have already been awake for several hours. They may have had a bad start to the day or be holding on to other experiences or memories from the evening before. We also have to remember that children cannot be expected to do heavy thinking on top of heavy thoughts. Relaxation sessions can teach very important skills that the children will transfer to the enquiry. They will also build on the classroom bonding process that P4C develops. As Joanna Haynes (2001) writes:

> Knowledge and skill in physical and mental relaxation promote
> healthy self-maintenance, greater self-control and personal autonomy.
> Regular relaxation practice can contribute to the development of
> mindfulness and meta-cognitive ability.

Mindfulness is simply the ability we have to notice without effort and, beyond this, to be aware of the opinions and judgements we make. Further training in mindfulness allows us to notice our own and others' judgements without automatically reacting to them: our default state becomes one of reflection and considered action. Philosophical enquiry and mindfulness reinforce one another and lead us away from any tendency to a knee-jerk reflex of opinion or impulsive action.

Relaxation activities to prepare for deeper thinking

Relaxation is a state of non-effort: a simple letting go of any attempt to do anything (or indeed trying not to do anything!). Because the mind and the body work together, mental relaxation has profound and beneficial physical effects, and vice versa. This is not to say that nothing happens during relaxation. The brain switches to the so-called 'alpha state', also known as the state of relaxed alertness, wherein attention can be fine-focused or diffused, and where attention can be sustained easily for long periods of time. In alpha state, the analytical, conscious part of the mind and the holistic, Big Picture, symbol-speaking subconscious are more closely connected and can communicate more effectively. The 'meaning-making' process which lies at the heart of all creativity and learning is enhanced under such circumstances, although accessing the alpha state can also be used as an end in itself – for pure enjoyment – or as a precursor to more consciously oriented endeavours, such as philosophical enquiry.

Two key features of relaxation training are:

- regularity of practice
- anchoring.

To begin training the children to access the alpha state, choose a particular time of day and make this a regular feature of what goes on in your classroom. Position yourself in the same spot each time as you lead children through the relaxation process (we are reluctant to use the phrase 'relaxation exercises'– although some term has to be coined in describing the individual techniques!). Establish further associations, for instance by playing the same piece of music as a lead-in to relaxation practice. (Choose a gentle instrumental piece, naturally.) Another anchor might take the form of an object that children can gaze at as they relax, or something they can hold – a small stone or shell, for example. When these links become familiar, any one of them can then trigger the alpha state, even outside the usual time and place where relaxation practice occurs.

A number of relaxation 'exercises' are suggested below. Use what works for you, and be aware also that different techniques are likely to work for different children. With this in mind, take a creative approach to the training and be prepared to adapt and play with the exercises singly and in combination to achieve the most beneficial results. Having said that, we suggest using the following activity (or should that be 'lack of activity'?) as a starter.

Starter activity

Having chosen your time, place and anchors, take a little while to allow the children to become more aware of their own bodies. Tell them to notice the position of their bodies as they sit at their tables. Notice physical sensations, feelings, even thoughts as they drift by. Just notice these things; there's no need to do anything more.

Now draw the children's attention to colours in the room, to the shapes of things, to little details. Be aware of sounds and smells. Are there any sounds coming from far away? What are the smallest sounds that can be heard? What are the nearest sounds? Let the children's attention expand and contract like a gently flexing lens. No need to hurry this or be too prescriptive. If a child is fidgety or says they are bored, just tell them that's fine, and ask them simply to notice the fidgeting and the feelings of boredom. And how interesting that is – just to step back in your mind and be aware of these things going on.

After a while, have the children look at an object you have chosen for this purpose, or ask them to become aware of a small object they are holding. Again, take time to let them absorb the details of its size, shape, weight, texture, temperature, and any associations with it that arise in the mind.

Then suggest that the children gaze at a blank spot on the wall or close their eyes. Ask them to let their thoughts come together to create an impression (a picture, if you like) of the room as they remember it. Just notice what thoughts appear – there's no need to try to remember what the room is like. Suggest that the children can play with this picture; they can add bits and change bits and take bits away. Maintain a sense of playfulness and good humour throughout: if your suggestions and voice tones reinforce this, it will be a further powerful association with the alpha state.

Now ask the children's wonderful imaginations to create a pleasant, safe and comfortable place in their minds. Be 'artfully vague' in your suggestions – avoid supplying much detail, but make sure the children have a definite task to do. So, you might say, 'And now you can notice many colours in this place, and be really pleased and maybe a bit surprised by just how many different colours come into your mind ... And I don't know if this will happen right now or in a few moments' time, but you will find that you'll notice some new and interesting things in this place ... I wonder what you'll notice first...'

Be assured that you don't need to keep talking throughout. Suggesting things in this rather vague and fuzzy manner stimulates the children's subconscious resources and allows rich scenarios to unfold spontaneously with little or no conscious effort. Most children are happy just to drift along in this daydreamy way for as long as you want them to – and often enough they will be reluctant to return to the busy world of 'normal waking consciousness' – 'Oh, I was really enjoying that! It was really nice. Do I have to open my eyes and do work now?'

To close the session, tell the children that the special place they have created in their mind will always be there for them, but now it's time to leave it. Bring their attention back to their own bodies, then tell them to open their eyes (if they're closed) and come fully awake and feeling brilliant as they look at you – now.

If children spontaneously come out of alpha state before the end of relaxation time, that's fine. Just ask them to sit patiently, or even look at a book. If a child becomes upset during a relaxation, it may be because an unpleasant thought or memory has come to mind. (The subconscious will sometimes do this when people are consciously relaxed, as a way of asking the logical, analytical conscious part of the mind to help deal with the material.) If you notice that a child looks upset, you can either ask them to put those thoughts away for now – because they have earned this relaxation time and can enjoy it – or you might deal with the issue immediately. If you have another adult in the room who can continue the session, that's ideal, as you take the upset child out to resolve matters. (For techniques for developing children's emotional capabilities, see Steve Bowkett's *Self-Intelligence*.)

Individual relaxation exercises

Balloon breathing

Breathing in a controlled manner produces calmness and tranquillity. Not only does it develop the child's self-awareness, but when the whole class participates it can break down negative energies that may exist within the group.

Ensure children have enough space to lie comfortably; all in a circle with feet in the middle and heads on the outside works well as it allows you to walk around the perimeter, checking on breathing. Remind the children that this exercise should be done seriously and that they should aim to be completely focused on your words and their own breathing. Ensure children have their arms resting on the ground, a little way from the body, palms up. Legs should be shoulder-width apart; feet relaxed and rolling out to the side. Then give instructions as follows:

- Place one hand gently on your tummy, close your eyes and imagine that your tummy is a soft, coloured balloon.

- Breathe in slowly through your nose, imagining that the balloon is inflating – rising slowly and gently to the sky. Make sure you do not push the balloon, but just let it rise gently with your breath.

- Now breathe out slowly, letting the air out of your nose and visualizing the balloon emptying and returning to its soft, deflated form. Make sure you do this slowly and stay in control.

Repeat this sequence five times.

This exercise can also be done sitting up, either cross-legged, or in the lotus position for those who are able. Ensure that spines are straight and tall, but not locked rigid.

Muddy feet

This exercise relaxes the body through breathing and correcting posture, which in turn relieves tension in the head, shoulders and spine.

Start with the feet hip-width apart. Make sure the spine is kept straight but not locked, neck level with the spine. The head should be light and floaty. Ask the children to feel that their feet are level and that they have equal weight on each leg. Then give instructions as follows:

- Breathe in and out gently and slowly through your nose.

- Now close your eyes and imagine that your feet are sinking into thick, warm mud. Let your feet sink while breathing slowly, quietly and deeply.

- Wriggle your toes, imagining the warm mud between them.

- Now try and lift just your big toes, keeping all the other toes still.

- Now lift all your small toes while keeping your big toes on the ground. Keep breathing slowly and deeply, concentrating fully on your toes.

- Next, slowly raise one foot above the mud and hold it a few centimetres above the ground. Hold the balance for a count of five. Gently place your foot down, imagining that you are putting it down into a bowl of warm water. Repeat with the other foot.

- End the exercise by wriggling all your toes in the imaginary bowl of water.

During the exercise, you can move quietly around the group, checking for relaxed shoulders. Simply placing your hands on a tense child's shoulders can help them relax.

Tree pose

- Stand with your legs hip-width apart. Feel your feet and legs strong like the trunk of a tree.

- Breathe in deeply and slowly through your nose, and raise your arms above your head. Hold your breath for 3 seconds, then exhale slowly through a slightly open mouth to make a small sighing noise. Imagine that this is the sound of the gentle breeze in the branches of the tree. Lower the arms.

- Repeat this three times.

- Now make the tree stronger by joining your legs together to make one strong tree trunk.

- Inhale through your nose and bring your arms above your head.

- Focus on one person opposite in the circle. Keep your eyes on that person the whole time. Now carefully raise one leg up to the inside of the knee of the other leg. By concentrating hard you will be able to balance much better. Hold the balance for a count of five. Gently lower the leg and arms.

- Repeat with the other leg.

Praise good balance and focus. This exercise can be extended for those who have developed good balance by asking them to bring their hands in front of the upper abdomen in the prayer position. Older children could also turn the raised leg out to the side. Check that children maintain calm, even breathing throughout this exercise.

Relaxation in pairs

The following exercises can be used at any time in the school day, and work especially well after playtimes. Find a piece of slow piano music to use for all these exercises.

For each exercise, ask children to find a partner. Alternatively, consider pairing children with someone they don't usually work with, as this develops new relationships and trust.

Piano partners

- Sit cross-legged on the floor facing your partner.
- Decide which of you will be the piano and which the piano player. If you are the piano, hold both hands in front of you at waist height – palms up, fingers long. Your fingers are the piano keys.
- If you are the player, place your fingers palm down on top of your partner's fingers – the piano keys. Concentrating on their fingers, gently press the keys in time to the music. Try to play all the keys.

After about 2 minutes, children swap roles. At the end of the exercise, ask the children to bow to their partners, smile and say thank you.

When they can do this exercise with confidence and using all the fingers, encourage them to maintain eye contact with their partner.

Drawing partners

- Sit cross-legged on the floor, one in front of the other and both facing the same way.

- Both close your eyes and concentrate on the gentle, calming music.

- If you are sitting behind your partner, draw a pattern on their back that matches the music. Keep your finger straight and firm so that your partner can feel the movement.

After a few minutes, children swap roles. At the end of the exercise, ask the children to say thank you to their partners and talk about how it felt to be drawn on.

As the children perform this exercise, you can walk around the group, checking all children have a straight but not rigid back, and a relaxed posture in the neck and shoulders.

It might be helpful to model a variety of patterns the children could use beforehand, for example spirals, circles, straight lines, hearts and stars.

Puppet partners

Tell the children that they are going to pretend to be puppets – so they will only be able to move their bodies if their strings are pulled.

First, ask them to watch as you demonstrate. Holding an imaginary string above your head, gently and slowly turn your head to the side as you pull the string in the same direction. Return your head in a controlled manner to the centre and repeat the other way. Then demonstrate a gentle but pronounced nod, tucking the head onto the chest, and return.

Then show how you can tilt the head to each side, always passing and pausing in a central position. Finally, demonstrate the same kind of actions with your arms and legs.

Then ask the children to try the same with their own arms. Tell them to pull the imaginary string to lift their own arm, hold it still and then bounce it gently. Then tell them to release the string, making sure that the limb falls loosely with no resistance. When they have got the idea, ask them to pair up for the exercise.

- Stand facing each other, legs hip-width apart.
- Decide who will be the puppeteer and who will be the puppet.
- If you are the puppet, imagine that your head is held up by a string coming out of the very top of your head. Keep your spine straight and your head on a long, relaxed neck. Remember that you can only move when your strings are pulled. Watch the puppeteer and be ready to move.
- If you are the puppeteer, gently lift the puppet's limb using the invisible string, bounce it gently and then release it. Puppet, as you move, make sure you stay floppy and relaxed. You must both concentrate hard on each other's movements.

After a few minutes, children swap roles.

As the children become more confident and able to do this exercise with arms and legs, build in movement of the back.

Relaxation through visualization

Once children feel comfortable with the relaxation and breathing exercises, visual imagery and simple meditation techniques can be introduced.

You can explain to the children that meditation is simply a way of keeping their minds quiet and still. It is a form of relaxation and a way of emptying the mind of all thoughts to create a clear, quiet space. Emphasize to the children that this is something they have complete control over, and in training their mind to be calm and focused they are learning a very important skill.

Fingertips (catch your heart)

Children sit in a circle, cross-legged and relaxed. Explain to the children that they will be able, with practice, to feel their heart moving around their body.

- Place your hands in front of your tummy with the very tips of all fingers and thumbs touching. Close your eyes.

- Breathe in and out, slowly and steadily, through your nose.

- Now press your fingertips together firmly and try to imagine you can feel your heartbeat in your fingertips.

- As you breathe in and out, focus on the pulse movement. Now try to visualize your heart travelling in a circle around the body. The more you concentrate on this, the more strongly you will feel the heartbeat in your fingers.

Practise this for a few minutes each day. If the children are unable to detect their pulse, encourage them to raise their hands above their head until they can feel it.

The sweet jar exercise

Children sit in a circle, spines straight and relaxed, hands placed softly in their laps.

- Close your eyes and imagine a jar of sweets in your head. You can decide what shape, size and colour they are, but you must not tell anyone what they look like.

- Now see the sweets slowly turning black. When all the sweets are black, see them start to disappear as you breathe. See a few more vanish with each breath you take. Keep breathing in and out slowly and steadily through your nose.

- Soon the jar will be empty. As a reward for careful breathing and concentrating, imagine the jar very gradually filling up again with new sweets. Try to visualize the appearance of each new sweet with every breath. Imagine its size, colour, texture, shape and smell. But remember, no talking to others.

- Now see the jar completely full up. Choose one sweet and imagine you are eating it. Concentrate on the flavour, smell and texture. Carry on breathing slowly and deeply.

- Now choose another sweet and make a picture in your head of someone you would like to give it to – but do not tell anyone whom you have chosen.

Then hand each child a small piece of paper and a pencil. Ask them to draw their sweet and then place it in a pile in the middle of the circle, keeping silent all the while. When they have all returned to their places in the circle, hand out the sweet pictures randomly. Ask the children to make a picture in their mind of the sweet they have been given, and give them a couple of minutes to imagine themselves eating it. End the exercise by allowing them to talk to their neighbours about the taste, shape, texture, smell and colour of that sweet.

Special places

This exercise is done to some relaxing music, with children in a circle, sitting in a relaxed position.

- Close your eyes and listen to the music.

- While you listen, think of a place where you would always feel happy and safe, and imagine you are there. Perhaps you are on a beach, or flying in the sky, or at home, or in a wood ... or somewhere else.

- Make a picture in your head of where you are and what you can see. And visualize who you can see. Can you see your friends or people in your family, or perhaps your pets?

- Imagine that you feel warm and light as a feather. What can you hear? What can you smell?

- Now visualize what you are doing. Remember that you are feeling happy and safe.

- Now it is time to return to the classroom. Imagine yourself walking back through the classroom door, and in your mind see yourself sitting on the carpet again. When you are ready, you can open your eyes.

Throughout this exercise, ensure that children stay focused, with eyes and mouths closed. Afterwards, allow the children to draw their special place in their thinking journal. With the music playing, encourage them to draw the scene in silence. When it is finished, praise the children for their concentration and calm, and allow them to show their picture to a neighbour, giving a verbal description of it.

Games and activities to develop philosophical thinking and talking

The following games and activities can serve several purposes. They can be used to start or punctuate a philosophy session. They could also be used before a session to stimulate or further develop discussion – or afterwards to set up starting points for another session. They develop key skills that are used in P4C:

- a sense of community and turn-taking

- questioning skills

- making connections

- decision making

- dialogue skills.

Some of these games have been developed and adapted from ideas devised by Karin Murris, Joanna Haynes and Roger Sutcliffe; the rest have been developed with the children in Philosophy Club at Chapel Break. It is important that the children understand why they are doing these games and activities so that they engage with the philosophical element as well as having fun. Before each activity, ask the children to really think about which skills they will be practising and how they transfer to a P4C session.

A sense of community and turn-taking

These games and activities serve to demonstrate to the children the importance of working as a class in the sessions. The very nature of P4C means that the children have to work as a class to decide what they want to discuss and explore. This means working towards an atmosphere of trust and safety so every child feels confident that their views will be listened to and their ideas valued, even where there is disagreement. In every class there will be children who find it difficult to take turns, and this domination by a few can be intimidating for others in the group. Equally, there might be others who lack confidence or feel embarrassed to speak out. The following games can help children at both these extremes.

> He who is unable to live in society, or who has no need because he is sufficient for himself, must be either a beast or a god.
>
> ARISTOTLE

With these games that rely on co-operation, it is very important that no member of the class is made to feel they have let the group down. Avoid mentioning names and put the emphasis on the whole class working together.

Thoughts in the wind

This activity can be played purely as a turn-taking game, but can also be used to develop philosophical thinking as the children become more confident and literate.

Version 1 – for very young children. Arrange the class in a circle. Give each child a small square of paper and ask them to draw their face or write their name on it. Explain to the children that this paper represents their personal thoughts. The aim of the game is for everybody to throw their thoughts into the middle of the circle, one at a time. If two or more pieces of paper are thrown at the same time, the papers have to be picked up and the game starts again. Encourage the children to do this in silence.

In this activity, the children must become aware of their peers and discover how to tune in to what they are doing. They have to develop heightened awareness of the movements of those around them and be willing to wait to throw their thought.

Version 2 – for older children. This version of the game is extended to encourage the children to start discussing their thoughts and using the language of dialogue: 'I agree', 'I disagree' and 'I'm not sure'. The game could be used at the start of a session to revisit concepts covered in a previous session or as an introduction to new concepts that will be discussed in the current session. It could also serve as a useful round-up (where are we in our thinking?) at the end of a session.

Start by presenting a statement to the class, for example 'It is always wrong to tell a lie'. Then ask the children to draw a symbol to indicate whether they agree (tick) or disagree (cross) with the statement, or are not sure (question mark). Older and more able children could write the words instead. They can also choose whether they put their name on the paper.

Everyone must then throw their thoughts into the middle of the circle, in the same way as in version 1. When all the papers have been successfully thrown, children each pick up a paper from the middle, one at a time, trying to avoid picking up their own. If the children have written their responses and put their names, you can extend the activity by asking a few children to read or describe what is on the paper they have picked up. The person who dropped that thought is then invited to say why they chose to agree or disagree. A mini-dialogue can be created in this way.

Stand up / sit down

This is Karin Murris' wonderful activity. Arrange the class in a circle. The aim of the game is that each child will stand up in turn; if two or more people stand at the same time, all must sit down and start again.

When the class have achieved this, they repeat the procedure in reverse – this time aiming for all to be sitting. To make it even harder, try the activity with eyes closed. (Remember to nominate one person to oversee by keeping their eyes open!)

The purpose of this game is to build the skills of the community. Learning to become aware of each other and take turns will enhance the way they work together within the community of enquiry.

Same as

Arrange the class in a circle and include one extra chair or space within it. Explain to the children that you or a nominated member of the group will choose a category of children who must then move across the circle, for example 'Find a new place to stand/sit if you have shirt buttons undone.' The catch is that the children who have to move must do so one at a time. This means that they have to take turns to fill the place vacated by the person who has moved just before.

The exercise can be repeated as many times as you like, choosing a variety of different categories. To develop this further, you could ask children to fill the empty space if they agree with a given statement, for example 'You are the same person when you are old.' You can interchange the words 'agree' and 'disagree'. Children have to be ready to justify their answer if asked.

Questioning skills and making connections

The following activities are designed to develop the idea that questions and statements may have several links and connections. Our brains make sense of the world by creating connections. Through time we establish in our heads what might be called a 'map of reality' – an amazingly complex network of links and associations. This map is not reality, of course, for no map is the actual territory it represents. Furthermore, it is constantly being updated as we absorb more and more information – and here we think it is useful to consider 'information' as 'in-formation', stuff that we can manipulate in various ways to help enrich the map and increase our understanding.

There is a direct link between what we think, say and feel and the way neural networks in our brains are 'wired up'. In other words, connections between brain cells are the physical analogue of the thoughts we think and the words we speak to express our own reality. Such neural connections form what has been called the *brainscape*. All of our brainscapes have features in common, but many individual differences exist that contribute to our uniqueness. The mental expression of the brain's activities might be termed the *thoughtscape*: the rich and varied complex of beliefs, ideas and understandings that allow us to engage with the world in a purposeful way. The patterns of language we employ to articulate our thoughts (mentally using our own 'inner voices' and outwardly through speech) form the *wordscape*, one very significant feature of which is the range of metaphors we use to understand and describe our reality.

> **An intellectual is someone whose mind watches itself.**
>
> ALBERT CAMUS

There are three immediate implications that arise from these ideas:

- Activities which are integrative, that encourage the creation of links and associations, mirror the brain's natural processes and boost learning.

- Reflecting upon the meanings we make and being curious about the words and metaphors we use increases our ability to process information and consolidate our understandings.

- Noticing how we define and describe reality strengthens our metacognitive skills (our capacity to think about and influence the thinking we do). Accelerated learning theory has long recognized that 'doing metacognition' empowers children as learners.

The very act of learning implies making connections. We can help our children to be better learners by raising their awareness of this process and by giving them strategies for gaining greater control over it. The linking games that follow can act as precursors to the activities under the heading Thinking skills and dialogue (page 131) that have a more direct application to P4C.

The simile game

This is a useful way of raising children's awareness of how their minds work. Begin by saying something like 'The mind is a like a spider's web because ... ?' and allow the group to come up with comparisons. (The 'because' suggests and encourages reasoned comparisons.) Continue perhaps with:

- The mind is like a map because ...
- The mind is like a garden because ...
- The mind is like music because ...
- The mind is like a rocket ship because ...

And so on. Become more adventurous by noticing objects in the classroom to use as the basis for similes. Subsequently, invite the children to generate entire similes for themselves. Conclude a session by making the point (in this case) that the mind is like all of these things, and many more.

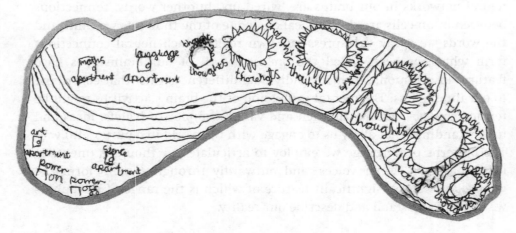

The bisociation game

Links between two previously unrelated things are called *bisociations*. This habit of thought can be encouraged by using a 6 x 6 grid filled with pictures, or a mixture of words and pictures. Try to include both objects and abstract ideas, for example:

a castle	a hole in the ground	an axe	the sun	a dragon	a two-headed dog
a king	a flower	falling rocks	a winged horse	a backwards-walking man	a ring
a picture frame	a whirlpool	a chain	a loaf of bread	a storm	a mask
a dog	three friends	a shooting star	some leaves	an explosion	the moon
mountains	a book	a cave	an ear of wheat	a forest	a princess
a river	a pair of eyes	a wise old man	a fairy	a dream	a cloak

Begin by saying to the children, 'I'm going to pick two things from this grid. As soon as I've told you the two things, notice how your mind puts them together to make a new idea.'

Encourage simple links – many children assume they have to start making up a story using the two items. So you might choose, for example, the *dragon* and the *backwards-walking man*. Responses to this pair might include:

- The man was walking backwards away from the dragon.
- The dragon was the man's pet.
- The man was walking backwards and was going to fall into a hole, and the dragon saved him.
- The man was the dragon's pet!
- The man was looking for the dragon.
- The man was hunting the dragon.

And so on. Subsequently, choose items randomly by rolling dice. This element of the unexpected adds a sense of enjoyable anticipation to the game.

The three-column game

This activity encourages more complex linkings (*trisociations*). Create a grid of three columns and eleven rows like the one below. Number the rows 2 to 12. Fill each column with words and/or pictures from a different subject area. For example, in the first column you could have features of the landscape and weather; in the second column, motifs from a familiar fairy tale; in the third column, concepts from mathematics.

	Features of the landscape	Motifs from traditional tales	Maths motifs
2	river	wolf	measure
3	mountains	home	size
4	forest	path	compare
5	woods	family	three
6	hills	Red Riding Hood	(not) enough
7	shore	temptation	(too) much / little
8	sky	gift	(too) many / few
9	lake	mirror	about the same
10	meadow	wheel	(just) over
11	cliffs	opposites	(just) under
12	valley	Grandma	half

Tell the children that you will choose something from each column, and ask them to notice how quickly their mind puts the three things together to form an idea. Roll two dice together to choose an item from each column. For example, on the grid shown responses could include:

- Little Red Riding Hood was crossing the hills carrying three cakes.

- The wolf asked for half of the cakes for himself when he met Little Red Riding Hood by the river.

- Grandma said she had too much food and would give some of the cakes to the birds that lived in the forest.

And so on. Notice how these links tend to be richer and more complex than bisociations. They are also seedbeds for philosophical enquiry, and can easily be developed into original variations of old stories.

It is through practice that children learn to see connections. Once they can do this, they are more able to see the philosophical concepts and bigger issues that these connections illustrate. It is when connections are made that the children edge further towards understanding what these questions

First 4 Letters of Last Name

S	M	i	T

Last 4 digits of Learning Centre No

3	6	5	O

Item must be issued before leaving Key Text Area.

↑------------------------------------↑

Adsetts

To renew items online at

http://catalogue.shu.ac.uk/patroninfo

☎ 0114 225 2116

Sheffield
Hallam University

SHARPENS YOUR THINKING

are really asking, which in turn helps them build on their ideas. These activities also help promote discussion among the group, and the game format means that children who are less vocal in enquiry sessions may well feel more confident about sharing their views.

Skipping-rope connections

Prepare a set of questions on cards. You could use questions from the list below, or use selected questions from the sessions or other good open-ended questions of your own. Provide each child with a skipping rope or piece of string and a card with a question. Explain that everyone must move around the space, reading their question aloud to each person they meet. If they meet someone who has a question that they feel is connected in some way with their own, then they should join up by giving the other person the other end of their rope. The idea is to join with as many people as possible, using the skipping ropes. The connections can be as tenuous as they like, as long as they can justify the connection. If there are any children who have not been able to join a rope, you can ask the children to listen to that question and see if anyone can provide a link. At any point in this activity you can move among the groups, asking children to explain their reasons for connection.

Skipping-rope connections questions

- Why do people want money?
- Why are some people more important than others?
- Why did Red Riding Hood visit her granny?
- Is there magic in the world?
- Does money bring happiness?
- Why did Goldilocks steal the porridge?
- Was Pinocchio real?
- Why was Jack scared of the giant?
- Was it right for Jack to take the giant's harp?
- Were the magic beans really magic?
- Why didn't the stepmother like Cinderella?
- Was Sleeping Beauty dreaming it all?
- How did Beauty fall in love with the Beast?
- What is love?
- Do we choose who we fall in love with?
- Should the three pigs' mother have sent them off by themselves?
- What's the difference between stealing and borrowing?
- Why are stepmothers in fairy tales always horrible?
- Why wasn't Jack told off for taking all that gold?
- What is a conscience?
- Is revenge right?

You could also do this activity using picture cards or objects. Fairy-tale characters are ideal.

CASE STUDY

Skipping-rope connections

These connections were made in a game of Skipping-rope connections by a Reception class. They were given a selection of fairy-tale characters and examples of questions they had raised and discussed.

- The princess is connected to the prince because they are married and are both good. (Questions: Can you marry someone different to you? Can a good prince marry a bad princess?)

- The queen, the fairy and the princess are all beautiful and nice. (Questions: What is beauty? Can you be beautiful and not nice?)

- The witch, the fairy and the wizard can all do magic. (Questions: What is magic? Is magic real? What's the difference between a trick and magic?)

- The dragon, the stepmother, the bad queen, the giant and the witch are all bad and angry. (Questions: Can you be good and angry? Were these characters born bad?)

- The beast, the giant, the frog and the seven dwarfs are opposites in size. (Questions: Does difference matter? Is big better or more powerful than small?)

Are beautiful Princesses nice?

- The beast and the dragon are both good on the inside (Lois thought the dragon was good because he had eaten a good prince). (Questions: Do we have 'good' inside us. What is inside us? What is it that makes us who we are?)

Philosophical Connect Four

Make a grid on a large sheet of paper: the best format is seven squares across and six down. You will also need four different sets of picture cards, each set a different colour. The list below gives some ideas for pictures.

The children work in two teams. The aim is to be the first team to get four connecting cards in a row, horizontally, diagonally or vertically on the grid. The two teams line up, seated in a queue. Each member of the team is given a colour-coded picture card (for example red for team A; blue for team B). The players then take it in turns to stick their card on the grid (use sticky tack). Turns must be taken in strict order, from alternate teams and moving from the front of the team line to the back. When a card is placed on the grid next to another card of the same colour, a connection must be made and justified if it is to be allowed to stay there. Members of the same team can try and think of a connection if their team-mate struggles. Players can also challenge a member of the opposing team if no connection is offered. It is up to the class to debate and justify any dubious connections. You could elect a judge who has the deciding vote. The first team to achieve a line of four cards wins.

This game can be done in the same way with children placing themselves on a giant grid on the floor or playground.

Philosophical Connect Four pictures

• a fish	• a tap	• an umbrella
• a bucket	• a hat	• a tree
• a flower	• a bird	• a coin
• a windmill	• a mouse	• a house
• a cup	• an apple	• a cage
• a policeman	• a knife	• a heart
• a wand	• an egg	• a dice
• a fossil	• a bone	• a newspaper
• a fire	• a robber	• an old lady
• a man	• a baby	

When choosing objects, try and include some that symbolize abstract and philosophical themes (for example a heart representing love). This will throw up connections that may have a philosophical consequence.

This is also fun to play with a set of fairy-tale cards.

Fairy-tale Connect Four pictures

• Snow White	• a fairy godmother	• an evil queen
• a frog	• a prince	• a wicked witch
• a huntsman	• a wolf	• a grandma
• a pig	• Red Riding Hood	• a giant
• a queen	• a princess	• a goblin
• a monster	• a mermaid	• a bear
• a dragon	• the Gingerbread Man	• a king

The connections that the children make between the figures involve the elements of story such as power, revenge, trust, love, hate, belief, ethics and social conventions. These can be discussed briefly during the game or in greater depth after the game is finished.

Think quick

This is another active game, based on the playground game, Duck, duck, goose.

The children stand in a circle. One person is chosen to walk around the outside of the circle (the chaser) and touch the children's heads in turn. The chaser touches each head silently until they get to the person they want to race with. When they touch that person's head, they call out a word they have been given by the teacher from the list below. The chaser and the person chosen must now chase each other back to the chosen child's place. The winner is usually the chaser, so they stay in the place in the circle and the new chaser carries on around the circle touching heads. (You might decide to make them swap places even if the chaser doesn't win.) When the new chaser gets to the person they want to chase, they must now say aloud a new concept word – one that connects with the previous one. The two children then race each other as before. Each new chaser has to think of a connecting word. The idea is to see how many connecting words can be made.

A simpler version of this is to whisper to each new chaser a secret concept word. When a person is touched on the head and presented with this word, they can only be allowed to chase if they can think of a word that connects.

Concepts that could be used include:

Think quick concepts

• greed	• anger	• friendship
• sad	• happy	• big
• stealing	• fairness	• God
• me	• brain	• real
• bully	• prison	• police
• heaven	• parents	• time

But Why?

Philosophical consequences

This game is a quiet activity which could be used as a preparation for a P4C session or as a calming down, reflective activity to end a dialogue.

You could use the questions and statements from the 'Let's pretend' section (page 134) or invent your own with the children.

The children sit in a circle. The facilitator or a child starts by giving a conjecture such as:

> If money grew on trees …

The next person in the circle has to repeat their conjecture and add a consequence, for example:

> If money grew on trees, people with no gardens would be poor.

The next person has to turn that consequence into another conjecture, and also add the consequence, for example:

> If people who had no gardens were poor, they would steal from the rich.

And so on:

> If the poor stole from the rich, then all the poor would be in jail.
>
> If all the poor were in jail, the rich would all be equal.
>
> If all rich people were equal, there would be no need for the rich to work.
>
> If the rich did not work, only the poor would work.
>
> If only the poor worked, then they would be the only ones being paid.
>
> If only the poor were paid, they would become richer than the rich.
>
> If the poor became richer than the rich, then we would run out of money.
>
> If we ran out of money, we would plant more trees.
>
> If we planted more trees, then there would be no spare land.
>
> If there was no spare land, we could not build more houses.
>
> If we could not build more houses, we would live in the trees.
>
> If we lived in the trees, we would become like monkeys.
>
> If we became like monkeys, we would groom each other for fleas.

When the sequence has gone round the circle, the final consequence can be joined to the first conjecture – which might produce something either serious or silly. So in this case:

> If money grew on trees, we would groom each other for fleas!

Rapunzel's magic mirror

This activity is designed to encourage children to ask questions. Explain to the children that when the prince reached the top of the tower, he fell madly in love with Rapunzel and asked her to leave the tower and come away with him. Rapunzel was anxious about doing this as she had no knowledge of the world outside her tower, other than what she could see or hear just outside. The understanding prince rushed away to find Snow White's stepmother's magic mirror. He presented it to Rapunzel, saying that she could ask it any question she liked about the world and life itself!

The children then take it in turns or work in small groups to think of questions they would like the mirror to answer. Initially, younger children will almost certainly ask factual questions, but they will usually be open-ended, especially if you explain that the mirror cannot say 'yes' or 'no'. You could also work with these questions as a classifying exercise. As the children become more experienced, they can be asked to make their questions more abstract and therefore more potentially philosophical.

Year 3 and 4 children asked:

- Are there other people who look like me?
- Why do people laugh?
- What are animals?
- What is the grass?
- Who will I be friends with?
- Who will look after me?
- Can I do what I want?
- Will I have to have a job?
- How big is the world?
- Where do people come from?
- Are people ever sad?
- Why do you love me?

You could display the mirror on the wall, and write up the children's questions around it. The mirror can then be used as an interactive activity for the children to practise question-making in their play. You could also put up a label saying 'Come and ask the magic mirror a question'. You might also leave a large sheet of paper pinned up next to the mirror so the children can write, or ask someone to scribe, any other questions they might want to ask during independent play.

Thinking skills and dialogue
Stuck in the (philosophical) mud

Version 1 – the crawling one. Choose one catcher – or two for a larger class. Provide the catcher(s) with three or four statements about debatable points, for example 'Boys can wear pink'. You could use some from the Pathways list on page 133 or, better still, compile a list with the children. The children then run around, chased by the catchers. (Setting a 1-minute running time can help avoid too much chaos.) If a child is caught, they are given a statement card and must stand in the traditional 'stuck-in-the-mud' pose, with legs apart and a hand raised to indicate that they need help. When all statements have been given out, stop the running. Ask all the children to listen carefully while you move among the group reading out the statements. With younger children who may not be able to read the card, make sure they can remember their statement. On your command, all the other children (including the chasers) must try and free all the captured people.

> If a man will begin with certainties, he will end in doubts; but if he will be content to begin with doubts, he shall end in certainties.
>
> FRANCIS BACON

The idea is that the class work together to free the stuck people as quickly as possible. Several rescuers may group round each stuck person, who reads out their statement. The rescuers have to find a way to agree with that statement and justify their answer. For the example, this could be: I agree, because boys like pink because they really like strawberry ice cream and that's pink.

When someone has found a justification, they can then crawl through the stuck person's legs to release them. If, however, they disagree with the statement, they must state why and move on, leaving the other person stuck in the mud.

You can freeze the action during this time and ask any children in the process of rescuing to share the process with the rest of the class. In this case, invite other children to give their opinions, thus prompting mini-dialogues and discussions. If you notice that any children are having problems being released, use one of these breaks to ask the class to support each other and try and think of a way to agree. Again it can be contentious, tenuous or even impossible, as long as it can be justified. When you have listened to a few examples (one or two each time) move the game on again, giving out different statement cards and choosing new catchers.

Version 2 – the more sedate one! The same basic rules apply. Use the prepared statements, but this time code the cards with four colours, for example red, pink, yellow and green. Spread them all face down in the space. Ask the children to move among the cards. At a given signal, they have to move to the nearest card, pick it up and read it. The facilitator then calls out a colour, for example 'pink'. All those with a pink card are then 'stuck', and have to hold up their card. It is the job of the others to free as many of these people as they can by agreeing and justifying their position. If they disagree, they must also be able to say why. When all the stuck people have been released, return all the cards, face down, to a different place and repeat, calling a different colour.

Connecting brain cells

Choose two children with opposing views on a concept and explain that each is a single brain cell. Choose a floating cell (a member of the class who is a good thinker) and invite each of the 'cells' to put forward one reason for their argument. The floating cell has to decide which side to join. Then it is their turn to develop the argument and present it to another floating cell. The idea is to see which brain grows the largest. Cells are allowed to move if they change their thinking at any point. Using a timer to limit the time for the opposing brains to give their arguments (say 30 seconds) encourages children to think quickly and increases the pace and excitement of the game.

Pathways (or Corners)

This has been adapted from a game devised by Karin Murris and Roger Sutcliffe.

You will need some prepared statements; you could choose from the list on pages 133–134 or, better still, compile a list with the children. Also, make four large signs as follows, adding symbols for use with younger children.

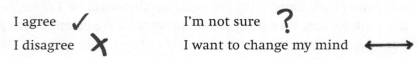

I agree ✓   I'm not sure ?

I disagree ✗   I want to change my mind ⟷

Place the first three signs in three corners of the room (these could be hung over the back of a chair to make them easier to see) and put the last sign (I want to change my mind) at your feet.

Have all the children stand on a mat in the middle of the room, and ensure they all know which sign is which. Read out a statement twice, then ask the children to go to the sign that describes how they feel about it. Emphasize the importance of individual thought, and ask some children to tell you why they have gone to that particular sign. When you have taken some examples, give the children an opportunity to move again if they have changed their minds. Anyone who wishes to do so must first go to the sign at your feet and give their reason before moving on.

- We can come alive again.
- Pinocchio was real.
- Your dreams are real.
- The strongest people should be leaders.
- There should be no rules.
- You must never steal.
- Animals can dream.
- You should always do as you are told.
- You are the same person when you are old.
- You are a different person if you change your name.
- Eating meat is wrong.
- You should never lie.
- We should do what we like.

- We have free choice in our lives.
- If you are invisible you are not real.
- Slugs have feelings.
- If you swapped brains with your friend you would be them.
- It is always wrong to hurt somebody.
- We choose whom we love.
- Boys should wear pink.
- Punishment is always right.
- Only clever children should go to school.
- Ugly people are nasty.
- Beautiful people are good and kind.

'Let's pretend' dialogue games

This activity challenges children's assumptions and encourages them to revisit their first thoughts. It also develops problem-solving skills and creative-thinking processes.

You will need a box or something similar in which you place several strips of paper containing the 'let's pretend' statements. You could use some from the list below, or invent some of your own.

You will also need three bags, clearly marked as follows:

- 'Good thing because ...' and the smiley face symbol
- 'Bad thing because ...' and a sad face symbol
- 'I don't know because ...' and a question mark.

Each child will need a pencil and a small piece of paper to write their name on.

Ask children to divide a page in their thinking journal into two by drawing a vertical line down the middle. On one side of the line, they draw a symbol for 'good thing' (for example, a smiley face) and on the other a symbol for 'bad thing' (for example, a sad face).

Ask one child to pick a 'let's pretend' statement from the box, read it aloud to the class and then stick it to the top of a large sheet of paper. Explain to the children that they will have a few moments' silent thinking time in which they can think about the consequences of the statement, and decide whether it would be a good or a bad thing. After this, ask them to draw a picture in their journals – either on the 'good' side or the 'bad' side – to show what would happen. If they are not sure, they must draw a picture to illustrate any good or bad points they can think of.

During this time, move among the group, talking to the children and scribing any written explanations they offer. Next, explain that they must write their name on their small piece of paper and post it into the bag which is most appropriate to their thinking. Allow the children to post their votes into the bags a few at a time. Ensure that all children are aware which bag is which, and remind them to place their slip in the bag with the symbol that matches the one above their journal drawing – not necessarily the bag their friend may have chosen. When voting is finished, tip out the bags and record the initials of those in each. Start a dialogue by asking one child to explain what they voted and why. After some dialogue, you may decide to have another vote. First recap the main points of the dialogue, and explain to the children that they may change their minds, but will have to justify their decision.

Let's pretend statements

Let's pretend …

it was always Christmas.	you had a birthday every day.
you knew everything.	it never rained.
it rained every day.	we could all do magic.
toys came alive.	we had no fingers.
everyone was a boy.	there were no numbers.
we grew every day.	people were as small as ants.
it was never cold.	nothing was round.
there was no such thing as love.	there were no grown-ups.
we could see what people were thinking.	we could stay up all night.
people could fly.	children swapped places with teachers.
there was no money.	all people looked the same.
nobody could talk.	there was no sun.
there was no time.	babies hatched from eggs.
there were no schools.	money grew on trees.
nobody ever got told off.	there were no police.
dreams came true.	we lived in zoos.
chickens laid golden eggs.	there was no electricity.

Let's pretend

CASE STUDY

In another session, the same Reception class were given the statement:

- Let's pretend there was no such thing as electricity.

After drawing in their journals, they voted this time by moving into a designated area instead of posting votes into bags. Then they started the dialogue:

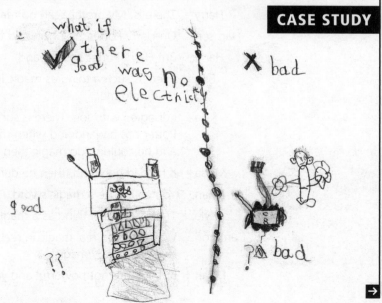

CASE STUDY

Billy:	If there was no such thing as electricity, all the houses would have no lights on. And if a person was cooking, the food wouldn't get cooked.
Joe:	You would have to eat sandwiches and salad every day.
Harry:	If you ate the same food every day, you might get sick and your teeth would get all dirty and you might not like salad.
Kaomi:	You'd be all skinny.
Joanna:	You couldn't have a cup of tea because there's no hot water.
Leah:	If there's no hot water, you couldn't have a bath
Billy:	You could have a cold bath or shower.
Joe:	Or you could wash yourself in watery food like drink.
Harry:	I disagree 'cos you'd probably still be dirty.
Samuel:	I disagree 'cos you'd be really smelly.
Dylan:	I think you need hot water 'cos if you bath yourself in cold water it would make you freezing like ice and you'd freeze to death.
Facilitator:	Can anyone see any other problems or good things?
Billy:	The clouds would go all black because the electricity has got something in it what is dangerous and powerful. So if there's not electricity, the clouds wouldn't go black.
Harrison:	I agree with Billy because the powerful stuff in electricity does make the clouds go black. Electricity can hurt you. If you touch it you get badly hurt.
Harry:	Yes, you get electric shocks.
Billy:	If there was no electricity, there'd be no TV. My mum and Peter couldn't watch *EastEnders* when I go to bed. That would be good because I can't get to sleep.
Kyle:	You wouldn't go to the cinema either. That would be a bad thing.
Kelsie:	You couldn't watch any movies.
Maria:	You would have to read a book instead.
Joanna:	You could find your favourite film book and make it move by magic.
Joe:	I disagree, there's no such thing as magic.
Harry:	There is. My brother can do magic.
Harrison:	On Harry Potter, his uncle said there's no such thing as magic.
Harry:	But Harry Potter has a wand.
Billy:	There is such a thing as magic in Harry Potter but not in real life. My mum told me.
Kyle:	I disagree with Joe. There is such a thing as magic, because Harry Potter has a wand and when the snakes came out it broke his wand and he couldn't do magic then.
Maria:	If he had no wand, then he definitely couldn't do magic.
Dylan:	You could use a magic sword.
Kyle:	There's no such thing as a magic sword. I've never seen one in real life.
Cameron:	Well I've seen real magic in real life at Disneyland and it made my brain and body magic.
Dylan:	But you are not powerful and you haven't got magic in your hands.

Cameron:	One day you will see some!
Dylan:	I've seen real magic. I got a magic game for Christmas and my dad did a cup and ball trick and then the ball was gone.
Billy:	Did it disappear?
Dylan:	No, it went under the floor.
Harry:	Dylan's dad didn't do real magic, 'cos it might have just rolled under the chair.
Facilitator:	If there is such a thing as magic, are you born magic or do you buy it?
Harry:	You buy it from magic shops.
Dylan:	No, you are born magic, you get powers.
Kyle:	But people don't get powers. They just trick you to think you are magic, but you're not.
Cameron:	I have powers because I have special electricity in me.
Billy:	I think if you had real electricity in you, you would die.

Having turned full circle with this dialogue, the main points were recapped and the class voted again.

Philosophy games and activities through stories

Points of view

Choose a character from a book stimulus and ask the children what they think would be the beliefs and views of that character; for example what are his/her/its views on love, war, the monarchy, raising children, God and religion, immigrants? Encourage the children to back up their ideas with reasons. Make a list of as many views as possible. The responses could also be recorded on a mind map for future use.

Would you rather?

This activity is inspired by John Burningham's book *Would You Rather?* and can be used as a starter for a session or as a stand-alone game to develop thinking and talking skills. It is a great stimulus to get children to think about making choices and decisions where they have to choose between the 'lesser of two evils' or the 'cream of the crop'. It is also a useful activity for developing the skills of a facilitator.

Prepare a set of dilemma cards, each with three or four choices, for example:

> Imagine that you have been kidnapped by an evil troll. However, he has a moment of generosity after his meal and decides to let you choose where you will be kept prisoner. Would you rather be imprisoned in:
>
> a) a bird cage?
> b) a lift?
> c) a submarine?
> d) a school?

You may wish to use some of the dilemma examples given on page 140, or write some of your own with the children.

The idea of the activity is that all the children have to make a choice and justify their decision. Divide the room into areas a, b, c and d, and designate them with signs. Choose a dilemma yourself, or get the children to draw one out of the hat, then read it. If appropriate, write it up on the board as well. To begin with, it may help if you explain the dilemmas to the children by putting them into a context where they have to pretend.

Ask the children to make their choice and to go to the appropriate area: a, b, c or d. You will then need to develop the children's answers and seek out paths which could lead into philosophical discussion. Encourage the children to see flaws in other people's reasoning: can they find any contradictions or negative points in each other's arguments? Can they be persuaded to challenge their own thinking?

Further the discussion by considering the choices they did *not* make, as well as the ones they did. Consider, for example, the following dilemma:

> You are stranded in the sea after a shipwreck. You can choose to swim to one of four nearby islands. Each island has only one of these food groups. Which island will you go to? Would you rather survive by eating:
>
> a) insects?
> b) plants and fruit?
> c) animals?
> d) humans?

It is unlikely that any of the children will choose to survive by eating other human beings. This negative choice is in itself an interesting point for discussion. People in other times and cultures have eaten human flesh. Why is eating human flesh so different to eating animal flesh? Does the 'right choice' change according to the situation? If no one was to see or judge us, would that make it all right?

In thinking carefully about this type of scenario, children will be discussing important issues such as human and animal rights, justice, identity, power and authority, the environment and genetics.

Dilemmas

Would you rather be chosen to:

a) go into space?

b) captain the national football team?

c) have your own TV show?

d) be the winner of *Pop Idol*?

Would you rather be lost:
a) at sea?

b) in space?

c) on a desert island?

d) in a crowded city?

Would you rather win:
a) a million pounds?

b) eternal youth?

c) happiness for the rest of your life?

d) free sweets every day of your life?

Would you rather live:
a) a long, lonely life?
b) a short, happy life?
c) a short life with endless money?
d) a long life with no money?

Would you rather meet:
a) God?

b) your great, great, great, great grandparents?

c) the cleverest person in the world?

d) your favourite football player?

Would you rather find:
a) a living dinosaur?

b) a real fairy?

c) a purse that never empties?

d) a doorway into a different world?

Would you rather be born again as:
a) a bird?

b) a tortoise?

c) a fish?

d) a lion?

Would you rather live with:
a) the big bad wolf?

b) Goldilocks?

c) Peter Pan?

d) the seven dwarfs?

Would you rather live without:
a) your hands?

b) your feet?

c) your eyes?

d) your ears?

If there was only one rule in the world, would you rather it was:
a) everybody must only ever wear school uniform?

b) everybody must smile at all times?

c) nobody is allowed to spend any money?

d) nobody is allowed to tell any kind of lie?

Would you rather people were not allowed to be:
a) angry?

b) sad?

c) scared?

d) silly?

Would you rather look like:
a) a kitten?

b) a monkey?

c) a frog?

d) a tiger?

Would you rather live:
a) on the moon?

b) under the sea?

c) in a jungle?

d) underground?

Would you rather be:
a) as small as an ant?

b) as big as a giant?

c) as beautiful as a princess?

d) as scary as a monster?

Part 5

Using the picture books

It is our hope that the previous chapters will have facilitated an understanding of what P4C is, why it is worth doing, and how it can be introduced into the classroom and beyond. If doing philosophy with children is new to you, we hope that you now feel ready and eager to start your own journey through P4C.

This part of the book looks specifically at the use of the three stimulus picture books in the *But Why?* pack. (Use of *Philosophy Bear and the Big Sky* as an introduction to P4C is covered in Part 3.) It includes some worked examples of use in a classroom to provide an insight to the kinds of questions, ideas and dialogues they might produce.

Pinocchio

The story of *Pinocchio* is anchored in the ancient traditions of folklore and dark morality tales, where meanness and evil are punished swiftly by unseen forces, but where goodness, truth and altruism bring positive rewards. In a sense, the 'straight and narrow path' (a common feature of such stories) is clearly marked (the consequences of straying are dire) but the resolution is usually satisfying – 'they all lived happily ever after'. *Pinocchio* raises a wealth of fascinating issues, such as the extent to which we have or should have free will, and what are the 'mysterious forces' that more or less explicitly or coercively guide our way? Is this thing we call 'conscience' of human making? To what extent is it genetically determined, and how far is it culturally influenced? Most profoundly perhaps, what exactly does it mean to be 'real'? Exploring the multifaceted jewel of this tale produces some interesting reflections on the way that we ourselves function as human beings in the world.

The case study lessons using *Pinocchio* illustrate the progression between a Year 1 and a Year 2 class, using the same stimulus.

CASE STUDY

Using *Pinocchio* – making secondary questions

This was a lesson with a class of 18 Year 1 pupils, some of whom were in their second year of philosophy and some of whom had had very limited philosophical experience. Many of the children had reached the stage where they could ask open-ended questions but were not yet able to take them away from the stimulus to make secondary questions.

The role of the facilitator was therefore to model and help the children understand this process and to encourage dialogue about the concepts highlighted. One child with very limited philosophical experience was still at the stage of offering a statement, but was able to express the area of interest and comment on it in the session. The children were asked to listen carefully to other people's questions and to stand up if they thought their question was the same or if there was a link or connection. The majority of the children could do this with minimal support. The more experienced children participated more in this exercise, offering connections that other children had missed. The questions were written down in groups of connected questions to make it easier for the class to see what each set of connected questions was asking.

The questions offered were:

1 Why did Pinocchio tell a lie?

2 Why did Pinocchio tell a big lie?

3 Why did Pinocchio's nose grow big when he told a lie?

4 Was Pinocchio a real person or was he just a piece of wood? Why was Pinocchio wood first?

5 Why did Pinocchio listen to the cat and the fox?

6 Why did the cat and the fox trick Pinocchio?

7 Why didn't Pinocchio listen to the cricket? Could he hear him?

8 Was the cricket dead?

9 Why did he hit the cricket?

10 Did Pinocchio kill the cricket?

11 Why did he hammer the cricket?

12 Why did Pinocchio not get in school?

13 Why didn't Pinocchio go to school?

14 He was digging a hole 'cos the cat and the fox told him.

As the children looked at finding out what the sets of questions were asking, they could tell that the first set (questions 1, 2 and 3) were about lies, but found it difficult to come up with a new question about not

---

telling the truth. I explained to them that this skill – making secondary questions – was the next thing they were going to learn. They were given an example of a secondary question and asked to decide whether it was asking the same thing as the original set of questions? The secondary question was:

- Why do people tell lies?

The children were then asked to explain any other connections they could see in the questions. They grouped questions 7 and 8, and explained that that these were about people not being very nice and playing tricks. When I asked if anybody could talk about why they thought the cat and fox were nasty, one child offered the idea that they had told Pinocchio a lie.

James:	They were lying to him because there's no such things as money trees. It's only pretend.
Joanna:	But there is such things as magic trees 'cos I've read them in my book.
Nicole:	Yes, and tooth fairies live in magic trees too.
Liam:	There is tooth fairies.
Facilitator:	How do we know they are real?
Liam:	Because I stayed awake all night and I felt a little tiny hand under my pillow.
Georgia:	But it could have been your mum tricking you.
Facilitator:	I wonder if tricking someone is the same as telling a lie?
Kieran:	No, tricking is just pretend. You do tricks for fun to your friends and dad sometimes. Lying is bad and naughty. You get told off for that.
Facilitator:	Are all tricks fun then? Were the cat and the fox tricking or lying?
Jake:	I think they were tricking him to be mean.
Facilitator:	So if you can have good tricks and bad tricks, can you also have good lies and bad lies?

(The children were thoughtful, but no responses of note were offered.)

Facilitator:	OK, stand up if you would like to tell us if you have ever told a lie?
	(Most of the class stood.)
Facilitator:	Is anyone brave enough to tell us what they have lied about?
James:	I once lied that I had a tenner, but I only had a fiver.
Facilitator:	Can you remember why you told that lie?
James:	I don't really know. My sister Erica had more holiday money than me, so I said I had more.
Facilitator:	Do you think maybe you were a bit jealous or wished you had more money? Or was it something else, do you think?
James:	I wanted more.
Kieran:	Yeah, it's good to have loads of money.
Facilitator:	Actually, if we think back to the story, I can see a connection with tricking and money. Does anyone else want to talk about that?
Anoushka:	The fox wanted more money so he tricked Pinocchio. Only not very nice people have lots of money.

CASE STUDY

Liam: I agree. Having lots of money makes you nasty 'cos that's greedy.

Facilitator: But lots of people are very rich – are they all nasty people? What about the Queen? She is very rich – is she nasty?

(General discussion followed with divided responses.)

Facilitator: Let's pretend that the people who live next door to you have a huge house, lots of cars and lots of money and you live in a broken-down house with not many toys and not much to eat. Do you think they should give you some money? Stand up if you think they should.

(12 stood; 4 remained seated.)

Facilitator: Billy, you didn't stand up. Can you explain why?

Billy: Well, maybe they earned their money and they will say, 'No it's my money. You have to earn your own money.'

Facilitator: Some people, like the Queen, are born with millions of pounds without earning it. Is that fair, do you think?

Kieran: No! She has loads of guards and my dad knows where she lives – it's Sandringham – and he's been there and the Queen has guards that do all her jobs like feed the horses and do the fields and clean stuff and she just sits on her bum and has a cigarette!

Nicole: Yeah, she has loads of money to look beautiful and nice dresses and hairstyles.

Georgia: But it's not her fault she was born with money. She can do what she likes with it like buy loads of sweets if she wants, because it is hers.

As this dialogue shows, the children were easily able to apply a traditional tale to their lives in a modern situation.

Using *Pinocchio* – connecting questions

In this lesson with 24 Year 2 pupils who had done P4C for two years, it can be seen that given the same stimulus, more experienced children are able to make better connections, to discuss what the questions were actually asking and to begin changing questions into secondary questions.

After being read the story, the children were given time to look at the book and chat with their neighbours about what questions they were interested in asking and any interesting comments they wanted to share. They were then asked to illustrate or write their questions in their journals in an atmosphere of quiet, reflective thinking. Back in the group, they volunteered their questions. The children were asked to listen carefully to all the questions as they were offered, and to think about whether any were the same or connected with their own questions, and if so how?

Their questions included:

1   Why didn't Pinocchio like being a donkey?

2   How did Pinocchio go to life?

3   How did the boys turn into donkeys?

4   Why did the farmer make Pinocchio do all the work instead of doing it himself?

5   If we are all made from puppets first, how did we get flesh?

6   Why in Playland is there only allowed boys?

7   Why didn't Pinocchio go to school?

8   Why did Pinocchio go to the puppet theatre?

9   How did he go in the whale's mouth?

10   Why didn't Pinocchio tell his father the truth?

11   Why did Pinocchio tell his dad a lie?

12   Why did Pinocchio squash the cricket?

13   Why didn't Pinocchio obey his father?

14   Why didn't Pinocchio listen to the cricket?

When using this stimulus with children with just one more year's experience, it was noticeable that they could make better connections and start discussing what the questions were actually asking. Several children changed questions into secondary questions as follows:

- From connecting questions 7, 10, 11 and 13 – Why do people tell lies?

- From connecting questions 2 and 5 – How do we come to exist? and Are we real?

- From connecting questions 7 and 8 (through the concept of choice) – Do we really have a choice about anything?

- From connecting questions 3, 7, 8, 10, 11, 12, 13 and 14 (through the idea of being bad) – Why do people want to be bad? and Why are people bad?

CASE STUDY

In relation to the last set of secondary questions, the group discussed the difference in meaning between the two questions with very similar wording. At this point the children were buzzing with the idea of what made people bad, and had moved on to the nature/nurture debate. They were asked to move to the left side of the room if they thought people were *born* bad, or to the right side if they thought people *wanted* or *chose* to be bad, or to stay in the middle if they were not sure. Five people stayed in the middle. One of the reasons given for uncertainty was the question about whether in fact it could be both. Another reason given by one child was that people might be born good but then taught to be bad. The children were regrouped into the circle and asked to hold those ideas in their head. The dialogue then built on questions about how people might come to be bad:

- Do people learn to be bad?
- Are people born bad and therefore cannot be responsible for their actions?
- Do some people just enjoy being bad, and if so why?

Facilitator: George, you weren't quite sure were you? You stood in the middle.

George: Well, I think it could be both.

Facilitator: Can you say why?

George: Well, some people have bad parents and they are nice children but their bad parents tell them to be bad.

Facilitator: That's an interesting idea.

Lewis: Maybe if the parents are bad, they could teach their children to be bad.

Thomas: Or they could be born bad.

Mark: How do you know people who have got born bad though? If you are born bad, do you know you are bad? I don't think there are many people who have been born bad in this class. I think they would be stealing something.

Facilitator: Would you like to stand up if you've ever been bad?

(All the children stood up except George.)

Facilitator: Ever been bad George? Would your parents agree?

(George stood up.)

Facilitator: OK, sit down. I think most people just stood up didn't they? But does that mean that because you have been bad that you *are* bad?

Lewis: You could be bad because you are getting bored and you want to get sent to your bedroom.

Facilitator: So you can choose to be bad – is that what you are saying? You can choose to be bad because …? Why do *you* choose to be bad, Lewis?

Lewis: Because if you are bored and you want to go somewhere – maybe you've got a wardrobe in your bedroom with games in it – you could go up to your bedroom and play the games.

Facilitator: Can anyone else think of a reason why they have been bad?

Farrah: Because I just feel like it.

Facilitator: Why would you just feel like it, though?

But Why?

Farrah:	Because I'm annoyed?
Facilitator:	OK, but what is it that makes you bad? Is it your brain deciding to be bad or is it something else?
Danielle:	Well, I think that when I'm bad, it's usually because somebody's been nasty to me.
Bryony:	Yes, that happens to me.
Facilitator:	Can you help it? Can you stop yourself being bad back to people?
	Well, is it better to be good, then, or better to be bad? If you think about robbers, do you think that they think, 'Oh, it's much better to rob something and then I could end up with a new video, or whatever.'?
Tom:	Yeah, but what if the police saw him robbing something? Then they wouldn't have it, would they?
Farrah:	If they went out, then you could have one of those things that you do the numbers and then the video goes in.
Facilitator:	Do you mean a safe?
Thomas:	Yeah, my mum's got one of those.
Facilitator:	Robbers, burglars, then – they make a choice. We don't know yet. They're either born bad – that makes them want to go and steal things – or somebody teaches them to be bad. They must understand that if they are caught, they are going to be punished. So why do you think that they still do it, even though they might get punished?
Lewis:	Maybe because they want to go in jail?
Bryony:	It might be about your feelings, how you feel.
Facilitator:	That you are not worried about going to prison?
Bryony:	I am.
Facilitator:	Why do burglars still burgle, even if they know they are going to end up in prison?
Lewis:	'Cos they get stuff if they don't get caught sometimes.
Farrah:	Years ago in Italy, if somebody was naughty and that, then they got fed to the lions.
Facilitator:	But did that used to stop people being naughty then?
Farrah:	In Italy they could have put them near the volcano instead, but then they would have probably killed themselves.
Mark:	And they might think that if they set fire to something … 'cos I watched a programme where someone set fires. They might think that they could get away with it – but in the fire someone could have died.
Danielle:	But how would they know that they would get away with it?
Thomas:	America is a really rich country, that's why.
Tom:	They've got all the money.
Lewis:	They might get away with it because they might have a really fast car and the police car might not be really fast.
Facilitator:	Well they might think, 'I've got a fast car and the police will never catch me.'
George:	But what if they don't have a fast car?
Facilitator:	Well, exactly – something might go wrong with the car.

But Why?

CASE STUDY

Mark:	And then they'd be in trouble.
Facilitator:	OK, I'm just going to stop that there because I'm just going to give a chance to anyone who didn't give me a question just to write some more questions down. So has anyone got a different question from *Pinocchio* that you haven't had a chance to ask yet? Ryan?
Ryan:	How come we can't see our conscience?
Facilitator:	That's a good philosophical question because it's not about Pinocchio, as such, is it? Even people who haven't read the story of Pinocchio might be able to think about that question, wouldn't they, Ryan?
Ryan:	Yes.
Facilitator:	(to another child) What was your question?
Mark:	Why was a cricket the conscience?
Charlie:	What is a conscience?
Facilitator:	Great! Another philosophical question.
George:	I know what a conscience is.
Facilitator:	Do you? What is it George?
George:	I think it's something in your head. Something in your brain that tells you what you should do right and what you think is wrong. It's something that tells you what you should do right and what you should do wrong
Facilitator:	So are you born with a conscience, George, or is it something that you learn?
George:	We are born with it.
Facilitator:	So right from when we are babies, we know what is right and wrong, do we?
Farrah:	No!
George:	Well, the conscience … When we are babies, we don't know things – we just don't know anything about the world.
Facilitator:	So that's why we need a conscience, then, do we?
George:	We need a conscience to know what to do.
Facilitator:	Do you think bad people have consciences, then, George?
George:	Yes, they do, but their conscience is a bad conscience.
Facilitator:	What's the difference between a good conscience and a bad conscience?
George:	Well, if a good conscience tells you things that are right, a bad conscience tells you bad things.
Jordan:	A bad person's conscience works differently. It's kind of mixed up, isn't it?
Thomas:	Yes, it's opposite.
Facilitator:	Yes, that's a good word. So when you do something bad, a bad person's conscience says, 'Yeah, that's great!' but a good person's conscience says, 'Oh no, that's terrible! Don't do that!'
Samara:	Yes, well, when my little brother fell down and he broke his bone, he didn't know what to do.
Facilitator:	He didn't understand what was going to happen, did he? OK, anyone else who hasn't given me their question?

→

Mark:	Why are people bad when they grow up?
Facilitator:	This is coming from the conscience thing, isn't it?
Farrah:	You are not always bad when you grow up, 'cos you can get something called ADHD, which is when you just want more attention from teachers and people.

In this sample of dialogue the children continued to explore the concept of good and bad, even though the three questions covered were different, showing their developing ability to build upon previous ideas.

If I Were a Spider

If I Were a Spider speaks of grand dreams but suggests the ultimate limitations of simple wishful thinking. The best ideas and solutions are often those that can be applied practically in life. This is not to deny the value of considering the impossible! Albert Einstein's famous 'thought experiments' are a case in point. What would the universe look like, Einstein daydreamed, if I could ride on a light beam? That poetical and powerful leap of the imagination created insights which allowed Einstein to make further progress in developing his theories of relativity.

Similarly, technological innovations are often preceded by the desire to get there – the wish comes before the action. Humankind's ancient desire to rise above the world and travel, for example, to the moon has its written origins in ancient Greece, and then more recently in the works of Jules Verne, H.G. Wells and many others. Pioneering scientists and technologists in various fields have had their imaginations fired by fantasy. As the old saying goes, inspiration comes before aspiration. So how would the line: 'If I were a spider I'd build a web to the moon' translate into the language of twenty-first-century technology?

The three case studies showing use of the spider poem show progression according to experience rather than age. With less experienced children, you might consider reading the poem and then tackling just one or two verses and pictures in each session.

Using *If I Were a Spider* – with a Reception group

The poem was read to a Reception class who had been doing philosophy for about five months. After being read the text and shown the illustrations, the children were asked to think about which pages most interested them. The page the children had focused on particularly in this session was:

- If I were a sound, I'd be a beautiful tune.

Facilitator:	What is a beautiful sound?
Chloe:	A beautiful sound can't look like anything. It is just a beautiful sound, like this – (whistles a tune).
Tom:	But beautiful can be lots of nice sounds.

Hayden:	It's singing. My granddad can sing and he is a policeman.
Jordan:	A sound will have colours, like blue and rainbow colours.
Tom:	Sounds are beautiful because they have sweet voices, like fairies and ballerinas.
Danielle:	When I am six, I'll have a beautiful tune because I'm having singing lessons and colours will come from my mouth.
Jade:	Colours can't come from your mouth because colours are just like colouring pencils, and they'll only come out if you chew the pencils.
Bryony:	No, if you swallow a sweet that is blue or red. But only red stays in you because of your blood.
Hayden:	And blue because of your veins.
Danielle:	And pink because of your heart.
Jade:	Not green, because that's for a peacock.
Dylan:	When you are sick … Once I was sick and yellow came out of my mouth, and then when I was five I was sick and it was all red.
Hayden:	When you drink or eat something, all the colours go inside you.
Sam:	Colour red came out of my toe because I ran outside and cut my toe and it was bleeding.
Bryony:	You have a singing voice in your throat, and that's got colours in it.
Facilitator:	Can you see colours when you hear a sound?
Danielle:	Yes, you see them in your head and then when you close your eyes they are there.

(At this point all the children were asked to close their eyes and listen to a short piece of music.)

Jade:	I saw pink and purple and gold.

(Lots of examples of colours were given by other children.)

Facilitator:	How can you see colour when your eyes are shut?
Matthew:	It is like a dream. You get colour in your eyes.
Tom:	The colour was behind my eyes.
Matthew:	My colours were in the back of my head.
Sean:	No, in front of your eyes.
Jade:	But how can you see that if your eyes were shut? Were you peeping?
Danielle:	No, it's like when I close my eyes, I can still see you but I'm not looking.
Jade:	Like we take photos of our keywords and put them in our head?
Sean:	But keywords are not colours are they?
Tom:	I know, but there are things in your head that you can see all the time, and stuff you can't, like other words.
Facilitator:	Do you think blind people can see colours in their heads?

Unfortunately the session had to stop as it was past time for lunch. Other questions that could have been asked by the facilitator include:

- What does a sound look like?
- Do your ears hear the same sound as mine?

But Why?

- What is beauty?
- Is beautiful the same for everyone?
- How can a person who has always been blind know what 'red' is?
- Can a blind person visualize anything if they have no visual knowledge?
- Can touch ever be the same as sight?
- Why can we visualize things inside our head?

The following week, the session focused on another verse that had interested the children: 'If I were a spider I'd build a web to the moon.' After the book had been read again, the children were invited to offer questions or statements about this part of the poem.

The main question that arose was:

- How did the spider get to the moon?

Facilitator:	How do you think the spider got to the sky?
Sean:	The spider got there 'cos he used his legs to climb the web.
Dylan:	No, he used the web from his hands to stretch to the moon.
Jordan:	He could have got a lift from a bird who jumps him up and flies him to the moon.
Megan:	He might have climbed a ladder, because I climbed a ladder once and I touched the sky.
Facilitator:	But where do you think the sky begins?
Ryan:	Above our heads.
Facilitator:	Whose head?
Ryan:	The tallest person in the class.
Jade:	But what about the mummies and daddies? Taller than them?
Dylan:	No, I think it must start at the top of the trees, or houses, or tall towers.

At this point the children were given some thinking time to draw where they thought the sky began.

CASE STUDY

One child had drawn a plane in his picture.

Facilitator:	At what point did the plane enter the sky?
Ryan:	Well, planes work by gravity. When it is on the ground, it is not in the sky. When you turn the engine on, it is hovering, so that must be flying and then it goes straight up. When it is up it's in the sky.
Sean:	Yes, sky is up. It's where the clouds are.
Danielle:	It has to be higher than us.
Bryony:	It is as high as where God is.
Dylan:	I think God must have lifted the spider up, then.
Tom:	He couldn't have, because God hasn't got real hands.
Matthew:	He has, otherwise how would he make the mummies and daddies?
Dylan:	If my dad had a ladder and because my house is medium-sized, my dad could go up and stand on the roof and then he could touch the sky.
Facilitator:	What do you think might fill the gap between the Earth and the sky that lots of you have drawn?
Hayden:	I think the middle part is fresh air.
Ryan:	Yes, all around us is what we breathe in.
Sean:	Fresh air is just like water – it is in your mouth and you can blow up balloons.
Hayden:	Fresh air used to be in the sky, and now it's come down to Earth.
Matthew:	But how can it come down to earth, because the air can't even go up in the sky?
Danielle:	It was in the olden days, but now it has come back down to Earth.
Matthew:	If the air was in the sky, you couldn't pull it down because Jesus put it there and only Jesus can get it down.
Hayden:	Yes, he doesn't like fresh air and we do.

Below are some further examples of facilitator questions that could be used to help develop the children's philosophical thinking when using some of these illustrations.

If I were a path I'd go the right way.

Ideas about choice can be built on here.

- Do we have choice in our lives? Are our lives mapped out for us, or do we control everything in them?
- Is the right path the easiest or the hardest?
- How can we know whether we are on the right path, and whether our choice was right or not?
- How do we define right and wrong? How are right and wrong decided, by whom/what and why?

If I were a smile I'd be full of good cheer.

Ideas about the nature of happiness could be considered.

- Does smiling really mean you are happy?
- What is happiness?
- Is happiness the same for everyone?
- Where does happiness come from?
- Can we measure happiness?
- Can we ever be genuinely happy?
- Could we live a life without happiness?

If I were the sun I'd shine every day.

Start off by asking the children whether it would be good or bad if the sun shone every day?

- If you were the sun and you got the chance to shine every day, would you do so even if its consequences were not for the good of everything?
- If you have the ability to make others happy using a talent or gift that you possess, do you have a duty to use it?
- Is your first duty to others or to yourself?
- What social responsibilities do we have?
- What social responsibilities should we have?
- Who decides what societies' rules are, and how can we ensure we live together fairly?

If I were a butterfly I'd grow as big as a kite.

This leads to thinking about concepts of size and power.

- Are big things better than small things?
- Can you give examples of big things that are harmful to humans and small things that are harmful to humans?
- Can small things have big consequences? (the butterfly effect)
- Can anything ever get too big?
- Are bigger things always more powerful?
- Can size change anything?

If I were a thought I'd be as big as the sky.

This could be used to explore the nature of thinking. Ask the children where they think their thoughts come from.

- Do we control our thoughts or are we controlled by them?
- Can we ever have no thoughts about anything?
- Are thoughts always good?
- Can our thoughts change things?
- Do our thoughts change as we get older? If so why?
- Does 'thinking big' matter?
- Are thoughts the same as daydreams?
- Could we have thoughts without a brain?

CASE STUDY	Using *If I Were a Spider* – with a Year 1 group

If I Were a Spider was used with a Year 1 class, most of whom had been participating in philosophy for a year and a half. The poem was read through twice and the children allowed 2 minutes talking time with a partner or in a group. They were then asked to come up with a question and to illustrate their thinking. The children were given a further 5 minutes to do this. They were then asked to walk around the space, joining up with other children who had asked questions or drawn pictures about the same page of the poem as they had. Once groups had been formed, they were asked to reform the circle but stay grouped.

Questions were then collected in as follows:

- How did the flowers grow?
- How do flowers get their colours?
- Why do flowers grow?
- Why do flowers open when the sun comes out?
- I like rainbows – they are beautiful.
- Why are rainbows beautiful?
- Why did the rainbow glitter all night?
- Why do spiders make webs?
- Why did the spider want to build a web to the moon?
- Why do spiders float in space?
- How can the sun shine all the time?
- Why do suns flash all day?
- Why are paths zig-zaggy?
- If I was a smiley face, would I be happy?
- Why do rivers go to the sea?
- How do we think?

The dialogue was started by asking the child who suggested 'Why are rainbows beautiful?' if she could say why she thought the rainbow was beautiful.

Before she could answer, several boys showed they were in disagreement about this. The children were asked to stand up if they agreed with the statement that rainbows are beautiful. All the girls stood up but only one boy joined them.

Then the children were asked to make a list of things that people say are beautiful. ('What beautiful ...!') They came up with the following list:

- flowers, pictures, butterflies, shoes, hair, eyes, weather, girls, ladies

Facilitator:	Are boys not beautiful, then?
Harrison:	Yes, boys can be beautiful if they have nice clothes.
Facilitator:	Can you be beautiful and wear horrible clothes?
Nadia:	If your clothes are dirty, you are not beautiful.
Joe:	I agree, because you will be dirty and you need a bath.
Facilitator:	Can you ever make something beautiful?

(The children continued to discuss the bathing and clothes issue without building constructively upon the idea of beauty.)

Facilitator:	Can you think of any examples of ugly people in stories? Are all ugly people nasty?
Kyle:	No, just because you are ugly doesn't mean you are nasty.
Harry:	Well, they can be and cannot, you don't know if they are nice or bad, even beautiful people like princesses.
Facilitator:	So what is it that makes people beautiful, then? Is it more than just their clothes, do you think?
Sophie:	You have to be polite and kind and helpful.
Kyle:	But you can be not beautiful and still be kind, like Beauty and the Beast. It isn't always what you look like, is it?
Kirsten:	You can wear make-up – then you will be beautiful. My mum always wears make-up. But boys don't, so they can't be beautiful.
Billy:	Some boys wear make-up. I've seen them on the television with make-up on.
Sophie:	Yes, but you don't because you are normal boys, but some do.
Joe:	Some men wear make-up when they are in movies.
Facilitator:	So are they wearing it for a reason, then?
Maria:	To look beautiful.
Sophie:	You can be beautiful in all different ways. At a party we didn't wear make-up, but Maria's dad did.
Maria:	He had a purple top on and a hat.
Facilitator:	I wonder why some ladies say that they can't go out unless they have got their make-up on?
Kelsie:	My mum says that, but I don't think she's different.
Facilitator:	Do you mean she doesn't look different or seem different in another way, Kelsie?
Kelsie:	Well, she is still the same. I mean, she is still my mum all the time.
Maya:	When my mum comes to school, she doesn't wear make-up and I still know she is my mum.
Kelsie:	I think I'm ugly because I wear glasses.
Sophie:	You're not. It doesn't matter what you look like. My dad has glasses and he looks great.
Harry:	I don't like my glasses. I have to clean them and they itch my ears.
Sophie:	You both look OK with glasses and without.
Harry:	I look like my cousin with my glasses off.
Facilitator:	If your best friend came to school covered with purple spots, scaly skin and red eyes, would you still like them? Stand up if you think you would still be best friends with them looking that ugly.

(Only three children stood.)

Facilitator:	Let me ask any of the three standing, why?
Billy:	I would still like them as a person. We could still play the same stuff at playtime.
Sophie:	Well, I think I wouldn't be friends, because I would be a bit scared of them if they looked like that.

CASE STUDY

Kyle:	They would still be the same inside though.
Sophie:	Or probably not – if people were always scared of you and ran away, you would have no friends and then you wouldn't be nice any more.
Maria:	Yes, even though you should know, you don't know how they feel and they don't know how you feel.
Sophie:	If we said we liked them, they would probably feel happy.

This was the end of the session. The session was closed by reviewing what we had been trying to work out: what is the nature of' beautiful'. A homework question was set from the lesson:

- What makes something beautiful?

Points to consider:

- Is beauty in the eye of the beholder?
- Are beautiful things always good?
- Can you make something beautiful by changing it?

CASE STUDY

Using *If I Were a Spider* – with a Year 2 group

With a more experienced Year 2 class, the poem was read through twice before the children were asked to focus on finding a question that related to what the poem was trying to say (in other words, picking out the metaphors and applying a philosophical slant to them). The difference in the quality of the questions produced by these more experienced children is apparent. After talking and thinking time, the children were again encouraged to group up with other children who had similar questions. This time, groups worked together to negotiate new questions based on their original questions. The questions were collected as follows:

- What is so good about being a child?
- What can reach the sky?
- What is so good about going the right way?
- Why can't we stay like a child for ever?
- What is a thought?
- Is there another solar system?
- If I was a thought, why would I be as big as the sky?
- What if the sun ran out of light?
- What if the rain ran out of wetness?
- Can rainbows really gleam all night?
- Why do we have rainbows?

The children were then asked if they could decide which of the questions were scientific and which were philosophical. They decided that the questions about space and rainbows were the most obviously scientific. They were then asked whether they could explain the difference between a scientist and a philosopher.

Ryan:	Well, a scientist has a job and it's his job to find out the real answer.
Facilitator:	So if a scientist told you how the world began, would you believe him or her?
George:	Well, I know how the world began. It was with a big bang, and then loads of micro-things joined together to make the planet.
Facilitator:	How do we know this is true, then? Do we know anyone who saw this?
George:	Well, it was aliens from another planet.
Farrah:	No, I disagree, God made the world.
Facilitator:	Now this is interesting. You have come up with the world's biggest philosophy-versus-science argument, probably since time began.

The children's dialogue continued to debate the nature of evolution, with three themes being dominant: one that the earth came from the big bang, another that it was God's creation and the third that it was caused by alien intervention.

When the discussion reached a stage where ideas were not being effectively built upon, another question was introduced.

Facilitator:	Is it science or coincidence that the sun rises every day?
Thomas:	Well, it must be science because it's to do with the planets.
Facilitator:	A philosopher might argue that just because the sun has come out every day for a few million years, it may not always be so in the future.
Molly:	The sun doesn't come out every day – it's not sunny now.
Ryan:	But it is still there – it's just sometimes in the clouds.
Bryony:	But the sun isn't there at night.
Danielle:	It's still in the sky though.
Charlie:	But there isn't any sun at night or in winter.
Facilitator:	So if we can't see it, does that mean its not there?
Thomas:	We don't have to see it. We know our house is still there, even though we can't see it right now.
Ryan:	Ahh, but how do we know it just doesn't disappear or fly up into space or get up and walk away – like on *The Simpsons* – as soon as we get to school and then comes back when it's home time!

(Laughter)

Facilitator:	Well, actually, Ryan could be making a good point. We are fairly certain that houses can't walk – why is that?
Molly:	They aren't alive?
George:	But robots aren't alive and they can walk.
Ryan:	The house on *The Simpsons* is a robot house.
Mark:	They don't have legs or wheels, and houses can't think, 'Let's go for a walk' because they have no brain either.
Facilitator:	OK, so at the moment could we say that it is impossible for a house to vanish and reappear frequently? Stand up if you agree with that statement.

(All the children stood.)

CASE STUDY

Facilitator: OK, so now let me ask you another. Are rainbows *definitely and always* caused by the sun and the rain coming out at the same time, as Charlie said earlier? Has it been scientifically proven? How do we know it's not just a coincidence? Could the rainbow appear because of any other reason?

Thomas: Well, maybe it could be a spaceship with coloured lights?

Facilitator: Maybe, a long time ago, before scientists said how rainbows were discovered, people might have believed that and put things they didn't understand down to other reasons – like thunder was God being angry in the sky. Do you think science is always absolutely right?

Lewis: Well, sometimes science is wrong. Like they said the earth was flat first off, didn't they? And then they found it wasn't.

The community of enquiry proceeded to discuss changes in scientific knowledge, and I explained to them that science developed from philosophy and that there is still ongoing argument between the two schools of thinking. This brought the session to a close. The homework question was to discuss whether we could always trust what we are told by scientists. Several children remained to continue discussing their thoughts with the facilitator at the end of the session. I asked Lewis what he felt about science and philosophy. He replied, 'I think philosophers must be cleverer than scientists, because they never think they are right and so people can still think stuff and we can still find out new things.'

Dojen the Wanderer

Dojen the Wanderer draws his joy and the power of his wisdom from a close observation of the simple things in nature. He has become sensitive to the essential rightness of the world, which he perceives moment-by-moment with a childlike delight and sense of awe. For Dojen, all things are glowing with 'firstness' (to use a term coined by the educationalist and teacher Margaret Meek). His discoveries, insights, intuitions are first hand: he is a true authority because he has found out for himself. He is also able to transfer his wisdoms and help other people to apply them in their own lives, especially when they have realized the power of metaphor. Like the philosophy of the Tao, Dojen uses water as his central metaphor, and this allows him to resolve the long-standing conflict between Kuo-Chin and the Stone King (whose name itself is a metaphor). Dojen's achievement is to let the world unfold and to go along with that unfolding. In this he is neither passive nor a victim, but applies natural forces artfully and with a gentle elegance. In this uncomplicated philosophy of life, Dojen finds his happiness.

As an overtly philosophical story, this is an interesting text to use with older children who have experience of P4C and are used to questioning. Although we have argued strongly for the use of 'ordinary' stories and other stimuli in P4C, we believe there is also a place for the explicitly philosophical text. *Dojen the Wanderer* was trialled extensively with a Year 3 class, most of whom had had experience of P4C since starting school. It was found that the philosophical nature of the text helped these more skilled but still young children to 'cut to the chase'. They found the use of metaphor intriguing and recognized the philosophical thinking. The quality of questions was good and led to discussions that the class had not had in such depth previously.

Below are some examples of the sorts of questions the children came up with and the route they took to dialogue over the first few chapters.

Using *Dojen the Wanderer* – with a Year 3 group

CASE STUDY

A Year 3 class used *Dojen the Wanderer* in their philosophy sessions, working on a chapter a week and building on the ideas previously raised each time.

In week 1, the questions offered included:

- How did Dojen become wise?
- Why didn't Dojen stop pouring the tea?
- Why, if Dojen was thirsty, did he take two sips of tea and then leave it?
- Why did he (Kuo-Chin) say he would chop off Dojen's hands?
- Why did soldiers come with the King to the tea shop?
- Why does he (Kuo-Chin) want to defeat the Stone King?
- How did everyone know Dojen?
- Why did the Stone King want to defeat the Emperor?
- Why did everyone want to know the secret of happiness?
- Why are people scared of the Stone King?
- What did Dojen mean by 'you are too full of your own opinions'?

The facilitator collected in the questions and then went through them with the children, making sure that everyone knew what each one meant. She also asked the children to classify them into closed, open-ended, scientific or philosophical questions. The children decided that the question 'Why didn't Dojen stop pouring the tea?' was closed, but Megan argued against this, saying that the overflowing of the tea was actually a metaphor for something else. She pointed to part of the text that said the Emperor's head was like the tea cup, so full of his own opinions that there was no room for other thoughts. This led to a mini-dialogue about the nature of knowledge and wisdom. The themes discussed were: Can you ever be too wise? Can you ever know everything? It was noticeable that the children did not have to look too hard to discover what themes they were working on, and could participate to a fairly high level on these subjects.

In week 2, the facilitator refreshed the plot of the first chapter and read the second. She then revisited the previous week's questions and put them on display for the children to look at. They were asked to think about the two chapters so far, and to make new questions or make previous ones

CASE STUDY

more philosophical. They were encouraged to do this by summing up what the questions were really asking with another question.

As the questions were collected, the children were encouraged to think about connections with questions they wanted to offer, and also to help the community make sure the questions were as philosophical as they could be. One child offered:

- How do some people become wise?
- Why does the queen think she is more important than us?

This was turned into a secondary question by another child who asked whether he meant:

- Why do some people have power?

Which in turn was changed into:

- What is power?

This question also led to the questions: Why do we have to have a king and queen at all? and Why should we bow to the queen? This led to the more philosophical question of why can we not all be equal? A mini-dialogue ensued about the pros and cons of a monarchy, and what would happen without a ruler. The children were asked to consider the difference between the prime minister and the queen, as leaders. They offered opinions as to whether it was fair that some people are born into leadership while others had to work hard to be chosen. Most children came to the agreement that society would eventually break down if there was no system of leadership, and that we should actually have a queen. The next question to be recorded was:

- Why do people who are poor give food to others?

From this question emerged the idea that some people are selfless and willing to put others before themselves. This led to a discussion about leadership, linked to the previous one. One child stated that if kings and queens were selfless, then the world would be a better place. At this point, the facilitator explained the theory of utilitarianism: basing your acts upon doing the greatest good for the greatest amount of people. The same child then said that she had a question linked with this idea:

- Why do people want to take over other countries?

When asked to explain what she meant by this question, she said that it seemed unnecessary to need more than one country and have to kill people in the process. This led to a discussion about the nature of war and whether there is ever such a thing as a just war. The children were mostly agreed that there is, and talked about the need to fight to protect your own people and defend your country, but agreed that it was not right to kill or hurt people outside the confines of war.

What was interesting about this dialogue was the ease with which the children were able to take the story and transfer their feelings about it, making it relevant to their previous studies on the Second World War and current affairs in Iraq. They were also able to make the connection that war is about power and greed. There was a very strong feeling that it is always the enemies who are wrong. The facilitator brought up the example of the freedom fighters: 'One man's terrorist is another man's freedom fighter.' She asked the children to think about whether there is a difference between a soldier and a murderer. The children were asked to stand up if they agreed with the statement: soldiers have the right to kill. The class were split about this. Some went with their gut feeling that killing is morally wrong; others agreed with the statement, citing reasons of protection against enemies.

The final question was then offered:

- Why did the Emperor obey Dojen?

One child said that it was because he was lying; another said that he wasn't lying but pretending. The facilitator asked the children to consider whether pretending is the same as lying. The class then discussed and built upon the idea of whether lying could ever be a good thing, especially in the case of someone like Dojen, who was trying to change things for the better and make someone else understand the consequences of their actions. The children also made the connection with a previous dialogue they had had on the nature of slavery, and realized they had turned almost full circle again, back to the concept of power.

Afterword

We hope that this book – and in particular the extracts of dialogue presented in the case studies – will convince you that practising philosophy with children is incredibly powerful. Every time I facilitate a session, I feel privileged to be able to share the children's amazing insights and perceptions, and it is so rewarding to see their progress into the realms of deep and knowledgeable thinking. Their ideas excite and move me, and make me wonder at what point we as adults start blindly believing everything we are told. It is so refreshing to listen to young children unlocking closed doors and offering so many alternatives to our very grown-up way of thinking. I will finish the book with a wonderful extract from a philosophy journal written by Harvey Boyer's dad. The class had been working on *The Last Noo-Noo* by Jill Murphy, and the homework question was: Should grown-ups behave differently to children?

Here were the points to consider, along with the responses offered by Harvey's dad.

1.	Can grown-ups have their birthday parties at McDonald's?	I phoned McDonald's; they said 'no'!
2.	Do we have to grow up?	McDonald's said I should!
3.	Who decides how grown-ups should behave?	Ronald McDonald, apparently!
4.	Why do we have to behave differently?	As you get older you naturally gain more responsibilities. These require a more mature attitude. However you should never take yourself too seriously or forget your carefree childhood (see 1–3).

As you can see, we get a lot of enjoyment from doing philosophy – and working with children can prevent you from taking life too seriously. Have fun!

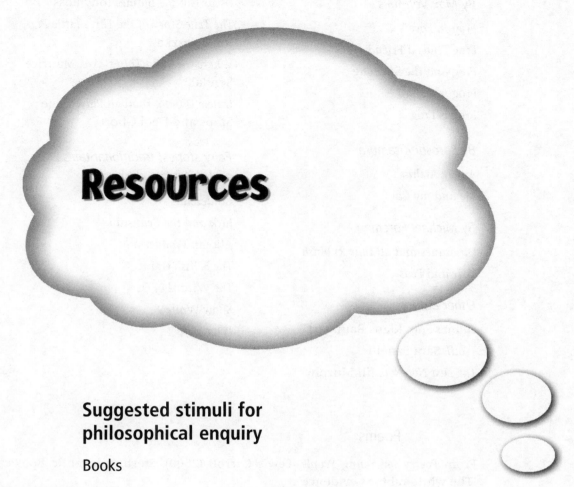

Resources

Suggested stimuli for philosophical enquiry

Books

By Anthony Browne

Piggybook

The Tunnel

Hansel and Gretel

Voices in the Park

The Visitors Who Came to Stay

Through the Magic Mirror

Zoo

Gorilla

Bear Goes to Town

Changes

The Night Shimmy

By John Burningham

Cloudland

Whaddyamean

Grandpa

Aldo

Would You Rather?

By David McKee

Not Now Bernard

Tusk Tusk

The Hill and the Rock

By Colin Thompson

The Paradise Garden

The Paperbag Prince

How to Live Forever

Looking For Atlantis

The Tower to The Sun

Falling Angels

The Last Alchemist

By Max Velthuijs

Frog in Love

Frog Finds a Friend

Frog and the Birdsong

Frog is a Hero

Frog is Frog

By Satoshi Kitamura

Angry Arthur

Me and my Cat

By Michael Foreman

Dinosaurs and all that Rubbish

War and Peas

Other authors

Laura's Star, Klaus Baungart

Wolf!, Sara Fanelli

The Last Noo-Noo, Jill Murphy

Oscar Got the Blame, Tony Ross

The True Story of the Three Little Pigs, Jon Scieszka

Where the Wild Things Are, Maurice Sendak

Dulcie Dando, Football Player, Sue Stops and Debi Gliori

Fairy stories, traditional tales and children's classics

Cinderella

Jack and the Beanstalk

Alice in Wonderland

The Selfish Giant

The Wizard of Oz

Snow White

Peter Pan

Poems

From *Poetry for Young People,* Lewis Carroll (2000), Sterling Juvenile Books: 'The white rabbit's evidence'

From *Ghosts Galore,* haunting verse edited by Robert Fisher (1986), Faber and Faber: 'Uncle Fred', by Robert Fisher

From *One Hundred and One Favourite Poems,* chosen by John Foster (2003), Collins: 'The prime minister is ten today' by David Harrison, 'Growing up' by Daphne Kitching

From *All the Best,* selected poems of Roger McGough (2004), Puffin: 'The kleptomaniac', 'Give and take', 'A poem just for me'

From *Because a Fire Was in My Head: 101 Poems to Remember,* edited by Michael Morpurgo (2001), Faber and Faber: 'The Pied Piper' by Robert Browning, 'Back in the playground' by Adrian Mitchell

From *Quick Let's Get Out of Here,* Michael Rosen (1985), Puffin: 'Unfair', 'Lizzie', 'I wake up'

From *Where the Sidewalk Ends,* Shel Silverstein (2004), HarperCollins: 'The unicorn', 'Point of view', 'Listen to the mustn'ts'

From *The Day I Fell Down the Toilet,* Steve Turner (1997), Lion: 'Who made the world?', 'Who was I before I was born?', 'The worst school in the world'

From *Talking Turkeys,* Benjamin Zephaniah (1995), Puffin: 'Heroes', 'A killer lies'

Music

'The Ugly Duckling' from *Hans Christian Andersen*

The Carnival of Animals, by Camille Saint-Saëns: compare two sections, for example 'The swan' and 'The elephant'

Extract(s) from John Williams' *Harry Potter* soundtrack (invite questions about the film content as well as musical interpretations)

Disney soundtrack songs and lyrics offer good starting points for philosophy, for example:

> *The Little Mermaid*: 'Part of Your World', 'Poor Unfortunate Souls'
>
> *Pinocchio*: 'Give a Little Whistle'
>
> *Beauty and the Beast*: 'The Mob Song'
>
> *Robin Hood*: 'The Phony King of England'

Disney song lyrics can be found at:

> www.fpx.de/fp/Disney/Lyrics/

Useful websites

www.P4C.net
An extremely useful site with lists of resources, discussion groups, and events from all over the world.

www.simnet.is/heimspekiskolinn/icpic.html
International Council for Philosophical Inquiry with Children – the largest and most respected P4C organisation in the world.

www.sapere.net
Society for the Advancement of Philosophical Enquiry and Reflection in Education – this is the UK section of ICPIC, and is great for contacts and information. Very approachable; also offers excellent training.

www.dialogueworks.co.uk
Karin Murris' and Roger Sutcliffe's consultancy (founding members of SAPERE). Excellent resources and training, including *Newswise*, an internet educational resource based on topical news stories.

www.childrenthinking.co.uk
Practice-based training, advice and support for teachers, particularly those starting out with P4C. Also the base for the Teacher's Philosophy Forum – the East Anglia branch of SAPERE.

http://ubertas.infosys.utas.edu.au/tea_party
The Philosophers' Tea Party. A Tasmanian-based interactive philosophy site with ongoing dialogues from adult and child philosophers around the world.

www.philosophyslam.org
A teachers' resource site with lots of useful links.

Further reading for facilitators

Craig, Edward (2002) *Philosophy: A Very Short Introduction*, Oxford Paperbacks

Gaarder, Jostein (1995), *Sophie's World*, Orion

Grayling, A.C. (2001) *The Meaning of Things: Applying Philosophy to Life*, Weidenfeld & Nicolson

Haynes, Joanna (2001), *Children as Philosophers: Learning through Enquiry and Dialogue in the Primary Classroom*, Routledge Falmer

Haynes, Joanna and Murris, Karin (2000), *Storywise: Thinking through Stories*, Dialogueworks

Law, Stephen and Postgate, Daniel (2002), *The Philosophy Files*, Orion

Law, Stephen (2003), *The Philosophy Gym: 25 Short Adventures in Thinking*, Headline

Nagel, Thomas (1989), *What Does It All Mean? A Very Short Introduction to Philosophy*, Oxford University Press

Splitter, Laurance J. and Sharp, Ann M. (1995), *Teaching for Better Thinking*, ACER

Stevenson, Jay (2002), *The Complete Idiot's Guide to Philosophy*, Alpha

Warburton, Nigel (2004), *Philosophy: The Basics*, Routledge

Warburton, Nigel (2000), *Thinking From A to Z*, Routledge

Weate, Jeremy (1998), *A Young Person's Guide to Philosophy*, Dorling Kindersley

References

Bowkett, Stephen (1999), *Self-Intelligence: A Handbook for Developing Confidence, Self-Esteem and Interpersonal Skills*, Network Educational Press

Blake, Quentin (2001), *Tell Me A Picture*, Lincoln

Haynes, Joanna (2001), *Children as Philosophers: Learning through Enquiry and Dialogue in the Primary Classroom*, Routledge Falmer

Smith, Alistair and Call, Nicola (1999), *The Alps Approach: Accelerated Learning in Primary Schools*, Network Educational Press

Index

Titles from Network Educational Press

Able and talented children collection

Effective Provision for Able and Talented Children by Barry Teare
Effective Resources for Able and Talented Children by Barry Teare
More Effective Resources for Able and Talented Children by Barry Teare
Challenging Resources for Able and Talented Children by Barry Teare
Enrichment Activities for Able and Talented Children by Barry Teare
Parents' and Carers' Guide to Able and Talented Children by Barry Teare

Learning to learn

Let's Learn How to Learn: Workshops for Key Stage 2 by UFA National Team
Brain Friendly Revision by UFA National Team
Creating a Learning to Learn School by Toby Greany & Jill Rodd
Teaching Pupils How to Learn by Bill Lucas, Toby Greany, Jill Rodd & Ray Wicks

Accelerated learning series

Accelerated Learning: A User's Guide by Alistair Smith, Mark Lovatt & Derek Wise
Accelerated Learning in the Classroom by Alistair Smith
Accelerated Learning in Practice by Alistair Smith
The ALPS Approach: Accelerated Learning in Primary Schools by Alistair Smith &
  Nicola Call
The ALPS Approach Resource Book by Alistair Smith & Nicola Call
ALPS StoryMaker by Stephen Bowkett
MapWise by Oliver Caviglioli & Ian Harris
Creating an Accelerated Learning School by Mark Lovatt & Derek Wise

Thinking for Learning by Mel Rockett & Simon Percival
Reaching out to all learners by Cheshire LEA
Coaching Solutions by Will Thomas & Alistair Smith

Primary resources

But Why: Developing philosophical thinking in the classroom by Sara Stanley
 with Steve Bowkett
Foundations of Literacy by Sue Palmer & Ros Bayley
Help Your Child To Succeed by Bill Lucas & Alistair Smith
Help Your Child To Succeed – Toolkit by Bill Lucas & Alistair Smith
That's English! by Tim Harding
That's Maths! by Tim Harding
That's Science! by Tim Harding
The Thinking Child by Nicola Call with Sally Featherstone
The Thinking Child Resource Book by Nicola Call with Sally Featherstone
Numeracy Activities Key Stage 2 by Afzal Ahmed & Honor Williams
Numeracy Activities Key Stage 3 by Afzal Ahmed, Honor Williams & George
 Wickham

Creative thinking

Think it–Map it! by Ian Harris & Oliver Caviglioli
Thinking Skills & Eye Q by Oliver Caviglioli, Ian Harris & Bill Tindall
Reaching out to all thinkers by Ian Harris & Oliver Caviglioli
With Drama in Mind by Patrice Baldwin
Imagine That... by Stephen Bowkett
Self-Intelligence by Stephen Bowkett
StoryMaker Catch Pack by Stephen Bowkett

Effective learning and leadership

Effective Heads of Department by Phil Jones & Nick Sparks
Leading the Learning School by Colin Weatherley
Closing the Learning Gap by Mike Hughes
Strategies for Closing the Learning Gap by Mike Hughes with Andy Vass
Transforming Teaching & Learning by Colin Weatherley with Bruce
 Bonney, John Kerr & Jo Morrison
Effective Learning Activities by Chris Dickinson
Tweak to Transform by Mike Hughes
Making Pupil Data Powerful by Maggie Pringle & Tony Cobb
Raising Boys' Achievement by Jon Pickering
Effective Teachers by Tony Swainston
Effective Teachers in Primary Schools by Tony Swainston

Effective personnel management

*The Well Teacher – management strategies for beating stress, promoting staff health
 & reducing absence* by Maureen Cooper

Managing Challenging People – dealing with staff conduct by Maureen Cooper & Bev Curtis

Managing Poor Performance – handling staff capability issues by Maureen Cooper & Bev Curtis

Managing Recruitment and Selection – appointing the best staff by Maureen Cooper & Bev Curtis

Managing Allegations Against Staff – personnel and child protection issues in schools by Maureen Cooper & Bev Curtis

Visions of education series

The Power of Diversity by Barbara Prashnig
The Brain's Behind It by Alistair Smith
Wise Up by Guy Claxton
The Unfinished Revolution by John Abbott & Terry Ryan
The Learning Revolution by Gordon Dryden & Jeannette Vos

Emotional intelligence

Becoming Emotionally Intelligent by Catherine Corrie
Lend Us Your Ears by Rosemary Sage
Class Talk by Rosemary Sage
A World of Difference by Rosemary Sage
Best behaviour and *Best behaviour FIRST AID* by Peter Relf, Rod Hirst, Jan Richardson & Georgina Youdell
Best behaviour FIRST AID also available separately

Display material

Move It: Physical movement and learning by Alistair Smith
Bright Sparks by Alistair Smith
More Bright Sparks by Alistair Smith
Leading Learning by Alistair Smith

Newly qualified teachers

Lessons are for Learning by Mike Hughes
Classroom Management by Philip Waterhouse & Chris Dickinson
Getting Started by Henry Liebling

School governors

Questions School Governors Ask by Joan Sallis
Basics for School Governors by Joan Sallis
The Effective School Governor by David Marriott (including audio tape)

For more information and ordering details, please consult our website
www.networkpress.co.uk

FINANCIAL ACCOUNTING

Visit the *Financial Accounting: An Introduction, fifth edition* Companion Website at **www.pearsoned.co.uk/weetman** to find valuable **student** learning material including:

- Multiple choice questions to test your learning
- Extensive links to valuable resources on the web
- An online glossary to explain key terms

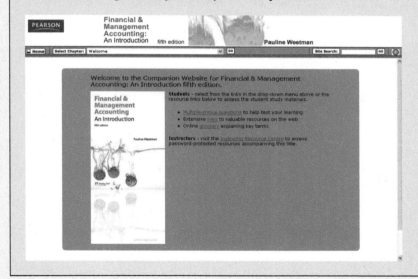

Fifth Edition

FINANCIAL ACCOUNTING
An Introduction

Pauline Weetman
Professor of Accounting
University of Edinburgh

Financial Times
Prentice Hall
is an imprint of

Harlow, England • London • New York • Boston • San Francisco • Toronto • Sydney • Singapore • Hong Kong
Tokyo • Seoul • Taipei • New Delhi • Cape Town • Madrid • Mexico City • Amsterdam • Munich • Paris • Milan

**To my parents,
Harry and Freda Weetman**

Pearson Education Limited
Edinburgh Gate
Harlow
Essex CM20 2JE
England

and Associated Companies throughout the world

Visit us on the World Wide Web at:
www.pearsoned.co.uk

First edition published under the
Financial Times Pitman Publishing imprint in 1996
Second edition 1999
Third edition 2003
Fourth edition 2006
Fifth edition published 2011

© Pearson Education Limited 1996, 1999, 2003, 2006, 2011

ISBN: 978-0-273-71840-6

British Library Cataloguing-in-Publication Data
A catalogue record for this book is available from the British Library

Library of Congress Cataloging-in-Publication Data
Weetman, Pauline.
       / Pauline Weetman. – 5th ed.
    p.   cm.
  ISBN 978-0-273-71840-6 (pbk.)
1.   Accounting.   2. Accounting–Problems, exercises, etc.   I. Title.
  HF5636.W44 2010
  657–dc22
                                          2010029147

10 9 8 7 6 5 4 3 2
15 14 13 12 11

Typeset in 9.5/12pt Palatino by 35
Printed and bound by Rotolito Lombarda, Italy

Contents in brief

Contents

FINANCIAL ACCOUNTING

Part 1 A conceptual framework: setting the scene

Part 2   Reporting the transactions of a business

Supporting resources

Visit **www.pearsoned.co.uk/weetman** to find valuable online resources.

Companion Website for students

- Multiple choice questions to test your learning
- Extensive links to valuable resources on the web
- An online glossary to explain key terms

For instructors

- Complete Instructor's Manual
- PowerPoint slides that can be downloaded and used for presentations

Also: The Companion Website provides the following features:

- Search tool to help locate specific items of content
- E-mail results and profile tools to send results of quizzes to instructors
- Online help and support to assist with website usage and troubleshooting

For more information please contact your local Pearson Education sales representative or visit **www.pearsoned.co.uk/weetman**.

Preface to the fifth edition

Introduction

Preparers and users of financial statements have now become familiar with the impact of the implementation of International Financial Reporting Standards (IFRS) in the UK from January 2005. Those involved in accounting education have set an aim of ensuring that our students understand and can apply the approach represented in IFRS while still being aware that many organisations in the UK will continue to follow the UK tradition as set out in company law and UK accounting standards. For listed companies, in their group accounts, IFRS are mandatory. For all other companies the use of IFRS is a matter of choice with the alternative being to cling to the UK tradition. For unincorporated businesses the prospect of IFRS-related practice is coming closer as the UK ASB considers whether to adopt the version of IFRS published for small and medium-sized entitites from 2012. For the public sector in the UK, IFRS-related practice has arrived with effect from fiscal year 2009/10.

This book uses the international framework and IFRS as its primary focus. This enables students in their early stages of study to understand and analyse the published annual reports and financial statements of our largest businesses. However, it also explains the UK tradition, where this differs from the IFRS, so that students will also understand and appreciate small business accounts where the traditions of UK GAAP continue to be applied.

The book is written for the first level of undergraduate degree study in accounting and business studies, or equivalent introductory accounting courses for any professional training where an understanding of accounting is a basic requirement. Regulation does not stand still and all UK companies now operate under the Companies Act 2006 which has been phased into practice over the period 2006 to 2009. The International Accounting Standards Board revised the standard IAS 1 *Presentation of Financial Statements* to take effect from 2009. This fifth edition is thoroughly revised to reflect these regulatory changes. All 'Real World' case studies at the start of each chapter have been updated to reflect changing conditions and particularly the note of caution over financial statements that has emerged from the banking and credit crisis of 2008–09. The underlying pedagogy of previous editions has been retained in response to encouraging comments from reviewers and from users of the book.

As institutions come under increasing scrutiny for the quality of the teaching and learning experience offered, a textbook must do more than present the knowledge and skills of the chosen subject. It must make explicit to the students what targets are to be achieved and it must help them to assess realistically their own achievements of those targets. It must help the class lecturer prepare, deliver, explain and assess the knowledge and skills expected for the relevant level of study. This is achieved by stating learning outcomes at the start of each chapter and by ensuring that the chapter headings and the end-of-chapter questions address the stated outcomes.

An accompanying website at **www.pearsoned.co.uk/weetman** provides the lecturer with a complete resource pack for each chapter. Student handouts containing a skeleton outline of each chapter, leaving slots for students to complete; overhead-projector masters that match the lecture handouts, additional multiple-choice questions and further graded questions in application of knowledge and in problem solving; all are features for this fifth edition.

End-of-chapter questions are graded according to the skills being assessed. There are tests of retained knowledge, tests of application of knowledge in straightforward situations and tests of problem solving and evaluation using the acquired knowledge in less familiar situations.

Overall the aim of the fifth edition is to provide an introduction to financial accounting which engages the interest of students and encourages a desire for further study. It also contributes to developing the generic skills of application, problem solving, evaluation and communication, all emphasised by employers.

Subject coverage

Financial reporting is an essential component in the process of communication between a business and its stakeholders. The importance of communication increases as organisations become larger and more complex. Reporting financial information to external stakeholders not involved in the day-to-day management of the business requires a carefully balanced process of extracting the key features while preserving the essential core of information. The participants in the communication process cover a wide range of expertise and educational background, so far as accounting is concerned. The range begins with those who prepare financial statements, who may have a special training in accounting techniques, but it ends with those who may be professional investors, private investors, investment advisers, bankers, employee representatives, customers, suppliers and journalists.

First-level degree courses in accounting are increasingly addressed to this broad base of potential interest and this book seeks to provide such a broad base of understanding while also supplying a sound technical base for those intending to pursue specialised study of the subject further. In particular it makes use of the *Framework for the Preparation and Presentation of Financial Statements* which is used by the International Accounting Standards Board in developing and reviewing accounting standards. That *Framework* is intended to help preparers, users and auditors of financial statements to understand better the general nature and function of information reported in financial statements.

Aim of the book

The fifth edition has been updated throughout. It aims to provide a full understanding of the key aspects of the annual report, concentrating in particular on companies in the private sector but presenting principles of wider application which are relevant also to organisations operating in the public sector.

In particular

An international perspective reflects the convergence in accounting standards across the European Union for listed companies. *Features specific to the UK* are retained where these continue to be relevant to other enterprises.

Concepts of financial accounting are identified by applying the principles enunciated by the International Accounting Standards Board in its *Framework for the Preparation and Presentation of Financial Statements*. The *Framework* emphasises the desirability of meeting the needs of users of financial statements and it takes a balance sheet-oriented approach. That approach is applied consistently throughout the book, with some indication of the problems which may arise when it is clear that the established emphasis on the matching of revenues and costs may give a more rational explanation of existing practice. The *Framework* is under review in stages but until that review is complete it is more consistent for students to continue to refer to the complete version.

User needs are explained in every chapter and illustrated by including first-person commentary from a professional fund manager, holding a conversation with an audit manager. The conversations are based on the author's research in the area of communication through the annual report.

The *accounting equation* is used throughout the financial accounting section for analysis and processing of transactions. It is possible for students who do not seek a technical specialism to complete the text without any reference to debit and credit bookkeeping. It is, however, recognised that particular groups of students may wish to understand the basic aspects of debit and credit bookkeeping and for this purpose the end-of-chapter supplements revisit, on a debit and credit recording basis, material already explored in the chapter. Debit and credit aspects of management accounting are not covered since these are regarded as best reserved for later specialist courses if the student so chooses.

Practical illustration is achieved by drawing on the financial information of a fictitious major listed company, taking an overview in early chapters and then developing the detailed disclosures as more specific matters are explored.

Interpretation of financial statements is a feature of all financial reporting chapters, formally brought together in Chapters 13 and 14. The importance of the wider range of corporate communication is reinforced in Chapter 14. This chapter also includes a discussion of some *current developments* that are under debate in the context of international convergence.

A *running example* of the fictitious company Safe and Sure plc provides illustration and interpretation throughout the chapters. Safe and Sure plc is in the service sector. The website contains a parallel example, Craigielaw plc, in the manufacturing sector. On the website there are questions on Craigielaw to accompany most of the chapters.

Self-evaluation is encouraged by setting learning outcomes at the start of each chapter and reviewing these in the chapter summaries. Activity questions are placed at various stages throughout each chapter. Self-testing questions at the end of the chapter may be answered by referring again to the text. Further end-of-chapter questions provide a range of practical applications. Group activities are suggested at the end of each chapter with the particular aim of encouraging participation and interaction. Answers are available to all computational questions, either at the end of the book or on the website.

A *sense of achievement* is engendered in the reader of the financial accounting section by providing a general understanding of the entire annual report by the end of Chapter 7. Thereafter specific aspects of the annual report are explored in Chapters 8–12. Lecturers who wish to truncate a first-level course or leave specific aspects to a later level will find Chapters 8–12 may be used on a selective basis.

A *spreadsheet* approach to financial accounting transactions is used in the body of the relevant chapters to show processing of transactions using the accounting equation. The author is firmly convinced, after years of trying every conceivable approach, that the spreadsheet encourages students to apply the accounting equation analytically, rather than trying to memorise T-account entries. Furthermore students now use spreadsheets as a tool of analysis on a regular basis and will have little difficulty in applying suitable software in preparing spreadsheets. In the bookkeeping supplementary sections, the three-column ledger account has been adopted in the knowledge that school teaching is moving increasingly to adopt this approach which cuts out much of the bewilderment of balancing T-accounts. Computerised accounting systems also favour the three-column presentation with continuous updating of the balance.

Flexible course design

There was once a time when the academic year comprised three terms and we all knew the length of a typical course unit over those three terms. Now there are semesters, trimesters, modules and half-modules so that planning a course of study becomes an exercise in critical path analysis. This text is written for one academic year comprising two semesters of 12 weeks each but may need selective guidance to students for a module of lesser duration.

In financial accounting, Chapters 1–4 provide an essential conceptual framework which sets the scene. For a general appreciation course, Chapters 5 and 6 are practical so that one or both could be omitted, leading directly to Chapter 7 as a guide to published accounts. Chapters 8–12 are structured so that the explanation of principles is contained early in each chapter, but the practical implementation is later in each chapter. For a general appreciation course, it would be particularly important to refer to the section of each chapter which analyses users' needs for information and discusses information provided in the financial statements. However, the practical sections of these chapters could be omitted or used on a selective basis rather than attempting full coverage. Chapters 13 and 14 are important to all readers for a sense of interpretation and awareness of the range of material within corporate reports. Chapter 15 takes the reader through a cash flow statement item-by-item with the emphasis on understanding and interpretation.

Approaches to teaching and learning

Learning outcomes

Targets for student achievement in relation to knowledge and understanding of the subject are specified in learning outcomes at the head of each chapter. The achievements represented by these learning outcomes are confirmed against graded questions at the end of each chapter. The achievement of some learning outcomes may be confirmed by Activities set out at the appropriate stage within the chapter.

Skills outcomes

The end-of-chapter questions test not only subject-specific knowledge and technical skills but also the broader general skills that are transferable to subsequent employment or further training.

Graded questions

End-of-chapter questions are graded and each is matched to one or more learning outcomes. Where a solution is provided to a question this is shown by an **[S]** after the question number.

A series questions: test your understanding

The A series questions confirm the application of technical skills. These are skills specific to the subject of accounting which add to the specialist expertise of the student. More generally they show the student's capacity to acquire and apply a technical skill of this type.

The answers to these questions can be found in relevant sections of the chapter, as indicated at the end of each question.

B series questions: application

The B series questions apply the knowledge gained from reading and practising the material of the chapter. They resemble closely in style and content the technical material of the chapter. Confidence is gained in applying knowledge in a situation that is very similar to that illustrated. Answers are given in Appendix II or on the website. These questions test skills of problem solving and evaluation that are relevant to many subjects and many activities in life, especially in subsequent employment. Some initiative is required in deciding how to apply relevant knowledge and in solving problems.

C series questions: problem solving and evaluation

The C series questions apply the knowledge gained from reading the chapter, but in a varied style of question. Problem solving skills are required in selecting relevant data or in using knowledge to work out what further effort is needed to solve the problem. Evaluation means giving an opinion or explanation of the results of the problem-solving exercise. Some answers are given in Appendix II but others are on the website so that they can be used in tutorial preparation or class work.

Group and individual cases

Cases apply knowledge gained from the chapter but they also test communication skills. Communication may involve writing or speaking, or both. It may require, for example, explanation of a technical matter to a non-technical person, or discussion with other students to explore a controversial issue, or presentation of a report to a business audience.

S series questions in supplementary sections

The S series questions test knowledge of the accounting records system (bookkeeping entries) to confirm understanding by those who have chosen to study the supplementary bookkeeping sections.

Website

A website is available at **www.pearsoned.co.uk/weetman** by password access to lecturers adopting this book. It contains additional problem questions for each chapter, with full solutions to these additional questions as well as any solutions not provided in the book. The website includes basic tutorial instructions and overhead-projector masters to support each chapter.

Target readership

This book is targeted at a broad-ranging business studies type of first-level degree course. It is intended to support the equivalent of one semester of 12 teaching weeks. There is sufficient basic bookkeeping (ledger accounts) in the end-of-chapter supplements to make the book suitable for those intending to pursue a specialised study of accounting beyond the first level but the bookkeeping material is optional for those who do not have such special intentions. The book has been written with undergraduate students particularly in mind, but may also be suitable for professional and postgraduate business courses where financial reporting is taught at an introductory level.

Acknowledgements

I am grateful to academic colleagues and to reviewers of the text for helpful comments and suggestions. I am also grateful to undergraduate students of five universities who have taken my courses and thereby helped in developing an approach to teaching and learning the subject. Professor Graham Peirson and Mr Alan Ramsay of Monash University provided a first draft of their text based on the conceptual framework in Australia which gave valuable assistance in designing the structure of this book, which was also guided from the publishing side by Pat Bond and Ron Harper.

Professor Ken Shackleton of the University of Glasgow helped plan the structure of the management accounting chapters. The Institute of Chartered Accountants of Scotland gave permission for use of some of the end-of-chapter questions.

Subsequently I have received valuable support in successive editions from the editorial staff at Pearson Education. For this latest edition I am grateful to colleagues and students who have used the book in their teaching and learning. I have also been helped by constructive comments from reviewers and by guidance from Matthew Smith, Acquisitions Editor, and Tim Parker, Senior Desk Editor.

Guided tour of the book

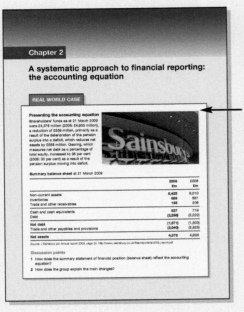

Chapter contents provide a quick and easy reference to the following section.

Real world case studies at the beginning of each chapter are designed to exemplify a typical situation in which financial or management accounting can be helpful.

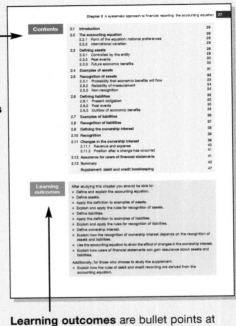

Learning outcomes are bullet points at the start of each chapter to show what you can expect to learn from that chapter, highlighting the core coverage.

Key terms and **definitions** are emboldened where they are first introduced, with a definition box to provide a concise explanation where required.

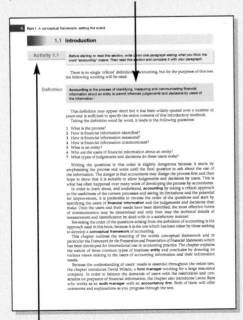

Figures and Tables, at frequent intervals throughout most chapters, provide clear explanations of key points and calculations.

Colour coding provides a clear and accessible guide to key aspects of accounting equations.

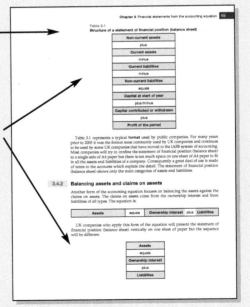

Activities appear throughout each chapter to encourage self-evaluation and help you to think about the application of the subject in everyday life.

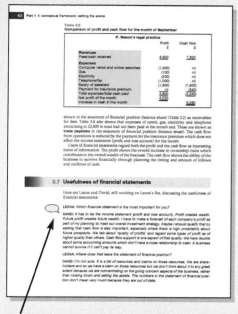

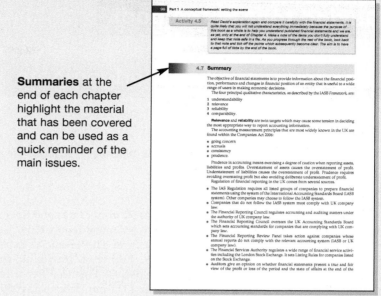

Summaries at the end of each chapter highlight the material that has been covered and can be used as a quick reminder of the main issues.

A conversation between two managers (**consultants**) appears at intervals throughout the text to provide a valuable insight into the type of interpretative comment which you may find more taxing. These conversations allow a more candid discussion of issues and problems within the subject.

Application (Series B) questions are questions that ask you to apply the knowledge gained from reading and practising the material in the chapter, and closely resemble the style and content of the technical material. Answers are given at the end of the book or in the Resources for Tutors on the Companion Website at **www.pearsoned.co.uk/weetman**.

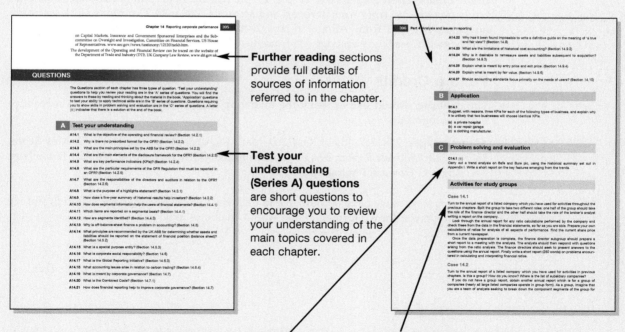

Further reading sections provide full details of sources of information referred to in the chapter.

Test your understanding (Series A) questions are short questions to encourage you to review your understanding of the main topics covered in each chapter.

Problem solving and evaluation (Series C) questions require problem solving skills to select relevant data in order to work out what further effort is needed to solve the problem. Evaluation questions ask for your opinion surrounding the results of the problem solving exercise. Some solutions are found at the end of the book but others are in the Resources for Tutors section on the Companion Website at **www.pearsoned.co.uk/weetman**, for use in tutorial preparation or class work.

Activities for study groups at the end of most chapters are designed to help you apply the accounting skills and knowledge you have acquired from the chapter to the real world.

Publisher's acknowledgements

We are grateful to the following for permission to reproduce copyright material:

Text

Case Study on page 50 from Marks and Spencer plc Annual report 2009 p.16; Case Study on page 51 from BAA Annual report 2004/5, p.34; BAA Annual report 2004/5, p.34; Case Study on page 73 from The Financial Reporting Review Panel Press Notice PN 123, 9 December 2009, http:www.frc.org.uk/frrp/press/pub2189.html; Figure 4.1 from Statement of Principles for Financial Reporting p.34, 1999 , Accounting Standards Board; Case Study on page 133 from Debenhams 2009 Annual report, p.19, http://www.investis.com/debenhams/pdfs/ar2009_new.pdf; Case Study on pages 160–1 from Home Retail Group, Annual Report 2009, http://www.homeretailgroup.com/home/investors; Figure 7.1 from Statement of Principles for Financial Reporting p.34, 1999, Accounting Standards Board; Case Study on pages 200–1 from Annual Report, 01/01/2009, Halfords Group plc, http://halfordscompany.com; Case Study on pages 238–9 from Annual report, 01/01/2008, Cadbury plc, http:www.cadburyinvestors.com; Case Study on page 268 from Annual report, and Directors' report p.39, Carphone Warehouse plc; Case Study on pages 287–8 from Annual report 2008 p. 158, BP plc, BP plc Annual Report and Accounts, 2008; Case Study on page 340 from Annual report and accounts 2009 p.87, Thorntons plc; Case Study on pages 399–400 from Annual report 2009, Chloride plc, www.chloridepower.com; Dutch Shell; Case Study on page 688 from Business Wire, 3/09/2009.

Picture Credits

The publisher would like to thank the following for their kind permission to reproduce their photographs:

Alamy Images: 238, 367, Justin Kase 200, Mark Richardson 4, Superstock 73; **Alex Segre:** 26, 287, 340; **Chloride Power:** 399; **Chris Batson:** 268; **Getty Images:** 50, 104, 133, Bloomberg 309; **Roger G Howard Photography:** 160

In some instances we have been unable to trace the owners of copyright material, and we would appreciate any information that would enable us to do so.

FINANCIAL ACCOUNTING

Part 1

A conceptual framework: setting the scene

Chapter 1

Who needs accounting?

REAL WORLD CASE

Meeting users' needs

Extracts from annual report 2008 (pp. 1 and 26)

Key results (p. 1)

		2008 £m	2007 £m
Gross sales including VAT and travel agency sales	Up 15%	10,435	9,075
Revenue before premiums ceded to reinsurers	Up 13%	9,399	8,289
Operating profit before significant items	Up 11%	393	355
Operating profit after significant items	Up 60%	275	173
Profit before payments to and on behalf of members	Up 11%	218	196
Payments to and on behalf of members Members' funds	Up 122% Up 4%	102 3,933	46 3,797

Directors' responsibilities (extract)

Directors are expected to exercise their judgement when making decisions in the best interests of the Society as a whole, mindful of their responsibilities to members and other stakeholders. (p. 26)

What is a co-operative? (from the website)

Unlike lots of other businesses, a co-operative doesn't have tradeable shares like a plc whose values can fluctuate. A co-operative, however, is owned equally and fairly by its members – people like you! We'd far rather give our profits back to our members and the community than to faceless shareholding institutions. You know that twice-yearly payment you get from us? That's actually a share of our profits! And the more you spend with us, the more of a profit you get back! How neat is that? Your dividend is linked to how much profit we make. Not many businesses give back that sort of money to their customers.

Values in action (from the website)

Our family of businesses has a set of social goals which underpin everything we do, called our values and principles. We have asked members what is important to them and they have told us. By exercising their democratic rights, members make sure that we have long standing agreements with Fairtrade producers, that we do not deal with arms traders, that we can offset the carbon that is produced when we fly, and that we do give back to the communities in which we trade. That is pretty special.

Source: The Cooperative Group, http://www.co-operative.coop/, December 2009. http://www.co-operative.coop/en/corporate/corporatepublications/Annual-Report-and-Accounts/Annual-Report-archive/

Discussion points

1 Who might be included in the stakeholders to whom the directors are responsible?

2 To what extent do the 'key results' meet the needs of users of financial statements?

Contents

Learning outcomes

After studying this chapter you should be able to:

- Define, and explain the definition of, accounting.
- Explain what is meant by a *conceptual framework*.
- Explain the distinguishing features of a sole trader, a partnership and a limited company.
- List the main users of financial information and their particular needs.
- Discuss the usefulness of financial statements to the main users.

Additionally, for those who choose to study the supplement:

- Define the basic terminology of business transactions.

1.1 Introduction

Before starting to read this section, write down one paragraph stating what you think the word 'accounting' means. Then read this section and compare it with your paragraph.

There is no single 'official' definition of accounting, but for the purposes of this text the following wording will be used:

Definition
Accounting is the process of identifying, measuring and communicating financial information about an entity to permit informed judgements and decisions by users of the information.[1]

This definition may appear short but it has been widely quoted over a number of years and is sufficient to specify the entire contents of this introductory textbook.

Taking the definition word by word, it leads to the following questions:

1 What is the process?
2 How is financial information identified?
3 How is financial information measured?
4 How is financial information communicated?
5 What is an entity?
6 Who are the users of financial information about an entity?
7 What types of judgements and decisions do these users make?

Writing the questions in this order is slightly dangerous because it starts by emphasising the process and waits until the final question to ask about the use of the information. The danger is that accountants may design the process first and then hope to show that it is suitable to allow judgements and decisions by users. This is what has often happened over many years of developing the process by accountants.

In order to learn about, and understand, **accounting** by taking a critical approach to the usefulness of the current processes and seeing its limitations and the potential for improvement, it is preferable to reverse the order of the questions and start by specifying the users of **financial information** and the judgements and decisions they make. Once the users and their needs have been identified, the most effective forms of communication may be determined and only then may the technical details of measurement and identification be dealt with in a satisfactory manner.

Reversing the order of the questions arising from the definition of accounting is the approach used in this book, because it is the one which has been taken by those seeking to develop a **conceptual framework** of accounting.

This chapter outlines the meaning of the words conceptual framework and in particular the *Framework for the Preparation and Presentation of Financial Statements* which has been developed for international use in accounting practice. The chapter explains the nature of three common types of business **entity** and concludes by drawing on various views relating to the users of accounting information and their information needs.

Because the understanding of users' needs is essential throughout the entire text, the chapter introduces David Wilson, a **fund manager** working for a large insurance company. In order to balance the demands of users with the restrictions and constraints on preparers of financial information, the chapter also introduces Leona Rees who works as an **audit manager** with an **accountancy firm**. Both of them will offer comments and explanations as you progress through the text.

Activity 1.2

How does this section compare with your initial notions of what accounting means? If they are similar, then it is likely that the rest of this book will meet your expectations. If they are different, then it may be that you are hoping for more than this book can achieve. If that is the case, this may be a useful point at which to consult your lecturer, tutor or some other expert in the subject to be sure that you are satisfied that this book will meet your personal learning outcomes.

1.2 The development of a conceptual framework

A **conceptual framework** for accounting is a statement of principles which provides generally accepted guidance for the development of new reporting practices and for challenging and evaluating the existing practices. Conceptual frameworks have been developed in several countries around the world, with the UK arriving a little late on the scene. However, arriving late does give the advantage of learning from what has gone before. It is possible to see a pattern emerging in the various approaches to developing a conceptual framework.

The conceptual frameworks developed for practical use by the **accountancy profession** in various countries all start with the common assumption that **financial statements** must be useful. The structure of most conceptual frameworks is along the following lines:

- Who are the users of financial statements?
- What are the information needs of users?
- What types of financial statements will best satisfy their needs?
- What are the characteristics of financial statements which meet these needs?
- What are the principles for defining and recognising items in financial statements?
- What are the principles for measuring items in financial statements?

The most widely applicable conceptual framework is the *Framework for the Preparation and Presentation of Financial Statements* produced by the International Accounting Standards Board (IASB). This *Framework* was issued in 1989 and either reflects, or is reflected in, national conceptual frameworks of the USA, Canada, Australia and the UK. Since 2006 the *Framework* has been under review for updating but it seems unlikely that a revised version will be issued until after some challenging accounting issues have been addressed. The thinking in all those documents can be traced to two discussion papers of the 1970s in the UK and the USA. In the UK, *The Corporate Report*[2] was a slim but highly influential document setting out the needs of users and how these might be met. Two years earlier the *Trueblood Report*[3] in the USA had taken a similar approach of identifying the needs of users, although perhaps coming out more strongly in support of the needs of shareholders and creditors than of other user groups. In the UK, various documents on the needs of users have been prepared by individuals invited to help the process[4] or those who took it on themselves to propose radical new ideas.[5]

Since January 2005, all **listed** companies in member states of the European Union (EU) have been required by an accounting regulation called the IAS regulation[6] to use a system of international financial reporting standards set by the International Accounting Standards Board. The UK ASB has been influential in the development of these international reporting standards and, over a period of years, has been moving UK accounting practice closely into line with the international standards. For **unlisted** companies and other organisations not covered by the IAS regulation of the EU, the UK ASB has a conceptual framework of its own, called the *Statement of Principles*.[7] This document has many similarities to the IASB's *Framework*.

1.3 Framework for the preparation and presentation of financial statements

The IASB's Framework has seven main sections.

1 Introduction – purpose of the *Framework*, users and their information needs.
2 The objective of financial statements.
3 Underlying assumptions.
4 Qualitative characteristics of financial statements.
5 The elements of financial statements.
6 Recognition of the elements of financial statements.
7 Measurement of the elements of financial statements.

Sections 1 and 2 of the *Framework* are written at a general level and a reader would find no difficulty in reviewing these at an early stage of study, to gain a flavour of what is expected of financial statements. The remaining sections are a mixture of general principles, which are appropriate to first-level study of the subject, and some quite specific principles which deal with more advanced problems. Some of those problems need an understanding of accounting which is beyond a first level of study. This book will refer to aspects of the various sections of the *Framework*, as appropriate, when particular issues are dealt with. You should be aware, however, that this book concentrates on the basic aspects of the *Framework* and does not explore every complexity.

A conceptual framework is particularly important when practices are being developed for reporting to those who are not part of the day-to-day running of the business. This is called **external reporting** or **financial accounting** and is the focus of the *Financial Accounting* half of this book. For those who are managing the business on a day-to-day basis, special techniques have been developed and are referred to generally as **internal reporting** or **management accounting**. That is the focus of the management accounting half of this book.

Before continuing with the theme of the conceptual framework, it is useful to pause and consider the types of business for which accounting information may be required.

1.4 Types of business entity

The word **entity** means 'something that exists independently'. A business entity is a business that exists independently of those who own the business. There are three main categories of business which will be found in all countries, although with different titles in different ones. This chapter uses the terminology common to the UK. The three main categories are: **sole trader**, **partnership** and **limited liability company**. This list is by no means exhaustive but provides sufficient variety to allow explanation of the usefulness of most accounting practices and their application.

Activity 1.5

Before reading the next sections, take out a newspaper with business advertisements or a business telephone directory, or take a walk down your local high street or drive round the trading estate. Write down the names of five businesses, shops or other organisations. Then read the sections and attempt to match your list against the information provided in each.

1.4.1 Sole trader

An individual may enter into business alone, either selling goods or providing a service. Such a person is described as a **sole trader**. The business may be started because the sole trader has a good idea which appears likely to make a profit, and has some cash to buy the equipment and other resources to start the business. If cash is not available, the sole trader may borrow from a bank to enable the business to start up. Although this is the form in which many businesses have started, it is one which is difficult to expand because the sole trader will find it difficult to arrange additional finance for expansion. If the business is not successful and the sole trader is unable to meet obligations to pay money to others, then those persons may ask a court of law to authorise the sale of the personal possessions, and even the family home, of the sole trader. Being a sole trader can be a risky matter and the cost of bank borrowing may be at a relatively unfavourable rate of interest because the bank fears losing its money.

From this description it will be seen that the sole trader's business is very much intertwined with the sole trader's personal life. However, for accounting purposes, the business is regarded as a separate economic entity, of which the sole trader is the owner who takes the risk of the bad times and the benefit of the good times. Take as an example the person who decides to start working as an electrician and advertises their services in a newspaper. The electrician travels to jobs from home and has no business premises. Tools are stored in the loft at home and the business records are in a cupboard in the kitchen. Telephone calls from customers are received on the domestic phone and there are no clearly defined working hours. The work is inextricably intertwined with family life.

For accounting purposes that person is seen as the owner of a business which provides electrical services and the business is seen as being separate from the person's other interests and private life. The owner may hardly feel any great need for accounting information because they know the business very closely, but accounting information will be needed by other persons or entities, mainly the government (in the form of **HM Revenue and Customs**) for tax collecting purposes. It may also be required by a bank for the purposes of lending money to the business or by another sole trader who is intending to buy the business when the existing owner retires.

1.4.2 Partnership

One method by which the business of a sole trader may expand is to enter into **partnership** with one or more people. This may permit a pooling of skills to allow more efficient working, or may allow one person with ideas to work with another who has the money to provide the resources needed to turn the ideas into a profit. There is thus more potential for being successful. If the business is unsuccessful, then the consequences are similar to those for the sole trader. Persons to whom money is owed by the business may ask a court of law to authorise the sale of the personal property of the partners in order to meet the obligation. Even more seriously, one partner may be required to meet all the obligations of the partnership if the other partner does not have sufficient personal property, possessions and cash. This is described in law as **joint and several liability** and the risks have to be considered very carefully by those entering into partnership.

Partnership may be established as a matter of fact by two persons starting to work together with the intention of making a profit and sharing it between them. More often there is a legal agreement, called a **partnership deed**, which sets out the rights and duties of each partner and specifies how they will share the profits. There is also **partnership law**, which governs the basic relationships between partners and which they may use to resolve their disputes in a court of law if there is no partnership deed, or if the partnership deed has not covered some aspect of the partnership.

For accounting purposes the partnership is seen as a separate economic entity, owned by the partners. The owners may have the same intimate knowledge of the business as does the sole trader and may therefore feel that accounting information is not very important for them. On the other hand, each partner may wish to be sure that they are receiving a fair share of the partnership profits. There will also be other persons requesting accounting information, such as HM Revenue and Customs, banks who provide finance and individuals who may be invited to join the partnership so that it can expand even further.

1.4.3   Limited liability company

The main risk attached to either a sole trader or a partnership is that of losing personal property and possessions, including the family home, if the business fails. That risk would inhibit many persons from starting or expanding a business. Historically, as the UK changed from a predominantly agricultural to a predominantly industrial economy in the nineteenth century, it became apparent that owners needed the protection of **limited liability**. This meant that if the business failed, the owners might lose all the money they had put into the business but their personal wealth would be safe.

There are two forms of limited liability company. The **private limited company** has the word 'Limited' (abbreviated to 'Ltd') in its title. The **public limited company** has the abbreviation 'plc' in its title. The private limited company is prohibited by law from offering its **shares** to the public, so it is a form of limited liability appropriate to a family-controlled business. The public limited company is permitted to offer its shares to the public. In return it has to satisfy more onerous regulations. Where the shares of a public limited company are bought and sold on a **stock exchange**, the public limited company is called a **listed company** because the shares of the company are on a list of share prices.

In either type of company, the owners are called **shareholders** because they share the ownership and share the profits of the good times and the losses of the bad times (to the defined limit of liability). Once they have paid in full for their shares, the owners face no further risk of being asked to contribute to meeting any obligations of the business. Hopefully, the business will prosper and the owners may be able to receive a share of that prosperity in the form of a cash **dividend**. A cash dividend returns to the owners, on a regular basis and in the form of cash, a part of the profit created by the business.

If the company is very small, the owners may run the business themselves. If it is larger, then they may prefer to pay someone else to run the business. In either case, the persons running the business on a day-to-day basis are called the **directors**.

Because limited liability is a great privilege for the owners, the company must meet regulations set out by Parliament in the form of a **Companies Act**. At present the relevant law is the Companies Act 2006.

For accounting purposes the company is an entity with an existence separate from the owners. In the very smallest companies the owners may not feel a great need for accounting information, but in medium- or large-sized companies, accounting information will be very important for the shareholders as it forms a report on how well the directors have run the company. As with other forms of business accounting information must be supplied to HM Revenue and Customs for tax-collecting purposes. The list of other users will expand considerably because there will be a greater variety of sources of finance, the company may be seeking to attract more **investors**, employees will be concerned about the well-being of the business and even the customers and suppliers may want to know more about the financial strength of the company.

Although the law provides the protection of limited liability, this has little practical meaning for many small family-controlled companies because a bank lending money to the business will ask for personal guarantees from the shareholder directors. Those personal guarantees could involve a mortgage over the family home, or an interest in life assurance policies. The potential consequences of such personal guarantees, when a company fails, are such that the owners may suffer as much as the sole trader whose business fails.

Table 1.1 summarises the differences between a partnership and a limited liability company that are relevant for accounting purposes.

Table 1.1
Differences between a partnership and a limited liability company

	Partnership	Limited liability company
Formation	Formed by two or more persons, usually with written agreement but not necessarily in writing.	Formed by a number of persons registering the company under the Companies Act, following legal formalities. In particular there must be a written **memorandum** and **articles of association** setting out the powers allowed to the company.
Running the business	All partners are entitled to share in the running of the business.	Shareholders must appoint **directors** to run the business (although shareholders may appoint themselves as directors).
Accounting information	Partnerships are not obliged to make accounting information available to the wider public.	Companies must make accounting information available to the public through the **Registrar of Companies**.
Meeting obligations	All members of a general partnership are jointly and severally liable for money owed by the firm.	The personal liability of the owners is limited to the amount they have agreed to pay for shares.
Powers to carry out activities	Partnerships may carry out any legal business activities agreed by the partners.	The company may only carry out the activities set out in its **memorandum** and **articles of association**.
Status in law	The partnership is not a separate legal entity (under English law), the partnership property being owned by the partners. (Under Scots law the partnership is a separate legal entity.)	The company is seen in law as a separate person, distinct from its members. This means that the company can own property, make contracts and take legal action or be the subject of legal action.

Table 1.2 identifies the differences between the public limited company and the private limited company that are relevant for accounting purposes.

Table 1.2
Brief comparison of private and public companies

	Public company	Private company
Running the business	Minimum of two directors.	Minimum of one director.
	Must have a company secretary who holds a relevant qualification (responsible for ensuring the company complies with the requirements of company law).	The sole director may also act as the company secretary and is not required to have a formal qualification.
Ownership	Shares may be offered to the public, inviting subscription.	Shares must not be offered to the public. May only be sold by private arrangements.
	Minimum **share capital** £50,000.	No minimum share capital.
Accounting information	Extensive information required on transactions between directors and the company.	Less need for disclosure of transactions between directors and the company.
	Information must be made public through the Registrar of Companies.	
	Provision of financial information to the public is determined by size of company, more information being required of medium- and large-sized companies.	
	Accounting information must be sent to all shareholders.	

Activity 1.6

Look at the list of five organisations which you prepared before reading this section. Did the list match what you have just read? If not, there are several possible explanations. One is that you have written down organisations which are not covered by this book. That would apply if you have written down 'museum', 'town hall' or 'college'. These are examples of public sector bodies that require specialised financial statements not covered by this text. Another is that you did not discover the name of the business enterprise. Perhaps you wrote down 'Northern Hotel' but did not find the name of the company owning the hotel. If your list does not match the section, ask for help from your lecturer, tutor or other expert in the subject so that you are satisfied that this book will continue to meet your personal learning outcomes.

1.5 Users and their information needs

Who are the users of the information provided by these reporting entities? This section shows that there is one group, namely the **management** of an organisation, whose information needs are so specialised that a separate type of accounting has evolved called **management accounting**. However, there are other groups, each of which may believe it has a reasonable right to obtain information about an organisation, that do not enjoy unrestricted access to the business and so have to rely on management to supply suitable information. These groups include the owners, where the owners are not also the managers, but extend further to employees, lenders, suppliers, customers, government and its branches and the public interest. Those in the wider interest groups are sometimes referred to as **stakeholders**.

<table>
<tr><td>Definition</td><td>**Stakeholder** A general term to indicate all those who might have a legitimate interest in receiving financial information about a business because they have a 'stake' in it.</td></tr>
</table>

1.5.1 Management

Many would argue that the foremost users of accounting information about an organisation must be those who manage the business on a day-to-day basis. This group is referred to in broad terms as **management**, which is a collective term for all those persons who have responsibilities for making judgements and decisions within an organisation. Because they have close involvement with the business, they have access to a wide range of information (much of which may be confidential within the organisation) and will seek those aspects of the information which are most relevant to their particular judgements and decisions. Because this group of users is so broad, and because of the vast amount of information potentially available, a specialist branch of accounting has developed, called management accounting, to serve the particular needs of management.

It is management's responsibility to employ the resources of the business in an efficient way and to meet the objectives of the business. The information needed by management to carry out this responsibility ought to be of high quality and in an understandable form so far as the management is concerned. If that is the case, it would not be unreasonable to think that a similar quality (although not necessarily quantity) of information should be made available more widely to those stakeholders who do not have the access available to management.[8] Such an idea would be regarded as somewhat revolutionary in nature by some of those who manage companies, but more and more are beginning to realise that sharing information with investors and other stakeholders adds to the general atmosphere of confidence in the enterprise.

1.5.2 Owners as investors

Where the owners are the managers, as is the case for a sole trader or a partnership, they have no problem in gaining access to information and will select information appropriate to their own needs. They may be asked to provide information for other users, such as HM Revenue and Customs or a bank which has been approached to provide finance, but that information will be designed to meet the needs of those particular users rather than the owners.

Where the ownership is separate from the management of the business, as is the case with a limited liability company, the owners are more appropriately viewed as investors who entrust their money to the company and expect something in return, usually a **dividend** and a growth in the value of their investment as the company prospers. Providing money to fund a business is a risky act and investors are concerned with the **risk** inherent in, and **return** provided by, their investments. They need information to help them decide whether they should buy, hold or sell.[9] They are also interested in information on the entity's financial performance and financial position that helps them to assess both its cash-generation abilities and the stewardship of management.[10]

Much of the investment in shares through the Stock Exchange in the UK is carried out by **institutional investors**, such as pension funds, insurance companies, unit trusts and investment trusts. The day-to-day business of buying and selling shares is carried out by a **fund manager** employed by the institutional investor. Private investors are in the minority as a group of investors in the UK. They will often take the advice of an

equities analyst who investigates and reports on share investment. The fund managers and the equities analysts are also regarded as users of accounting information.

The kinds of judgements and decisions made by investors could include any or all of the following:

(a) Evaluating the performance of the entity.
(b) Assessing the effectiveness of the entity in achieving objectives (including compliance with **stewardship** obligations) established previously by its management, its members or owners.
(c) Evaluating managerial performance, efficiency and objectives, including investment and dividend distribution plans.
(d) Ascertaining the experience and background of company directors and officials including details of other directorships or official positions held.
(e) Ascertaining the economic stability and vulnerability of the reporting entity.
(f) Assessing the **liquidity** of the entity, its present or future requirements for additional **working capital**, and its ability to raise long-term and short-term finance.
(g) Assessing the capacity of the entity to make future reallocations of its resources for economic purposes.
(h) Estimating the future prospects of the entity, including its capacity to pay **dividends**, and predicting future levels of investment.
(i) Making economic comparisons, either for the given entity over a period of time or with other entities at one point in time.
(j) Estimating the value of present or prospective interests in or claims on the entity.
(k) Ascertaining the ownership and control of the entity.[11]

That list was prepared in 1975 and, while it is a valid representation of the needs of investors, carries an undertone which implies that the investors have to do quite a lot of the work themselves in making estimates of the prospects of the entity. Today there is a stronger view that the management of a business should share more of its thinking and planning with the investors. The list may therefore be expanded by suggesting that it would be helpful for investors (and all external users) to know:

(a) the entity's actual performance for the most recent accounting period and how this compares with its previous plan for that period;
(b) management's explanations of any significant variances between the two; and
(c) management's financial plan for the current and forward accounting periods, and explanations of the major assumptions used in preparing it.[12]

If you look through some **annual reports** of major listed companies you will see that this is more a 'wish list' than a statement of current practice, but it is indicative of the need for a more progressive approach. In the annual reports of large companies you will find a section called the Operating and financial review (or similar title). This is where the more progressive companies will include forward-looking statements which stop short of making a forecast but give help in understanding which of the trends observed in the past are likely to continue into the future.

1.5.3 Employees

Employees and their representatives are interested in information about the stability and profitability of their employers. They are also interested in information that helps them to assess the ability of the entity to provide remuneration, retirement benefits and employment opportunities.[13] Employees continue to be interested in their employer after they have retired from work because in many cases the employer provides a pension fund.

The matters which are likely to be of interest to past, present and prospective employees include: the ability of the employer to meet wage agreements; management's intentions regarding employment levels, locations and working conditions; the pay, conditions and terms of employment of various groups of employees; job security; and the contribution made by employees in other divisions of the organisation. Much of this is quite specialised and detailed information. It may be preferable to supply this to employees by means of special purpose reports on a frequent basis rather than waiting for the annual report, which is slow to arrive and more general in nature. However, employees may look to financial statements to confirm information provided previously in other forms.

1.5.4 Lenders

Lenders are interested in information that enables them to determine whether their loans, and the related interest, will be paid when due.[14]

Loan **creditors** provide finance on a longer-term basis. They will wish to assess the economic stability and vulnerability of the borrower. They are particularly concerned with the risk of **default** and its consequences. They may impose conditions (called **loan covenants**) which require the business to keep its overall borrowing within acceptable limits. The financial statements may provide evidence that the loan covenant conditions are being met.

Some lenders will ask for special reports as well as the general financial statements. Banks in particular will ask for **cash flow projections** showing how the business plans to repay, with interest, the money borrowed.

1.5.5 Suppliers and other trade creditors

Suppliers of goods and services (also called trade creditors) are interested in information that enables them to decide whether to sell to the entity and to determine whether amounts owing to them will be paid when due. Suppliers (trade creditors) are likely to be interested in an entity over a shorter period than lenders unless they are dependent upon the continuation of the entity as a major customer.[15] The amount due to be paid to the supplier is called a trade payable or an account payable.

Trade creditors supply goods and services to an entity and have very little protection if the entity fails because there are insufficient assets to meet all **liabilities**. They are usually classed as **unsecured creditors**, which means they are a long way down the queue for payment. So they have to exercise caution in finding out whether the business is able to pay and how much risk of non-payment exists. This information need not necessarily come from accounting statements; it could be obtained by reading the local press and trade journals, joining the Chamber of Trade, and generally listening in to the stories and gossip circulating in the geographic area or the industry. However, the financial statements of an entity may confirm the stories gained from other sources.

In recent years there has been a move for companies to work more closely with their suppliers and to establish 'partnership' arrangements where the operational and financial plans of both may be dovetailed by specifying the amount and the timing of goods and services required. Such arrangements depend heavily on confidence, which in turn may be derived partly from the strength of financial statements.

1.5.6 Customers

Customers have an interest in information about the continuance of an entity, especially when they have a long-term involvement with, or are dependent upon, its prosperity.[16] In particular, customers need information concerning the current and future supply of goods and services offered, price and other product details, and conditions of sale. Much of this information may be obtained from sales literature or from sales staff of the enterprise, or from trade and consumer journals.[17]

The financial statements provide useful confirmation of the reliability of the enterprise itself as a continuing source of supply, especially when the customer is making payments in advance. They also confirm the capacity of the entity in terms of **non-current assets** (also called **fixed assets**) and working **capital** and give some indication of the strength of the entity to meet any obligations under guarantees or warranties.[18]

1.5.7   Governments and their agencies

Governments and their agencies are interested in the allocation of resources and, therefore, in the activities of entities. They also require information in order to regulate the activities of entities, assess taxation and provide a basis for national income and economic statistics.[19]

Acting on behalf of the UK government's Treasury Department, HM Revenue and Customs collects taxes from businesses based on profit calculated according to commercial accounting practices (although there are some specific rules in the taxation legislation which modify the normal accounting practices). HM Revenue and Customs has the power to demand more information than appears in published financial statements, but will take these as a starting point.

Other agencies include the regulators of the various utility companies. Examples are Ofcom[20] (the Office of Communications) and Ofgem[21] (the Office of Gas and Electricity Markets). They use accounting information as part of the package by which they monitor the prices charged by these organisations to consumers of their services. They also demand additional information designed especially to meet their needs.

1.5.8   Public interest

Enterprises affect members of the public in a variety of ways. For example, enterprises may make a substantial contribution to the local economy by providing employment and using local suppliers. Financial statements may assist the public by providing information about the trends and recent developments in the prosperity of the entity and the range of its activities.[22]

A strong element of public interest has been aroused in recent years by environmental issues and the impact of companies on the environment. There are costs imposed on others when a company pollutes a river or discharges harmful gases into the air. It may be perceived that a company is cutting corners to prune its own reported costs at the expense of other people. Furthermore, there are activities of companies today which will impose costs in the future. Where an oil company has installed a drilling rig in the North Sea, it will be expected one day to remove and destroy the rig safely. There is a question as to whether the company will be able to meet that cost. These costs and future liabilities may be difficult to identify and quantify, but that does not mean that companies should not attempt to do so. More companies are now including descriptions of environmental policy in their annual reports, but regular accounting procedures for including environmental costs and obligations in the financial statements have not yet been developed.

Activity 1.7	*Look back to the list of users of financial statements which you prepared earlier in this chapter. How closely does your list compare with the users described in this section? Did you have any in your list which are not included here? Have you used names which differ from those used in the chapter? Are there users in the chapter which are not in your list? If your list does not match the section, ask for help from your lecturer, tutor or other expert in the subject so that you are satisfied that this book will continue to meet your personal learning outcomes.*

1.6 General purpose or specific purpose financial statements?

Some experts who have analysed the needs of users in the manner set out in the previous section have come to the conclusion that no single set of **general purpose financial statements** could meet all these needs. It has been explained in the previous section that some users already turn to special reports to meet specific needs. Other experts hold that there could be a form of general purpose financial statements which would meet all the needs of some user groups and some of the needs of others.

This book is written on the assumption that it *is* possible to prepare a set of general purpose financial statements which will have some interest for all users. The existence of such reports is particularly important for those who cannot prescribe the information they would like to receive from an organisation. That is perhaps because they have no bargaining power, or because they are many in number but not significant in economic influence.

Preparers of general purpose financial statements tend to regard the owners and long-term lenders as the primary users of the information provided. There is an expectation or hope that the interests of these groups will overlap to some extent with the interests of a wider user group and that any improvements in financial statements will be sufficient that fewer needs will be left unmet.[23]

The primary focus of the *Framework* is on general purpose financial statements.[24] It takes the view that many users have to rely on the financial statements as their major source of financial information. Financial statements should be prepared with their needs in mind. The *Framework* assumes that if financial statements meet the needs of investors, they will also meet the needs of most other users.[25]

1.7 Stewards and agents

In an earlier section, the needs of investors as users were listed and the word 'stewardship' appeared. In the days before an industrial society existed, stewards were the people who looked after the manor house and lands while the lord of the manor enjoyed the profits earned. Traditionally, accounting has been regarded as having a particular role to play in confirming that those who manage a business on behalf of the owner take good care of the resources entrusted to them and earn a satisfactory profit for the owner by using those resources.

As the idea of a wider range of users emerged, this idea of the 'stewardship' objective of accounting was mentioned less often (although its influence remains strong in legislation governing accounting practice). In the academic literature it has been reborn under a new heading – that of **agency**. Theories have been developed about the relationship between the owner, as 'principal', and the manager, as 'agent'. A conscientious manager, acting as an agent, will carry out their duties in the best interest of the owners, and is required by the law of agency to do so. However, not all agents will be perfect in carrying out this role and some principals will not trust the agent entirely. The principal will incur costs in monitoring (enquiring into) the activities of the agent and may lose some wealth if the interests of the agent and the interests of the principal diverge. The view taken in **agency theory** is that there is an inherent conflict between the two parties and so they spend time agreeing contracts which will minimise that conflict. The contracts will include arrangements for the agent to supply information on a regular basis to the principal.

While the study of agency theory in all its aspects could occupy a book in itself, the idea of conflicts and the need for compromise in dealing with pressures of demand for, and supply of, accounting information may be helpful in later chapters in understanding why it takes so long to find answers to some accounting issues.

1.8 Who needs financial statements?

In order to keep the flavour of debate on accounting issues running through this text, two people will give their comments from time to time. The first of these is David Wilson, a fund manager of seven years' experience working for an insurance company. He manages a UK equity **portfolio** (a collection of company shares) and part of his work requires him to be an equities analyst. At university he took a degree in history and has subsequently passed examinations to qualify as a chartered financial analyst (CFA).[26]

The second is Leona Rees, an audit manager with a major accountancy firm. She has five years' experience as a qualified accountant and had previously spent three years in training with the same firm. Her university degree is in accounting and economics and she has passed the examinations to qualify for membership of one of the major accountancy bodies.

David and Leona had been at school together but then went to different universities. More recently they have met again at workout sessions at a health club, relaxing afterwards at a nearby bar. David is very enthusiastic about his work, which demands long hours and a flexible attitude. He has absorbed a little of the general scepticism of audit which is expressed by some of his fund manager colleagues.

Leona's main role at present is in company audit and she is now sufficiently experienced to be working on the audit of one listed company as well as several private companies of varying size. For two years she worked in the corporate recovery department of the accountancy firm, preparing information to help companies find sources of finance to overcome difficult times. She feels that a great deal of accounting work is carried out behind the scenes and the careful procedures are not always appreciated by those who concentrate only on the relatively few well-publicised problems.

We join them in the bar at the end of a hectic working week.

DAVID: *This week I've made three visits to companies, attended four presentations of preliminary announcements of results, received copies of the projector slides used for five others that I couldn't attend, and collected around 20 annual reports. I have a small mound of brokers' reports, all of which say much the same thing but in different ways. I've had to read all those while preparing my monthly report to the head of Equities Section on the performance of my fund and setting out my strategy for three months ahead consistent with in-house policy. I think I'm suffering from information overload and I have reservations about the reliability of any single item of information I receive about a company.*

LEONA: *If I had to give scores for reliability to the information crossing your desk, I would give top marks to the 20 annual reports. They have been through a very rigorous process and they have been audited by reputable audit firms using established standards of auditing practice.*

DAVID: *That's all very well, but it takes so long for annual reports to arrive after the financial year-end that they don't contain any new information. I need to get information at the first available opportunity if I'm to keep up the value of the share portfolio I manage. The meetings that present the preliminary announcements are held less than two months after the accounting year-end. It can take another six weeks before the printed annual report appears. If I don't manage to get to the meeting I take a careful look at what the company sends me in the way of copies of projector slides used.*

LEONA: *Where does accounting information fit in with the picture you want of a company?*

DAVID: *It has some importance, but accounting information is backward-looking and I invest in the future. We visit every company in the portfolio once a year and I'm looking for a confident management team, a cheerful-looking workforce and a general feeling that things are moving ahead. I'll also ask questions about prospects: how is the order book; which overseas markets are expanding; have prices been increased to match the increase in raw materials?*

LEONA: *Isn't that close to gaining insider information?*

DAVID: *No – I see it as clarification of information which is already published. Companies are very careful not to give an advantage to one investor over another – they would be in trouble with the Stock Exchange and perhaps with the Financial Services Authority if they did give price-sensitive information. There are times of the year (running up to the year-end and to the half-yearly results) when they declare a 'close season' and won't even speak to an investor.*

LEONA: *So are you telling me that I spend vast amounts of time auditing financial statements which no one bothers to read?*

DAVID: *Some people would say that, but I wouldn't. It's fairly clear that share prices are unmoved by the issue of the annual report, probably because investors already have that information from the preliminary announcement. Nevertheless, we like to know that there is a regulated document behind the information we receive – it allows us to check that we're not being led astray. Also I find the annual report very useful when I want to find out about a company I don't know. For the companies I understand well, the annual report tells me little that I don't already know.*

LEONA: *I'll take that as a very small vote of confidence for now. If your offer to help me redecorate the flat still stands, I might try to persuade you over a few cans of emulsion that you rely on audited accounts more than you realise.*

Activity 1.8

As a final activity for this chapter, go back to the start of the chapter and make a note of every word you have encountered for the first time. Look at the glossary at the end of the book for the definition of each technical word. If the word is not in the glossary it is probably in sufficiently general use to be found in a standard dictionary.

1.9 Summary

This chapter has explained that accounting is intended to provide information that is useful to a wide range of interested parties (stakeholders).

Key points are:

- **Accounting** is the process of identifying, measuring and communicating financial information about an entity to permit informed judgements and decisions by users of the information.

- A **conceptual framework** for accounting is a statement of principles which provides generally accepted guidance for the development of new reporting practices and for challenging and evaluating the existing practices.

- The *Framework* of the IASB provides broad principles that guide accounting practice in many countries.

- The *Statement of Principles* of the UK ASB has many similarities to the IASB's *Framework*.
- Since January 2005, all **listed companies** in member states of the EU have been required by an accounting regulation to use a system of international financial reporting standards (IFRS) set by the IASB.
- Business **entities** in the UK are either **sole traders**, **partnerships** or **limited liability** companies.
- **Users** of accounting information include management, owners, employees, lenders, suppliers, customers, governments and their agencies and the public interest.
- **Stakeholders** are all those who might have a legitimate interest in receiving financial information about a business because they have a 'stake' in it.
- General purpose **financial statements** aim to meet the needs of a wide range of users.
- The relationship between the owner, as 'principal', and the manager, as 'agent' is described in the theory of **agency** relationships. Accounting information helps to reduce the potential conflicts of interest between principal and agent.

Further reading

ASSC (1975), *The Corporate Report*, Accounting Standards Steering Committee.

Beattie, V. (ed.) (1999), *Business Reporting: The Inevitable Change?*, Research Committee of The Institute of Chartered Accountants of Scotland.

IASB (1989), *Framework for the Preparation and Presentation of Financial Statements*, International Accounting Standards Board.

ICAS (1988), *Making Corporate Reports Valuable*, discussion paper of the Research Committee of The Institute of Chartered Accountants of Scotland.

Marston, C. (1999), *Investor Relations Meetings: Views of Companies, Institutional Investors and Analysts*, Research Committee of The Institute of Chartered Accountants of Scotland.

Weetman, P. and Beattie, A. (eds) (1999), *Corporate Communication: Views of Institutional Investors and Lenders*, Research Committee of The Institute of Chartered Accountants of Scotland.

QUESTIONS

The Questions section of each chapter has three types of question. 'Test your understanding' questions to help you review your reading are in the 'A' series of questions. You will find the answers to these by reading and thinking about the material in the book. 'Application' questions to test your ability to apply technical skills are in the 'B' series of questions. Questions requiring you to show skills in problem solving and evaluation are in the 'C' series of questions. A letter [S] indicates that there is a solution at the end of the book.

A Test your understanding

A1.1 Define 'accounting' and identify the separate questions raised by the definition. (Section 1.1)

A1.2 The following technical terms appear for the first time in this chapter. Check that you know the meaning of each. (If you can't find them again in the text, there is a glossary at the end of the book.)

- agency
- annual report
- broker
- business entity
- capital
- cash flow projections
- conceptual framework
- directors
- entity
- equities analyst
- external reporting
- financial accounting
- financial information
- financial reporting standards
- financial statements
- fund manager
- general purpose financial statements
- HM Revenue and Customs
- limited liability company
- liquidity
- loan covenants
- management accounting
- partnership
- portfolio of shares
- Registrar of Companies
- share capital
- shareholders
- sole trader
- specific purpose financial statements
- stakeholders
- stewardship
- unsecured creditors

B Application

B1.1
Brian and Jane are planning to work in partnership as software consultants. Write a note (100–200 words) to explain their responsibilities for running the business and producing accounting information about the financial position and performance of the business.

B1.2
Jennifer has inherited some shares in a public company which has a share listing on the Stock Exchange. She has asked you to explain how she can find out more about the financial position and performance of the company. Write a note (100–200 words) answering her question.

B1.3
Martin is planning to buy shares in the company that employs him. He knows that the directors of the company are his employers but he wonders what relationship exists between the directors and the shareholders of the company. Write a note (100–200 words) answering his question.

C Problem solving and evaluation

C1.1
The following extracts are typical of the annual reports of large listed companies. Which of these extracts satisfy the definition of 'accounting'? What are the user needs that are most closely met by each extract?

(a) Suggestions for improvements were made by many employees, alone or in teams. Annual savings which have been achieved total £15m. The best suggestion for improvement will save around £0.3m per year for the next five years.
(b) As of 31 December, 3,000 young people were learning a trade or profession with the company. This represents a studentship rate of 3.9%. During the reporting period we hired 1,300 young people into training places. This is more than we need to satisfy our employment needs in the longer term and so we are contributing to improvement of the quality of labour supplied to the market generally.
(c) During the year to 31 December our turnover (sales) grew to £4,000 million compared to £2,800 million last year. Our new subsidiary contributed £1,000 million to this increase.
(d) It is our target to pay our suppliers within 30 days. During the year we achieved an average payment period of 33 days.
(e) The treasury focus during the year was on further refinancing of the group's borrowings to minimise interest payments and reduce risk.

(f) Our plants have emission rates that are 70% below the national average for sulphur dioxide and 20% below the average for oxides of nitrogen. We will tighten emissions significantly over the next ten years.

C1.2

Explain how you would class each of the following – as a sole trader, partnership or limited company. List any further questions you might ask for clarification about the nature of the business.

(a) Miss Jones works as an interior decorating adviser under the business name 'U-decide'. She rents an office and employs an administrative assistant to answer the phone, keep files and make appointments.

(b) George and Jim work together as painters and decorators under the business name 'Painting Partners Ltd'. They started the business ten years ago and work from a rented business unit on a trading estate.

(c) Jenny and Chris own a hotel jointly. They operate under the business name 'Antler Hotel Company' and both participate in the running of the business. They have agreed to share profits equally.

Activities for study groups (4 or 5 per group)

Obtain the annual report of a listed company. Each member of the group should choose a different company. Most large companies will provide a copy of the annual report at no charge in response to a polite request – or you may know someone who is a shareholder and receives a copy automatically. Many companies have websites with a section for 'Investor Relations' where you will find a document file containing the annual report.

1 Look at the contents page. What information does the company provide?

2 Find the financial highlights page. What are the items of accounting information which the company wants you to note? Which users might be interested in this highlighted information, and why?

3 Is there any information in the annual report which would be of interest to employees?

4 Is there any information in the annual report which would be of interest to customers?

5 Is there any information in the annual report which would be of interest to suppliers?

6 Find the auditors' report. To whom is it addressed? What does that tell you about the intended readership of the annual report?

7 Note the pages to which the auditors' report refers. These are the pages which are regulated by company law, accounting standards and Stock Exchange rules. Compare these pages with the other pages (those which are not regulated). Which do you find more interesting? Why?

8 Each member of the group should now make a five-minute presentation evaluating the usefulness of the annual report examined. When the presentations are complete the group should decide on five criteria for judging the reports and produce a score for each. Does the final score match the initial impressions of the person reviewing it?

9 Finally, as a group, write a short note of guidance on what makes an annual report useful to the reader.

Notes and references

1. AAA (1966), *A Statement of Basic Accounting Theory*, American Accounting Association, p. 1.
2. ASSC (1975), *The Corporate Report*, Accounting Standards Steering Committee.
3. AICPA (1973), *Report of a Study Group on the Objectives of Financial Statements* (The Trueblood Committee), American Institute of Certified Public Accountants.
4. Solomons, D. (1989), *Guidelines for Financial Reporting Standards*, Research Board of The Institute of Chartered Accountants in England and Wales.

5. ICAS (1988), *Making Corporate Reports Valuable*, Research Committee of The Institute of Chartered Accountants of Scotland.
6. The IAS Regulation (2002), see Chapter 4.
7. ASB (1999), *Statement of Principles for Financial Reporting*, Accounting Standards Board.
8. ICAS (1988), para. 3.3.
9. IASB (1989), para. 9(a).
10. IASB (1989), para. 14.
11. ASSC (1975), para. 2.8.
12. ICAS (1988), para. 3.12.
13. IASB (1989), para. 9(b).
14. *Ibid.*, para. 9(c).
15. *Ibid.*, para. 9(d).
16. *Ibid.*, para. 9(e).
17. ASSC (1975), para. 2.25.
18. *Ibid.*, para. 2.26.
19. IASB (1989), para. 9(f).
20. www.ofcom.org.uk
21. www.ofgem.gov.uk
22. IASB (1989), para. 9(g).
23. ICAS (1988), para. 3.7.
24. IASB (1989), Introduction, para. 6.
25. IASB (1989), para. 10. Similar views are expressed in para OB11 of the exposure draft: *An improved conceptual framework for financial reporting: Chapter 1 The objective of financial reporting*, issued by the IASB in May 2008.
26. www.cfainstitute.org

Introduction to the terminology of business transactions

The following description explains the business terminology which will be encountered frequently in describing transactions in this textbook. The relevant words are highlighted in bold lettering. These technical accounting terms are explained in the Financial accounting terms defined *section at the end of the book.*

Most businesses are established with the intention of earning a **profit**. Some do so by selling goods at a price greater than that paid to buy or manufacture the goods. Others make a profit by providing a service and charging a price greater than the cost to them of providing the service. By selling the goods or services the business is said to earn *sales revenue*.

Profit arising from transactions relating to the operation of the business is measured by deducting from sales revenue the expenses of earning that revenue.

Revenue from sales (often abbreviated to 'sales' and sometimes referred to as 'turnover') means the value of all goods or services provided to customers, whether for *cash* or for *credit*. In a *cash sale* the customer pays immediately on receipt of goods or services. In a *credit sale* the customer takes the goods or service and agrees to pay at a future date. By agreeing to pay in the future the customer becomes a **debtor** of the business. The amount due to be collected from the debtor is called a **trade receivable** or an **account receivable**. The business will send a document called a **sales invoice** to the credit customer, stating the goods or services provided by the business, the price charged for these and the amount owing to the business.

Eventually the credit customer will pay cash to settle the amount shown on the invoice. If they pay promptly the business may allow a deduction of discount for prompt payment. This deduction is called *discount allowed* by the business. As an example, if the customer owes £100 but is allowed a 5% discount by the business, he will pay £95. The business will record cash received of £95 and discount allowed of £5.

The business itself must buy goods in order to manufacture a product or provide a service. When the business buys goods it *purchases* them and holds them as an **inventory** of goods (also described as a 'stock' of goods) until they are used or sold. The goods will be purchased from a supplier, either for **cash** or for **credit**. In a **credit purchase** the business takes the goods and agrees to pay at a future date. By allowing the business time to pay, the supplier becomes a **creditor** of the business. The name creditor is given to anyone who is owed money by the business. The business will receive a purchase invoice from the supplier describing the goods supplied, stating the price of the goods and showing the amount owed by the business.

Eventually the business will pay cash to settle the amount shown on the purchase invoice. If the business pays promptly the supplier may permit the business to deduct a discount for prompt payment. This is called **discount received** by the business. As an example, if the business owes an amount of £200 as a **trade payable** but is permitted a 10% discount by the supplier, the business will pay £180 and record the remaining £20 as **discount received** from the supplier.

The purchase price of goods sold is one of the **expenses** of the business, to be deducted from sales revenue in calculating profit. Other expenses might include wages, salaries, rent, rates, insurance and cleaning. In each case there will be a document providing evidence of the expense, such as a wages or salaries slip, a landlord's bill for rent, a local authority's demand for rates, an insurance renewal note or a cleaner's time sheet. There will also be a record of the cash paid in each case.

Sometimes an expense is incurred but is not paid for until some time later. For example, electricity is consumed during a quarter but the electricity bill does not arrive until after the end of the quarter. An employee may have worked for a week but not yet have received a cash payment for that work. The unpaid expense of the business is called an *accrued expense* and must be recorded as part of the accounting information relevant to the period of time in which the expense was incurred.

On other occasions an expense may be paid for in advance of being used by the business. For example, a fire insurance premium covering the business premises is paid annually in advance. Such expenditure of cash will benefit a future time period and must be excluded from any profit calculation until that time. In the meantime it is recorded as a **prepaid expense** or a **prepayment**.

Dissatisfaction may be expressed by a customer with the quantity or quality of goods or service provided. If the business accepts that the complaint is justified it may replace goods or give a cash refund. If the customer is a credit customer who has not yet paid, then a cash refund is clearly inappropriate. Instead the customer would be sent a **credit note** for sales returned, cancelling the customer's debt to the business for the amount in dispute. The credit note would record the quantity of goods or type of service and the amount of the cancelled debt.

In a similar way the business would expect to receive a credit note from a supplier for *purchases returned* where goods have been bought on credit terms and later returned to the supplier because of some defect.

S   Test your understanding

S1.1   The following technical terms appear in this supplement. Check that you know the meaning of each.

- Profit
- Sales revenue
- Cash sale
- Credit sale
- Debtor
- Trade receivable
- Discount allowed
- Purchases
- Credit purchase

- Creditor
- Trade payable
- Discount received
- Expense
- Accrued expense
- Prepaid expense
- Credit note for sales returned
- Credit note for purchases returned

Chapter 2

A systematic approach to financial reporting: the accounting equation

Presenting the accounting equation

Shareholders' funds as at 21 March 2009 were £4,376 million (2008: £4,935 million), a reduction of £559 million, primarily as a result of the deterioration of the pension surplus into a deficit, which reduces net assets by £588 million. Gearing, which measures net debt as a percentage of total equity, increased to 38 per cent (2008: 30 per cent) as a result of the pension surplus moving into deficit.

Summary balance sheet at 21 March 2009

	2009 £m	2008 £m
Non-current assets	8,425	8,010
Inventories	689	681
Trade and other receivables	195	206
Cash and cash equivalents	627	719
Debt	(2,298)	(2,222)
Net debt	**(1,671)**	(1,503)
Trade and other payables and provisions	(3,040)	(2,825)
Net assets	**4,376**	4,935

Source: J Sainsbury plc Annual report 2009, page 20. http://www.j-sainsbury.co.uk/files/reports/ar2009_report.pdf

Discussion points

1 How does the summary statement of financial position (balance sheet) reflect the accounting equation?

2 How does the group explain the main changes?

Contents

Learning outcomes

After studying this chapter you should be able to:

- Define and explain the accounting equation.
- Define assets.
- Apply the definition to examples of assets.
- Explain and apply the rules for recognition of assets.
- Define liabilities.
- Apply the definition to examples of liabilities.
- Explain and apply the rules for recognition of liabilities.
- Define ownership interest.
- Explain how the recognition of ownership interest depends on the recognition of assets and liabilities.
- Use the accounting equation to show the effect of changes in the ownership interest.
- Explain how users of financial statements can gain assurance about assets and liabilities.

Additionally, for those who choose to study the supplement:

- Explain how the rules of debit and credit recording are derived from the accounting equation.

2.1   Introduction

Chapter 1 considered the needs of a range of users of financial information and summarised by suggesting that they would all have an interest in the resources available to the business and the obligations of the business to those outside it. Many of these users will also want to be reassured that the business has an adequate flow of cash to support its continuation. The owners of the business have a claim to the resources of the business after all other obligations have been satisfied. This is called the **ownership interest** or the **equity interest**. They will be particularly interested in how that ownership interest grows from one year to the next and whether the resources of the business are being applied to the best advantage.

Accounting has traditionally applied the term **assets** to the resources available to the business and has applied the term **liabilities** to the obligations of the business to persons other than the owner. Assets and liabilities are reported in a financial statement called a **statement of financial position** (also called a **balance sheet**). The statement of the financial position of the entity represents a particular point in time. It may be described by a very simple equation.

2.2   The accounting equation

The **accounting equation** as a statement of financial position may be expressed as:

Assets	minus	**Liabilities**		equals	**Ownership interest**

The ownership interest is the residual claim after liabilities to third parties have been satisfied. The equation expressed in this form emphasises that residual aspect.

Another way of thinking about an equation is to imagine a balance with a bucket on each end. In one bucket are the assets (A) minus liabilities (L). In the other is the ownership interest (OI).

If anything happens to disturb the assets then the balance will tip unevenly unless some matching disturbance is applied to the ownership interest. If anything happens to disturb the liabilities then the balance will tip unevenly unless some matching disturbance is applied to the ownership interest. If a disturbance applied to an asset is applied equally to a liability, then the balance will remain level.

2.2.1   Form of the equation: national preferences

If you have studied simple equations in a maths course you will be aware that there are other ways of expressing this equation. Those other ways cannot change the magnitudes of each item in the equation but can reflect a different emphasis being placed on the various constituents. The form of the equation used in this chapter is the sequence which has, for many years, been applied in most statements of financial position (balance sheets) reported to external users of accounting information in the UK. The statements of financial position that have been reported to external users in some Continental European countries are better represented by another form of the equation:

The 'balance' analogy remains applicable here but the contents of the buckets have been rearranged.

A disturbance on one side of the balance will require a corresponding disturbance on the other side if the balance is to be maintained.

2.2.2 International variation

The International Accounting Standards Board (IASB) has developed a set of accounting standards which together create an accounting system which in this book is described as the **IASB system**. The IASB offers no indication as to which of the above forms of the accounting equation is preferred. That is because of the different traditions in different countries. Consequently, for companies reporting under the IASB system, the form of the equation used in any particular situation is a matter of preference related to the choice of presentation of the statement of financial position (balance sheet). That is a communication issue which will be discussed later. This chapter will concentrate on the nature of the various elements of the equation, namely assets, liabilities and ownership interest.

Activity 2.1

Make a simple balance from a ruler balanced on a pencil and put coins on each side. Satisfy yourself that the ruler only remains in balance if any action on one side of the balance is matched by an equivalent action on the other side of the balance. Note also that rearranging the coins on one side will not disturb the balance. Some aspects of accounting are concerned with taking actions on each side of the balance. Other aspects are concerned with rearranging one side of the balance.

2.3 Defining assets

An **asset** is defined as: *'a resource controlled by the entity as a result of past events and from which future economic benefits are expected to flow to the entity'.*[1]

To understand this definition fully, each phrase must be considered separately.

2.3.1 Controlled by the entity

Control means the ability to obtain the economic benefits and to restrict the access of others. The items which everyone enjoys, such as the benefit of a good motorway giving access to the business or the presence of a highly skilled workforce in a nearby town, provide benefits to the business which are not reported in financial statements because there would be considerable problems in identifying the entity's share of the benefits. If there is no control, the item is omitted.

The condition of control is also included to prevent businesses from leaving out of the statement of financial position (balance sheet) some items which ought to be in there. In past years, practices emerged of omitting an asset and a corresponding liability from a statement of financial position on the grounds that there was no effective obligation remaining in respect of the liability. At the same time, the business carefully retained effective control of the asset by suitable legal agreements. This practice of omitting items from the statement of financial position was felt to be unhelpful to users because it was concealing some of the resources used by the business and concealing the related obligations.

The strongest form of control over an asset is the right of ownership. Sometimes, however, the entity does not have ownership but does have the right to use an item. This right may be very similar to the right of ownership. So far as the user of accounting information is concerned, what really matters is the availability of the item to the entity and how well the item is being used to earn profits for the business. Forms of **control** may include an agreement to lease or rent a resource, and a licence allowing exclusive use of a resource.

2.3.2 Past events

Accounting depends on finding some reasonably objective way of confirming that the entity has gained control of the resource. The evidence provided by a past transaction is an objective starting point. A transaction is an agreement between two parties which usually involves exchanging goods or services for cash or a promise to pay cash. (The supplement to Chapter 1 explains basic business transactions in more detail.) Sometimes there is no transaction but there is an event which is sufficient to give this objective evidence. The event could be the performance of a service which, once completed, gives the right to demand payment.

2.3.3 Future economic benefits

Most businesses use resources in the expectation that they will eventually generate cash. Some resources generate cash more quickly than others. If the business manufactures goods in order to sell them to customers, those goods carry a future economic benefit in terms of the expectation of sale. That benefit comes to the entity relatively quickly. The business may own a warehouse in which it stores the goods before they are sold. There is a future economic benefit associated with the warehouse because it helps create the cash flow from sale of the goods (by keeping them safe from damage and theft) and also because at some time in the future the warehouse could itself be sold for cash.

The example of the warehouse is relatively easy to understand, but in other cases there may be some uncertainty about the amount of the future economic benefit. When goods are sold to a customer who is allowed time to pay, the customer becomes a **debtor** of the business (a person who owes money to the business) and the amount of the **trade receivable** is regarded as an asset. There may be some uncertainty as to whether the customer will eventually pay for the goods. That uncertainty does not prevent the trade receivable being regarded as an asset but may require some caution as to how the asset is measured in money terms.

Activity 2.2

Write down five items in your personal possession which you regard as assets. Use the definition given in this section to explain why each item is an asset from your point of view. Then read the next section and compare your list with the examples of business assets. If you are having difficulty in understanding why any item is, or is not, an asset you should consult your lecturer, tutor or other expert in the subject area for a discussion on how to apply the definition in identifying assets.

2.4 Examples of assets

The following items are commonly found in the assets section of the statement of financial position (balance sheet) of a company:

- land and buildings owned by the company
- buildings leased by the company on a 50-year lease
- plant and machinery owned by the company
- equipment leased (rented) by the company under a finance lease
- vehicles
- raw materials
- goods for resale
- finished goods
- work in progress
- trade receivables (amounts due from customers who have promised to pay for goods sold on credit)
- prepaid insurance and rentals
- investments in shares of other companies
- cash held in a bank account.

Do all these items meet the definition of an asset? Tables 2.1 and 2.2 test each item against the aspects of the definition which have already been discussed. Two tables have been used because it is conventional practice to separate assets into current assets and non-current assets. **Current assets** are held with the intention of converting them into cash within the business cycle. **Non-current assets**, also called **fixed assets**, are held for continuing use in the business. The business cycle is the period (usually 12 months) during which the peaks and troughs of activity of a business form

Table 2.1

Analysis of some frequently occurring non-current assets (fixed assets)

	Controlled by the entity by means of	Past event	Future economic benefits
Land and buildings owned by the company	Ownership.	Signing the contract as evidence of purchase of land and buildings.	Used in continuing operations of the business; potential for sale of the item.
Buildings leased (rented) by the company on a 50-year lease	Contract for exclusive use as a tenant.	Signing a lease agreeing the rental terms.	Used in continuing operations of the business.
Plant and machinery owned by the company	Ownership.	Purchase of plant and equipment, evidenced by receiving the goods and a supplier's invoice.	Used in continuing operations of the business.
Equipment used under a finance lease	Contract for exclusive use.	Signing lease agreeing rental terms.	Used in continuing operations of the business.
Vehicles owned by the company	Ownership.	Purchase of vehicles, evidenced by taking delivery and receiving a supplier's invoice.	Used in continuing operations of the business.

Table 2.2
Analysis of some frequently occurring current assets

	Controlled by the entity by means of	Past event	Future economic benefits
Raw materials	Ownership.	Receiving raw materials into the company's store, evidenced by goods received note.	Used to manufacture goods for sale.
Goods purchased from supplier for resale	Ownership.	Receiving goods from supplier into the company's store, evidenced by the goods received note.	Expectation of sale.
Finished goods (manufactured by the entity)	Ownership.	Transfer from production line to finished goods store, evidenced by internal transfer form.	Expectation of sale.
Work in progress (partly finished goods)	Ownership.	Evaluation of the state of completion of the work, evidenced by work records.	Expectation of completion and sale.
Trade receivables (amounts due from customers)	Contract for payment.	Delivery of goods to the customer, obliging customer to pay for goods at a future date.	Expectation that the customer will pay cash.
Prepaid insurance premiums	Contract for continuing benefit of insurance cover.	Paying insurance premiums in advance, evidenced by cheque payment.	Expectation of continuing insurance cover.
Investments in shares of other companies	Ownership.	Buying the shares, evidenced by broker's contract note.	Expectation of dividend income and growth in value of investment, for future sale.
Cash held in a bank account	Ownership.	Depositing cash with the bank, evidenced by bank statement or certificate.	Expectation of using the cash to buy resources which will create further cash.

a pattern which is repeated on a regular basis. For a business selling swimwear, production will take place all winter in preparation for a rush of sales in the summer. Painters and decorators work indoors in the winter and carry out exterior work in the summer. Because many businesses are affected by the seasons of the year, the business cycle is normally 12 months. Some of the answers are fairly obvious but a few require a little further comment here.

First, there are the items of buildings and equipment which are rented under a lease agreement. The benefits of such leases are felt to be so similar to the benefits of ownership that the items are included in the statement of financial position (balance sheet) as assets. Suitable wording is used to describe the different nature of these items so that users, particularly **creditors**, are not misled into believing that the items belong to the business.

Second, it is useful to note at this stage that partly finished items of output may be recorded as assets. The term 'work in progress' is used to describe work of the business which is not yet completed. Examples of such work in progress might be: partly finished items in a manufacturing company; a partly completed motorway being built by a construction company; or a continuing legal case being undertaken by a firm of lawyers. Such items are included as assets because there has been an event in the partial completion of the work and there is an expectation of completion and eventual payment by a customer for the finished item.

Finally, it is clear that the relative future economic benefits of these assets have a wide variation in potential risk. This risk is a matter of great interest to those who use accounting information, but there are generally no accounting techniques for reporting this risk in financial statements. Consequently, it is very important to have adequate descriptions of assets. Accounting information is concerned with the words used to describe items in financial statements, as well as the numbers attributed to them.

Definitions

An **asset** is a resource controlled by the entity as a result of past events and from which future economic benefits are expected to flow.[2]

A **current asset** is an asset that satisfies any of the following criteria:

(a) it is expected to be realised in, or is intended for sale or consumption in, the entity's normal operating cycle;
(b) it is held primarily for the purpose of being traded;
(c) it is expected to be realised within 12 months after the reporting period;
(d) it is cash or a cash equivalent.[3]

A **non-current asset** is any asset that does not meet the definition of a current asset.[4] Non-current assets include tangible, intangible and financial assets of a long-term nature. These are also described as **fixed assets**.[5]

2.5 Recognition of assets

When an item has passed the tests of definition of an asset, it has still not acquired the right to a place in the statement of financial position (balance sheet). To do so it must meet further tests of recognition. **Recognition** means reporting an item by means of words and amounts within the main financial statements in such a way that the item is included in the arithmetic totals. An item which is reported in the notes to the accounts is said to be **disclosed** but *not* **recognised**.

The conditions for recognition have been expressed as in the following definition.

Definition

An **asset** is **recognised** in the statement of financial position (balance sheet) when:

it is probable that the future economic benefits will flow to the entity and the asset has a cost or value that can be measured reliably.[6]

2.5.1 Probability that economic benefits will flow

To establish probability needs evidence. What evidence is sufficient? Usually more than one item of evidence is looked for. In the case of non-current assets (fixed assets) which have a physical existence, looking at them to make sure they do exist is a useful precaution which some auditors have in the past regretted not taking. Checking on physical existence is not sufficient, however, because the enterprise may have no control over the future economic benefit associated with the item. Evidence of the benefit from non-current assets may lie in: title deeds of property; registration documents for vehicles plus the purchase invoice from the supplier; invoices from suppliers of plant and equipment or office furniture; a written lease agreement for a computer or other type of equipment; and also the enterprise's internal forecasts of the profits it will make by using these non-current assets. This is the kind of evidence which the auditor seeks in forming an opinion on the financial statements.

For current assets the evidence of future benefit comes when the assets are used within the trading cycle. A satisfactory sales record will suggest that the present **inventory (stock)** of finished goods is also likely to sell. Analysis of the time that credit customers have taken to pay will give some indication of whether the **trade receivables** should be recognised as an asset. Cash can be counted, while amounts deposited in banks may be confirmed by a bank statement or bank letter. Internal projections of profit and cash flow provide supporting evidence of the expected benefit from using current assets in trading activities.

2.5.2 Reliability of measurement

Reliable measurement of assets can be quite a problem. For the most part, this book will accept the well-tried practice of measuring an asset at the cost of acquiring it, allowing for any reduction in value through use of the asset (depreciation) or through it falling out of fashion (obsolescence). The suitability of this approach to measurement will be discussed in Chapter 14 as one of the main unresolved problems of accounting.

2.5.3 Non-recognition

Consider some items which pass the definition test but do not appear in a statement of financial position balance sheet:

- the workforce of a business (a human resource)
- the strength of the management team (another human resource)
- the reputation established for the quality of the product
- the quality of the regular customers
- a tax refund which will be claimable against profits in two years' time.

These items all meet the conditions of rights or other access, future economic benefits, control and a past transaction or event. However, they all have associated with them a high level of uncertainty and it could be embarrassing to include them in a statement of financial position (balance sheet) of one year, only to remove them the following year because something unexpected had happened.

All these items fail one of the recognition tests and some fail both. The workforce as a whole may be reliable and predictable, but unexpected circumstances can come to all and the illness or death of a member of the management team in particular can have a serious impact on the perceived value of the business. A crucial member of the workforce might give notice and leave. In relation to the product, a reputation for quality may become well established and those who would like to include brand names in the statement of financial position (balance sheet) argue for the permanence of the reputation. Others illustrate the relative transience of such a reputation by bringing out a list of well-known biscuits or sweets of 30 years ago and asking who has heard of them today. Reliable customers of good quality are valuable to a business, but they are also fickle and may change their allegiance at a moment's notice. The tax refund may be measurable in amount, but will there be taxable profits in two years' time against which the refund may be claimed?

It could be argued that the assets which are not recognised in the financial statements should be reported by way of a general description in a note to the accounts. In practice, this rarely happens because accounting tries to avoid raising hopes which might subsequently be dashed. This cautious approach is part of what is referred to more generally as **prudence** in accounting practice.

2.6　Defining liabilities

A **liability** is defined as: 'a present obligation of the entity arising from past events, the settlement of which is expected to result in an outflow from the entity of resources embodying economic benefits'.[7] This wording reads somewhat tortuously but has been designed to mirror the definition of an asset.

The most familiar types of liabilities arise in those situations where specific amounts of money are owed by an entity to specific persons called creditors. There is usually no doubt about the amount of money owed and the date on which payment is due. Such persons may be **trade creditors**, the general name for those suppliers who have provided goods or services in return for a promise of payment later. Amounts due to **trade creditors** are described as **trade payables**. Other types of creditors include bankers or other lenders who have lent money to the entity.

There are also situations where an obligation is known to exist but the amount due is uncertain. That might be the case where a court of law has found an entity negligent in failing to meet some duty of care to a customer. The company will have to pay compensation to the customer but the amount has yet to be determined.

Even more difficult is the case where an obligation might exist if some future event happens. Neither the existence nor the amount of the obligation is known with certainty at the date of the financial statements. An example would arise where one company has guaranteed the overdraft borrowing of another in the event of that other company defaulting on repayment. At the present time there is no reason to suppose a default will occur, but it remains a possibility for the future.

The definition of a liability tries to encompass all these degrees of variation and uncertainty. It has to be analysed for each separate word or phrase in order to understand the full implications.

2.6.1　Present obligation

A legal obligation is evidence that a liability exists because there is another person or entity having a legal claim to payment. Most liabilities arise because a legal obligation exists, either by contract or by statute law.

However, a legal obligation is not a necessary condition. There may be a commercial penalty faced by the business if it takes a certain action. For example, a decision to close a line of business will lead to the knowledge of likely redundancy costs long before the employees are actually made redundant and the legal obligation becomes due. There may be an obligation imposed by custom and practice, such as a condition of the trade that a penalty operates for those who pay bills late. There may be a future obligation caused by actions and events of the current period where, for example, a profit taken by a company now may lead to a taxation liability at a later date which does not arise at this time because of the wording of the tax laws.

2.6.2　Past events

A decision to buy supplies or to acquire a new non-current asset is not sufficient to create a liability. It could be argued that the decision is an event creating an obligation, but it is such a difficult type of event to verify that accounting prefers not to rely too much on the point at which a decision is made.

Most liabilities are related to a transaction. Normally the transaction involves receiving goods or services, receiving delivery of new non-current assets such as vehicles and equipment, or borrowing money from a lender. In all these cases there is documentary evidence that the transaction has taken place.

Where the existence of a liability is somewhat in doubt, subsequent events may help to confirm its existence at the date of the financial statements. For example, when a company offers to repair goods under a warranty arrangement, the liability exists from the moment the warranty is offered. It may, however, be unclear as to the extent of the liability until a pattern of customer complaints is established. Until that time there will have to be an estimate of the liability. In accounting this estimate is called a **provision**. Amounts referred to as **provisions** are included under the general heading of liabilities.

2.6.3 Outflow of economic benefits

The resource of cash is the economic benefit transferable in respect of most obligations. The transfer of property in settlement of an obligation would also constitute a transfer of economic benefits. More rarely, economic benefits could be transferred by offering a resource such as labour in settlement of an obligation.

Activity 2.3

Write down five items in your personal experience which you regard as liabilities. Use the definition given in this section to explain why each item is a liability from your point of view. Then read the next section and compare your list with the examples of business liabilities. If you are having difficulty in understanding why any item is, or is not, a liability you should consult your lecturer, tutor or other expert in the subject area for a discussion on how to apply the definition in identifying liabilities.

2.7 Examples of liabilities

Here is a list of items commonly found in the liabilities section of the statements of financial position (balance sheets) of companies:

- bank loans and overdrafts
- trade payables (amounts due to suppliers of goods and services on credit terms)
- taxation payable
- accruals (amounts owing, such as unpaid expenses)
- provision for deferred taxation
- long-term loans.

The first five items in this list would be classified as **current liabilities** because they will become due for payment within one year of the date of the financial statements. The last item would be classified as **non-current liabilities** because they will remain due by the business for longer than one year.

Definitions

A **liability** is a present obligation of the entity arising from past events, the settlement of which is expected to result in an outflow from the entity of resources embodying economic benefits.[8]

A **current liability** is a liability which satisfies any of the following criteria:

(a) it is expected to be settled in the entity's normal operating cycle;
(b) it is held primarily for the purpose of being traded;
(c) it is due to be settled within 12 months after the reporting period.[9]

A **non-current liability** is any liability that does not meet the definition of a current liability.[10] Non-current liabilities are also described as **long-term liabilities.**

2.8 Recognition of liabilities

As with an asset, when an item has passed the tests of definition of a liability it may still fail the test of recognition. In practice, because of the concern for prudence, it is much more difficult for a liability to escape the statement of financial position (balance sheet).

The condition for recognition of a liability uses wording which mirrors that used for recognition of the asset. The only difference is that the economic benefits are now expected to flow *from* the enterprise. The conditions for recognition have been expressed in the following way:

Definition

A **liability** is **recognised** in the statement of financial position (balance sheet) when:

- it is probable that an outflow of resources embodying economic benefits will result from the settlement of a present obligation and
- the amount at which the settlement will take place can be measured reliably.[11]

What kind of evidence is acceptable? For current liabilities there will be a payment soon after the date of the financial statements and a past record of making such payments on time. For non-current liabilities (long-term liabilities) there will be a written agreement stating the terms and dates of repayment required. The enterprise will produce internal forecasts of cash flows which will indicate whether the cash resources will be adequate to allow that future benefit to flow from the enterprise.

Reliable measurement will normally be based on the amount owing to the claimant. If goods or services have been supplied there will be an invoice from the supplier stating the amount due. If money has been borrowed there will be a bank statement or some other document of a similar type, showing the lender's record of how much the enterprise owes.

In cases which fail the recognition test, the documentary evidence is likely to be lacking, probably because there is not sufficient evidence of the existence or the measurable amount. Examples of liabilities which are not recognised in the statement of financial position (balance sheet) are:

- a commitment to purchase new machinery next year (but not a firm contract)
- a remote, but potential, liability for a defective product, where no court action has yet commenced
- a guarantee given to support the bank overdraft of another company, where there is very little likelihood of being called upon to meet the guarantee.

Because of the prudent nature of accounting, the liabilities which are not recognised in the statement of financial position (balance sheet) may well be reported in note form under the heading **contingent liabilities**. This is referred to as **disclosure** by way of a note to the accounts.

Looking more closely at the list of liabilities which are not recognised, we see that the commitment to purchase is not legally binding and therefore the outflow of resources may not occur. The claim based on a product defect appears to be uncertain as to occurrence and as to amount. If there has been a court case or a settlement out of court then there should be a provision for further claims of a similar nature. In the case of the guarantee the facts as presented make it appear that an outflow of resources is unlikely. However, such appearances have in the past been deceiving to all concerned and there is often interesting reading in the note to the financial statements which describes the contingent liabilities.

An analysis of some common types of liability is given in Table 2.3.

Table 2.3
Analysis of some common types of liability

Type of liability	Obligation	Transfer of economic benefits	Past transaction or event
Bank loans and overdrafts (repayable on demand or in the very short term)	The entity must repay the loans on the due date or on demand.	Cash, potentially within a short space of time.	Receiving the borrowed funds.
Trade payables (amounts due to suppliers of goods and services)	Suppliers must be paid for the goods and services supplied, usually about one month after the supplier's invoice is received.	Cash within a short space of time.	Taking delivery of the goods or service and receiving the supplier's invoice.
Taxation payable (tax due on company profits after the financial year-end date)	Cash payable to HMRC. Penalties are charged if tax is not paid on the due date.	Cash.	Making profits in the accounting year and submitting an assessment of tax payable.
Accruals (a term meaning 'other amounts owing', such as unpaid bills)	Any expense incurred must be reported as an accrued liability (e.g. electricity used, gas used, unpaid wages), if it has not been paid at the financial year-end date.	Cash.	Consuming electricity or gas, using employees' services, receiving bills from suppliers (note that it is not necessary to receive a gas bill in order to know that you owe money for gas used).
Provision for deferred taxation (tax due in respect of present profits but having a delayed payment date allowed by tax law)	Legislation allows companies to defer payment of tax in some cases. The date of future payment may not be known as yet.	Cash eventually, but could be in the longer term.	Making profits or incurring expenditure now which meets conditions of legislation allowing deferral.
Long-term loans (sometimes called debenture loans)	Statement of financial position will show repayment dates of long-term loans and any repayment conditions attached.	Cash.	Received borrowed funds.

2.9 Defining the ownership interest

The ownership interest is defined in the Framework as equity. **Equity** is the residual interest in the assets of the entity after deducting all its liabilities.[12]

The term **net assets** is used as a shorter way of saying 'total assets less total liabilities'. Because the ownership interest is the residual item, it will be the owners of the business who benefit from any increase in assets after liabilities have been met. Conversely it will be the owners who bear the loss of any decrease in assets after liabilities have been met. The ownership interest applies to the entire net assets. It is sometimes described as the owners' wealth, although economists would take a view that the owners' wealth extends beyond the items recorded in a statement of financial position (balance sheet).

If there is only one owner, as in the sole trader's business, then there is no problem as to how the ownership interest is shared. In a partnership, the partnership agreement will usually state the profit-sharing ratio, which may also be applied to the net assets shown in the statement of financial position (balance sheet). If nothing is said in the partnership agreement, the profit sharing must be based on equal shares for each partner.

In a company the arrangements for sharing the net assets depend on the type of ownership chosen. The owners may hold **ordinary shares** in the company, which entitle them to a share of any dividend declared and a share in net assets on closing down the business. The ownership interest is in direct proportion to the number of shares held.

Some investors like to hold **preference shares**, which give them a preference (although not an automatic right) to receive a dividend before any ordinary share dividend is declared. The rights of preference shareholders are set out in the articles of association of the company. Some will have the right to share in a surplus of net assets on winding up, but others will only be entitled to the amount of capital originally contributed.

Definitions

> The **ownership interest** is called **equity** in the IASB *Framework*.
>
> **Equity** is the residual interest in the assets of the entity after deducting all its liabilities.
>
> **Net assets** means the difference between the total assets and the total liabilities of the business: it represents the amount of the ownership interest in the entity.

2.10 Recognition

There can be no separate recognition criteria for the ownership interest because it is the result of recognising assets and recognising liabilities. Having made those decisions on assets and liabilities the enterprise has used up its freedom of choice.

2.11 Changes in the ownership interest

It has already been explained that the owner will become better off where the net assets are increasing. The owner will become worse off where the net assets are decreasing. To measure the increase or decrease in net assets, two accounting equations are needed:

At time t = 0	**Assets$_{(t0)}$ – Liabilities$_{(t0)}$**	equals	**Ownership interest$_{(t0)}$**
At time t = 1	**Assets$_{(t1)}$ – Liabilities$_{(t1)}$**	equals	**Ownership interest$_{(t1)}$**

Taking one equation away from the other may be expressed in words as:

Change in (assets – liabilities)	equals	Change in ownership interest

or, using the term 'net assets' instead of 'assets – liabilities':

Change in net assets	equals	Change in ownership interest

The change in the ownership interest between these two points in time is a measure of how much better or worse off the owner has become, through the activities of the business. The owner is better off when the ownership interest at time $t = 1$ is higher than that at time $t = 0$. To calculate the ownership interest at each point in time requires knowledge of all assets and all liabilities at each point in time. It is particularly interesting to know about the changes in assets and liabilities which have arisen from the day-to-day operations of the business.

The term **revenue** is given to any increase in the ownership interest arising from the operations of the business and caused by an increase in an asset which is greater than any decrease in another asset (or increase in a liability). The term **expense** is given to any reduction in the ownership interest arising from the operations of the business and caused by a reduction in an asset to the extent that it is not replaced by a corresponding increase in another asset (or reduction in a liability).

The owner or owners of the business may also change the amount of the ownership interest by deciding to contribute more cash or other resources in order to finance the business, or deciding to withdraw some of the cash and other resources previously contributed or accumulated. The amount contributed to the business by the owner is usually referred to as **capital**. Decisions about the level of capital to invest in the business are financing decisions. These financing decisions are normally distinguished separately from the results of operations.

So another equation may now be derived as a subdivision of the basic accounting equation, showing analysis of the changes in the ownership interest.

Change in ownership interest	equals	Capital contributed/withdrawn by the ownership plus Revenue minus Expenses

The difference between revenue and expenses is more familiarly known as profit. So a further subdivision of the basic equation is:

Profit	equals	Revenue minus Expenses

2.11.1 Revenue and expense

Revenue is created by a transaction or event arising during the operations of the business which causes an increase in the ownership interest. It could be due to an increase in cash or trade receivables, received in exchange for goods or services. Depending on the nature of the business, revenue may be described as sales, turnover, fees, commission, royalties or rent.

An **expense** is caused by a transaction or event arising during the operations of the business which causes a decrease in the ownership interest. It could be due to an outflow or depletion of assets such as cash, inventory (stock) or non-current assets (fixed assets). It could be due to a liability being incurred without a matching asset being acquired.

Definitions

> **Revenue** is created by a transaction or event arising during the ordinary activities of the entity which causes an increase in the ownership interest. It is referred to by a variety of different names including sales, fees, interest, dividends, royalties and rent.[13]
>
> An **expense** is caused by a transaction or event arising during the ordinary activities of the business which causes a decrease in the ownership interest.[14]

2.11.2 Position after a change has occurred

At the end of the accounting period there will be a new level of assets and liabilities recorded. These assets and liabilities will have resulted from the activities of the business during the period, creating revenue and incurring expenses. The owner may also have made voluntary contributions or withdrawals of capital as a financing decision. The equation in the following form reflects that story:

Assets minus **Liabilities** at the end of the period	equals	**Ownership interest at the start of the period** plus **Capital contributed/ withdrawn in the period** plus **Revenue of the period** minus **Expenses of the period**

2.12 Assurance for users of financial statements

The definitions of assets and liabilities refer to expected flows into or out of the business. The recognition conditions refer to the evidence that the expected flows in or out will occur. The directors of a company are responsible for ensuring that the financial statements presented by them are a faithful representation of the assets and liabilities of the business and of the transactions and events relating to those assets and liabilities. Shareholders need reassurance that the directors, as their agents, have carried out this responsibility with sufficient care. To give themselves this reassurance, the shareholders appoint a firm of auditors to examine the records of the business and give an opinion as to whether the financial statements correspond to the accounting records and present a true and fair view. (Chapter 1 explained the position of directors as agents of the shareholders. Chapter 4 explains the regulations relating to company financial statements and the appointment of auditors.)

Meet David and Leona again as they continue their conversation on the work of the auditor and its value to the shareholder as a user of accounting information provided by a company.

DAVID: *I've now coated your ceiling with apple green emulsion. In return you promised to convince me that I rely on audited accounting information more than I realise. Here is your chance to do that. I was looking today at the annual report of a company which is a manufacturing business. There is a production centre in the UK but most of the production work is carried out in Spain where the operating costs are lower. The distribution operation is carried out from Swindon, selling to retail stores all over the UK. There is an export market, mainly in France, but the company has only scratched the surface of that market. Let's start with something easy – the inventories (stocks) of finished goods which are held at the factory in Spain and the distribution depot in Swindon.*

LEONA: *You've shown right away how limited your understanding is, by choosing the asset where you need the auditor's help the most. Everything can go wrong with inventories (stocks)! Think of the accounting equation:*

Assets – Liabilities = Ownership interest

If an asset is overstated, the ownership interest will be overstated. That means the profit for the period, as reported, is higher than it should be. But you won't know that because everything will appear to be in order from the accounts. You have told me repeatedly that you buy the future, not the past, but I know you look to the current profit and loss account as an indicator of future trends of profit. And so do all your friends.

DAVID: *How can the asset of finished goods inventories be overstated? It's quite a solid item.*

LEONA: *There are two types of potential error – the physical counting of the inventory and the valuation placed on it. There are two main causes of error, one being carelessness and the other an intention to deceive. I've seen situations where the stocktakers count the same stack of goods twice because they don't have a marker pen to put a cross on the items counted. I've also heard of situations where items are counted twice deliberately. We always attend the end-of-year counting of the inventory and observe the process carefully. I wish there weren't so many companies with December year-ends. Counting inventory on 2 January is never a good start to the new year.*

DAVID: *I suppose I can believe that people lose count but how does the valuation go wrong? All companies say that they value inventories at cost as the usual rule. How can the cost of an item be open to doubt?*

LEONA: *Answering that question needs a textbook in itself. The subject comes under the heading of 'management accounting'. Take the goods that you know are manufactured in Spain. There are costs of materials to make the goods, and labour to convert raw materials into finished goods. There are also the running costs of the production unit, which are called the overheads. There is an unbelievable variety of ways of bringing those costs together into one item of product. How much does the company tell you about all that? I know the answer – nothing.*

DAVID: *Well, I could always ask them at a briefing meeting. I usually ask about the profit margin on the goods sold, rather than the value of the goods unsold. But I can see that if the inventories figure is wrong then so is the profit margin. Do you have a systematic procedure for checking each kind of asset?*

LEONA: *Our magic word is **CEAVOP**. That stands for:*

*   *Completeness of information presented.*
*   *Existence of the asset or liability at a given date.*
*   *Amount of the transaction is correctly recorded.*
*   *Valuation reported for assets and liabilities is appropriate.*
*   *Occurrence of the transaction or event took place in the period.*
*   *Presentation and disclosure is in accordance with regulations and accounting standards or other comparable regulations.*

Every aspect of that list has to be checked for each of the assets and liabilities you see in the statement of financial position. We need good-quality evidence of each aspect before we sign off the audit report.

DAVID: *I probably believe that you do a great deal of work with your CEAVOP. But next time I come round to paint your kitchen I'll bring a list of the situations where the auditors don't appear to have asked all the questions in that list.*

2.13 Summary

This chapter has set out the accounting equation for a situation at any one point in time:

Assets	minus	**Liabilities**	equals	**Ownership interest**

Key points are:

- An **asset** is a resource controlled by the entity as a result of past events and from which future economic benefits are expected to flow.
- A **current asset** is an asset that satisfies any of the following criteria:
  - (a) it is expected to be realised in, or is intended for sale or consumption in, the entity's normal operating cycle;
  - (b) it is held primarily for the purpose of being traded;
  - (c) it is expected to be realised within 12 months after the date of the financial year-end;
  - (d) it is cash or a cash equivalent.[15]
- A **non-current asset** is any asset that does not meet the definition of a current asset. Non-current assets include tangible, intangible and financial assets of a long-term nature. These are also described as **fixed assets**.
- A **liability** is a present obligation of the entity arising from past events, the settlement of which is expected to result in an outflow from the entity of resources embodying economic benefits.
- A **current liability** is a liability which satisfies any of the following criteria:
  - (a) it is expected to be settled in the entity's normal operating cycle;
  - (b) it is held primarily for the purpose of being traded;
  - (c) it is due to be settled within 12 months after the date of the financial year-end.
- A **non-current liability** is any liability that does not meet the definition of a current liability. Non-current liabilities are also described as **long-term liabilities**.
- The **ownership interest** is called **equity** in the IASB *Framework*.
- **Equity** is the residual interest in the assets of the entity after deducting all its liabilities.
- **Net assets** means the difference between the total assets and the total liabilities of the business: it represents the amount of the ownership interest in the entity.
- **Recognition** means reporting an item in the financial statements, in words and in amounts, so that the amounts are included in the arithmetic totals of the financial statements. Any other form of reporting by way of note is called disclosure. The conditions for recognition of assets and liabilities are similar in wording.
- At the end of an accounting period the assets and liabilities are reported in a statement of financial position (balance sheet). Changes in the assets and liabilities during the period have caused changes in the ownership interest through revenue and expenses of operations. The owner may also have voluntarily added or withdrawn capital. The final position is explained on the left-hand side of the equation and the movement to that position is explained on the right-hand side:

Assets minus **Liabilities** at the end of the period	equals	**Ownership interest at the start of the period** plus **Capital contributed/ withdrawn in the period** plus **Revenue of the period** minus **Expenses of the period**

- As with any equation, it is possible to make this version more complex by adding further details. That is not necessary for the purpose of explaining the basic processes, but the equation will be revisited later in the book when some of the problems of accounting are opened up. The helpful aspect of the accounting equation is that it can always be used as a basis for arguing a feasible answer. The limitation is that it cannot give an opinion on the most appropriate answer when more than one option is feasible.

In Chapter 3 there is an explanation of how the information represented by the accounting equation is displayed in a form which is useful to the user groups identified in Chapter 1.

Further reading

IASB (1989), *Framework for the Preparation and Presentation of Financial Statements*, section 5 'The Elements of Financial Statements' and section 6 'Recognition of the Elements of Financial Statements', International Accounting Standards Board.

QUESTIONS

The Questions section of each chapter has three types of question. 'Test your understanding' questions to help you review your reading are in the 'A' series of questions. You will find the answers to these by reading and thinking about the material in the book. 'Application' questions to test your ability to apply technical skills are in the 'B' series of questions. Questions requiring you to show skills in problem solving and evaluation are in the 'C' series of questions. A letter [S] indicates that there is a solution at the end of the book.

A   Test your understanding

A2.1   Write out the basic form of the accounting equation. (Section 2.2)

A2.2   Define an asset and explain each part of the definition. (Section 2.3)

A2.3   Give five examples of items which are assets. (Section 2.4)

A2.4   Use the definition to explain why each of the items in your answer to A.2.3 is an asset. (Section 2.4)

A2.5   Explain what 'recognition' means in accounting. (Section 2.5)

A2.6   State the conditions for recognition of an asset. (Section 2.5)

A2.7   Explain why an item may pass the definition test but fail the recognition test for an asset. (Section 2.5)

A2.8   Give three examples of items which pass the definition test for an asset but fail the recognition test. (Section 2.5)

A2.9   Some football clubs include the players in the statement of financial position (balance sheet) as an asset. Others do not. Give the arguments to support each approach. (Section 2.5)

A2.10 Define a liability and explain each part of the definition. (Section 2.6)

A2.11 Give five examples of items which are liabilities. (Section 2.7)

A2.12 Use the definition to explain why each of the items in your answer to A2.11 is a liability. (Section 2.7)

A2.13 State the conditions for recognition of a liability. (Section 2.8)

A2.14 Explain why an item may pass the definition test but fail the recognition test for a liability. (Section 2.8)

A2.15 Define the term 'equity'. (Section 2.9)

A2.16 Explain what is meant by 'net assets'. (Section 2.9)

A2.17 Set out the accounting equation for a change in the ownership interest. (Section 2.11)

A2.18 Define 'revenue' and 'expenses'. (Section 2.11.1)

A2.19 Set out the accounting equation which represents the position after a change has occurred. (Section 2.11.2)

A2.20 Explain the auditor's approach to giving assurance about assets and liabilities. (Section 2.12)

B Application

B2.1 [S]
Classify each of the items in the following list as: asset; liability; neither an asset nor a liability.

(a) cash at bank
(b) loan from the bank
(c) letter from the bank promising an overdraft facility at any time in the next three months
(d) trade receivable (an amount due from a customer who has promised to pay later)
(e) trade receivable (an amount due from a customer who has promised to pay later but has apparently disappeared without leaving a forwarding address)
(f) trade payable (an amount due to a supplier of goods who has not yet received payment from the business)
(g) inventory of finished goods (fashion clothing stored ahead of the spring sales)
(h) inventory of finished goods (fashion clothing left over after the spring sales)
(i) investment in shares of another company where the share price is rising
(j) investment in shares of another company where the share price is falling
(k) lender of five-year loan to the business
(l) customer to whom the business has offered a 12-month warranty to repair goods free of charge
(m) a motor vehicle owned by the business
(n) a motor vehicle rented by the business for one year
(o) an office building owned by the business
(p) an office building rented by the business on a 99-year lease, with 60 years' lease period remaining.

B2.2 [S]
Explain whether each of the items from question B.2.1 above which you have identified as assets and liabilities would also meet the conditions for recognition of the item in the statement of financial position (balance sheet).

B2.3 [S]
Explain why each of the following items would not meet *either* the definition *or* the recognition conditions of an asset of the business:

(a) a letter from the owner of the business, addressed to the bank manager, promising to guarantee the bank overdraft of the business
(b) a list of the customers of the business
(c) an order received from a customer
(d) the benefit of employing a development engineer with a high level of 'know-how' specifically relevant to the business
(e) money spent on an advertising campaign to boost sales
(f) structural repairs to a building.

C Problem solving and evaluation

C2.1
The following information has been gathered from the accounting records of Pets Parlour:

Assets and liabilities at 31 December Year 4

	£
Cash at bank	500
Borrowings	6,000
Trade receivables (debtors)	5,000
Property, plant and equipment	29,000

Revenue and expenses for the year ended 31 December Year 4

	£
Fees charged for work done	20,000
Interest paid on borrowings	1,000
Administration costs incurred	1,500
Salaries paid to employees	14,000

Required

Using the accounting equation, calculate:

(a) The amount of ownership interest at 31 December Year 4.
(b) The amount of net profit for the year.
(c) The amount of the ownership interest at 1 January Year 4.

Activities for study groups

Obtain the annual report of a listed company. From the statement of financial position (balance sheet) list the items shown as assets and liabilities. (This will require you to look in detail at the notes to the accounts using the references on the face of the statement of financial position (balance sheet). Share out the list of assets and liabilities so that each person has four or five assets and four or five liability items.

1 Separately, using the definitions and recognition criteria, prepare a short statement explaining why each item on your list passes the tests of definition and recognition. State the evidence you would expect to see, as auditor, to confirm the expected future inflow of economic benefit from any asset and the expected future outflow of benefit from any liability.

2 Present your explanations to the group and together prepare a list of assets and a separate list of liabilities in order of the uncertainty which attaches to the expected future benefit.

3 Read the 'contingent liability' note, if there is one, to find examples of liabilities which have not been recognised but have been disclosed. Why will you not find a 'contingent asset' note?

Notes and references

1. IASB (1989), *Framework for the Preparation and Presentation of Financial Statements*, para. 49(a).
2. IASB (1989), *Framework for the Preparation and Presentation of Financial Statements*, para. 49(a).
3. IAS 1 (2009), para. 66.
4. IAS 1 (2009), para. 66.
5. IAS 1 para. 67 permits the use of alternative descriptions for non-current assets provided the meaning is clear.
6. IASB (1989), *Framework*, para. 89.
7. IASB (1989), *Framework*, para. 49(b).
8. IASB (1989), *Framework*, para. 49(b).
9. IAS 1 (2009), para. 69.
10. *Ibid.*
11. IASB (1989), *Framework*, para. 91.
12. IASB (1989), *Framework*, para. 49(c).
13. IASB (1989), *Framework*, para. 74.
14. IASB (1989), *Framework*, para. 78.
15. IAS 1 (2004), para. 57.

Debit and credit bookkeeping

You do not have to read this supplement to be able to progress through the rest of the textbook. In the main body of each chapter the explanations are all given in terms of changes in elements of the accounting equation. However, for those who would like to know how debits and credits work, each chapter will have a supplement putting into debit and credit form the material contained in the chapter.

Recording in ledger accounts

The double-entry system of bookkeeping records business transactions in ledger accounts. It makes use of the fact that there are two aspects to every transaction when analysed in terms of the accounting equation.

A ledger account accumulates the increases and reductions either in a category of business activities such as sales or in dealings with individual customers and suppliers.

Ledger accounts may be subdivided. Sales could be subdivided into home sales and export sales. Separate ledger accounts might be kept for each type of non-current asset, e.g. buildings and machinery. The ledger account for machinery might be subdivided as office machinery and production machinery.

Ledger accounts for rent, business rates and property insurance might be kept separately or the business might instead choose to keep one ledger account to record transactions in all of these items, giving them the collective name administrative expenses. The decision would depend on the number of transactions in an accounting period and on whether it was useful to have separate records.

The managers of the business have discretion to combine or subdivide ledger accounts to suit the information requirements of the business concerned.

Using the accounting equation

Before entries are made in ledger accounts, the double entry system of bookkeeping assigns to each aspect of a business transaction a **debit** or a **credit** notation, based on the analysis of the transaction using the accounting equation.

In its simplest form the accounting equation is stated as:

Assets minus **Liabilities**	equals	**Ownership interest**

To derive the debit and credit rules it is preferable to rearrange the equation so that there is no minus sign.

Assets	equals	**Liabilities** plus **Ownership interest**

There are three elements to the equation and each one of these elements may either *increase* or *decrease* as a result of a transaction or event. The six possibilities are set out in Table 2.4.

Table 2.4
Combinations of increases and decreases of the main elements of transactions

Left-hand side of the equation		
Assets	Increase	Decrease

Right-hand side of the equation		
Liabilities	Decrease	Increase
Ownership interest	Decrease	Increase

The double-entry bookkeeping system uses this classification (which preserves the symmetry of the equation) to distinguish debit and credit entries as shown in Table 2.5.

Table 2.5
Rules of debit and credit for ledger entries, basic accounting equation

	Debit entries in a ledger account	Credit entries in a ledger account
Left-hand side of the equation		
Asset	Increase	Decrease
Right-hand side of the equation		
Liability	Decrease	Increase
Ownership interest	Decrease	Increase

It was shown in the main body of the chapter that the ownership interest may be increased by:

● earning revenue; and
● new capital contributed by the owner;

and that the ownership interest may be decreased by:

● incurring expenses; and
● capital withdrawn by the owner.

So the 'ownership interest' section of Table 2.5 may be expanded as shown in Table 2.6.

That is all you ever have to know about the rules of bookkeeping. All the rest can be reasoned from this table. For any transaction there will be two aspects. (If you find there are more than two, the transaction needs breaking down into simpler steps.) For each aspect there will be a ledger account. Taking each aspect in turn you ask yourself: *Is this an asset, a liability, or an aspect of the ownership interest?* Then you ask yourself: *Is it an increase or a decrease?* From Table 2.6 you then know immediately whether to make a debit or a credit entry.

Examples of the application of the rules of debit and credit recording are given in the supplement to Chapter 5 for a service business and in the supplement to Chapter 6 for a manufacturing business. They will also be used in later chapters to explain how particular transactions are reported.

Table 2.6

Rules of debit and credit for ledger entries, distinguishing different aspects of ownership interest

	Debit entries in a ledger account	Credit entries in a ledger account
Left-hand side of the equation		
Asset	Increase	Decrease
Right-hand side of the equation		
Liability	Decrease	Increase
Ownership interest	Expense	Revenue
	Capital withdrawn	Capital contributed

S   Test your understanding

(The answer to each of the following questions is either **debit** or **credit**)

S2.1   What is the bookkeeping entry for an increase in an asset?

S2.2   What is the bookkeeping entry for a decrease in a liability?

S2.3   What is the bookkeeping entry for an increase in an expense?

S2.4   What is the bookkeeping entry for a withdrawal of owner's capital?

S2.5   What is the bookkeeping entry for an increase in revenue?

Chapter 3

Financial statements from the accounting equation

Cash flows

Extracts from management reviews within annual reports

Marks and Spencer plc

We took a number of actions to improve our cash flow in 2008/09. In addition to reducing capital expenditure to £652m from over £1bn in the previous year, we generated a working capital inflow of £194.0m and raised £58.3m from the disposal of non-trading stores. As a result we generated a net cash inflow of £107.5m after paying interest, tax, dividend and share buy back of £661.2m. In addition we agreed certain changes to the property partnership with the pension fund that provide us with discretion around the annual payments from the partnership to the fund. This gives us additional cash flow flexibility and reclassifies the obligation from debt to equity. As a result of our good cash flow management and the changes to the property partnership, net debt at year-end was down to £2.5bn from £3.1bn at the end of 2007/08.

Source: Marks and Spencer plc Annual report 2009, p. 16.

First Group plc

The Group continues to generate strong cash flows which are used to enhance shareholder value and pay down debt. Throughout the year we repaid £1,062m of existing short-term acquisition debt from new equity of £231m, new medium- to long-term debt and cash generation. Subsequent to year-end we successfully issued a 12 year £350m bond, the proceeds of which were used to prepay the remaining balance on short-term acquisition debt and to reduce drawings under our bank revolving facilities. The Group's debt maturity profile has been significantly improved during the period with the average duration increasing to 4.6 years (2008: 3.5 years). Following the issue of the £350m bond, the average debt duration has further increased to 6.0 years. The next major facilities do not fall due until February 2012. Liquidity under committed bank facilities is strong with £583m available at the year-end. The flexible nature of our businesses together with the actions we have implemented on costs and a strong focus on budgetary discipline will ensure that the Group is well placed to deliver our plans for cash generation and to continue to reduce net debt.

Source: First Group plc Annual report 2009, p. 26.

Discussion points

1 What do we learn about cash flow from the information provided by Marks and Spencer (a retail business) and First Group (a transport business).

2 Why are both companies placing emphasis on reduction of net debt (external borrowing minus cash and short-term investments)?

Cash flow

After deducting interest, tax and dividend payments, £467 million of operating cash flow was available to fund our capital investment programme, demonstrating BAA's continued strong conversion of operating profit to cash. The APP joint venture and the other investment property sales generated a further cash inflow of £625 million. The balance of the £1,403 million capital investment during the year was funded by increased net debt. The table below summarises the Group's cash flow movements during the year.

Summary cash flow (£ million)

	2005	2004
Cash flow from operating activities	**957**	853
Interest, tax and dividends	**(490)**	(447)
Net cash flow from operations	**467**	406
Capital expenditure and investment	**(1,433)**	(1,266)
Cash impact of property transactions	**625**	(7)
Other	**31**	15
Increase in net debt (net of issue costs)	**(310)**	(825)

Source: BAA Annual Report 2004/5, p. 34.

Discussion points

1 What do we learn about cash flow from the information in the table?

2 How does the description in words help the user to understand the information in the table?

After studying this chapter you should be able to:

- Explain the benefits and problems of producing annual financial statements.
- Explain the purpose and structure of the statement of financial position (balance sheet).
- Explain the purpose and structure of the income statement (profit and loss account).
- Explain the purpose and structure of the statement of cash flows.
- Comment on the usefulness to users of the financial statements prepared.

Additionally for those who choose to study the supplement:

- Apply the debit and credit form of analysis to the transactions of a short period of time, summarising them in a list which may be used for preparation of simple financial statements.

3.1 Introduction

In the previous chapter the accounting equation was developed as a representation of the relationships among key items of accounting information: assets, liabilities and the ownership interest. An understanding of the accounting equation and the various elements of the equation provides a systematic approach to analysing transactions and events, but it gives no guidance as to how the results should be communicated in a manner which will be helpful and meaningful to users. The accounting equation is used in this chapter as a basis for explaining the structure of financial statements. Ideas beyond the accounting equation are required as to what qualities are expected of financial statements.

The various financial statements produced by enterprises for the owners and other external users are derived from the accounting equation. The *Framework* identifies the purposes of financial reporting as producing information about the financial position, performance and financial adaptability of the enterprise. The three most familiar **primary financial statements**, and their respective purposes, are:

Primary financial statement	*Purpose is to report*
Statement of financial position (balance sheet)	Financial position
Income statement (Profit and loss account)	Financial performance
Statement of cash flows	Financial adaptability

This chapter explains the general shape and content of each of these financial statements.

3.2 Who is in charge of the accounting system?

Since 2005 two different accounting systems have existed for companies in the UK, depending on the type of company. When you look at the name of a company listed on the Stock Exchange, such as Vodaphone, BskyB, Burberry and Marks and Spencer, you are really looking at a family group of companies all owned by one parent company. One set of financial statements represents all the companies in the group. Under the law of the European Union (EU), these group financial statements for listed companies must apply the accounting system set out by the International Accounting Standards Board (**IASB system**). Other companies in the UK may choose to follow the

IASB system of standards but there is no requirement to do so. All companies in the UK that do not apply the IASB system must apply the accounting system set out by the UK Accounting Standards Board (ASB). The ASB's system is also used by many bodies in the UK public sector such as town and city councils, hospital trusts and universities.

Fortunately for those studying the subject, the ASB and the IASB have been working closely together for many years and there are relatively few differences between the two systems. However, there is a potential difference in the appearance and the wording of financial statements. Companies applying the UK ASB's accounting system must use specifications of the sequence and content of items (called **formats** of financial statements) set out in UK company law which is based on EU directives. Companies applying the IASB's system to their listed group reporting have a choice in how they present their financial statements. As a consequence we are now seeing variety in the content and sequence of financial statements published in the annual reports of groups listed on the Stock Exchange. This chapter gives you a flavour of the formats that you might see in financial statements. Where there are differences in words used, this chapter gives the wording of the IASB system first, followed by the wording of UK company law and ASB standards in brackets. As an example, the description:

income statement (profit and loss account)

means that the IASB system uses **income statement** in its illustrations of a profit statement, while UK law and ASB standards use **profit and loss account** in their illustrations of a profit statement.

3.3 The accounting period

In the far-away days of traders sailing out of Italian ports on three-year voyages, the **accounting period** was determined by the date of return of the ship, when the accounts could be prepared for the whole voyage. That rather leisurely view of the scale of time would not be tolerated in an industrial and commercial society where there is always someone demanding information. The convention is that businesses should prepare financial statements at least once in every calendar year. That convention is a requirement of law expressed in the Companies Act 2006 in the case of limited liability companies. Where companies have a Stock Exchange listing they are required to produce an interim report six months into the accounting year. Some companies voluntarily produce quarterly reports to shareholders, reflecting the practice of listed companies in the USA. For internal management accounting purposes, a business may produce reports more frequently (e.g. on a monthly or a weekly basis).

Businesses may choose their accounting date as a time convenient to their activities. Many companies choose 31 December for the year-end, but others (including many of the utility companies which were formerly owned by the government) use 31 March. Some prefer a September or October date after the peak of the summer sales has passed. Whatever the choice, companies are expected to keep the same date from one year to the next unless there is a strong reason for changing.

The use of a 12-month accounting period should not be too much of a problem where the trading cycle fits neatly into a year. If the business is seasonal, there will be a peak of production to match the seasonal peak of sales and the pattern will be repeated every year. There could be a few technical problems of deciding exactly how to close the door on 31 December and whether transactions towards the end of the year are to be included in that year or carried to the next period. These problems can be dealt with by having systematic 'cut-off' rules. There is a bigger problem for those companies whose trading cycle is much longer. It could take two years to build a section of a motorway or three years to build a bridge over a wide river estuary. Such a company will have to subdivide the work on the main contract so that some can be reported each year.

The use of the 12-month accounting period also causes problems for recognition of assets and liabilities. Waiting for the ship to arrive was much safer evidence for the Venetian traders than hoping it was still afloat or relying on reported sightings. For today's business the equivalent situation would be waiting for a property to be sold or for a large customer to pay the amount due as a debt. However, in practice the statement of financial position (balance sheet) cannot wait. Notes to the accounts give additional explanations to help users of financial statements evaluate the risk, but it is all quite tentative.

3.4 The statement of financial position (balance sheet)

The **statement of financial position (balance sheet)** reflects the accounting equation. Both descriptions are used in this textbook because you will find both in use. The International Accounting Standards Board prefers the term 'statement of financial position' while company law in the UK uses the term 'balance sheet'. You saw in Chapter 2 that there is more than one way to write the accounting equation. That means there is more than one way to present a statement of financial position (balance sheet). You will find throughout your study of accounting that there is often more than one approach to dealing with an activity or solving a problem. This is the first time but there will be more. It means that you need to be flexible in your approach to reading and using financial statements.

3.4.1 Focus on the ownership interest

One form of the accounting equation focuses on the ownership interest as the result of subtracting liabilities from assets. The equation is as follows:

Assets	minus	**Liabilities**	equals	**Ownership interest**

UK companies who apply this form of the equation will present the statement of financial position (balance sheet) in a narrative form, reading down the page, as follows:

Assets
minus
Liabilities
equals
Ownership interest

The assets are subdivided into current assets and non-current assets (defined in Chapter 2), while the liabilities are subdivided into current liabilities and non-current liabilities (also defined in Chapter 2). The ownership interest may also be subdivided to show separately the capital contributed or withdrawn and the profit of the period. Because current assets and current liabilities are closely intertwined in the day-to-day operations of the business, they are grouped close to each other in the statement of financial position (balance sheet) (Table 3.1).

Table 3.1
Structure of a statement of financial position (balance sheet)

Non-current assets
plus
Current assets
minus
Current liabilities
minus
Non-current liabilities
equals
Capital at start of year
plus/minus
Capital contributed or withdrawn
plus
Profit of the period

Table 3.1 represents a typical **format** used by public companies. For many years prior to 2005 it was the format most commonly used by UK companies and continues to be used by some UK companies that have moved to the IASB system of accounting. Most companies will try to confine the statement of financial position (balance sheet) to a single side of A4 paper but there is not much space on one sheet of A4 paper to fit in all the assets and liabilities of a company. Consequently a great deal of use is made of notes to the accounts which explain the detail. The statement of financial position (balance sheet) shows only the main categories of assets and liabilities.

3.4.2 Balancing assets and claims on assets

Another form of the accounting equation focuses on balancing the assets against the claims on assets. The claims on assets come from the ownership interest and from liabilities of all types. The equation is:

Assets	equals	**Ownership interest**	plus	**Liabilities**

UK companies who apply this form of the equation will present the statement of financial position (balance sheet) vertically on one sheet of paper but the sequence will be different:

Assets
equals
Ownership interest
plus
Liabilities

In some countries there is a preference for lining up the statement of financial position (balance sheet) horizontally to match the accounting equation even more closely.

	Ownership interest
Assets	plus
	Liabilities

Activity 3.1

Before reading further, make sure that you can explain why each item in the accounting records is an asset or a liability, as shown in the foregoing list. If you have any doubts, read Chapter 2 again before proceeding with this chapter.

3.4.3 Example of presentation

The following list of assets and liabilities of P. Mason's legal practice was prepared from the accounting records of transactions summarised at 30 September Year 5:

	£
Land and buildings	250,000
Office furniture	30,000
Receivables (debtors) for fees	1,200
Prepayment of insurance premium	540
Cash at bank	15,280
Total assets (A)	**297,020**
Trade payables (creditors)	2,800
Long-term loan	150,000
Total liabilities (L)	**152,800**
Ownership interest (A − L)	**144,220**

Table 3.2 shows how this would appear in a statement of financial position (balance sheet) based on the 'ownership interest' form of the equation. Table 3.3 shows how the same information would appear in a statement of financial position (balance sheet) based on the 'claims on assets' form of the equation.

The statement of financial position (balance sheet) in Table 3.2 is more informative than the list of assets and liabilities from which it was prepared because it has been arranged in a helpful format. The first helpful feature is the use of headings (shown in Table 3.2 in bold) for similar items grouped together, such as non-current assets, current assets, current liabilities and non-current liabilities. The second helpful feature is the use of **subtotals** (identified in Table 3.2 by descriptions in italics and shaded) for similar items grouped together. The subtotals used in this example are those for: total non-current assets; total current assets; and current assets less current liabilities. There are no standard rules on use of subtotals. They should be chosen in a manner most appropriate to the situation.

A person using this statement of financial position (balance sheet) can see at a glance that there is no problem for the business in meeting its current liabilities from its resources of current assets. The financing of the business is split almost equally between the non-current liabilities and the ownership interest, a split which would not be regarded as excessively risky by those who lend to businesses. The non-current assets used as a basis for generating profits from one year to the next are collected together as a group, although the statement of financial position (balance sheet) alone

Table 3.2
Statement of financial position (balance sheet): Assets minus liabilities equals ownership interest

P. Mason's legal practice Statement of financial position (balance sheet) at 30 September Year 5	£	£
Non-current assets		
Land and buildings		250,000
Office furniture		30,000
Total non-current assets		280,000
Current assets		
Receivables (debtors) for fees	1,200	
Prepayment of insurance premium	540	
Cash at bank	15,280	
Total current assets	17,020	
Current liabilities		
Trade payables (creditors)	(2,800)	
Current assets less current liabilities		14,220
		294,220
Non-current liabilities		
Long-term loan		(150,000)
Net assets		144,220
Ownership interest		144,220

Table 3.3
Statement of financial position (balance sheet): Assets equal ownership interest plus liabilities

P. Mason's legal practice Statement of financial position (balance sheet) at 30 September Year 5	£	£
Non-current assets		
Land and buildings		250,000
Office furniture		30,000
Total non-current assets		280,000
Current assets		
Receivables for fees		1,200
Prepayment of insurance premium		540
Cash at bank		15,280
Total current assets		17,020
Total assets		297,020
Ownership interest		144,220
Non-current liabilities		
Long-term loan		150,000
Current liabilities		
Trade payables		2,800
Total ownership interest plus liabilities		297,020

cannot show how effectively those assets are being used. For that, an income statement (profit and loss account) is needed.

The statement of financial position (balance sheet) in Table 3.3 is again more informative than the list of assets and liabilities from which it was prepared because it has been arranged in a helpful format. It offers a helpful feature in the use of headings (in bold) for similar items grouped together. It is also helpful in providing subtotals (identified by descriptions in italics and shaded) for similar items grouped together. The subtotals used in this example are those for: total non-current assets and total current assets. There could also be subtotals for the current assets less current liabilities. There are no standard rules on use of subtotals. They should be chosen in a manner most appropriate to the situation.

A person using this statement of financial position (balance sheet) can again see at a glance that there is no problem for the business in meeting its current liabilities from its resources of current assets. The financing of the business is split almost equally between the non-current liabilities and the ownership interest, a split which would not be regarded as excessively risky by those who lend to businesses. The non-current assets used as a basis for generating profits from one year to the next are collected together as a group, although the statement of financial position (balance sheet) alone cannot show how effectively those assets are being used.

3.5 The income statement (profit and loss account)

For many years in the UK, **profit and loss account** was the only title used for the financial statement reporting profit of the period. From 2005 many of those listed groups following the IASB's system have chosen to follow an example given by the IASB which uses the heading **income statement**, found more commonly in US company reports. It is not compulsory for listed group companies to use 'income statement' and some retain the 'profit and loss account' heading. The income statement (profit and loss account) reflects that part of the accounting equation which defines profit:

Profit	equals	**Revenue** minus **Expenses**

The expenses of a period are matched against the revenue earned in that period. This is described as the application of the **matching concept** in accounting.

As with the statement of financial position (balance sheet), it is presented in a vertical form so that it can be read down the page as a narrative (Table 3.4).

Table 3.4
Structure of an income statement (profit and loss account)

Revenue
minus
Expenses
equals
Profit

3.5.1 Example of presentation

The accounting records of P. Mason's legal practice at 30 September Year 5 showed that the ownership interest could be explained as follows (using brackets to show negative items):

	£
Increases in ownership interest	
Capital contributed at start of month	140,000
Fees	8,820
Decreases in ownership interest	
Computer rental and online searches	(1,500)
Gas	(100)
Electricity	(200)
Telephone/fax	(1,000)
Salary of assistant	(1,800)
Ownership interest at end of month	144,220

The statement of profit is quite simple, as shown in Table 3.5.

Table 3.5
Financial statement of profit, in a useful format

P. Mason's legal practice Income statement (profit and loss account) for the month of September		
	£	£
Revenues		
Fees		8,820
Expenses		
Computer rental and online searches	(1,500)	
Gas	(100)	
Electricity	(200)	
Telephone/fax	(1,000)	
Salary of assistant	(1,800)	
Total expenses		(4,600)
Net profit of the month		4,220

3.5.2 Comment

The income statement (profit and loss account) improves on the mere list of constituent items by providing headings (shown in bold) for each main category. As this is a very simple example, only two headings and one subtotal are required. Headings and subtotals are most useful where there are groups of items of a similar nature. The resulting net profit shows how the revenues and expenses have contributed overall to increasing the ownership interest during the month.

Activity 3.2

Taking each item of the income statement (profit and loss account) in turn, explain to an imaginary friend why each item of revenue and expense is regarded as increasing or decreasing the ownership interest. If necessary, look back to the definitions of revenue and expense in Chapter 2. Make sure that you feel confident about the income statement (profit and loss account) before you move on.

3.6 The statement of cash flows

It was shown in Chapter 1 that liquidity is of interest to more than one user group, but of particular interest to creditors of the business.

Liquidity is measured by the cash and near-cash assets and the change in those assets, so a financial statement which explains cash flows should be of general interest to user groups:

Cash flow	equals	**Cash inflows to the enterprise** minus **Cash outflows from the enterprise**

The **statement of cash flows** will appear in a vertical form:

Cash inflows
minus
Cash outflows
equals
Change in cash assets

In a business there will be different factors causing the inflows and outflows of cash. The enterprise will try to make clear what the different causes are. Subdivisions are commonly used for operating activities, investing activities and financing activities:

- *Operating activities* are the actions of buying and selling goods, or manufacturing goods for resale, or providing a service to customers.
- *Investing activities* are the actions of buying and selling non-current assets for long-term purposes.
- *Financing activities* are the actions of raising and repaying the long-term finance of the business.

Table 3.6 sets out the basic structure of a basic statement of cash flows.

Table 3.6
Structure of a statement of cash flows

Operating activities **Cash inflows** minus
Cash outflows
plus
Investing activities **Cash inflows** minus **Cash outflows**
plus
Financing activities **Cash inflows** minus **Cash outflows**
equals
Change in cash assets

3.6.1   Example of presentation

The cash transactions of P. Mason's legal practice for the month of September were recorded as follows:

Accounting records

Year 5   £
Cash received
Sept. 1   Capital contributed by P. Mason   140,000
Sept. 1   Loan from bank   150,000
Sept. 19   Fees received from clients   7,620
                   Total cash received   297,620

Cash paid
Sept. 1   Land and buildings   250,000
Sept. 5   Prepayment of insurance premium   540
Sept. 26   Supplier for office furniture   30,000
Sept. 30   Salaries   1,800
                   Total cash paid   282,340
                   Cash remaining at 30 September   15,280

The statement of cash flows would be presented as shown in Table 3.7.

Table 3.7
Financial statement showing cash flows of an enterprise

P. Mason's legal practice	
Statement of cash flows for the month of September Year 5	
Operating activities	£
Inflow from fees	7,620
Outflow to insurance premium	(540)
Outflows to salaries	(1,800)
Net inflow from operations	5,280
Investing activities	
Payment for land and building	(250,000)
Payment for office furniture	(30,000)
Net outflow for investing activities	(280,000)
Financing activities	
Capital contributed by owner	140,000
Five-year loan from bank	150,000
Net inflow from financing activities	290,000
Increase in cash at bank over period	15,280

3.6.2   Comment

The cash flows, listed at the start of section 3.5.1 in the accounting records for the legal practice, relate to three different types of activity which are brought out more clearly in the statement of cash flows by the use of headings and subtotals. The headings are shown in bold and the subtotals are highlighted by italics and shading. The story emerging from the statement of cash flows is that the owner put in £140,000 and the bank lent £150,000, providing a total of £290,000 in start-up finance. Of this amount, £280,000 was used during the month to pay for non-current assets. That left £10,000 which, when added to the positive cash flow from operations, explains why the cash resources increased by £15,280 over the month.

It is quite common to compare the increase in ownership claim caused by making a profit with the increase in the cash resources of a business caused by operations. In this case the profit is £4,220 (Table 3.5) but the operations have added £15,280 to the cash assets of the business.

To make the comparison, Table 3.8 takes the income statement (profit and loss account) of Table 3.5 and sets alongside it the cash flows relating to operations.

Table 3.8 shows that the cash flow from fees was £1,200 less than the fee revenue earned because some customers had not paid at the month end. This is the amount

Table 3.8
Comparison of profit and cash flow for the month of September

P. Mason's legal practice		
	Profit £	Cash flow £
Revenues		
Fees/cash received	8,820	7,620
Expenses		
Computer rental and online searches	(1,500)	nil
Gas	(100)	nil
Electricity	(200)	nil
Telephone/fax	(1,000)	nil
Salary of assistant	(1,800)	(1,800)
Payment for insurance premium	nil	(540)
Total expenses/total cash paid	4,600	(2,340)
Net profit of the month	4,220	
Increase in cash in the month		5,280

shown in the statement of financial position (balance sheet) (Table 3.2) as receivables for fees. Table 3.8 also shows that expenses of rental, gas, electricity and telephone amounting to £2,800 in total had not been paid at the month end. These are shown as **trade payables** in the statement of financial position (balance sheet). The cash flow from operations is reduced by the payment for the insurance premium which does not affect the income statement (profit and loss account) for the month.

Users of financial statements regard both the profit and the cash flow as interesting items of information. The profit shows the overall increase in ownership claim which contributes to the overall wealth of the business. The cash flow shows the ability of the business to survive financially through planning the timing and amount of inflows and outflows of cash.

3.7 Usefulness of financial statements

Here are Leona and David, still working on Leona's flat, discussing the usefulness of financial statements.

LEONA: *Which financial statement is the most important for you?*

DAVID: *It has to be the income statement (profit and loss account). Profit creates wealth. Future profit creates future wealth. I have to make a forecast of each company's profit as part of my planning to meet our overall investment strategy. Maybe I should qualify that by adding that cash flow is also important, especially where there is high uncertainty about future prospects. We talk about 'quality of profits' and regard some types of profit as of higher quality than others. Cash flow support is one aspect of that quality. We have doubts about some accounting amounts which don't have a close relationship to cash. A business cannot survive if it can't pay its way.*

LEONA: *Where does that leave the statement of financial position?*

DAVID: *I'm not sure. It is a list of resources and claims on those resources. We are share-holders and so we have a claim on those resources but we don't think about it to any great extent because we are concentrating on the going concern aspects of the business, rather than closing down and selling the assets. The numbers in the statement of financial position don't mean very much because they are out of date.*

LEONA: *We studied research at university which suggested that cash flow is the answer and income statements (profit and loss accounts) are too difficult to understand. It was suggested that the statement of financial position (balance sheet) should show what the assets could be sold for. I don't think the ideas had caught on in practice, but they seemed to have some merits.*

DAVID: *I like to know the dynamics of the business. I like to see the movements of different aspects and the interactions. I think I would feel that cash flow alone is concentrating on only one aspect of the wealth of the business. I suppose the statement of financial position is a useful check on the position which has been reached as a result of making profits for the period. One thing we do look at in the statement of financial position is how much has been borrowed for use in the business. We don't like to see that become too high in comparison with the ownership interest.*

LEONA: *At least you are admitting to seeing something in the financial statements. I still have to persuade you that the auditors are important in giving you the reassurance you obviously obtain.*

Activity 3.3	*Analyse your own view of wealth and changes in wealth. Which items would you include in your personal statement of financial position (balance sheet) today? Which items would you include in your personal 'profit or loss' calculation for the past year? Which items would you include in your personal statement of cash flows? Has your view of 'wealth' been modified as a result of reading these first three chapters? If so, how have your views changed?*

3.8 Summary

This chapter has explained the structure of the main financial statements produced by business and non-business entities.

Key points are:

- An **accounting period** of 12 months is common for financial reporting.
- The **primary financial statements** produced by a wide range of entities are the statement of financial position (balance sheet), the income statement (profit and loss account) and the statement of cash flows.
- A **statement of financial position (balance sheet)** presents financial position at a point in time. The **format** of the statement of financial position (balance sheet) will vary depending on which version of the accounting equation is preferred by the entity preparing the statement.
- An **income statement** (profit and loss account) presents the performance over a period of time. The income statement (profit and loss account) presents financial performance by **matching** revenue and expenses to arrive at a profit of the period.
- A **statement of cash flows** presents the financial adaptability over a period of time. It explains changes in the cash position over a period caused by operating cash flows, investing cash flows and financing cash flows.
- Since 2005 two different accounting systems (consisting of **accounting standards** and legislation) have existed for companies in the UK, depending on the type of company. The **IASB system** applies to the group financial statements of listed companies. Other companies may choose voluntarily to follow the IASB system. The **UK ASB system**, based on UK law and the standards of the UK ASB, applies to all companies that do not follow the IASB system.
- The **accounting standards** of the UK ASB are very similar to those of the IASB.

QUESTIONS

The Questions section of each chapter has three types of question. 'Test your understanding' questions to help you review your reading are in the 'A' series of questions. You will find the answers to these by reading and thinking about the material in the book. 'Application' questions to test your ability to apply technical skills are in the 'B' series of questions. Questions requiring you to show skills in problem solving and evaluation are in the 'C' series of questions. A letter [S] indicates that there is a solution at the end of the book.

A Test your understanding

A3.1 Explain why an accounting period of 12 months is used as the basis for reporting to external users of financial statements. (Section 3.3)

A3.2 Explain how the structure of the statement of financial position (balance sheet) corresponds to the accounting equation. (Section 3.4)

A3.3 Explain how the structure of the income statement (profit and loss account) represents a subsection of the accounting equation. (Section 3.5)

A3.4 Explain how the structure of the statement of cash flows represents another subsection of the accounting equation. (Section 3.6)

A3.5 List three features of a statement of financial position (balance sheet) which are particularly useful in making the format helpful to readers. (Section 3.4.3)

A3.6 List three features of an income statement (profit and loss account) format which are particularly useful in making the format helpful to readers. (Section 3.5.1)

A3.7 List three features of a statement of cash flows which are particularly useful in making the format helpful to readers. (Section 3.6.1)

B Application

B3.1 [S]
John Timms is the sole owner of Sunshine Wholesale Traders, a company which buys fruit from farmers and sells it to supermarkets. All goods are collected from farms and delivered to supermarkets on the same day, so no inventories (stocks) of fruit are held. The accounting records of Sunshine Traders at 30 June Year 2, relating to the year then ended, have been summarised by John Timms as follows:

	£
Fleet of delivery vehicles, after deducting depreciation	35,880
Furniture and fittings, after deducting depreciation	18,800
Trade receivables	34,000
Bank deposit	19,000
Trade payables (creditors)	8,300
Sales	294,500
Cost of goods sold	188,520
Wages and salaries	46,000
Transport costs	14,200
Administration costs	1,300
Depreciation of vehicles, furniture and fittings	1,100

Required
(a) Identify each item in the accounting records as either an asset, a liability, or ownership interest (identifying separately the expenses and revenues which contribute to the change in the ownership interest).

(b) Prepare a statement of financial position (balance sheet) at 30 June Year 2.

(c) Prepare an income statement (profit and loss statement) for the year ended 30 June Year 2.

B3.2 [S]

Prepare a statement of financial position (balance sheet) from the following list of assets and liabilities, regarding the ownership interest as the missing item.

	£
Trade payables (creditors)	43,000
Cash at bank	9,000
Inventories (stocks) of goods for resale	35,000
Land and buildings	95,000
Wages due to employees but not paid	2,000
Vehicles	8,000
Five-year loan from a bank	20,000

Explain how the statement of financial position (balance sheet) will change for each of the following transactions:

(a) The wages due to the employees are paid at £2,000.

(b) One-quarter of the inventory (stock) of goods held for resale is destroyed by fire and there is no insurance to cover the loss.

(c) Goods for resale are bought on credit at a cost of £5,000.

There are no questions in the C series for this chapter.

Activities for study groups

Return to the annual reports your group obtained for the exercise in Chapter 1. Find the statement of financial position (balance sheet), income statement (profit and loss account) and statement of cash flows. Use the outline formats contained in this chapter to identify the main areas of each of the published statements. Work together in preparing a list of features which make the formats useful to the reader. Note also any aspects of the presentation which you find unhelpful at this stage. (It may be useful to look back on this note at the end of the course as a collective check on whether your understanding and awareness of annual report items has improved.)

Using the accounting equation to analyse transactions

In the main body of the chapter the transactions of P. Mason's legal practice are set out in summary form and are then presented in financial statements. This supplement goes back one stage and looks at the transactions and events for the month of September which resulted in the summary and financial statements shown in the chapter.

The list of transactions and events is as follows:

Sept. 1	P. Mason deposits £140,000 in a bank account to commence the business under the name *P. Mason's legal practice*.
Sept. 1	P. Mason's legal practice borrows £150,000 from a finance business to help with the intended purchase of a property for use as an office. The loan is to be repaid in five years' time.
Sept. 1	A property is purchased at a cost of £75,000 for the land and £175,000 for the buildings. The full price is paid from the bank account.
Sept. 3	Office furniture is purchased from Stylecraft at a cost of £30,000. The full price is to be paid within 90 days.
Sept. 5	An insurance premium of £540 is paid in advance. The insurance cover will commence on 1 October.
Sept. 8	An applicant is interviewed for a post of legal assistant. She agrees to start work on 10 September for a salary of £24,000 per annum.
Sept. 11	Invoices are sent to some clients for work done in preparing contracts for them. The total of the invoiced amounts is £8,820. Clients are allowed up to 30 days to pay.
Sept. 19	Cheques received from clients in payment of invoices amount to £7,620.
Sept. 26	Payment is made to Stylecraft for the amount due for office furniture, £30,000.
Sept. 28	Bills are received as follows: for computer rental and online searches, £1,500; gas, £100; electricity, £200; and telephone/fax, £1,000.
Sept. 30	Legal assistant is paid salary of £1,800 for period to end of month.

In the supplement to Chapter 2 a table was prepared, based on the accounting equation, showing the classification used for debit and credit bookkeeping entries. As a reminder, the form of the equation used to derive the debit and credit rules is:

Assets	equals	Liabilities	plus	Ownership interest

As a further reminder, the rules are set out again in Table 3.9. Each of the transactions of P. Mason's legal practice for the month of September is now analysed in terms of the effect on the accounting equation and the resulting debit and credit entries which would be made in the accounting records.

Table 3.9
Rules for debit and credit recording

	Debit entries in a ledger account	Credit entries in a ledger account
Left-hand side of the equation		
Asset	Increase	Decrease
Right-hand side of the equation		
Liability	Decrease	Increase
Ownership interest	Expense	Revenue
	Capital withdrawn	Capital contributed

Analysis of each transaction

Sept. 1   P. Mason deposits £140,000 in a bank account to commence the business under the name *P. Mason's legal practice*.

The business acquires an asset (cash in the bank) and an ownership interest is created through contribution of capital.

Transaction number: 1	Debit	Credit
Asset	Bank £140,000	
Ownership interest		Capital contributed £140,000

Sept. 1   P. Mason's legal practice borrows £150,000 from a finance business to help with the intended purchase of a property for use as an office. The loan is to be repaid in five years' time.

The business acquires an asset of cash and a long-term liability is created.

Transaction number: 2	Debit	Credit
Asset	Bank £150,000	
Liability		Long-term loan £150,000

Sept. 1   A property is purchased at a cost of £75,000 for the land and £175,000 for the buildings. The full price is paid from the bank account.

The business acquires an asset of land and buildings (£250,000 in total) and the asset of cash in the bank is reduced.

Transaction number: 3	Debit	Credit
Asset	Land and buildings £250,000	Bank £250,000

Sept. 3   Office furniture is purchased from Stylecraft at a cost of £30,000. The full price is to be paid within 90 days.

The business acquires an asset of furniture and also acquires a liability to pay the supplier, Stylecraft. The liability is called a trade payable (creditor).

Transaction number: 4	Debit	Credit
Asset	Furniture £30,000	
Liability		Trade payable (Stylecraft) £30,000

Sept. 5   An insurance premium of £540 is paid in advance. The insurance cover will commence on 1 October.

The business acquires an asset of prepaid insurance (the benefit of cover exists in the future) and the asset of cash at bank is reduced.

Transaction number: 5	Debit	Credit
Asset	Prepayment £540	Bank £540

Sept. 8   An applicant is interviewed for a post of legal assistant. She agrees to start work on 10 September for a salary of £24,000 per annum.

The successful outcome of the interview is an *event* and there is an expected future benefit from employing the new legal assistant. The employee will be controlled by the organisation through a contract of employment. The organisation has a commitment to pay her the agreed salary. It could be argued that the offer of employment, and acceptance of that offer, create an asset of the human resource and a liability equal to the future salary. That does not happen because the *recognition* conditions are applied and it is felt too risky to recognise an asset when there is insufficient evidence of the future benefit. Commercial prudence dictates that it is preferable to wait until the employee has done some work and pay her at the end of the month for work done during the month. The accounting process is similarly prudent and no accounting recognition takes place until the payment has occurred. Even then it is the expense of the past which is recognised, rather than the asset of benefit for the future.

Sept. 11   Invoices are sent to some clients showing fees due for work done in preparing contracts for them. The total of the invoiced amounts is £8,820. Clients are allowed up to 30 days to pay.

Earning fees is the main activity of the legal practice. Earning fees makes the owner better off and is an example of the more general activity *of increasing the ownership interest* by creating revenue. The clients have not yet paid and therefore the business has an asset called a **trade receivable (debtor)**.

Transaction number: 6	Debit	Credit
Asset	Trade receivables £8,820	
Ownership interest (revenue)		Fees for work done £8,820

Sept. 19   Cheques received from clients in payment of invoices amount to £7,620.

When the customers pay, the amount due to the business from debtors will be decreased. So the asset of trade receivables decreases and the asset of cash in the bank increases.

Transaction number: 7	Debit	Credit
Asset	Bank £7,620	Trade receivables £7,620

Sept. 26   Payment is made to Stylecraft for the amount due for office furniture, £30,000.

The asset of cash in the bank decreases and the liability to Stylecraft decreases to nil.

Transaction number: 8	Debit	Credit
Asset		Bank £30,000
Liability	Trade payable (Stylecraft) £30,000	

Sept. 28   Bills are received as follows: for computer rental and online searches, £1,500; gas, £100; electricity, £200; and telephone/fax £1,000 (total £2,800).

The computer rental, online searches, gas, electricity and telephone have been used up during the period and are all expenses which reduce the ownership interest. They are unpaid and, therefore, a liability is recorded.

Transaction number: 9	Debit	Credit
Liability		Trade payables £2,800
Ownership interest	Expenses £2,800	

Sept. 30   Legal assistant is paid salary of £1,800 for period to end of month.

The asset of cash at bank decreases and the salary paid to the legal assistant is an expense of the month.

Transaction number: 10	Debit	Credit
Asset		Bank £1,800
Ownership interest	Expense £1,800	

Summarising the debit and credit entries

The formal system of bringing together debit and credit entries is based on ledger accounts. These are explained in the supplement to Chapter 5. For the present it will be sufficient to use a spreadsheet (Table 3.10) to show how the separate debit and credit entries analysed in this supplement lead to the list of items used in the main part of the chapter as the basis for the financial statements presented there.

In the spreadsheet there are dates which correspond to the dates of the foregoing ten separate analyses of transactions. The debit and credit entries are shown with Dr or Cr alongside to distinguish them. For each column all the debit entries are totalled

Table 3.10
Spreadsheet of transactions for P. Mason's legal practice, during the month of September

	Assets					Liabilities		Ownership interest		
Date	Land and buildings £	Office furniture £	Trade receivables £	Pre-payments £	Cash at bank £	Trade payables £	Bank loan £	Revenue £	Expenses £	Owner's capital contributed £
1 Sept.					140,000 Dr					140,000 Cr
1 Sept.					150,000 Dr		150,000 Cr			
1 Sept.	250,000 Dr				250,000 Cr					
3 Sept.		30,000 Dr				30,000 Cr				
5 Sept.				540 Dr	540 Cr					
11 Sept.			8,820 Dr					8,820 Cr		
19 Sept.			7,620 Cr		7,620 Dr					
26 Sept.					30,000 Cr	30,000 Dr				
28 Sept.						2,800 Cr			2,800 Dr	
30 Sept.					1,800 Cr				1,800 Dr	
Total debit entries in each column										
	250,000 Dr	30,000 Dr	8,820 Dr	540 Dr	297,620 Dr	30,000 Dr	nil	nil	4,600 Dr	nil
Total credit entries in each column										
	nil	nil	7,620 Cr	nil	282,340 Cr	32,800 Cr	150,000 Cr	8,820 Cr	nil	140,000 Cr
Surplus of debits over credits (or credits over debits)										
	250,000 Dr	30,000 Dr	1,200 Dr	540 Dr	15,280 Dr	2,800 Cr	150,000 Cr	8,820 Cr	4,600 Dr	140,000 Cr

and all the credit entries are totalled separately. The surplus of debits over credits (or credits over debits) is calculated and shown in the final line. This allows a summarised list to be prepared as shown in Table 3.11.

A spreadsheet is useful where there are not too many entries, but ledger accounts become essential when the volume of information increases.

Table 3.11
Summary of debit and credit entries for each category of asset, liability and ownership interest

	Debit	Credit
	£	£
Assets		
Land and buildings	250,000	
Office furniture	30,000	
Trade receivables (debtors)	1,200	
Prepayment	540	
Cash at bank	15,280	
Liabilities		
Trade payables (creditors)		2,800
Long-term loan		150,000
Ownership interest		
Revenue		8,820
Expenses	4,600	
Capital contributed		140,000
Totals	*301,620*	*301,620*

Note: The totals of each column have no particular meaning, but they should always be equal because of the symmetry of the debit and credit records, and so are useful as an arithmetic check that no item has been omitted or recorded incorrectly.

Turning the spreadsheet back to a vertical listing, using the debit column for items where the debits exceed the credits, and using the credit column for items where the credits exceed the debits, the list becomes as in Table 3.11. You will see that this list is the basis of the information provided about P. Mason's legal practice in the main body of the chapter, except that the debit and credit notation was not used there.

Activity 3.4

The most serious problem faced by most students, once they have understood the basic approach, is that of making errors. Look back through this Supplement and think about the errors which might have been made. What type of error would be detected by finding totals in Table 3.11 which were not in agreement? What type of error would not be detected in this way because the totals would be in agreement despite the error? Types of error will be dealt with in the supplement to Chapter 5.

S Test your understanding

S3.1 [S] Analyse the debit and credit aspect of each transaction listed at (a), (b) and (c) of question B3.2.

S3.2 Prepare a spreadsheet similar to that presented in Table 3.10, setting out on the first line the items contained in the list of assets and liabilities of question B3.2 and then on lines 2, 3 and 4 adding in the transactions (a), (b) and (c). Calculate the totals of each column of the spreadsheet and show that the accounting equation remains equal on both sides.

Chapter 4

Ensuring the quality of financial statements

REAL WORLD CASE

The Financial Reporting Review Panel

Press notice: The Financial Reporting Review Panel announces priority sectors for 2010/11

The Financial Reporting Review Panel today announced that its review activity in 2010/11 will focus on the following sectors:

Commercial property
Advertising
Recruitment
Media
Information technology

Banking, house-builders and travel and leisure have featured as priority sectors for the last two years. As companies enter the next stage of the recession where the outlook for corporate spending is uncertain, the Panel is turning its attention to sectors that rely heavily on discretionary spend and which might be stretched in the short term.

Advertising, media, recruitment and technology all featured in the Panel's priority list last year as deserving attention but this year they take centre stage.

Annual reports and accounts will continue to be selected from across the full range of companies within the Panel's remit and will also be selected for review on the basis of company-specific factors and complaints.

Recent economic pressures on companies have led some to make changes to the way in which they do business, particularly where this helps them to manage their cash flow. These companies may need to take a fresh look at their accounting policies that impact on the measurement of earnings, such as revenue recognition and the expensing of costs, to ensure that they remain appropriate. The reporting and accounting impact of changes to business models is likely to be a focus of the Panel's work for 2010/11.

Commenting on areas of reporting where this might be reflected, Bill Knight, Chairman of the Panel said:

Companies who are seeing their business models develop to meet the challenges of the recession will need to reconsider their revenue recognition policies to ensure that they still reflect their business activities. The Panel will pay particular attention to the accounts of those companies which appear to apply aggressive policies compared with their peers.

Source: Financial Reporting Review Panel Press Notice PN 123, 9 December 2009; http://www.frc.org.uk/frrp/press/pub2189.html.

Discussion points

1 Is it a good idea for the Financial Reporting Review Panel to focus on particular industry sectors in monitoring the quality of financial reporting?

2 Why is it more likely that the industries listed for attention could face more 'challenges' in recognising revenues and in expensing costs?

Contents

Learning outcomes

After studying this chapter you should be able to:

- List and explain the qualitative characteristics desirable in financial statements.
- Explain the approach to measurement used in financial statements.
- Explain why there is more than one view on the role of prudence in accounting.
- Understand and explain how and why financial reporting is regulated or influenced by external authorities.
- Be aware of the process by which financial statements are reviewed by an investor.

4.1   Introduction

The previous chapter used the accounting equation as a basis for explaining the structure of financial statements. It showed that design of formats for financial statements is an important first step in creating an understandable story from a list of accounting data.

The objective of financial statements is to provide information about the financial position, performance and changes in financial position of an entity that is useful to a wide range of users in making economic decisions.[1]

Information about financial position is provided in a **statement of financial position (balance sheet)**. Information about performance is provided in an **income statement** (profit and loss account).[2] Information about changes in the cash position is provided in a **statement of cash flows**. These three statements were explained in outline in Chapter 3. Information about changes in equity is also provided in a separate statement, described in Chapter 12. Notes to the financial statements provide additional information relevant to the needs of users. These notes may include information about risks and uncertainties relating to assets, liabilities, revenue and expenses.[3]

4.2   Qualitative characteristics of financial statements

The IASB *Framework* sets out qualitative characteristics that make the information provided in financial statements useful to users. The four principal qualitative characteristics are:

- understandability
- relevance
- reliability
- comparability.[4]

The principal qualitative characteristics of relevance and reliability have further subheadings:

- relevance
  - materiality
- reliability
  - faithful representation
  - substance over form
  - neutrality
  - prudence
  - completeness.

Each of these characteristics is now described.

4.2.1   Understandability

It is essential that the information provided in financial statements is readily **understandable** by users.[5] Users are assumed to have a reasonable knowledge of business and economic activities and accounting, and a willingness to study the information with reasonable diligence. Information on complex matters should not be omitted from financial statements merely on the grounds that some users may find it difficult to understand.

Relevance

Information has the quality of **relevance** when it influences the economic decisions of users by helping them evaluate past, present or future events or confirming, or correcting, their past evaluations.[6]

Information has a predictive role in helping users to look to the future. Predictive value does not necessarily require a forecast. Explaining unusual aspects of current performance helps users to understand future potential. Information also has a confirmatory role in showing users how the entity has, or has not, met their expectations.[7]

Materiality

Information is **material** if its omission or misstatement could influence the economic decisions of users taken on the basis of the financial statements. Materiality depends on the size of the item or error judged in the particular circumstances of its omission or misstatement.[8]

The IASB *Framework* takes the view that materiality is a cut-off point in deciding whether information is important to users. The description of an item may make it material. The amount of an item may make it material.

For example, the statement of financial position (balance sheet) of a business shows inventories of raw materials and inventories of finished goods as two separate items. That is because the users of financial statements are interested in the types of inventory held as well as the amount of each. The risks of holding raw materials are different from the risks of holding finished goods. However, the inventory of finished goods is not separated into the different types of finished goods because that would give too much detail when the risks of holding finished goods are relatively similar for all items.

4.2.3 ## Reliability

Information has the quality of **reliability** when it is free from material error and bias and can be depended upon by users to represent faithfully what it either purports to represent or could reasonably be expected to represent.[9]

Information may be relevant but so unreliable that it could be misleading (e.g. where a director has given a highly personal view of the value of an investment). On the other hand, it could be reliable but quite non-relevant (e.g. the information that a building standing in the centre of a major shopping street was bought for 50 guineas some 300 years ago).

Faithful representation

Faithful representation is important if accounting information is to be reliable. Faithful representation involves the words as well as the numbers in the financial statements. Sometimes it may be difficult for the managers of an entity to find the right words to describe a transaction and convey the problems of making reliable measurement. In such cases it will be important to disclose the risk of error surrounding recognition and measurement.[10]

Substance over form

If information is to meet the test of faithful representation, then the method of accounting must reflect the **substance** of the economic reality of the transaction and not merely its **legal form**.

For example, a company has sold its buildings to a bank to raise cash and then pays rent for the same buildings for the purpose of continued occupation. The company carries all the risks and problems (such as repairs and insurance) that an owner would carry. One view is that the commercial substance of that sequence of transactions is comparable to ownership. Another view is that the legal form of the transaction is a sale. The characteristic of substance over form requires that the information in the financial statements should show the commercial substance of the situation.[11]

Neutrality

The information contained in financial statements must be **neutral**. This is also described as being 'free from bias'. Financial statements are not neutral if, by the selection and presentation of information, they influence the making of a decision or judgement in order to achieve a predetermined result or outcome.[12]

This condition is quite difficult to enforce because it has to be shown that the entity producing the financial statements is trying to influence the decisions or judgements of all members of a class of users of the information. It would be impractical to know the decision-making process of every individual user.

Prudence

The preparers of financial statements have to contend with uncertainty surrounding many events and circumstances. The existence of uncertainties is recognised by the disclosure of their nature and extent and by the exercise of **prudence** in the preparation of the financial statements. Prudence is the inclusion of a degree of caution in the exercise of the judgements needed in making the estimates required under conditions of uncertainty, such that gains and assets are not overstated and losses and liabilities are not understated.[13]

Completeness

It almost goes without saying that information cannot be reliable if it is not **complete**. The information in financial statements must be complete, within the bounds of materiality and cost. An omission can cause information to be false or misleading and thus to lack reliability and relevance.[14]

4.2.4   Comparability

Comparability means that users must be able to compare the financial statements of an enterprise over time to identify trends in its financial position and performance. Users must also be able to compare the financial statements of different enterprises to evaluate their relative financial position, performance and changes in financial position.[15] Financial statements should show corresponding information for the previous period.[16]

Consistency

This concerns the measurement and display of the financial effect of like transactions and other events being carried out in a consistent way throughout an entity within each accounting period and from one period to the next, and also in a consistent way by different entities.[17]

However, the need for **consistency** should not be allowed to become an impediment to the introduction of improved accounting practices. Consistency does not require absolute uniformity.[18]

Disclosure of accounting policies

This is another important aspect of **comparability**. **Disclosure** means that users of financial statements must be informed of the accounting policies employed in the preparation of financial statements. Managers must also disclose changes in accounting policies and the effect of those changes.[19]

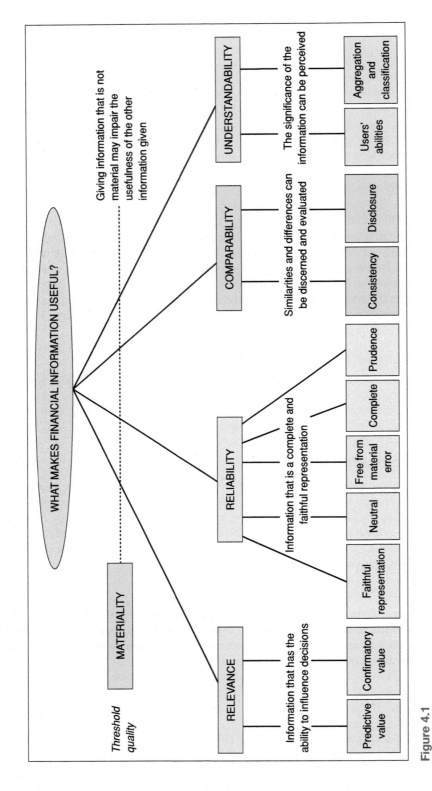

Figure 4.1

UK ASB: relationships of the qualitative characteristics of financial information

Source: ASB (1999), *Statement of Principles for Financial Reporting*, p. 34. Reproduced with the permission of the Accounting Standards Board.

The annual report of a company will usually have a separate section headed 'Accounting policies'. It will be located immediately after the primary financial statements, leading into the detailed notes to the accounts. The statement of accounting policies is essential reading for any user of the annual report.

4.2.5 Constraints on relevant and reliable information

Relevance and **reliability** are twin targets which may cause some tension in deciding the most appropriate way to report accounting information. There is a trade-off between relevance and reliability when it comes to ensuring that information is delivered in a timely manner so that it is still relevant, and when it comes to deciding whether the costs of producing further information exceed the benefits.

Timeliness

If information is provided in a timely way, the reliability may be less than 100% because some aspects of a transaction are not yet complete. If reporting is delayed until all aspects of a transaction are known then the relevance may be less than 100% because investors have become tired of waiting. The balance of **timeliness** is achieved by considering how best to serve the needs of users in making economic decisions.[20]

Benefit and cost

The benefits derived from information should be greater than the costs of providing it. The analysis is complicated because the benefits fall mainly on the users, while the costs fall mainly on the provider. It is important for standard-setters to consider the benefits and costs as a whole.[21]

4.2.6 Revising the conceptual framework

The IASB is in the process of revising its conceptual framework but the date of publication is still some way into the future. Phase A focuses on the objective and qualitative characteristics and has been under debate since 2006 as a Discussion Paper and since 2008 as an Exposure Draft.[22] The most controversial recommendation is to focus the objective of decision usefulness rather than emphasise stewardship (careful use of the resources of the business). Many commentators think stewardship is an important objective of financial reporting. The IASB thinks that stewardship is assumed within decision usefulness. Another provisional decision is to cease to refer to 'reliability' and instead use the term 'faithful representation' to refer to the characteristic that is labelled 'reliability' in the existing framework. The IASB has also clarified that it thinks the components of faithful representation (neutrality, completeness and freedom from error) are not absolutes. For example, the phrase freedom from error is not intended to imply that financial statements must be 100% accurate. There is an intention to continue to classify verifiability, comparability, timeliness and understandability as enhancing characteristics. It is also intended to continue to describe materiality and cost as constraints on financial reporting.

4.2.7 UK ASB

The UK ASB's representation of the relationships between the various qualitative characteristics is set out in Figure 4.1.[23]

In many ways the ideas of the UK ASB reflect those of the IASB which were written ten years earlier. However, during that ten-year period the ASB had time to benefit by thinking about ways of clarifying some aspects of the IASB's ideas. One difference in presentation is that the ASB suggests that materiality is a test to be applied at the threshold of considering an item. If any information is not material, it does not need to be considered further.

4.3 Measurement in financial statements

You have seen in Chapter 2, sections 2.5 and 2.8, that the recognition of assets and liability requires reliability of measurement. You have seen in Chapter 3 the methods of presentation of accounting information containing numbers that represent measurement. We now need to know more about the accounting measurement principles that establish reliability and about the disclosure of information that allows users of financial statements to understand the measurement process.

The accounting measurement principles that are most widely known in the UK are found within the Companies Act 2006:[24]

- going concern
- accruals
- consistency
- prudence.

The IASB *Framework* describes the accrual basis and going concern as 'underlying assumptions' in the preparation of financial statements. It describes **prudence** as a 'constraint' on relevance and reliability. Consistency is an aspect of comparability.

4.3.1 Going concern

Definition

The financial statements are normally prepared on the assumption that an entity is a **going concern** and will continue in operation for the foreseeable future. Hence, it is assumed that the entity has neither the intention nor the need to liquidate or curtail materially the scale of its operations; if such an intention or need exists the financial statements may have to be prepared on a different basis and, if so, the basis used is disclosed.[25]

The UK Companies Act statement on **going concern** is rather like a crossword clue, in being short and enigmatic. It states: 'The company shall be presumed to be carrying on business as a going concern.'

The Financial Reporting Council provides a practical guide for directors in *Going Concern and Liquidity Risk: Guidance for Directors of UK Companies 2009*, published in October 2009. It took effect for accounting periods ending on or after 31 December 2009. The guidance is based on three principles covering: the process which directors should follow when assessing going concern; the period covered by the assessment; and the disclosures on going concern and liquidity risk. The guidance applies to all companies and in particular addresses the statement about going concern that must be made by directors of listed companies in their annual report and accounts.

Directors should plan their assessment of going concern as early as practicable including deciding on the processes, procedures, information, analyses and board papers that will be needed. These plans should also address the evidence to be obtained, including identifying any potential remedial actions that may need to be addressed, to support their conclusion prior to their approval of the annual or half-yearly financial statements.

The practical effect will usually be that directors of UK companies will adopt a review period of not less than 12 months from the date of approval of annual and half-yearly financial statements but, in rare cases, when they do not they should explain why.

Directors of listed companies incorporated in the UK are required by the Listing Rules to include in their annual financial report a statement that the business is a going concern, together with supporting assumptions or qualifications as necessary, that has been prepared in accordance with the Guidance.

The auditor is required to consider the disclosures about going concern and liquidity risk made in the financial statements. If the auditor concludes that the disclosures are not adequate to meet the requirements of accounting standards and CA 2006, including the need for financial statements to give a true and fair view, the auditor is required to qualify its opinion and to provide its reasons for doing so.

4.3.2   Accruals (also called 'matching')

Definition

> Under the **accruals** basis, the effects of transactions and other events are recognised when they occur (and not as cash or its equivalent is received or paid) and they are recorded in the accounting records and reported in the financial statements of the periods to which they relate.[26]

The IASB explains that financial statements prepared on the accruals basis are useful for stewardship purposes because they report past transactions and events but are also helpful to users for forward-looking information because they show obligations to pay cash in the future and resources that represent cash to be received in the future.

The UK Companies Act explains the accruals concept as a requirement that all income and charges (i.e. expenses) relating to the financial year shall be taken into account, without regard to the date of receipt or payment.

The word 'accrue' means 'to fall due' or 'to come as a natural result'. If, during a year, a company sells £100m of goods but collects only £80m from customers, it records sales as £100m in the profit and loss account. The cash yet to be collected from customers is reported as an asset called 'debtor' in the statement of financial position (balance sheet). If, during the year, it uses electricity costing £50m but has only paid £40m so far, it records the expense of £50m in the profit and loss account. The unpaid electricity bill is reported as a liability called 'accruals' in the statement of financial position (balance sheet).

The idea of matching is also used in applying the idea of accruals. Matching has two forms, matching losses or gains against time and matching expenses against revenue. Time matching occurs when a gain or loss is spread over the relevant period of time, such as receiving interest on a loan or paying rent on a property. Matching of revenues and expenses occurs when costs such as labour are matched against the revenue earned from providing goods or services.

4.3.3   Consistency

Consistency is described in the IASB *Framework* as an aspect of comparability (see section 4.2.4). The UK Companies Act requires that accounting policies shall be applied consistently within the same accounts and from one period to the next.

4.3.4 Prudence

The Companies Act does not define prudence but uses the word prudent in relation to measurement. It requires that the amount of any item shall be determined on a prudent basis, and in particular:

(a) only profits realised at the date of the financial year-end shall be included in the profit and loss account; and

(b) all liabilities and losses which have arisen or are likely to arise in respect of the financial year shall be taken into account, including those which only become apparent between the date of the financial year-end and the date on which it is signed by the board of directors.

The UK ASB has said that decisions about recognition of income or assets and of expenses or liabilities require evidence of existence and reliability of measurement. Stronger evidence and greater reliability of measurement are required for assets and gains than for liabilities and losses.[27]

4.3.5 Realisation

There is no clear statement of the conditions that will make a profit **realised**. It is not specifically defined in the IASB system. It is an example of an idea that is so widely used that it appears to be almost impossible to explain. If you turn to a dictionary you will find 'realise' equated to 'convert into cash'. The accounting standard FRS 18[28] confirms that it is the general view that profits shall be treated as realised when evidenced in the form of cash or other assets whose cash **realisation** is reasonably certain. However, the standard avoids linking realisation to 'prudence', explaining that a focus on cash does not reflect more recent developments in financial markets. Evidence of 'reasonable certainty' in such markets does not necessarily require cash. It is based on confidence in the reliable operation of the market.

Activity 4.2

Take a piece of paper having two wide columns. Head the left-hand column 'My thoughts on measurement in accounting' and head the right-hand column 'What the book tells me about measurement'. Fill in both columns and then exchange your paper with a fellow student. Discuss with each other any similarities and differences in the left-hand column and relate these to your personal views and prior experience. Discuss with each other any similarities and differences in the right-hand column and evaluate the extent to which different people see books differently. Finally, discuss with each other the extent to which reading this section has changed your views on measurement as a subject in accounting.

4.4 Views on prudence

The Companies Act 2006 makes an explicit link between prudence and realisation that reflects UK accounting practice when the previous Companies Act 1985 was written. The IASB's *Framework* avoids mentioning realisation and describes prudence in terms of 'a degree of caution'.[29] From the UK ASB, the standard FRS 18 acknowledges the meaning of realisation but breaks the link between realisation and prudence.[30] It appears that FRS 18 has not changed the entrenched conservatism of accounting practice which tends towards understatement on grounds of caution. Where does that leave the student of accounting who wants to understand the meaning of prudence?

The most important message for students of accounting (and for many practitioners) is contained in the IASB's *Framework*:[31]

the exercise of prudence does not allow . . . the deliberate understatement of assets or income, or the deliberate overstatement of liabilities or expenses, because the financial statements would not be neutral and, therefore, not have the quality of reliability.

Why are there different views on understatement and overstatement, depending on the item being reported? Here is your first chance to use the accounting equation to solve a problem:

Assets minus **Liabilities**	equals	**Capital contributed/withdrawn** plus **Profit**

Profit	equals	**Revenue** minus **Expenses**

<table>
<tr><td>**Activity 4.3**</td><td>*Ask yourself what will happen to profit in the accounting equation if the amount of an asset is increased while the liabilities and the capital contributed remain the same. Then ask yourself what will happen to profit in the accounting equation if the amount of a liability is decreased while the assets and the capital contributed remain the same. Next ask yourself what will happen to profit if revenue is overstated. Finally ask yourself what will happen to profit if expenses are understated.*</td></tr>
</table>

Assuming that capital contributed/withdrawn remains constant, overstating assets will overstate profit. Understating liabilities will overstate profit. Overstating revenue will overstate profit. Understating expenses will overstate profit.

Examples

A market trader buys £100 of stock on credit, promising to pay the supplier at the end of the day. The trader sells three-quarters of the stock at a price of £90 and takes the rest home to keep for next week's market. At the end of the day the trader has £90 in cash, one-quarter of the stock which cost £25, and owes £100 to the supplier. How much profit has the trader made? The answer is that the profit is £15 (£90 received for the sale of stock less the cost of the items sold, £75, being three-quarters of the stock purchased). The accounting equation is:

Assets minus **Liabilities** at the end of the period	equals	**Ownership interest at the start of the period** plus **Capital contributed/ withdrawn** plus **Revenue of the period** minus **Expenses of the period**
stock £25 + cash £90 – liability £100	equals	nil + nil + revenue £90 – expenses £75
£15	equals	£15

1 Supposing the trader 'forgets' part of the liability and thinks it is only £84 owing, rather than £100. The assets remain at stock £25 + cash £90, which equals £115. The liability is now thought to be £84 and therefore the equation becomes:

£25 + £90 – £84	equals	nil + nil + revenue £90 – expenses £75 + [?] £16 [?]
£31	equals	£31

For the equation to be satisfied there must be a total of £31 on both sides. The total of £31 is therefore written in. The recorded profit is still only £15, calculated as revenue £90 minus expenses £75, so there is a 'hole' amounting to £16 on the right-hand side of the equation. The accounting equation has to balance so the extra £16 is written in, surrounded by question marks, on the right-hand side. It is assumed on the right-hand side that the trader has either forgotten to record revenue of £16 or has recorded too much expense, so that the amount appears to represent an unexplained profit. Thus *understating a liability will overstate profit*. That favourable news might mislead a competitor or investor. It might be bad news when HMRC demands tax on profit of £31. Also there is the unpaid supplier who may not be entirely patient when offered £84 rather than £100.

2 Supposing instead that the trader 'forgets' there is some unsold inventory left. The only recorded asset would be the cash at £90 and there would be a liability of £100. This gives negative net assets of (£10) and, because the accounting equation has to balance, suggests that there is a 'forgotten' expense of £25 on the right-hand side. The equation then becomes:

£90 – £100	equals	nil + nil + £90 – £75 – [?] £25 [?]
(£10)	equals	(£10)

This would cause HMRC to ask a lot of questions as to why there was no record of stock remaining, because they know that omitting inventory from the record is a well-tried means of fraudulently reducing profits and therefore reducing tax bills. *Understating an asset will understate profit*.

These two examples have illustrated the meaning of the warning that deliberate understatement or overstatement is not acceptable. The general message of prudence is: *avoid overstating profit*. In down-to-earth terms, don't raise the readers' hopes too high, only to have to tell them later that it was all in the imagination.

4.5 Regulation of financial reporting

Because the external users of accounting information do not have day-to-day access to the records of the business, they rely on the integrity and judgement of management to provide suitable information of a high quality. But will the management be honest, conscientious and careful in providing information? In an ideal world there should be no problem for investors in a company because, as shareholders, they appoint the directors and may dismiss them if dissatisfied with the service provided. However, the world is not ideal. Some companies are very large and they have many shareholders whose identity changes as shares are bought and sold. Over the years it has been found that regulation is needed, particularly for financial reporting by companies. The general regulation of companies in the UK is provided by parliamentary legislation, through the Companies Act 2006.

However, since 2005 the regulation of financial reporting by UK companies has taken two separate routes depending on the type of company.

The group financial statements of listed companies must comply with the IAS Regulation set by the European Commission. The IAS Regulation takes precedence over the relevant sections of the Companies Act. The IAS Regulation was issued in 2002, requiring listed group financial statements from 2005 to apply approved International Financial Reporting Standards (IFRS) (previously called International Accounting Standards, IAS). The UK government subsequently permitted individual companies and non-listed groups to choose to apply IFRS. Any companies not taking up this choice must continue to apply the relevant sections of the Companies Act and follow the accounting standards set by the UK Accounting Standards Board (ASB). Other organisations that are not companies (such as sole traders, partnership, public sector bodies) have to look to the regulations that govern their operations to decide which accounting guidance to follow.

So how can we tell which accounting system has been applied in any situation? Look first for the audit report, if there is one. That will include a paragraph starting 'In our opinion'. In that paragraph the auditors will specify the accounting system on which their opinion is based. If there is no auditors' report, look for the Note on Accounting Policies. There will usually be a paragraph stating the accounting system that has been applied.

4.5.1   The IAS Regulation

In 2002 the European Commission issued the *IAS Regulation* which took effect from 1 January 2005. Its purpose is to harmonise the financial information presented by public listed companies in order to ensure a high degree of transparency and comparability of financial statements. The Regulation is relatively short but has been extended and clarified by a trail of subsequent documents. The European Commission publishes all documents on its website[32] in the languages of all member states but that is more detail than is necessary for a first-year course.

A Regulation is directly applicable in member states. It has a higher status than a Directive, which is an instruction to member states on the content of their national laws. Before the Regulation was issued, the company law of member states was harmonised by following the Fourth and Seventh Directives on company law. Companies in member states did not need to know the Directives because the national company law applied the Directives. Now that the IAS Regulation is directly applicable, member states must ensure that they do not seek to apply to a company any additional elements of national law that are contrary to, conflict with or restrict a company's compliance with IASs.

The Commission decides on the applicability of IFRS within the Community. It is assisted by an Accounting Regulatory Committee and is advised by a technical group called the European Financial Reporting and Accounting Group (EFRAG).[33] The tests for adoption of IFRS are that the standards:

(a) do not contradict specific principles of the Fourth and Seventh Directive,
(b) are conducive to the European public good, and
(c) meet the criteria of understandability, relevance, reliability and comparability required of financial information needed for making economic decisions and assessing the stewardship of management.

A standard that is adopted is said to be **endorsed**. If a standard is awaiting endorsement, or is rejected, it may be used as guidance if it is not inconsistent with endorsed standards. If a rejected standard is in conflict with adopted standards, it may not be used. When the European Commission first announced the endorsement process there were fears expressed that this would be used to create 'European IFRS' by selecting some IFRS and rejecting others. The Commission's reply was that the EU cannot give its powers to a body (the IASB) that is not subject to EU jurisdiction, and it is necessary for the EU to endorse standards as part of its duty in setting laws for member states.

4.5.2   UK company law

Companies Act 2006

The Companies Act 2006 sets many rules to protect those investing in companies and to guide those operating companies. Parts of the Act cover the information presented in financial statements. For companies and other organisations that do not follow the IAS Regulation, the Companies Act 2006, by means of Statutory Instruments, prescribes formats of presentation of the statement of financial position (balance sheet) and profit and loss account. Companies must select one of the permitted formats. It also prescribes methods of valuation of the assets and liabilities contained in the statement of financial position (balance sheet), broadly expecting that normally these items will be recorded at their cost at the date of acquisition, subject to diminutions in value since that date. Some other approaches to valuation are permitted, but these are carefully regulated and are subject to requirements for prudence, consistency and an expectation that the business is a going concern (i.e. will continue for some time into the future). The UK legislation places strong emphasis on the requirement to present a **true and fair view** in financial statements.

Since the early 1980s company law on financial reporting has been harmonised with that of other Member States in the EU through the Fourth and Seventh Directives of the EU (see Chapter 7).

The directors are responsible for the preparation of company accounts. Exhibit 4.1 sets out the statement made by directors of one major public company regarding their responsibilities in these matters. This type of statement will be found in the annual reports of most of the large listed companies. It is regarded as an important aspect of giving reassurance to investors and others that there is a strong system of corporate governance within the company. It is also intended to clarify any misunderstandings the shareholders may have about the work of directors as distinct from the work of the auditors (see below).

The Companies (Audit, Investigations and Community Enterprise) Act, 2004 made changes intended to improve the reliability of financial reporting, the independence of auditors and disclosure to auditors. In particular it required a statement to be inserted in the directors' report confirming that there is no relevant information that has not been disclosed to the auditors. The role of the Financial Reporting Review Panel was strengthened by giving it new powers to require documents. HM Revenue and Customs was authorised to pass information about companies to the FRRP.

4.5.3 The Financial Reporting Council

The Financial Reporting Council (FRC)[34] describes itself as the UK's independent regulator for corporate reporting and governance. It is recognised in its regulatory role by the Department of Trade and Industry. The government effectively delegates responsibility to an independent body but maintains close interest in the strategy and operations of the FRC.

The FRC's aim is to promote confidence in corporate reporting and governance. To achieve this aim it sets itself five key objectives, in promoting:

- high-quality corporate reporting
- high-quality auditing
- high standards of corporate governance
- the integrity, competence and transparency of the accountancy profession
- its effectiveness as a unified independent regulator.

The FRC is one regulator but it has a wide range of functions:

- setting, monitoring and enforcing accounting and auditing standards
- statutory oversight and regulation of auditors
- operating an independent investigation and discipline scheme for public interest cases
- overseeing the regulatory activities of the professional accountancy bodies
- promoting high standards of corporate governance.

Exhibit 4.1

Statement of directors' responsibilities as expressed in the annual report of a public limited company

---

Directors' responsibilities

The following statement, which should be read in conjunction with the auditors' statement of auditors' responsibilities set out in their report, is made with a view to distinguishing for shareholders the respective responsibilities of the Directors and of the auditors in relation to the financial statements.

The Directors are responsible for preparing the Annual Report and Accounts and Directors' Remuneration Report in accordance with applicable law and regulations. The Directors are required to prepare financial statements for the Group in accordance with International Financial Reporting Standards (IFRS) and have also elected to prepare the parent company financial statements in accordance with IFRS. Company law requires the Directors to prepare such financial statements for each financial year in accordance with IFRS, as adopted by the European Union, the Companies Act 2006 and Article 4 of the IAS Regulation.

International Accounting Standard 1 requires that financial statements present fairly for each financial period the Company's financial position, financial performance and cash flows. This requires the faithful representation of the effects of transactions, other events and conditions in accordance with the definitions and recognition criteria for assets, liabilities, income and expenses set out in the International Accounting Standards Board's 'Framework for the preparation and presentation of Financial Statements'. In virtually all circumstances, a fair presentation will be achieved by compliance with all applicable International Financial Reporting Standards. The Directors are also required to:

- properly select and apply accounting policies;
- present information, including accounting policies, in a manner that provides relevant, reliable, comparable and understandable information; and
- provide additional disclosures when compliance with the specific requirements in IFRS is insufficient to enable users to understand the impact of particular transactions, other events and conditions on the entity's financial position and financial performance.

The Directors are responsible for keeping proper accounting records that are sufficient to show and explain the company's transactions and disclose with reasonable accuracy at any time the financial position of the Group and Company, and enable them to ensure that the financial statements comply with the Companies Act 2006. They are also responsible for safeguarding the assets, for taking reasonable steps for the prevention and detection of fraud and other irregularities and for the preparation of a Directors' Report and Directors' Remuneration Report which comply with the requirements of the Companies Act 2006.

The Directors are responsible for the maintenance and integrity of the corporate and financial information included on the Company's website. Legislation in the United Kingdom governing the preparation and dissemination of financial statements may differ from legislation in other jurisdictions.

Directors' responsibility statement

We confirm to the best of our knowledge:

1 the financial statements, prepared in accordance with International Financial Reporting Standards as adopted by the EU, give a true and fair view of the assets, liabilities, financial position and profit or loss of the company and the undertakings included in the consolidation taken as a whole; and
2 the management report, which is incorporated into the directors' report, includes a fair review of the development and performance of the business and the position of the company and the undertakings included in the consolidation taken as a whole, together with a description of the principal risks and uncertainties that they face.

By order of the board
(signed)   Chief Executive Officer,   Chief Financial Officer
Date

There are six operating bodies (subsidiaries of the FRC) to carry out these functions.

1 Accounting Standards Board
2 Auditing Practices Board
3 Board for Actuarial Standards (relevant to the actuarial profession)
4 Professional Oversight Board

5 Financial Reporting Review Panel

6 Accountancy and Actuarial Discipline Board.

The five relevant to the accountancy profession are now described.

4.5.4 UK Accounting Standards Board

Traditionally, professions in the UK have been expected to regulate their own affairs and control their members. The accounting profession satisfied this expectation between 1970 and 1990 by forming the Accounting Standards Committee (ASC) and requiring members of each professional body to apply accounting standards or face disciplinary action. Over a period of years there was growing dissatisfaction with this pure self-regulatory model because the disciplinary aspects appeared to be applied only rarely and the existence of potential conflicts of self-interest was pointed to by some critics as weakening the standard-setting process. Consequently, in 1990 the purely self-regulatory approach was abandoned in favour of an independent regime having statutory backing, but retaining some self-regulatory features. The independent standard-setting body was created as the Accounting Standards Board (ASB).

Since 1990 the ASB has published Financial Reporting Standards (FRSs) setting standards of practice which go beyond the requirements of company law in particular problem areas. In the period from 1970 to 1990 the standards set by the ASC were called Statements of Standard Accounting Practice (SSAPs). Those SSAPs which remained valid were adopted by the ASB and are gradually being replaced. SSAPs and FRSs collectively are referred to as 'accounting standards'. The Accounting Standards Board (ASB) is recognised as a standard-setting body under a Statutory Instrument of the Companies Act 2006.

The UK ASB is gradually harmonising its standards with those of the IASB so that eventually all companies will apply the same accounting standards, irrespective of whether they present financial statements under the IAS Regulation or the Companies Act. Until that happens there will continue to be some differences between ASB standards and IASB standards but in general this need not be of concern in a first year of study.

The ASB collaborates with accounting standard-setters from other countries and the IASB both in order to influence the development of international standards and to ensure that its standards are developed with due regard to international developments.

The ASB has up to ten Board members, of whom two (the Chairman and the Technical Director) are full-time, and the remainder, who represent a variety of interests, are part-time. ASB meetings are also attended by three observers. Under the ASB's constitution, votes of seven Board members (six when there are fewer than ten members) are required for any decision to adopt, revise or withdraw an accounting standard. Board members are appointed by a Nominations Committee comprising the chairman and fellow directors of the Financial Reporting Council (FRC).

The Accounting Standards Board is independent in its decisions on issuing standards. Before doing so the Board consults widely on all its proposals.

4.5.5 Auditing Practices Board

The Auditing Practices Board (APB) was established in April 2002, and replaces a previous APB which had been in place since 1991. APB is a part of the Financial Reporting Council. The APB is committed to leading the development of auditing practice in the UK and the Republic of Ireland so as to establish high standards of auditing, meet the developing needs of users of financial information and ensure public confidence in the auditing process.

4.5.6   Professional Oversight Board

The Professional Oversight Board (POB) contributes to the achievement of the Financial Reporting Council's own fundamental aim of supporting investor, market and public confidence in the financial and governance stewardship of listed and other entities by:

- independent oversight of the regulation of the auditing profession by the recognised supervisory and qualifying bodies;
- monitoring the quality of the auditing function in relation to economically significant entities;
- independent oversight of the regulation of the accountancy profession by the professional accountancy bodies.

4.5.7   Financial Reporting Review Panel

When the Accounting Standards Board was established in 1990 it was felt to be important that there was a mechanism for enforcing accounting standards. An effective mechanism had been lacking in the previous process of setting standards. Accordingly the Financial Reporting Council established a Financial Reporting Review Panel (FRRP) which enquires into annual accounts where it appears that the requirements of the Companies Act, including the requirement that annual accounts shall show a true and fair view, might have been breached. The FRRP has the power to ask companies to revise their accounts where these are found to be defective. If companies do not voluntarily make such a revision, the FRRP may take proceedings in a court of law to require the company to revise its accounts. These powers are awarded under the Companies Act 2006 and delegated to the FRRP by the Secretary of State for Trade and Industry. So far the FRRP has not found it necessary to resort to legal action, having found its powers of persuasion were sufficient.

The FRRP, (referred to as 'the Panel') considers whether the annual accounts of public companies and large private companies comply with the requirements of the Companies Act 2006, including applicable accounting standards. The Panel does not offer advice on the application of accounting standards or the accounting requirements of the Companies Act 2006.

The Panel can ask directors to explain apparent departures from the requirements. If it is not satisfied by the directors' explanations it aims to persuade them to adopt a more appropriate accounting treatment. The directors may then voluntarily withdraw their accounts and replace them with revised accounts that correct the matters in error. Depending on the circumstances, the FRRP may accept another form of remedial action – for example, correction of the comparative figures in the next set of annual financial statements. Failing voluntary correction, the Panel can exercise its powers to secure the necessary revision of the original accounts through a court order. The FRRP has enjoyed a long and successful record in resolving all cases brought to its attention without having to apply for a court order. The Panel maintains a legal costs fund of £2m for this purpose. Also, if the case concerns accounts issued under listing rules, the Panel may report to the Financial Services Authority.

4.5.8   Accountancy and Actuarial Discipline Board

The Accountancy and Actuarial Discipline Board (AADB) is the independent disciplinary body for accountants in the UK. It has up to eight members. The AADB is responsible for operating and administering an independent disciplinary scheme ('the Scheme') covering members of the major professional bodies.

The AADB deals with cases which raise or appear to raise important issues affecting the public interest in the UK and which need to be investigated to determine whether or not there has been any misconduct by an accountant or accountancy firm.

4.5.9 Committee on Corporate Governance

The Committee on Corporate Governance works to satisfy the FRC's responsibility for promoting high standards of corporate governance. It aims to do so by:

- maintaining an effective Combined Code on Corporate Governance and promoting its widespread application;
- ensuring that related guidance, such as that on internal control, is current and relevant;
- influencing EU and global corporate governance developments;
- helping to promote boardroom professionalism and diversity; and
- encouraging constructive interaction between company boards and institutional shareholders.

4.5.10 The Financial Services Authority

Under the Financial Services and Markets Act 2000, the Financial Services Authority (FSA) is a single regulator with responsibility across a wide range of financial market activity. It is required to maintain confidence in the UK financial system, to promote public understanding of the financial system, to secure protection for consumers and to reduce the scope for financial crime. The FSA is an independent, non-governmental body and receives no funds from government. It reports annually to Parliament through the Treasury.

The FSA regulates listing of companies' shares on the UK stock exchange. The work is carried out by a division called the UK Listing Authority (UKLA). When a company first has its shares listed, it must produce a prospectus, which is normally much more detailed than the annual report. The regulations covering the content of a prospectus are set by the UKLA. Once a company has achieved a listing, it must keep up with ongoing obligations under the Listing Rules, which includes providing accounting information to the market in the annual report and press releases. Details of the Listing Rules are not necessary for first-year study but if you are interested you can read them on the FSA's website: www.fsa.gov.uk.

4.5.11 Auditors

The shareholders of companies do not have a right of access to the records of the day-to-day running of the business, and so they need someone to act on their behalf to ensure that the directors are presenting a true and fair view of the company's position at a point in time and of the profits generated during a period of time. To achieve this reassurance, the shareholders appoint a firm of auditors to investigate the company's financial records and give an opinion on the truth and fairness of the financial information presented. Exhibit 4.2 sets out the wording of a typical audit report to the

Exhibit 4.2
Sample audit report

Independent auditor's report to the shareholders of XYZ plc

We have audited the financial statements of (name of entity) for the year ended . . . which comprise the Group income statement, the Group statement of comprehensive income, the Group and parent Company statements of financial position, the Group and parent Company statements of cash flows, the Group and parent Company statements of changes in equity, and the related notes. The financial reporting framework that has been applied in their preparation is applicable law and International Financial Reporting Standards (IFRSs) as adopted by the European Union.

This report is made solely to the company's members, as a body, in accordance with sections 495, 496 and 497 of the Companies Act 2006. Our audit work has been undertaken so that we might state to the company's members those matters we are required to state to them in an auditors' report and for no other purpose. To the fullest extent permitted by law, we do not accept or assume responsibility to anyone other

Exhibit 4.3 continued

than the company and the company's members as a body, for our audit work, for this report, or for the opinions we have formed.

Respective responsibilities of Directors and Auditors

As explained more fully in the Directors' Responsibilities Statement, the directors are responsible for the preparation of the financial statements and for being satisfied that they give a true and fair view. Our responsibility is to audit the financial statements in accordance with applicable law and International Standards on Auditing (UK and Ireland). Those standards require us to comply with the Auditing Practices Board's Ethical Standards for Auditors.

Scope of the audit of the financial statements

An audit involved obtaining evidence about the amounts and disclosures in the financial statements sufficient to give reasonable assurance that the financial statements are free from material misstatement, whether caused by fraud or error. That includes an assessment of: whether the accounting policies are appropriate to the group's and parent company's circumstances and have been consistently applied and adequately disclosed; the reasonableness of significant accounting estimates made by the directors; and the overall presentation of the financial statements.

Opinion on the financial statements

In our opinion:

- the financial statements give a true and fair view of the state of the Group's and of the parent company's affairs as at .... and of the Group's profit for the year then ended;
- the financial statements have been properly prepared in accordance with IFRSs as adopted by the European Union;
- the financial statements and the part of the Remuneration report to be audited have been prepared in accordance with the Companies Act 2006 and, as regards the Group financial statements, Article 4 of the IAS Regulation; and

Separate opinion in relation to IFRSs as issued by the IASB

As explained in Note xx to the group financial statements, the group in addition to complying with its legal obligation to comply with IFRSs as adopted by the European Union, has also applied IFRSs as issued by the International Accounting Standards Board (IASB).

In our opinion the group financial statements comply with IFRSs as issued by the IASB.

Opinion on other matters prescribed by the Companies Act 2006

In our opinion:

- the part of the Directors' Remuneration Report to be audited has been properly prepared in accordance with the Companies Act 2006; and
- the information given in the Directors' Report for the financial year for which the financial statements are prepared is consistent with the financial statements.

Matters on which we are required to report by exception

We have nothing to report in respect of the following:

Under the Companies Act 2006 we are required to report to you if, in our opinion:

- adequate accounting records have not been kept by the parent company, or returns adequate for our audit have not been received from branches not visited by us; or
- the parent company financial statements and the part of the Directors' Remuneration Report to be audited are not in agreement with the accounting records and returns; or
- certain disclosures of directors' remuneration specified by law are not made; or
- we have not received all the information and explanations we require for our audit.

Under the Listing Rules we are required to review:

- the directors' statement [set out on page . . .], in relation to going concern; and
- the part of the Corporate Governance Statement relating to the company's compliance with the nine provisions of the [2006] [June 2008] 27 Combined Code specified for our review.

Signed [Name of partner] Senior Statutory Auditor
For and on behalf of [Name of firm]
Chartered Accountants and Statutory Auditors, name and address
Date

shareholders of a public company. You will see that there are separate opinions on the financial statements and on other aspects of the accounting information recorded or provided by the company.

You will note that the auditors do not look at all the pages of the annual report. The earlier part of the annual report is important to the companies in setting the scene and explaining their businesses. These earlier pages are reviewed by the auditors to ensure that anything said there is consistent with the information presented in the audited financial statements. You will also note that the auditors have their own code of practice, referred to as International Standards for Auditing (ISAs). The ISAs are prepared by the International Auditing and Assurance Standards Board (IAASB) which operates under a body called the International Financial Accounting Committee (IFAC). The standards are then adopted by national standard-setters. In the UK the national standard-setter is the Auditing Practices Board (APB) which is one of the arms of the Financial Reporting Council.

What surprises some readers is the phrase 'reasonable assurance that the accounts are free from material misstatement'. The auditors are not expected to be totally certain in their opinion and they are only looking for errors or fraud which is material. The meaning of the word 'material' has proved difficult to define and it tends to be a matter left to the judgement of the auditor. The best guidance available is that an item is material if its misstatement or omission would cause the reader of the annual report (shareholder or creditor) to take a different decision or view based on the financial statements.

4.5.12 The tax system

Businesses pay tax to HM Revenue and Customs (HMRC) (as the tax-collecting agent of the government) based on the profits they make. Sole traders and partnerships pay income tax on their profits while companies pay corporation tax. There are differences in detail of the law governing these two types of taxes but broadly they both require as a starting point a calculation of profit using commercial accounting practices. The law governing taxation is quite separate from the law and regulations governing financial reporting, so in principle the preparation of financial statements is not affected by tax matters. That is very different from some other countries in the EU where the tax law stipulates that an item must be in the financial accounting statements if it is to be considered for tax purposes. Those countries have an approach to financial reporting which is more closely driven by taxation matters.

In the UK the distinction may be blurred in practice in the case of sole traders because HMRC is the main user of the financial statements of the sole trader. Similarly, tax factors may influence partnership accounts, although here the fairness of sharing among the partners is also important. The very smallest companies, where the owners also run the business, may in practice have the same attitude to tax matters as does the sole trader or partnership. For larger companies with a wider spread of ownership, the needs of shareholders will take priority.

4.5.13 Is regulation necessary?

There are those who would argue that all this regulatory mechanism is unnecessary. They take the view that in a market-based economy, competitive forces will ensure that those providing information will meet the needs of users. It is argued that investors will not entrust their funds to a business which provides inadequate information. Banks will not lend money unless they are provided with sufficient information to answer their questions about the likelihood of receiving interest and eventual repayment of the loan. Employee morale may be lowered if a business appears non-communicative regarding its present position and past record of performance. Suppliers may not wish to give credit to a business which appears secretive or has a reputation for producing poor-quality information. Customers may be similarly doubtful.

Against that quite attractive argument for the abolition of all regulations stand some well-documented financial scandals where businesses have failed. Employees have lost their jobs, with little prospect of finding comparable employment elsewhere; suppliers have not been paid and have found themselves in financial difficulties as a result. Customers have lost a source of supply and have been unable to meet the requirements of their own customers until a new source is found. Those who have provided long-term finance for the business, as lenders and investors, have lost their investment. Investigation shows that the signs and warnings had existed for those who were sufficiently experienced to see them, but these signs and warnings did not emerge in the published accounting information for external use.

Such financial scandals may be few in number but the large-scale examples cause widespread misery and lead to calls for action. Governments experience pressure from the electorate and lobby groups; professional bodies and business interest groups decide they ought to be seen to react; and new regulations are developed which ensure that the particular problem cannot recur. All parties are then reasonably satisfied that they have done their best to protect those who need protection against the imbalance of business life, and the new practices are used until the next scandal occurs and the process starts over again.

There is no clear answer to the question 'Is regulation necessary?' Researchers have not found any strong evidence that the forces of supply and demand in the market fail to work and have suggested that the need for regulation must be justified by showing that the benefits exceed the costs. That is quite a difficult challenge but is worth keeping in mind as you explore some of the more intricate aspects of accounting regulation.

Activity 4.4	*Look back through this section and, for each subheading, make a note of whether you were previously aware that such regulation existed. In each case, irrespective of your previous state of knowledge, do you now feel a greater or a lesser sense of confidence in accounting information? How strong is your confidence in published accounting information? If not 100%, what further reassurance would you require?*

4.6 Reviewing published financial statements

If you look at the annual report of any large listed company you will find that it has two main sections. The first part contains a variety of diagrams and photographs, a statement by the chairman, a report by the chief executive and, in many cases, an Operating and Financial Review which may extend to a considerable number of pages. Other aspects of the business, such as its corporate governance and environmental policy, may also be explained. This first part is a mixture of unregulated and broadly regulated material. There are many sources of influence on its contents, some of which will be explained in later chapters of this book.

The second part contains the financial statements, which are heavily regulated. As if to emphasise this change of status, the second part of the annual report will often have a different appearance, perhaps being printed on a different colour or grade of paper, or possibly having a smaller print size. Appendix I to this book contains extracts from the financial statements of a fictitious company, Safe and Sure plc, which will be used for illustration in this and subsequent chapters.

Relaxing after a hard workout at the health club, David Wilson took the opportunity to buy Leona a drink and tell her something about Safe and Sure prior to a visit to the company's headquarters to meet the finance director.

DAVID: *This is a major listed company, registered in the UK but operating around the world selling its services in disposal and recycling, cleaning and security. Its name is well known and its services command high prices because of the company's reputation gained over many years. Basically it is a very simple business to understand. It sells services by making contracts with customers and collects cash when the service is performed.*

In preparation for my visit I looked first at the performance of the period. This company promises to deliver growth of at least 20% in revenue and in profit before tax so first of all I checked that the promise had been delivered. Sure enough, at the front of the annual report under 'Highlights of the year' there was a table showing revenue had increased by 22.4% and profit before tax had increased by 20.4%. I knew I would need to look through the profit and loss account in more detail to find out how the increases had come about, but first of all I read the operating review (written by the chief executive) and the financial review (written by the finance director). The chief executive gave more details on which areas had the greatest increase in revenue and operating profit and which areas had been disappointing. That all helps me in making my forecast of profit for next year.

The chief executive made reference to acquisitions during the year, so I knew I would also need to think whether the increase in revenue and profits was due to an improvement in sales and marketing as compared with last year or whether it reflected the inclusion of new business for the first time.

In the financial review, the finance director explained that the business tries to use as little working capital as possible (that means they try to keep down the current assets and match them as far as possible with current liabilities). I guessed I would need to look at the statement of financial position to confirm that, so I headed next for the financial statements at the back of the annual report, pausing to glance at the auditors' report to make sure there was nothing highlighted by them as being amiss.

The financial statements are quite detailed and I wanted a broad picture so I noted down the main items from each in a summary format which leaves out some of the detail but which I find quite useful.

4.6.1 Income statement (profit and loss account)

Safe and Sure plc
Summary income statement (profit and loss account) with comparative figures

	Notes	Year 7 £m	Year 6 £m
Continuing operations			
Revenue		714.6	589.3
Cost of sales		(491.0)	(406.3)
Gross profit		223.6	183.0
Expenses and interest		(26.1)	(26.0)
Profit before tax		197.5	157.0
Tax on profit		(62.2)	(52.4)
Profit for the period from continuing operations		135.3	104.6
Discontinued operations			
Loss for the period from discontinued operations		(20.5)	(10.0)
Profit for the period attributable to ordinary shareholders		114.8	94.6

DAVID: *It is part of my job to make forecasts of what the next reported profit of the company is likely to be (i.e. the profit of Year 8). This is March Year 8 now so there are plenty of current signs I can pick up, but I also want to think about how far Year 7 will be repeated or improve during Year 8. A few years ago I would have made a rough guess and then phoned the finance director for some guidance on whether I was in the right area. That's no longer allowed because the Financial Services Authority tightened up the rules on companies giving information to some investors which is not available to others, especially where that information could affect the share price.*

One easy way out is for me to collect the reports which come in from our stockbrokers. Their analysts have specialist knowledge of the industry and can sometimes work out what is happening in a business faster than some of the management. However, I like to form my own opinion using other sources, such as trade journals, and I read the annual report to give me the background structure for my forecast. The company has helpfully separated out the effect of continuing and discontinued operations, which helps me in making a forecast.

When I meet the finance director next week I'll have with me a spreadsheet analysing revenue and profit before tax – so far as I can find the data – by product line and for each of the countries in which the company trades. I'll also ask the following questions:

1 *Although the revenue has increased, the ratio of gross profit to revenue on continuing operations has increased only very slightly, from 31.1% in Year 6 to 31.3% in Year 7. That suggests that the company has increased revenue by holding price rises at a level matching the increase in operating costs. I would like to see the company pushing ahead with price rises but does the company expect to see a fall in demand when its prices eventually rise?*

2 *The tax charge on continuing operations has decreased from approximately 33% to 31.5%, slightly higher than the rate which would be expected of UK companies. I know that this company is trading overseas. You say in your financial review that the tax charge is 30% in the UK and rates on overseas profits will reduce, so am I safe in assuming that 30% is a good working guide for the future in respect of this company?*

3 *With all this overseas business there must be an element of foreign exchange risk. You say in your financial review that all material foreign currency transactions are matched back into the currency of the group company undertaking the transaction. You don't hedge the translation of overseas profits back into sterling. You also say that using Year 6 exchange rates the Year 7 profit, including the effect of the discontinued operations, would have been £180.5m rather than the £177.0m reported. That seems a fairly minimal effect but are these amounts hiding any swings in major currencies where large downward movements are offset by correspondingly large upward movements?*

4 *Your increase in revenue, comparing £714.6m to £589.9m, is 21.1% which is meeting the 20% target you set yourself. However, elsewhere in the financial statements I see that the acquisitions in Year 7 contributed £13.5m to revenue. If I strip that amount out of the total revenue I'm left with an increase in respect of activities continuing from Year 6 which is only 19%. When the scope for acquisitions is exhausted, will you be able to sustain the 20% target by organic growth alone?*

4.6.2   Statement of financial position (balance sheet)

DAVID: *Looking at the statement of financial position, this is a fairly simple type of business. It is financed almost entirely by equity capital (shareholders' funds), so there are none of the risks associated with high levels of borrowings which might be found in other companies.*

Again, I have summarised and left out some of the details which aren't significant in financial terms.

Safe and Sure plc
Summarised statement of financial position (balance sheet)
(with comparative amounts)

	Notes	Year 7 £m	Year 6 £m
Non-current assets			
Property, plant and equipment		137.5	121.9
Intangible assets		260.3	237.6
Investments		2.8	2.0
Taxation recoverable		5.9	4.9
		406.5	366.4
Current assets			
Inventories (stocks)		26.6	24.3
Amounts receivable (debtors)		146.9	134.7
Six-month deposits		2.0	–
Cash and cash equivalents		105.3	90.5
		280.8	249.5
Current liabilities			
Amounts payable (creditors)		(159.8)	(157.5)
Bank overdraft		(40.1)	(62.6)
		(199.9)	(220.1)
Net current assets		80.9	29.4
Total assets less current liabilities		487.4	395.8
Non-current liabilities			
Amounts payable (creditors)	9	(2.7)	(2.6)
Bank and other borrowings	10	(0.2)	(0.6)
Provisions	11	(20.2)	(22.2)
Net assets		464.3	370.4
Capital and reserves			
Shareholders' funds		464.3	370.4

DAVID: *By far the largest non-current (fixed) asset is the intangible asset of goodwill arising on acquisition. It reflects the fact that the group has had to pay a price for the future prospects of companies it has acquired. Although the company reports this in the group's statement of financial position, and I like to see whether the asset is holding its value from the group's point of view, I have some reservations about the quality of the asset because I know it would vanish overnight if the group found itself in difficulties.*

The other non-current assets are mainly equipment for carrying out the cleaning operations and vehicles in which to transport the equipment. I've checked in the notes to the accounts that vehicles are being depreciated over four to five years and plant and equipment over five to ten years, all of which sounds about right. Also, they haven't changed the depreciation period, or the method of calculation, since last year so the amounts are comparable. Estimated useful lives for depreciation are something I watch closely. There is a great temptation for companies which have underperformed to cut back on the depreciation by deciding the useful life has extended. (Depreciation is explained more fully in Chapter 8.)

I think I might ask a few questions about working capital (the current assets minus the current liabilities of the business). Normally I like to see current assets somewhat greater than current liabilities – a ratio of 1.5 to 1 could be about right – as a cushion to ensure the liabilities are met as they fall due. However, in this company the finance director makes a point of saying that they like to utilise as little working capital as possible, so I'm wondering why it increased from £29.4m in Year 6 to more than £80m in Year 7. There appear to be two effects working together: current assets went up and current liabilities went down. Amounts receivable (trade debtors) increased in Year 7 in absolute terms but that isn't as bad as it looks when allowance is made for the increase in revenue. Amounts receivable in Year 7 are 20.6% of continuing revenue, which shows some control has been achieved when it is compared with the Year 6 amount at 22.8% of revenue. My questions will be:

1 Mostly, the increase in the working capital (net current assets) appears to be due to the decrease in bank borrowing. Was this a voluntary action by the company or did the bank insist?
2 The second major cause of the increase in the working capital is the increase in the balance held in the bank account. Is that being held for a planned purpose and, if so, what?
3 The ratio of current assets to current liabilities has increased from last year. What target ratio are you aiming for?

I always shudder when I see 'provisions' in a statement of financial position. The notes to the financial statements show that these are broadly:

	£m
For treating a contaminated site	12.0
For restructuring part of the business	4.2
For tax payable some way into the future	4.0
Total	20.2

I shall want to ask whether the estimated liability in relation to the contaminated site is adequate in the light of any changes in legislation. I know the auditors will have asked this question in relation to existing legislation but I want to think also about forthcoming legislation.

I am always wary of provisions for restructuring. I shall be asking more about why the restructuring is necessary and when it will take place. I want to know that the provision is sufficient to cover the problem, but not excessive.

The provision for tax payable some way into the future is an aspect of prudence in accounting. I don't pay much attention unless the amount is very large or suddenly changes dramatically. (An explanation of deferred taxation is contained in Chapter 10.)

4.6.3 Statement of cash flows

DAVID: *Cash is an important factor for any business. It is only one of the resources available but it is the key to survival. I've summarised the totals of the various main sections of the cash flow statement. 'Net cash' means the cash less the bank borrowings.*

Safe and Sure plc
Summary statement of cash flows (with comparative amounts)
Consolidated statement of cash flows for the years ended 31 December

	Notes	Year 7	Year 6
		£m	£m
Net cash from operating activities		143.0	116.3
Net cash used in investing activities		(98.3)	(85.3)
Net cash used in financing activities		(10.2)	(46.4)
Net increase/(decrease) in cash and cash equivalents*		34.5	(15.4)

What I'm basically looking for in the cash flow statement is how well the company is balancing various sources of finance. It generated £143m from operating activities and that was more than sufficient to cover its investing activities in new fixed assets and acquisitions. There was also enough to cover the dividend of £29.5m, which is a financing activity but that was partly covered by raising new loan finance. This is why the cash used in financing activities is only £10.2m. I come back to my earlier question of why they are holding so much cash.

Read David's explanation again and compare it carefully with the financial statements. It is quite likely that you will not understand everything immediately because the purpose of this book as a whole is to help you understand published financial statements and we are, as yet, only at the end of Chapter 4. Make a note of the items you don't fully understand and keep that note safe in a file. As you progress through the rest of the book, look back to that note and tick off the points which subsequently become clear. The aim is to have a page full of ticks by the end of the book.

4.7 Summary

The objective of financial statements is to provide information about the financial position, performance and changes in financial position of an entity that is useful to a wide range of users in making economic decisions.

The four principal qualitative characteristics, as described by the IASB *Framework*, are:

1 understandability
2 relevance
3 reliability
4 comparability.

Relevance and **reliability** are twin targets which may cause some tension in deciding the most appropriate way to report accounting information.

The accounting measurement principles that are most widely known in the UK are found within the Companies Act 2006:

- going concern
- accruals
- consistency
- prudence.

Prudence in accounting means exercising a degree of caution when reporting assets, liabilities and profits. Overstatement of assets causes the overstatement of profit. Understatement of liabilities causes the overstatement of profit. Prudence requires avoiding overstating profit but also avoiding deliberate understatement of profit.

Regulation of financial reporting in the UK comes from several sources.

- The IAS Regulation requires all listed groups of companies to prepare financial statements using the system of the International Accounting Standards Board (IASB system). Other companies may choose to follow the IASB system.
- Companies that do not follow the IASB system must comply with UK company law.
- The Financial Reporting Council regulates accounting and auditing matters under the authority of UK company law.
- The Financial Reporting Council oversees the UK Accounting Standards Board which sets accounting standards for companies that are complying with UK company law.
- The Financial Reporting Review Panel takes action against companies whose annual reports do not comply with the relevant accounting system (IASB or UK company law).
- The Financial Services Authority regulates a wide range of financial service activities including the London Stock Exchange. It sets Listing Rules for companies listed on the Stock Exchange.
- Auditors give an opinion on whether financial statements present a true and fair view of the profit or loss of the period and the state of affairs at the end of the

period. They are professionally qualified accountants with auditing experience who are members of a recognised professional body.

● The UK tax system charges corporation tax on company profits. Her Majesty's Revenue and Customs (HMRC) start with the accounting profit in calculating the amount of tax payable but there are some special rules of accounting for tax purposes.

Further reading

Please note that the International Accounting Standards Board (IASB) indicated in September 2009 its intention to change its name to the International Financial Reporting Standards Board ('IFRS Board' or 'IFRSB') and asked for opinions. The responses indicated support.

IASB (1989), *Framework for the Preparation and Presentation of Financial Statements*, International Accounting Standards Board.

Paterson, R. (2002), 'Whatever happened to Prudence?', *Accountancy*, January, p. 105.

The website of the Financial Reporting Council explains the methods and nature of regulation of financial reporting and the accountancy profession: www.frc.org.uk.

QUESTIONS

The Questions section of each chapter has three types of question. 'Test your understanding' questions to help you review your reading are in the 'A' series of questions. You will find the answers to these by reading and thinking about the material in the book. 'Application' questions to test your ability to apply technical skills are in the 'B' series of questions. Questions requiring you to show skills in problem solving and evaluation are in the 'C' series of questions. A letter [S] indicates that there is a solution at the end of the book.

A   Test your understanding

A4.1   Explain what is meant by each of the following: (Section 4.2)

(a) relevance;
(b) reliability;
(c) faithful representation;
(d) neutrality;
(e) prudence;
(f) completeness;
(g) comparability;
(h) understandability; and
(i) materiality.

A4.2   Explain the accounting measurement principles of each of the following: (Section 4.3)

(a) going concern;
(b) accruals;
(c) consistency;
(d) the concept of prudence.

A4.3   Explain why companies should avoid overstatement of assets or understatement of liabilities. (Section 4.4)

A4.4   Explain the responsibilities of directors of a company towards shareholders in relation to the financial statements of a company. (Section 4.5.2)

A4.5 Explain the impact on financial statements of each of the following: (Section 4.5)

(a) company law;
(b) the International Accounting Standards Board; and
(c) the UK tax law.

A4.6 Explain how the monitoring of financial statements is carried out by each of the following: (Section 4.5)

(a) the auditors; and
(b) the Financial Reporting Review Panel.

B   Application

B4.1 [S]
Explain each of the following:

(a) The IAS Regulation
(b) The Financial Reporting Council
(c) The Auditing Practices Board

B4.2 [S]
Explain any two accounting measurement principles, explaining how each affects current accounting practice.

B4.3 [S]
Discuss the extent to which the regulatory bodies explained in this chapter have, or ought to have, a particular concern for the needs of the following groups of users of financial statements:

(a) shareholders;
(b) employees;
(c) customers; and
(d) suppliers.

C   Problem solving and evaluation

C4.1
Choose one or more characteristics from the following list that you could use to discuss the accounting aspects of each of the statements 1 to 5 and explain your ideas:

- Relevance
- reliability
- comparability

- understandability
- materiality
- neutrality

- completeness
- prudence
- faithful representation

1 Director: 'We do not need to tell shareholders about a loss of £2,000 on damaged stock when our operating profit for the year is £60m.'
2 Shareholder: 'I would prefer the statement of financial position (balance sheet) to tell me the current market value of land is £20m than to tell me that the historical cost is £5m, although I know that market values fluctuate.'
3 Analyst: 'If the company changes its stock valuation from average cost to FIFO, I want to hear a good reason and I want to know what last year's profit would have been on the same basis.'
4 Regulator: 'If the company reports that it has paid "*commission on overseas sales*", I don't expect to discover later that it really meant bribes to local officials.'
5 Director: 'We have made a profit on our drinks sales but a loss on food sales. In the Notes to the Accounts on segmental results I suggest we combine them as "food and drink". It will mean the annual report is less detailed for our shareholders but it will keep competitors in the dark for a while.'

C4.2

Choose one or more accounting measurement principles from the following list that you could use to discuss the accounting aspects of each of the problems 1–5 and explain your ideas.

- going concern
- accruals
- consistency
- prudence.

1 Director: 'The fixed assets of the business are reported at depreciated historical cost because we expect the company to continue in existence for the foreseeable future. The market value is much higher but that is not relevant because we don't intend to sell them.'

2 Auditor: 'We are insisting that the company raises the provision for doubtful debts from 2% to 2.5% of debtor amount. There has been recession among the customer base and the financial statements should reflect that.'

3 Analyst: 'I have great problems in tracking the depreciation policy of this company. It owns several airports. Over the past three years the expected useful life of runways has risen from 30 years to 50 years and now it is 100 years. I find it hard to believe that the technology of tarmacadam has improved so much in three years.'

4 Auditor: 'We have serious doubts about the ability of this company to renew its bank overdraft at next month's review meeting with the bank. The company ought to put shareholders on warning about the implications for the financial statements.'

5 Shareholder: 'I don't understand why the company gives a profit and loss account and a cash flow statement in the annual report. Is there any difference between profit and cash flow?'

Activities for study groups

Continuing to use the annual reports of a company that you obtained for Chapter 1, look for the evidence in each report of the existence of the directors, the auditors and the various regulatory bodies.

In your group, draw up a list of the evidence presented by companies to show that the annual report has been the subject of regulation. Discuss whether the annual report gives sufficient reassurance of its relevance and reliability to the non-expert reader.

Notes and references

1. IASB (1989), *Framework*, para. 12.
2. *Ibid.*, para. 20.
3. *Ibid.*, para. 21.
4. *Ibid.*, para. 24.
5. *Ibid.*, para. 25.
6. *Ibid.*, para. 26.
7. *Ibid.*, paras. 27–8.
8. *Ibid.*, paras. 29–30.
9. *Ibid.*, para. 31.
10. *Ibid.*, paras. 33–4.
11. *Ibid.*, para. 35.
12. *Ibid.*, para. 36.
13. *Ibid.*, para. 37.
14. *Ibid.*, para. 38.
15. *Ibid.*, para. 39.
16. *Ibid.*, para. 42.
17. *Ibid.*, para. 39.
18. *Ibid.*, para. 41.
19. *Ibid.*, para. 40.
20. *Ibid.*, para. 43.
21. *Ibid.*, para. 44.
22. http://www.fasb.org/project/cf_phase-a.shtml.
23. ASB (1999), *Statement of Principles*, p. 34.
24. Under the Companies Act 2006, detailed accounting requirements are contained in Statutory Instruments. The accounting principles are specified in paras 11-15 of SI 2008/410 *The Large and*

Medium-sized Companies and Groups (Accounts and Reports) Regulations 2008. Listed groups in the UK follow the International Financial Reporting Standards, where the same accounting measurement principles apply. http://www.opsi.gov.uk/si/si2008/uksi_20080410_en_5.

25. IASB (1989), *Framework*, para. 23.
26. IASB (1989), *Framework*, para. 23.
27. ASB (1999), Appendix III, paras 21–3.
28. ASB (2000), Financial Reporting Standard 18 (FRS 18) *Accounting Policies*, Accounting Standards Board, para. 28.
29. IASB (1989), *Framework*, para. 37.
30. ASB (2000), Appendix IV, paras 12 to 20.
31. IASB (1989), *Framework*, para. 27.
32. http://europa.eu.int/comm/internal_market/accounting/index_en.htm.
33. www.efrag.org/.
34. www.frc.org.uk/.

Part 2

Reporting the transactions of a business

Chapter 5

Accounting information for service businesses

Employees as assets of a service business

The following extracts are taken from the annual reports of two companies that rely heavily on a skilled workforce. Although the workforce is not recognised in the statement of financial position (balance sheet) it is clearly a valuable but risky resource which is costly to maintain.

Apple Inc.

Extract from Annual report, 2009.

The Company's success depends largely on the continued service and availability of key personnel.

Much of the Company's future success depends on the continued availability and service of key personnel, including its CEO, its executive team and highly skilled employees in technical, marketing and staff positions. Experienced personnel in the technology industry are in high demand and competition for their talents is intense, especially in the Silicon Valley, where most of the Company's key personnel are located. There can be no assurance that the Company will continue to attract and retain key personnel.

In addition, the Company has relied on equity awards in the form of stock options and restricted stock units as one means for recruiting and retaining highly skilled talent. Significant adverse volatility in the Company's stock price could result in a stock option's exercise price exceeding the underlying stock's market value or a significant deterioration in the value of restricted stock units granted, thus lessening the effectiveness of stock-based awards for retaining employees.

Source: Extract from Annual report on Form 10-K for the fiscal year ended September 26, 2009; http://www.apple.com/investor/.

Hewlett Packard

Extract from Annual report, 2008.

In order to be successful, we must attract, retain and motivate key employees, and failure to do so could seriously harm us.

In order to be successful, we must attract, retain and motivate executives and other key employees, including those in managerial, technical, sales, marketing and IT support positions. Hiring and retaining qualified executives, engineers, skilled solutions providers in the IT support business and qualified sales representatives are critical to our future, and competition for experienced employees in the IT industry can be intense. The failure to hire executives and key employees or the loss of executives and key employees could have a significant impact on our operations.

Source: Hewlett Packard Inc. Annual Report 2008; http://media.corporate-ir.net/media_files/irol/71/71087/HewlettPackard_2008_AR.pdf.

Discussion points

1 What are the costs to each company of maintaining the 'people' assets that will not appear in the statement of financial position (balance sheet)?
2 What are the risks to a service business of strong reliance on its 'people' resource?

Contents		

Learning outcomes

After studying this chapter you should be able to:

- Explain how the accounting equation is applied to transactions of a service business.
- Analyse the transactions of a service business during a specific period of time, using the accounting equation.
- Prepare a spreadsheet analysing the transactions and show that the results of the spreadsheet are consistent with the financial statements provided by the organisation.
- Explain the main aspects of the statement of cash flows, income statement (profit and loss account) and statement of financial position (balance sheet) of a service business.

Additionally, for those who read the supplement:

- Analyse the transactions of a service business using the rules of debit and credit bookkeeping.
- Prepare, from a list of transactions of an organisation, ledger accounts and a trial balance which could be used to prepare the financial statements provided by the organisation.

5.1 Introduction

A person who starts a service business intends to offer a service based on personal skills for which other people will be willing to pay a fee. The most important asset of the service business is the person or people providing the service. Despite that, the workforce as an asset never appears in an accounting statement of financial position (balance sheet). That is because, although it satisfies all the conditions of the definition, it is too difficult to measure objectively and so does not meet the conditions for recognition. (See Chapter 2 for the definition of an asset and the conditions for recognition of an asset.)

The service business will have other assets which accounting is able to record: for example, the taxi driver may own a taxi; the electrician will have electrical tools; the joiner will have a workbench and joinery tools; the car mechanic will have a repair garage and equipment; the lawyer will have an office and a word-processor. The service business will also buy materials for use in any particular job and the customer will be asked to pay for these materials as well as for the labour time involved. Moreover, it will have liabilities to suppliers of goods and services used by the business itself.

There will be an owner or owners having an ownership interest in the business. The service business will make profits for the owner (and thus increase the ownership interest) by charging a price for services which is greater than the cost of labour and materials used in providing the service.

All these aspects of the service business may be analysed and recorded on the basis of the accounting equation as specified in Chapter 2. This chapter will discuss the analysis of transactions using the accounting equation and will then apply that analysis to the transactions of a doctor providing a service of medical health screening for managerial and secretarial staff.

Activity 5.1	*Choose a service business and write down the main activity of that business. Then write down the types of expense you would expect to find in the income statement (profit and loss account) of such a business. Write down the types of asset you would expect to find in the statement of financial position (balance sheet). Exchange your list with a fellow student. What are the similarities and what are the differences? Keep your list safe and when you have finished the chapter compare your list with the example in the chapter. Ask yourself, at that point, whether you would be able to apply what you have learned to the business you have chosen.*

5.2 Analysing transactions using the accounting equation

Three main categories of accounting elements in the accounting equation have been defined in Chapter 2: **asset**, **liability** and **ownership interest**. Any one of these elements may increase or decrease during a period of time but the ownership interest may conveniently be subdivided. There will be increases and decreases caused by the decision of the owner(s) to make further contributions of capital or to withdraw capital. There will be increases and decreases due to the activity of the business, with **revenues** increasing the ownership claim and **expenses** decreasing it.

Decrease in ownership interest	Increase in ownership interest
Withdrawals of capital by the owner	Contributions of capital by the owner
Expenses	Revenues

Consequently there are several aspects to consider when transactions are analysed according to the accounting equation.

The accounting equation will be used in this chapter in the form:

Assets minus **Liabilities**	equals	**Ownership interest**

When one item in the equation increases, an upward arrow will be used and when one item decreases a downward arrow will be used:

Assets ↓   denotes a decrease in an asset.

Liabilities ↑   denotes an increase in a liability.

For further emphasis, **bold** highlighting will be used for the elements of the equation which are changed as a result of the transaction or event.

Each business transaction has two aspects in terms of the accounting equation. These aspects must be considered from the viewpoint of the *business*. Table 5.1 sets out a list of some common types of transaction encountered in a service business. Each transaction is then analysed using the accounting equation.

Table 5.1
List of transactions for a service business

Transaction
1　Receive cash from the owner.
2　Buy a vehicle for cash.
3　Receive a bill for gas consumed.
4　Pay the gas bill in cash.
5　Buy materials for cash.
6　Buy materials on credit terms.
7　Sell services for cash.
8　Sell services on credit terms.
9　Pay wages to an employee.
10　Pay cash to the owner for personal use.

Transaction 1: receive cash from the owner

In this transaction the business *acquires* an **asset** (cash) and must note the **ownership interest** *created* by this contribution of capital from the owner:

Assets ↑ – Liabilities	equals	**Ownership interest ↑**

The equation remains in balance because an increase to the left-hand side is exactly matched by an increase to the right-hand side.

Transaction 2: buy a vehicle for cash

In this transaction the business *acquires* a new **asset** (the vehicle) but gives up another **asset** (cash):

Assets ↑↓ – Liabilities	equals	**Ownership interest**

Transaction 3: receive a bill for gas consumed

The business becomes aware that it has a **liability** to pay for gas consumed and also knows that the **ownership interest** has been *reduced* by the expense of using up gas in earning revenue for the business:

Assets – **Liabilities ↑**	equals	**Ownership interest ↓ (expense)**

Transaction 4: pay the gas bill in cash

The **asset** of cash is *reduced* and the **liability** to the gas supplier is *reduced*:

Assets ↓ – **Liabilities ↓**	equals	Ownership interest

Transaction 5: buy materials for cash

When the materials are acquired they will create an asset of inventory (stock), for future use. The **asset** of inventory (stock) will therefore *increase* and the **asset** of cash will *decrease*:

Assets ↓↑ – Liabilities	Equals	Ownership interest

Transaction 6: buy materials on credit terms

Again, materials are acquired which cause an *increase* in the **asset** of inventory (stock). Obtaining goods on credit means that there is a **liability** *created* for amounts owing to the supplier:

Assets ↑ – Liabilities ↑	equals	Ownership interest

Transaction 7: sell services for cash

The cash received from the customer causes an *increase* in the **asset** of cash, while the act of selling services *increases* the **ownership interest** through earning revenue:

Assets ↑ – Liabilities	equals	Ownership interest ↑ (revenue)

Transaction 8: sell services on credit terms

The sale of services creates an *increase* in the **ownership interest** through earning revenue, but also creates an *increase* in the **asset** of trade receivables (debtors):

Assets ↑ – Liabilities	equals	Ownership interest ↑ (revenue)

Transaction 9: pay wages to an employee

The **asset** of cash *decreases* when the wage is paid and there is a *decrease* in the **ownership interest** because the business has used up the service provided by the employee (an expense has been incurred):

Assets ↓ – Liabilities	equals	Ownership interest ↓ (expense)

This is a transaction which often causes problems to those new to accounting. They would like to argue that paying wages creates an asset, rather than an expense, because there is an expected future benefit to be gained from the services of the employee. The answer to that argument is that, while there is no disputing the expected future benefit from the services of most employees, the wages paid are for work *already done* and so there can be no future expectations about that particular week's or month's work. The question of whether the workforce as a whole should be recognised as an asset of the business is one of the unresolved problems of accounting.

Transaction 10: pay cash to the owner for personal use

The **asset** of cash *decreases* and the **ownership interest** *decreases* because the owner has made a voluntary withdrawal of capital:

Assets ↓ – Liabilities	equals	Ownership interest ↓ (voluntary withdrawal)

Write down the transactions of Table 5.1 in a different order and put the piece of paper away for two days. Then take it out and practise the analysis of each transaction without looking at the answers in the book. If your answers are all correct, is it the result of memory or of genuine understanding? If your answers are not entirely correct, can you decide where the problem lies? It is very important that you can analyse transactions correctly using the accounting equation. It is also important that you use your powers of reasoning and not your powers of memory. You cannot possibly memorise the accounting treatment of every transaction you will meet.

5.3 Illustration of accounting for a service business

We now move on to an example which considers the private medical practice of Dr Lee. At the start of October Dr Lee commenced a new medical practice offering a general health screening service to managerial and secretarial staff at a standard fee of £500 per examination. Where patients make personal arrangements they will be asked to pay cash on the day of the examination. If the patient's employer has agreed to pay for the screening, Dr Lee will send an invoice to the employer, requiring payment within 30 days.

In Table 5.2 there is a list of transactions for Dr Lee's medical practice during the month of October. Try to work out the effect on the accounting equation of each transaction listed. Do this before you read the rest of this section. Then compare your answers and your reasoning with that in the rest of this section. Being able to reason correctly at this stage will reduce the likelihood of error later.

Oct. 1   When Dr Lee provides the practice with cash in a bank account to allow the business to start, the business *acquires* an **asset** of cash at bank and the transaction *creates* an **ownership interest** by Dr Lee in the assets of the business. This means that the business now has the use of £50,000, but, if the business ceases immediately, that £50,000 must be returned to Dr Lee. The accounting equation is satisfied because an increase in an asset is matched by an increase in the ownership interest:

Assets ↓ – Liabilities	equals	Ownership interest ↓

Oct. 2   The medical practice now becomes the business entity so far as accounting is concerned (although it is fairly clear that Dr Lee is making all the decisions as the manager of the business as well as being the owner). The entity *acquires* an **asset** of medical equipment in exchange for an equal *decrease* in the amount of an **asset** of cash. The accounting equation is satisfied because the increase in one asset is exactly equal to the decrease in another.

Assets ↑↓ – Liabilities	equals	Ownership interest

Oct. 2   The medical practice pays one month's rent in advance. At the moment of paying the rent, an asset is acquired representing the benefit to be gained from the use of the consulting rooms for the month ahead. However, this benefit only lasts for a short time and will have expired at the end of the accounting period (which has been chosen as one month for the purpose of this example). Once the benefit of an asset has expired, the business

becomes worse off and the ownership interest decreases. That decrease is called an expense of the business. To save the time and trouble of recording such transactions as assets and then re-naming them as expenses at the end of the accounting period, the short-cut is taken of calling them expenses from the outset. There needs to be a check on such items at the end of the accounting period to ensure that there is no part of the benefit remaining which could still be an asset.

Table 5.2
Transactions of Dr Lee's medical practice for the month of October

Date	Business transactions of the entity (nature of the entity: medical practice)	Amount
		£
Oct. 1	Dr Lee provides the practice with cash to allow business to start.	50,000
Oct. 2	The entity acquires medical equipment for cash.	30,000
Oct. 2	One month's rent is paid in advance for consulting rooms.	1,900
Oct. 2	Office furniture is purchased on two months' credit from Office Supplies Company.	6,500
Oct. 7	The practice purchases medical supplies on credit from P. Jones and receives an invoice.	1,200
Oct. 8	Dr Lee pays the medical receptionist for one week's work, 2 to 8 October.	300
Oct. 10	Four patients are examined, each paying £500 cash.	2,000
Oct. 11	The business pays P. Jones in cash for the goods it acquired on credit.	1,200
Oct. 14	The business pays an electricity bill in cash.	100
Oct. 15	Dr Lee pays the medical receptionist for one week's work, 9 to 15 October.	300
Oct. 17	Three patients are examined, their employer (Mrs West) being sent an invoice requesting payment of £500 for each.	1,500
Oct. 22	Dr Lee pays the medical receptionist for one week's work, 16 to 22 October.	300
Oct. 23	The employer (Mrs West) pays in cash for the examination of three patients.	1,500
Oct. 24	Four patients are examined, their employer (Mr East) being sent an invoice requesting payment of £500 for each.	2,000
Oct. 28	Dr Lee draws cash from the business for personal use.	1,000
Oct. 29	Dr Lee pays the medical receptionist for one week's work, 23 to 29 October.	300
Oct. 31	The medical equipment and office furniture is estimated by Dr Lee to have fallen in value over the month.	250
Oct. 31	Dr Lee checks the inventory (stock) of medical supplies and finds that items costing £350 have been used during the month.	350

In terms of the accounting equation there is a *decrease* in the **ownership interest** due to an expense of the business. There is a corresponding *decrease* in the **asset** of cash.

Assets ↑ – Liabilities	equals	**Ownership interest ↓ (expense)**

Oct. 2   The entity acquires an asset of office furniture. It does not pay cash on this occasion, having been given two months to pay. Looking over the rest of the transactions for October it is clear that there has been no payment by the end of the month. At the moment of taking delivery of the asset, the business incurs a liability to the supplier, Office Supplies Company. The accounting equation is satisfied because the *increase* in an **asset** is exactly equal to the *increase* in a **liability**.

Assets ↑ – Liabilities ↑	equals	Ownership interest

Oct. 7   The practice purchases medical supplies on credit from P. Jones and receives an invoice. This is very similar to the previous transaction. An **asset** *is acquired* and a **liability** to a supplier is *created*. The liability is recognised when the practice accepts delivery of the goods because that is the moment of accepting legal liability. For convenience, accounting procedures normally use the arrival of the invoice as the occasion for recording the liability but, even if the invoice failed to arrive, the liability must be recognised in relation to accepting the goods.

Assets ↑ – Liabilities ↑	equals	Ownership interest

Oct. 8   The medical receptionist has worked for one week and is paid for the work done. The amount paid in wages is an expense of the business which *decreases* the **ownership interest** because the benefit of that work has been used up in providing support for the medical practice. There is a *decrease* in the **asset** of cash.

Assets ↓ – Liabilities	equals	**Ownership interest ↓ (expense)**

Oct. 10   The medical practice now begins to carry out the activities which increase the wealth of the owner by earning revenue. The patients pay cash, so there is an *increase* in the **asset** of cash, and the owner becomes better off so there is an *increase* in the **ownership interest**.

Assets ↑ – Liabilities	equals	**Ownership interest ↑ (revenue)**

Oct. 11   The business pays P. Jones in cash for the goods it acquired on credit. Payment of cash *decreases* the **asset** of cash and *decreases* the **liability** to the supplier. Because the supplier is paid in full, the liability is extinguished.

Assets ↓ – Liabilities ↓	equals	Ownership interest

Oct. 14 The business pays an electricity bill in full. The business has enjoyed the use of the electricity but there is no benefit remaining. This is an **expense** of the business which causes a *decrease* in the **ownership interest**. There is a *decrease* in the **asset** of cash.

Assets ↓ − Liabilities	equals	Ownership interest ↓ (expense)

Oct. 15 The payment to the medical receptionist is similar in effect to the payment made on 8 October, causing a further **expense** which *decreases* the **ownership interest** and causes a *decrease* in the **asset** of cash.

Assets ↓ − Liabilities	equals	**Ownership interest ↓ (expense)**

Oct. 17 There is an increase in the **ownership interest** which arises from the operations of the business and so is termed **revenue**. On this occasion the business *acquires* an **asset** of a trade receivable (debtor), showing that an amount of money is owed by the employer of these patients.

Assets ↑ − Liabilities	equals	**Ownership interest ↑ (revenue)**

Oct. 22 The payment to the medical receptionist causes a further **expense** and a *decrease* in the **asset** of cash.

Assets ↓ − Liabilities	equals	**Ownership interest ↓ (expense)**

Oct. 23 The cash received from the employer of the three patients examined on 17 October causes an *increase* in the **asset** of cash and a *decrease* in the **asset** of the trade receivable (debtor). Because the amount is paid in full, the asset of the trade receivable (debtor) is reduced to nil.

Assets ↑↓ − Liabilities	equals	Ownership interest

Oct. 24 Again the business carries out the activities intended to make the owner better off. The accounting effect is similar to that of 17 October, with an *increase* in the **ownership interest** and an *increase* in the **asset** of cash.

Assets ↑ − Liabilities	equals	**Ownership interest ↑ (revenue)**

Oct. 28 The owner of a sole trader business does not take a salary or wage as an employee would, but nevertheless needs cash for personal purposes. Taking cash for personal use is called taking 'drawings' and is recorded in terms of the accounting equation as a *decrease* in the **ownership interest** and a *decrease* in the **asset** of cash.

Assets ↓ − Liabilities	equals	**Ownership interest ↓ (drawings)**

Oct. 29 Paying wages causes an **expense** and a *decrease* in the **asset** of cash.

Assets ↓ − Liabilities	equals	**Ownership interest ↓ (expense)**

Oct. 31   The medical equipment and the office furniture are non-current (fixed) assets of the business. They are expected to have some years' useful life in the business but they will eventually be used up. In accounting, the term 'depreciation' is applied to this gradual using up and there are various ways of deciding how much of the fixed asset has been 'used up' in any period. (Chapter 8 gives more information on depreciation.) For this example the owner's estimate of depreciation is sufficient. There is a *decrease* in the non-current (fixed) **assets** which is not matched by an increase in any other asset and so there is a *decrease* in the **ownership interest** due to the operations of the business. **Depreciation** is an **expense** of the business.

Assets ↓ – Liabilities	equals	Ownership interest ↓ (expense)

Oct. 31   Dr Lee checks the inventory (stock) of medical supplies and finds that items costing £350 have been used during the month. When these medical supplies were received on 7 October, they were all treated as an asset of the business. It appears now that the asset has been reduced from £1,200 to £850 and that the items used up have caused a decrease of £350 in the ownership interest. This decrease is the expense of medical supplies which will appear in the income statement (profit and loss account) of the month. The two aspects of this event are therefore a *decrease* in the **ownership interest** and a *decrease* in the **asset** of inventory (stock) of medical supplies.

Assets ↓ – Liabilities	equals	Ownership interest ↓ (expense)

This analysis has been set out in some detail to show that each transaction must first of all be considered, in order to establish the nature of the two aspects of the transaction, before any attempt is made to deal with the monetary amounts. The next section uses the analysis based on the accounting equation to produce a spreadsheet which can be totalled to give a summary picture of the transactions of the month in terms of the accounting equation.

5.4 A process for summarising the transactions: a spreadsheet

In Table 5.3 the transactions are repeated in the left-hand column but the relevant money amounts are shown in columns which correspond to the assets, liabilities and ownership interest, using brackets to show a negative amount. (It would be equally acceptable to use a minus sign but minus signs tend to disappear or be confused with unintentional blobs on the paper, so brackets are frequently used in accounting in order to ensure clarity.)

Taking the first line as an example, the analysis of the transaction showed that there was an increase in the asset of cash and an increase in the ownership interest. Thus the amount of £50,000 is written in the spreadsheet column for cash and again in the spreadsheet column for ownership interest. In the second line, the asset of cash decreases by £30,000 and the asset of medical equipment increases by £30,000. A similar pattern follows down the spreadsheet for each transaction.

It may be seen that where there are more than a few transactions during the month, a spreadsheet of the type shown in Table 5.3 would need to be much larger and use more columns.

Table 5.3

Spreadsheet analysing transactions into the elements of the accounting equation

Date	Business transactions of the entity (nature of the entity: medical practice)	Assets				Liabilities	Ownership interest		
		Cash and bank £	Trade rec'ble (debtor) £	Inventory (stock) £	Fixed assets £	Liabilities £	Capital contributed or withdrawn £	Revenue + £	Expenses − £
Oct. 1	Dr Lee provides the practice with cash to allow business to start	50,000					50,000		
Oct. 2	The entity acquires medical equipment for cash	(30,000)			30,000				
Oct. 2	One month's rent is paid in advance for consulting rooms	(1,900)							1,900
Oct. 2	Office furniture is purchased on two months' credit from Office Supplies Company				6,500	6,500			
Oct. 7	The practice purchases medical supplies on credit from P. Jones and receives an invoice			1,200		1,200			
Oct. 8	Dr Lee pays the medical receptionist for one week's work, 2 to 8 October	(300)							300
Oct. 10	Four patients are examined, each paying £500 cash	2,000						2,000	
Oct. 11	The business pays P. Jones in cash for the goods it acquired on credit	(1,200)				(1,200)			
Oct. 14	The business pays an electricity bill in cash	(100)							100
Oct. 15	Dr Lee pays the medical receptionist for one week's work, 9 to 15 October	(300)							300
Oct. 17	Three patients are examined, their employer (Mrs West) being sent an invoice requesting payment of £500 for each		1,500					1,500	
Oct. 22	Dr Lee pays the medical receptionist for one week's work, 16 to 22 October	(300)							300
Oct. 23	The employer (Mrs West) pays in cash for the examination of three patients	1,500	(1,500)						
Oct. 24	Four patients are examined, their employer (Mr East) being sent an invoice requesting payment of £500 for each		2,000					2,000	
Oct. 28	Dr Lee draws cash from the business for personal use	(1,000)					(1,000)		
Oct. 29	Dr Lee pays the medical receptionist for one week's work, 23 to 29 October	(300)							300
Oct. 31	The medical equipment and office furniture is estimated by Dr Lee to have fallen in value over the month				(250)				250
Oct. 31	Dr Lee checks the inventory (stock) of medical supplies and finds that items costing £350 have been used during the month			(350)					350
	Totals	18,100	2,000	850	36,250	6,500	49,000	5,500	3,800

57,200   50,700

At the foot of the spreadsheet in Table 5.3 there is a total for each column. Those totals from Table 5.3 are used in Table 5.4, which represents the accounting equation, to show the state of the accounting equation at the end of the month. It may be used to explain to Dr Lee how the ownership interest has changed over the month. The owner contributed £50,000 at the start of the month and has a claim of £50,700 at the end of the month. The ownership interest was increased by earning revenue of £5,500 but reduced by incurring expenses of £3,800 and withdrawing £1,000 for personal use.

Table 5.4
Summary of transactions analysed into the elements of the accounting equation

Assets	minus	Liabilities	=	Ownership interest at start of period	plus	Capital contributed/ withdrawn	plus	Revenue	minus	Expenses
£57,200	–	£6,500		nil	+	£49,000	+	£5,500	–	£3,800
└─── £50,700 ───┘				└─────────────── £50,700 ───────────────┘						

5.5 Financial statements as a means of communication

This chapter has established the approach taken in accounting towards analysing and classifying transactions in such a way that Dr Lee as the owner of a business knows how much better or worse off she has become during a period. There is sufficient information contained in Table 5.3 and it is possible to write an interpretation based on Table 5.4. However, this presentation is not particularly informative or easy on the eye.

The process of communication requires some attention to a clear style of presentation. Accounting practice has evolved the statement of cash flows, the income statement (profit and loss account) and the statement of financial position (balance sheet) to give the owner a more informative presentation of the information contained in Tables 5.3 and 5.4.

Chapter 3 set out the structure of the financial statements of a business. These ideas are now applied to Dr Lee's medical practice. Don't worry too much about how the information is transferred from Table 5.3 to these financial statements, but look back to the table and satisfy yourself that you can find the corresponding pieces of information.

5.5.1 Statement of cash flows

Medical Practice of Dr Lee
Statement of cash flows for the month of October Year 20xx

	£
Operating activities	
Inflow from fees	3,500
Outflow: rent paid	(1,900)
payment to supplier (P. Jones)	(1,200)
wages	(1,200)
electricity	(100)
Net outflow from operations	(900)
Investing activities	
Payment for equipment	(30,000)
Net outflow for investing activities	(30,000)
Financing activities	£
Capital contributed by owner	50,000
Capital withdrawn as drawings	(1,000)
Net inflow from financing activities	49,000
Increase in cash at bank over period	18,100

Comment. All the amounts for this statement are taken from the 'Cash at bank' column of Table 5.3 but are regrouped for the three headings of operating activities, investing activities and financing activities. The statement shows that the business had a net outflow of cash of £900 due to operations and an outflow of cash amounting to £30,000 due to purchase of medical equipment. The owner contributed £50,000 at the start of the month but took drawings of £1,000 at the end, resulting in a net inflow of £49,000 from financing. The overall effect was an increase in cash over the period amounting to £18,100.

5.5.2 Income statement (profit and loss account)

Medical Practice of Dr Lee
Income statement (profit and loss account)
for the month of October Year 20xx

	£	£
Fees charged		5,500
Medical supplies used	(350)	
Wages	(1,200)	
Rent	(1,900)	
Electricity	(100)	
Depreciation	(250)	
		(3,800)
Profit		1,700

Comment. The total fees charged constitute the total revenue of the period as may be seen in the column in Table 5.3 headed 'revenue'. The expenses of the period amount to £3,800 and are taken from the final column of Table 5.3. The difference between revenue and expenses is the profit of £1,700. This is the amount by which the owner-ship interest has increased to make the owner of the business better off.

Some students ask at this point why the owner's drawings are not included in the income statement (profit and loss account). The answer is that making drawings of cash has nothing to do with the operations of the business. It is a voluntary action taken by the owner, who is also the manager, balancing the owner's personal need for cash against the needs of the business for cash to ensure continued smooth running. Where the owner is the only person working in the business, the owner may regard the drawings as being closer to wages. The amount taken may represent wages in economic terms. However, accounting ignores this economic reality and reports all amounts withdrawn by the owner as drawings.

Activity 5.3

The medical practice of Dr Lee has made a profit of £1,700 over the month but the cash flow caused by operations is an outflow of £900. How can a business make a profit and yet see an outflow of cash caused by operations? This question is asked all too often in reality. You can provide the answer by comparing the cash flow due to operating activities and the calculation of net profit. If you are not sure how to make the comparison, look back to Chapter 3 where the financial statements of P. Mason's legal practice were analysed (Table 3.7).

5.5.3   Statement of financial position (balance sheet)

Medical Practice of Dr Lee
Statement of financial position (balance sheet)
at 31 October Year 20xx

	£	£
Non-current (fixed) assets		
Medical equipment at cost		30,000
Office furniture		6,500
		36,500
Depreciation		(250)
Depreciated cost of fixed assets		36,250
Current assets		
Medical supplies	850	
Trade receivables (debtors)	2,000	
Cash at bank	18,100	
	20,950	
Current liabilities		
Trade payables (creditors)	(6,500)	
Current assets less current liabilities		14,450
Net assets		50,700
Capital at start		50,000
Add: profit		1,700
Less: drawings		(1,000)
Total ownership interest		50,700

Comment. The statement of financial position (balance sheet) follows the pattern of the accounting equation. The non-current (fixed assets) are presented first of all, showing the resources available to the business over a longer period of time. The depreciation is deducted to leave an amount remaining which is probably best described as the 'depreciated cost' but is often labelled 'net book value' or 'written down value'. Chapter 8 contains more information on the procedures for measuring and recording depreciation and the limitations of using the word 'value' in relation to those procedures.

The next section contains the **current assets** which are expected to be converted into cash within a 12-month period. The medical supplies shown are those which have not yet been used and therefore remain as a benefit for the next month. Trade receivables (debtors) are those customers who are expected to pay in the near future. The other current asset is the cash held at the bank, which is very accessible in the short term.

The only liability is the amount of £6,500 owing to the Office Supplies Company, due for payment at the start of December. This is a **current liability** because it is due for payment within 12 months.

It is felt to be helpful in the statement of financial position (balance sheet) to set out subtotals which may guide the reader. These have been shaded in the statement of financial position (balance sheet). The total of fixed assets is interesting as the long-term asset base used to generate profits. The difference between the current assets and the current liabilities is sometimes called the **working capital**. At the moment the current assets look rather high in relation to the need to cover current liabilities. This is because the amount of cash held is quite high in relation to the apparent needs of the business. It is possible that Dr Lee has plans to use the cash for business purposes quite soon but, in the absence of such plans, Dr Lee ought to consider investing it to earn interest or else withdrawing it for other uses.

The amount for total assets less total liabilities (A – L) is usually called the **net assets** of the business. (The word 'net' means 'after taking something away' – in this case, after taking away the liabilities.) There is not much to say here except to note that it equals the ownership interest as would be expected from the accounting equation. The ownership interest has increased over the period through making a profit of £1,700 but decreased by £1,000 through making drawings, so that the resulting increase is £700 overall.

Activity 5.4	Compare the financial statements of Dr Lee's medical practice with the information collected in the spreadsheet of Table 5.3. Take a pencil and, very lightly, place a tick against each amount in the financial statements and a tick against each amount in the spreadsheet, as you match them together. If you are able to work backwards in this way from the financial statements to the spreadsheet then you will be well on the way to understanding how the financial statements are related to the original list of transactions.

5.6 Summary

The first stage in recording a transaction is to think about its effect on the accounting equation.

Assets minus **Liabilities**	equals	**Ownership interest**

A transaction must have at least two effects on the accounting equation. For example, when cash is contributed by the owner there is an *increase* in the **asset** of cash and an *increase* in the **ownership interest**:

Assets $\uparrow$ **– Liabilities**	equals	**Ownership interest** $\uparrow$

Accounting transactions may be recorded in a spreadsheet where the columns record the assets and liabilities and the rows record each transaction. The totals at the foot of all columns contain the information for the statement of financial position (balance sheet) at the end of the period. The columns for revenue and expenditure allow the profit or loss to be calculated. The bank or cash column provides information for the statement of cash flows.

QUESTIONS

The Questions section of each chapter has three types of question. 'Test your understanding' questions to help you review your reading are in the 'A' series of questions. You will find the answers to these by reading and thinking about the material in the book. 'Application' questions to test your ability to apply technical skills are in the 'B' series of questions. Questions requiring you to show skills in problem solving and evaluation are in the 'C' series of questions. A letter [S] indicates that there is a solution at the end of the book.

A Test your understanding

A5.1   [S] The following list of transactions relates to a television repair business during the first month of business. Explain how each transaction affects the accounting equation: (Section 5.2)

(a) Owner puts cash into the business.
(b) Buy a vehicle for cash.

(c) Receive a bill for electricity consumed.
(d) Purchase stationery for office use, paying cash.
(e) Pay the electricity bill in cash.
(f) Pay rental for a computer, used to keep customer records.
(g) Buy spare parts for cash, to use in repairs.
(h) Buy spare parts on credit terms.
(i) Pay garage service bills for van, using cash.
(j) Fill van with petrol, using credit account at local garage, to be paid at the start of next month.
(k) Carry out repairs for cash.
(l) Carry out repairs on credit terms.
(m) Pay wages to an employee.
(n) Owner takes cash for personal use.

A5.2 [S] Which of the items in the list of transactions in question A5.1 will have an effect on an income statement (profit and loss account)?

A5.3 [S] Which of the items in the list of transactions in question A5.1 will have an effect on a statement of cash flows?

A5.4 [S] Which of the items in the list of transactions in question A5.1 will have an effect on a statement of financial position (balance sheet)?

A5.5 [S] Analyse each of the following transactions to show the two aspects of the transaction: (Section 5.3)

Apr. 1	Jane Gate commenced her dental practice on 1 April by depositing £60,000 in a business bank account.
Apr. 1	Rent for a surgery was paid, £800, for the month of April.
Apr. 2	Dental equipment was purchased for £35,000, paying in cash.
Apr. 3	Dental supplies were purchased for £5,000, taking 30 days' credit from a supplier.
Apr. 4	Fees of £1,200 were collected in cash from patients and paid into the bank account.
Apr. 15	Dental assistant was paid wages for two weeks, £700.
Apr. 20	Jane Gate withdrew £500 cash for personal use.
Apr. 21	Fees of £2,400 were collected in cash from patients and paid into the bank.
Apr. 29	Dental assistant was paid wages for two weeks, £700.
Apr. 29	Invoices were sent to patients who are allowed 20 days' credit, for work done during April amounting to £1,900.
Apr. 30	Telephone bill for April was paid, £80.
Apr. 30	Dental supplies unused were counted and found to be worth £3,500, measured at cost price.

B   Application

B5.1 [S]
(a) Using the list of transactions at question A5.5 prepare a spreadsheet similar to that presented in Table 5.3.
(b) Show that the spreadsheet totals satisfy the accounting equation.

B5.2 [S]
Using the totals from the columns of the spreadsheet of question B5.1, prepare for the dental practice in the month of April:

(a) a statement of cash flows;
(b) a statement of financial position (balance sheet); and
(c) an income statement (profit and loss account).

There are no questions in the C series for this chapter.

Recording transactions in ledger accounts – a service business

In the supplement to Chapter 2 it was shown that the rules for debit and credit bookkeeping may be summarised in terms of the elements of the accounting equation as shown in Table 5.5.

Table 5.5
Rules for debit and credit entries in ledger accounts

	Debit entries in a ledger account	Credit entries in a ledger account
Left-hand side of the equation		
Asset	Increase	Decrease
Right-hand side of the equation		
Liability	Decrease	Increase
Ownership interest	Expense	Revenue
	Capital withdrawn	Capital contributed

In the supplement to Chapter 3 a spreadsheet was used to show that a series of transactions could be analysed and summarised in tabular form. That spreadsheet format is becoming increasingly used as the basis for computer-based recording of transactions but the more conventional approach to analysing transactions is to collect them together in ledger accounts. This supplement takes the transactions of Chapter 5 and analyses them in debit and credit form in order to produce a trial balance as a basis for the preparation of financial statements.

In Table 5.1 some common transactions of a service business were listed and then analysed using the accounting equation. They will now be analysed in terms of where the debit and credit entries would be made in a ledger account. Test yourself by trying out the answer before you look at the answer in Table 5.6 below. Once you are satisfied that you could produce the correct answer for the transactions in Table 5.1, you are ready to deal with Dr Lee's medical practice.

Illustration: Dr Lee's medical practice

The first transaction in Table 5.2 reads:

> Oct. 1   Dr Lee provides the practice with cash, £50,000.

The two aspects of this transaction were identified as:

1 Acquisition of an asset (cash).
2 Increasing the ownership interest (voluntary contribution).

The bookkeeping system requires two ledger accounts in which to record this transaction. One ledger account is called Cash and the other is called Ownership interest.

Table 5.6

Analysis of service business transactions (from Table 5.1) to identify two aspects of each

Transaction	Aspects of the transaction	Debit entry in	Credit entry in
Receive cash from the owner	Acquisition of an asset (cash)	Cash	
	Acceptance of ownership interest		Ownership interest
Buy a vehicle for cash	Acquisition of an asset (vehicle)	Vehicle	
	Reduction in an asset (cash)		Cash
Receive a bill for gas consumed	Incur an expense (gas consumed)	Gas expense	
	Incur a liability (to the gas supplier)		Supplier
Pay the gas bill in cash	Decrease a liability (to the gas supplier)	Supplier	
	Reduction in an asset (cash)		Cash
Buy materials for cash	Increase in an asset (inventory of materials)	Inventory (stock)	
	Decrease in an asset (cash)		Cash
Buy materials on credit	Acquisition of an asset (inventory of materials)	Inventory (stock)	
	Incur a liability (to the supplier)		Supplier
Sell services for cash	Acquisition of an asset (cash)	Cash	
	Earn revenue		Sales
Sell services on credit	Acquisition of an asset (trade receivables)	Trade receivables (debtors)	
	Earn revenue		Sales
Pay wages to an employee	Incur an expense (cost of wages)	Wages expense	
	Decrease in asset (cash)		Cash
Pay cash to the owner for personal use	Reduction in the ownership interest	Ownership interest	
	Reduction in an asset (cash)		Cash

There will be a *debit* entry of £50,000 in the Cash ledger account showing that the business has acquired an asset of £50,000 cash. There will be a *credit* entry of £50,000 in the Ownership interest ledger account showing that the business acknowledges the claim of the owner for eventual return of the amount contributed.

The second transaction in Table 5.2 reads:

> Oct. 2 The entity acquires medical equipment for cash, £30,000.

The two aspects of this transaction were identified as:

1 Acquisition of an asset (medical equipment).
2 Decrease of an asset (cash).

Table 5.7

Analysis of debit and credit aspect of each transaction of the medical practice

Date	Business transactions of medical practice	Amount	Debit	Credit
		£		
Oct. 1	Dr Lee provides the practice with cash to allow business to start.	50,000	Cash	Owner
Oct. 2	The entity acquires medical equipment for cash.	30,000	Equipment	Cash
Oct. 2	One month's rent is paid in advance for consulting rooms.	1,900	Rent	Cash
Oct. 2	Office furniture is purchased on two months' credit from Office Supplies Company.	6,500	Furniture	Office Supplies Company
Oct. 7	The practice purchases medical supplies on credit from P. Jones and receives an invoice.	1,200	Inventory (stock)	P. Jones
Oct. 8	Dr Lee pays the medical receptionist for one week's work, 2 to 8 October.	300	Wages	Cash
Oct. 10	Four patients are examined, each paying £500 cash.	2,000	Cash	Patients' fees
Oct. 11	The business pays P. Jones in cash for the goods it acquired on credit.	1,200	P. Jones	Cash
Oct. 14	The business pays an electricity bill in cash.	100	Electricity	Cash
Oct. 15	Dr Lee pays the medical receptionist for one week's work, 9 to 15 October.	300	Wages	Cash
Oct. 17	Three patients are examined, their employer (Mrs West) being sent an invoice requesting payment of £500 for each.	1,500	Mrs West	Fees
Oct. 22	Dr Lee pays the medical receptionist for one week's work, 16 to 22 October.	300	Wages	Cash
Oct. 23	The employer (Mrs West) pays in cash an invoice requesting payment of £500 for each.	1,500	Cash	Mrs West
Oct. 24	Four patients are examined, their employer (Mr East) being sent an invoice requesting payment of £500 for each.	2,000	Mr East	Fees
Oct. 28	Dr Lee draws cash from the business for personal use.	1,000	Owner	Cash
Oct. 29	Dr Lee pays the medical receptionist for one week's work, 23 to 29 October.	300	Wages	Cash
Oct. 31	The medical equipment and office furniture is estimated by Dr Lee to have fallen in value over the month.	250	Depreciation	Equipment and furniture
Oct. 31	Dr Lee checks the inventory (stock) of medical supplies and finds that items costing £350 have been used during the month.	350	Medical supplies expense	Inventory (stock)

The bookkeeping system requires two ledger accounts in which to record this transaction. One ledger account is called Medical equipment and the other is called Cash.

There will be a *debit* entry of £30,000 in the Medical equipment ledger account showing that the business has acquired an asset of £30,000 medical equipment.

There will be a *credit* entry of £30,000 in the Cash ledger account showing that the business has reduced its asset of cash by £30,000 to pay for the medical equipment.

Analysing the debit and credit entries for each transaction

Table 5.7 takes the information contained in Table 5.2 and analyses it under debit and credit headings showing the ledger accounts in which each entry will be made.

Ledger accounts required to record these transactions are:

L1 Cash	L8 Inventory (stock) of medical supplies
L2 Ownership interest	L9 P. Jones
L3 Medical equipment and office furniture	L10 Electricity
L4 Office Supplies Company	L11 Mrs West
L5 Rent	L12 Mr East
L6 Wages	L13 Depreciation
L7 Patients' fees	L14 Expense of medical supplies

Form of ledger accounts

There is no single standard form of ledger account rulings in which to record debit and credit transactions. Historically, ledger accounts were recorded in what were called 'T' accounts where all the debit entries were on the left-hand side and all the credit entries on the right-hand side. This was designed to minimise arithmetic errors by avoiding subtractions in systems which were dealt with manually.

Form of a 'T' ledger account

Page number and name of the account

Debit entries   **Credit entries**

Date	Particulars	Page	£ p	Date	Particulars	Page	£ p

This type of layout requires a wide page if it is to be read clearly. In recent years ledger accounts have more frequently been prepared in a 'three-column' ruling which keeps a running total. This book will use the three-column ruling throughout. You will see by comparison of the column headings that the different types of rulings use the same information. If you have an opportunity to look at business ledgers you will probably come across yet more varieties, but they will all require the inclusion of this basic set of information.

Three-column ruling

Date	Particulars	Page	Debit	Credit	Balance
			£ p	£ p	£ p

Features are:

- The left-hand column will show the date of the transaction.
- The 'particulars' column will show essential narrative, usually confined to the name of the ledger account which records the other aspect of the transaction.
- The 'page' column will show the ledger account page number of the ledger account where the other aspect of the transaction is recorded.
- The amount of the transaction will be entered in the debit or credit column as appropriate.
- The 'balance' column will keep a running total by treating all debit entries as positive and all credit entries as negative. A credit balance will be shown in brackets as a reminder that it is negative. Some ledger systems print the letters 'dr' or 'cr' against the balance.

Illustration

The first transaction of Table 5.7 may now be shown in the appropriate ledger accounts. It will require a *debit* entry in a cash account to indicate an increase in the asset of cash and a *credit* entry in the ownership interest account to indicate an increase in the owner's claim.

L1 Cash

Date	Particulars	Page	Debit	Credit	Balance
			£	£	£
Oct. 1	Ownership interest	L2	50,000		50,000

L2 Ownership interest

Date	Particulars	Page	Debit	Credit	Balance
			£	£	£
Oct. 1	Cash	L1		50,000	(50,000)

Ledger accounts for Dr Lee's medical practice

The full ledger account record for the transactions in Table 5.7 is now set out. Leona Rees comments on each ledger account, showing how she interprets ledger accounts in her work of auditing and accounting.

L1 Cash

Date	Particulars	Page	Debit	Credit	Balance
			£	£	£
Oct. 1	Ownership interest	L2	50,000		50,000
Oct. 2	Medical equipment	L3		30,000	20,000
Oct. 2	Rent	L5		1,900	18,100
Oct. 8	Wages	L6		300	17,800
Oct. 10	Patients' fees	L7	2,000		19,800
Oct. 11	P. Jones	L9		1,200	18,600
Oct. 14	Electricity	L10		100	18,500
Oct. 15	Wages	L6		300	18,200
Oct. 22	Wages	L6		300	17,900
Oct. 23	Mrs West	L11	1,500		19,400
Oct. 28	Ownership interest taken as	L2		1,000	18,400
Oct. 29	Wages	L6		300	18,100

LEONA's comment: *The amount of £50,000 put into the business at the start is quickly eaten into by spending cash on medical equipment and paying rent in advance. Further items such as paying a supplier, paying the electricity account and the assistant's wages took the cash balance down further but it remained quite high throughout the month. With the benefit of hindsight the owner might not have needed to put so much cash into the business at the outset. Up to £18,000 could have been invested on a short-term basis to earn interest, either for the business or for Dr Lee.*

L2 Ownership interest

Date	Particulars	Page	Debit	Credit	Balance
			£	£	£
Oct. 1	Cash contributed	L1		50,000	(50,000)
Oct. 28	Cash drawn	L1	1,000		(49,000)

LEONA's comment: *The ownership interest is created when the owner contributes cash or resources to the business. In this case it was cash. The sole trader in business may withdraw cash for personal use at any time – it is called owner's drawings – but the desirability of that action depends on how useful cash is to the owner when compared to how useful it might have been if left in the business. The owner of this business has a claim remaining equal to £49,000 after making the drawing.*

L3 Medical equipment and office furniture

Date	Particulars	Page	Debit £	Credit £	Balance £
Oct. 2	Cash	L1	30,000		30,000
Oct. 2	Office Supplies Company	L4	6,500		36,500
Oct. 31	Depreciation	L13		250	36,250

LEONA's comment: *This ledger account is particularly useful as a reminder that some very valuable assets are owned by the business. Having a record in the ledger account encourages the owner to think about continuing care for the medical equipment and office furniture and also to review their value against the amount recorded. If Dr Lee intended to have a large number of fixed asset items it is possible to have a separate ledger account for each, but that seems a long-distant prospect at the moment.*

Depreciation is a way of showing that the original cost of the asset has to be spread over its useful life. If the estimate of depreciation is correct, this ledger account should reduce to nil on the day the equipment and furniture ceases to be of use. In reality, things usually are not quite so straightforward. (Depreciation of non-current (fixed) assets is dealt with in more detail in Chapter 8.)

L4 Office Supplies Company

Date	Particulars	Page	Debit £	Credit £	Balance £
Oct. 2	Office furniture	L3		6,500	(6,500)

LEONA's comment: *When the office furniture was purchased from the Office Supplies Company, an invoice was received from that company showing the amount due. That invoice was used to make the credit entry on 2 October showing that the business had a liability. The liability remained owing at 31 October, but that is acceptable because the supplier allowed two months' credit.*

L5 Rent

Date	Particulars	Page	Debit £	Credit £	Balance £
Oct. 2	Cash	L1	1,900		1,900

LEONA's comment: *This payment in advance starts by being an asset and gradually turns into an expense as the benefit is used up. For bookkeeping purposes, a debit entry records both an asset and an expense so it is only at the end of the month that some care is needed in thinking about the nature of the debit balance. In this case it is clear that the benefit is used up but there could be a situation where part of the benefit remained to be reported as an asset.*

L6 Wages

Date	Particulars	Page	Debit	Credit	Balance
			£	£	£
Oct. 8	Cash	L1	300		300
Oct. 15	Cash	L1	300		600
Oct. 22	Cash	L1	300		900
Oct. 29	Cash	L1	300		1,200

LEONA's comment: *This is a straightforward account in which to accumulate all wages expenses. A very enthusiastic accountant would estimate the liability for the final two days of the month and add these on, but there is a very useful idea in accounting called 'materiality' which, broadly interpreted, means the extra information provided would not justify the extra amount of work involved.*

L7 Patients' fees

Date	Particulars	Page	Debit	Credit	Balance
			£	£	£
Oct. 10	Cash	L1		2,000	(2,000)
Oct. 17	Credit: Mrs West (as employer)	L11		1,500	(3,500)
Oct. 24	Credit: Mr East (as employer)	L12		2,000	(5,500)

LEONA's comment: *This is a revenue account so credit entries are expected. The balance column shows the total patients' fees earned in the month were £5,500. This could be described as 'turnover' or 'sales' but both of those words sound rather out of place when a professional service is being described.*

L8 Inventory (stock) of medical supplies

Date	Particulars	Page	Debit	Credit	Balance
			£	£	£
Oct. 7	P. Jones	L9	1,200		1,200
Oct. 31	Expense of medical supplies	L14		350	850

LEONA's comment: *This is an asset account so when the medical supplies were acquired on credit from P. Jones the entire amount was recorded as an asset. These medical supplies will be quite small items and it would not be appropriate for Dr Lee to have to count every cotton wool swab, hypodermic needle or sample bottle used in each examination. It is sufficient for accounting purposes to count up what is left at the end of the period (we call it 'taking stock') and assume that the difference represents the amount used during the period. As an auditor, I might start to ask questions about possible errors, fraud or theft if the amounts of supplies used did not look sensible when compared with the number of examinations carried out on patients.*

L9 P. Jones

Date	Particulars	Page	Debit £	Credit £	Balance £
Oct. 7	Inventory (stock) of medical supplies	L8		1,200	(1,200)
Oct. 11	Cash	L1	1,200		nil

LEONA's comment: *When the medical supplies were delivered to Dr Lee, the business took on a liability to pay P. Jones. That liability was recorded by a credit entry in the ledger account for P. Jones and was extinguished on 11 October when the medical practice paid £1,200 to P. Jones.*

L10 Electricity

Date	Particulars	Page	Debit £	Credit £	Balance £
Oct. 14	Cash	L1	100		100

LEONA's comment: *This is a very straightforward expense account. The balance on this account will show the total expense of electricity consumed during the period.*

L11 Mrs West

Date	Particulars	Page	Debit £	Credit £	Balance £
Oct. 17	Patients' fees	L7	1,500		1,500
Oct. 23	Cash	L1		1,500	nil

L12 Mr East

Date	Particulars	Page	Debit £	Credit £	Balance £
Oct. 24	Patients' fees	L7	2,000		2,000

LEONA's comment: *The credit sale to the employees of Mrs West and Mr East made them trade receivables (debtors) of the business and so there is a debit entry. By the end of October Mr East had not paid, so remains a debtor, denoted by a debit balance. Mrs West has paid during October and a nil balance is the result.*

L13 Depreciation

Date	Particulars	Page	Debit £	Credit £	Balance £
Oct. 31	Medical equipment and office furniture	L3	250		250

LEONA's comment: *This is another expense account showing an item which has decreased the ownership interest through a decrease in the recorded amount of some assets. This is where accounting begins to look slightly complicated because no cash has changed hands. Recording depreciation is the accounting way of expressing caution as to the expected future benefits from an asset. These will be eroded as the asset is used up. Depreciation is a way of acknowledging that erosion.*

L14 Expense of medical supplies					
Date	Particulars	Page	Debit	Credit	Balance
			£	£	£
Oct. 31	Inventory (stock) of medical supplies	L8	350		350

LEONA's comment: *This account continues the story from L8 where the inventory (stock) of medical supplies was found to have dwindled through use in examining patients. It is assumed that the difference between the amount purchased and the amount held at the end of the month represents the expense of using the asset during the month.*

Checking the accuracy of double-entry records

At periodic intervals it may be considered necessary for a number of reasons to check the accuracy of the entries made in ledger accounts. For instance, the omission of an entry on the debit side of a customer's ledger account for goods sold on credit terms could result in a failure to issue reminders for payment of an amount owed to the business.

There are methods in double-entry bookkeeping of discovering these and other errors. One such method is the use of the *trial balance*.

If a debit entry and a credit entry have been made in the appropriate ledger accounts for each business transaction, then the total money amount of all the debit entries will equal the total money amount of all the credit entries. If a debit entry has been made without a corresponding credit entry (or vice versa), then the totals will not agree.

In the ledger accounts shown in this example, the balances have been kept as running totals. It would be possible to add up all the debit and all the credit entries in each ledger account but the same arithmetic proof will be obtained by listing all the debit balances and all the credit balances. It was explained earlier in this supplement that brackets are used in the ledger accounts to show credit balances. The list of balances on all the ledger accounts for Dr Lee's medical practice is set out in Table 5.8.

Error detection using the trial balance

The calculation of the totals of each column of the trial balance is a useful precaution which will reveal some, but not all, of the errors it is possible to make in a debit and credit recording system. Think first about the errors you might make and then check against the following list:

Table 5.8
Trial balance at 31 October for Dr Lee's medical practice

Ledger account title	Debit	Credit
	£	£
L1 Cash	18,100	
L2 Ownership interest		49,000
L3 Medical equipment and office furniture	36,250	
L4 Office Supplies Company		6,500
L5 Rent	1,900	
L6 Wages	1,200	
L7 Patients' fees		5,500
L8 Inventory (stock) of medical supplies	850	
L9 P. Jones		nil
L10 Electricity	100	
L11 Mrs West	nil	
L12 Mr East	2,000	
L13 Depreciation	250	
L14 Expense of medical supplies	350	
Totals	61,000	61,000

Errors which will be detected by unequal totals in the trial balance

● Omitting one aspect of a transaction (e.g. a debit entry but no credit entry).
● Writing incorrect amounts in one entry (e.g. debit £290 but credit £209).
● Writing both entries in one column (e.g. two debits, no credit).
● Incorrect calculation of ledger account balance.

Errors which will leave the trial balance totals equal

● Total omission of a transaction.
● Errors in both debit and credit entry of the same magnitude.
● Entering the correct amount in the wrong ledger account (e.g. debit for wages entered as debit for heat and light).

Preparing the financial statements

The main part of this chapter set out the statement of financial position (balance sheet) and income statement (profit and loss account) of Dr Lee's medical practice for the month of October. If you compare the amounts in the trial balance with the amounts in the financial statements you will see they are the same. The normal practice in accounting is to use the trial balance to prepare the statement of financial position (balance sheet) and income statement (profit and loss account).

In this case it would be a little easier to use the trial balance for this purpose if it were arranged so that all the statement of financial position (balance sheet) items are

Table 5.9
Rearranging the trial balance into statement of financial position (balance sheet) items and income statement (profit and loss account) items

Ledger account title	£	£
L3 Medical equipment and office furniture	36,250	
L8 Inventory (stock) of medical supplies	850	
L12 Mr East	2,000	
L11 Mrs West	nil	
L1 Cash at bank	18,100	
L4 Office Supplies Company		6,500
L9 P. Jones		nil
L2 Ownership interest		49,000
Subtotal X	57,200	55,500
Difference: profit of the month (57,200 − 55,000)		1,700
L7 Patients' fees		5,500
L14 Expense of medical supplies	350	
L6 Wages	1,200	
L5 Rent	1,900	
L10 Electricity	100	
L13 Depreciation	250	
Subtotal Y	3,800	5,500
Difference: profit of the month (5,500 − 3,800)	1,700	
Total of ledger balances in each column X + Y	61,000	61,000

together and all the income statement (profit and loss account) items are together. This is done in Table 5.9.

This form of trial balance will be used in later chapters as the starting point for the preparation of financial statements.

By way of providing further help in preparing the income statement (profit and loss account) and statement of financial position (balance sheet), subtotals are calculated for each part of the trial balance in Table 5.9. The difference between the subtotals in each section gives the profit amount. That is because the exhibit has been subdivided according to two equations, each of which leads to profit:

Assets	*minus*	Liabilities	*minus*	Capital contributed/withdrawn	*equals*	Profit

Revenue	*minus*	Expenses	*equals*	Profit

S Test your understanding

S5.1 Prepare ledger accounts for the transactions of Jane Gate's dental practice, listed in question A5.5.

S5.2 Which of the following errors would be detected at the point of listing a trial balance?

(a) The bookkeeper enters a cash sale as a debit of £49 in the cash book and as a credit of £94 in the sales account.

(b) The bookkeeper omits a cash sale of £23 from the cash book and from the sales accounts.

(c) The bookkeeper enters cash received of £50 from Peter Jones as a debit in the cashbook but enters the credit of £50 in the ledger account of Roger Jones.

(d) The bookkeeper enters a cash sale as a credit of £40 in the cash book and as a debit of £40 in the sales account.

Chapter 6

Accounting information for trading businesses

REAL WORLD CASE

Sales, margin and costs

The Group's gross transaction value grew by 0.2% during the 52 weeks ended 29 August 2009 to £2,339.7 million (2008: £2,336.0 million) and revenue was up by 4.2% to £1,915.6 million (2008: £1,839.2 million). These increases were primarily from our own bought ranges, including our exclusive Designers at Debenhams offer, and were supported by, good sales performances in new stores. During the year we have seen trading space being converted from concession to own bought ranges and the introduction of a number of new brands and departments. However, like-for-like sales declined by 3.6% in the financial year, reflecting the difficult trading environment and disruption to sales in the fourth quarter arising out of the space move programme.

Continued growth was achieved from our internet business, with sales increasing 31% to £55.1 million (2008: £42.1 million) during the year. At the same time we have changed our fulfilment partner and we expect to be able to deliver new functionality and cost savings from this transfer.

The international business has continued to grow and over the past 12 months we opened 11 new stores. At the year end we were represented in 17 countries with a total of 52 franchise stores with sales of £63.3 million, up 13.6% on the previous financial year (2008: £55.7 million).

Gross margin increased by 70 basis points over the previous financial year. This was driven by the higher mix of own bought sales, the tight management of costs and stocks and historically low levels of terminal stock, which resulted in lower markdown during sale periods. The effect of our 18-month hedging policy has also reduced the impact of US dollar movement during the year.

Control of costs is critical, particularly in the current economic environment, and further significant cost savings have been made during the financial year in addition to those achieved during the second half of last year. Overall store operational costs increased, primarily due to new store openings, but like-for-like stores saw a decrease in costs of 0.4%. This combined to generate gross profit during the financial year of £264.9 million (2008: £267.6 million).

Distribution costs decreased by £4.7 million, due to tighter control of stocks and transport schedules alongside warehouse labour efficiencies. Administration costs were also down £4.1 million reflecting the full year impact of changes implemented last year and the ongoing challenges to the cost base.

Operating profit in the financial year ending 29 August 2009 increased to £182.2 million (2008: £176.1 million) and profit before taxation grew to £120.8 million (2008: £105.9 million).

Source: Debenhams 2009 Annual Report, p. 19; http://www.investis.com/debenhams/pdfs/ar2009_new.pdf.

Discussion points

1 How does the company describe its trading performance?

2 How does the company measure trends in operating performance?

Contents

Learning outcomes

After studying this chapter you should be able to:

- Explain the application of the accounting equation to transactions involving the buying and selling of inventory (trading stock).
- Explain the application of the accounting equation to transactions involving the manufacture and sale of products.
- Analyse transactions of a trading or manufacturing business during a specific period of time, using the accounting equation.
- Prepare a spreadsheet analysing the transactions, and show that the results of the spreadsheet analysis are consistent with financial statements provided by the organisation.
- Explain the main aspects of the statement of cash flows, profit and loss account and statement of financial position (balance sheet) of a trading or a manufacturing business.

Additionally, for those who choose to study the supplement:

- Analyse the transactions of a trading or a manufacturing business using the rules of debit and credit bookkeeping.
- Prepare, from a list of transactions of an organisation, ledger accounts and a trial balance which could be used to confirm the financial statements provided by the organisation.

6.1 Introduction

Chapter 5 has shown in detail the application of the accounting equation to the analysis of transactions in service businesses. The same approach applies in the case of trading businesses, but with one significant addition. Businesses which engage in trading have either purchased or manufactured a product with the intention of selling that product to customers. It is the purchase or manufacture of a product and the act of selling the product which must be analysed carefully in terms of the accounting equation. This chapter first analyses the transactions and events occurring when goods are purchased for resale and sold to a customer. Secondly, it analyses the transactions and events occurring when goods are manufactured and then sold to a customer. Finally, there is a worked example which takes one month's transactions of a trading business and shows the resulting financial statements.

6.2 Goods purchased for resale

A trading business which buys goods for resale (e.g. a wholesaler buying goods from a manufacturer for distribution to retailers) makes a profit by selling the goods at a price which is higher than the price paid. The difference between the selling price and the purchase price is called the **gross profit** of the business. The gross profit must be sufficient to cover all the costs of running the business (e.g. administration, marketing and distribution costs) and leave a net profit which will increase the ownership interest in the business.

6.2.1 Analysis of transactions

Consider the transactions of a trading company set out in Table 6.1, relating to buying and selling goods.

Table 6.1
Transactions of a trading company

		£
Apr. 1	Purchase goods from manufacturer, 100 items at £2 each, paying in cash, and store in warehouse.	200
Apr. 4	Remove 70 items from warehouse to meet a customer's request. Those 70 items cost £2 each on 1 April. They are delivered to the customer, who accepts the delivery.	140
Apr. 4	The customer pays in cash. Selling price is £2.50 per item.	175

What is the profit on the sale of 70 items? Each one cost £2.00 and is sold for £2.50, so there is a profit of 50 pence per item or £35 for 70 items. In accounting, that calculation might be set out as follows:

	£
Sale of goods (70 items)	175
Cost of goods sold (70 items)	(140)
Gross profit	35

There is an asset of unsold goods (30 items) which cost £2 each or £60 in total. Since that item is an asset, it will appear in the statement of financial position (balance sheet).

That is a statement of the gross profit and of the monetary amount of the asset of unsold goods, using common sense and intuition to arrive at an answer. Now look at how a systematic analysis is undertaken in accounting.

6.2.2   Analysis of transactions and events

Apr. 1	Purchase goods from manufacturer, 100 items at £2 each, paying in cash, and store in warehouse	£200

This transaction has two aspects in terms of the accounting equation. It *increases* the **asset** of inventory (stock of goods) and it *decreases* the **asset** of cash. One asset increases, another decreases by an equal amount and there is no effect on the ownership interest.

Assets ↑↓ – Liabilities	equals	Ownership interest

Apr. 4	Remove 70 items from warehouse to meet customer's request. Those 70 items cost £2 each on 1 April. They are delivered to the customer, who accepts the delivery.	£140

This is an event which is not a transaction. The goods which are in the store are removed to a more convenient place for sale to the customer. In this case they are removed to a delivery van and transported to the customer. The moment of delivery to, and acceptance by, the customer is the event which transforms the goods from an asset to an expense. By that event, ownership is transferred to the customer, who either pays cash immediately or agrees to pay in the future. The expense is called **cost of goods sold**.

It should be noted at this point that the acts of physical removal and transport are events which financial accounting does not record, because at that point there is not sufficient evidence for recognition that a sale has taken place. In management accounting you will find that quite a different attitude is taken to events which involve moving goods from one location to another. In management accounting, such movements are recorded in order to help the managerial process of control.

In terms of the accounting equation there is a *decrease* in the **asset** of inventory (stock) because it is no longer owned by the business and there can be no future benefit from the item. The benefit has occurred on this day, creating a sale by the act of delivery and acceptance.

If an asset has decreased then the **ownership interest** must also have *decreased* through an expense. The expense is called cost of goods sold.

Assets ↓ – Liabilities	equals	**Ownership interest ↓** **(expense: cost of goods sold)**

Apr. 4	The customer pays in cash. Selling price is £2.50 per item.	£175

The final transaction is the payment of cash by the customer. In timing, it will occur almost simultaneously with the delivery and acceptance of the goods. In accounting it is nevertheless analysed separately. The business receives an *increase* in the **asset** of cash and the **ownership interest** *is increased* by an act which has earned **revenue** for the business.

Assets ↑ – Liabilities	equals	**Ownership interest ↑ (revenue)**

Activity 6.1	Return to Table 6.1 and change the cost price to £3 and the selling price to £3.50. Calculate the profit if the customer receives (a) 70 items, (b) 80 items, (c) 90 items and (d) 100 items. How many items remain in inventory (stock) in each of these four cases? What can you say about the pattern of profit which appears from the four calculations you have carried out? Now write down the effect on the accounting equation for each of these four separate situations. Doing this will help you to test your own understanding before you proceed further.

6.2.3 Spreadsheet summarising the transactions

It is possible to bring the analysis together in a spreadsheet similar to that used in Chapter 5, but containing column headings which are appropriate to the assets involved in these transactions. Table 6.2 shows the spreadsheet. Table 6.3 summarises the impact of the accounting equation, showing that the assets remaining at the end of the period, £35 in total, equal the sum of the opening capital at the start (nil in this case) plus revenue, £175, minus expenses, £140.

Table 6.2
Spreadsheet analysing transactions and events into elements of the accounting equation

Date	Transaction or event	Assets		Ownership interest	
		Cash £	Inventory (stock) £	Revenue + £	Expense − £
Apr. 1	Purchase goods from manufacturer, paying in cash, 100 items at £2 each, and place in warehouse.	(200)	200		
Apr. 4	Remove 70 items from warehouse to meet customer's request. Those 70 items cost £2 each on Apr. 1. They are delivered to the customer, who accepts the delivery.		(140)		140
Apr. 4	The customer pays in cash. Selling price is £2.50 per item.	175		175	
	Totals at end of period	(25)	60	175	140

└── 35 ──┘

Table 6.3
Summary of transactions analysed into the elements of the accounting equation

Assets	minus	Liabilities	=	Ownership interest at start of period	plus	Capital contributed/ withdrawn	plus	Revenue	minus	Expenses
£35	−	nil	=	nil	+	nil	+	£175	−	£140

6.3 Manufacturing goods for resale

The manufacture of goods for resale requires the purchase of raw materials which are used in production of the finished goods. There are several stages here where the business may hold an asset of one type or another. Any unused raw materials will represent a benefit for the future and therefore be treated as an asset. Any finished goods which are not sold will also represent a benefit for the future and therefore be treated as an asset. Less obvious than these two items is the expected future benefit of partly completed goods that may be in the production process at the accounting date. That is also regarded as an asset, called work in progress. If the manufacturing process is rapid, then at any date there will be relatively little work in progress. If the manufacturing process is slow, there could be significant amounts of work in progress at an accounting date.

6.3.1 Analysis of transactions

Consider the transactions of a manufacturing company which are set out in Table 6.4. The company buys breakfast trays and customises them to designs requested by catering outlets.

Table 6.4
Transactions of a manufacturing company

		£
July 1	Purchase raw materials from supplier, 100 trays at £2 each, paying in cash, and place in raw materials store.	200
July 3	Remove 80 trays from raw materials store to meet production department's request (cost £2 each).	160
July 4	Carry out labour work and use production facilities to convert raw materials into finished goods. Additional costs incurred for labour and use of facilities were £1.50 per tray processed.	120
July 5	Finished goods are transferred to finished goods store. The job has cost £3.50 per tray in total (80 trays × £3.50 = £280).	280
July 10	60 trays, which cost £3.50 each to manufacture, are delivered to a customer.	210
July 10	The customer pays a price of £5 cash per tray immediately on delivery.	300

What is the profit on the sale of 60 trays? Each one cost £3.50 to manufacture and is sold for £5.00 so there is a profit of £1.50 per item or £90 for 60 items.

The business retains an inventory (stock) of 20 unsold finished trays which cost £3.50 each to manufacture (a cost of £70 in total) and an inventory (stock) of unused raw materials (20 basic trays costing £2 each which is a total cost of £40).

That is a statement of the position using common sense and intuition to arrive at an answer. Now look at how a systematic analysis is undertaken in accounting.

6.3.2 Analysis of transactions and events

July 1	Purchase raw materials from supplier, 100 trays at £2 each, paying in cash, and place in raw materials store.	£200

The business experiences an *increase* in the **asset** of inventory (stock) of raw materials and a *decrease* in the **asset** of cash. In terms of the accounting equation there is an increase in one asset matched by a decrease in another and there is no effect on the ownership interest.

Assets ↑↓ **– Liabilities**	equals	Ownership interest

July 3	Remove 80 trays from raw materials store to meet production department's request (cost £2 each).	£160

Next, some of the raw materials are removed for use in production. This is an event, rather than a transaction, but is recorded because it creates a possible asset of work in progress. The **asset** of work in progress *increases* and the **asset** of raw materials *decreases*. There is no effect on the ownership claim.

Assets ↑↓ **– Liabilities**	equals	Ownership interest

July 4	Carry out labour work and use production facilities to convert raw materials into finished goods. Additional costs incurred for labour and use of facilities were £1.50 per tray processed.	£120

The next stage is that some work is done to convert the raw materials into the product desired by customers. The work involves labour cost and other costs of using the production facilities. (You will find in management accounting that the other costs of using production facilities are usually described as **production overheads**.) This payment for labour and use of production facilities is adding to the value of the basic tray and so is adding to the value of the asset of work in progress (which will eventually become the asset of finished goods). So there is an *increase* in the **asset** of work in progress and a *decrease* in the **asset** of cash. There is no effect on the ownership interest.

Assets ↑↓ **– Liabilities**	equals	Ownership interest

July 5	Finished goods are transferred to finished goods store. The job has cost £3.50 per tray in total (80 trays × £3.50 = £280).	£280

When the work in progress is complete, it becomes finished goods and is transferred to the store. The **asset** of work in progress *decreases* and the **asset** of finished goods *increases*. A measure of the value of the asset is the cost of making it which, in this case, is £3.50 per item or £280 for 80 items. Again, there is no effect on the ownership interest.

Assets ↑↓ **– Liabilities**	equals	Ownership interest

July 10	60 trays, which cost £3.50 each to manufacture, are delivered to a customer.	£210

The customer now requests 60 trays and these are delivered from the store to the customer. At the moment of acceptance by the customer, the 60 trays cease to be an asset of the business. There is a *decrease* in an **asset** and a *decrease* in the **ownership interest** which is recorded as an **expense** of cost of goods sold.

Assets ↑↓ **– Liabilities**	equals	**Ownership interest** ↓ **(expense: cost of goods sold)**

The owner's disappointment is momentary because the act of acceptance by the customer results in immediate payment being received from the customer (or in some cases a promise of future payment).

July 10	The customer pays a price of £5 cash per tray immediately on delivery.	£300

When the customer pays immediately for the goods, there is an *increase* in the **asset** of cash and a corresponding *increase* in the **ownership interest**, recorded as **revenue** of the business.

Assets ↑↓ – Liabilities	equals	**Ownership interest ↑ (revenue)**

Activity 6.2

Return to Table 6.4. Without looking to the rest of the section, write down the effect of each transaction on the accounting equation. At what point in the sequence of events in Table 6.4 is the ownership interest affected? Why is it not affected before that point in the sequence? How would the ownership interest have been affected if, on 5 July, there had been a fire as the goods were being transferred to the finished goods store and one-quarter of the finished trays were destroyed?

6.3.3 Spreadsheet summarising the transactions

Table 6.5 brings the analysis together in a spreadsheet similar to that used in Table 6.2, showing the effect of each transaction separately and also the overall effect on the accounting equation. Table 6.6 sets out the accounting equation at the end of the period and shows that the assets remaining at the end of the period are equal to the owner-ship interest at the start (which is taken as nil in this example) plus the profit of the period.

Once you have understood the analysis up to this point, you are ready to embark on the financial statements of a trading business.

6.4 Illustration of accounting for a trading business

This example considers the business of M. Carter, wholesale trader. At the start of May, M. Carter commenced a trading business as a wholesaler, buying goods from manufacturers and storing them in a warehouse from which customers could be supplied. All the customers are small shopkeepers who need the services of the whole-saler because they are not sufficiently powerful in purchasing power to negotiate terms directly with the manufacturers.

In Table 6.7 (on page 142) there is a list of transactions for M. Carter's whole-saling business during the month of May. In section 6.4.1 each transaction is analysed using the accounting equation.

Activity 6.3

Before reading section 6.4.1, analyse each transaction in Table 6.7 using the accounting equation. (If necessary look back to Chapter 5 for a similar pattern of analysis.) Then compare your answer against the detail of section 6.4.1. If there is any item where you have a different answer, consult your lecturer, tutor or other expert before proceeding with the rest of the chapter.

Table 6.5
Spreadsheet analysing transactions and events into elements of the accounting equation

Date	Transaction or event	Assets				Ownership interest	
		Cash at bank £	Raw materials inventory (stock) £	Work in progress £	Finished goods £	Revenue + £	Expenses – £
July 1	Purchase raw materials from supplier, paying in cash, trays at £2 each, and place 100 in raw materials store.	(200)	200				
July 3	Remove 80 trays from raw materials store to meet production department's request (cost £2 each).		(160)	160			
July 4	Carry out labour work and use production facilities to convert raw materials into finished goods. Additional costs incurred for labour and use of facilities were £1.50 per tray processed.	(120)		120			
July 5	Finished goods are transferred to finished goods store. The job has cost £3.50 per tray in total (80 trays × £3.50 = £280).			(280)	280		
July 10	60 trays, which cost £3.50 each to manufacture, are delivered to a customer.				(210)		210
July 10	The customer pays a price of £5 cash per tray immediately on delivery.	300				300	
	Totals at the end of the period.	(20)	40	nil	70	300	210

└────── 90 ──────┘

Table 6.6
Summary of transactions analysed into the elements of the accounting equation

Assets	minus	Liabilities	=	Ownership interest at start of period	plus	Capital contributed/ withdrawn	plus	Revenue	minus	Expenses
£90	–	nil	=	nil	+	nil	+	£300	–	£210

Table 6.7
Transactions of the business of M. Carter, wholesaler, for the month of May

Date	Business transactions and events (nature of the entity: wholesale trader)	Amount £
May 1	The owner pays cash into a bank account for the business.	50,000
May 2	The business acquires buildings for cash.	30,000
May 4	The business acquires equipment for cash.	6,000
May 6	The business purchases an inventory (stock) of goods for cash.	6,500
May 7	The business purchases an inventory (stock) of goods on credit from R. Busby and receives an invoice.	5,000
May 11	The business pays R. Busby in cash for the goods it acquired on credit.	5,000
May 14	The business pays an electricity bill in cash.	100
May 17	Items costing £3,500 are removed from the store because sales have been agreed with customers for this date.	3,500
May 17	The business sells items costing £2,000 to customers for a cash price of £4,000.	4,000
May 17	The business sells items costing £1,500 on credit to R. Welsby and sends an invoice for the price of £3,000.	3,000
May 24	R. Welsby pays in cash for the goods obtained on credit.	3,000
May 28	The owner draws cash from the business for personal use.	1,000
May 30	The business pays wages to an employee for the month, in cash.	2,000
May 31	The business discovers that its equipment has fallen in value over the month.	250

6.4.1 Explanation of the analysis of each transaction

May 1   When M. Carter provides the business with cash in a bank account to allow the company to proceed, the business *acquires* an **asset** of cash and the transaction *creates* an **ownership interest** for M. Carter on the assets of the business. Using the symbols of the accounting equation:

Assets ↑ – Liabilities	equals	**Ownership interest ↑ (contribution of capital)**

May 2   The wholesale business now becomes the business entity so far as accounting is concerned (although M. Carter may still be making the decisions as an owner/manager of the business). The entity acquires an asset of buildings in exchange for an asset of cash. There is an *increase* in one **asset** and a *decrease* in another **asset**. There is no impact on the ownership interest.

Assets ↑↓ – Liabilities	equals	Ownership interest

May 4   The entity acquires an asset of equipment in exchange for an asset of cash. There is an *increase* in the **asset** of equipment and a *decrease* in the **asset** of cash. There is no impact on the ownership interest.

Assets ↑↓ – Liabilities	equals	Ownership interest

May 6   The entity acquires an asset of inventory (stock) of goods in exchange for an asset of cash. There is an *increase* in the **asset** of inventory (stock) and a *decrease* in the **asset** of cash. There is no impact on the ownership interest.

Assets ↑↓ – Liabilities	equals	Ownership interest

May 7   The entity again acquires an asset of inventory (stock) of goods but this time it is related to the acquisition of a liability to R. Busby. There is an *increase* in the **asset** of inventory (stock) and an *increase* in the **liability** of receivables (creditors). There is no impact on the ownership interest.

Assets ↑ – **Liabilities** ↑	equals	Ownership interest

May 11   When payment is made to R. Busby there is a *decrease* in the **asset** of cash and a *decrease* in the **liability** to R. Busby.

Assets ↓ – **Liabilities** ↓	equals	Ownership interest

May 14   When the electricity bill is paid, the benefit of using the electricity has been consumed. There is a *decrease* in the **asset** of cash and a *decrease* in the **ownership interest**, reported as an expense.

Assets ↓ – Liabilities	equals	**Ownership interest ↓ (expense)**

May 17   At the moment of acceptance by the customer, the goods cease to be an asset of the business. There is a *decrease* in the **ownership interest** (recorded as an **expense** of cost of goods sold) and a *decrease* in the **asset** of inventory (stock).

Assets ↓ – Liabilities	equals	**Ownership interest ↓ (cost of goods sold)**

May 17   The owner's wealth is then immediately restored or enhanced because some customers pay cash for the goods. There is an *increase* in the **asset** of cash and a corresponding *increase* in the **ownership interest**, recorded as revenue of the business. The information about cost of goods sold has been dealt with in the previous equation.

Assets ↑ – Liabilities	equals	**Ownership interest ↑ (revenue)**

May 17   The owner's wealth is similarly restored by a promise from the customer to pay at a future date. This creates the asset of a trade receivable (debtor) which, in accounting, is regarded as acceptable in the overall measure of shareholder wealth. There is an *increase* in the **asset** of trade receivable (debtor) and a corresponding *increase* in the **ownership interest**, recorded as

revenue of the business. The information about cost of goods sold has been dealt with in the earlier equation.

Assets ↑ – Liabilities	equals	Ownership interest ↑ (revenue)

May 24   R. Welsby is a credit customer of the business, called a 'trade receivable' or a 'debtor'. When a credit customer makes payment to the business there is an *increase* in the **asset** of cash and a *decrease* in the **asset** of trade receivable (debtor). There is no effect on the ownership interest.

Assets ↑↓ – Liabilities	equals	Ownership interest

May 28   As was explained in Chapter 5, the owner of a sole trader business does not take a salary or wage as an employee would, but needs cash for personal purposes. Taking cash for personal use is called **drawings** and is recorded in terms of the accounting equation as a *decrease* in the **ownership interest** and a *decrease* in the **asset** of cash.

Assets ↓ – Liabilities	equals	Ownership interest ↓ (withdrawal of capital)

May 30   Paying wages is similar in effect to paying the electricity bill. The benefit of the employee's work has been consumed. There is a *decrease* in the **asset** of cash and a *decrease* in the **ownership interest**, reported as an **expense**.

Assets ↓ – Liabilities	equals	Ownership interest ↓ (expense)

May 31   All fixed assets will eventually be used up by the business, after several years of useful life. Depreciation is a recognition of the *decrease* in the **asset** and the *decrease* in the **ownership interest**, reported as an **expense**. (There is more on **depreciation** in Chapter 8.)

Assets ↓ – Liabilities	equals	Ownership interest ↓ (expense)

6.5 A process for summarising the transactions: a spreadsheet

In Table 6.8 the transactions of Table 6.7 are repeated at the left-hand side and are analysed into columns headed for assets, liabilities and ownership interest using brackets to show a negative amount. It would be equally acceptable to use a minus sign but minus signs tend to disappear or be confused with unintentional blobs on the paper, so brackets are frequently used in accounting in order to ensure clarity.

At the foot of the spreadsheet in Table 6.8 there is a total for each column. Those totals are used in Table 6.9 to show the state of the accounting equation at the end of the month. It may be used to explain to M. Carter how the ownership interest has changed over the month. The owner contributed £50,000 at the start of the month and has a claim of £50,150 at the end of the month. The ownership interest was increased by earning revenue of £7,000 but reduced by incurring expenses of £5,850 and withdrawing £1,000 for personal use.

Table 6.8
Spreadsheet analysing transactions into the elements of the accounting equation

Date	Business transactions	Assets Cash at bank £	Assets Inventory (stock) of goods £	Assets Fixed assets and trade receivables (debtors) £	Liabilities Trade payables (creditors) £	Ownership interest Capital contributed/ withdrawn £	Ownership interest Revenue + £	Ownership interest Expenses − £
May 1	The owner provides the business with cash.	50,000				50,000		
May 2	The business acquires buildings for cash.	(30,000)		30,000				
May 4	The business acquires equipment for cash.	(6,000)		6,000				
May 6	The business purchases an inventory (stock) of goods for cash.	(6,500)	6,500					
May 7	The business purchases an inventory (stock) of goods on credit from R. Busby and receives an invoice.		5,000		5,000			
May 11	The business pays R. Busby in cash for the goods it acquired on credit.	(5,000)			(5,000)			
May 14	The business pays an electricity bill in cash.	(100)						100
May 17	Some of the goods purchased for resale (items costing £3,500) are removed from the store because sales have been agreed with customers for this date.		(3,500)					3,500
May 17	The business sells some of the purchased goods for cash.	4,000					4,000	
May 17	The business sells the remaining purchased goods on credit to R. Welsby and sends an invoice.			3,000			3,000	
May 24	R. Welsby pays in cash for the goods obtained on credit.	3,000		(3,000)				
May 28	The owner draws cash from the business for personal use.	(1,000)				(1,000)		
May 30	The business pays wages to an employee for the past month, in cash.	(2,000)						2,000
May 31	The business discovers that its equipment has fallen in value over the month.			(250)				250
	Totals at the end of the period	6,400	8,000	35,750	nil	49,000	7,000	5,850

—— 50,150 ——

Table 6.9
Summary of transactions analysed into the elements of the accounting equation

Assets	minus	Liabilities	=	Capital contributed/ withdrawn	plus	Revenue	minus	Expenses
£50,150	–	nil	=	£49,000	+	£7,000	–	£5,850
	£50,150					£50,150		

How has the ownership interest changed over the month? The owner contributed £50,000 at the start of the month and has a claim of £50,150 at the end of the month. The ownership interest was increased by earning revenue of £7,000 but reduced by incurring expenses of £5,850 and withdrawing £1,000 for personal use.

6.6 Financial statements of M. Carter, wholesaler

The transactions in Table 6.8 may be summarised in financial statements for use by interested parties. The first user will be the owner, M. Carter, but others such as the Inland Revenue may ask for a copy. If the owner seeks to raise additional finance by borrowing from a bank, the bank manager may ask for a copy of the financial statements.

There are no regulations regarding the format of financial statements for a sole trader, but it is good practice to try to match, as far as possible, the more onerous requirements imposed on limited liability companies. The financial statements presented in this section follow the general formats set out in Chapter 3.

6.6.1 Statement of cash flows

M. Carter, wholesaler
Statement of cash flows for the month of May Year 20xx

	£
Operating activities	
Cash from customers	7,000
Outflow: payment for goods	(6,500)
payment to supplier (R. Busby)	(5,000)
wages	(2,000)
electricity	(100)
Net outflow from operations	(6,600)
Investing activities	
Payment for buildings	(30,000)
Payment for equipment	(6,000)
Net outflow for investing activities	(36,000)
Financing activities	
Capital contributed by owner	50,000
Capital withdrawn as drawings	(1,000)
Net inflow from financing activities	49,000
Increase in cash at bank over period	6,400

Comment. The operating activities caused a drain on cash with a net effect that £6,600 flowed out of the business. A further £36,000 cash flow was used for investing activities. The owner contributed £50,000 at the start of the month but withdrew £1,000 at the end of the month. Cash in the bank increased by £6,400 over the month.

6.6.2 Income statement (profit and loss account)

M. Carter, wholesaler
Income statement (profit and loss account)
for the month of May Year 20xx

	£	£
Sales		7,000
Cost of goods sold		(3,500)
Gross profit		3,500
Other expenses		
Wages	(2,000)	
Electricity	(100)	
Depreciation	(250)	
		(2,350)
Net profit		1,150

Comment. This profit and loss account differs slightly from that presented for the service business in Chapter 5. It has a subtotal for gross profit. The difference between sales and the cost of purchasing or manufacturing the goods sold is regarded as an important indicator of the success of the business in its particular product line. The gross profit is sometimes referred to as the **margin** or **gross margin** and is a piece of information which is much explored by professional investors and analysts.

Making a subtotal for **gross profit** means that the final line needs a different label and so is called **net profit**. The word 'net' means 'after taking everything away', so in this case the net profit is equal to sales minus all expenses of the operations of the business.

Activity 6.4

The business of M. Carter, wholesaler, has made a profit of £1,150 from operations during the month but the cash flow due to operating activities has been negative to the extent of £6,600. Make a comparison of the cash flow from operating activities and the profit from operations. From your comparison, explain how a business can make a profit and yet see its cash drain away. Then make some recommendations about reducing the outflow of cash without affecting profit.

6.6.3 Statement of financial position (balance sheet)

M. Carter, wholesaler
Statement of financial position (balance sheet)
at 31 May Year 20xx

	£
Non-current (fixed) assets	
Buildings	30,000
Equipment	6,000
	36,000
Depreciation	(250)
Depreciated cost of fixed assets	35,750
Current assets	
Inventory (stocks)	8,000
Cash at bank	6,400
	14,400
Net assets	50,150
Ownership interest	
Capital at start	50,000
add: profit	1,150
less: drawings	(1,000)
Total ownership interest	50,150

Comment. There are no liabilities at the end of the month and so the net assets are the same as the total of fixed assets and current assets. That somewhat artificial situation arises from keeping the example fairly simple and manageable. The depreciation has been recorded for the equipment but many businesses would also depreciate buildings. The useful life of a building is much longer than that of equipment and so the depreciation for any single month would be a negligible amount in relation to other information for the period. The amount of £35,750 has been described here as depreciated cost but could also be called the **net book value** or the **written down value**.

The statement of financial position (balance sheet) is a statement of position and, on its own, is of limited usefulness. Companies which publish accounting information will present the previous year's amounts alongside the current year's data so that comparisons may be made. Some companies provide, in addition, five- or ten-year summaries which allow comparison over a longer period.

6.7 Summary

The following sequence summarises the effect on the accounting equation of buying goods and then selling them to customers.

1 Inventory (stock) is acquired for cash.

Assets ↑↓ – Liabilities	equals	Ownership interest

2 When the inventory is sold an expense of cost of goods sold is recorded.

Assets ↓ – Liabilities	equals	**Ownership interest ↓ (expense: cost of goods sold)**

3 At the same time the sale of the inventory increases an asset of cash or trade receivable (debtor) and creates revenue.

Assets ↑ – Liabilities	equals	**Ownership interest ↑ (revenue)**

The following sequence summarises the effect on the accounting equation of buying raw materials, converting them to finished products and then selling these to customers.

1 The asset of raw materials is converted to an asset of work in progress.

Assets ↑↓ – Liabilities	equals	Ownership interest

2 The asset of work in progress becomes an asset of finished goods.

Assets ↑↓ – Liabilities	equals	Ownership interest

3 When the finished goods are sold an expense of cost of goods sold is created.

Assets ↓ – Liabilities	equals	**Ownership interest ↓ (expense: cost of goods sold)**

4 At the same time the sale of the inventory increases an asset of cash or trade receivable (debtor) and creates revenue.

Assets ↑ – Liabilities	equals	Ownership interest ↑ (revenue)

QUESTIONS

The Questions section of each chapter has three types of question. 'Test your understanding' questions to help you review your reading are in the 'A' series of questions. You will find the answers to these by reading and thinking about the material in the book. 'Application' questions to test your ability to apply technical skills are in the 'B' series of questions. Questions requiring you to show skills in problem solving and evaluation are in the 'C' series of questions. A letter [S] indicates that there is a solution at the end of the book.

A   Test your understanding

A6.1 [S] On 1 May the Sea Traders Company purchased 200 spare parts for fishing boats, costing £20 each. On 5 May, 60 of these spare parts were sold to a customer at a price of £25 each. The customer paid in cash immediately.

(a) Calculate the profit made on this transaction.
(b) Explain the impact of each transaction on the accounting equation.

A6.2 [S] Summarise the transactions of question A6.1 in a spreadsheet and show that the totals of the spreadsheet satisfy the accounting equation.

A6.3 [S] The following transactions relate to Toy Manufacturers Company during the month of June.

Date	Business transactions	£
June 1	Purchase toy components from supplier, 100 items at £3 each, paying in cash, and place in raw materials store.	300
June 3	Remove 70 components from raw materials store to meet production department's request (cost £3 each).	210
June 5	Carry out labour work and use production facilities to convert components into finished goods. Additional costs incurred for labour and use of facilities were £2.50 per toy processed.	175
June 6	Finished goods are transferred to finished goods store. Each toy has cost £5.50 in total (70 toys × £5.50 = £385).	385
June 11	50 toys, which cost £5.50 each to manufacture, are delivered to a customer.	275
June 14	The customer pays a price of £8 cash per toy immediately on delivery.	400

(a) Calculate the profit on sale.
(b) Explain the effect of each transaction on the accounting equation.
(c) Prepare a spreadsheet summarising the transactions.

A6.4 [S] The following list of transactions relates to the business of Peter Gold, furniture supplier, during the month of April. Analyse each transaction to show the two aspects of the transaction.

Date	Business transactions and events (nature of the entity: wholesale trader)	Amount £
Apr. 1	The owner pays cash into a bank account for the business.	60,000
Apr. 2	The business acquires buildings for cash.	20,000
Apr. 4	The business acquires equipment for cash.	12,000
Apr. 6	The business purchases an inventory (stock) of goods for cash.	8,500
Apr. 7	The business purchases an inventory (stock) of goods on credit from R. Green and receives an invoice.	7,000
Apr. 11	The business pays R. Green in cash for the goods it acquired on credit.	7,000
Apr. 14	The business pays a gas bill in cash.	400
Apr. 17	Items costing £5,500 are removed from the store because sales have been agreed with customers for this date.	5,500
Apr. 17	The business sells some of the goods removed from store for cash of £6,000.	6,000
Apr. 17	The business sells the remainder of the goods removed from store on credit to P. Weatherall and sends an invoice.	4,200
Apr. 24	P. Weatherall pays in cash for the goods obtained on credit.	4,200
Apr. 28	The owner draws cash from the business for personal use.	2,700
Apr. 29	The business pays wages to employees for the past month, in cash.	2,800
Apr. 30	The business discovers that its equipment has fallen in value over the month.	550

B Application

B6.1 [S]
(a) Using the list of transactions at question A6.4 above, prepare a spreadsheet similar to that presented in Table 6.8.
(b) Show the resulting impact on the accounting equation and demonstrate that it remains in balance.

B6.2 [S]
Using the total from the columns of the spreadsheet of question B6.1(a), prepare for the business in the month of April:

(a) a statement of cash flows;
(b) a statement of financial position (balance sheet); and
(c) a profit and loss account.

There are no questions in the C series for this chapter. These skills are tested in specific situations in Chapters 8 to 12.

Recording transactions in ledger accounts: a trading business

The supplement starts with a reminder of the rules of debit and credit bookkeeping, set out in Table 6.10.

Table 6.10
Rules of debit and credit

	Debit entries in a ledger account	Credit entries in a ledger account
Left-hand side of the equation		
Asset	Increase	Decrease
Right-hand side of the equation		
Liability	Decrease	Increase
Ownership interest	Expense	Revenue
	Capital withdrawn	Capital contributed

Activity 6.5

It might be a useful test of your understanding of the chapter if you try to write down the debit and credit entries before looking at Table 6.11. If you find your answers don't agree with that table then you should go back to the analysis contained in the chapter and think about the various aspects of the accounting equation. Debit and credit entries do nothing more than follow the analysis based on the accounting equation so you should not have a problem if you have followed the analysis.

Table 6.1 presented a short list of transactions for a trading company, relating to the purchase and sale of goods. That list of transactions is repeated in Table 6.11 but showing in the final two columns the ledger accounts in which debit and credit entries would be made. Compare Table 6.11 with Table 6.2 to see that the analysis of transactions and the analysis of debit and credit entries follow similar patterns.

Table 6.4 presented a short list of transactions for a manufacturing company. These are repeated in Table 6.12 with the ledger accounts for debit and credit entries being shown in the final two columns. Again, you should try this first and then check your answer against Table 6.12.

Table 6.11
Transactions of a trading company: debit and credit entries

		£	Debit	Credit
Apr. 1	Purchase goods from manufacturer, 100 items at £2 each, paying in cash, and store in warehouse.	200	Inventory (stock)	Cash
Apr. 4	Remove 70 items from warehouse to meet a customer's request. Those 70 items cost £2 each on 1 April. They are delivered to the customer who accepts the delivery.	140	Cost of goods sold	Inventory (stock)
Apr. 4	The customer pays in cash. Selling price is £2.50 per item.	175	Cash	Revenue

Table 6.12
Transactions of a manufacturing company: debit and credit entries

		£	Debit	Credit
July 1	Purchase raw materials from supplier, 100 trays at £2 each, paying in cash, and place in raw materials store.	200	Raw materials inventory (stock)	Cash
July 3	Remove 80 trays from raw materials store to meet production department's request (cost £2 each).	160	Work in progress	Raw materials inventory (stock)
July 4	Carry out labour work and use production facilities to convert raw materials into finished goods. Additional costs incurred for labour and use of facilities were £1.50 per tray processed.	120	Work in progress	Cash
July 5	Finished goods are transferred to finished goods store. The job has cost £3.50 per tray in total (80 trays × £3.50 = £280).	280	Finished goods	Work in progress
July 10	60 trays, which cost £3.50 each to manufacture, are delivered to a customer.	210	Cost of goods sold	Finished goods
July 10	The customer pays a price of £5 cash per tray immediately on delivery.	300	Cash	Revenue

M. Carter, wholesaler: analysing the debit and credit entries

Table 6.13 takes the information contained in Table 6.8 and analyses it under debit and credit headings showing the ledger accounts in which each entry will be made. Ledger accounts required to record these transactions are:

L1 Cash	L2 Owner	L3 Buildings	L4 Equipment
L5 Inventory (stock) of goods	L6 R. Busby	L7 Electricity	L8 Wages
L9 Cost of goods sold	L10 Sales	L11 R. Welsby	L12 Depreciation

The full ledger account records for the transactions in Table 6.13 are set out. Leona Rees has commented on each one, to show how she interprets them when she is carrying out work of audit or investigation.

L1 Cash

Date	Particulars	Page	Debit	Credit	Balance
			£	£	£
May 1	Owner's capital	L2	50,000		50,000
May 2	Buildings	L3		30,000	20,000
May 4	Equipment	L4		6,000	14,000
May 6	Inventory (stock) of goods	L5		6,500	7,500
May 11	R. Busby	L6		5,000	2,500
May 14	Electricity	L7		100	2,400
May 17	Sales	L10	4,000		6,400
May 24	R. Welsby	L11	3,000		9,400
May 28	Ownership interest drawn out	L2		1,000	8,400
May 30	Wages	L8		2,000	6,400

LEONA's comment: *The amount of £50,000 put into the business at the start is quickly swallowed up by spending cash on buildings, equipment, buying an inventory (stock) of goods and paying the supplier who gave credit. Paying the electricity account £100 took the cash balance down to £2,400 and it was only the sale of some goods which allowed the business to continue. If the sale of goods had not taken place, the owner might have needed to put more cash into the business at that point, or else ask the bank manager to make a loan to the business. With the benefit of hindsight, the owner might have waited a few days before paying R. Busby for goods supplied. It's not a good idea to delay paying the electricity bill in case there is a disconnection, and failing to pay wages usually means the employee does not return. It might have helped cash flow to have bought the buildings and equipment using a loan, but borrowing money has a cost in interest payments and perhaps the owner prefers not to start with a high level of borrowing.*

L2 Ownership interest

Date	Particulars	Page	Debit	Credit	Balance
			£	£	£
May 1	Cash contributed	L1		50,000	(50,000)
May 28	Cash drawn	L1	1,000		(49,000)

Table 6.13

Analysis of transactions for M. Carter, wholesaler

Date	Business transactions	Amount	Debit	Credit
		£		
May 1	The owner provides the business with cash.	50,000	Cash	Owner
May 2	The business acquires buildings for cash.	30,000	Buildings	Cash
May 4	The business acquires equipment for cash.	6,000	Equipment	Cash
May 6	The business purchases an inventory (stock) of goods for cash.	6,500	Inventory (stock)	Cash
May 7	The business purchases an inventory (stock) of goods on credit from R. Busby and receives an invoice.	5,000	Inventory (stock)	R. Busby
May 11	The business pays R. Busby in cash for the goods it acquired on credit.	5,000	R. Busby	Cash
May 14	The business pays an electricity bill in cash.	100	Electricity	Cash
May 17	Items costing £3,500 are removed from the store because sales have been agreed with customers for this date.	3,500	Cost of goods sold	Inventory (stock)
May 17	The business sells goods for cash.	4,000	Cash	Sales
May 17	The business sells goods on credit to R. Welsby and sends an invoice.	3,000	R. Welsby	Sales
May 24	R. Welsby pays in cash for the goods obtained on credit.	3,000	Cash	R. Welsby
May 28	The owner draws cash from the business for personal use.	1,000	Owner	Cash
May 30	The business pays wages to an employee for the past month, in cash.	2,000	Wages	Cash
May 31	The business discovers that its equipment has fallen in value over the month.	250	Depreciation	Equipment

LEONA's comment: *The ownership interest is created when the owner contributes cash or resources to the business. In this case, it was cash. The sole trader in business may withdraw cash for personal use at any time – it is called owner's drawings – but the desirability of that action depends on how useful it is to the owner when compared to how useful it might have been if left in the business. The owner of this business has a claim remaining equal to £49,000 after making the drawing.*

L3 Buildings					
Date	Particulars	Page	Debit	Credit	Balance
			£	£	£
May 2	Cash	L1	30,000		30,000

LEONA's comment: *This ledger account is particularly useful as a reminder that a very valuable asset is owned by the business. Having a record in the ledger account encourages the owner to think about continuing care for the buildings and also to review their value against the amount recorded.*

L4 Equipment

Date	Particulars	Page	Debit	Credit	Balance
			£	£	£
May 4	Cash	L1	6,000		6,000
May 31	Depreciation	L12		250	5,750

LEONA's comment: *The equipment cost £6,000 but is being gradually used up over its life in the business. Depreciation is a way of showing that the original cost of the asset has to be spread over its useful life. If the estimate of depreciation is correct, this ledger account should reduce to nil on the day the equipment ceases to be of use. In reality things usually are not quite so straightforward. (Depreciation of fixed assets is dealt with in more detail in Chapter 8.)*

L5 Inventory (stock) of goods

Date	Particulars	Page	Debit	Credit	Balance
			£	£	£
May 6	Cash	L1	6,500		6,500
May 7	R. Busby	L6	5,000		11,500
May 17	Cost of goods sold	L9		3,500	8,000

LEONA's comment: *The balance on this ledger account at any point in time should equal the cost price of the goods held in the warehouse. So at the end of May, if the owner goes to the warehouse and carries out an inventory count (stock count), there should be goods to a total cost of £8,000. Checking the presence of an inventory (stock) of unsold goods which agrees with the ledger account is an important part of my work as an auditor. If they don't agree, I start to ask a lot of questions.*

L6 R. Busby

Date	Particulars	Page	Debit	Credit	Balance
			£	£	£
May 7	Inventory (stock) of goods	L5		5,000	(5,000)
May 11	Cash	L1	5,000		nil

LEONA's comment: *When the goods were purchased from R. Busby, the supplier, an invoice was received from that supplier showing the amount due. That invoice was used to make the credit entry on May 7 showing that the business had a liability. The liability was extinguished on May 11 by a payment to R. Busby, so at the end of May the business owes that supplier nothing.*

L7 Electricity

Date	Particulars	Page	Debit	Credit	Balance
			£	£	£
May 14	Cash	L1	100		100

LEONA's comment: *This is a very straightforward expense account. The balance on this account will show the total expense of electricity consumed during the period.*

L8 Wages

Date	Particulars	Page	Debit	Credit	Balance
			£	£	£
May 30	Cash	L1	2,000		2,000

LEONA's comment: *Another very straightforward account in which to accumulate all wages expenses.*

L9 Cost of goods sold

Date	Particulars	Page	Debit	Credit	Balance
			£	£	£
May 17	Inventory (stock) of goods	L5	3,500		3,500

LEONA's comment: *This is an expense account showing the cost of the goods sold during the month. The total sales are shown in ledger account L10 as £7,000 and the cost of goods sold is shown here as £3,500, so there is a profit ('margin') of 50% on sales before taking into account the expenses of electricity, wages and depreciation. As an auditor I have considerable interest in the profit margin on sales. It tells me a great deal about the business.*

L10 Sales

Date	Particulars	Page	Debit	Credit	Balance
			£	£	£
May 17	Cash	L1		4,000	(4,000)
May 17	R. Welsby	L11		3,000	(7,000)

LEONA's comment: *This is a revenue account, so credit entries are expected. The balance column shows the total sales of the month were £7,000.*

L11 R. Welsby

Date	Particulars	Page	Debit	Credit	Balance
			£	£	£
May 17	Sales	L10	3,000		3,000
May 24	Cash	L1		3,000	nil

LEONA's comment: *The credit sale to R. Welsby made him a trade receivable (debtor) of the business and so the first entry is a debit entry. When R. Welsby paid this extinguished the debt, by the end of the month R. Welsby owed nothing to the business.*

L12 Depreciation

Date	Particulars	Page	Debit	Credit	Balance
			£	£	£
May 31	Equipment	L4	250		250

LEONA's comment: *This is another expense account showing an item which has decreased the ownership interest through a decrease in the recorded amount of an asset. This is where accounting begins to look slightly complicated because no cash has changed hands. Recording depreciation is the accounting way of expressing caution as to the expected future benefits from the asset. These will be eroded as the asset is used up. Depreciation is a way of acknowledging that erosion.*

Checking the accuracy of double-entry records

In Chapter 5, the process of listing all ledger account balances in a trial balance was explained.

The trial balance for the accounting records of M. Carter, wholesaler, at 31 May year 1, is as shown in Table 6.14. This is a basic list summarising the transactions of the month. If you compare it with the financial statements in the main part of the chapter you will see that all the amounts correspond.

Table 6.14
Trial balance at 31 May for M. Carter, wholesaler

Ledger account title	£	£
L1 Cash	6,400	
L2 Ownership interest		49,000
L3 Buildings	30,000	
L4 Equipment	5,750	
L5 Inventory (stock) of goods	8,000	
L6 R. Busby		nil
L7 Electricity	100	
L8 Wages	2,000	
L9 Cost of goods sold	3,500	
L10 Sales		7,000
L11 R. Welsby	nil	
L12 Depreciation	250	
Totals	56,000	56,000

As was the case in the supplement to Chapter 5, it is rather easier to use the trial balance if it is arranged so that all the statement of financial position (balance sheet) items are together and all the profit and loss account items are together. This is done in Table 6.15. The unshaded lines are not part of the trial balance but take advantage of the various forms of the accounting equation to calculate profit in two different ways. In the first part of the table:

Profit	equals	Assets – Liabilities – Owner's capital at the start and any changes during the period

In the second part of the table:

Profit	equals	Revenue – Expenses

Table 6.15
Rearranging the trial balance into statement of financial position (balance sheet) items and profit and loss account items

Ledger account title	£	£
L3 Buildings	30,000	
L4 Equipment	5,750	
L5 Inventory (stock) of goods	8,000	
L11 R. Welsby	nil	
L1 Cash	6,400	
L6 R. Busby		nil
L2 Ownership interest		49,000
Subtotal X	50,150	49,000
Difference: profit of the month 50,150 – 49,000		1,150
L10 Sales		7,000
L9 Cost of goods sold	3,500	
L7 Electricity	100	
L8 Wages	2,000	
L12 Depreciation	250	
Subtotal Y	5,850	7,000
Difference: profit of the month 7,000 – 5,850	1,150	
Total of ledger balances in each column X + Y	56,000	56,000

The form of trial balance shown in Table 6.15 will be used in later chapters as the starting point for the preparation of financial statements.

S Test your understanding

S6.1 Prepare ledger accounts for the transactions of Peter Gold, furniture supplier, listed in question A6.4.

Part 3

Recognition in financial statements

Chapter 7

Published financial statements

Who we are and what we do

We are the UK's leading home and general merchandise retailer. Argos and Homebase are two of the UK's leading retail brands, with large customer bases across the UK and Ireland. Between them, our retail brands have more than 60 years of market heritage and consumer awareness. Argos was founded in 1973 and Homebase in 1981. They have been shaping modern retailing ever since.

Group four-year summary

Income statement	52-week period to 28 Feb 2009 £m	52-week period to 1 Mar 2008 £m	52-week pro forma to 3 Mar 2007 £m	52-week pro forma to 4 Mar 2006 £m
Argos	4,281.9	4,320.9	4,164.0	3,858.8
Homebase	1,513.2	1,568.5	1,594.2	1,559.0
Financial services	102.3	95.4	93.2	92.5
Sales	5,897.4	5,984.8	5,851.4	5,510.3
Argos	303.6	376.2	325.0	297.0
Homebase	14.9	45.1	53.4	51.4
Financial services	6.1	5.5	5.0	6.1
Central activities	(24.2)	(28.8)	(24.0)	(22.7)
Benchmark operating profit	300.4	398.0	359.4	331.8
Net financing income	29.7	33.3	16.6	9.5
Share of post-tax (loss)/profit of joint ventures and associates	(2.4)	1.6	0.7	(4.2)
Benchmark PBT	327.7	432.9	376.7	337.1

Extracts from notes

Pro forma information

The change in both the year-end and the Group's capital structure on demerger in 2006 resulted in statutory reported results that are non-comparable. To assist with analysis and comparison, certain pro forma information has therefore been provided in respect of the comparative periods to eliminate the distortions of these two impacts on the performance of the Group (p. 119).

Benchmark profit before tax (PBT)

The Group uses the term benchmark PBT as a measure which is not formally recognised under IFRS. Benchmark PBT is defined as profit before amortisation of acquisition intangibles, store impairment and onerous lease charges, exceptional items, costs related to demerger incentive schemes, financing fair value remeasurements, financing impact on retirement benefit balances, the discount unwind on non-benchmark items and taxation. This measure is considered useful in that it provides investors with an alternative means to evaluate the underlying performance of the Group's operations (p. 81).

Source: Home Retail Group, Annual Report 2009; http://www.homeretailgroup.com/home/investors/.

Discussion points

1 Which activities are the main contributors to the profit of the Home Retail Group?
2 What does the four-year summary tell us about the group?

Contents

Learning outcomes

After reading this chapter you should be able to:

- Explain the key international influences that affect accounting practice in the UK.
- Explain the structure of company reporting as set out in the *Framework* and in UK guidance.
- Explain the main contents of (a) the balance sheet, (b) the income statement (profit and loss account) and (c) the cash flow statement as presented by larger companies.
- Define 'parent company' and 'subsidiary company' and explain how a group is structured.
- Explain the main features of group financial statements.
- Explain the nature of, and reason for, other forms of communication beyond the annual report.

7.1 Introduction

It is explained in Chapters 1 and 4 that in the case of sole traders and partnerships the groups of persons who have an interest in the financial statements are limited to the owners themselves, HM Revenue and Customs and organisations such as banks which are asked to provide finance for the company. For limited liability companies the list of potential users widens and the access to internal information becomes restricted. Even the owners of a limited liability company, called the equity holders (shareholders) are not permitted access to the day-to-day records of the company and are treated as being outsiders of (external to) the company they own. The quality and amount of information communicated to these users who are external to the company becomes a matter which is too important to be left entirely to the discretion of the directors running the company.

Chapter 4 outlined the various regulatory authorities which exist to establish the quality and quantity of information to be published by limited liability companies. There are over one million limited liability companies in the UK, although only a few thousand are listed on the Stock Exchange and of these only around 500 have their shares bought and sold regularly. The number of major listed companies, and their importance to the economy in terms of the funds invested in them, means it is appropriate to take them as the benchmark for current practice in external reporting. The practices applied by larger limited liability companies set a good example as a starting point for smaller ones and for organisations that are not limited liability companies, such as charitable trusts or public sector bodies.

In this chapter, and in Chapters 8 to 12, there is mention only of **limited liability companies** because the aim of this book is to provide an understanding of the accounting information published by companies. The more general word **enterprise** (meaning a business activity or commercial project) could be substituted throughout for limited liability company. Most of what is said in these chapters applies to all enterprises because the principles and practice described here have a wider application beyond companies, although modifications may be necessary when the needs of the users and the purposes of the enterprise are different from those relevant to a limited liability company.

7.2 International influences

Chapter 3 explained that, since January 2005, two different accounting systems have existed for companies in the UK, depending on the type of company. For the group financial statements of a listed company the accounting system set out by the International Accounting Standards Board (IASB) must be applied. All other companies, and the separate companies in the group, may choose to follow IASB standards but there is no requirement to do so. Companies that do not choose to follow the international accounting standards must continue to follow the rules of UK company law and the UK ASB's accounting standards.

For many years there has been a strong international influence on and from UK accounting practice so the change to international accounting standards in 2005 did not bring many surprises. The UK accounting standard-setting body was a founder member of the International Accounting Standards Committee (IASC), set up in 1973, and has been closely involved in its work since that date. In 2001, with an organisational change, the IASC became the IASB but the close similarity between international accounting standards and UK accounting standards continued. The UK ASB has worked continuously towards matching UK standards to IFRS.

Since 1980 the law regulating financial reporting in the UK (now contained in the Companies Act 2006 and related legislation) has reflected its membership of the European Union (EU) and the work of regulators across the EU to harmonise aspects of financial reporting. From 2005 the law governing financial reporting in the UK has been split into two routes. One route is the rule of UK company law influenced by the EU. The other route is the IASB system of accounting as endorsed by the EU.

7.2.1 The European Union

The UK is a member state of the EU and is required to develop its laws so as to harmonise with those of other member states of the EU. There are two procedures by which the EU influences the accounting practices of UK-based companies.

1 The European Commission, which is the permanent secretariat and staff of the EU, issues a Regulation which overrides national laws and applies to all companies specified in the Regulation.
2 The European Commission issues Directives which are incorporated in national laws of member states.

The IAS Regulation

In 2002 the European Commission issued the first IAS Regulation. The IAS Regulation is a direct instruction to companies in all member states. It required that, by 2005, all **listed** companies in the European Union would use IASB standards in preparing their **group** financial statements. This was intended to cause convergence ('bringing together') of accounting practices, and so improve the movement of capital across the stock markets of the EU. The Commission, which prepares and implements the legislation of the European Parliament, has established procedures for giving European approval to each of the IASB Standards. It takes advice from the European Financial Reporting Advisory Group (EFRAG), a team of experts that includes a UK member. The final recommendation to the Commission is made by the Accounting Regulatory Committee, which includes representatives of all member states. The process of approving IASB standards for use in the EU is called **endorsement**.

Harmonisation through Directives

For many aspects of regulation within the EU, the process of harmonisation starts when a **Directive** is issued by the European Commission, setting out the basic rules which should be followed in each member state's national laws. For limited liability companies in the UK, two such Directives have been particularly important. These are the Fourth Directive and the Seventh Directive. Together they specify the content of the Companies Act 2006. One important aspect of Directives is that they specify **formats** for the financial statements (see section 7.3.2) which ensure that all companies produce documents that are similar in appearance and present items in a systematic order. The idea of having standard formats was not a familiar concept in the UK before the Directives became effective in the 1980s, but became accepted during the 1980s and 1990. Having standard formats makes it easier for the reader to find the starting point in reading the financial statements. In later chapters we will see that having standard formats does not solve all the problems of comparability and understandability. For companies that do not apply IFRS these formats continue to apply. For companies using the IFRS there is potentially more flexibility of presentation.

Activity 7.1   *From your general interest reading, or perhaps from your study of law, make a list of other areas of activity in which the UK law is harmonised with that of other countries in the EU.*

7.2.2   IASB

The International Accounting Standards Board (IASB) is an independent body that sets International Financial Reporting Standards (IFRS). It was formed in 2000 as the successor to the International Accounting Standard Committee (IASC) which had been setting International Accounting Standards (IAS) since 1973. These IAS have been adopted by the IASB and will gradually be revised as IFRS. In the meantime the description 'IFRS' is used as a collective name for all forms of international accounting standard, whatever the precise title of the standard.

The IASB's objective is to bring about convergence of national accounting standards and international accounting standards to high-quality solutions. This will help participants in the world's capital markets and other users to make economic decisions.

There are many similarities between the UK accounting standards and the IASB Standards. There are also some differences where the UK standard-setter believes a particular approach is justified, or where historical developments have a strong influence. The UK Accounting Standards Board works on projects with the IASB, as do other countries' standard-setting bodies, all seeking to develop international convergence.

7.3 Accounting framework

Chapter 1, section 1.3 has explained that the IASB has developed a *Framework* of principles and definitions that are used in setting accounting standards. The UK ASB has also issued a *Statement of Principles*. There are many similarities between these documents because the UK ASB benefited from the earlier work of the IASB. The explanations in this chapter draw mainly on the IASB *Framework*, adding more information where this is needed to understand the separate ideas of the UK ASB.

7.3.1   The primary financial statements

The IASB requires a complete set of financial statements to comprise:[1]

- a statement of financial position (balance sheet) at the end of the period
- an income statement (showing the profit or loss for the period), as part of a larger statement of comprehensive income (see Chapter 12)
- a statement of changes in equity for the period
- a statement of cash flows, and
- notes that summarise the accounting policies and give other explanations.

The IASB also gives general guidance on how to prepare and present the financial statements but stops short of giving precise rules on presentation. There is discretion for companies to present information in a way that best suits the company and those who are likely to use the information.

The UK ASB requires the same four primary statements but with some differences of names. The income statement is called a profit and loss account. The statement of changes in equity is replaced by two items: a statement of total recognised gains and losses and a note of changes in share capital and reserves (explained in Chapter 12 of this book). The Companies Act 2006 sets out formats of financial statements (see section 7.3.2) which give detailed rules on the sequence of information. These formats apply to companies that do *not* follow the IFRS.

A comparison of the primary statements in the IASB and UK ASB systems is shown in Table 7.1.

Table 7.1
Primary statements – IASB and UK ASB compared

IASB system	UK ASB and company law
Statement of financial position	Balance sheet
Income statement	Profit and loss account
Statement of cash flows	Cash flow statement
Statement of changes in equity	
● Statement of recognised income and expense *plus*	● Statement of total recognised gains and losses *plus*
● *Transactions with equity holders (e.g. dividends paid) *plus*	● Reconciliation of movements in shareholders' funds[†]
● *Changes in the retained earnings (accumulated profit or loss) *plus*	
● *Changes in each class of equity and each reserve	

* May be shown on the face of the statement of changes in equity or in notes.
[†] Shown with primary statements or in notes.

The IASB's *Framework* explains that the objective of financial statements is to provide information about the financial position, performance and changes in financial position of an entity that is useful to a wide range of users in making economic decisions.[2]

Financial position

Information about financial position is reported primarily in a statement of financial position (balance sheet). It reports economic resources controlled by the company, its financial structure, its liquidity and its solvency. Information about economic resources held by the entity allows users of the information to estimate future cash flows from those resources. Information about financial structure is useful in predicting future needs for borrowing or for raising new equity finance. Liquidity refers to the availability of cash in the near future after taking account of commitments in the same period. Solvency refers to the availability of cash to meet financial commitments as they fall due. The balance sheet is not a statement of the value of the company because there are limitations in the measurement process and also because not all items which are of value to the company are included in the balance sheet.

Performance

Information about the performance of an entity is primarily provided in an income statement (profit and loss account). Performance is indicated by profitability and changes in profitability. Information about performance is useful in evaluating how well the resources of the entity have been used to generate profit. Statements of financial performance are seen as providing an account of the stewardship of management and also as helping readers to check the accuracy of previous estimates they may have made about the expected outcome of the period.

Changes in financial position

Information about changes in financial position of an entity is useful to help assess the operating, investing and financing activities of the period. It is usually found in a statement of cash flows.

7.3.2   Formats for financial statements

The word **format** means 'shape'. A format for a financial statement sets out the shape of the document. It sets out the items to be reported and the sequence in which they are reported. Section 7.2.1 explains that EU Directives have guided the formats used by UK companies for many years, as set out in company law and UK accounting standards. Since 2005 the group financial statements of listed companies have followed the IASB system of reporting. The IASB system does not specify formats. It does provide some lists of items to be included in financial statements but there is no requirement to present these items in any particular sequence. This means that companies have choices in the shape of their financial statements. This book describes the shapes of financial statements that you are likely to see in company reports but you will need to be flexible in understanding that companies do have choices.

7.3.3   Categories of financial information

The primary financial statements are the core of a much wider range of sources of financial information which users may obtain about a company. The relative position of the primary financial statements is shown in Figure 7.1.

Activity 7.2

Write down three items of accompanying information about a company which you feel would be useful in the annual report of a company. Exchange lists with other members of the group and establish the similarities and differences across the group. To what extent would one general set of financial statements with notes and accompanying information meet your collective expectations?

7.3.4   Notes and accompanying information

The annual report contains the primary financial statements, notes to the financial statements and accompanying information.

Notes to the financial statements

Notes to the financial statements are essential in amplifying and explaining the primary financial statements. They may contain additional information that is relevant to the needs of users about the items in the balance sheet, income statement and cash flow statement. The notes and the primary financial statements form an integrated whole. The wording of the notes is as important as the numbers if ambiguity is to be avoided.

For companies that do not follow the IFRS, many of these notes are required by regulations such as the Companies Act 2006 or relevant UK accounting standards. The ASB also warns that notes to the accounts are not the place to correct or justify a misrepresentation in the primary financial statements. That potential misrepresentation should be dealt with by amending the financial statement to eliminate the problem.

Accompanying information

Accompanying information is any other information additional to the primary financial statements and notes. It could be information which is highly relevant but of lower reliability than the financial statements and notes. It could be information which will only interest a particular group of users. Such accompanying information may not be subject to the audit process which is compulsory for the primary financial statements and notes. The IASB does not give a view on the accompanying information beyond the notes to the financial statements. The view of the UK ASB is that such accompanying information may be very important, one example being the Operating and Financial Review now presented by large companies as management's explanation of

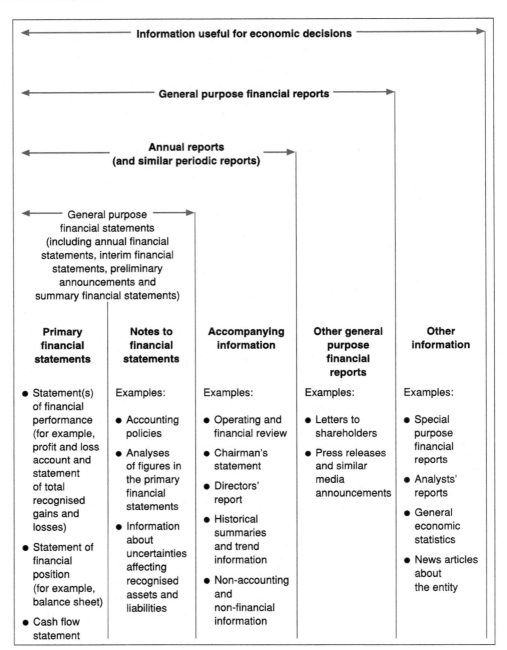

Figure 7.1
Categories of financial information

Source: ASB (1999) *Statement of Principles for Financial Reporting*, Accounting Standards Board, Introduction. Reproduced with the permission of the Accounting Standards Board.

the information given in the financial statements (see Chapter 14). Accompanying information may include disclosures of a voluntary or evolutionary nature.

Many annual reports include highlights pages showing amounts, ratios and other calculations that distil a great deal of information into a few key items. The UK ASB agrees that highlights can be useful but warns against focusing attention exclusively on one or two measures. You cannot read about financial statements for long without meeting the phrase 'the bottom line'. That refers to the line in the income statement (profit and loss account) which reports the profit attributable to the equity holders (ordinary shareholders). It may be described as **earnings** for equity holders (ordinary shareholders). When this amount is divided by the number of shares which have been issued by the company it becomes the **earnings per share**. Investors, financial journalists and brokers' analysts have traditionally paid great attention to the earnings per share. The standard-setters (both the IASB and the UK ASB) would prefer to discourage this narrow focus and encourage instead a 'building block' approach where the company produces information in such a way that the user of the annual statement can create useful arrangements and combinations of information.

Companies also produce accompanying information for specialised needs. Regulated industries (such as gas, electricity, telecommunications and water) provide supplementary information about their regulated activities. Some companies give non-financial performance indicators (such as speed of answering customer enquiries, or level of customer satisfaction). Graphs, charts, diagrams and even photographs are all ways of providing accompanying information which adds to users' understanding of a document.

7.4 Statement of financial position (balance sheet)

7.4.1 What items must be reported?

Companies that follow the IASB system of accounting in presenting a statement of financial position (balance sheet) have choices in the way they present their balance sheet. There is no particular **format** required[3] but some items are listed in the relevant standard as a minimum set of disclosures (see Supplement 7.1 to this chapter). Companies choose the form of layout for items in the balance sheet.

Companies that do not follow the IASB system of accounting must comply with the Companies Act 2006 and the UK accounting standards. The Companies Act 2006 contains more detail of the format that must be used. The details are set out in Supplement 7.2 to this chapter.

7.4.2 What formats are used?

Companies applying the IASB system do not have to follow any particular format but it is likely that any balance sheet you see will resemble one of the three formats described in this section because they will retain some of the traditions of the UK system that has existed for more than 20 years.

Companies that do not apply the IASB system of accounting must follow the requirements of the Companies Act 2006 and the standards of the UK ASB. The Companies Act 2006 permits two different formats of statement of financial position (balance sheet), each conforming to the accounting equation but permitting different layouts on the page. The word format means 'shape' so it covers the items to be reported and the sequence in which they are reported. The most commonly used format in the UK is Format 1, which uses the accounting equation to create a vertical format as shown in Exhibit 7.1.

Exhibit 7.1
Vertical format of statement of financial position (balance sheet)

Assets
minus
Liabilities
equals
Ownership interest

Format 2 uses the accounting equation to create a horizontal format as shown in Exhibit 7.2.

Exhibit 7.2
Horizontal form of statement of financial position (balance sheet)

		Ownership interest
Assets	equal	plus
		Liabilities

Format 2 is observed more commonly in the financial statements of continental European countries where the horizontal format is preferred.

Some companies use a variation on Format 2 which stacks the assets on top and the ownership interest and liabilities underneath (see Exhibit 7.3).

Exhibit 7.3
Assets above, ownership interest plus liabilities below

Assets
equals
Ownership interest
plus
Liabilities

When you read a statement of financial position (balance sheet) you should first of all look at the overall structure to see where the main sections of **assets**, **liabilities** and **ownership interest** are placed. Then you can begin to look at each section in more detail. The process is something like seeing a landscape painting for the first time. You stand back to look at the overall impression of the landscape and the main features first. Then you step forward to look at some of the details in different parts of the painting. Finally if you are very enthusiastic you move in closer and start to examine the details of the texture, brush strokes and shading.

7.4.3 Descriptions in the statement of financial position (balance sheet)

You will see from the Supplement that the statement of financial position (balance sheet) formats contain some words you will recognise but also many new words. Non-current assets (fixed assets) are separated from current assets. Current liabilities (due in less than one year) are separated from non-current liabilities (due in more than one year). Some of the items under the Companies Act headings A to J may look rather strange at this stage (particularly A, D, I and J). Do not worry about that at present. If they are appropriate to first-level study they will be explained at some point in this text. If they are not explained, then they are relatively rare in occurrence and the time taken to explain them will outweigh the benefits you would gain from understanding.

The ownership interest is shown at heading K as **capital** and **reserves**. The word **capital** here means the claim which owners have because of the number of shares they own, and the word **reserves** means the claim which owners have because the company has created new wealth for them over the years. Various labels are used to describe the nature of that new wealth and how it is created. Some of the new wealth is created because new investors pay more than a specified amount for the shares. Paying more is referred to as paying a **premium**, so this kind of ownership interest is labelled the **share premium**. Some of the new wealth is created because the fixed assets held by the company increase in value and that new valuation is recorded. This kind of ownership interest is labelled the **revaluation reserve**. Some of the new wealth is created by making profits through operating activities. This kind of ownership interest is labelled the **retained earnings** reserve.

7.4.4   Subtotals

Subtotals in financial statements help to group information within financial statements into useful sections. There are no rules about the placing of subtotals in either the IASB lists or the Companies Acts formats. Companies have to decide for themselves where to place subtotals and totals in presentation of the list of items in the format. You will need to be flexible in reading statements of financial position (balance sheets) and using the subtotals provided.

Activity 7.3

Read again the format for the balance sheet. How many of the items there came as no surprise to you? How many looked unfamiliar? Make a note of these and check that you find out about them in later chapters.

7.4.5   Illustration

The remainder of this chapter explores the published financial statements of a hypothetical listed company, Safe and Sure plc, which operates in a service industry. There is a parent company called Safe and Sure plc and it owns some subsidiary companies that together make up a 'group'. Buildings and vehicles are the main fixed assets. The Safe and Sure Group sells recycling and cleaning services to customers based on the high reputation of the company's products and name. The Safe and Sure Group follows the IASB system of accounting and has chosen a format that is similar to Format 1 (see Exhibit 7.1).

The following illustration sets out the balance sheet of the Safe and Sure Group plc for Year 7 with comparative amounts alongside for the previous year. The balance sheet is followed by a comment on matters of particular interest.

Safe and Sure Group plc Consolidated statement of finacial position (balance sheet) at 31 December

	Notes	Year 7 £m	Year 6 £m
Non-current assets			
Property, plant and equipment	1	137.5	121.9
Intangible assets	2	260.3	237.6
Investments	3	2.8	2.0
Taxation recoverable	4	5.9	4.9
		406.5	366.4
Current assets			
Inventories (stocks)	5	26.6	24.3
Amounts receivable (debtors)	6	146.9	134.7
Six-month deposits		2.0	–
Cash and cash equivalents		105.3	90.5
		280.8	249.5

	Notes	Year 7 £m	Year 6 £m
Current liabilities			
Amounts payable (creditors)	7	(159.8)	(157.5)
Bank overdraft	8	(40.1)	(62.6)
		(199.9)	(220.1)
Net current assets		80.9	29.4
Total assets less current liabilities		487.4	395.8
Non-current liabilities			
Amounts payable (creditors)	9	(2.7)	(2.6)
Bank and other borrowings	10	(0.2)	(0.6)
Provisions	11	(20.2)	(22.2)
Net assets		464.3	370.4
Capital and reserves (ownership interest)			
Called-up share capital	12	19.6	19.5
Share premium account	13	8.5	5.5
Revaluation reserve	14	4.6	4.6
Retained earnings	15	431.6	340.8
Equity holders' funds		464.3	370.4

7.4.6 Discussion

The first feature to note is the title, *Consolidated statement of financial position (balance sheet)*. Companies listed on the Stock Exchange are generally using one name as an umbrella for a group of several companies linked together under one parent. It is thought to be more useful to the shareholders of the parent company to see all the assets controlled by that company within the single financial statement. The word **control** is important here. The parent company owns the other companies. They each own their separate assets. The parent company controls the use of those assets indirectly by controlling the companies it owns. The statement of financial position (balance sheet) as presented here represents a group where the parent company owns 100% of all the other companies in the group (called its subsidiary undertakings). A similar consolidated balance sheet would be produced if the parent owned less than 100%, provided it had the same element of control. The only additional item would be a **minority interest** in the ownership claim to indicate the proportion of the equity interest in subsidiaries held by shareholders outside the group. The minority interest is also called a **non-controlling interest**.

The second feature to note in the statement of financial position (balance sheet) as presented is that there are two columns of figures. Companies are required to present the figures for the previous year, in order to provide a basis for comparison.

The statement of financial position (balance sheet) follows the accounting equation and this company has helpfully set out in the left-hand margin the main elements of the equation. There are some phrases in the statement of financial position (balance sheet) which you are meeting for the first time but you should not feel intimated by new titles when you can work out what they mean if you think about the ordinary meanings of words.

Intangible assets means assets which may not be touched – they have no physical existence. Examples are the goodwill of a business or the reputation of a branded product.

Tangible non-current (fixed) assets is another phrase which you are seeing here for the first time, but again you can work out the meaning. You know from Chapter 2 what **non-current assets** are and you know that tangible means 'something that may be touched'. So you would not be surprised to find that note 2 to the accounts gives more detail on land and buildings, plant, equipment, vehicles and office equipment.

Investments here means shares in other companies which are not subsidiary undertakings within the group.

The *taxation recoverable* is an amount of tax which has been paid already but may be reclaimed in 18 months' time because of events that have occurred to reduce the tax due, after the tax was paid.

Current assets comprise inventories (stocks), receivables (debtors) and cash. They are set out in order of increasing liquidity. Inventories (stocks) are the least readily convertible into cash while amounts receivable (debtors) are closer to collection of cash. Cash itself is the most liquid asset. The notes to the accounts contain more detailed information. Take as an example note 4, relating to inventories (stocks). It appears as follows:

Note 4	Year 7	Year 6
Inventories (stocks)	£m	£m
Raw materials	6.2	5.4
Work in progress	1.9	1.0
Finished products	18.5	17.9
	26.6	24.3

The notes are shown in full in Appendix I at the end of this book. There is a note relating to amounts receivable (debtors), mainly relating to trade receivables (trade debtors). Amounts payable (creditors) has a similar type of note to the balance sheet.

The *non-current liabilities* include long-term borrowings, which are quite low in amount compared with those of many other companies of this size. The provisions relate to future obligations caused by: treating a contaminated site; reorganisation of part of the business; and future tax payable.

That stage of the statement of financial position (balance sheet) concludes with the net assets, defined as all assets minus all liabilities. Drawing a total at this point is not a requirement of any format, but is used by many companies as the point which creates a pause in the balance sheet before moving on to the ownership interest.

For a company the *ownership interest* is described as *capital and reserves*. The ownership interest in a company is specified in company law as comprising the claim created through the shares owned by the various equity holders (shareholders) and the claim representing additional reserves of wealth accumulated since the company began. That wealth is accumulated by making profits year after year. The claim is reduced when the owners take dividends from the company. (Further information on the reporting of share capital, reserves and dividends is contained in Chapter 12.)

The ownership interest is the part of the statement of financial position (balance sheet) which causes greatest confusion to most readers. It is purely a statement of a legal claim on the assets after all liabilities have been satisfied. The word *reserves* has no other significance. There is nothing to see, touch, count or hold. To add to the potential confusion, company law delights in finding names for various different kinds of ownership interest. If you are the kind of person who takes a broad-brush view of life you will not worry too much about share premium account, revaluation reserve and retained earnings. They are all part of accounting terminology which becomes important to a company lawyer when there is a dispute over how much dividend may be declared, but are less important to the investor who says 'How much is my total claim?'

7.5 Income statement (profit and loss account)

7.5.1 What items must be reported?

Companies that follow the IASB system of accounting in presenting an income statement must report the profit or loss for the period. There is no particular format required[4] but some items are listed in the relevant standard as a minimum set of disclosures (see Supplement 7.4 to this chapter). Companies choose the form of layout of the items in the income statement.

Companies that do not follow the IASB system of accounting must comply with the Companies Act 2006 and the UK accounting standards. The Companies Act 2006 contains more detail of the items to be reported and the format that must be used. The details are set out in Supplement 7.3 to this chapter.

7.5.2 What formats are used?

Companies applying the IASB system do not have to follow any particular format but it is likely that any income statement (profit and loss account) you see will resemble one of the formats described in this section because they will retain some of the traditions of the UK system that has existed for more than 20 years.

Companies that do not apply the IASB system of accounting must follow the requirements of the Companies Act 2006 and the standards of the UK ASB. The Companies Act 2006 permits four different formats of profit and loss account but the version most frequently observed in the UK is format 1 (see supplement 7.4).

7.5.3 Illustration

The published income statements (profit and loss accounts) of most major companies are very similar to the illustration set out here for Safe and Sure plc.

Safe and Sure Group plc
Consolidated income statement (profit and loss account)
for the years ended 31 December

	Notes	Year 7 £m	Year 6 £m
Continuing operations			
Revenue	16	714.6	589.3
Cost of sales	16	(491.0)	(406.3)
Gross profit		223.6	183.0
Distribution costs		(2.2)	(2.5)
Administrative expenses	17	(26.2)	(26.5)
Profit from operations		195.2	154.0
Interest receivable (net)	18	2.3	3.0
Profit before tax	19	197.5	157.0
Tax	20	(62.2)	(52.4)
Profit for the period from continuing operations		135.3	104.6
Discontinued operations			
Loss for the period from discontinued operations	21	(20.5)	(10.0)
Profit for the period attributable to equity holders		114.8	94.6
Earnings per share	22	11.74	9.71

7.5.4 Discussion

The first point to note is the heading. This is a consolidated income statement (profit and loss account) bringing together the results of the activities of all the companies in the group during the year. The individual companies will also produce their own separate profit and loss accounts and these are added together to produce the consolidated picture. Where one company in the group sells items to another in the group, the sale and purchase are matched against each other on consolidation so that the results reported reflect only sales to persons outside the group.

The second point to note is that the income statement (profit and loss account) as presented by the company is more informative than the lists contained in Supplements 7.3 or 7.4 might suggest. That is partly because the company has used subtotals to break up the flow and make it digestible for the reader. One very common subtotal is the **gross profit** calculated as revenue minus the cost of the goods or services sold as revenue.

Starting at the top of the income statement we see that the word *revenue* is used to describe the sales of goods or services. **Revenue** is sometimes described as **turnover** or **sales**. Revenue (turnover) represents sales to third parties outside the group of companies. The **cost of sales** is the total of the costs of materials, labour and overheads which relate closely to earning the sales. The gross profit is sometimes referred to as the **gross margin** and is monitored closely by those who use the financial statements to make a judgement on the operations of the company. Within any industry the gross profit as a percentage of revenue (or turnover, or sales) is expected to be within known limits. If that percentage is low then the company is either underpricing its goods or else taking the market price but failing to control costs. If the percentage is high, then the company is perhaps a market leader which can command higher prices for its output because of its high reputation. However, it might also be seen by customers and competitors as charging too much for its goods or services.

The next item in the income statement (profit and loss account) is *distribution costs,* which would include the costs of delivering goods to customers. For this company the distribution costs are low because it provides services by contract and does not carry out much distribution work. For many users the trends in an amount are more interesting than the actual amount. They might ask why the amount has decreased. On the other hand, it is not a particularly significant component of the overall picture and the users might show little interest. They would pay more attention to the *administrative expenses,* a collective term for all those costs which have to be incurred in order to keep the business running but which are less closely related to the direct activity of creating revenue (making sales). The directors' salaries, head office costs and general maintenance of buildings and facilities are the kinds of details brought together under this heading. Directors' salaries are always a matter of some fascination and companies are expected to give considerable detail in the notes to the accounts about how much each director is paid and what other benefits are provided.

The *profit from operations* is the end of the first stage of the income statement (profit and loss account), where the story of the business operations is complete. The rest of the profit and loss account is concerned with the cost of financing the company.

Interest is paid on loans and received on investments, usually brought together in one net amount which shows, in this case, an excess of interest receivable over interest payable. That suggests a fairly cash-rich company with relatively low levels of borrowing. Next comes the *corporation tax*, which all companies must pay as a percentage of the profit before tax. The percentage is a standard percentage applied to the profit calculated according to the tax rules. Because the tax rules are not identical to the accounting rules, the percentage appears to vary when the reader looks at the profit and loss account. Helpful companies will explain the tax charge in the Operating and Financial Review, as well as providing more detailed notes to the accounts on the tax charge.

That information ends with the profit for the period from continuing operations. Investors or analysts who want to make a forecast of future profits may decide to use this figure as a starting point because the activities will continue. Separately below this line the group shows the results in this period of operations that have been discontinued. Usually operations are discontinued because they are performing poorly so it is no great surprise to see a loss here. The loss is part of the performance of the period but investors can see that the bad news of this operation will not continue in future. Finally the equity holders (ordinary shareholders) see the profit for the period attributable to them.

They do not see here any mention of a reward in the form of a dividend which returns to them some of the wealth created by the company during the period. That information will appear in a statement of changes in equity which is explained in Chapter 12.

7.6 Statement of cash flows

The presentation of cash flow statements by companies is guided by IAS 7, *Statement of Cash Flows*. (There is a UK standard, FRS 1, which sets out a different form of cash flow statement,[5] but in this chapter the version required by IAS 7 is used because it is more likely that you will find this one in published financial statements.)

The benefits of cash flow information are explained in IAS 7.[6] A statement of cash flows, when used in conjunction with the rest of the financial statements, provides users with information on solvency and liquidity. It shows how cash is generated in the business and helps users to understand how much flexibility is available to adapt to changing circumstances and opportunities.

7.6.1 What items must be reported?

The statement of cash flows presents three classifications of cash flows.[7] These are:

- operating activities
- investing activities
- financing activities.

Definitions

Operating activities are the principal revenue-producing activities of the entity and other activities that are not investing or financing activities.

Investing activities are the acquisition and disposal of long-term assets and other investments not included in cash equivalents.

Financing activities are activities that result in changes in the size and composition of the contributed equity and borrowings of the entity.

Safe and Sure uses these classifications, as shown in the next section. We need two more definitions of terms in the cash flow statement. These are **cash** and **cash equivalents**.

Definitions

Cash comprises cash on hand and demand deposits.

Cash equivalents are short-term, highly liquid investments that are readily convertible to known amounts of cash and which are subject to an insignificant risk of changes in value.[8]

7.6.2 Illustration

Safe and Sure Group plc
Consolidated statement of cash flows for the years ended 31 December

	Notes	Year 7 £m	Year 6 £m
Cash flows from operating activities			
Cash generated from operations	23	196.7	163.5
Interest paid		(3.1)	(2.4)
UK corporation tax paid		(20.1)	(18.3)
Overseas tax paid		(30.5)	(26.5)
Net cash from operating activities		143.0	116.3

Cash flows from investing activities

Purchase of tangible non-current assets		(60.0)	(47.5)
Sale of tangible non-current assets		12.0	10.1
Purchase of companies and businesses	25	(27.7)	(90.1)
Sale of a company		3.1	–
Movement in short-term deposits		(30.7)	36.3
Interest received		5.0	5.9
Net cash used in investing activities		(98.3)	(85.3)
Cash flows from financing activities			
Issue of ordinary share capital	27	3.1	2.0
Dividends paid to equity holders		(29.5)	(24.4)
Net loan movement (excluding overdraft)	26	16.2	(24.0)
Net cash used in financing activities		(10.2)	(46.4)
Net increase/(decrease) in cash and cash equivalents*		34.5	(15.4)
Cash and cash equivalents at the beginning of the year		27.9	45.3
Exchange adjustments		2.8	(2.0)
Cash and cash equivalents at the end of the year	29	65.2	27.9

* Cash on demand and deposits of maturity less than three months, net of overdrafts.

Note 23 Cash flow from operating activities
Reconciliation of operating profit to net cash flow from operating activities

	Year 7 £m	Year 6 £m
Profit before tax from continuing operations	195.2	154.0
Loss from discontinued operations	(20.5)	(10.0)
Profit from operations	174.7	144.0
Depreciation charge	33.2	30.1
Increase in inventories (stocks)*	(1.9)	(1.1)
Increase in trade receivables (debtors)*	(7.4)	(5.3)
Decrease in trade payables (creditors)*	(0.4)	(3.6)
Net cash inflow from continuing activities	198.2	164.1
Cash outflow in respect of discontinued item	(1.5)	(0.6)
Net cash inflow from operating activities	196.7	163.5

* *Note*: It is not possible to reconcile these figures with the balance sheet information because of the effect of acquisitions during the year.

7.6.3 Discussion

The first line of the statement of cash flows is *cash flows from operating activities*, highlighted by the company as an important feature. Note 23 to the accounts explains why this is not the same as operating profit. When a company makes a profit it earns revenue which is greater than the expenses. Some of the revenue is collected as cash but some will be collected later when the credit customers pay. When expenses are incurred, some are paid for immediately but others relate to goods and services taken from suppliers. Note 23 to the accounts is set out above and shows that cash is generated by profits but is used when inventory (stock) levels increase and when trade receivables (debtors) increase. Allowing inventories (stocks) to increase will use up cash because more has to be paid for them. Allowing trade receivables (debtors) to increase means that credit customers are not paying the cash so fast and therefore the cash is not coming in. That will diminish cash flow. Allowing trade payables (creditors) to decrease is a further way of diminishing cash flow because it means that suppliers are being paid faster.

There is one other line in note 23 which gives pause for thought. That is the fourth line, *depreciation charge*. **Depreciation** is a measure of how much a non-current (fixed) asset has been used up. It is an amount which is deducted from profits as a measure of using up the cost of the non-current (fixed) asset in the accounting period. It does not of itself generate cash, but it stops the owners removing so much cash from the company that they are unable to replace a non-current (fixed asset) at the end of its useful life. Since it is not a cash item it has to be added back to the reported profit. By way of illustration, suppose a company pays £100 for goods and sells them for £150. It has generated £50 cash. In the profit and loss account £10 is deducted for depreciation, so the reported profit becomes £40. The reconciliation of profit to cash flow from operations will be written as:

	£
	£
Operating profit	40
add Depreciation	10
Cash inflow from operating activities	50

There is more about depreciation in Chapter 8 and more about cash flow in Chapter 14.

The cash generated from operations is used first of all to pay interest on loans, as a reward to lenders, and to pay taxation to the government. Deducting these items leaves the net cash from operating activities. This is the amount left over for long-term investment.

In the next section we find the cash flows from investing activities. The purchase of tangible non-current (fixed) assets is also called **capital expenditure**. Cash is paid to purchase new businesses and cash is received from selling companies or businesses no longer required. Safe and Sure has put some of its cash into short-term deposits to earn interest. In Year 6, Safe and Sure reduced the amount on short-term deposit, converting it back to cash that was available for spending, but in Year 7 it increased the amount on deposit, reducing the amount of cash available to spend in other ways. The final item in this investment section is interest received which is the reward for investment.

The third section shows the cash flows from financing activities. For some companies the cash inflow from operating activities may be insufficient to cover all the investment requirements for capital expenditure and acquisitions, so more finance has to be raised from external sources. Safe and Sure is not in such a difficult position because the cash generated from operations is greater than the cash paid out for investing activities. However, there is one further important outflow in the dividends paid to equity holders (shareholders). Dividend is the reward to equity holders (shareholders) for investing in the company. For the particular cash flow statement presented here, the broad story is that the company generated sufficient cash from its operations to cover loan interest, to pay the tax due, meet its investment needs and pay dividends. Despite that positive amount, the company has increased its loans by £16.2m and marginally increased its share capital by £3.1m, so that a total of £34.5m has been added to cash and deposits repayable on demand.

The company explained its cash flow management as follows in the Operating and Financial Review: 'The group's businesses are structured to use as little fixed and working capital as is consistent with the profit and earnings growth objective in order to produce a high cash flow.'

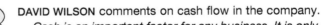

DAVID WILSON comments on cash flow in the company.

Cash is an important factor for any business. It is only one of the resources available but it is the key to survival.

What I'm basically looking for in the cash flow statement is how well the company is balancing various sources of finance. It generated £196.7m from operating activities. The servicing of investment cost £3.1m in loan interest and the company paid taxes of £50.6m. That left net cash from operations amounting to £143.0m. That was used to cover its investing activities in new non-current (fixed) assets costing £48m (£60m less £12m) and acquisitions costing £24.6m after allowing for the sale of a company. Cash was used to increase short-term deposits by £30.7m. Interest received was £5m. The net cash used for investing activities amounted to £98.3m. If I deduct this from the £143m cash flow generated there is an increase in cash of £44.7m. The company had to pay a dividend of £29.5m, leaving

£15.2m surplus cash. There was no immediate need for any long-term financing flows with a healthy cash flow like that. Nevertheless the company raised £3.1m in cash through an issue of shares to the employees' share option scheme and, perhaps surprisingly, there was an increase of £16.2m in short-term loans. Add the £15.2m to the £3.1m and £16.2m and you arrive at £34.5m which is the increase in cash and cash equivalents of the period. That brings me back to my earlier question of why they are holding so much cash and short-term deposits.

The company in this example has told me that it carries out its financial management by recognising that the tax bill has to be paid first of all. Then it plans its investment in non-current (fixed) assets and its programme of disposals. Once the investment has been decided the company aims to pay a dividend which will satisfy the expectations of investors. Surplus cash after that is available for acquisition of other companies and, because this company is always looking for good opportunities to expand, it will borrow ahead of time so that it is in a position to move quickly when a target presents itself. The company does not agree with IAS 7's requirement to separate out the bank deposits which had more than three months to run when they were made. The deposits are placed largely for six months, so that many have less than six months to run at the balance sheet date. It is all very accessible cash and the company sees it all as one pool.

In the Operating and Financial Review the finance director explains the company's view of cash flow as follows:

The Group's businesses are structured to utilise as little fixed and working capital as is consistent with the profit and earnings growth objective in order to produce a high cash flow. The impact of working capital on cash flow was held to an increase in Year 7 of £9.7m (Year 6: £10.0m).

A net cash flow of £196.7m was generated from operating activities. That was boosted by other amounts of cash from interest received. After paying interest and tax, the Group had £143.0m remaining. Fixed assets required £48.0m after allowing for the proceeds of selling some of our vehicle fleet in the routine replacement programme. That left £95m from which £24.6m was required to pay for acquisitions. The remaining £70.4m covered dividends of £29.5m leaving £40.9m. We received £5m interest on investments and raised £3.1m in ordinary share capital to give a net inflow of liquid funds in the year of £49.0m. Out of that amount, short-term deposits have increased by £14.5m, leaving an increase in cash of £34.5m.

You can see there are lots of different ways of interpreting the information in the cash flow statement. What is important is that the information is available.

7.7 Group structure of companies

Most major companies in the UK operate using a group structure. Within a group there is a **parent** company which controls **subsidiary** companies undertaking various different aspects of the operations of the business. It would in theory be possible to have all the operations located within one company but in practice, because company law draws very tight boundaries around a single company, there is some safety for the organisation in having different parts of the business packaged separately. If something goes seriously wrong with one subsidiary company, that company may be allowed to fail without irreparable damage to the total group. This approach has not always worked out in practice because very often the banks which lend money to a subsidiary will request guarantees from other companies in the group. So if one subsidiary fails in a spectacular way, it may drag the rest of the group with it.

Other reasons for retaining separate subsidiaries include: employee loyalty, product reputation, taxation legislation and overseas operations. When a new company is taken into the group, a sense of pride in the formerly independent company may be retained by continuing to use the traditional company name. The company name may be linked to a reputation for a high-quality product so that it is desirable to perpetuate the benefit of that reputation. Tax legislation applies to individual companies and not to the group as a whole. Efficient use of the tax laws may require different types of business to operate in different companies. Operations located in other countries will come under the legal systems of those countries and may be required to have a separate legal identity.

For accounting purposes the group as a whole is the economic entity for which financial statements are prepared. An entity should prepare and publish financial statements if there is a legitimate demand for the information that its financial statements would provide and it is a cohesive economic unit.[9] The process of combining all the financial statements of the companies within a group is called **consolidation**. This chapter will explain sufficient aspects of the preparation of consolidated financial statements to allow an understanding of annual reports of groups of companies. The full complexities of consolidation and the wider aspects of group accounting may be found in advanced textbooks.

Definition | **Consolidated** financial statements are the financial statements of a group presented as those of a single economic entity.[10]

Consolidated financial statements recognise the parent's control of its subsidiaries. Consolidation is a process that aggregates the total assets, liabilities and results of all companies in the group. The consolidated balance sheet brings together all the assets controlled by the parent and shows all the liabilities to be satisfied from those assets. The consolidated income statement (profit and loss account) brings together all the revenues and costs of the companies in the group.

7.7.1 Defining a group

The smallest group consists of two companies. A group is created when one company (the **parent**) has **control** of another company (the **subsidiary**). There is no upper limit to the number of companies which may form a group.

The International Accounting Standards Board has defined a group as a parent and all its subsidiaries.[11] A parent is an entity that has one or more subsidiaries.[12] A subsidiary is an entity, including an unincorporated entity such as a partnership, that is controlled by another entity (known as the **parent**).[13] **Consolidated** financial statements must include all **subsidiaries** of the parent.[14]

Control is the power to govern the financial and operating policies of an entity so as to obtain benefits from its activities.[15] Control is presumed to exist when the parent owns, directly or indirectly, more than half of the voting power of an entity. Control also exists where the parent owns half or less than half of the voting power of an entity where there is:[16]

(a) power over more than half of the voting rights by virtue of an agreement with other investors;
(b) power to govern the financial and operating policies of the entity under a statute or an agreement;
(c) power to appoint or remove the majority of the members of the board of directors or equivalent governing body;
(d) power to cast the majority of votes at a meeting of the board of directors or equivalent governing body.

7.7.2   The importance of control

Control describes the highest degree of influence that an investor can have over its investee. If an investor (the parent) controls its investee (the subsidiary), it has the ability to direct the investee's operating and financial policies with a view to gaining economic benefit from its activities. The parent becomes fully accountable for the risks and rewards arising from its subsidiary's activities and obtains access to any benefits generated by the subsidiary's activities.

Whatever the percentage holding, the concept of control is the guiding principle which allows the consolidated balance sheet to report *all* the assets and *all* the liabilities of the combined companies. The consolidated profit and loss account reports *all* the profit generated by those assets and liabilities.

7.7.3   The parent company's balance sheet

In some annual reports the parent company may choose to continue to produce its own balance sheet, showing as an asset the cost of the investment in the subsidiary, but this information is not regarded as being particularly useful. The investment in the subsidiary is reported by the parent company as a single-line item but the consolidated balance sheet shows all the assets and all the liabilities of the group under each separate heading. The group balance sheet is more useful to readers. In previous chapters, where the financial statements of Safe and Sure plc have been discussed, the group accounts have been used.

7.7.4   Acquisition

The general term **business combination** may be applied to any transaction whereby one company becomes a subsidiary of another. The most common form of business combination is an **acquisition** where one party (the **acquirer**) is clearly the dominant entity and the other (the **acquiree**) is seen to be under new control. The method of accounting used to produce consolidated financial statements in an acquisition is called the **acquisition method**[17] (sometimes described as the **purchase method**). In this introductory text you do not need to worry about the details of the method of producing consolidated financial statements. All you need to do is recognise the descriptions used and be aware that when you see these words you are reading information about a group of companies combined.

Activity 7.4	*Check your understanding of the terms: parent, subsidiary, control, acquisition. Write down a definition of each and then look back through this section to test your definition against that in the text.*

7.8   Group financial statements

This section explains how the acquisition of a subsidiary affects the balance sheet of the parent company. It shows how the group's balance sheet and income statement (profit and loss account) are created. It also explains the nature of goodwill arising on acquisition and it outlines the nature and treatment of associated companies.

7.8.1   The parent company's balance sheet

When an acquisition takes place, the parent company acquires shares in the subsidiary in exchange for cash or for shares in the parent. The parent company will offer cash if it has adequate cash resources to make the offer and it appears that those selling the shares would prefer to take cash for investment elsewhere. The parent company will offer its own shares in exchange where it may not have sufficient cash resources available or where it thinks it can persuade those selling their shares in the target company of the desirability of acquiring shares in the new parent. Many deals offer a mixture of shares and cash.

For a cash purchase the effect on the parent company's balance sheet, in terms of the accounting equation, is:

For a share exchange, the effect on the parent company's balance sheet is to increase the assets and increase the ownership interest. In terms of the accounting equation:

7.8.2 The group's consolidated balance sheet

In the group's consolidated balance sheet the parent company's assets and liabilities are added to the assets and liabilities of the subsidiary companies. The assets and liabilities of the subsidiary take the place of the parent company's investment in the subsidiary. Figure 7.2 shows the net assets of P and S separately. The arrows indicate the net assets of S moving in to take the place of P's investment in S. Removing the investment in S from the balance sheet of P and replacing it with the net assets of S leads to the group's consolidated balance sheet. Figure 7.3(a) shows the resulting amalgamation. The assets and liabilities in Figure 7.3(a) are then rearranged under each asset and liability category to result in Figure 7.3(b).

7.8.3 The group income statement (profit and loss account)

Investors and their advisers may wish to use the income statement (profit and loss account) of the group to make predictions of the future profitability of the group. To be able to do this, they must know how much of the current year's profit relates to continuing operations and how much relates to changes during the year. The illustration of the income statement of Safe and Sure plc in section 7.5.3 shows how the consolidated profit and loss is subdivided into continuing activities and discontinued activities.

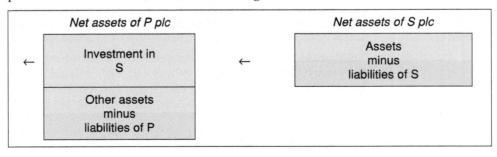

Figure 7.2
Separate net assets of parent and subsidiary

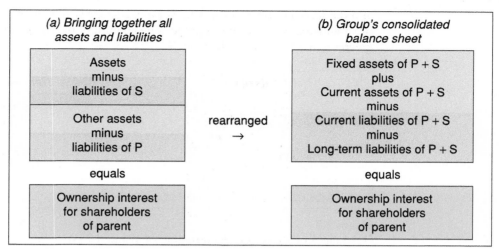

Figure 7.3
Completing the process of consolidation

One rule of acquisition accounting is that, where a subsidiary is acquired part-way through the year, only the profits earned after the date of acquisition may be included in the group profit and loss account. The analyst seeking to make a forecast for the year ahead will be helped by a note to the accounts showing what the profit would have been from a full 12-month contribution.

Groups are not required to present separately the parent company's income statement (profit and loss account). It is not felt to be particularly interesting to users as, generally, the parent company's main income comprises the dividends received from its investments in subsidiaries. Usually it is the subsidiaries which carry out the operations generating profit. It is far more interesting to know about the underlying operating profits which allow those dividends to be paid to the parent.

Activity 7.5	*P plc pays cash of £6m for an investment in net assets of S Ltd having a net book value (equal to fair value) of £6m. Explain how this transaction will affect the balance sheet of P plc as the parent company and explain how it will affect the group balance sheet of P Group plc, whose only subsidiary is S Ltd.*

7.8.4   Goodwill on acquisition

In the illustration presented in Figure 7.2 and Figure 7.3 the net assets of the subsidiary were shown as being of the same magnitude as the amount of the investment in the subsidiary so that the substitution of the former for the latter was a neat replacement process. That situation is unlikely to apply in real life because the price paid for an investment will rarely depend solely on the net assets being acquired. The purchaser will be looking to the future expectations from the investment and the seller will be seeking a reward for all that has been built into the business which cannot readily be quantified in terms of tangible assets. The future expectations will rest upon the reputation of the product or service, the quality of the customers, the skills of the workforce and the state of the order book, amongst many other things. The price negotiated for the business will include some recognition of all these qualities under the global heading of **goodwill**.

In these circumstances the price paid for the investment in the subsidiary will be greater than the amount of the net assets of the subsidiary. When the consolidation into the group balance sheet is attempted, a space will appear. Figure 7.4 shows the separate net assets of P plc and S plc. The amount of the cost of the investment in S is greater than the net assets of S plc.

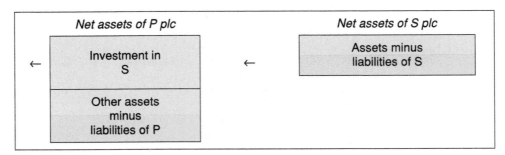

Figure 7.4
Net assets of the separate companies P plc and S plc

Figure 7.5 shows the resulting consolidation. The space shaded is equal to the difference between the amount of the investment in S and the net assets of S. This space is, in arithmetic terms, nothing more than a **difference on consolidation** but has traditionally been called **goodwill** because it is explained in terms of paying for something more than the underlying net assets.

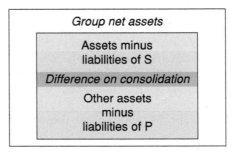

Figure 7.5
Group net assets of the P group

Definition **Goodwill** is defined as an asset representing the future economic benefits arising from other assets acquired in a business combination that are not individually identified and separately recognised.[18]

Goodwill is recognised in the balance sheet as an asset and is measured as the excess of the cost of the business combination over the fair value of the net assets acquired.[19]

The existence of a difference on consolidation is an inescapable consequence of the process of combining the balance sheets of parent and subsidiary. For many years it caused one of the most difficult problems facing the accounting standard-setters. The questions asked were: 'How should this consolidation difference be reported in the balance sheets of succeeding years?' and 'Is it an asset?'

After a great deal of international debate and disagreement, the IASB has taken the view that acquisition goodwill is an asset that should be tested regularly by means of an **impairment test** which asks, 'Can the business expect to recover the carrying value of the intangible asset, through either using it or selling it?' If the answer is 'no' then the asset is impaired and its value must be reduced. An expense of impairment will appear in the income statement (profit and loss account). If the answer is 'yes' then the asset value should remain in the balance sheet.

Definition | **Impairment** means 'damaged' or 'spoiled'. Where the carrying value of goodwill cannot be recovered through sale or use, it is said to be 'impaired'. The asset value in the balance sheet must be reduced.

Activity 7.6 | *P pays cash of £8m for an investment in net assets of S Ltd having a net book value (equal to fair value) of £6m. Explain how this transaction will affect the balance sheet of P plc as the parent company and explain how it will affect the group balance sheet of P Group plc, whose only subsidiary is S Ltd.*

7.8.5   Associated companies

Where company P holds less than a controlling interest in company A, it may nevertheless have a significant influence over company A. Such significant influence would involve the power to participate in the financial and operating policy decisions of company A. Significant influence is presumed to exist when one company or a group of companies holds 20% or more of the ordinary shareholders' voting rights of another company, unless the facts indicate that significant influence is not possible.[20]

Where significant influence over a company exists, that company is called an **associated company**. The group must show in its balance sheet the group's share of the net assets of the associated company as a single-line item, and must show in the income statement (profit and loss account) the group's share of the profits or losses of the associated company.

This treatment of an investment in an associated company is called **equity accounting** because it reports the parent's and the group's share of the investment in the ownership interest (also referred to as the equity).

For investments which do not meet the conditions of being reported as associated companies, the accounting treatment is to record the investment at cost in the balance sheet and to record in the profit and loss account of the group only the dividend income received from the associate.

7.9   Small and medium-sized entities (SMEs)

7.9.1   Definitions

The amount of detail in the information presented by companies depends on their size. The Companies Act 2006 defines small and medium-sized companies. The definitions are based on turnover, balance sheet totals and average number of employees. Currently the limits for a small company are satisfying two or more of the conditions: turnover not more than £5.6m, balance sheet total not more than £2.8m and employees not more than 50 (section 382). The limits for a medium-sized company are satisfying two or more of the conditions: turnover not more than £22.8m, balance sheet total not more than £11.4m and employees not more than 250 (section 465). The amounts for turnover and balance sheet totals are altered from time to time by Statutory Instrument to keep pace with inflation, so it is perhaps easiest to take as a 'rule of thumb' the employee limits of 50 for a small company and 250 for a medium-sized company. For these companies there are substantial exemptions from requirements to publish information (although they must still provide details to shareholders if asked to do so). Generally they are not listed companies and so are not required to meet the obligations placed on listed companies. Most of these small and medium-sized companies are currently presenting financial statements based on UK ASB standards and company law. Section 7.9.2 explains proposals for change that will affect these companies.

During the 1980s, concerns were expressed about the 'burden' of regulation for small companies. This burden was seen as falling from all directions, including tax laws, employment laws, product protection laws, health and safety laws and accounting regulation. The government of the time committed itself to reducing this burden. One consequence was that the UK Accounting Standards Board introduced a Financial Reporting Standard for Smaller Entities (FRSSE). This condenses into one standard the essential aspects of all the separate accounting standards for larger companies. It reduces disclosure requirements but maintains standards for measurement. Small companies may choose either to apply the FRSSE in full or to comply with the full range of separate standards.

The Companies Act 2006 permits small and medium-sized companies to file 'abbreviated' financial statements with the Registrar of Companies. The word 'abbreviated' can be explained as 'cutting down the detail' but views have been expressed that this has gone too far and that abbreviated financial statements do not provide useful information about small companies. It allows them, for example, to maintain confidentiality of profit margins. During discussions on law reform leading to the Companies Act 2006, the White Paper of 2005[21] acknowledged this concern but noted that the option was popular with many companies. It said that the Government intended to retain the option for abbreviated financial statements but would require small and medium-sized companies to disclose revenue (turnover).

7.9.2 IFRS for SMEs and the future of UK GAAP

After many years of discussion the IASB issued a shortened form of accounting standards called *International Financial Reporting Standards for Small and Medium-sized Entities* (IFRS for SMEs).[22]

It maintains measurement principles that are consistent with the full IFRS but is a considerably shorter document. It achieves this in several ways. Firstly, topics not relevant to SMEs are omitted. Secondly, where the full IFRSs allow accounting policy choices, the IFRS for SMEs specifies one choice only and selects the least difficult one. Thirdly, while the measurement principles are consistent with full IFRS, the SME version simplifies the principles for recognising and measuring assets, liabilities, income and expenses. Fourthly, the required disclosures are significantly reduced in number. Finally, the standard has been written in clear language that can be translated relatively easily.

Until 2009 there was a need for UK GAAP where standards were maintained by the UK ASB for those companies that do not use the full IFRS. However, the need for continuing UK GAAP seems less clear now there is the IFRS for SMEs. Accordingly the UK ASB issued a discussion paper in 2009 asking whether, and how soon, UK SMEs could move to the IFRS for SMEs. The tentative target is 2012.

As explained in section 7.9.1, there is a separate document called the Financial Reporting Standard for Small Entities (FRSSE) which has been issued for several years by the UK ASB. The ASB thinks this document could be retained for the very smallest companies.

The accounting standards used would be:

- Tier 1, EU adopted IFRS, to be applied by listed group companies (including the Alternative Investment Market) and publicly accountable unlisted companies.
- Tier 2 IFRS for SMEs to be applied by entities that are not publicly accountable.
- Tier 3 FRSSE, to be applied by the smallest UK companies.

7.10 Beyond the annual report

The annual report is a regulated base of information on which a reporting cycle is built. The cycle begins when the company makes its first announcement of the results of the financial year. This announcement is made in a manner dictated by Stock Exchange rules and is called a 'preliminary announcement' because it is a preliminary to the issue of the full annual report. It is also called a 'press release' because it forms the basis of the information which first appears in the financial press.

The cycle continues with reports being issued in the period between annual reports. These are called 'interim reports'. The London Stock Exchange requires half-yearly reports. The regulators of the US stock exchanges require quarterly reports. All UK listed companies provide half-yearly reports and some voluntarily provide quarterly reports.

Other questions arising beyond the annual report are:

- What help exists for small and medium-sized companies to reduce the burden of communication for regulatory purposes?
- How do larger companies avoid information overload for their shareholders?
- Can users have confidence in additional information provided beyond the annual report?
- What developments is the UK government currently implementing or planning?

This section outlines developments on these issues.

7.10.1 Preliminary announcements

The **preliminary announcement** is the first external communication of the financial performance and position of a company in relation to the financial year most recently completed. When the year-end results and half-yearly results are ready for publication, a preliminary announcement of key information is made in a manner set out by the Stock Exchange which aims at fair and equal access for all investors. The preliminary announcement is usually accompanied by a press release, giving the information to the media, and by meetings with professional investors and brokers' analysts at which key personnel in the company (usually the chairman, chief executive and finance director) will make speeches and answer questions.

The institutional shareholders and their advisers will form expectations about the position and performance in advance of the announcement. They look carefully at the preliminary announcement in comparison with their expectations.

Company law does not prescribe the content of the preliminary announcement or the interim report. The Company Law Review report of 2001 recommended that regulation of the preliminary announcement was best carried out by the market regulator rather than by parliamentary legislation. The report did suggest that company law should require that the preliminary announcement be published on the company's website, with electronic notification to shareholders. However, that recommendation was not taken up in the Company Law Reform Bill of 2005. Instead the Bill included a general provision that companies may use electronic communication of documents providing the recipient agrees.

The content of the preliminary statement is influenced by guidance to listed companies, formerly provided by the Stock Exchange but transferred to the Financial Services Authority in 2000. The guidance leaves scope for flexibility in disclosure and measurement. That has caused the UK ASB to write non-mandatory guidance on good practice. There is no obligation on companies to send these preliminary announcements to shareholders, although most companies make the information available on their websites, normally by a press release.

Reliability is a key requirement of the preliminary announcement. The Stock Exchange requires the company's auditors to agree to the release of the preliminary announcement. There is an expectation that the information in the preliminary announcement will be consistent with the annual report when it eventually appears.

The rules of the Financial Services Authority and the Stock Exchange do not regulate the content of the preliminary announcement other than the requirement for profit and loss information and any significant information necessary for the purpose of assessing the results being announced. In practice many of these announcements include more information than the profit and loss account. The ASB recommends a narrative commentary, a summarised profit and loss account, a summarised balance sheet and a summarised cash flow statement. Increasingly it is found that companies are using the text of the Operating and Financial Review as the basis for the narrative comment in the preliminary announcement.

In general the ASB wishes to improve the timeliness, quality, relevance and consistency of preliminary announcements within the constraints of reliability. It could be that in the longer term the preliminary announcement would increasingly take over the role of the annual report. The delay in publishing the annual report is related to the need to publish a paper-based document. The Company Law Review report recommends that electronic means of communication could speed up the process considerably.

7.10.2 Interim reports

Interim reports are issued by companies as updating bulletins in between annual reports. They are mainly used by listed companies in response to the requirements of market regulators. Some market regulators ask for half-yearly reports. Others ask for quarterly reports. The international accounting standard IAS 34[23] provides guidance on interim reporting.

One interesting accounting question is how to measure the results of half a year. One view is that the results of half a year should represent the actual events of that half-year. This is called the 'discrete' method. A different view is that the result for six months should represent half of the results of the full year. This is called the 'integral' method. Why does this make a difference? Imagine a company which manufactures and sells fireworks. The costs will fall evenly through the year but most of the sales will arise in the months leading to 5 November. Using the discrete method, the first six months of the calendar year will show low profits or perhaps losses. The second six months will show relatively high profits. Using the integral method each half-year will show the same profit at 50% of the total figure of the year.

IAS 34 requires the discrete method to be used as far as possible. Some expense items, such as taxation, may have to be spread evenly over the year.

In matters of disclosure the IASB recommends that the interim report should include a balance sheet, income statement, statement of changes in equity and cash flow, together with explanatory notes and comments.

Activity 7.7

Obtain the interim report and the annual report of a major listed company. Compare the interim report with the annual report. What are the information items in the interim report? How do they compare with the full year in the annual report? What statements of accounting policy are made in the interim report?

7.10.3 Prospectus

When a major company wants to raise significant amounts of finance through selling shares on the Stock Market, it issues a **prospectus**. The contents of the prospectus are regulated by the UK Listing Authority, backed up on some items by the Companies

Act 2006. The document is often several hundred pages in length and quite formidable in appearance. It contains more detail than the annual report. The prospectus is a public document but there is no central archive of prospectuses so it is useful in research projects to retain copies as they appear. Some business libraries retain copies.

7.10.4   Avoiding information overload

Even the very largest companies may take advantage of the rule which allows them to publish summary financial statements. These are usually very much shorter than the full annual report and are offered to shareholders as an alternative to the full report. There is a short form of the balance sheet, profit and loss account and cash flow statement, no notes to the accounts but usually an accompanying commentary by the company directors. Shareholders are reminded of the existence of the full report and invited to ask for a copy if desired.

7.10.5   Additional non-GAAP measures

A survey undertaken by the accountancy firm Deloitte[24] showed widespread use in 2008 and 2009 of additional non-GAAP measures of performance reported on the face of the income statement. Such additional measures are encouraged by IAS 1 when they are relevant to an understanding of the financial performance of the company. One criticism made by Deloitte is that some of the companies do not define their non-GAAP measures so that it is difficult for readers to understand why they are being used. The most common adjustment observed was the exclusion of the costs of fundamental reorganisation from non-GAAP performance measures. Other exclusions covered impairment, amortisation, asset disposal and items relating to changes in value of financial assets and liabilities. A common form of presentation observed was the use of the word 'exceptional' to describe such costs, locating them in a separate column on the income statement or in a separate box that can be removed from the performance measures.

Two different views may be taken of this flexible approach. One is that it allows a company to provide a better understanding of its financial performance. The other is that it allows a company to confuse investors by presenting performance in a way that favours the company and distracts the reader from the overall picture.

7.10.6   'Pro forma' financial statements

'Pro forma' financial statements represent a recent development in company reporting that is causing some confusion among users of accounting information, and some concern among the regulators. According to the dictionary, the phrase 'pro forma' means 'as a matter of form'. The underlying accounting meaning is 'outside the normal reporting regulations'. It usually involves selective editing from a larger body of information that has been prepared under accounting rules, or the inclusion of some items that would not be permitted under the accounting standards applied. The risk is that the selective information may not, by itself, represent a true and fair view. This does not necessarily mean that the information is bad or misleading, but it does mean that the investor is deprived of the full protection of regulation. An example is provided in the Real World case study at the start of this chapter. The company was formed by a demerger from a larger group, changing the capital structure and changing the accounting year-end. To preserve comparability the company adjusted the figures for earlier years to be presented on a basis consistent with more recent years. This company also defines its own 'benchmark' profit measures which are not specified in accounting standards. It claims the pro forma and benchmark information helps readers better to understand the performance of the group.

7.10.7	**Electronic publication of documents**

One conclusion of the Company Law Review, leading to the Companies Act 2006, was that the law allows financial reporting to be a slow process that could be speeded up by use of electronic delivery. The Companies Act now confirms that a document supplied in electronic form will be validly delivered if that form has been agreed by the intended recipient (or the intended recipient had not replied when asked for a preference). However, shareholders and others having a right to receive information are able to ask for a paper copy of a document.

7.11 Summary

- Company law in the UK includes sections that implement EU Directives. This means that UK company accounting has for many years been harmonised with company accounting in other member states of the EU, but mainly in matters of disclosure. Member states have continued to require or permit different measurement practices.

- From 2005 listed groups of companies in EU member states have been required to follow the IASB system of reporting. Individual companies and unlisted groups have the choice of the IASB system or UK company law and UK ASB standards.

- The primary financial statements under both systems include a balance sheet, income statement (profit and loss account) and cash flow statement. Under the IASB system a statement of changes in equity is required. Under the UK ASB standards a statement of recognised gains and losses is required and a note of movements on reserves.

- Formats set out the content and layout of financial statements. Under UK company law there are detailed formats required for the balance sheet and profit and loss account. The IASB system is more flexible on layout but provides lists of essential items.

- A group of companies consists of a parent and subsidiaries. All must be included. A subsidiary is defined by the control exercised by the parent. Control is commonly evidenced by the parent holding more than half of the voting power in the subsidiary. Control may be evidenced in other kinds of agreements relating to shareholdings or to the board of directors.

- A consolidated balance sheet contains the total assets and liabilities of the group of companies, after eliminating any amounts receivable and payable between group companies.

- A consolidated income statement (profit and loss account) contains the total revenues and expenses of the group of companies, after eliminating any transactions and profits made between group companies.

- A consolidated cash flow statement contains the total cash flows of the group of companies, after eliminating any cash flows between group companies.

- Goodwill arising on acquisition is calculated by comparing the fair value of the payment for the subsidiary with the fair value of net assets acquired. It represents future economic benefits arising from assets that are not capable of being individually identified and separately recognised.

- Goodwill is recognised as an asset in the balance sheet and is tested annually for impairment.

- Beyond the annual report there is a range of corporate communications – often found most readily by visiting a company's website.

- For small companies special disclosure rules apply to reduce the burden of providing information.

Further reading

Deloitte LLP provide regular surveys of the content of annual report, published on the website www.deloitte.co.uk/audit.

IAS 1 (2009), *Presentation of Financial Statements*. International Accounting Standards Board. This is a detailed standard, some of which is beyond a first-level course, but the examples of financial statements given in the Appendix show the types of presentation that companies might use or adapt.

IFRS 3 (2009), *Business Combinations*. International Accounting Standards Board. (This is a very detailed standard which is beyond a first-level course but the definitions in the Appendix may be useful in explaining terms encountered in financial statements.)

Useful websites

International Accounting Standards Board: www.iasb.org

UK Accounting Standards Board: www.asb.org.uk

London Stock Exchange: www.londonstockex.co.uk

Financial Services Authority: www.fsa.gov.uk

QUESTIONS

The Questions section of each chapter has three types of question. 'Test your understanding' questions to help you review your reading are in the 'A' series of questions. You will find the answers to these by reading and thinking about the material in the book. 'Application' questions to test your ability to apply technical skills are in the 'B' series of questions. Questions requiring you to show skills in problem solving and evaluation are in the 'C' series of questions. A letter [S] indicates that there is a solution at the end of the book.

A   Test your understanding

A7.1   What is a Directive? (Section 7.2.1)

A7.2   What is the IAS Regulation? (Section 7.2.1)

A7.3   What is the role of the IASB? (Section 7.2.2)

A7.4   Name the primary financial statements and explain the purpose of each. (Section 7.3.1)

A7.5   The following technical terms appear in this chapter. Check that you know the meaning of each. (If you cannot find them again in the text, they are defined at the end of the book.)

    (a)   revenue
    (b)   capital
    (c)   non-current asset
    (d)   depreciation
    (e)   directors
    (f)   earnings for equity holders (ordinary shareholders)
    (g)   earnings per share

(h) external users (of financial statements)
(i) financial position
(j) gross
(k) gross margin
(l) gross profit
(m) net
(n) net assets
(o) primary financial statements
(p) reserves
(q) revaluation reserve
(r) share premium
(s) tangible fixed assets
(t) turnover

A7.6 How do companies report: (Section 7.3.1)

(a) financial position;
(b) performance; and
(c) changes in financial position?

A7.7 What are the main headings to be found in most company balance sheets? (Section 7.4)

A7.8 In the Companies Act formats, what is the reason for the order of items under heading C: current assets? (Section 7.4)

A7.9 What are the main headings to be found in most company income statements (profit and loss accounts)? (Section 7.5)

A7.10 What are the main sections of a cash flow statement prepared according to IAS 7? (Section 7.6)

A7.11 Why does depreciation appear as a line item in the reconciliation of operating profit with cash flow? (Section 7.6.3)

A7.12 Explain why groups of companies are formed. (Section 7.7)

A7.13 Explain the purpose of consolidated financial statements. (Section 7.7)

A7.14 Define the terms: (Section 7.7.1)

(a) group;
(b) parent company; and
(c) subsidiary.

A7.15 Explain, using the accounting equation, the effect on the parent company's balance sheet of a cash payment for an investment in a subsidiary company. (Section 7.8.1)

A7.16 Explain, using the accounting equation, the effect on the parent company's balance sheet of a share issue in exchange for shares in the subsidiary company. (Section 7.8.1)

A7.17 Explain what is meant by goodwill on acquisition. (Section 7.8.4)

A7.18 What is an associated company? (Section 7.8.5)

A7.19 Apart from the annual report, what other documents do companies use to communicate financial statement information to investors, creditors and other users of financial statements? (Section 7.9)

B Application

B7.1 [S]
Write a letter to the financial controller of a company advising on the factors which a company should take into consideration when deciding how to arrange information in financial statements.

B7.2 [S]

Write a note for financial analysts explaining how the published income statement (profit and loss account) provides a useful indication of the financial performance of a company.

B7.3 [S]

What features are likely to make a balance sheet helpful to users?

B7.4 [S]

Could a cash flow statement be presented as the only financial statement reported by a company? Explain your view.

C | Problem solving and evaluation

C7.1 [S]

A listed company is of the view that shareholders might welcome a statement of highlights and supplementary information as a leaflet to be inserted in the annual report. Give advice on the principles to be followed in making such information useful to users.

Activities for study groups

Continuing to use the annual reports of companies which you obtained for Chapters 1 and 4, find the financial statements (balance sheet, profit and loss account and cash flow statement) and the notes to the accounts.

1   Compare the financial statements with the formats and presentations shown in this chapter, and note any differences which you observe. Look at the notes to the accounts for items which are required by the regulations but are included in the notes rather than the main financial statements.

2   Find the Operating and Financial Review (sometimes named the finance director's review) and compare the cash flow discussion there with the FRS 1 presentation. Form a view on how readily the discussion may be related to the financial statement.

3   In your group, take the list of qualitative characteristics listed at section 4.2 and use the financial statements as a means of illustrating how the company has met those characteristics. If you have a set of different annual reports, each member of the group should take the role of a finance director pointing out the qualitative characteristics of their own company's financial statements. The group together should then decide on a ranking with a view to nominating one of the annual reports for an award of 'Communicator of the Year'.

Notes and references

1. IAS 1 (2009), *Presentation of Financial Statements*, para. 10.
2. IASB *Framework*, para. 12.
3. The Appendix to IAS 1 (2009) gives an illustration which is not compulsory.
4. The Appendix to IAS 1 (2009) gives an illustration which is not compulsory.
5. ASB (1996), Financial Reporting Standard (FRS 1), *Cash Flow Statements*, Accounting Standards Board (revised from 1991 version).
6. IASB (2009), IAS 7 *Statement of Cash Flows*, para. 4.
7. IAS 7 (2009), para. 6.
8. IAS 7 (2009), para. 6.
9. ASB (1999), ch. 2, 'The reporting entity', Principles section.
10. IAS 27 (2009), *Consolidated and separate financial statements*, para. 4.
11. IAS 27 (2009), para. 4.
12. IAS 27 (2009), para. 4.
13. IAS 27 (2009), para. 4.

14. IAS 27 (2009), para. 12.
15. IAS 27 (2009), para. 4.
16. IAS 27 (2009), para. 13.
17. IFRS 3 (2009), para. 4.
18. IFRS 3 (2009), Appendix A.
19. IFRS 3 (2009), para. 32. In this section it is assumed in the explanations that fair value equals book value of net assets of subsidiary.
20. IAS 28 (2009), *Investments in Associates*, paras 2 and 6.
21. DTI Company Law Reform 2005, http://www.bis.gov.uk/files/file13958.pdf
22. IASB (2009), *International Financial Reporting Standard for Small and Medium-sized Entities*, http://www.iasplus.com/standard/ifrsforsmes.htm.
23. IASB (2009), IAS 34 *Interim Financial Reporting*.
24. *Finishing (in) Figures: Surveying financial statements in annual reports*. Deloitte LLP, www.deloitte.co.uk/audit.

Information to be presented on the face of the balance sheet, as required by IAS 1

Note that this is a list of items, not a format, so a company could choose to present the items in a different sequence.

There must be separate headings for current and non-current assets, and current and non-current liabilities.[1]

As a minimum the face of the balance sheet must include the following line items:[2]

(a) Property, plant and equipment
(b) Investment property
(c) Intangible assets
(d) Financial assets
(e) Investments accounted for using the equity method
(f) Biological assets
(g) Inventories
(h) Trade and other receivables
(i) Cash and cash equivalents
(j) The total of assets classified as 'held for sale'
(k) Trade and other payables
(l) Provisions
(m) Financial liabilities (excluding items shown under (k) and (l))
(n) Liabilities and assets for current tax
(o) Deferred tax assets and deferred tax liabilities
(p) Liabilities included in disposal groups classified as held for sale
(q) Non-controlling (minority) interests within equity (ownership interest)
(r) Issued capital and reserves attributable to equity holders of the parent.

An entity must disclose further subclassifications of these line items, classified in a manner appropriate to the entity's operations. These further subclassifications may be presented either on the face of the balance sheet or in notes.[3]

1. IAS 1 (2003), para. 60.
2. IAS 1 (2009), para. 54.
3. IAS 1 (2003), para. 77.

Information to be presented on the face of the Income Statement as required by IAS 1

As a minimum, the face of the income statement must include line items that present the following amounts for the period:[1]

(a) revenue
(b) finance costs
(c) share of the profit or loss of associates and joint ventures accounted for using the equity method
(d) tax expense
(e) a single amount comprising the total of (i) the after-tax profit or loss of discontinued operations and (ii) the after-tax gain or loss recognised on disposal of the discontinued operation
(f) profit or loss.

If there is a non-controlling (minority) interest in a subsidiary (where the parent holds less than 100% of the share capital of the subsidiary) then the profit or loss attributable to the non-controlling interest must be disclosed separately from the profit or loss attributable to equity shareholder in the parent.[2]

An entity must disclose additional line items, headings and subtotals on the face of the income statement when such presentation is relevant to an understanding of the entity's financial performance.[3]

1. IAS 1 (2009), para. 82.
2. IAS 1 (2009), para. 83.
3. IAS 1 (2009), para. 85.

UK Companies Act profit and loss account format 1 – list of contents

1 Turnover
2 Cost of sales
3 Gross profit
4 Distribution costs
5 Administrative expenses
6 Other operating income
7 Income from shares in group undertakings
8 Income from participating interests (excluding group undertakings)
9 Income from other fixed asset investments
10 Other interest received and similar income
11 Amounts written off investments
12 Interest payable and similar charges
13 Tax on profit or loss of ordinary activities
14 Profit or loss on ordinary activities after taxation
15 Extraordinary income
16 Extraordinary charges
17 Extraordinary profit or loss
18 Tax on extraordinary profit or loss
19 Other taxes not shown under the above items
20 Profit or loss for the financial year

Chapter 8

Non-current (fixed) assets

Our stores

The Group operates from 466 stores and the strategic focus remains in the development of the two formats of choice, the superstore and the smaller format Compact store, previously referred to as Neighbourhood. Compact stores provide a comprehensive Halfords offer, carrying some 6,000 of the 10,000 lines available within an average superstore, to smaller catchments where a full superstore would not be viable (p. 6).

Finance director's report – operating leases

All of the Group's stores are occupied under operating leases, the majority of which are on standard lease terms, typically with a 15-year term at inception. The Group has a total commitment under noncancellable operating leases of £778.5m (2008: £818.6m), (p. 20).

Note 11. Property, plant and equipment

	Short leasehold land and buildings £m	Fixtures, fittings and equipment £m	Payments on account and assets in course of construction £m	Total £m
Net book value at 3 April 2009	28.3	79.0	0.2	107.5
Net book value at 28 March 2008	29.2	86.6	0.4	116.2

(p. 73).

Accounting policy – Property, plant and equipment

Property, plant and equipment are held at cost less accumulated depreciation and any impairment in value. Depreciation of property, plant and equipment is provided to write-off the cost, less residual value, on a straight-line basis over their useful economic lives as follows:

- Leasehold premises with lease terms of 50 years or less are depreciated over the remaining period of the lease;
- Motor vehicles are depreciated over 3 years;
- Store fixtures are depreciated over the period of the lease to a maximum of 25 years;
- Fixtures, fittings and equipment are depreciated over 4 to 10 years according to the estimated life of the asset;
- Computer equipment is depreciated over 3 years; and
- Land is not depreciated.

Residual values, remaining useful economic lives and depreciation periods and methods are reviewed annually and adjusted if appropriate (p. 62).

Source: extracts from Halfords Group plc, Annual report 2009; http://www.halfordscompany.com/hal/ir/fininfo/reports/rep2009/ar2009/ar2009.pdf.

Discussion points

1 Why is it important for the company to give descriptive information about the investment in stores?

2 What is the largest non-current asset category by net book value? Is it what you would expect for a business of this kind?

Contents

After studying this chapter you should be able to:

- Define a non-current (fixed) asset and apply the definition.
- Explain the recognition conditions that are applied to tangible non-current (fixed) assets, intangible non-current (fixed) assets and non-current (fixed) asset investments.
- Explain users' needs for information about non-current (fixed) assets.
- Describe and explain the non-current (fixed) asset information provided in annual reports of companies.
- Evaluate the usefulness of published information about non-current (fixed) assets.
- Explain the nature of depreciation.
- Calculate depreciation, record the effect on the accounting equation and report the result in financial statements.

Additionally, for those who choose to study the supplement:

- Record non-current (fixed) assets and depreciation in ledger accounts.

8.1 Introduction

If you have progressed through Chapters 1 to 7 you are now familiar with the accounting equation and the analysis of transactions or events using that equation. You know what is meant by the terms asset, liability, revenue, expense and ownership interest. You are aware of the structure of the primary financial statements and the way in which they seek to provide information which is relevant and reliable.

This chapter starts a new phase of the text which will help you to develop a critical awareness of some of the component items in the financial statements. Chapters 8 to 12 progress through the main sections of the statement of financial position (balance sheet). Inevitably, they also cover relevant aspects of the income statement (profit and loss account) and the statement of cash flows because transactions involving the statement of financial position (balance sheet) will sometimes have an effect in the other financial statements.

It is important at this stage not to become so enthusiastic for the intricacies of accounting procedures as to lose sight of the importance of user needs, which were set out in Chapter 1. That chapter set out, in section 1.2, the structure of most conceptual frameworks, which provides a sequence for each of Chapters 8 to 12, as follows:

- What are the principles for defining and recognising these items?
- What are the information needs of users in respect of the particular items?
- What information is currently provided by companies to meet these needs?
- Does the information show the desirable qualitative characteristics of financial statements?
- What are the principles for measuring, and processes for recording, these items?

That analysis is applied to non-current (fixed) assets in this chapter.

8.2 Definitions

The following definition of an asset was provided in Chapter 2.

Definition

An **asset** is a resource controlled by the entity as a result of past events and from which future economic benefits are expected to flow.[1]

The following definitions explain the nature of tangible and non-tangible non-current assets. The word 'tangible' means 'able to be touched'. So 'intangible' means 'not able to be touched'.

Definitions

A **non-current asset** is any asset that does not meet the definition of a current asset.[2] Non-current assets include tangible, intangible and financial assets of a long-term nature. These are also described as **fixed assets**.[3]

Tangible non-current (fixed) assets are assets that have physical substance and are held for use in the production or supply of goods or services, for rental to others, or for administrative purposes on a continuing basis in the reporting entity's activities.[4]

An **intangible** asset is an identifiable non-monetary asset without physical substance.[5]

These definitions are taken from different sources because the definitions have been developed and discussed at different times for different purposes. The IASB and the UK ASB have both spent many years in discussion over the subjects of accounting for tangible and intangible non-current assets because these are complex matters.

8.2.1 Examples of non-current (fixed) assets

The following is a sample of the non-current (fixed) assets found in a company's statement of financial position (balance sheet).

Tangible non-current (fixed) assets

Companies following the International Financial Reporting Standards (IFRS) will typically use a general heading of 'Property, plant and equipment'. This general heading might include:

- Land and buildings owned by the entity
- Buildings leased by the entity
- Plant and equipment (owned or leased)
- Vehicles (owned or leased)
- Office equipment
- Assets under construction
- Telecommunications network
- Airport runways
- Water pipes and sewers
- Oil and mineral reserves.

Definition[6]

Property, plant and equipment includes intangible items that:

(a) are held for use in the production or supply of goods or services, for rental to others, or for administrative purposes; and

(b) are expected to be used during more than one period.

Intangible non-current (fixed) assets

- Newspaper titles and publishing rights
- Patents
- Trade marks
- Goodwill purchased
- Brand names purchased.

Investments

- Long-term investments in subsidiary companies
- Long-term investments in other companies.

That sample was taken from only 10 annual reports of leading companies. Looking at more companies would soon extend the list considerably. The potential variety and the likelihood of encountering something new is one reason why definitions are essential.

8.2.2 Cost of a non-current (fixed) asset

There is one issue which is not as straightforward as it seems. That is the question of measuring the cost of a non-current (fixed) asset. When a toffee manufacturer buys a new toffee-shaping machine, the purchase price will be known from the supplier's invoice and the manufacturer's catalogue, but should the costs of delivery and installation be added to the amount recorded as the asset cost? When an insurance company buys a new head office, the purchase price will be shown in the contract, but should the legal costs be added to the amount recorded as the asset cost? When a new head office building is under development and interest is being paid on the funds borrowed to finance the development, should the interest paid on the borrowed funds be added to the cost of the development as part of the asset value?

The answer in all three cases is 'yes', although the third example causes greatest discussion and debate. The general principle is that the cost of a non-current (fixed) asset is the purchase price or the amount spent on its production together with any other expenditure incurred in bringing the non-current (fixed) asset to working condition for its intended use at its intended location.

Definition

> The **cost** of a non-current (fixed) asset is the purchase price or the amount spent on its production together with any costs directly attributable to bringing the non-current (fixed) asset to working condition for its intended use at its intended location.

8.2.3 Repairs and improvements

There are sometimes problems in deciding whether a payment for a repair to a non-current (fixed) asset should be treated as an expense of the business or an asset. The key lies in the words of the definition of an asset and the phrase *future economic benefits*. If the payment relates to some act which merely preserves the existing life of the asset and the existing expectations of benefit from the asset, then the payment is treated as a repair and reported as an **expense**. The asset of cash decreases and there is a decrease in the ownership interest caused by the expense.

If the payment relates to some act which significantly extends the useful life of the asset, or increases the future economic benefit expected from the asset, then the payment is treated as an **improvement** and reported as an asset. It may be reported as a separate asset but, more usually, the amount will be added to the cost or value recorded for the asset which has been improved. The asset of cash decreases and is replaced by an asset of improvements. There is no effect on the ownership interest.

The following are examples of improvements and repairs.

Improvements

- Extensions to a building which increase the operating capacity of the business.
- A new roof which gives a building an extra ten years of life.
- A new engine for a delivery van which is more powerful than the existing engine and allows faster delivery in hilly districts.
- Renewing the fittings and interior decoration of a hotel to attract international visitors instead of the traditional local customers.

Repairs

- A new roof, required because of storm damage, which will keep the building weatherproof for the remainder of its estimated life.
- A new engine for a delivery van which replaces an existing damaged engine.
- Redecorating inside a building to preserve the existing standards of cleanliness and appearance.

Activity 8.1	*Imagine you are the owner of a big hotel in the centre of town. Make a list of the items you would expect to include in your business statement of financial position (balance sheet) as non-current (fixed) assets. Make a list of the types of repair which would be classed as 'improvements'. Use the definition of a non-current (fixed) asset to show that your list includes items which are correctly classified.*

8.3 Recognition

This section outlines the recognition issues faced in reporting non-current assets in the separate categories of tangible assets, intangible assets and investment assets.

8.3.1 Tangible non-current (fixed) assets

Tangible non-current (fixed) assets are those items which can be touched, seen or heard and meet the conditions set out in the definition of a non-current (fixed) asset. **Recognition** by reporting in the statement of financial position (balance sheet) presents no problem where the future benefit can be identified and the cost of the asset can be measured. (Look back to section 2.5 for an explanation of recognition.) The evidence of cost is usually a purchase invoice. Some tangible non-current (fixed) assets are recorded at a valuation made subsequent to the purchase. Revaluations are discussed in Chapter 12.

As the list in the previous section indicates, there is considerable variety in tangible non-current (fixed) assets. The common feature is that they all have a limited life expectancy. They may wear out, be used up, go out of fashion, break down or be sold for scrap. Whatever the reason, the effect is the same and is called **depreciation**. Users have many questions to ask about tangible non-current (fixed) assets, such as:

- What kinds of tangible fixed assets are in use?
- How old are they?
- How has the company measured the depreciation?
- Where is the depreciation recorded?

Answering those questions will take up most of the remainder of this chapter.

8.3.2 Intangible non-current (fixed) assets

An intangible non-current (fixed) asset is an item which meets the definition of a non-current (fixed) asset but has no physical substance. It cannot be touched, seen or heard.

The evidence of its existence is the benefit flowing from it. For many years, items such as patents, trademarks and licences to manufacture products have been bought and sold between companies. The purchase has been recorded as a non-current (fixed) asset and depreciated over the estimated life of the patent, trademark or licence. The estimated life is decided by law (for patents and trademarks) or by legal contract (for licences). The depreciation of intangible non-current (fixed) assets is usually referred to as **amortisation** (in which you may recognise the French word *mort* meaning *death*).

The intangible non-current (fixed) asset which has attracted most accounting-related comment in recent years has been the brand name of a company's product. When a company works over many years to develop the reputation of its product, that reputation creates an expected future benefit for the company and meets the definition of an **asset** as set out in Chapter 2. However, the generally held view is that it should not be recognised in the statement of financial position (balance sheet) because it fails the **recognition** test of Chapter 2. The conventional argument is that there is no measurable **cost** of the reputation gained by the brand name and the value cannot be measured with reliability.

That is the generally held view which was challenged in the mid-1980s by a number of leading companies. Some had bought other companies which had developed brand names. The new owners argued that they were buying the other company purely because of the quality of the brand name and they wanted to show that brand name in the new statement of financial position (balance sheet). They had a reasonable argument because they had paid a price in the market and could show the cost of the brand name acquired. Other companies who had developed their own brand names did not want to be left behind and so paid expert valuers to calculate a value for their home-grown brands. A new professional specialism of brand valuation gained prominence and the experts claimed they could measure the value of a home-grown brand with reliability.

The companies which reported brand names in the statement of financial position (balance sheet) argued that the brand had a long life and did not require amortisation. This argument gave them the advantage of expanding the statement of financial position (balance sheet) without the disadvantage of amortisation appearing in the income statement (profit and loss account).

The IASB has issued a standard, IAS 38, covering accounting for intangible assets. Internally generated brand names must *not* be recognised as intangible assets. This rule applies to similar assets such as publishing titles, customer lists, or newspaper titles. Purchased brand names or trademarks or patents may be reported in a statement of financial position (balance sheet) if they meet the conditions for recognition. Recognition requires that it is probable that the expected economic benefit will flow to the entity, and the cost of the asset can be measured reliably.

If the intangible asset has a finite life it must be amortised over its useful life. The method of amortisation must reflect the pattern of use of the asset.

Activity 8.2	*A company which has manufactured a well-known brand of brown bread for many years has decided that the brand name is so well known that it should appear in the statement of financial position (balance sheet). Write down two arguments in favour of this, to be made by the company's finance director, and two arguments against, which will appear in a newspaper article.*

8.3.3   Investments

Investments exist in many different forms but the essential feature is an ability to generate future economic benefits so that the wealth of the owner increases. This increase in wealth may arise because the value of the investment increases, or may arise because the investment creates income for the owner in the form of a distribution such as interest paid or dividends. Companies may hold investments for a variety of reasons. A non-current (fixed asset) investment is one which is held for long-term purposes, such as shares in another company which has close trading links with the investing company.

The number of shares held may be such as to give direct control of the investment or may be of a lesser amount which indicates a long-term relationship, without direct control, in a similar line of business.

Non-current (fixed) asset investments may be held so that resources are available to meet a long-term obligation, such as the payment of pensions. Such non-current (fixed) assets are normally found in the statements of financial position (balance sheets) of insurance companies or pension funds, rather than in the balance sheet of the company employing staff.

The features which make investments different as non-current (fixed) assets are the importance of the increase in value of the investment itself and the fact that they are not used in the production or service process. Both features require a different kind of accounting treatment from that given to other non-current (fixed) assets. Those special treatments are advanced accounting matters and will not be dealt with in any detail in this text. What you should look for in accounts is the existence of non-current (fixed) asset investments and the information provided about them. The questions users will ask are: 'How well is this investment keeping up its value?' and 'How important is the income from this investment to the overall profit of the company?'

8.4 Users' needs for information

Activity 8.3

Before you read this section, make a list of the information about non-current (fixed) assets which would be useful to you if you wished to learn more about a specific company. Then read the section and compare it with your list. How far-thinking are you in respect of accounting information?

Analysts who write reports for professional and private investors have a particular interest in the non-current (fixed) assets because these are the base from which profits are generated. They want to know what types of assets are held, how old they are and what plans the company has for future investment in non-current (fixed) assets.

The analysts also want to know about the impact of the depreciation charge on the profit of the year. They are aware that detailed aspects of calculations of depreciation may vary from one year to the next and this may affect the comparability of the profit amounts.

To estimate the remaining life of the assets, analysts compare the accumulated depreciation with the total cost (or value) of the non-current (fixed) assets. If the accumulated depreciation is relatively low, then the non-current (fixed) assets are relatively new. Other companies in the industry will be used for comparison. The analysts also compare the depreciation charge for the year with the total cost (or value) of the assets and expect to see a similar relationship from one year to the next. A sudden change will cause them to ask more questions about a change in the basis of calculation.

8.5 Information provided in the financial statements

In Chapter 7 the statement of financial position (balance sheet) of Safe and Sure plc was presented. The statement of financial position (balance sheet) showed a single line of information on tangible non-current (fixed) assets. This section shows how that single line becomes understandable when read in conjunction with the notes to the accounts, the statement of accounting policy and the finance director's review.

8.5.1 Statement of financial position (balance sheet)

	Notes	Year 7 £m	Year 6 £m
Non-current assets			
Property, plant and equipment	1	137.5	121.9

8.5.2 Notes to the statement of financial position (balance sheet)

In the notes to the statement of financial position (balance sheet) there is considerably more information:

Note 1 Property, plant and equipment

	Land and buildings £m	Plant and equipment £m	Vehicles £m	Total £m
Cost or valuation				
At 1 January Year 7	28.3	96.4	104.8	229.5
Additions at cost	3.9	18.5	37.8	60.2
On acquisitions	0.3	1.0	0.7	2.0
Disposals	(0.6)	(3.1)	(24.7)	(28.4)
At 31 December Year 7	31.9	112.8	118.6	263.3
Aggregate depreciation				
At 1 January Year 7	2.2	58.8	46.6	107.6
Depreciation for the year	0.5	13.5	19.2	33.2
On acquisitions	0.1	0.7	0.6	1.4
Disposals	(0.2)	(2.8)	(13.4)	(16.4)
At 31 December Year 7	2.6	70.2	53.0	125.8
Net book value at 31 December Year 7	29.3	42.6	65.6	137.5
Net book value at 31 December Year 6	26.1	37.6	58.2	121.9

Analysis of land and buildings at cost or valuation

	Year 7 £m	Year 6 £m
At cost	10.4	7.1
At valuation	21.5	21.2
	31.9	28.3

The majority of the group's freehold and long-term leasehold properties were revalued during Year 5 by independent valuers. Valuations were made on the basis of the market value for existing use. The book values of the properties were adjusted to the revaluations and the resultant net surplus was credited to the revaluation reserve.

Analysis of net book value of land and buildings

	Year 7 £m	Year 6 £m
Freehold	24.5	21.0
Leasehold:		
Over 50 years unexpired	2.1	2.4
Under 50 years unexpired	2.7	2.7
	29.3	26.1

If the revalued assets were stated on the historical cost basis the amounts would be:

	Year 7 £m	Year 6 £m
Land and buildings at cost	15.7	14.5
Aggregate depreciation	(2.2)	(1.9)
	13.5	12.6

It is clear from the extensive nature of note 2 to the statement of financial position (balance sheet) that tangible non-current (fixed) assets are regarded as important by those who regulate the information. All companies present a detailed note of this kind because the information is required by IAS 16, *Property, Plant and Equipment*.

8.5.3 Statement of accounting policy

In addition the company is required, by the accounting standard IAS 1, *Presentation of Financial Statements*, to disclose its significant accounting policies. For this company the wording of the accounting policy statement is as follows:

Freehold and leasehold property
Freehold and leasehold land and buildings are stated either at cost or at their revalued amounts less depreciation. Full revaluations are made at five-year intervals with interim valuations in the intervening years, the most recent being in Year 0.

Provision for depreciation of freehold land and buildings is made at the annual rate of 1% of cost or the revalued amounts. Leasehold land and buildings are amortised in equal annual instalments over the periods of the leases subject to a minimum annual provision of 1% of cost or the revalued amounts. When properties are sold the difference between sales proceeds and net book value is dealt with in the income statement (profit and loss account).

Other tangible non-current (fixed) assets
Other tangible non-current assets are stated at cost less depreciation. Provision for depreciation is made mainly in equal annual instalments over the estimated useful lives of the assets as follows:

4 to 5 years	*vehicles*
5 to 10 years	*plant, machinery and equipment*

8.5.4 Operating and financial review

There is also a comment in the finance director's report, as a contribution to the operating and financial review:

Capital expenditure
The major items of capital expenditure are vehicles, equipment used on customers' premises and office equipment, particularly computers. Disposals during the year were mainly of vehicles being replaced on a rolling programme.

Activity 8.4

Find the annual report of a company of your choice. This may be through access to the website, or by requesting a printed copy of the annual report through the website www.ft.com, or by using the free annual reports offer on the London Stock Exchange page of the Financial Times.

In the annual report find the information that corresponds to the extracts from Safe & Sure given in section 8.5. What are the similarities and differences? What do you learn about the non-current (fixed) asset base of your chosen company?

8.6 Usefulness of published information

Here is David Wilson to explain how useful he sees the information provided by companies about their tangible non-current (fixed) assets. If you look back to Chapter 4 you will see that he was about to visit the company and had made a preliminary list of questions. He has now made the visit and has a better understanding of what is reported in the statement of financial position (balance sheet). He talks to Leona in a break at a workout session.

DAVID: *I told you that in making my review before visiting the company I looked closely at the type of tangible non-current (fixed) assets held and the estimated useful life. I also checked that the depreciation period and method of calculation had not changed from previous years.*

As I was making a site visit I took the opportunity to look at the various non-current (fixed) assets. This is a group of companies, expanding by acquisition of other companies, and each acquisition brings in more land and buildings. Some of these assets are recorded at valuation rather than original cost. The company has to review the valuation on a regular basis. That is quite a common practice and I have confidence in the firm of valuers used.

Plant and equipment has an aggregate depreciation of £70.2m which is 62% of the cost of the assets at £112.8m. It seems to me that must be saying that the plant and equipment is more than halfway through its estimated life. The finance director wasn't too enthusiastic about this interpretation. He pointed out that when another company is acquired the non-current (fixed) assets may be quite old and have to be brought into the group statement of financial position, but once they are in group control there is a strict policy of evaluation and replacement. He views the depreciation policy as being at the prudent end of the spectrum, so the realistic life remaining might be marginally over half, but discretion and the fast-moving nature of the industry requires an element of caution. He called in the plant manager who showed me the replacement schedules for plant and equipment for the next three years. It certainly reassured me that risk of obsolescence is probably not a serious worry. I also met the vehicle fleet supervisor who showed me similar replacement schedules for the vehicles.

I saw how the vehicle fleet is managed so that every vehicle is idle for the minimum time. Each vehicle is assigned to a group of cleaning operatives, whose shifts are scheduled so that the vehicle's use is maximised. Plant and equipment are the responsibility of area managers who have to look after security, maintenance and efficiency of usage. I thought it was all really quite impressive.

The depreciation charge for the plant and equipment in Year 7 is £13.5m which is 12% of the cost of £112.8m and suggests an estimated life of just over eight years is being applied. That is within the range of five to ten years stated as the company's accounting policy. I think the wording 'five to ten years' is too vague. Using five years would double the depreciation charge compared with ten. I tried to pin down the finance director so that I can get a good figure for my forecast but all he would say was that there is no reason to suppose there are any unusual features in the amount in the accounts. The depreciation charge for vehicles is £19.2m which is 16% of the cost of £118.6m. That suggests an estimated life of just over six years is being applied. I asked the finance director how that squared with the accounting policy statement of estimated useful lives of four to five years for vehicles. He did seem to sigh a little at that point but was quite patient in explaining that there are some fully depreciated vehicles still in use (because they are quite prudent in their estimates of depreciation) and so the depreciation charge is not the 20% to 25% I was looking for. I'll need to think about that one but I might move my estimate for next year closer to 20%.

You asked me how this company's information measures up to the qualitative characteristics (set out in Chapter 4). Relevance I would rate highly, because there is plenty of information in the notes which I can use to ask questions about the effective use of non-current (fixed) assets and the impact on income statement (profit and loss account) through the depreciation charge. Reliability, faithful representation and neutrality are qualities I leave to the auditors. Prudence is something which seems to come out strongly in conversation with the finance director. The detailed schedule of assets which I saw suggests that completeness is not a problem. Comparability is fine because there are amounts for the previous year and the standard format allows me to make comparison with other companies in the industry. Understandability is perhaps more of a problem than I thought. Those fully depreciated assets caught me out.

LEONA: *Well, I have now heard you admit that there is some value in having auditors. Shall I tell you how much you have missed? You could have asked more searching questions about the way in which they measure the cost of plant and equipment. Does it include delivery charges and installation costs? You could have asked whether a technical expert inside the company estimates and reviews the asset lives used, or whether the finance director makes a guess. Did you ask whether they are perhaps verging on being over-prudent so that surprises come later when the depreciation charge is less than expected? You could have asked how the interim valuations are carried out. These are all questions we ask as auditors so that you may treat the information as being reliable and a faithful representation.*

Hopefully you now have a feeling for the information provided by companies on tangible non-current (fixed) assets and how it is used by the professional investor. The nature and recording of depreciation is now explained.

8.7 Depreciation: an explanation of its nature

Activity 8.5

Before you read this section, write down what you think 'depreciation' means. Then read the section and compare it with your initial views. Depreciation is a very subjective matter and there are different views of its purpose, so your answer may be interesting even if it does not match the text. You should consult your lecturer, tutor or other expert in the area to understand why your perceptions may be different.

Definitions[7]

Depreciation is the systematic allocation of the depreciable amount of an asset over its useful life.

The **depreciable amount** is the cost of an asset, or other amount substituted for cost, less its residual value.

Residual value is the estimated amount that an entity would currently obtain from disposal of the asset, after deducting the estimated cost of disposal, if the asset were already of the age and in the condition expected at the end of its useful life.

The asset may be an item of plant or equipment which is wearing out through being used. It may be a payment made by a company for the right to become a tenant of a property. That payment purchases a lease which reduces in value through the passage of time. The asset may be a computer system which becomes out of date in a very short space of time because of obsolescence. It may be a machine which produces goods for which demand falls because of changing market conditions.

The definition shows that depreciation is a device used in accounting to allocate (spread) the cost of a non-current (fixed) asset over its useful life. The process of spreading cost over more than one accounting period is called **allocation**.

In terms of the accounting equation, the useful life of the non-current (fixed) asset is being reduced and this will reduce the ownership interest.

	Assets		**Liabilities**		**Ownership** interest
Year		−		=	
1	↓				↓
2	↓				↓
3	↓				↓
etc.					

As the asset becomes older, the depreciation of one year is added to the depreciation of previous years. This is called the **accumulated depreciation** or **aggregate depreciation**. The accumulated depreciation at the end of any year is equal to the accumulated depreciation at the start of the year plus the depreciation charge for that year.

Deducting the accumulated depreciation from the original cost leaves the **net book value**. The net book value could also be described as the cost remaining as a benefit for future years.

Showing the effect of depreciation by use of arrows and the accounting equation is relatively easy. Deciding on the amount of depreciation each year is much more difficult because there are so many different views of how to calculate the amount of asset used up in each period.

8.7.1 Calculation of depreciation

Calculation of depreciation requires three pieces of information:

1 the cost of the asset;
2 the estimated useful life; and
3 the estimated residual value.

The total depreciation of the non-current (fixed) asset is equal to the cost of the non-current (fixed) asset minus the estimated residual value. The purpose of the depreciation calculation is to spread the total depreciation over the estimated useful life.

The first point at which differences of opinion arise is in the estimation of the useful life and residual value. These are matters of judgement which vary from one person to the next.

Unfortunately the differences do not stop at those estimates. There is also no agreement on the arithmetical approach to spreading the total depreciation over the useful life. Some people are of the opinion that a non-current (fixed) asset is used evenly over time and that the depreciation should reflect the benefit gained from its use. Others argue that the non-current (fixed) asset declines in value most in the early years and so the depreciation charge should be greater in earlier years.

8.7.2 Straight-line method

Those who are of the opinion that a non-current (fixed) asset is used evenly over time apply a method of calculation called straight-line depreciation. The formula is:

$$\frac{\text{Cost} - \text{Expected residual value}}{\text{Expected life}}$$

To illustrate the use of the formula, take a non-current (fixed) asset which has a cost of £1,000 and an estimated life of five years. The estimated residual value is nil. The calculation of the annual depreciation charge is:

$$\frac{£1,000 - \text{nil}}{5} = £200 \text{ per annum}$$

The depreciation rate is sometimes expressed as a percentage of the original cost. In this case the company would state its depreciation policy as follows:

Accounting policy:
Depreciation is charged on a straight-line basis at a rate of 20% of cost per annum.

Table 8.1
Pattern of depreciation and net book value over the life of an asset

End of year	Depreciation of the year (a) £	Total depreciation (b) £	Net book value of the asset (£1,000 – b) £
1	200	200	800
2	200	400	600
3	200	600	400
4	200	800	200
5	200	1,000	nil

The phrase 'straight-line' is used because a graph of the net book value of the asset at the end of each year produces a straight line. Table 8.1 sets out the five-year pattern of depreciation and net book value for the example used above.

Figure 8.1 shows a graph of the net book value at the end of each year. The graph starts at the cost figure of £1,000 when the asset is new (Year 0) and reduces by £200 each year until it is zero at the end of Year 5.

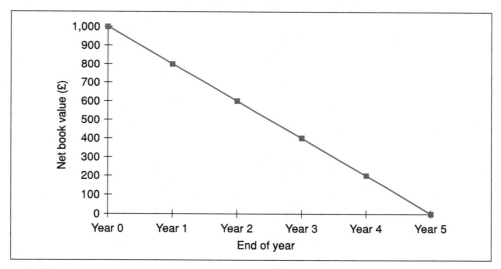

Figure 8.1
Graph of net book value over Years 1 to 5, for the straight-line method of depreciation

8.7.3 Reducing-balance method

Those who believe that the asset depreciates most in earlier years would calculate the depreciation using the formula:

Fixed percentage × Net book value at the start of the year

Take the example of the asset costing £1,000. The fixed percentage applied for the reducing-balance method might be as high as 50%. The calculations would be as shown in the table in Table 8.2.

You will see from the table in Table 8.2 that under the reducing-balance method there is always a small balance remaining. In this example, the rate of 50% is used to bring the net book value to a relatively small amount. The formula for calculating the exact rate requires a knowledge of compound interest and may be found at the end of the Supplement to this chapter. For those whose main interest is in understanding and interpreting accounts it is not necessary to know the formula, but it is useful to be aware that a very much higher percentage rate is required on the reducing-balance method as compared with the straight-line method. As a useful guide, the reducing-balance rate must be at least twice the rate of the straight-line calculation if the major part of the asset is to be depreciated over its useful life.

Table 8.2
Calculation of reducing-balance depreciation

Year	Net book value at start of year (a) £	Annual depreciation (b) = 50% of (a) £	Net book value at end of year (a – b) £
1	1,000	500	500
2	500	250	250
3	250	125	125
4	125	63	62
5	62	31	31

A graph of the net book value at the end of each year under the reducing-balance method is shown in Figure 8.2. The steep slope at the start shows that the net book value declines rapidly in the early part of the asset's life and then less steeply towards the end when most of the benefit of the asset has been used up.

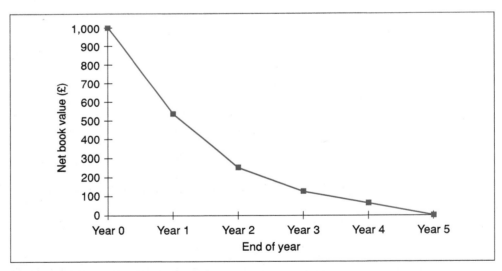

Figure 8.2
Graph of net book value over Years 1 to 5, for the reducing-balance method of depreciation

8.7.4 Which method to choose?

The separate recording of asset at cost and accumulated depreciation is accounting information provided in many countries. The UK practice at a general level is consistent with the IASB standard. Country-specific factors may lead to differences in matters of detail such as the choice of depreciation method or the estimated life of non-current (fixed) assets. In some countries, the depreciation expense in the accounting income statement (profit and loss account) must match that used for the purposes of calculating taxable profit. This may encourage the use of the reducing-balance method, giving a higher expense (and so a lower profit) in the early years of the asset's life. In the UK there are separate rules in tax law for calculating depreciation, and so this has no effect on accounting profit.

The choice of depreciation method should be based on the expected pattern of usage of the asset. If the usage is evenly spread then the straight-line method is appropriate. If the usage is heaviest in early years then the reducing-balance method is the best representation of the economic activity. In practice, it is found that most UK companies use straight-line depreciation. In some other countries, particularly those where tax rules and accounting laws are closely linked, the reducing-balance method is commonly observed. So it appears that there are different international practices that may reflect different conditions in the respective countries. David and Leona discuss the problem.

DAVID: *The choice of depreciation method may have a significant impact on reported profit. Companies that are actively investing in non-current (fixed) assets will do so in the expectation of increased profits. However, it may take some time for such profits to emerge. If, in the meantime, there is a relatively high charge to income statement (profit and loss account) through reducing-balance depreciation, profits may fall in the short term. In contrast the use of straight-line depreciation will have a less dramatic impact on reported profit immediately following the new investment, so the company avoids a dip in profits.*

LEONA: *I can't accept that as a valid argument to give to the auditor. I ask the company what the pattern of usage is. If the company tells me that the asset produces benefit evenly over its useful life, I can accept straight-line depreciation. If, on the other hand, I hear that the asset is more productive in its early years of life, I expect to see reducing-balance depreciation.*

DAVID: *Well let me try your social conscience. I came across a case of a UK company that had been taken over by a German parent company. The UK company had always used straight-line depreciation and was making small profits each year. The parent company had always used reducing-balance depreciation and so changed the accounting method of the UK subsidiary. Small profits turned into large losses and the parent company said that there would have to be a reduction in the workforce to cut costs. The employee representatives said that nothing had changed except that the accountants had redefined the game. They blamed the accountants for the resulting job losses and increased unemployment.*

LEONA: *My role is confined to giving an opinion on the accounting information. If a particular accounting process is detrimental to the public interest then it is the job of government to legislate.*

Activity 8.6   *Consider the discussion between David and Leona. Do you share the concern of the employee representatives as described by David? Do you agree with Leona that the economic impact of accounting information is not a problem for the auditor? What is your view on the social responsibility attached to financial reporting?*

8.7.5 Retaining cash in the business

Suppose that the policy of the owner is to take all the available profits as drawings for personal use. Take a company that has fee income of £120,000 and pays wages and other costs of £58,000. If the company did not recognise the expense of depreciation the owner's drawings could be as high as £62,000. Suppose now that depreciation of non-current (fixed) assets is calculated as £10,000. The net profit after depreciation becomes £52,000. The owner can still see £62,000 in the bank account but knows £10,000 of that amount represents using up non-current (fixed) assets. Leaving the £10,000 in the bank will allow the business to save cash for asset replacement. The owner should withdraw no more than £52,000.

It is often said that depreciation limits the amount of profits available for cash drawings by the owner and encourages saving for asset replacement. However, there is nothing to stop the business spending the £10,000 on some purpose other than replacement of non-current (fixed) assets. We can only say that cash withheld from shareholders *may* be used to replace assets at the end of the asset life.

8.8 Reporting non-current (fixed) assets and depreciation in financial statements

This section moves step by step through the recording process. First, it looks at a situation of straight-line depreciation with no residual value for the asset. Then it takes in the additional complication of an estimated residual value.

8.8.1 Straight-line depreciation, no residual value

When a retail company wants new premises, it must either buy a shop or rent one. Renting is referred to as **leasing**. When the rent agreement is signed, the tenant may pay an agreed price for the privilege of having the lease. This is called the initial payment for the lease. It is paid in addition to the annual rental payment. The initial payment to acquire the lease provides a benefit of occupation for the entire period of the lease and so is a non-current (fixed) asset. Because the lease has a known life, it must be depreciated.

On 1 January Year 2 Electrical Instruments purchased a three-year lease of a shop for a payment of £60,000. Using the straight-line method of depreciation the amount of depreciation each year will be calculated on a straight-line basis as £20,000 (one-third of the cost of the lease). The income statement (profit and loss account) will report this amount as an expense in each of the three years of the lease. The statement of financial position (balance sheet) will show on one line the original cost of £60,000 and, on a second line, the accumulated depreciation to be subtracted at the end of each year.

The financial statements over the period of three years will show the following information relating to this lease:

Income statement (profit and loss account) (extract)			
Year ended 31 December	Year 2	Year 3	Year 4
	£000s	£000s	£000s
Depreciation expense	(20)	(20)	(20)

Statement of financial position (balance sheet) (extract)			
At 31 December	Year 2	Year 3	Year 4
	£000s	£000s	£000s
Lease at cost	60	60	60
Less accumulated depreciation	20	40	60
Net book value	40	20	nil

8.8.2 Straight-line depreciation with a residual value

In the case of Electrical Instruments the lease had no residual value. Take now the example of The Removals Company which commences business on 1 January Year 2 by paying cash for a van costing £60,000. It is estimated to have a useful life of three years and is estimated to have a residual value of £6,000. On 31 December Year 2 the owner calculates annual depreciation of the van as £18,000, using the formula:

$$\frac{Cost - Estimated\ residual\ value}{Estimated\ life}$$

During each year of operating the van, the company collected £120,000 in cash from customers and paid £58,000 in cash for drivers' wages, fuel and other running costs.

These transactions and events may be summarised using the accounting equation and a spreadsheet similar to that used in Chapter 5 (Table 5.3). In Table 8.3 there is a spreadsheet for the first year of the use of the van by the company. The assets section of the spreadsheet has three columns, one of which is for cash but two of which are for the van. The two columns for the van keep a separate record of the original cost and the accumulated depreciation. The original cost is the positive part of the asset but the accumulated depreciation is the negative part of the asset. Taking the accumulated depreciation from the original cost leaves the net book value. That is the amount of cost not yet amortised which acts as a measure of the benefit remaining in the asset for the future. In Table 8.4 the information collected together by Table 8.3 is presented in the form of a statement of financial position (balance sheet) and an income statement (profit and loss account).

8.8.3 Continuing to use the non-current (fixed) asset

So far, the accounting entries have related to the first year of the business so that there was no need to ask any questions about the position at the start of the period. To show the full impact of the progressive depreciation of the asset, the spreadsheet and financial

Table 8.3

Spreadsheet analysing transactions and events of The Removals Company into the elements of the accounting equation

	Transaction or event	Assets			Ownership interest	
		Van at cost	Accumulated depreciation of van	Cash	Capital contributed or withdrawn	Profit = revenue minus (expenses)
Year 2		£	£	£	£	£
1 Jan.	Owner contributes cash			60,000	60,000	
1 Jan.	Purchase furniture van	60,000		(60,000)		
All year	Collected cash from customers			120,000		120,000
All year	Paid for wages, fuel, etc.			(58,000)		(58,000)
31 Dec.	Calculate annual depreciation		(18,000)			(18,000)
	Totals	60,000	(18,000)	62,000	60,000	44,000

└──── 104,000 ────┘   └──── 104,000 ────┘

Table 8.4
The Removals Company: Statement of financial position (balance sheet) at end of Year 2 and Income statement (profit and loss account) for Year 2

The Removals Company
Statement of financial position (balance sheet) at 31 December Year 2

	£
Non-current (fixed) assets	
Furniture van at cost	60,000
Accumulated depreciation	(18,000)
Net book value	42,000
Current assets	
Cash	62,000
Total assets	104,000
Ownership interest	
Ownership interest at the start of the year	nil
Capital contributed during the year	60,000
Profit of the year	44,000
	104,000

The Removals Company
Income statement (profit and loss account)
for the year ended 31 December Year 2

	£	£
Revenue		
Fees for removal work		120,000
Expenses		
Wages, fuel and other running costs	(58,000)	
Depreciation	(18,000)	
		(76,000)
Net profit		44,000

Table 8.5
Spreadsheet analysis of transactions of The Removals Company, Year 3

	Transaction or event	Assets			Ownership interest		
		Van at cost	Accumulated depreciation of van	Cash	Ownership interest at start of year	Capital contributed or withdrawn	Profit = revenue minus (expenses)
Year 3		£	£	£	£	£	£
1 Jan.	Amounts brought forward at start of year	60,000	(18,000)	62,000	104,000		
All year	Collected cash from customers			120,000			120,000
All year	Paid for wages, fuel, etc.			(58,000)			(58,000)
31 Dec.	Calculate annual depreciation		(18,000)				(18,000)
	Totals	60,000	(36,000)	124,000	104,000		44,000

— 148,000 —   — 148,000 —

Table 8.6
The Removals Company statement of financial position (balance sheet) at end of Year 3 and Income statement (profit and loss account) for Year 3

The Removals Company
Statement of financial position (balance sheet) at 31 December Year 3

	£
Non-current (fixed) assets	
Furniture van at cost	60,000
Accumulated depreciation	(36,000)
Net book value	24,000
Current assets	
Cash	124,000
Total assets	148,000
Ownership interest	
Ownership interest at the start of the year	104,000
Profit of the year	44,000
	148,000

The Removals Company
Income statement (profit and loss account)
for the year ended 31 December Year 3

	£	£
Revenue		
Fees for removal work		120,000
Expenses		
Wages, fuel and other running costs	(58,000)	
Depreciation	(18,000)	
		(76,000)
Net profit		44,000

statements are now presented for Year 3. Table 8.5 sets out the spreadsheet and Table 8.6 sets out the financial statements. It is assumed that for Year 3 the amounts of cash collected from customers and the amounts paid in cash for running costs are the same as for Year 2. No further capital is contributed by the owner and no new vans are acquired.

The first line of the spreadsheet in Table 8.5 shows the position at the start of the year. The asset columns show the amounts as they were at the end of the previous year. The ownership interest shows the amount resulting at the end of the previous year, as seen in the Year 2 statement of financial position (balance sheet). The columns for revenue and expenses are empty at the start of the year, awaiting the transactions and events of Year 3.

8.8.4   Disposing of the non-current (fixed) asset

During Year 4 the amounts of cash received from customers and cash paid for running costs are the same as they were in Year 3. Table 8.7 sets out the spreadsheet for the transactions and events.

Now suppose that the van is sold for £6,000 in cash on the final day of December Year 4. The spreadsheet contained in Table 8.7 requires further attention, the additional accounting impact of the sale being seen in Table 8.8.

The disposal of the van must be analysed in stages:

1 collecting cash;
2 transferring ownership of the vehicle;
3 removing the vehicle from the accounting records.

Table 8.7
Spreadsheet analysis of transactions of The Removals Company, Year 4

	Transaction or event	Assets			Ownership interest		
		Van at cost	Accumulated depreciation of van	Cash	Ownership interest at start of year	Capital contributed or withdrawn	Profit = revenue minus (expenses)
Year 4		£	£	£	£	£	£
1 Jan.	Amounts brought forward at start of year	60,000	(36,000)	124,000	148,000		
All year	Collected cash from customers			120,000			120,000
All year	Paid for wages, fuel, etc.			(58,000)			(58,000)
31 Dec.	Calculate annual depreciation		(18,000)				(18,000)
	Totals	60,000	(54,000)	186,000	148,000		44,000

└──── 192,000 ────┘   └──── 192,000 ────┘

Table 8.8
Spreadsheet analysis of transactions of The Removals Company, Year 4, including sale of non-current (fixed) asset

	Transaction or event	Assets			Ownership interest		
		Van at cost	Accumulated depreciation of van	Cash	Ownership interest at start of year	Capital contributed or withdrawn	Profit = revenue minus (expenses)
Year 4		£	£	£	£	£	£
1 Jan.	Amounts brought forward at start of year	60,000	(36,000)	124,000	148,000		
All year	Collected cash from customers			120,000			120,000
All year	Paid for wages, fuel, etc.			(58,000)			(58,000)
31 Dec.	Calculate annual depreciation		(18,000)				(18,000)
31 Dec.	Van disposal	(60,000)	54,000	6,000			
	Totals	nil	nil	192,000	148,000		44,000

└──── 192,000 ────┘   └──── 192,000 ────┘

When the vehicle is removed from the record, two columns must be reduced to zero. These are the *van at cost* column and the *accumulated depreciation* column. The van at cost column shows the original cost of £60,000 and the accumulated depreciation shows the amount of £54,000 which has to be deducted to show the amount of the net book value. The asset of cash increases by £6,000. In terms of the accounting equation:

Assets		–	Liabilities	=	Ownership interest
	£		no change		no change
Increase in cash	6,000				
Decrease van:					
At cost	60,000				
Accumulated depreciation	(54,000)				
	6,000				

The resulting statement of financial position (balance sheet) and income statement (profit and loss account) are shown in Table 8.9.

Table 8.9
The Removals Company: statement of financial position (balance sheet) at end of Year 4 and Income statement (profit and loss account) for Year 4

The Removals Company
Statement of financial position (balance sheet)
at 31 December Year 4

	£
Non-current (fixed) assets	Nil
Current assets	
Cash	192,000
Total assets	192,000
Ownership interest	
Ownership interest at the start of the year	148,000
Profit of the year	44,000
	192,000

The Removals Company
Income statement (profit and loss account)
for the year ended 31 December Year 4

	£	£
Revenue		
Fees for removal work		120,000
Expenses		
Wages, fuel and other running costs	(58,000)	
Depreciation	(18,000)	
		(76,000)
Net profit		44,000

8.8.5 Selling for a price which is not equal to the net book value

The previous illustration was based on selling the van for £6,000, an amount equal to the net book value. Suppose instead it was sold for £9,000. There is a gain on disposal of £3,000. This gain is reported in the income statement (profit and loss account).

Assets		−	Liabilities	=	Ownership interest
	£				
Increase cash	9,000		no change		Increase by £3,000
Decrease van:					
At cost	60,000				
Accumulated depreciation	(54,000)				
	6,000				

If the amount of the gain or loss on disposal is relatively small, it may be deducted from the depreciation charge. In that situation the income statement (profit and loss account) would appear as shown in Table 8.10 where bold printing highlights the difference when compared with the income statement (profit and loss account) in Table 8.9. If the gain or loss is **material** it will be reported separately.

Table 8.10
Income statement (profit and loss account) for Year 4 when proceeds of sale exceed net book value of non-current (fixed) asset

The Removals Company Income statement (profit and loss account) for the year ended 31 December Year 4		
	£	£
Revenue		
Fees for removal work		120,000
Expenses		
Wages, fuel and other running costs	(58,000)	
Depreciation (18,000 – 3,000)	**(15,000)**	
		(73,000)
Net profit		47,000

8.8.6 A table of depreciation expense

To test your understanding of the impact of depreciation you may wish to use a table of the type shown in Table 8.11. It shows that, whatever the proceeds of sale of the asset, the total expense in the income statement (profit and loss account) will always be the same but the amount of expense each year will vary.

If you compare the two tables (a) and (b) you will see that:

- total depreciation over the three years is the same in both cases;
- total net profit after depreciation over the three years is the same in both cases;
- annual depreciation in Years 1 and 2 is lower in table (b);
- net profit after depreciation in Years 1 and 2 is higher in table (b);
- net book value of the asset at the end of Years 1 and 2 is higher in table (b);
- the depreciation charge in Year 3 is higher in table (b);
- the net profit after depreciation in Year 3 is lower in table (b).

This is an example of what is referred to in accounting as an **allocation** problem (a 'sharing' problem). The expense is the same in total but is allocated (shared) differently across the years of the asset's life. As a result, there are different amounts

Table 8.11
Table of depreciation charge

(a) A van cost £60,000, was estimated to have a useful life of three years and a residual value of £6,000. It was sold for £9,000 on the last day of Year 3. Net profit before depreciation is £62,000.

Year	Net profit before depreciation	Depreciation expense of the year	Net profit after depreciation	Cost less accumulated depreciation	Net book value
	£	£	£	£	£
1	62,000	18,000	44,000	60,000 – 18,000	42,000
2	62,000	18,000	44,000	60,000 – 36,000	24,000
3	62,000	15,000	47,000	60,000 – 54,000	6,000
Total depreciation charge		51,000			
Total reported net profit			135,000		

Proceeds of sale exceed net book value by £3,000. This gain is deducted from the depreciation expense of £18,000 leaving £15,000 as the expense of the year.

(b) A van cost £60,000, was estimated to have a useful life of three years and a residual value of £9,000. The annual depreciation was calculated as £17,000. The van was sold for £9,000 on the last day of Year 3. Net profit before depreciation is £62,000.

Year	Net profit before depreciation	Depreciation expense of the year	Net profit after depreciation	Cost less accumulated depreciation	Net book value
	£	£	£	£	£
1	62,000	17,000	45,000	60,000 – 17,000	43,000
2	62,000	17,000	45,000	60,000 – 34,000	26,000
3	62,000	17,000	45,000	60,000 – 51,000	9,000
Total depreciation charge		51,000			
Total reported net profit			135,000		

Net book value equals proceeds of sale so the depreciation charge of Year 3 is the same as that of previous years.

in the income statement (profit and loss account) for each year but the total profit over the longer period is the same.

8.8.7 Impairment

An asset is impaired when the business will not be able to recover the amount shown in the statement of financial position (balance sheet), either through use or through sale. If the enterprise believes that impairment may have taken place, it must carry out an **impairment review**. This requires comparison of the net book value with the cash-generating ability of the asset. If the comparison indicates that the recorded net book value is too high, the value of the asset is reduced and there is an expense in the income statement (profit and loss account).[8]

The impairment test may be applied to intangible non-current (fixed) assets such as goodwill, in order to justify non-amortisation. If no impairment is detected it may be argued that the asset has maintained its value and so amortisation is not necessary. If there has been impairment of the historical cost net book value, then the loss in asset value becomes an expense for the income statement (profit and loss account).

8.9 Summary

- A **non-current asset** is any asset that does not meet the definition of a current asset.[9] Non-current assets include tangible, intangible and financial assets of a long-term nature. These are also described as **fixed assets**.

- **Tangible non-current (fixed) assets** are assets that have physical substance and are held for use in the production or supply of goods or services, for rental to others, or for administrative purposes on a continuing basis in the reporting entity's activities.

- An **intangible asset** is an identifiable non-monetary asset without physical substance.

- Users need information about the cost of an asset and the aggregate (accumulated) depreciation as the separate components of net book value. Having this detail allows users to estimate the proportion of asset life remaining to be used. This information will be reported in the notes to the statement of financial position (balance sheet).

- Users also need information about the accounting policy on depreciation and its impact on the reported asset values. This information will be found in the notes to the accounts on accounting policies and the notes. There may also be a description and discussion in the Operating and Financial Review, including a forward-looking description of intended capital expenditure.

- **Depreciation** is estimated for the total life of the asset and then allocated to the reporting periods involved, usually annual reporting. No particular method of depreciation is required by law. Preparers of financial statements have to exercise choices. Companies in the UK commonly use straight-line depreciation. An alternative is reducing-balance depreciation. This is found more commonly in some other countries. Choice of depreciation method affects the comparability of profit.

Further reading

The following standards are too detailed for a first level course but the definitions sections may be helpful.

IASB (2009), IAS 38, *Intangible Assets*, International Accounting Standards Board.

IASB (2009), IAS 16, *Property, Plant and Equipment*, International Accounting Standards Board.

QUESTIONS

The Questions section of each chapter has three types of question. 'Test your understanding' questions to help you review your reading are in the 'A' series of questions. You will find the answers to these by reading and thinking about the material in the book. 'Application' questions to test your ability to apply technical skills are in the 'B' series of questions. Questions requiring you to show skills in problem solving and evaluation are in the 'C' series of questions. A letter [S] indicates that there is a solution at the end of the book.

A   Test your understanding

A8.1   State the definition of a non-current (fixed) asset and explain why each condition is required. (Section 8.2)

A8.2   Explain the categories: (Section 8.2.1)

(a) tangible non-current (fixed) assets;
(b) intangible non-current (fixed) assets; and
(c) non-current (fixed) asset investments;

and give an example of each.

A8.3   What do users of financial statements particularly want to know about non-current (fixed) assets? (Section 8.4)

A8.4   What type of information would you expect to find about non-current (fixed) assets in the financial statements and notes of a major UK listed company? (Section 8.4)

A8.5   State the definition of depreciation. (Section 8.7)

A8.6   What is meant by accumulated depreciation (also called aggregate depreciation)? (Section 8.7)

A8.7   What information is needed to calculate annual depreciation? (Section 8.7.1)

A8.8   What is the formula for calculating straight-line depreciation? (Section 8.7.2)

A8.9   How is reducing-balance depreciation calculated? (Section 8.7.3)

A8.10   How does depreciation help to retain cash in a business for asset replacement? (Section 8.7.5)

A8.11   Why does the net book value of a non-current (fixed) asset not always equal the proceeds of sale? (Section 8.8.5)

A8.12   Why is depreciation said to cause an **allocation** problem in accounting? (Section 8.8.6)

A8.13   How should the cost of a non-current (fixed) asset be decided? (Section 8.2.2)

A8.14   [S] What are the matters of judgement relating to non-current (fixed) assets which users of financial statements should think about carefully when evaluating financial statements?

A8.15   What is meant by **impairment**? (Section 8.8.7)

B   Application

B8.1 [S]
On reviewing the financial statements of a company, the company's accountant discovers that expenditure of £8,000 on repair to factory equipment has been incorrectly recorded as a part of the cost of the machinery. What will be the effect on the income statement (profit and loss account) and statement of financial position (balance sheet) when the error is corrected?

B8.2
On 1 January Year 1, Angela's Employment Agency was formed. The owner contributed £300,000 in cash which was immediately used to purchase a building. It is estimated to have a 20-year life and a residual value of £200,000. During Year 1 the agency collects £80,000 in fee income and pays £60,000 in wages and other costs. Record the transactions and events of Year 1 in an accounting equation spreadsheet. (See Table 8.3 for an illustration.) Prepare the statement of financial position (balance sheet) at the end of Year 1 and the income statement (profit and loss account) for Year 1.

B8.3

Assume that fee income and costs are the same in Year 2 as in Year 1. Record the transactions and events of Year 2 in an accounting equation spreadsheet. Prepare the statement of financial position (balance sheet) at the end of Year 2 and the income statement (profit and loss account) for Year 2.

B8.4

Angela's Employment Agency sells the building for £285,000 on the final day of December Year 3. Record the transactions and events of Year 3 in an accounting equation spreadsheet. (See Table 8.7 for an illustration.) Assume depreciation is calculated in full for Year 3.

B8.5

Explain how the accounting equation spreadsheet of your answer to question B8.4 would alter if the building had been sold for £250,000.

B8.6

On 1 January Year 1, Company A purchased a bus costing £70,000. It was estimated to have a useful life of three years and a residual value of £4,000. It was sold for £8,000 on the last day of Year 3.

On 1 January Year 1, Company B purchased a bus also costing £70,000. It was estimated to have a useful life of three years and a residual value of £7,000. It was sold for £8,000 on the last day of Year 3.

Both companies have a net profit of £50,000 before depreciation. Calculate the depreciation charge and net profit of each company for each of the three years. Show that over the three years the total depreciation charge for each company is the same. (See Table 8.11 for an example.)

C   Problem solving and evaluation

C8.1 [S]

The Biscuit Manufacturing Company commenced business on 1 January Year 1 with capital of £22,000 contributed by the owner. It immediately paid cash for a biscuit machine costing £22,000. It was estimated to have a useful life of four years and at the end of that time was estimated to have a residual value of £2,000. During each year of operation of the machine, the company collected £40,000 in cash from sale of biscuits and paid £17,000 in cash for wages, ingredients and running costs.

Required
(a) Prepare spreadsheets for each of the four years analysing the transactions and events of the company.
(b) Prepare a statement of financial position (balance sheet) at the end of Year 3 and an income statement (profit and loss account) for that year.
(c) Explain to a non-accountant how to read and understand the statement of financial position (balance sheet) and income statement (profit and loss account) you have prepared.

C8.2 [S]

The biscuit machine in question C8.1 was sold at the end of Year 4 for a price of £3,000.

Required
(a) Prepare the spreadsheet for Year 4 analysing the transactions and events of the year.
(b) Prepare the statement of financial position (balance sheet) at the end of Year 4 and the income statement (profit and loss account) for Year 4.
(c) Explain to a non-accountant the accounting problems of finding that the asset was sold for £3,000 when the original expectation was £2,000.

C8.3 [S]

The Souvenir Company purchased, on 1 January Year 1, a machine producing embossed souvenir badges. The machine cost £16,000 and was estimated to have a five-year life with a residual value of £1,000.

Required

(a) Prepare a table of depreciation charges and net book value over the five-year life using straight-line depreciation.

(b) Make a guess at the percentage rate to be used in the reducing-balance calculation, and prepare a table of depreciation charges and net book value over the five years using reducing-balance depreciation.

(c) Using the straight-line method of depreciation, demonstrate the effect on the accounting equation of selling the asset at the end of Year 5 for a price of £2,500.

(d) Using the straight-line method of depreciation, demonstrate the effect on the accounting equation of disposing of the asset at the end of Year 5 for a zero scrap value.

Activities for study groups

Turn to the annual report of a listed company which you have used for activities in previous chapters. Find every item of information about non-current (fixed) assets. (Start with the financial statements and notes but look also at the operating and financial review, chief executive's review and other non-regulated information about the company.)

As a group, imagine you are the team of fund managers in a fund management company. You are holding a briefing meeting at which each person explains to the others some feature of the companies in which your fund invests. Today's subject is *non-current (fixed) assets*. Each person should make a short presentation to the rest of the team covering:

1 the nature and significance of non-current (fixed) assets in the company;

2 the asset lives stated in the accounting policies for depreciation purposes;

3 the asset lives estimated by you from calculations of annual depreciation as a percentage of asset cost;

4 the remaining useful life of assets as indicated by comparing accumulated depreciation with asset cost;

5 the company's plans for future investment in non-current (fixed) assets.

Notes and references

1. IASB (1989), *Framework for the Preparation and Presentation of Financial Statements*, para. 49(a) 6.
2. IASB (2009), IAS 1 paras 66 and 67.
3. IASB (2009), IAS 1 para. 67 permits the use of alternative descriptions for non-current assets provided the meaning is clear.
4. ASB (1999), FRS 15, *Measurement of Tangible Fixed Assets*, para. 2.
5. IASB (2009), IAS 38, *Intangible Assets*, para. 8.
6. IASB (2009), IAS 16, *Property, Plant and Equipment*, para 6.
7. IASB (2009), IAS 16, *Property, Plant and Equipment*, para. 6.
8. There remain international differences on the precise method of estimating cash-generating ability. There are detailed rules in IAS 38 but these are beyond a first-level text.
9. IASB (2009), IAS 1 paras 66 and 67.

Recording non-current (fixed) assets and depreciation

The rules for debit and credit entries in a ledger account should by now be familiar but are set out again in Table 8.12 for convenience. If you still feel unsure about any aspect of Exhibit 8.14 you should revisit the supplements of earlier chapters before attempting this one.

In this supplement you will concentrate primarily on the ledger accounts for the non-current (fixed) assets. It takes The Removals Company of the main chapter as the example for illustration.

Table 8.12
Rules for debit and credit entries in ledger accounts

	Debit entries in a ledger account	Credit entries in a ledger account
Left-hand side of the equation		
Asset	Increase	Decrease
Right-hand side of the equation		
Liability	Decrease	Increase
Ownership interest	Expense	Revenue
	Capital withdrawn	Capital contributed

Information to be recorded

The Removals Company commences business on 1 January Year 2 by paying cash for a van costing £60,000. The cash was contributed by the owner. The van is estimated to have a useful life of three years and is estimated to have a residual value of £6,000. On 31 December Year 2 the owner calculates annual depreciation of the van as £18,000, using the formula:

$$\frac{\text{Cost} - \text{Estimated residual value}}{\text{Estimated life}}$$

During each year of operating the van, the company collected £120,000 in cash from customers and paid £58,000 in cash for drivers' wages, fuel and other running costs.

The transactions of Year 2 have been analysed in Table 8.3 for their impact on the accounting equation. That same list may be used to set out the debit and credit book-keeping entries, as shown in Table 8.13.

Table 8.13
Analysis of transactions for The Removals Company, Year 2

Date	Transaction or event	Amount	Dr	Cr
Year 2		£		
1 Jan.	Owner contributes cash	60,000	Cash	Ownership interest
1 Jan.	Purchase furniture van	60,000	Van at cost	Cash
All year	Collected cash from customers	120,000	Cash	Sales
All year	Paid for running costs	58,000	Running costs	Cash
31 Dec.	Calculate annual depreciation	18,000	Depreciation	Accumulated depreciation

Ledger accounts required to record transactions of Year 2 are as follows:

L1　Ownership interest	L4　Accumulated depreciation of van
L2　Cash	L5　Sales
L3　Van at cost	L6　Running costs
	L7　Depreciation of the year

L1 Ownership interest

Date	Particulars	Page	Debit	Credit	Balance
Year 2			£	£	£
Jan. 1	Cash	L2		60,000	(60,000)

LEONA's comment: *This ledger account shows the opening contribution to the start of the business which establishes the ownership interest.*

L2 Cash

Date	Particulars	Page	Debit	Credit	Balance
Year 2			£	£	£
Jan. 1	Ownership interest	L1	60,000		60,000
Jan. 1	Van	L3		60,000	nil
Jan.–Dec.	Sales	L5	120,000		120,000
Jan.–Dec.	Running costs	L6		58,000	62,000

LEONA's comment: *For convenience in this illustration all the sales and running costs have been brought together in one amount for the year. In reality there would be a large number of separate transactions recorded throughout the year. The balance at the end of the year shows that there is £62,000 remaining in the bank account.*

L3 Van at cost

Date	Particulars	Page	Debit £	Credit £	Balance £
Year 2					
Jan. 1	Cash	L2	60,000		(60,000)

LEONA's comment: *The van is recorded by a debit entry and this entry remains in the ledger account for as long as the van is in use by the company. A separate ledger account is maintained for the cost of the asset because it is regarded as a useful piece of information for purposes of financial statements.*

L4 Accumulated depreciation of van

Date	Particulars	Page	Debit £	Credit £	Balance £
Year 2					
Dec. 31	Depreciation of the year	L7		18,000	(18,000)

LEONA's comment: *The accumulated depreciation account completes the story about the van. It has an original cost of £60,000 and an accumulated depreciation at the end of Year 2 equal to £18,000. The accumulated depreciation account will always show a credit balance because it is the negative part of the asset. Deducting accumulated depreciation from cost gives a net book value of £42,000.*

L5 Sales

Date	Particulars	Page	Debit £	Credit £	Balance £
Year 2					
Jan.–Dec.	Cash	L2		120,000	(120,000)

LEONA's comment: *For convenience all the sales transactions of the year have been brought together in one single amount, but in reality there would be many pages of separate transactions.*

L6 Running costs

Date	Particulars	Page	Debit £	Credit £	Balance £
Year 2					
Jan.–Dec.	Cash	L2	58,000		58,000

LEONA's comment: *As with the sales transactions of the year, all running costs have been brought together in one single amount, but in reality there will be several pages of separate transactions recorded over the year.*

L7 Depreciation of the year

Date	Particulars	Page	Debit	Credit	Balance
Year 2			£	£	£
Dec. 31	Depreciation of year 2	L4	18,000		18,000

LEONA's comment: *The depreciation of the year is a debit entry because it is an expense. The process of depreciation is continuous but that is not convenient for ledger account recording, so companies prefer a single calculation at the end of the year.*

At this point a trial balance may be prepared, as explained in the supplement to Chapter 5, and shown in Table 8.14.

Table 8.14
Trial balance at the end of Year 2 for The Removals Company

Ledger account title	£	£
L1 Ownership interest		60,000
L2 Cash	62,000	
L3 Van at cost	60,000	
L4 Accumulated depreciation of van		18,000
L5 Sales		120,000
L6 Running costs	58,000	
L7 Depreciation	18,000	
Totals	198,000	198,000

Closing at the end of Year 2 and starting the ledger accounts for Year 3

At the end of the year the balances on asset and liability accounts are *carried forward* to the next year. The phrase 'carried forward' means that they are allowed to remain in the ledger account at the start of the new year. The balances on revenue and expense accounts are treated differently. After the trial balance has been prepared and checked, the amounts on each revenue account and expense account are *transferred to an income statement (profit and loss account)*. Transferring a balance requires an entry of the opposite type to the balance being transferred. A debit entry is made to transfer a credit balance. A credit entry is made to transfer a debit balance. Matching but opposite entries are made in the income statement (profit and loss account). This is called 'closing' the expense or revenue account.

L5 Sales

Date	Particulars	Page	Debit	Credit	Balance
Year 2			£	£	£
Jan.–Dec.	Cash	L2		120,000	(120,000)
Dec. 31	Transfer to profit and loss account	L8	120,000		nil

LEONA's comment: *The ledger account for sales shows a credit balance of £120,000 for the total transactions of the year. This is transferred to the income statement (profit and loss account) by making a debit entry of similar amount, so that the balance of the sales account is reduced to nil.*

L6 Running costs

Date	Particulars	Page	Debit	Credit	Balance
Year 2			£	£	£
Jan.–Dec.	Cash	L2	58,000		58,000
Dec. 31	Transfer to income statement (profit and loss account)	L8		58,000	nil

LEONA's comment: *The ledger account for running costs shows a debit balance of £58,000 for the total transactions of the year. This is transferred to the income statement (profit and loss account) by making a credit entry of similar amount, so that the balance of the running costs account is reduced to nil.*

L7 Depreciation of the year

Date	Particulars	Page	Debit	Credit	Balance
Year 2			£	£	£
Dec. 31	Depreciation of Year 2	L4	18,000		18,000
Dec. 31	Transfer to income statement (profit and loss account)	L8		18,000	nil

LEONA's comment: *The ledger account for depreciation expense shows a debit balance of £18,000 for the depreciation charge of the year. This is transferred to the income statement (profit and loss account) by making a credit entry of similar amount, so that the balance of the depreciation expense account of the year is reduced to nil.*

L8 Income statement (profit and loss account)

Date	Particulars	Page	Debit	Credit	Balance
Year 2			£	£	£
Dec. 31	Sales	L5		120,000	(120,000)
Dec. 31	Running costs	L6	58,000		(62,000)
Dec. 31	Depreciation of the year	L7	18,000		(44,000)

LEONA's comment: *The income statement (profit and loss account) in ledger form shows all items of revenue in the credit column and all items of expense in the debit column. The balance in the third column shows, at the end of the ledger account, the profit of £44,000 for the year. There is one final entry to be made, and that is to transfer the £44,000 balance of the income statement (profit and loss account) to the ownership interest account. That requires a debit entry in the income statement (profit and loss account) to remove the credit balance.*

L8 Income statement (profit and loss account)

Date	Particulars	Page	Debit	Credit	Balance
Year 2			£	£	£
Dec. 31	Sales	L5		120,000	(120,000)
Dec. 31	Running costs	L6	58,000		(62,000)
Dec. 31	Depreciation	L7	18,000		(44,000)
Dec. 31	Transfer to ownership interest	L1	44,000		nil

L1 Ownership interest

Date	Particulars	Page	Debit	Credit	Balance
Year 2			£	£	£
Jan. 1	Cash	L2		60,000	(60,000)
Dec. 31	Transfer from income statement (profit and loss account)	L8		44,000	(104,000)

LEONA's comment: *The transfer from the income statement (profit and loss account) is shown as a credit entry in the ledger account for the ownership interest. That credit entry matches the debit entry, removing the balance from the ledger account. As a check on the common sense of the credit entry, go back to the table at the start of this Supplement (Table 8.12), which shows that a credit entry records an increase in the ownership interest. In the ledger account the credit entry of £44,000 increases the ownership interest from £60,000 to £104,000.*

Subsequent years

The income statement (profit and loss account)s for Year 3 and Year 4 are identical to that for Year 2. The cash account flows on in a pattern similar to that of Year 2. These ledger accounts are therefore not repeated here for Years 3 and 4. Attention is concentrated on the asset at cost and the accumulated depreciation.

L3 Van at cost

Date	Particulars	Page	Debit	Credit	Balance
Year 2			£	£	£
Jan. 1	Cash	L2	60,000		60,000
Year 3	Balance	b/fwd			60,000
Year 4	Balance	b/fwd			60,000

LEONA's comment: *The asset continues in use from one year to the next and so the ledger account remains open with the balance of £60,000 remaining. At the start of each new year the balance on each asset account is brought forward (repeated) from the previous line to* show clearly that this is the amount for the start of the new accounting year. Because this is merely a matter of convenience in tidying up at the start of the year, the abbreviation 'b/fwd' (for 'brought forward') is entered in the 'page' column to show that there are no debit or credit entries for transactions on this line.

L4 Accumulated depreciation

Date	Particulars	Page	Debit	Credit	Balance
Year 2			£	£	£
Dec. 31	Depreciation of Year 2	L7		18,000	(18,000)
Year 3					
Dec. 31	Depreciation of Year 3	L7		18,000	(36,000)
Year 4					
Dec. 31	Depreciation of Year 4	L7		18,000	(54,000)

LEONA's comment: *The accumulated depreciation account is now showing more clearly what the word 'accumulated' means. Each year it is building in a further amount of £18,000 annual depreciation to build up the total shown in the 'balance' column. After three years the accumulated depreciation has built up to £54,000.*

L7 Depreciation of the year: Year 3

Date	Particulars	Page	Debit	Credit	Balance
Year 3			£	£	£
Dec. 31	Depreciation of Year 3	L4	18,000		18,000
Dec. 31	Transfer to income statement (profit and loss account)	L8		18,000	nil

L7 Depreciation of the year: Year 4

Date	Particulars	Page	Debit	Credit	Balance
Year 4			£	£	£
Dec. 31	Depreciation of Year 4	L4	18,000		18,000
Dec. 31	Transfer to income statement (profit and loss account)	L8		18,000	nil

LEONA's comment: *The depreciation of the year is an income statement (profit and loss account) item and so is transferred to the income statement (profit and loss account) each year in Years 3 and 4 in the manner explained earlier for Year 2.*

Disposal of the asset

At the end of Year 4 the asset is sold for a cash price of £6,000. To remove the asset requires entries in the 'Van at cost' account (L3), the 'Accumulated depreciation' account (L4) and the 'Cash' account (L2). The corresponding debit and credit entries are recorded in a 'Non-current (fixed) asset disposal' account (L9).

Table 8.15 shows the breakdown of the sale transaction into the removal of the asset at cost, the removal of the accumulated depreciation, and the collection of cash. The entry required to remove a balance on a ledger account is the opposite to the amount of the balance. So in the 'Van at cost' account (L3) a credit entry of £60,000 is required to remove a debit balance of £60,000. In the 'Accumulated depreciation' account (L4) a debit entry is required to remove a credit balance of £54,000. In the 'Cash' account (L2) there is a debit entry of £60,000 to show that the asset of cash has increased. In each case the 'Disposal' account (L9) collects the matching debit or credit.

Table 8.15
Analysis of debit and credit aspects of sale of a fixed asset

Date	Transaction or event	Amount	Dr	Cr
Year 4		£		
Dec. 31	Removal of asset at cost	60,000	Disposal	Van at cost
Dec. 31	Accumulated depreciation	54,000	Accumulated depreciation	Disposal
Dec. 31	Cash	6,000	Cash	Disposal

L3 Van at cost

Date	Particulars	Page	Debit	Credit	Balance
Year 2			£	£	£
Jan. 1	Cash	L2	60,000		60,000
Year 3	Balance	b/fwd			60,000
Year 4	Balance	b/fwd			60,000
Dec. 31	Disposal	L9		60,000	nil

L4 Accumulated depreciation

Date	Particulars	Page	Debit	Credit	Balance
Year 2			£	£	£
Dec. 31	Depreciation of Year 2	L7		18,000	(18,000)
Year 3					
Dec. 31	Depreciation of Year 3	L7		18,000	(36,000)
Year 4					
Dec. 31	Depreciation of Year 4	L7		18,000	(54,000)
Dec. 31	Disposal	L9	54,000		nil

L9 Non-current (fixed) asset disposal account

Date	Particulars	Page	Debit	Credit	Balance
Year 4			£	£	£
Dec. 31	Van at cost	L3	60,000		60,000
Dec. 31	Accumulated depreciation	L4		54,000	6,000
Dec. 31	Cash	L2		6,000	nil

LEONA's comment: *The disposal account is a very convenient way of bringing together all the information about the disposal of the van. The first two lines show the full cost and accumulated depreciation. The balance column, on the second line, shows that the difference between these two items is the net book value of £6,000. Collecting cash of £6,000 is seen to match exactly the net book value, which means that there is no depreciation adjustment on disposal.*

Sale for an amount greater than the net book value

In the main text of this chapter there is a discussion of the consequences of selling the van for £9,000 cash. There would be no problem in recording that in the bookkeeping system. Everything explained in the previous section would be unchanged except for the amount of the cash received. The Disposal account would now be recorded as:

L9 Non-current (fixed) asset disposal account

Date	Particulars	Page	Debit	Credit	Balance
Year 4			£	£	£
Dec. 31	Van at cost	L3	60,000		60,000
Dec. 31	Accumulated depreciation	L4		54,000	6,000
Dec. 31	Cash	L2		9,000	(3,000)
Dec. 31	Transfer to income statement (profit and loss account)	L8	3,000		nil

The income statement (profit and loss account) for Year 4 would be recorded as:

L8 Income statement (profit and loss account)

Date	Particulars	Page	Debit	Credit	Balance
Year 4			£	£	£
Dec. 31	Sales	L5		120,000	(120,000)
Dec. 31	Running costs	L6	58,000		(62,000)
Dec. 31	Depreciation of the year	L7	18,000		(44,000)
Dec. 31	Gain on disposal	L9		3,000	(47,000)

LEONA's comment: *This income statement (profit and loss account) in ledger form matches the income statement (profit and loss account) presented at Table 8.10 in the main text as a financial statement, although you will see that the latter is much more informative.*

Formula for calculating percentage rate for reducing-balance depreciation

The rate of depreciation to be applied under the reducing-balance method of depreciation may be calculated by the formula:

$$\text{rate} = (1 - \sqrt[n]{(R/C)}) \times 100\%$$

where: n = the number of years of useful life
R = the estimated residual value
C = the cost of the asset.

For the example given in the main chapter:

N = 5 years
C = £1,000
R = £30 (The residual value must be of reasonable magnitude. To use an amount of nil for the residual value would result in a rate of 100%.)

$$\text{rate} = (1 - \sqrt[5]{(30/1,000)}) \times 100\%$$

To prove that the rate is 50% you will need a scientific calculator or a suitable computer package. You may know how to calculate a fifth root using logarithms. Otherwise, if you have a very basic calculator it may be easier to use trial-and-error methods.

S   Test your understanding

S8.1   Prepare ledger accounts to report the transactions and events of questions C8.1 and C8.2.

S8.2   Write a short commentary on each ledger account prepared in S1, to enable a non-accountant to understand their purpose and content.

Chapter 9

Current assets

REAL WORLD CASE

Current assets of a manufacturing company

This case extracts information from the annual report of Cadbury plc to show how the company explains its management of current assets.

Current assets: balance sheets at 31 December 2008

Note		2008 £m	2007 £m
19	Inventories	767	821
	Short-term investments	247	2
20	Trade and other receivables	1,067	1,197
	Tax recoverable	35	41
	Cash and cash equivalents	251	493
27	Derivative financial instruments	268	46
		2,635	2,600

Annual report 2008, p. 84.

19. Inventories

	2008 £m	2007 £m
Raw materials and consumables	228	255
Work in progress	92	69
Finished goods and goods for resale	447	497
	767	821

The cost of inventories recognised as an expense for the period ended 31 December 2008 total £2,870 million (2007: £2,504 million).

Annual report 2008, p. 109.

Accounting policy note (r) Inventories

Inventories are recorded at the lower of average cost and estimated net realisable value. Cost comprises direct material and labour costs together with the relevant factory overheads (including depreciation) on the basis of normal activity levels. Amounts are removed from inventory based on the average value of the items of inventory removed.

Annual report 2008, p. 94.

Accounting policy note – transactional exposures

The Group is exposed to changes in prices of its raw materials, certain of which are subject to potential short and long-term fluctuations. In respect of such commodities the Group enters into derivative contracts in order to provide a stable cost base for marketing finished products. The use of commodity derivative contracts enables the Group to obtain the benefit of guaranteed contract performance on firm priced contracts offered by banks, the exchanges and their clearing houses. In principle these derivatives may qualify as 'cash flow hedges' of future forecast transactions. To the extent that the hedge is deemed effective, the movement in the fair value of the derivative would be deferred in equity and released to the income statement as the cash flows relating to the underlying transactions are incurred.

Annual report 2008, p. 96.

Working with our suppliers

We use a wide range of raw materials in manufacturing our confectionery products, the main ones being cocoa beans, sugar and other sweeteners (including polyols and artificial sweeteners such as aspartame), dairy products (including fresh milk), gumbase, fruit and nuts. Our supplier base is diverse. Our sustainability review sets out some of the initiatives we use to ensure ethical and sustainable sourcing, particularly through our Cadbury Cocoa Partnership. More details can be found online [website reference]. In addition, our supply chain team develops individual strategies, audit programmes and development plans to help manage risk within our supply base.

Annual report 2008, p. 25, *Vision into Action Business Plan*.

Source for all extracts: Cadbury plc. Annual report 2008; http://www.cadburyinvestors.com/.

Discussion points

1 What are the proportions of raw materials, work in progress and finished goods inventories?

2 How does the company deal with the volatile prices of cocoa and sugar?

Contents

Learning outcomes

After studying this chapter you should be able to:

- Define a current asset and apply the definition.
- Explain the operation of the working capital cycle.
- Explain the factors affecting recognition of inventories (stocks), receivables (debtors) and investments.
- Explain how the information presented in a company's statement of financial position (balance sheet) and notes, in relation to current assets, meets the needs of users.
- Explain the different approaches to measurement of inventories (stocks) and cost of goods sold.
- Analyse provisions for doubtful debts using a spreadsheet.
- Analyse prepayments using a spreadsheet.
- Explain the term 'revenue' and the application of principles of revenue recognition.

Additionally, for those who choose to study the supplement:

- Record receivables (debtors) and prepayments in ledger accounts.

9.1 Introduction

This chapter will continue the progress through the statement of financial position (balance sheet) which we began in Chapter 8. As in that chapter, the approach will be:

- What are the principles for defining and recognising these items?
- What are the information needs of users in respect of the particular items?
- What information is currently provided by companies to meet these needs?
- Does the information show the desirable qualitative characteristics of financial statements?
- What are the principles for measuring, and processes for recording, these items?

9.2 Definitions

Definitions were provided in Chapter 2. They are repeated here for convenience.

Definition

An **asset** is a resource controlled by the entity as a result of past events and from which future economic benefits are expected to flow.[1]

A **current asset** is an asset that satisfies any of the following criteria:

(a) it is expected to be realised in, or is intended for sale or consumption in, the entity's normal operating cycle;
(b) it is held primarily for the purpose of being traded;
(c) it is expected to be realised within twelve months after the reporting period;
(d) it is cash or a cash equivalent.[2]

The following list is a sample of the current assets found in most company statement of financial position (balance sheet)s:

- raw materials
- work in progress
- finished goods
- trade receivables (debtors)
- amounts owed by other companies in a group
- prepayments and accrued income
- investments held as current assets
- short-term bank deposits
- bank current account (also called 'cash at bank')
- cash in hand.

Activity 9.1

Using the definition provided, explain why each item in the foregoing list may be classed as a current asset. Could a plot of land ever be treated as a current asset?

The definition of a current asset refers to 'the entity's normal operating cycle'. The operating cycle experienced by many businesses lasts for 12 months, covering all the seasons of one year. One year is the reporting period most commonly used by most enterprises for reporting to external users of financial statements.

9.3 The working capital cycle

Working capital is the amount of long-term finance the business has to provide in order to keep **current assets** working for the business. Some short-term finance for current assets is provided by the suppliers who give credit by allowing time to pay, but that is not usually sufficient. Some short-term finance for current assets is provided by short-term bank loans but, in most cases, there still remains an excess of **current assets** over **current liabilities**.

The working capital cycle of a business is the sequence of transactions and events, involving current assets and current liabilities, through which the business makes a profit.

Figure 9.1 shows how the working capital cycle begins when suppliers allow the business to obtain goods on credit terms, but do not insist on immediate payment.

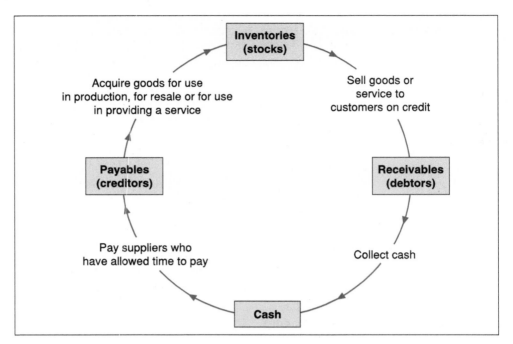

Figure 9.1
The working capital cycle for a manufacturing or service business

While they are waiting for payment they are called **trade creditors**. The amounts owing to suppliers as creditors are called **trade payables** in the statement of financial position (balance sheet). The goods obtained by the business are used in production, held for resale or used in providing a service. While the goods acquired are held by the business they are called the **inventories (stocks)** of the business. Any products manufactured from these goods and held for resale are also part of the inventories (stocks) of the business. The resulting product or service is sold to customers who may pay immediately in cash, or may be allowed time to pay. If they are allowed time to pay they become **debtors** of the business. Debtors eventually pay and the business obtains cash. In the statement of financial position (balance sheet) the amount due from **trade debtors** is described as **trade receivables**. **Cash** is a general term used to cover money held in the bank, and money held in notes and coins on the business premises. Cash held in the bank will be in an account such as a current account which allows immediate access. Finally the cash may be used to pay the suppliers who, as creditors, have been waiting patiently for payment.

Inventories (stocks), receivables (debtors) and cash are all current assets of the business and will be dealt with in this chapter. Creditors who have supplied goods to the business are current liabilities and will be dealt with in the next chapter.

Working capital is calculated as **current assets** minus **current liabilities**. If the working capital is low, then the business has a close match between current assets and current liabilities but may risk not being able to pay its liabilities as they fall due. Not all the current assets are instantly available in cash. There may be some delay in selling the inventories (stocks) of unsold goods. An impatient supplier or bank manager may cause difficulties if cash is not available when payment of a liability is due. On the other hand, if current assets are very much greater than current liabilities, then the business has a large amount of finance tied up in the current assets when perhaps that finance would be better employed in the acquisition of more fixed assets to expand the profit-making capacity of the operations.

Definition

> **Working capital** is the amount which a business must provide to finance the current
> assets of a business, to the extent that these are not covered by current liabilities.
> It is calculated by deducting current liabilities from current assets.

9.4 Recognition

The general conditions for recognition were set out in Chapter 2. An item that meets
the definition of an asset should be recognised if there is sufficient evidence that the
new asset has been created and the item can be measured at a monetary amount with
sufficient reliability. There is no doubt that inventories (stocks), receivables (debtors),
investments and cash are commonly recognised in a statement of financial position
(balance sheet) but it is useful to be aware of the element of doubt which may
be attached to the expectation of economic benefit which creates the asset and to the
reliability of measurement. That awareness is essential to understanding the level
of uncertainty which surrounds reported financial statements.

9.4.1 Inventories (stocks)

'Inventories' means lists of items. You might come across an inventory if you rent a
flat and the owner has a list of the contents that is checked at the start and end of your
tenancy. The pronunciation is *IN-ven-t'rees*, with stress on the first syllable 'IN' and not
INVENTOR-ees, which sounds like a collection of inventors.

Definition

> **Inventories** are assets:
>
> (a) held for sale in the ordinary course of business;
> (b) in the process of production for sale; or
> (c) in the form of materials or supplies to be consumed in the production process or in
>   the rendering of services.[3]

If a company is presenting its financial statements using the IASB's accounting system
you will probably see the description 'inventories'. If the company is following UK
company law and UK ASB standards then you will probably see the description 'stocks'.
The remainder of this chapter explains the IASB's system for reporting inventories.
The rules of UK law and standards are very similar. In business entities there are three
main categories of inventories: raw materials, work in progress and finished goods.
Consider these in reverse order.

Finished goods

The future economic benefit expected from finished goods is that they will be sold to
customers for a price which exceeds the cost of purchase or manufacture. That makes
a profit which increases the ownership interest. However, until the sale is agreed with
the customer, this expected benefit is uncertain and the qualitative characteristic of
prudence (explained in Chapter 4) dictates that it is safer not to anticipate that the
profit will arise. The value of the inventories of finished goods is therefore measured
at the **cost** of purchase or manufacture. In most cases that is a reliable measure
because it is based on recorded costs and is not anticipating an uncertain selling price.
Sometimes there may be a disappointment where goods are manufactured and then
it is found there is a lack of demand. Where there is strong doubt about the expected

selling price, such that it might be less than the cost of purchase or manufacture, the inventories (stock) of finished goods are valued at the net realisable value. This is defined as the estimated proceeds from sale of the items in question, less all costs to be incurred in marketing, selling and distributing these items.

The accounting policy note of most companies confirms this prudent approach. You will see in a later section of this chapter that Safe and Sure plc recognises inventories in its statement of financial position (balance sheet) at the lower of cost and net realisable value.

Work in progress

During the course of production the asset of finished goods is gradually being created. The expected future benefit of that activity is gradually building up as the work moves towards completion. A business could wait until the asset is totally finished, before recognising the asset in the statement of financial position (balance sheet). That would satisfy the qualitative characteristic of **prudence**, supported by the characteristic of **reliability**, but would run into problems with the characteristic of **relevance**. Where work in progress is a substantial aspect of the operations of the business, users need to know how much work in progress there is, whether it is increasing or decreasing, and what risks are attached. The risks attached to work in progress are often greater than those attached to finished goods because there is the risk of non-completion to add to all the risks faced when the goods are completed and awaiting sale. There is a reliable measurement, in the cost of work completed at the date of the financial year-end, but careful checking is required by the managers of the business to ensure that this is a reliable measure.

A particularly important type of **work in progress** is the construction contract (long-term contract) such as may be found in the engineering and building industries. A company building a bridge over three years will want to tell the shareholders about the progress being made in creating profit. Each year a portion of the total contract price will be reported as turnover and costs of the period will be matched against that turnover to calculate profit. The value of the work completed will be recognised as an asset in the statement of financial position (balance sheet), sometimes called work in progress. The reporting of profit on construction contracts (long-term contracts) is reviewed later in this chapter, in section 9.11.

Raw materials

The approach to recognition is the same as that for finished goods. Raw materials are expected to create a benefit by being used in the manufacture of goods for sale. On grounds of prudence the profit is not anticipated and the raw materials are measured at the lower of cost and net realisable value.

9.4.2 Receivables (debtors) and prepayments

Debtors are those persons who owe money to a business. Usually the largest amount shown under this heading relates to customers buying goods on credit. These are the **trade receivables (trade debtors)**. Additionally, the business may have lent money to another enterprise to help that enterprise in its activities. There may be loans to employees to cover removal and relocation expenses or advances on salaries. The business may be due to receive a refund of overpaid tax.

Trade receivables (debtors) meet the recognition conditions because there is an expectation of benefit when the customer pays. The profit on the sale of the goods is known because the customer has taken the goods or service and agreed the price. Trade receivables (debtors) are therefore measured at the selling price of the goods and the profit is recognised in the income statement (profit and loss account). There is a risk that the customer will not pay, but the view taken is that the risk of non-payment should be seen quite separately from the risk of not making a profit on a sale. The risk of non-payment is dealt with by reducing the reported value of the asset using an estimate for doubtful debts. That process is explained later in the chapter.

Prepayments are amounts of expenses paid in advance. Insurance premiums, rent of buildings, lease charges on a vehicle, road fund licences for the delivery vans and lorries, are all examples of items which have to be paid for in advance. At the date of the financial year-end some part of the future benefit may remain. This is recognised as the prepayment. Take the example of an insurance premium of £240 paid on 1 October to cover a 12-month period. At the company's year-end of 31 December, three months' benefit has expired but nine months' benefit remains. The statement of financial position (balance sheet) therefore reports a prepayment of £180.

Definition	**Prepayment** An amount paid for in advance for an benefit to the business, such as insurance premiums or rent in advance. Initially recognised as an asset, then transferred to expense in the period when the benefit is enjoyed.

9.4.3 Investments

Investments held as current assets are usually highly marketable and readily convertible into cash. The expectation of future economic benefit is therefore usually sufficient to meet the conditions of recognition. Measurement is more of a problem. There are two possible measures. One is the cost of the investment and the other is the market value. Recognising the investment at cost is prudent and reliable, but not as relevant as the current market value which is the amount of cash that could be released by sale of the investment. There is no agreed answer to this problem at the present time, although the issue has been debated in the standard-setting context. Most businesses report current asset investments at cost but a smaller number use the market value. Using the market value is called **marking to market**. It is a departure from the normal practice of recording assets at original cost but is justified in terms of the requirement of company law that financial statements should show a **true and fair view** (see Chapter 4). It is seen in companies whose business involves dealing in investments.

9.4.4 Cash

Recognising cash is no problem either in the expectation of benefit or in the measurement of the asset. The amount is known either by counting cash in hand or by looking at a statement from the bank which is holding the business bank account. The expectation of benefit lies in making use of the cash in future to buy fixed assets or to contribute to the working capital cycle so that the business earns a profit. In the meantime, cash which is surplus to immediate requirements should be deposited in such a way that it is earning interest. Where a company has substantial cash balances there should be indications in the income statement (profit and loss account) that investment income has been earned, to provide a benefit to the business.

Activity 9.2	*This section has covered in some detail the characteristics of various groups of current assets. Before reading the next section, write down what information you would expect to see, in respect of these groups of assets, in the statement of financial position (balance sheet) and notes to the accounts. Then read the section and consider similarities to, or differences from, the views given there.*

9.5 Users' needs for information

Investors have an interest in knowing that current assets are not overstated. If the assets are overstated the profit of the business will be overstated (see the explanation in Chapter 4, using the accounting equation). They will want to know particularly whether there has been allowance for inventories of goods which may not lead to sales and whether there has been allowance for customers who may not be able to pay the debts shown as due to the business. They may also want the reassurance that the auditors have established the existence of all the current assets, particularly ensuring that a very portable asset such as cash is where it ought to be in the ownership of the company.

The needs of users do not stop with the investors. The trade creditors who supply goods and services to the business are strongly reliant on the working capital cycle for their eventual payment. Employees look for their salaries and wages from the cash generated during the working capital cycle. They want to know that the cash will be there on the day it is required, rather than being tied up in inventories or receivables (debtors) awaiting release as cash. Tax collecting authorities, such as HMRC, have definite dates on which payments are required. All these persons have an interest in the working capital of the business and how it is managed. The concern of creditors and employees is primarily with the flow of cash and its availability on the day required. That information will not appear in the statement of financial position (balance sheet) but there will be some indications of flow in the statement of cash flows (outlined in Chapter 3).

9.6 Information provided in the financial statements

In Chapter 7 the statement of financial position (balance sheet) of Safe and Sure plc contained three lines relating to current assets:

	Notes	Year 2 £m	Year 1 £m
Current assets			
Inventories (stocks)	5	26.6	24.3
Amounts receivable (debtors)	6	146.9	134.7
Six-month deposits		2.0	–
Cash and cash equivalents		105.3	90.5
		280.8	249.5

There is more information provided in the notes to the statement of financial position (balance sheet).

9.6.1 Details in notes

There are two relevant notes, of which note 5 deals with inventories and note 6 with receivables (debtors):

Note 5	Year 2 £m	Year 1 £m
Inventories (stocks)		
Raw materials	6.2	5.4
Work in progress	1.9	1.0
Finished products	18.5	17.9
	26.6	24.3

This company is a service company so it is not surprising that stocks do not figure prominently in the overall collection of current assets. It is perhaps more surprising that there are inventories of finished products, but reading the description of the business shows that there is a Products Division which manufactures special cleaning chemicals under the company name.

The note on receivables (debtors) shows that the main category is trade receivables (debtors):

Note 6	Year 2	Year 1
Amounts receivable (debtors)	£m	£m
Trade receivables (trade debtors)	128.1	117.0
Other receivables (debtors)	10.9	9.8
Prepayments and accrued income	7.9	7.9
	146.9	134.7

There is no indication of the nature of 'other receivables (debtors)'. It could indicate employees who have received loans or advances of salaries. It could indicate a loan to a company which has trading links with the group but is not a full subsidiary. Prepayments are expenses paid in advance of gaining the benefit, as explained in the previous section of this chapter.

9.6.2 Accounting policy

It will be shown later in this chapter that the valuation of inventories is a matter of potential variation from one person to the next, so it is important to know that the company has followed an acceptable policy in its valuation of inventories. The accounting policy note of Safe and Sure provides that confirmation (see Exhibit 9.1). For the moment you will have to accept that this form of wording represents standard practice, but each phrase will be explained later in the chapter.

Exhibit 9.1
Accounting policy note

> **Safe and Sure plc Accounting policy**
>
> Inventories (stocks and work in progress) are stated at the lower of cost and net realisable value, using the first in first out principle. Cost includes all direct expenditure and related overheads incurred in bringing the inventories to their present condition and location.

9.6.3 Operating and financial review

The finance director of Safe and Sure commented as follows in his review:

> *The group's businesses are structured to utilise as little fixed and working capital as is consistent with the profit and earnings growth objective in order to produce a high cash flow.*

The focus on **working capital** is perhaps an indication of the importance seen in explaining how the company manages its current assets and current liabilities. It also shows that for this business the high cash flow is planned and is not an accident of events.

9.6.4 Analyst's view

DAVID WILSON comments: *This is a service business and so holds inventories of goods to be used in the service process. The note to the statement of financial position (balance*

sheet) does not actually say what the inventories are, so I asked when I made my visit. They tell me the raw materials are inventories of cleaning materials and chemicals for processes such as disinfecting. My main concern is to be assured that there is nothing in the inventories which could carry a risk of losing value through obsolescence or deterioration. There is not much problem of that with cleaning materials. The finished goods took me by surprise until I found out that there is a Products Division. It was actually the cleaning products that I knew best from years ago but I thought they had moved entirely into service contracts.

In any event, inventories are not all that important for this company. The receivables (debtors) amount is much larger. I know they have a relatively low risk of bad debts because most customers pay in advance for their contracts.

When I started as an analyst I worked alongside someone who had 20 years' experience. He told me that he had always used what he called 'the 10% test' when looking at inventories (stocks) and receivables (debtors) in a statement of financial position (balance sheet). He worked out what effect a 10% error in the inventories or receivables would have on the profit before tax. In this case a 10% error in inventories would be £2.7m. The profit from operations is £195.2m. A difference of £2.7m on £195.2m is 1.4%. An error of 1.4% in profit would not have a significant impact on the view of most investors. So in this company inventories is not a matter which needs time taken for questions. On the other hand, a 10% error in receivables (debtors) would be £14.7m. That is 7.5% of profit from operations. So receivables (debtors) are worth more attention. If this were a company I didn't know, I would ask about the quality of the asset and the type of customer who is given credit. In fact I do know the answer here. The finance director told me that when I met him. The receivables (debtors) are largely public sector bodies such as local authorities and hospitals who insist on paying after the work has been done to their satisfaction. There could be a risk of non-payment because of shoddy work but there is little risk of non-payment through default.

The final point to note in relation to current assets is that this company is a cash-generating business. I looked at the statement of cash flows for the past five years which shows that the group builds up cash balances, buys another company, and then generates even more cash. I suppose that can't go on for ever but there are no signs of problems at present.

LEONA: *I told you I would be looking for admissions of how much you rely on the auditor without knowing it. Your '10% test' is a very rough-and-ready example of the ratio analysis we carry out on a systematic basis as part of our analytical review of the financial statements. Maybe one day I'll tell you more about that. We have quite a long list of ratios which we calculate. We also look at interrelationships between ratios and relative changes in one compared with another.*

It is also an application of what we call 'materiality'. When we see an asset – in this case it is receivables (debtors) – where an error in estimation of the asset value could cause a serious impact on profit, we identify that as a matter for special attention. We would probably spend more time on receivables (debtors) than on inventories in our audit of this company but we would target the risk-related aspects of what is reported about each asset. For receivables (debtors) it is the risk of non-payment through either disputed debts or lack of funds. For inventories it is the risk of obsolescence or similar loss which is not covered by insurance.

Have you decided on how the company's information on current assets meets the list of desirable qualitative characteristics?

DAVID: *You're trying to get me to admit that I need the auditors. Reliability is in the auditors' hands as far as the numbers go, but I place a lot of reliance on my assessment of the qualities of senior management when I meet them. You can't audit that kind of feeling. It's all a matter of chemistry. Also, the main current asset is receivables (debtors) and I know they are reliable because the finance director told me what class of customer was involved. I didn't need the auditors for that. Relevance probably scores about eight out of ten* *because there aren't any complications here with unusual types of inventories. Faithful representation and neutrality are something I leave to the auditors for now but I'll be asking questions next year if the information in the financial statements turns out not to be neutral. Prudence, I know, is built into all aspects of accounting which uses historical cost measures. That sometimes works against relevance. Completeness is not a problem for current assets. The company is unlikely to leave anything out. They are more likely to include too much. I do expect the auditor to check that the assets are there. Comparability is a matter of presentation. This company has a five-year summary elsewhere in the annual report and gives the previous year's amounts in the financial statements. As for under-standability, I like to think that I can see my way around figures for inventories, receivables (debtors) and cash. I usually get the answers I want when I phone the financial controller.*

LEONA: *But don't you see that by admitting that you have to ask more questions to help you understand the amounts, there must be some further explanations which the company could give in the annual report so that your understanding may be shared by others?*

DAVID: *My fund manager colleagues would say that only the professional investors have the expertise. Even if more information were reported by companies, only the professionals would know how to use it.*

9.7 Measurement and recording

The basic measurement rule applying to all current assets is that they should be measured at the *lower* of **cost** and **net realisable value**.[4] The exception is receivables (debtors) which are measured at selling price because the related profit is earned when the sale is made and not when the credit customer chooses to pay.

The next three sections look at issues of measurement and recording, in relation to inventories, receivables (debtors) and current asset investments, which are essential to an understanding of how much variability and uncertainty lies behind the apparent confidence of the numbers reported in financial statements.

9.8 Inventories (stocks) of raw materials and finished goods

The analysis of transactions involving inventories of raw materials, work in progress and finished goods has been explained in detail in Chapter 6 and will not be repeated here. This section examines the problems created by the general rule that inventories must be valued at the lower of cost and net realisable value. This rule is a consequence of the **prudence** concept, based on not anticipating a sale until the goods are delivered to the customer.

Net realisable value means the estimated selling price in the ordinary course of business less the estimated costs of completion and the estimated costs necessary to make the sale. For example, damaged inventories are sold at auction for £10,000. The auctioneer charges selling commission of 20% which is £2,000. The amount received by the seller is £8,000, called the net realisable value.

Definition | **Net realisable value** is the estimated selling price in the ordinary course of business less the estimated costs of completion and the estimated costs necessary to make the sale.[5]

This section covers first of all the accounting equation in relation to the rule. It then looks at the meaning of cost and the allocation of overhead costs. Various specific models to deal with changing input prices are then discussed and the section concludes with the rules to be applied in financial reporting.

9.8.1 Lower of cost and net realisable value

Consider the example of a container of coffee beans purchased by a coffee manufacturer at a cost of £1,000. The beans are held for three months up to the date of the financial year-end. During that time there is a fall in the world price of coffee beans and the container of coffee beans would sell for only £800 in the market.

When the asset is acquired, the impact on the accounting equation is an increase of £1,000 in the asset of inventories and a decrease of £1,000 in the asset of cash.

At the end of the year the asset is found to be worth £800 and the ownership interest is reduced because the asset has fallen in value. The asset is reduced by £200 and an expense of loss of value in inventories value is reported in the income statement (profit and loss account).

If a business fails to report a fall in the value of the asset of inventories, the profit of the period will be overstated.

Where there are separate categories of inventories the rule of 'lower of cost and net realisable value' must be applied to each category separately. Suppose, for example, there is an inventory (stock) of paper at a cost of £2,000 with a net realisable value of £2,300 and an inventory (stock) of pens with a cost of £1,800 and a net realisable value of £1,400. The lower amount must be taken in each case, giving a value of £3,400 for inventories (calculated as £2,000 plus £1,400).

9.8.2 Meaning of cost

The **cost** of inventories comprises all costs of purchase, costs of conversion and other costs incurred in bringing the inventories to their present location and condition.[6] This expenditure will include not only the cost of purchase but also costs of converting raw materials into finished goods or services.

Costs of purchase include the price charged by the supplier, plus transport and handling costs, plus import duties and less discounts and subsidies.[7] Costs of conversion include items readily identifiable with the product, such as labour, expenses and subcontractors' costs directly related to the product. They also include production overheads and any other overheads directly related to bringing the product or service to its present condition and location. **Production overheads** are items such as depreciation of machines, service costs, rental paid for a factory, wages paid to supervisory and support staff, costs of stores control and insurance of production facilities.

Example

Take the example of a business which purchases 10 wooden furniture units for conversion to a customer's specification for installation in a hotel. The units cost £200 each and the labour cost of converting them is £100 each. Production overheads for the period are fixed at £3,500. Two units remain unsold at the end of the period. These two units will be recorded in the statement of financial position (balance sheet) at £1,300, calculated as £650 each (materials cost of £200 plus labour cost of £100 plus a share of the production overheads at £350 per item).

That was easy because there were 10 identical units to take equal shares of the production overheads. But suppose they had all been different and required different amounts of labour? Would it have been fair to share the overheads equally? Probably not. The problems of sharing out production overhead costs create a chapter in themselves and are studied further as part of management accounting. You need to be aware, in reading published accounting information, that there is considerable scope for discretion to be exercised by management in the allocation of overheads between completed goods and goods held in inventories. The general risk of overstatement of assets applies here. If the asset is overstated by having too much production overhead allocated, the profit of the period is also overstated because it is not bearing the share of production overheads which it should.

9.8.3 Costs when input prices are changing

One very tiresome problem faced by the accounts department in its record keeping is that suppliers change their prices from time to time. Goods held in store may have arrived at different times and at different unit prices. How does the accounts department decide on the unit price to be charged to each job when all the materials look the same once they are taken into store?

In some cases it may be possible to label the materials as they arrive so that they can be identified with the appropriate unit price. That is a very time-consuming process and would only be used for high-value low-volume items of materials. In other cases a convenient method is needed which gives an answer that is useful and approximately close to the true price of the units used. Some possibilities are shown in Table 9.1 using three options – first in first out (FIFO), last in first out (LIFO) and average cost. In each case, Table 9.1 takes a very simple approach, not complicated by having inventory at the start of the period. In real life the calculations can be even more tricky.

Table 9.1
Pricing the issue of goods to production

There are three parts to this illustration. Part (a) contains a table setting out the data to be used in the calculation. Part (b) defines the three bases of calculation. Part (c) uses the data from part (a) to illustrate each of the three bases.

(a) Data

Date	Received	Unit price	Price paid	Issued to production
	Units	£	£	Units
1 June	100	20	2,000	–
20 June	50	22	1,100	–
24 June	–	–	–	60
28 June	–	–	–	70
Total	150		3,100	130

Table 9.1 continued

(b) Bases of calculation

First in first out (FIFO)
Assume that the goods which arrived first are issued first.

Last in first out (LIFO)
Assume that the goods which arrived last are issued first.

Average cost
Assume that all goods are issued at the average price of the inventories held.

(c) Calculations

Basis	Date	Quantity and unit price	Issued to production £	Held in inventories £	Total £
FIFO					
	24 June	60 units at £20	1,200		
	28 June	40 units at £20			
		30 units at £22	1,460		
	30 June	20 units at £22		440	
Total			2,660	440	3,100
LIFO					
	24 June	50 units at £22			
		10 units at £20	1,300		
	28 June	70 units at £20	1,400		
	30 June	20 units at £20		400	
Total			2,700	400	3,100
Average					
	24 June	60 units at *£20.67	1,240		
	28 June	70 units at *£20.67	1,447		
	30 June	20 units at *£20.67		413	
Total			2,687	413	3,100

Note: *Weighted average [(100 × 20) + (50 × 22)]/150 = £20.67.

9.8.4 Approximation when dates are not recorded

In business there may not be time to keep the detailed records shown in the calculations in Table 9.1. In such cases the sales volume is known in total but the dates of sales are not recorded. The calculation then uses the best approximation available, which usually means working through the costs from the oldest date, for FIFO, or the most recent date, for LIFO, without attempting to match the various batches bought and sold during the year.

9.8.5   Choice of FIFO, LIFO or average cost

Look at table (c) of Table 9.1 and compare it with table (a) of that table. You will see from table (a) that the total amount spent on materials during the month was £3,100. You will see from table (c) that the total of the cost of goods issued to production, plus the cost of unsold goods, is always £3,100 irrespective of which approach is taken. All that differs is the allocation between goods used in production and goods remaining unsold. Cost can never be gained or lost in total because of a particular allocation process, provided the process is used consistently over time. The FIFO approach suffers the disadvantage of matching outdated costs against current revenue. The LIFO approach improves on FIFO by matching the most recent costs against revenue, but at the expense of an inventory value which becomes increasingly out of date. The average cost lies between the two and becomes more intricate to recalculate as more items come into inventory. In practice, the choice for internal reporting in management accounting is a matter of finding the best method for the purpose.

There is an effect on profit of the year which may influence management choice. When prices are rising and inventories volumes are steady or increasing, FIFO gives a lower cost of sales and so a higher profit than LIFO. If there were no regulations, companies that wished to show high profits (perhaps to impress investors buying shares in the company) might prefer FIFO. Companies that wished to show lower profits (perhaps to reduce tax bills) might prefer LIFO.

The IASB standard IAS 2 prohibits the use of LIFO. In the UK the tax authorities will not accept LIFO valuation. In the USA the LIFO method of valuation is permitted. Investors need to read the accounting policy note in the financial statements to find which approach a company has used.

Activity 9.3

Look back to Table 9.1 and write your own table of data for goods received, unit price, price paid and goods issued to production. Create calculations of cost of goods sold, using the various models in Table 9.1 (FIFO, LIFO and average price). Check that the value of goods issued to production, plus the value of goods held in stock, will always add up to the same answer in total.

9.9 Receivables (debtors)

The measurement of receivables (debtors) requires attention to bad and doubtful debts. A debt is described as a **bad debt** when there is no further hope of the customer paying the amount owed. This might be due to the customer being declared bankrupt or else disappearing without trace. If the customer is known to be in difficulties or there is some dispute over the amount owed, the debt is described as a **doubtful debt**. The company still hopes to recover the cash owed but realistically has some doubt. Evidence of doubtful debts may be seen in slow payment, partial payments, the need for several reminders or even rumours in the business community. A company will usually analyse the age of its debts to help identify those which may be doubtful.

Example

At the end of Year 1 the Garden Pond Company has a statement of financial position (balance sheet) comprising £2,000 receivables (debtors), £7,000 other assets and £9,000 ownership interest that consists of £1,800 ownership interest at the start of the period and £7,200 profit of the period. On the date of the financial year-end the manager of the company reviews the receivables (debtors) list and decides that debts amounting to £200 are doubtful because there are rumours of a customer not paying other suppliers in the trade. The statement of financial position (balance sheet) at the end of Year 1 is amended to show that the asset is of lower value than was thought and the ownership interest has consequently diminished.

Table 9.2 shows the spreadsheet for analysis set out to reflect the accounting equation. The new column is the one headed **provision for doubtful debts**. This is included in the assets section because it tells the user more about the asset of receivables (debtors), although it is the negative part of the asset. It causes some confusion to those who meet it for the first time because anything called a provision is usually reported under the heading of liabilities. However, on grounds of usefulness to readers and relevance to the provision of information about the asset, the provision for doubtful debts has special treatment in being included as a negative aspect within the asset section of the statement of financial position (balance sheet).

It is quite a difficult matter for a company to be prudent in expressing doubt about a debtor while still pursuing the non-payer with a view to collection of the debt. To remove the debt from the record would be to admit defeat. Even to show a separate provision among the liability headings might lead other customers to think, 'Why not me also?' Some companies therefore do not disclose a separate provision for doubtful debts in a company's statement of financial position (balance sheet). They deduct the provision from the full receivables (debtors)' list and report only the resulting net amount.

Table 9.2
Spreadsheet to analyse the effect of provision for doubtful debts at the end of Year 1, using the accounting equation

Date	Transaction or event	Assets			Ownership interest	
Year 1		Receivables (debtors)	Provision for doubtful debts	Other assets	Ownership interest at start	Profit of the period
		£	£	£	£	£
Dec. 31	Statement of financial position (balance sheet) first draft	2,000		7,000	1,800	7,200
Dec. 31	Recognition of doubtful debts		(200)			(200)
Dec. 31	Revised statement of financial position (balance sheet)	2,000	(200)	7,000	1,800	7,000

The statement of financial position (balance sheet) after incorporating a provision for the doubtful debt would appear as in Table 9.3.

There is no single method of calculating the provision for doubtful debts. Some companies consider separately the amount owed by each customer. To economise on time, most companies use previous experience to estimate a percentage of total receivables (debtors). A mixture of approaches could be used, with known problems being identified separately and a general percentage being applied to the rest.

Table 9.3
Statement of financial position (balance sheet) of Garden Pond Company showing the presentation of information on doubtful debts

Garden Pond Company Statement of financial position (balance sheet) at 31 December Year 1		
	£	£
Other assets		7,000
Receivables (debtors)	2,000	
Less: provision for doubtful debts	(200)	
		1,800
		8,800
Ownership interest at the start of the year		1,800
Profit of the year		7,000
		8,800

9.9.1   Change in a provision

During Year 2 matters take an upward turn and in July the customer who was showing signs of financial distress manages to pay the amount of £200 owed. The effect on the accounting equation is that the asset of cash is increased and the asset of debtor is reduced by £200. The provision for doubtful debts is now no longer required and could be transferred back to the income statement (profit and loss account), but in practice it tends to be left for tidying up at the end of the year.

The business continues and at the end of Year 2 the receivables (debtors) amount to £2,500. A review of the list of receivables (debtors) causes considerable doubt regarding an amount of £350. It is decided to create a new provision of £350. The old provision of £200 related to last year's receivables (debtors) and is no longer required.

Table 9.4 shows the spreadsheet at the end of Year 2, before and after recording the new provision for doubtful debts. It is assumed that the other assets have grown to £10,000 and there is a profit of £3,500 before amending the provision for doubtful debts.

Table 9.4
Spreadsheet to analyse the effect of provision for doubtful debts at the end of Year 2, using the accounting equation

Date	Transaction or event	Assets			Ownership	
Year 2		Receivables (debtors)	Provision for doubtful debts	Other assets	Ownership interest at start	Profit of the period
		£	£	£	£	£
Dec. 31	Statement of financial position (balance sheet) first draft	2,500	(200)	10,000	8,800	3,500
Dec. 31	Elimination of provision no longer required		200			200
Dec. 31	Creation of new provision		(350)			(350)
Dec. 31	Revised statement of financial position (balance sheet)	2,500	(350)	10,000	8,800	3,350

The income statement (profit and loss account) could show two separate entries, one being £200 increase in ownership interest and the other being £350 decrease in ownership interest. It is rather cumbersome in that form and most enterprises would report as an expense, in the income statement (profit and loss account), the single line:

Increase in provision for doubtful debts   £150

9.10 Prepayments

Prepayments arise when an item of expense is paid in advance of the benefit being received. A common example is the payment of an insurance premium. The payment is made in advance for the year ahead and the benefit is gradually used up as the year goes along. The statement of financial position (balance sheet) recognises the unexpired portion of the insurance premium as an asset, while the income statement (profit and loss account) reports the amount consumed during the period.

Example

On 1 October Year 1 a company paid £1,200 for one year's vehicle insurance. At the financial year-end date of 31 December there have been three months' benefit used up and there is a nine-month benefit yet to come. The transactions relating to insurance would be reported as in Table 9.5.

The effect of identifying the asset is to reduce the expense of the period from £1,200 to £300 and to hold the remaining £900 as a benefit for the next accounting period. In Year 2 the amount of £900 will be transferred from the prepayment column to the expense column, so that the decrease in the ownership interest is reported in the period in which it occurs.

Table 9.5
Spreadsheet recording prepayment of insurance at the financial year-end date

Date	Transaction or event	Assets		Ownership interest
Year 2		Cash £	Prepayment £	Expense £
Oct. 1	Payment of premium	(1,200)		(1,200)
Dec. 31	Identification of asset remaining as prepayment		900	900
		(1,200)	900	(300)

9.11 Revenue recognition

The sale of goods and services creates **revenue** for the business. Sometimes that revenue is referred to as **sales** or **turnover**. The term revenue may also be applied to rents received from letting out property, or interest received on investments made. In the conceptual frameworks of various countries, different views are held of the exact meaning and extent of the word *revenue*. The IASB defines revenue in terms of equity (ownership interest).

Definition

> **Revenue** is defined as the gross inflow of economic benefits during the period arising in the course of the ordinary activities of an enterprise when those inflows result in increases in equity, other than increases relating to contributions from equity participants.[8]

The main problem in recognition of revenue lies in the timing. Assets are recognised at a point in time but revenue is created over a period of time. What are the rules for deciding on the time period for which revenue should be reported? One suggestion has been that the **critical event** is the important factor.[9] When goods are produced or services are carried out, there is one part of the process which is critical to providing sufficient reassurance that the revenue has been earned by the efforts of the enterprise. For the sale of goods the point of delivery to the customer is the usual critical event which determines the date of revenue recognition. For a contract of service, the critical event is the production of the service.

9.11.1 Contract revenue

Where the service extends over more than one time period, the revenue may be split over the time periods involved. That may happen in a civil engineering or a building contract. In each year of the contract a portion of the revenue will be matched against costs of the period so as to report a portion of profit.

Take the example of a two-year bridge-building contract. The contract price is £60m. Two-thirds of the work has been completed in Year 1 and it is expected that the remainder will be completed in Year 2. The costs incurred in Year 1 are £34m and the costs expected for Year 2 are £17m.

The income statement (profit and loss account) of the business for Year 1 will report, in respect of this contract, turnover of £40m less costs of £34m giving profit of £6m. This gives a fair representation of the profit earned by the activity of the year (as two-thirds of the total). An independent expert, in this case an engineer, would confirm that the work had been completed satisfactorily to date. The effect on the accounting equation would be:

Assets ↑↓	–	Liabilities	=	Ownership interest ↑
+ £40m – £34m				+ £6m

Reporting contract revenue of £40m in Year 1 will increase the ownership interest by £40m. A matching asset will be reported, representing the value of the contract at that stage. The value of £40m shown for the construction contract represents the aggregate amount of costs incurred plus recognised profits to date.

In the income statement (profit and loss account) the expenses of £34m are reported in the usual way and a profit of £6m results. All being well, the income statement (profit and loss account) of Year 2 will report the remaining £20m of revenue minus £17m of expenses, leaving a profit of £3m. Over the two years the total profit of £9m will be reported.

Users of accounting information need to pay particular attention to contract revenue in a business and ask some careful questions. Has prudence been exercised in deciding what portion of revenue to report? Is there a risk that the future costs will escalate and there will be an overall loss? They should look carefully at the provisions section of the statement of financial position (balance sheet) (see Chapter 11).

Where the customer has paid money in advance as an instalment towards the final contract price, the effect on the accounting equation is to increase the asset of cash and create a liability towards the customer. These amounts received in advance from customers may be described as 'progress billings', 'payments on account', or 'payments in advance'. There is a liability because the business has an obligation to repay the customer if the contract is not completed on time or on specification. Although it might be expected that the liability towards the customer would appear in the current liabilities section of the statement of financial position (balance sheet), that does not happen. The liability in respect of payments made in advance is deducted from the value of the contract and the resulting net figure is reported as *construction contracts* in the current assets section of the statement of financial position (balance sheet). That may mean that, at first glance at the statement of financial position (balance sheet), the reader does not realise the true size of the contract being undertaken for the customer. There is no guarantee that any better information will be found anywhere else in the financial statements, because turnover is aggregated for all activities. For the analyst as an expert user, construction contracts (long-term contracts) require a great deal of careful questioning if the underlying details are to be understood.

9.11.2 A continuing debate

There are problems in revenue recognition that continue to be debated. Consider three examples. In the first, a film production company sells a programme to a television company which agrees to pay royalties every time the programme is broadcast. In the second, a farmer sells a cow to a neighbour in return for five sheep. In the third, a mobile phone company charges customers a start-up fee that is 24 times the monthly rental and service charge. There is no specific accounting standard to cover any of these situations. One approach to each is to ask, 'Has the revenue been earned?' The companies would all answer, 'Yes, we have completed our side of the transaction.' So perhaps revenue should be recognised in all three cases. Another approach is to ask, 'Are there any risks related to recognising revenue?' The answer is, 'Yes – the programme may never be broadcast; we are not sure about the exchange values between cows and sheep; and the telephone company may not be able to provide the service for the long period implied by the high initial charge.' So perhaps the revenue should not be reported until the risks are diminished. Both views are being applied, with the result that there has been some lack of clarity and comparability as new types of business have emerged. It is necessary to pay careful attention to the accounting policy on revenue recognition.

9.12 Summary

- A **current asset** is an asset that satisfies any of the following criteria:
  - (a) it is expected to be realised in, or is intended for sale or consumption in, the entity's normal operating cycle;
  - (b) it is held primarily for the purpose of being traded;
  - (c) it is expected to be realised within 12 months after the date of the financial year-end;
  - (d) it is cash or a cash equivalent.
- **Working capital** is the amount which a business must provide to finance the current assets of a business, to the extent that these are not covered by current liabilities. It is calculated by deducting current liabilities from current assets.
- Inventories (stocks), receivables (debtors), investments and cash are commonly **recognised** in a balance sheet. If there is doubt attached to the expectation of

economic benefit which creates the asset and to the reliability of measurement, then this is recognised by making a **provision** such as the provision for doubtful debts.

- Users need information about the working capital of the business to judge whether it is suitable to support the activities of the business. Information provided to help users includes: detailed notes of current assets and current liabilities; notes of accounting policy describing the valuation of current assets; and a discussion of working capital management in the operating and financial review.

- **Inventories** (stocks) are measured at the lower of cost and net realisable value.

- **Receivables** (debtors) are measured at the amount receivable on settlement less any provision for doubtful debts.

- **Prepayments** are amounts paid in advance for benefits expected. Prepayments are assets until the benefit is used up. The amount is then transferred from an asset to an expense.

- **Revenue** is defined as the gross inflow of economic benefits during the period arising in the course of the ordinary activities of an enterprise when those inflows result in increases in equity, other than increases relating to contributions from equity participants.

- If revenues are earned over more than one time period (e.g. on long-term contracts) then the revenue is allocated across time periods in proportion to the amount of work completed.

QUESTIONS

The Questions section of each chapter has three types of question. 'Test your understanding' questions to help you review your reading are in the 'A' series of questions. You will find the answers to these by reading and thinking about the material in the book. 'Application' questions to test your ability to apply technical skills are in the 'B' series of questions. Questions requiring you to show skills in problem solving and evaluation are in the 'C' series of questions. A letter [S] indicates that there is a solution at the end of the book.

A   Test your understanding

A9.1   What is the definition of a current asset? (Section 9.2)

A9.2   What is the working capital cycle? (Section 9.3)

A9.3   What are the features of raw materials, work in progress and finished goods which justify their recognition in a balance sheet? (Section 9.4.1)

A9.4   What information do users need about current assets? (Section 9.5)

A9.5   What is meant by FIFO, LIFO and the average cost method of pricing issues of goods? (Section 9.8.3)

A9.6   How is a provision for doubtful debts decided upon? (Section 9.9)

A9.7   What is a prepayment? (Section 9.10)

A9.8   What is meant by 'revenue recognition'? (Section 9.11)

A9.9   Why are there problems with revenue recognition? (Section 9.11.2)

A9.10 [S] The Sycamore Company has inventories which include the following four items:

Description	Purchase cost £	Selling price £	Cost of selling £
Engine	6,500	8,250	350
Chassis	2,000	1,800	200
Frame	4,800	4,900	300

What amount should be reported as total inventory in respect of these three items?

A9.11 [S] On reviewing the company's financial statements, the company accountant discovers that items of year-end inventory of goods which cost £18,000 have been omitted from the record. What will be the effect on the income statement (profit and loss account) and the statement of financial position (balance sheet) when this omission is rectified?

A9.12 [S] On reviewing the financial statements, the company accountant discovers that an amount of £154,000 owed by a customer will be irrecoverable because the customer has fled the country. What will be the effect on the income statement (profit and loss account) and the statement of financial position (balance sheet) when this event is recognised?

B Application

B9.1 [S]
During its first month of operations, a business made purchases and sales as shown in the table below:

Date	Number of units purchased	Unit cost	Number of units sold
Jan. 5	100	£1.00	
Jan. 10			50
Jan. 15	200	£1.10	
Jan. 17			150
Jan. 24	300	£1.15	
Jan. 30			200

All sales were made at £2 each.

Required
Calculate the profit for the month and the stock value held at the end of the month using:

(a) the FIFO approach to the issue of units for sale, where:
   (i) the calculation is carried out at the date of sale; and
   (ii) the calculation is carried out at the end of the month without regard for the date of sale; and
(b) the LIFO approach to the issue of units for sale, where:
   (i) the calculation is carried out at the date of sale; and
   (ii) the calculation is carried out at the end of the month without regard for the date of sale; and
(c) the average-cost approach to the issue of units for sale, making the calculation at the end of the month without regard for the date of sale.

B9.2 [S]
A company has a stock of goods consisting of four different groups of items. The cost and net realisable value of each group is shown in the table below.

Group of items	Cost £	Net realisable value £
A	1,000	1,400
B	1,000	800
C	2,100	1,900
D	3,000	3,100

Required
Calculate the amount to be shown as the value of the company's stock.

B9.3

At the end of Year 3 the Bed Company has a statement of financial position (balance sheet) comprising £3,000 receivables (debtors), £8,000 other assets and £11,000 ownership interest, consisting of £2,000 ownership interest at the start of the period and £9,000 profit of the period. On the date of the financial year-end the manager of the company reviews the receivables (debtors) list and decides that debts amounting to £450 are doubtful because the customers have not replied to repeated requests for payment.

Required

(a) Prepare an accounting equation spreadsheet to show the effect of the provision. (See Table 9.2 for an illustration.)
(b) Show the statement of financial position (balance sheet) information. (See Table 9.3 for an illustration.)

B9.4

The Bed Company continues trading during Year 4. The statement of financial position (balance sheet) at the end of Year 4, in its first draft, showed receivables (debtors) as £4,850 and the provision for doubtful debts unchanged from Year 3 at £450. Enquiry showed that during Year 4 some of the receivables (debtors) at the end of Year 3 had been confirmed as bad. They amounted to £250 but nothing had yet been recorded. The management wish to make the provision £550 at the end of Year 4. Other assets amount to £12,000, ownership interest at the start of Year 4 is £10,550 and the profit is £5,750.

Required

Prepare an accounting equation spreadsheet to show the effect of the bad debt being recognised and of the decision to make a provision at the end of Year 4. (See Table 9.4 for an illustration.)

B9.5

On 1 December Year 1 a company paid £2,400 as an insurance premium to give accident cover for the 12 months ahead. The accounting year-end is 31 December.

Required

Prepare an accounting equation spreadsheet to show the effect of the prepayment in the year ended 31 December Year 1.

C   Problem solving and evaluation

C9.1

A fire destroyed a company's detailed stock records and much of the merchandise held in stock. The company accountant was able to discover that stock at the beginning of the period was £40,000, purchases up to the date of the fire were £250,000, and sales up to the date of the fire were £400,000. In past periods, the company has earned a gross profit of 35% of sales.

Required

Calculate the cost of the stock destroyed by the fire.

C9.2

It is the policy of Seaton Ltd to make provision for doubtful debts at a rate of 10% per annum on all debtor balances at the end of the year, after deducting any known bad debts at the same date. The following table sets out the total receivables (debtors) as shown by the accounting records and known bad debts to be deducted from that total. There is no provision at 31 December Year 0.

Year-end	Debtor balances	Known bad debts
	£	£
31 Dec. Year 1	30,000	2,000
31 Dec. Year 2	35,000	3,000
31 Dec. Year 3	32,000	1,500
31 Dec. Year 4	29,000	1,000

Required

(a) Calculate the total expense in the income statement (profit and loss account) in respect of bad and doubtful debts.

(b) Set out the statement of financial position (balance sheet) information in respect of receivables (debtors) and provision for doubtful debts at each year-end.

Activities for study groups

Turn to the annual report of a listed company which you have used for activities in previous chapters. Find every item of information about current assets. (Start with the financial statements and notes but look also at the operating and financial review, chief executive's review and other non-regulated information about the company.)

As a group, imagine you are the team of fund managers in a fund management company. You are holding a briefing meeting at which each person explains to the others some feature of the companies in which your fund invests. Today's subject is current assets. Each person should make a short presentation to the rest of the team covering:

1 The nature and significance of current assets in the company.

2 The effect on profit of a 10% error in estimation of any one of the major categories of current asset.

3 The company's comments, if any, on its present investment in working capital and its future intentions.

4 The risks which might attach to the inventories of the company.

5 The liquidity of the company.

6 The trends in current assets since last year (or over five years if a comparative table is provided).

7 The ratio of current assets to current liabilities.

Notes and references

1. IASB (1989), *Framework for the Preparation and Presentation of Financial Statements*, para. 49(a).
2. IASB (2009), IAS 1, para. 66.
3. IASB (2009), IAS 2 *Inventories*, para. 6.
4. IASB (2009), IAS 2 *Inventories*, para. 9.
5. IASB (2009), IAS 2 *Inventories*, para. 6.
6. IASB (2009), IAS 2 *Inventories*, para. 10.
7. IASB (2009), IAS 2 *Inventories*, para. 11.
8. IASB (2009), IAS 18, *Revenue*, para. 7.
9. J. H. Myers (1959), 'The critical event and recognition of net profit', *Accounting Review*, **34**, pp. 528–32; and ASB (1999), *Statement of Principles for Financial Reporting*, ch. 5, paras 5.33–5.36.

Bookkeeping entries for (a) bad and doubtful debts; and (b) prepayments

The debit and credit recording aspects of inventories of raw materials and finished goods were explained in the supplement to Chapter 6. That leaves, for this supplement, the recording of bad and doubtful debts as a new area where potential care is needed. Prepayments are also illustrated here.

Provision for doubtful debts

The following ledger accounts illustrate the recording of the transactions analysed in section 9.9. Look back to that section for the description and analysis of the transactions. The debit and credit analysis is shown in Table 9.6. So that you will not be confused by additional information, the ledger accounts presented here show only sufficient information to illustrate the recording of transactions relating to doubtful debts. Leona comments on the main features.

Table 9.6
Analysis of debit and credit aspect of each transaction and event

Date		Debit	Credit
Year 1			
End of year	Manager identifies doubtful debts £200	Profit and loss account £200	Provision for doubtful debts £200
Year 2			
July	Customer who was doubtful pays £200 in full	Cash £200	Receivables (debtors) £200
End of year	Manager identifies new provision required £350	Profit and loss account £350	Provision for doubtful debts £350
End of year	Former provision no longer required	Provision for doubtful debts £200	Profit and loss account £200

The ledger accounts required are as follows:

L1	Receivables (debtors)	L3	Cash
L2	Provision for doubtful debts	L4	Profit and loss account

Also required to complete the double entry, but not shown here as a ledger account, is ledger account L5 Ownership interest.

The full list of transactions for the year would be too cumbersome to deal with here, so dots are used to show that the ledger account requires more information for completeness.

L1 Receivables (debtors)

Date	Particulars	Page	Debit	Credit	Balance
Year 1			£	£	£
	. . .		. . .		. . .
Dec. 31	Balance at end of year				2,000
Year 2					
	. . .		. . .		. . .
July	Cash from customer	L3		200	. . .
	. . .		. . .		. . .
Dec. 31	Balance at end of year				2,500

LEONA: *The ledger account for receivables (debtors) has no entries relating to doubtful debts. That is important because although there may be doubts from the viewpoint of the business, the customer still has a duty to pay and should be encouraged by all the usual means. Keeping the full record of amounts due is an important part of ensuring that all assets of the business are looked after.*

L2 Provision for doubtful debts

Date	Particulars	Page	Debit	Credit	Balance
Year 1			£	£	£
Dec. 31	Profit and loss account – new provision	L4		200	(200)
Year 2					
Dec. 31	Profit and loss account – old provision	L4	200		nil
Dec. 31	Profit and loss account – new provision	L4		350	(350)

LEONA: *The provision for doubtful debts is a credit balance because it is the negative part of an asset. It keeps a separate record of doubt about the full value of the asset. A credit entry in the ledger account increases the amount of the provision and a debit entry decreases the amount of the provision.*

L3 Cash

Date	Particulars	Page	Debit	Credit	Balance
Year 2			£	£	£
	. . .		. . .		. . .
July	Cash from debtor	L1	200		
	. . .		. . .		. . .

LEONA: *Receiving cash from the doubtful customer looks like any other transaction receiving cash. It is important that the cash is collected and the debt is removed by receiving the full amount due.*

L4 Profit and loss account

Date	Particulars	Page	Debit	Credit	Balance
Year 1			£	£	£
	. . .		. . .		. . .
Dec. 31	Balance before provision for doubtful debts				(7,200)
Dec. 31	Provision for doubtful debts	L2	200		(7,000)
Dec. 31	Transfer to ownership interest	L5	7,000		nil
Year 2					
	. . .		. . .		. . .
Dec. 31	Balance before provision for doubtful debts				(3,500)
Dec. 31	Removal of provision no longer required	L2		200	(3,700)
Dec. 31	New provision for doubtful debts	L2	350		(3,350)
Dec. 31	Transfer to ownership interest	L5	3,350		nil

LEONA: *In Year 1 of this example the provision is established for the first time so there is one debit entry to establish an expense which decreases the profit (as a part of the owner-ship interest). In Year 2 of this example the old provision is removed and a new provision created. The overall effect is that the provision increases by £150. Some people would take a shortcut and make one entry of £150 to increase the provision from £200 to £350 but I am not keen on shortcuts. They sometimes lead to disaster. Separate entries make me think carefully about the effect of each.*

Recording a doubtful debt which turns bad

Suppose that in July of Year 2 it was found that the doubtful debt turned totally bad because the customer was declared bankrupt. The effect on the accounting equation is that the asset of debtor is removed. That would normally reduce the ownership interest but on this occasion the impact on ownership interest was anticipated at the end of Year 1 and so the provision for doubtful debts is now used to match the decrease in the asset. The analysis of the transaction would be:

Date	Transaction or event	Debit	Credit
Year 2			
July	Doubtful debt becomes bad	Provision for doubtful debts £200	Receivables (debtors) £200

The consequence of using the provision for doubtful debts is that there is no impact on the income statement (profit and loss account) of Year 2 of a bad debt which was known to be likely at the end of Year 1. However, when the provision for doubtful debts is reviewed at the end of Year 2 there is no reversal of the £200 because that has already been used during the year. The charge of £350 for Year 2 relates solely to the provision for doubt in respect of receivables (debtors) owing money at the end of Year 2.

Prepayments

The prepayment transaction analysed in the chapter was as follows. On 1 October of Year 1 a company paid £1,200 for one year's vehicle insurance. At the financial year-end date of 31 December there have been three months' benefit used up and there is a nine-month benefit yet to come. (See Table 9.7.)

Table 9.7
Analysis of prepayment of insurance, Year 1

Date	Transaction or event	Debit	Credit
Year 2			
Oct. 1	Payment of premium £1,200	Expense (insurance)	Cash
Dec. 31	Identification of asset remaining as a prepayment £900	Asset (prepayment)	Expense (insurance)

Ledger accounts required to record the prepayment are:

L6   Expense of insurance
L7   Prepayment

Not shown, but necessary for completion of the debit and credit record, are:

L3   Cash
L4   Profit and loss account

L6 Expense of insurance

Date	Particulars	Page	Debit	Credit	Balance
Year 1			£	£	£
Oct. 31	Cash	L3	1,200		1,200
Dec. 31	Prepayment	L7		(900)	300
Dec. 31	Transfer to profit and loss account	L4		(300)	nil

LEONA: *Although it is known in October that there will be a balance remaining at the end of the year, it is usually regarded as more convenient to debit the entire payment as an expense of the period initially. The expense is reviewed at the end of the year and £900 is found to be an asset which benefits the future. It is transferred to the asset account for prepayments, leaving only the expense of £300 relating to this period, which is transferred to the income statement (profit and loss account).*

L7 Prepayment

Date	Particulars	Page	Debit	Credit	Balance
Year 1			£	£	£
Oct. 31	Insurance expense prepaid	L6	900		900

LEONA: *The prepayment account is an asset account and therefore the balance remains in the account until the benefit asset is used up. During Year 2 the benefit will disappear and the asset will become an expense. The bookkeeping treatment will be to credit the prepayment account and debit the insurance expense account.*

S   Test your understanding

S9.1   Record the transactions of question B9.3 in ledger accounts for L1 Receivables (debtors), L2 Provision for doubtful debts, L3 Cash and L4 Profit and loss account.

S9.2   Record the transactions of question B9.4 in ledger accounts for L1 Receivables (debtors), L2 Provision for doubtful debts, L3 Cash and L4 Profit and loss account.

S9.3   Record the transactions of question B9.5 in ledger accounts for L6 Expense of insurance and L7 Prepayment.

Chapter 10

Current liabilities

Trade payables and supplier payment

Supplier payment policy

The Group's policy is to agree terms of transactions, including payment terms, with suppliers and, provided that suppliers perform in accordance with the agreed terms, it is the Group's normal practice that payment is made accordingly. Details of the average credit period taken on trade payables are provided in note 20 to the financial statements.

Directors' Report, p. 39.

Note 20 Trade and other payables

	2009	2008
Current	£m	£m
Trade payables	77	520
Other taxes and social security costs	18	117
Other payables	13	111
Accruals and deferred income	159	335
Forward currency contracts (see note 22)	–	4
	267	1,087
Non-current		
Other payables	–	1

The average credit period taken on trade payables, calculated by reference to the amounts owed at the period end as a proportion of the amounts invoiced by suppliers in the period, adjusted to take account of the timing of acquisitions, was 21 days (2008: 48 days). The Directors consider that the carrying amount of trade and other payables approximates to their fair value.

Source: Carphone Warehouse Annual Report 2008; http://media.corporate-ir.net/media_files/irol/12/123964/AR09/CPW_AR09.pdf.

Discussion points

1 What do we learn about the group's policy of paying suppliers?
2 How significant is the amount of trade payables in the current liabilities?

Contents

Learning outcomes

After studying this chapter you should be able to:

- Define a liability and explain the distinguishing feature of current liabilities.
- Explain the conditions for recognition of liabilities.
- Explain how the information presented in a company's statement of financial position (balance sheet) and notes, in relation to liabilities, meets the needs of users.
- Explain the features of current liabilities and the approach to measurement and recording.
- Explain the terms 'accruals' and 'matching concept' and show how they are applied to expenses of the period.
- Explain how liabilities for taxation arise in companies.

Additionally, for those who choose to study the supplement:

- Prepare the ledger accounts to record accruals.

10.1 Introduction

The theme running through this textbook is the accounting equation:

Assets	minus	**Liabilities**	equals	**Ownership interest**

It was explained in Chapter 2 that the ownership interest is the residual amount found by deducting all liabilities of the company from total assets. Chapters 8 and 9 have taken you through aspects of non-current and current assets which are particularly significant to users of financial statements. Chapters 10 and 11 complete the left-hand side of the equation by providing a similar overview of current liabilities and non-current liabilities.

This chapter follows the approach established in Chapters 8 and 9:

- What are the principles for defining and recognising these items?
- What are the information needs of users in respect of the particular items?
- What information is currently provided by companies to meet these needs?
- Does the information show the desirable qualitative characteristics of financial statements?
- What are the principles for measuring, and processes for recording, these items?

10.2 Definitions

The definition of a liability, as provided in Chapter 2, is repeated here:

Definition

A **liability** is a present obligation of the entity arising from past events, the settlement of which is expected to result in an outflow from the entity of resources embodying economic benefits.[1]

A **current liability** is a liability which satisfies any of the following criteria:

(a) it is expected to be settled in the entity's normal operating cycle;
(b) it is held primarily for the purpose of being traded;
(c) it is due to be settled within twelve months after the reporting period.[2]

Supplement 7.1 to Chapter 7 sets out the information to be presented on the face of the statement of financial position (balance sheet) of companies using the IASB system in their financial statements. The only current liabilities listed there are item (j) trade and other payables, item (l) financial liabilities (where these are short-term loans) and (m) liabilities for current tax.

Supplement 7.2 to Chapter 7 sets out the information to be presented in the financial statements of companies that are using the UK Companies Act and UK ASB standards. There is one heading for current liabilities and a detailed list below. The list is as follows:

E Creditors: amounts falling due within one year
1 Debenture loans
2 Bank loans and overdrafts
3 Payments received on account
4 Trade creditors
5 Bills of exchange payable
6 Amounts owed to group undertakings
7 Amounts owed to undertakings in which the company has a participating interest
8 Other creditors including taxation and social security
9 Accruals and deferred income

Activity 10.1

Look back to Table 2.3, which analyses some common types of liability. Set up on a blank sheet a similar table with four columns and headings for: type of liability; obligation; transfer of economic benefits; and past transaction or event. Then close the book and write down any ten liabilities you have come across during your study. Fill in all the columns as a check that, at this stage, you really understand what creates a liability.

10.3 Recognition

The general conditions for recognition were set out in Chapter 2. An item that meets the definition of a liability should be recognised if there is sufficient evidence that the liability has been created and that the item has a cost or value that can be measured with sufficient reliability. In practice, recognition problems related to liabilities centre on ensuring that none is omitted which ought to be included. This is in contrast to the case of assets where there is a need, in practice, to guard against over-enthusiastic inclusion of items which do not meet the recognition conditions.

10.3.1 Risk of understatement of liabilities

The risk related to liabilities is therefore the risk of understatement. This is explained in Chapter 4 under the heading of prudence. The risk of understatement of liabilities is that it will result in overstatement of the ownership interest.

In recent years the standard-setting bodies have devoted quite strenuous efforts to discouraging companies from keeping liabilities (and related assets) off the statement of financial position (balance sheet). This problem is called **off-balance sheet finance** and will be explained in Chapter 14.

10.3.2 Non-recognition: contingent liabilities

There are some obligations of the company which fail the recognition test because there is significant uncertainty about future events that may cause benefits to flow from the company. The uncertainty may be about the occurrence of the event or about the measurement of the consequences. These are called **contingent liabilities** because they are contingent upon (depend upon) some future event happening. Examples are:

- A company is involved in legal action where a customer is seeking damages for illness allegedly caused by the company's product. If the customer is successful, there will be more claims. The company does not believe that the customer will succeed.
- A parent company has given guarantees to a bank that it will meet the overdraft and loans of a subsidiary company if that company defaults on repayment. At the present time there is no reason to suppose that any default will take place.
- A company is under investigation by the Competition Commission for possible price-fixing within the industry in contravention of an order prohibiting restrictive practices. If there is found to be a restrictive practice, a penalty may be imposed.
- The company has acquired a subsidiary in Australia where the tax authorities have raised an action for tax due on a disputed transaction which occurred before the subsidiary was acquired. The action is being defended strenuously.

In each of these examples, the company is convinced that it will not have a liability at the end of the day, but the users of the financial statements may wish to have some indication of the upper bounds of the liability if the company's optimism proves unfounded. There may, however, be a problem for the company in publishing an estimate of the amount of the possible liability because it may be seen as admitting liability and furthermore may require disclosure of commercially sensitive confidential information.

Where a **contingent liability** is identified, the obligation is not recognised in the statement of financial position (balance sheet) but it may be important that users of the financial statements are aware of the problem. There will therefore be a note to the statement of financial position (balance sheet) reporting the circumstances of the contingent liability and sometimes giving an indication of the amount involved. Because of the confidentiality aspect, companies tend to give little information about the financial effect of a contingent liability, but some will try to set the outer limits of the liability.

Definition

> A **contingent liability** is either:
>
> (a) a possible obligation that arises from past events and whose existence will be confirmed only by the occurrence of one or more uncertain future events not wholly within the control of the entity; or
> (b) a present obligation that arises from past events but is not recognised because:
>   (i) either it is not probable that a transfer of economic benefits will be required to settle the obligation;
>   (ii) or the amount of the obligation cannot be measured with sufficient reliability.[3]

A company should disclose a brief description of the nature of the contingent liability and, where practicable:

(a) an estimate of its financial effect;
(b) an indication of the uncertainties relating to the amount or timing of any outflow; and
(c) the possibility of any reimbursement.[4]

Rules about measurement are given in detail in the accounting standard. The detail is not necessary for an introductory course.

10.3.3 Changing thoughts on contingencies

In 2005 the IASB issued a proposal to eliminate the term 'contingent liability' because if the item cannot be recognised in a statement of financial position (balance sheet) then it cannot be a true liability. The proposal of the IASB was that items carrying an unconditional obligation should be recognised as a liability and measured at the best estimate. Any uncertain event affecting the measurement of the obligation would be explained in a note. Items that do not carry an unconditional obligation are seen as business risks. Such business risks would be reported as a note to the financial statements because they may have a significant effect on the carrying amount of assets and liabilities in the near future. These changing thoughts on contingencies do not change the overall amount of information to be disclosed about contingencies but the method of disclosure may change.

Activity 10.2

Consider the four examples of contingent liability given at the start of this section. Based on the definition, explain why each is a contingent liability.

10.4 Users' needs for information

There are two aspects of information in relation to liabilities. The first relates to the amount owed (sometimes called the **principal sum** or the **capital amount**) and the second relates to the cost of servicing the loan (usually the payment of **interest**).

In respect of current liabilities, other than a bank overdraft or bank loans repayable within the year, it is unlikely that interest will be payable, and so generally there will be no information about interest charges. The shareholders in the company will be concerned that there are adequate current assets to meet the current liabilities as they fall due. Those who supply goods and services will want to be reassured that payment will be made on the due date.

Owners of a company need to know how much the company owes to other parties because the owners are at the end of the queue when it comes to sharing out the assets of the company if it closes down. Many of those who supply goods and services are what is known as unsecured creditors, which means they come at the end of the list of creditors. They will also have an interest in the balance of long-term and current liabilities.

10.5 Information provided in the financial statements

The statement of financial position (balance sheet) of Safe and Sure plc, set out in Chapter 7, contains the following information in relation to current liabilities:

	Notes	Year 7 £m	Year 6 £m
Current liabilities			
Amounts payable (creditors)	7	(159.8)	(157.5)
Bank overdraft	8	(40.1)	(62.6)
		(199.9)	(220.1)

Notes to the statement of financial position (balance sheet) explain more about the statement of financial position (balance sheet) items. Note 7 lists the details of current liabilities.

Note 7 Current liabilities: amounts payable

	Year 7 £m	Year 6 £m
Deferred consideration on acquisition	1.1	4.3
Trade payables (trade creditors)	23.6	20.4
Corporation tax	31.5	26.5
Other tax and social security payable	24.5	21.2
Other payables (creditors)	30.7	23.8
Accruals and deferred income	48.4	61.3
	159.8	157.5

Note 8 gives information on bank overdrafts due on demand and confirms that the interest charges incurred on these loans are payable at commercial rates:

Note 8 Bank borrowings: current liabilities

	Year 7 £m	Year 6 £m
Bank overdrafts due on demand:	40.1	62.6

Interest on overdrafts is payable at normal commercial rates appropriate to the country where the borrowing is made.

The report of the finance director provides further insight into the currency spread of the bank borrowings:

Foreign currency: £35.2m of foreign currency bank borrowings have been incurred to fund overseas acquisition. The main borrowings were £26.8m in US dollars and £8.4m in Japanese yen. The borrowings are mainly from banks on a short-term basis, with a maturity of up to one year, and we have fixed the interest rate on $20m of the US dollar loans through to November, Year 7, at an overall cost of 4.46%.

All material foreign currency transactions are matched back into the currency of the group company undertaking the transaction.

David Wilson has already commented in Chapters 4 and 7 on some aspects of the liabilities in the financial statements of Safe and Sure plc. Here he is explaining to Leona, in the coffee bar at the health club, his views on current liabilities in particular.

DAVID: *Current liabilities are relatively similar in total to last year so there are no particular questions to ask there.*

Then I start to think about the limits of risk. There is £40m due for repayment to the bank within the year. Will the company have any problem finding this amount? With £105m in cash and cash, it seems unlikely that there could be a problem. The entire current liabilities are £199.9m, all of which could be met from the cash and cash equivalents and receivables (debtors).

There is another risk that £40m shown as owing to the banks may be the wrong measure of the liability if exchange rates move against the company. Whenever I see foreign borrowings I want to know more about the currency of borrowings. You know from your economics class the theory of interest rates and currency exchange rates. It backs up my rule of thumb that borrowing in currencies which are weak means paying high rates of interest. Borrowing in currencies which are strong will mean paying lower rates of interest but runs a greater risk of having to use up additional pounds sterling to repay the loan if the foreign currency strengthens more. Information about the currency mix of loans is something I can probably get from the company if I need it. In this case, the finance director's report is sufficiently informative for my purposes. In past years, before finance directors started providing explanations in the annual report, we were asking these questions at face-to-face meetings.

LEONA: *What you have described is similar in many respects to the analytical review carried out by the auditors. We do much more than merely check the bookkeeping entries and the paperwork. We are looking at whether the statement of financial position (balance sheet) makes sense and whether any items have changed without sufficient explanation.*

10.6 Measurement and recording

Liabilities are measured at the amount originally received from the lender of finance or supplier of goods and services, plus any additional charges incurred such as rolled-up interest added to a loan. This is generally agreed to be a useful measure of the obligation to transfer economic benefits from the company.

From the accounting equation it may be seen that an increase in a liability must be related either to an increase in an asset or a decrease in the ownership interest. Usually any related decrease in the ownership interest will be reported in the statement of financial position (balance sheet) as an expense.

The most significant current liabilities for most companies are bank borrowing and trade creditors. Both of these are essential sources of finance for small companies and are an important aspect, if not essential, for larger companies.

Activity 10.3

Write down the documentation you would expect to see as evidence of the money amount of the following liabilities:

- *bank overdraft;*
- *amount owing to a trade supplier.*

Now read the next sections and find whether your answer matches the information in the text.

10.6.1   Bank overdraft finance

Banks provide short-term finance to companies in the form of an overdraft on a current account. The advantage of an overdraft is its flexibility. When the cash needs of the company increase with seasonal factors, the company can continue to write cheques and watch the overdraft increase. When the goods and services are sold and cash begins to flow in, the company should be able to watch the overdraft decrease again. The most obvious example of a business which operates in this pattern is farming. The farmer uses the overdraft to finance the acquisition of seed for arable farming, or feed through the winter for stock farming and to cover the period when the crops or animals are growing and maturing. The overdraft is reduced when the crops or the animals are sold.

The main disadvantage of an overdraft is that it is repayable on demand. The farmer whose crop fails because of bad weather knows the problem of being unable to repay the overdraft. Having overdraft financing increases the worries of those who manage the company. The other disadvantage is that the interest payable on overdrafts is variable. When interest rates increase, the cost of the overdraft increases. Furthermore, for small companies there are often complaints that the rate of interest charged is high compared with that available to larger companies. The banks answer that the rates charged reflect relative risk and it is their experience that small companies are more risky.

10.6.2   Trade payables (trade creditors)

It is a strong feature of many industries that one enterprise is willing to supply goods to another in advance of being paid. Most suppliers will state terms of payment (e.g. the invoice must be paid within 30 days) and some will offer a discount for prompt payment. In the UK it has not been traditional to charge interest on overdue accounts but this practice is growing as suppliers realise there is a high cost to themselves of not collecting cash in good time. A supplier who is waiting to be paid is called a **trade creditor**.

Trade creditors rarely have any security for payment of the amount due to them, so that if a customer fails to pay the supplier must wait in the queue with other suppliers and hope for a share of some distribution. They are described as **unsecured creditors**. Some suppliers will include in the contract a condition that the goods remain the property of the supplier should the customer fail to pay. This is called retention of title (ROT) and will be noted in the statement of financial position (balance sheet) of a company which has bought goods on these terms. Retention of title may offer some protection to the unpaid supplier but requires very prompt action to recover identifiable goods in the event of difficulty.

Some suppliers send goods to a customer on a sale-or-return basis. If there are no conditions to prevent return then the goods will not appear as stock in the statement of financial position (balance sheet) of the customer and there will be no indication of a liability. This practice is particularly common in the motor industry where manufacturers send cars to showrooms for sale or return within a specified period of time. Omitting the inventories and the related potential liability is referred to as **off-balance-sheet finance**, a topic explored further in Chapter 14.

Suppliers send **invoices** to the customer showing the amount due for payment. These invoices are used in the customer's accounts department as the source of information for liabilities. At the end of the month the suppliers send statements as a reminder of unpaid invoices. Statements are useful as additional evidence of liabilities to suppliers.

Measurement of trade creditors is relatively straightforward because the company will know how much it owes to short-term creditors. If it forgets the creditors, they will soon issue a reminder.

Recording requires some care because omission of any credit transaction will mean there is an understatement of a liability. In particular, the company has to take some care at the end of the year over what are called **cut-off procedures**. Take the example of raw materials provided by a supplier. The goods arrive at the company's store by delivery van but the invoice for their payment arrives a few days later by mail. The accounts department uses the supplier's invoice as the document which initiates the *recording* of the asset of stock and the liability to the supplier. In contrast, the event which *creates* the liability is the acceptance of the goods. (It is difficult for the accounts department to use the delivery note as a record of the liability because it shows the quantities but not the price of the goods delivered.) So, at the end of the accounting year the accounts department has to compare the most recent delivery notes signed by the storekeeper with the most recent invoices received from the supplier. If goods have been received by the company, the statement of financial position (balance sheet) must include the asset of stock and the related liability. Using a similar line of reasoning, if a supplier has sent an invoice ahead of delivery of the goods, it should not be recorded as a liability because there is no related asset.

The recording of purchases of goods for resale is shown in Chapter 6. In the illustration of the process for recording the transactions of M. Carter there is a purchase of goods from the supplier, R. Busby, on credit terms. Payment is made later in the month. The purchase of the goods creates the asset of stock and the liability to the supplier. Payment to the supplier reduces the asset of cash and eliminates the liability to the supplier. The liability is described as an 'account payable'.

10.7 Accruals and the matching concept

At the financial year-end date there will be obligations of the company to pay for goods or services which are not contained in the accounting records because no document has been received from the supplier of the goods or services. It is essential that all obligations are included at the financial year-end date because these obligations fall under the definition of liabilities even although the demand for payment has not been received. The process of including in the statement of financial position (balance sheet) all obligations at the end of the period is called the accrual of liabilities and is said to reflect the **accruals basis** or accruals concept (see Chapter 4).

Definition | Under the **accruals basis**, the effects of transactions and other events are recognised when they occur (and not as cash or its equivalent is received or paid) and they are recorded in the accounting records and reported in the financial statements of the periods to which they relate.[5]

The argument contained in the previous paragraph is based on the definition of a liability, but some people prefer to arrive at the same conclusion using a different argument. They say that all expenses of the accounting period must be matched against the revenue earned in the period. If a benefit has been consumed, the effect must be recorded whether or not documentation has been received. This argument is referred to as the **matching concept**.

In the *Framework*, the IASB explains that in the income statement there is a direct association between the costs incurred and the earning of specific items of income. This process is called the matching of costs with revenues. As an example, the expenses that make up the cost of goods sold are recognised at the same time as the revenue derived from the sale of the goods.[6]

The accruals concept and the matching concept are, for most practical purposes, different ways of arriving at the same conclusion. (There are exceptions but these are well beyond the scope of a first-level text.)

10.7.1 The distinction between the expense of the period and the cash paid

A company starts business on 1 January Year 1. It has a financial year-end of 31 December Year 1. During Year 1 it receives four accounts for electricity, all of which are paid ten days after receiving them. The dates of receiving and paying the accounts are as follows:

Date invoice received	Amount of invoice £	Date paid
31 Mar. Year 1	350	10 Apr. Year 1
30 June Year 1	180	10 July Year 1
30 Sept. Year 1	280	10 Oct. Year 1
31 Dec. Year 1	340	10 Jan. Year 2
	1,150	

The company has used electricity for the entire year and therefore should match against revenue the full cost of £1,150. Only three invoices have been paid during the year, the final invoice not being paid until the start of Year 2. That is important for cash flow but is not relevant for the measurement of profit. The transactions during the year would be recorded as shown in Table 10.1. The arrival of the electricity invoice causes a record to be made of the increase in the liability and the increase in the expense (decreasing the ownership interest). The payment of the amount due requires a separate record to be made of the decrease in the liability and the decrease in the asset of cash.

Table 10.1
Spreadsheet analysis of transactions relating to the expense of electricity consumed, Year 1

Date	Transactions with electricity company	Asset	Liability	Ownership interest: profit of the period
		Cash	Electricity company	Electricity expense
Year 1		£	£	£
Mar. 31	Invoice received £350		350	(350)
Apr. 10	Pay electricity company £350	(350)	(350)	
June 30	Invoice received £180		180	(180)
July 10	Pay electricity company £180	(180)	(180)	
Sept. 30	Invoice received £280		280	(280)
Oct. 10	Pay electricity caompany £280	(280)	(280)	
Dec. 31	Invoice received £340		340	(340)
	Totals	(810)	340	(1,150)

The payment made to the electricity company in January Year 2 is not recorded in Table 10.1 because it is not a transaction of Year 1. It will appear in a spreadsheet for January Year 2. The totals at the foot of the spreadsheet show that the transactions of Year 1 have caused the cash of the company to decrease by £810. There remains a liability of £340 to the electricity company at the end of Year 1. The profit and loss account for the year will show an expense of £1,150. The spreadsheet satisfies the accounting equation because there is a decrease in an asset, amounting to £810, and an increase in a liability amounting to £340. These together equal the decrease of £1,150 in the ownership interest:

Asset ↓	–	Liability ↑	=	Ownership interest ↓
– £810		+ £340		– £1,150

That one needs a little careful thought because several things are happening at once. You might prefer to think about it one stage at a time. You know from earlier examples in Chapters 2, 5 and 6 that a decrease in an asset causes a decrease in the ownership interest. You also know that an increase in a liability causes a decrease in the owner-ship interest. Put them together and they are both working in the same direction to decrease the ownership interest.

10.7.2 Accrual where no invoice has been received

Now consider what might happen if the final electricity invoice for the year has not been received on 31 December Year 1. If no invoice has been received then there will be no entry in the accounting records. That, however, would fail to acknowledge that the electricity has been consumed and the company knows there is an obligation to pay for that electricity. In terms of the matching concept, only nine months' invoices are available to match against revenue when there has been twelve months' usage. The answer is that the company must make an *estimate* of the accrual of the liability for electricity consumed. Estimates will seldom give the true answer but they can be made reasonably close if some care is taken. If the company keeps a note of electricity meter readings and knows the unit charge, it can calculate what the account would have been.

The entries in the spreadsheet at the end of the month are shown in Table 10.2. They will be the same numerically as those in the final line of Table 10.1 but the item shown at 31 December will be described as an accrual.

Table 10.2
Spreadsheet entry for accrual at the end of the month

Date	Transactions with electricity company	Asset	Liability	Ownership interest: profit of the period
		Cash	Electricity company	Electricity expense
Year 1		£	£	£
Dec. 31	Accrual for three months		340	(340)

10.7.3 The nature of estimates in accounting

Making an accrual for a known obligation, where no invoice has been received, requires estimates. In the example given here it was a relatively straightforward matter to take a meter reading and calculate the expected liability. There will be other examples where the existence and amount of an expense are both known with reasonable certainty. There will be some cases where the amount has to be estimated and the estimate is later found to be incorrect. That is a normal feature of accounting, although not all users of financial statements realise there is an element of uncertainty about the information provided. If a liability is unintentionally understated at the end of a period, the profit will be overstated. In the next accounting period, when the full obligation becomes known, the expense incurred will be higher than was anticipated and the profit of that period will be lower than it should ideally be. If the error in the estimate is found to be such that it would change the views of the main users of financial statements, a prior year adjustment may be made by recalculating the profits of previous years and reporting the effect, but that is a relatively rare occurrence.

Activity 10.4	*Write down five types of transaction where you might expect to see an accrual of expense at the year-end. Against each transaction type write down the method you would use to estimate the amount of the accrued expense.*

10.8 Liabilities for taxation

In the statement of financial position (balance sheet) of a company there are two main categories of liability related directly to the company. The first is the **corporation tax** payable, based on the taxable profits of the period, the second is **deferred taxation**. Each of these will be discussed here. You will also see in the current liabilities section of a statement of financial position (balance sheet) the words 'other tax and social security payable'. This refers to the amounts deducted from employees' salaries and wages by the company on behalf of HMRC and paid over at regular intervals. In respect of such amounts the company is acting as a tax collecting agent of HMRC.

10.8.1 Corporation tax

Companies pay corporation tax based on the taxable profit of the accounting period (usually one year). The taxable profit is calculated according to the rules of tax law. That in itself is a subject for an entire textbook but one basic principle is that the taxable profit is based on profit calculated according to commercially accepted accounting practices. So, apart from some specific points of difference, the accounting profit is usually quite close to the taxable profit. Assume that the corporation tax rate is 30% of the taxable profit. (The tax rate each year is set by the Chancellor of the Exchequer.) Analysts will evaluate the tax charge in the profit and loss account as a percentage of taxable profit and start to ask questions when the answer is very different from 30%. The explanation could be that there are profits earned abroad where the tax rate is different, but it could also be that there has been some use of provisions or adjustments for accounting purposes which are not allowed for tax purposes. That will lead to more probing by the analysts to establish whether they share the doubts of the tax authorities.

Large companies must pay corporation tax by four quarterly instalments. A company with a year-end of 31 December Year 1 will pay on 14 July Year 1, 14 October Year 1, 14 January Year 2 and 14 April Year 2. The amount of tax due is estimated by making a forecast of the profit for the year. As the year progresses the forecast is revised and the tax calculation is also revised. This means that at the end of the accounting year there is a liability for half that year's tax bill. A 'large' company is any company that pays corporation tax at the full rate. Small companies, which have a special, lower, rate of corporation tax, pay their tax bill nine months after the end of the accounting period. The precise limits for defining 'large' and 'small' companies change with tax legislation each year. (You will be given the necessary information in any exercise that you are asked to attempt.) Suppose the taxable profit is £10m and the tax payable at 30% is £3m. During the year £1.5m is paid in total on the first two instalment dates. At the statement of financial position (balance sheet) date there will remain a liability of £1.5m to be paid in total on the final two instalment dates.

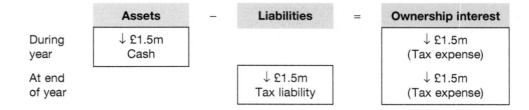

	Assets	–	Liabilities	=	Ownership interest
During year	↓ £1.5m Cash				↓ £1.5m (Tax expense)
At end of year			↓ £1.5m Tax liability		↓ £1.5m (Tax expense)

10.8.2 Deferred taxation liability

It was explained earlier in this section that the taxable profit is based on the accounting profit unless there are taxation rules which indicate otherwise. There are taxation rules which allow companies to defer the payment of some taxation on the full accounting profit. ('Deferring' means paying much later than the normal period of nine months.) The deferral period might be for a few months or it might be for a few years. The obligation to pay tax eventually cannot be escaped but the liability becomes long term. This is reflected, in terms of the accounting equation, by reporting the decrease in ownership claim in the profit and loss account but showing the deferred liability as a separate item under **non-current liabilities**.

10.9 Summary

- A **current liability** is a liability which satisfies any of the following criteria:
  - (a) it is expected to be settled in the entity's normal operating cycle;
  - (b) it is held primarily for the purpose of being traded;
  - (c) it is due to be settled within 12 months after the financial year-end date.
- The risk of understatement of liabilities is that it will result in overstatement of the ownership interest.
- **Off-balance sheet finance** means keeping liabilities (and related assets) off the statement of financial position (balance sheet).
- There are some obligations of the company which fail the recognition test because there is significant uncertainty about future events that may cause benefits to flow from the company. These are reported as **contingent liabilities** in the notes to the financial statements.
- Users need to know about the existence of liabilities, the amount and timing of expected repayments and interest charges payable on loans.
- Under the **accruals** basis, the effects of transactions and other events are recognised when they occur (and not as cash or its equivalent is received or paid) and they are recorded in the accounting records and reported in the financial statements of the periods to which they relate.
- Liabilities for unpaid expenses are often called **accruals**.
- The **matching concept** is the idea that all expenses of the accounting period must be matched against the revenue earned in the period. If a benefit has been consumed, the effect must be recorded whether or not documentation has been received.
- Companies pay corporation tax. The arrangements vary depending on the size of the company but there will usually be a liability for unpaid corporation tax in the current liabilities section of the statement of financial position (balance sheet). Where government policy allows payment to be delayed for more than 12 months the liability is described as **deferred taxation**.

QUESTIONS

The Questions section of each chapter has three types of question. 'Test your understanding' questions to help you review your reading are in the 'A' series of questions. You will find the answers to these by reading and thinking about the material in the book. 'Application' questions to test your ability to apply technical skills are in the 'B' series of questions. Questions requiring you to show skills in problem solving and evaluation are in the 'C' series of questions. A letter [S] indicates that there is a solution at the end of the book.

A   Test your understanding

A10.1   What is the definition of a liability? (Section 10.2)

A10.2   What is the distinction between a long-term liability and a current liability? (Section 10.2)

A10.3   What is the effect of understatement of liabilities? (Section 10.3.1)

A10.4   What is a contingent liability? (Section 10.3.2)

A10.5   What information do users of financial statements need to have concerning current liabilities of a company? (Section 10.4)

A10.6   How are the current liabilities for (a) bank overdraft and (b) trade creditors measured? (Section 10.6)

A10.7   What is meant by an accrual? How is it recorded? (Section 10.7)

A10.8   Explain what is meant by the matching concept. (Section 10.7)

A10.9   [S] On reviewing the financial statements, the company accountant discovers that a supplier's invoice for an amount of £10,000 has been omitted from the accounting records. The goods to which the invoice relates are held in the warehouse and are included in stock. What will be the effect on the profit and loss account and the statement of financial position (balance sheet) when this error is rectified?

A10.10   [S] On reviewing the financial statements, the company accountant discovers that a payment of £21,000 made to a supplier has been omitted from the cash book and other internal accounting records. What will be the effect on the profit and loss account and the statement of financial position (balance sheet) when this omission is rectified?

A10.11   [S] On reviewing the financial statements, the company accountant discovers that an invoice for the rent of £4,000 owed to its landlord has been recorded incorrectly as rent receivable of £4,000 in the company's accounting records. What will be the effect on the profit and loss account and the statement of financial position (balance sheet) when this error is rectified?

B   Application

B10.1 [S]
White Ltd commenced trading on 1 July Year 3 and draws up its accounts for the year ended 30 June Year 4. During its first year of trading the company pays total telephone expenses of £3,500. The three-month bill paid in May Year 4 includes calls of £800 for the quarter up to 30 April Year 4 and advance rental of £660 to 31 July Year 4. The bill received in August Year 4 includes calls of £900 for the quarter up to 31 July Year 4 and advance rental of £660 to 31 October Year 4.

Required
Show calculations of the telephone expense to be recorded in the profit and loss account of White Ltd for its first year of trading.

B10.2 [S]

Plastics Ltd pays rent for a warehouse used for storage. The quarterly charge for security guard services is £800. The security firm sends an invoice on 31 March, 30 June, 30 September and 31 December. Plastics Ltd always pays the rent five days after the invoice is received. The security services have been used for some years. Plastics Ltd has an accounting year-end of 31 December.

Required

Prepare a spreadsheet to show how the transactions of one year in respect of security services are recorded.

B10.3 [S]

The accountant of Brown Ltd has calculated that the company should report in its profit and loss account a tax charge of £8,000 based on the taxable profit of the period. Of this amount, £6,000 will be payable nine months after the accounting year-end but £2,000 may be deferred for payment in a period estimated at between three and five years after the accounting year-end. Using the accounting equation explain how this information will be reported in the financial statements of Brown Ltd.

C   Problem solving and evaluation

C10.1 [S]

The following file of papers was found in a cupboard of the general office of Green Ltd at the end of the accounting year. Explain how each would be treated in the financial statements and state the total amount to be reported as an accrued liability on the financial year-end date. The year-end is 31 December Year 1.

Item	Description	Amount £
1	Invoice dated 23 December for goods received 21 December.	260
2	Invoice dated 23 December for goods to be delivered on 3 January Year 2.	310
3	Foreman's note of electricity consumption for month of December – no invoice yet received from electricity supply company.	100
4	Letter from employee claiming overtime payment for work on 1 December and note from personnel office denying entitlement to payment.	58
5	Telephone bill dated 26 December showing calls for October to December.	290
6	Telephone bill dated 26 December showing rent due in advance for period January to March Year 2.	90
7	Note of payment due to cleaners for final week of December (to be paid in January under usual pattern of payment one week in arrears).	48
8	Invoice from supplier for promotional calendars received 1 December (only one-third have yet been sent to customers).	300
9	Letter dated 21 December Year 1 to customer promising a cheque to reimburse damage caused by faulty product – cheque to be sent on 4 January Year 2.	280
10	Letter dated 23 December promising donation to local charity – amount not yet paid.	60

Activities for study groups

Turn to the annual report of a listed company which you have used for activities in previous chapters. Find every item of information about current liabilities. (Start with the financial statements and notes but look also at the operating and financial review, chief executive's review and other non-regulated information about the company.)

Divide into two groups. One group should take on the role of the purchasing director and one should take on the role of a company which has been asked to supply goods or services to this company on credit terms.

- *Supplier group*: What questions would you ask to supplement what you have learned from the annual report?
- *Purchasing director*: What questions would you ask about the supplier? What might you learn about the supplier from the annual report of the supplier's company?

Notes and references

1. IASB (1989), *Framework*, para. 49(b).
2. IASB (2009), IAS 1, para. 69.
3. IASB (2009), IAS 37, *Provisions, Contingent Liabilities and Contingent Assets*, para. 10.
4. *Ibid.*, para. 86.
5. IASB (1989), *Framework*, para. 23.
6. IASB (1989), *Framework*, para. 95.

Bookkeeping entries for accruals

In the main part of the chapter the accruals for electricity were analysed. Now consider the debit and credit recording. The following transactions are to be recorded.

A company starts business on 1 January Year 1. It has a financial year-end of 31 December Year 1. During Year 1 it receives three accounts for electricity, all of which are paid ten days after receiving them. The dates of receiving and paying the accounts are as follows:

Amount of invoice £	Date invoice received	Date paid
350	31 Mar. Year 1	10 Apr. Year 1
180	30 June Year 1	10 July Year 1
280	30 Sept. Year 1	10 Oct. Year 1

At 31 December the final invoice for the year has not arrived because of delays in the mail but the amount due for payment is estimated at £340.

Activity 10.5	*Before you read further, attempt to write down the debit and credit entries for: each of the three invoices received; the payments of those three invoices; and the estimated amount due for payment at the end of the year. You may find help in looking back to Tables 10.1 and 10.2.*

Table 10.3 sets out the debit and credit aspect of each transaction and event. The amount of the liability to the supplier cannot be recorded until the invoice is received. The credit entry for the estimate of the amount owing to the supplier is therefore shown in a separate account called *accruals* which will be the basis for the amount shown in the statement of financial position (balance sheet) under that heading.

The ledger accounts required here are:

L1 Expense (electricity)
L2 Liability to supplier
L3 Accrual

Also required to complete the double entry, but not shown here as a ledger account, are:

L4 Cash
L5 Profit and loss account

Table 10.3
Analysis of debit and credit aspect of each transaction and event

Date	Transaction	Debit	Credit
Year 1			
Mar. 31	Receive invoice for electricity £350	Expense (electricity)	Liability to supplier
Apr. 10	Pay supplier £350	Liability to supplier	Cash
June 30	Receive invoice for electricity £180	Expense (electricity)	Liability to supplier
July 10	Pay supplier £180	Liability to supplier	Cash
Sept. 30	Receive invoice for electricity £280	Expense (electricity)	Liability to supplier
Oct. 10	Pay supplier £280	Liability to supplier	Cash
Dec. 31	Estimate amount owing to supplier £340	Expense (electricity)	Accruals

L1 Expense (electricity)

Date	Particulars	Page	Debit	Credit	Balance
Year 1			£	£	£
Mar. 31	Invoice from supplier	L2	350		350
June 30	Invoice from supplier	L2	180		530
Sept. 30	Invoice from supplier	L2	280		810
Dec. 31	Estimated accrual	L3	340		1,150
Dec. 31	Transfer to profit and loss account	L5		(1,150)	nil

LEONA: *The electricity account for the year shows a full 12 months' expense which is transferred to the profit and loss account at the end of the year.*

L2 Liability to supplier

Date	Particulars	Page	Debit	Credit	Balance
Year 1			£	£	£
Mar. 31	Invoice for electricity expense	L1		350	(350)
Apr. 10	Cash paid	L4	350		nil
June 30	Invoice for electricity expense	L1		180	(180)
July 10	Cash paid	L4	180		nil
Sept. 30	Invoice for electricity expense	L1		280	(280)
Oct. 10	Cash paid	L4	280		nil

LEONA: *The supplier's account is showing a nil liability because all invoices received have been paid. We know there is another invoice on the way but the bookkeeping system is quite strict about only making entries in the ledger when the documentary evidence is obtained. The document in this case is the supplier's invoice. Until it arrives the liability has to be recognised as an accrual rather than in the supplier's account.*

L3 Accruals

Date	Particulars	Page	Debit	Credit	Balance
Year 1			£	£	£
Dec. 31	Estimate of electricity expense	L1	340	(340)	

LEONA: *The statement of financial position (balance sheet) will record a nil liability to the supplier but will show an accrual of £340 for electricity. When the supplier's invoice arrives in January of Year 2, the debit and credit entries will be:*

Date	Transaction	Debit	Credit	
Year 2				
Jan. 4	Receive invoice for electricity £340	Accrual	Liability to supplier	

In this way the liability remaining from Year 1 is recorded without affecting the expense account for Year 2. The credit balance on the accrual account at the end of Year 1 is eliminated by being matched against the debit entry at the start of Year 2.

S | Test your understanding

S10.1 Prepare bookkeeping records for the information in question B10.1.

S10.2 Prepare bookkeeping records for the information in question B10.2.

S10.3 Prepare bookkeeping records for the information in question B10.3.

S10.4 Prepare bookkeeping records for the information in question C10.1.

Chapter 11

Provisions and non-current (long-term) liabilities

37 Provisions

				$ million
	Decommissioning	Environmental	Litigation and other	Total
At 1 January 2008	9,501	2,107	3,487	15,095
Exchange adjustments	(1,208)	(45)	(107)	(1,360)
New or increased provisions	327	270	2,059	2,656
Write-back of unused provisions	–	(107)	(513)	(620)
Unwinding of discount	202	43	42	287
Utilization	(402)	(512)	(1,424)	(2,338)
Deletions	(2)	(65)	–	(67)
At 31 December 2008	8,418	1,691	3,544	13,653
Of which				
– expected to be incurred within 1 year	322	418	805	1,545
– expected to be incurred in more than 1 year	8,096	1,273	2,739	12,108

The group makes full provision for the future cost of decommissioning oil and natural gas production facilities and related pipelines on a discounted basis on the installation of those facilities. The provision for the costs of decommissioning these production facilities and pipelines at the end of their economic lives has been estimated using existing technology, at current prices or long-term assumptions, depending on the expected timing of the activity, and discounted using a real discount rate of 2.0% (2007: 2.0%). These costs are generally expected to be incurred over the next 30 years. While the provision is based on the best estimate of

future costs and the economic lives of the facilities and pipelines, there is uncertainty regarding both the amount and timing of incurring these costs. Where BP has entered into a contract for the execution of decommissioning activity, these amounts are generally reported within accruals or other payables.

Provisions for environmental remediation are made when a clean-up is probable and the amount of the obligation can be reliably estimated. Generally, this coincides with commitment to a formal plan of action or, if earlier, on divestment or on closure of inactive sites. The provision for environmental liabilities has been estimated using existing technology, at current prices and discounted using a real discount rate of 2.0% (2007: 2.0%). The majority of these costs are expected to be incurred over the next 10 years. The extent and cost of future remediation programmes are inherently difficult to estimate. They depend on the scale of any possible contamination, the timing and extent of corrective actions, and also the group's share of the liability.

Included within the litigation and other category at 31 December 2008 are provisions for litigation of $1,446 million (2007: $1,737 million), for deferred employee compensation of $792 million (2007: $761 million) and for expected rental shortfalls on surplus properties of $251 million (2007: $320 million). To the extent that these liabilities are not expected to be settled within the next three years, the provisions are discounted using either a nominal discount rate of 2.5% (2007: 4.5%) or a real discount rate of 2.0% (2007: 2.0%), as appropriate. No additional provisions were made during 2008 in respect of the Texas City incident (in 2007 the provision was increased by $500 million). Disbursements to claimants in 2008 were $410 million (2007: $314 million) and the provision at 31 December 2008 was $46 million (2007: $456 million).

Source: BP Annual report 2008, p. 158.

Discussion points

1 Why is there a provision when the decommissioning will take place so far into the future?
2 What are the significant uncertainties in estimating the amounts of the provisions?

Contents

Learning outcomes	After studying this chapter you should be able to:

After studying this chapter you should be able to:

- Define a non-current (long-term) liability.
- Explain the needs of users for information about non-current (long-term) liabilities.
- Explain the different types of non-current (long-term) loan finance which may be found in the statements of financial position (balance sheets) of major companies.
- Understand the purpose of provisions and explain how provisions are reported in financial statements.
- Understand the nature of deferred income and explain how it is reported in financial statements.
- Know the main types of loan finance and capital instruments used by companies and understand the principles of reporting information in the financial statements.

Additionally, for those who choose to study the supplement to this chapter:

- Prepare the ledger accounts to record provisions and deferred income.

11.1 Introduction

Supplement 7.1 to Chapter 7 sets out the information to be presented on the face of the statement of financial position (balance sheet) of companies using the IASB system in their financial statements. The non-current liabilities listed there are item (k) provisions, (l) financial liabilities (where these are loans due in more than one year's time) and (n) deferred tax liabilities.

Supplement 7.2 to Chapter 7 sets out the information to be presented in the financial statements of companies that are using the UK Companies Act and UK ASB standards. There is one heading for non-current liabilities, with a detailed list below, as follows:

H Creditors: amounts falling due after more than one year
1 Debenture loans
2 Bank loans and overdrafts
3 Payments received on account
4 Trade creditors
5 Bills of exchange payable
6 Amounts owed to group undertakings
7 Amounts owed to undertakings in which the company has a participating interest
8 Other creditors including taxation and social security
9 Accruals and deferred income

Comparing Supplements 7.1 and 7.2 it could appear that companies using the IASB system face fewer detailed rules. However, those companies still produce a great deal of detailed information in practice because the IASB has other standards that require more detail.

In this chapter we follow the pattern established in earlier chapters by asking:

- What are the principles for defining and recognising these items?
- What are the information needs of users in respect of the particular items?
- What information is currently provided by companies to meet these needs?
- Does the information show the desirable qualitative characteristics of financial statements?
- What are the principles for measuring, and processes for recording, these items?

This chapter looks first at provisions, then turns to non-current (long-term) liabilities and finally covers deferred income. General principles of definition and recognition of liabilities are dealt with in Chapter 10 and you should ensure you have read and understood that chapter before embarking on this one. For convenience the definitions from Chapter 2 are repeated here.

Definitions

> A **liability** is a present obligation of the entity arising from past events, the settlement of which is expected to result in an outflow from the entity of resources embodying economic benefits.[1]
>
> A **current liability** is a liability which satisfies any of the following criteria:
>
> (a) it is expected to be settled in the entity's normal operating cycle;
> (b) it is held primarily for the purpose of being traded;
> (c) it is due to be settled within 12 months after the reporting period.[2]
>
> A **non-current liability** is any liability that does not meet the definition of a current liability.[3] Non-current liabilities are also described as **long-term liabilities**.

11.2 Users' needs for information

There are two aspects of information needed in relation to liabilities. The first relates to the amount owed (sometimes called the **principal sum** or the **capital amount**) and the second relates to the cost of servicing the loan (usually the payment of **interest**).

Owners of a company need to know how much the company owes to other parties because the owners are at the end of the queue when it comes to sharing out the assets of the company if it closes down. Lenders to the company want to know how many other lenders will have a claim on assets if the company closes down and how much the total claim of lenders will be. They may want to take a **secured loan**, where the agreement with the company specifies particular assets which may be sold by the lender if the company defaults on payment.

Cash flow is important to a range of users. Interest payments are an expense to be reported in the income statement (profit and loss account), but paying interest is a drain on cash as well as affecting the ownership interest by a reduction in profit. Owners of the company want to know if there will be sufficient cash left to allow them a **dividend** (or **drawings** for partnerships and sole traders) after interest has been paid. Lenders want to be reassured that the company is generating sufficient cash flow and profit to cover the interest expense.

Both owners and lenders want to see the impact of borrowing on future cash flows. They need to know the scheduled dates of repayments of loans (sometimes referred to as the **maturity profile of debt**), the currency in which the loan must be repaid and the structure of interest rates (e.g. whether the loan period is starting with low rates of interest which are then stepped up in future years).

Finally, owners and lenders are interested in the **gearing** of the company. This means the ratio of loan capital to ownership interest in the statement of financial position (balance sheet) or the ratio of interest payments to net profit in the income statement (profit and loss account). Chapter 13 will provide more detail on the calculation and interpretation of gearing.

Activity 11.1

Imagine you are a shareholder in a company which is financed partly by long-term loans. Write down the information needed by users in the order of importance to you as a shareholder and explain your answer.

11.3 Information provided in the financial statements

The statement of financial position (balance sheet) of Safe and Sure plc, set out in Chapter 7, contains the following information in relation to non-current (long-term) liabilities:

	Notes	Year 7 £m	Year 6 £m
Non-current liabilities			
Amounts payable (creditors)	9	(2.7)	(2.6)
Bank and other borrowings	10	(0.2)	(0.6)
Provisions	11	(20.2)	(22.2)
Net assets		464.3	370.4

Notes to the statement of financial position (balance sheet) explain more about each item. Note 9 gives some indication of the type of creditors due after more than one year.

Note 9 Non-current liabilities: payables (creditors)

	Year 7 £m	Year 6 £m
Deferred consideration on acquisition	0.6	–
Other payables (creditors)	2.1	2.6
	2.7	2.6

Note 10 distinguishes secured and unsecured loans among the borrowings due after one year and also gives a schedule of repayment over the immediate and medium-term or longer-term future. For this company, bank borrowings all mature within five years. Note 10 also confirms that commercial rates of interest are payable.

Note 10 Non-current liabilities: bank and other borrowings

	Year 7 £m	Year 6 £m
Secured loans	–	0.3
Unsecured loans	0.2	0.3
	0.2	0.6
Loans are repayable by instalments:		
Between one and two years	0.1	0.2
Between two and five years	0.1	0.4
	0.2	0.6

Interest on long-term loans, which are denominated in a number of currencies, is payable at normal commercial rates appropriate to the country in which the borrowing is made. The last repayment falls due in Year 11.

Note 11 gives information on provisions for liabilities which will occur at a future date, as a result of past events or of definite plans made.

Note 11 Provisions

	Year 7 £m	Year 6 £m
Provisions for treating contaminated site:		
At 1 January	14.2	14.5
Utilised in the year	(2.2)	(0.3)
At 31 December	12.0	14.2
Provisions for restructuring costs:		
At 1 January	4.2	–
Created in year	1.0	4.3
Utilised in year	(1.0)	(0.1)
At 31 December	4.2	4.2
Provision for deferred tax:		
At 1 January	3.8	2.7
Transfer to profit and loss account	0.5	1.2
Other movements	(0.3)	(0.1)
At 31 December	4.0	3.8
Total provision	20.2	22.2

Finally, note 33 sets out contingent liabilities. (Contingent liabilities are defined and explained in Chapter 10.) Two contingent items have the amount quantified. The impact of litigation (legal action) is not quantified. The company may think that to do so would be seen as an admission of legal liability.

Note 33 Contingent liabilities

The company has guaranteed bank and other borrowings of subsidiaries amounting to £3.0m (Year 6: £15.2m). The group has commitments, amounting to approximately £41.9m (Year 6: £28.5m), under forward exchange contracts entered into in the ordinary course of business.

Certain subsidiaries have given warranties for service work. These are explained in the statement on accounting policies. There are contingent liabilities in respect of litigation. None of the actions is expected to give rise to any material loss.

The accounting policy statement contains three items relevant to liabilities:

Accounting policies

Deferred tax
The provision for deferred tax recognises a future liability arising from past transactions and events. Tax legislation allows the company to defer settlement of the liability for several years.

Warranties
Some service work is carried out under warranty. The cost of claims under warranty is charged against the income statement (profit and loss account) of the year in which the claims are settled.

Deferred consideration
For acquisitions involving deferred consideration, estimated deferred payments are accrued in the statement of financial position (balance sheet). Interest due to vendors on deferred payments is charged to the income statement (profit and loss account) as it accrues.

In this extract the word 'charged' appears several times. In relation to interest or taxes, the use of the word **charge** describes the reduction in ownership interest reported in the income statement (profit and loss account) due to the cost of interest and tax payable.

Because the level of borrowing is low in this company, and therefore would not create any concern for investors or new lenders, the finance director has very little to say about it in his report. To some extent the chairman takes the initiative earlier in the annual report:

Finance

Once again, during Year 7 we had a strong operating cash flow, amounting to £196.7m (up from £163.5m in Year 6). This funded expenditure of £24.6m on acquisition of other companies and businesses (after allowing for £3.1m received from a disposal of a company) and the group still ended the year with an increase in its cash balances.

David Wilson has already commented in Chapters 4 and 7 on some aspects of the liabilities in the financial statements of Safe and Sure plc. Here he is explaining to Leona, in the coffee bar at the health club, his views on liabilities in particular.

DAVID: *Where do I start in explaining how I look at liabilities? Well, I always read the accounting policy notes before I look at any financial statements. This company provides three accounting policy notes relating to matters of liabilities. The policy on warranties is interesting because it confirms that the company does not record any expected liability on warranties. The first time I saw this in the annual report I was quite concerned about lack of prudence, but on my first visit to the company I was shown the warranty settlement file. There are very few claims under warranty because the company has lots of procedures which have to be followed by employees who carry out service work. Warranty claims are relatively unusual and unpredictable for this company so there is no previous pattern to justify setting up a liability in the form of a provision for future claims.*

The deferred consideration arises because this company has acquired another business and wants to look into all aspects of the newly acquired investment before making full payment.

Deferred tax provisions are common to many companies. They are an attempt to line up the accounting profit with the tax charge based on taxable profits, which are usually different. I don't understand the technical details but my test of importance is to look at the amount charged to the income statement (profit and loss account) for the year. It is less than 1% of the profit after tax, so I shan't be giving it much attention on this occasion.

Provisions for restructuring are my real headache. These are a measure of the costs expected when the company plans a restructuring such as changing the management structure with redefinition of the role of some employees and redundancy for others. It sounds reasonable to give warning of what all this will cost but the standard-setters have to be strict about the details because in the past the use of provisions has been linked to some creative accounting in the income statement (profit and loss account). Do you know anything about that?

LEONA: *Yes. On the one hand, you would like to know that a company is prudent in reporting in the income statement (profit and loss account) now the likely losses which will arise in future years because of a decision to reorganise. On the other hand, you would not like to think that a company has loaded the income statement with lots of bad news this year so that it can make next year look much better when the results are published. The accounting standard-setter has prevented companies from being excessively prudent. I could explain more but not at this time on a Friday night. What do you see in the statement of financial position (balance sheet) and the other information provided by the company?*

DAVID: *After reading and thinking about the items in the accounting policy notes I look to the breakdown between current liabilities and longer-term liabilities. I also look to the amount of long-term finance compared with the amount of the equity holders' funds. The borrowings in this company are relatively low in relation to equity-holders' funds, so there is not a high financial risk, but I still want to look for unexplained changes since the previous year. Again, there is nothing which springs to the eye.*

The contingent liability note is usually quite interesting. One of my senior colleagues says that you should start at the end of the annual report and read it backwards. Then you find the best parts first. The contingent liability note is always near the end. I would be asking lots of questions about the forward exchange contracts, if I had not already asked the financial controller. He confirmed in more detail what the finance director says rather briefly. The forward exchange contracts are used as part of prudent financial management to put a limit on any potential loss through adverse currency movements on transactions in different countries.

LEONA: *Much of what you say is reflected in what auditors carry out by way of analytical review. What we don't provide is a view to the future. What are your thoughts there?*

DAVID: *This is a cash-rich company and it has very little in the way of complicated financial structures. For a major company that is probably unusual, but it means I can concentrate on the operating aspects of the business and on whether it will continue to generate cash. It uses cash generated to buy other businesses and expand further, but I wonder what will happen when the scope for that expansion ceases. It is unlikely to be a problem in the near future because the company has a foothold in expanding markets in Asia. When that scope for expansion comes to an end the company may have to start borrowing to finance expansion rather than relying on internal cash flows.*

11.4 Provisions

Making a provision is an accounting process similar to that of making accrual for a known obligation.

Definition	A **provision** is a liability of uncertain timing or amount.[4]

The distinguishing feature of a provision often lies in the larger element of uncertainty which surrounds a provision. Such a provision will appear in the liabilities section of a statement of financial position (balance sheet). (This book has already considered in Chapter 8 the provision for depreciation and in Chapter 9 the provision for doubtful debts. These are examples of what is regarded as an adjustment to the reported value of an asset, rather than an adjustment for significant uncertainty. They are therefore reported as adjustments to the asset and do not appear in the liabilities section.) The following are examples of provisions which may be found in the liabilities sections of published accounts:

- losses on contracts
- obsolescence of stock
- costs related to closure of a division of the company
- costs of decommissioning an oil rig
- cost of landscaping a site at the end of the period of use
- warranties given for repair of goods.

Recording a **provision** is relatively straightforward. The ownership interest is reduced by an expense in the income statement (profit and loss account) and a liability is created under the name of the provision:

Assets – **Liabilities** ↑	equals	**Ownership interest ↓ (expense)**

When the provision is no longer required it is released to the income statement (profit and loss account) as an item of revenue which increases the ownership interest and the liability is reduced:

Assets – **Liabilities** ↓	equals	**Ownership interest** ↑

The provision may also be released to the income statement (profit and loss account) so as to match an expense which was anticipated when the provision was made. The effect on the accounting equation is an increase in the ownership interest – the same effect as results from regarding the release of the provision as an item of revenue.

Of the topics covered in this chapter, provisions give the greatest scope for international variation in accounting treatment. In countries where the accounting system and the tax system are linked, there may be specific rules about the level and nature of provisions allowed. In countries that have a strong culture of **conservatism** (strong **prudence**) the provisions may be used to understate profit. The problem with such an approach is that the unnecessary provision may then be released in a year when profits would otherwise be lower. This has the effect of 'smoothing out' the peaks and troughs of profit. Both the IASB and the UK ASB believe that provisions should only be used under carefully defined conditions. This approach also applies in the USA.

The IASB has proposed[5] to change the description of provisions to become 'non-financial liabilities'. It has taken longer than expected to bring this proposal to practice and a new standard is unlikely before the end of 2010. The IASB has proposed that any items satisfying the definition of a liability should be recognised unless they cannot be measured reliably. Any unconditional obligation would be recognised so there would no longer be a need to estimate the likelihood of the obligation being implemented. Uncertainty about the amount or timing of the economic benefits required to settle the non-financial liability would be recognised in the measurement of the liability.

Example of a provision

During the year ending 31 December Year 5, a company's sales of manufactured goods amounted to £1m. All goods carry a manufacturer's warranty to rectify any faults arising during the first 12 months of ownership. At the start of the year, based on previous experience, a provision of 2.5% of sales was made (estimating the sales to be £1m). During Year 5 repairs under warranty cost £14,000. There could be further repair costs incurred in Year 6 in respect of those items sold part-way through Year 5 whose warranty extends into Year 6.

Using the accounting equation, the effect of these events and transactions may be analysed. When the provision is established there is an increase in a liability and an expense to be charged to the income statement (profit and loss account):

Assets	–	**Liabilities** ↑	=	**Ownership interest** ↓ **(expense)**
		+ £25,000		– £25,000

As the repairs under warranty are carried out, they cause a decrease in the asset of cash and a decrease in the provision. They do not directly affect the income statement (profit and loss account) expense:

Assets ↓	–	**Liabilities** ↓	=	Ownership interest
– £14,000		– £14,000		

The overall effect is that the income statement (profit and loss account) will report an expense of £25,000 but the provision will only be used to the extent of £14,000, leaving £11,000 available to cover any further repairs in respect of Year 5 sales. The repairs, when paid for, decrease the asset of cash but are not seen as decreasing the ownership interest. They are seen as meeting a liability to the customer (rather like making a payment to meet a liability to a supplier). The creation of the provision establishes the full amount of the liability and the decrease in the ownership interest which is to be reported in the income statement (profit and loss account).

The spreadsheet for analysis is contained in Table 11.1.

Table 11.1
Spreadsheet for analysis of provision for warranty repairs

Date	Transaction or event	Asset	Liability	Ownership interest
		Cash	Provision	Profit and loss account
Year 5		£	£	£
Jan. 1	Provision for repairs		25,000	(25,000)
Jan.–Dec.	Repairs under warranty	(14,000)	(14,000)	
	Totals	(14,000)	11,000	(25,000)

Activity 11.2

Test your understanding of the previous section by analysing the following information and entering it in a spreadsheet to show analysis of the impact of the information on the accounting equation:

Jan. 1 Year 1   Make a provision for repairs, £50,000.
During Year 1   Spend £30,000 against the provision and carry the rest forward.
Jan. 1 Year 2   Make a further provision for repairs, £10,000.
During Year 2   Spend £25,000 against the provision and carry the rest forward.
Jan. 1 Year 3   Reduce the remaining provision to £3,000.

11.5 Deferred income

For companies located in areas of the country where there are particular problems of unemployment or a need to encourage redevelopment of the location, the government may award grants as a contribution to the operating costs of the company or to the cost of buying new fixed assets.

Consider the award of a government grant to a company, intended to help with the cost of training employees over the next three years. The asset of cash increases, but there is no corresponding effect on any other asset or liability. Consequently, the ownership interest is increased. The obvious label for this increase is **revenue**. However, the benefit of the grant will extend over three years and it would therefore seem appropriate to spread the revenue over three years to match the cost it is subsidising. The accounting device for producing this effect is to say that the cash received as an asset creates a liability called **deferred income**. This does not meet the definition of a liability stated at the start of this chapter because the practice of deferring income is dictated by the importance of **matching** revenues and costs in the income statement (profit and loss account). It is one of the cases where established custom and practice continues because it has been found to be useful although it does not fit neatly into the conceptual framework definitions.

Example

A company receives a grant of £30,000 towards the cost of employee retraining. The retraining programme will last for three years and the costs will be spread evenly over the three years.

The income statement (profit and loss account) will show revenue of £10,000 in each year. At the outset the deferred income will be recorded in the statement of financial position (balance sheet) as £30,000. By the end of Year 1 the deferred income will be reduced to £20,000. At the end of Year 2 the deferred income will be reduced to £10,000. At the end of Year 3 the deferred income is reduced to nil. The accounting records are shown in Table 11.2.

Where grants are received towards the acquisition of fixed assets there is a similar approach of spreading the grant over the period during which the company will benefit from use of the asset. Some companies show the revenue as a separate item in the income statement (profit and loss account) while others deduct it from the depreciation expense. This is a matter of presentation which makes no difference to the overall profit. The statement of financial position (balance sheet) treatment is more controversial. Some companies report separately the net book value of the asset and the deferred income. Others deduct the deferred income from the net book value of the asset. This does not affect the ownership interest but shows a lower amount in the fixed assets section of the statement of financial position (balance sheet). In consequence, the user who calculates profit as a percentage of fixed assets or a percentage of total assets will obtain a higher answer where a company shows the lower amount for net assets. Most companies report the asset and deferred income separately, but some argue for the **net** approach which sets one against the other. (Both methods are permitted by the international accounting standard and by the UK national standard. There is a view that the net approach may not be complying with the Companies Act 2006 and so relatively few UK companies have taken the net approach.) The choice will be set out in the notes on accounting policies. This is a useful illustration of the importance of reading the note on accounting policies.

Table 11.2
Recording deferred income and transfer to revenue

Date	Transaction or event	Asset	Liability	Ownership interest
		Cash	Deferred income	Revenue
Year 1		£	£	£
Jan. 1	Receiving the grant	30,000	30,000	
Dec. 31	Transfer to profit and loss account of first year's revenue		(10,000)	10,000
Year 2				
Dec. 31	Transfer to profit and loss account of second year's revenue		(10,000)	10,000
Year 3				
Dec. 31	Transfer to profit and loss account of third year's revenue		(10,000)	10,000

Activity 11.3

Consider a grant received as a contribution to staff retraining costs over the next three years. Write down three arguments in favour of reporting the entire grant in the income statement (profit and loss account) in the year it is received and write down three arguments in favour of spreading the grant across the period of retraining. Which set of arguments do you find more persuasive?

11.6 Non-current (long-term) liabilities

The statement of financial position (balance sheet) requires a separate heading for all liabilities payable after one year. Users of financial statements need information about when the liabilities will be due for repayment (the **maturity** pattern).

Users also need to know about the nature of the liability and any risks attaching to expected outflows of economic benefit from the liability. The risks lie in: the interest payable on the loan; the currency of the loan; and the eventual amount to be repaid to the lender. Interest payable may be at a fixed rate of interest or a variable rate of interest. The currency of borrowing is important when foreign exchange rates alter. Repayment amounts may equal the amount borrowed initially, in some cases. In other cases there may be a **premium** (an extra amount) payable in addition to the sum borrowed. There are some very complex accounting aspects to reporting non-current (long-term) liabilities, the technical aspects of which are well beyond the capacity of a first-level text, but they are all directed towards ensuring that liabilities are recorded in full and the matching concept is observed in relation to interest charges.

Users want to know about the risks of sacrificing particular assets if the loan is not repaid on the due date. A claim to a particular asset may be made by a creditor who has a loan **secured** on a particular asset or group of assets.

11.6.1 Recording and measurement

This section concentrates on the terminology of non-current (long-term) liabilities and the general issues of recording and measurement that they raise. The basic feature of non-current (long-term) loan finance is that it is:

● provided by a lender for a period longer than one year;
● who expects payment of interest at an agreed rate at agreed points in time; and
● expects repayment of the loan on an agreed date or dates.

The names given to loan capital vary depending on the type of lender, the possibility that the loan will be bought and sold like ordinary shares, the currency in which the loan has been provided and the legal form of the documents creating the loan. Some of the names you will see are: loan stock, debentures, bonds, commercial paper, loan notes and bank facility.

● **Loan stock.** The word **stock** is used in more than one context in accounting, which is potentially confusing. In Chapter 9 you saw the word used to describe goods held by a company for use or sale to customers. In the phrase **loan stock** it is used to describe an investment held by a lender. In the USA the problem has been avoided by using the word **inventories** to describe goods held for use or sale and using the word **bond** to describe loan stock. If a company shows loan stock in its statement of financial position (balance sheet) this usually indicates that the stock is available for purchase and sale, in a manner similar to the purchase and sale of shares in a company.
● **Debenture.** The legal meaning of the term **debenture** is a written acknowledgement of a debt. This means there will be a contract, in writing, between the company and

the lender. The contract is called the debenture deed and is held by a trustee who is required to look after the needs of the lenders. If the company does not pay interest, or repay capital, on the due date, the trustee must take action to recover what is owed to the lenders. Debentures may be secured or unsecured, depending on what is stated in the debenture deed.

- **Bond.** The term **bond** has been in common use in the USA for some time as a name for loan capital. It is now found increasingly frequently in the statements of financial position (balance sheets) of UK companies, particularly when they are raising finance in the international capital markets where the US terminology is more familiar.

- **Commercial paper**, **loan notes** and **bank facility**. These are all names of short- to medium-term financing provided by banks or similar organisations. The interest payable is usually variable and the loans are unsecured.

This is only a sample of the main variations of names given to loan finance. It is not exhaustive because the name does not matter greatly for the purposes of accounting records and interpretation. The essential information needed for the users of accounting information is the answer to five questions:

1 How much was borrowed (the **principal sum**)?
2 How much has to be repaid (the capital sum plus any additional interest charge)?
3 When is repayment required?
4 What are the interest payments required?
5 Has the lender sought any security for repayment of the interest and the principal sum?

For companies applying the IASB system of accounting, the relevant standard requires companies to provide information about the extent and nature of financial liabilities, including the significant terms and conditions and the timing of future cash flows. For companies that do not apply the IASB system, the UK Companies Act required disclosure of the total amount in respect of which any security has been given, and an indication of the nature of the security, plus the interest payable and terms of repayment for each category of loan.

Under either set of rules you will find detailed notes to tbe statement of financial position (balance sheet) setting out the interest costs and repayment conditions for loans reported as liabilities.

11.6.2 Secured and unsecured loans

- **Unsecured loan.** An **unsecured loan** is one where the lender has no first claim on any particular assets of the company and, in the event of default, must wait for payment alongside all the other unsecured creditors. If there is no wording to indicate that the loan is secured, then the reader of financial statements must assume it is unsecured.

- **Secured loan.** Where any loan is described as **secured**, it means that the lender has first claim to named assets of the company. Where a debenture is secured, and the company defaults on payment, the trustee for the debenture will take possession of the asset and use it to make the necessary repayment. In the event of the company not being able to pay all the amounts it owes, secured lenders come before unsecured lenders in the queue for repayment.

Activity 11.4

A financial weekly magazine contains the following sentence:

Telecoms plc this week raised cash by selling $1m bonds with five-year and ten-year maturities.

Explain each part of the sentence.

11.6.3 Loan having a range of repayment dates

When a loan is made to a business, conditions will be negotiated regarding the amount and date of repayment. Some banks are willing to offer a range of repayment dates, say any time between 10 and 15 years hence, with the company being allowed to choose when it will repay. If the company needs the money and the interest rate is favourable, the company will borrow for the longest period allowed under the contract. If the company finds it no longer needs the money, or else the interest rate is burdensome, the company will repay at the earliest possible opportunity. For statement of financial position (balance sheet) purposes the preparer of accounts has to decide which date to use as a basis for classification.

The general principle is that if there is an obligation to transfer economic benefits, there will be a liability in the statement of financial position (balance sheet). Where there is a range of possible dates for repayment, the maturity date will be taken as the earliest date on which the lender can require repayment.[6]

11.6.4 Change in the nature of finance source

Some types of finance provided to a business may be arranged so as to allow a change in the nature of the source during the period of financing. As an example, consider the case of convertible loans.

A **convertible loan** is a source of finance which starts its life as a loan but, at some point in the future, may be converted to ordinary shares in the company (e.g. the lender is promised five shares per £100 of loan capital). At the date of conversion, the lender becomes a **shareholder**. This kind of financial arrangement is attractive to those providing finance because it provides the reassurance of loan finance and a payment of interest in the early years of a new development, with the option of switching to shares if the project is successful. If the project is not successful and the share price does not perform as expected, then the lender will not convert and will look for repayment of the loan on the due date. For the company there are some tax advantages in issuing loan finance. Also, the rate of interest required by investors in a convertible loan is usually lower than that required for a straight (non-convertible) loan because investors see potential additional rewards in the convertible loan.

While a convertible loan remains unconverted it is reported as a loan. Companies are not allowed to say, 'We are almost certain there will be a conversion', and report the convertible loan as share finance from the outset. However, there is an awareness that the eventual conversion will dilute the existing shareholders' claim on future profits and so the company will report the earnings per share before and after taking into account the effect of this dilution. Consequently, you will see 'fully diluted earnings per share' at the foot of the income statement (profit and loss account).

11.6.5 Interest payable on the loan

Companies and their banks may negotiate a variety of patterns for interest payment on loans. The pattern of interest payment might be based on a low percentage charge in earlier years and a higher percentage charge in later years, because the company expects that profits will be low initially but will rise later to cover the higher interest payments. For many years the income statement (profit and loss account) would have reported the interest charge based on the amount paid in each year, but now the standard-setters require the interest charge to be reported as it would be if a compound interest rate were applied over the life of the loan. This is described as the **effective interest rate**.[7]

Definition

> The **effective interest rate** is the rate that exactly discounts estimated future cash payments or receipts through the expected life of the financial instrument.

The reasoning behind this approach is that, for purposes of reporting profit, the flexibility of negotiation of interest payment patterns makes comparability difficult to achieve. The banks will, however, ensure that they receive the overall compound interest they require and this gives a commercially relevant basis for comparability in the matching of interest charges against the profits of the period.

The general principle is that the amount shown as the expense of interest payable in the income statement (profit and loss account) should be based on the compound rate of interest applying over the entire period of the loan. This will not always be the same as the amount of interest paid in cash during the period. The spreading of interest charges over the period of the loan is an application of the accruals or matching concept. As an example, consider stepped bonds and deep discount bonds.

Stepped bonds

A **stepped bond** is a form of lending where the interest rate increases over the period of the loan. Take as an example a loan of £5m which carries a rate of interest of 8% per annum for the first three years, 10% per annum for the next three years and 13% per annum for the final four years. The cash payment for interest starts at £400,000 and by the tenth year has risen to £650,000. The overall payments may be shown to be equivalent to a compound rate of 10.06% per annum. Table 11.3 shows that the income statement (profit and loss account) charge of £503,000 would start higher than the cash amount, £400,000. By the final year the income statement (profit and loss account) charge of £517,000 would be lower than the cash amount, £650,000. The pattern followed on each line of Table 11.3 is to start with the amount owing, add interest at 10.06% and deduct the amount of the cash payment, leaving the amount owing at the end of the period which becomes the amount owing at the start of the next period. By the end of the ten years the amount owing is exactly £5,000,000, the amount required by the lender.

It may be seen from Table 11.3 that the expense charged in the income statement (income statement (profit and loss account)) has a smoother pattern than that of the cash payments. Over the life of the loan the total expense charged must equal the total of the cash payments. The accounting processes for recording these amounts are too complex for a first-level course. The important point to note is that all companies are required to use this approach in calculating the expense charged in calculating profit. The cash flow implications of interest payments may be quite different and it will be necessary to look to the cash flow statement for evidence of the cash flow effect.

Deep discount bonds

A **deep discount bond** is issued at a price lower than (at a 'discount' to) its repayment amount. The interest rate (**coupon**) paid during the life of the loan may be very low (a 'low coupon' bond) or there may be no interest paid at all during the period of the loan (a 'zero coupon' bond). As an example, consider a zero coupon bond issued at £28m with a redemption value of £41m in four years' time. The cash payments of interest are zero but the income statement (profit and loss account) would show an annual charge of 10% per annum (starting at £2.8m in Year 1 and rising to £3.73m by Year 4). If there were no pattern of annual interest the entire discount of £13m would be shown as an expense of Year 4, distorting the underlying pattern of trading profit. Table 11.4 shows the pattern of interest charges for the income statement (profit and loss account).

Table 11.3

Calculation of expense charged in income statement (profit and loss account) for interest based on compound interest calculation

Year	Loan at start	Expense charged	Cash payment record	
		Interest at 10.06%	Cash paid	Loan at end
	(a)	(b)	(c)	(a) + (b) − (c)
	£000s	£000s	£000s	£000s
1	5,000	503	400	5,103
2	5,103	513	400	5,216
3	5,216	525	400	5,341
4	5,341	537	500	5,378
5	5,378	541	500	5,419
6	5,419	545	500	5,464
7	5,464	550	650	5,364
8	5,364	540	650	5,254
9	5,254	529	650	5,133
10	5,133	517	650	5,000
Total		5,300	5,300	

Table 11.4

Schedule of interest charges for zero coupon bond

Year	Loan at start £m	Interest £m	Loan at end £m
1	28.00	2.80	30.80
2	30.80	3.08	33.88
3	33.88	3.39	37.27
4	37.27	3.73	41.00
Total		13.00	

In the statement of financial position (balance sheet) the amount recorded for the liability will start at £28m and rise to £41m as shown in the final column of Table 11.4, so that the liability at the end represents the total amount due.

Activity 11.5

A three-year loan of £100,000 will be repaid at the end of three years as £133,100. No interest is payable during the three-year period. The interest included in the loan repayment arrangement is equivalent to a compound annual charge of 10% per annum. Explain how this transaction would appear in the income statement (profit and loss account) and statement of financial position (balance sheet) over the three-year period.

11.6.6 **Complex capital instruments**

It is impossible to read the statement of financial position (balance sheet) of most major listed companies without realising rapidly that there is a bewildering array of capital instruments being used to raise money for business. The reasons are complex but lie in the need to provide conditions which are attractive to both borrower and lender when they may be based in different countries and may have different perspectives on interest rates and currency exchange rates. This section explains the term 'interest rate swaps', which are increasingly used by companies, and takes an illustration from a major company to indicate the variety of capital instruments (sources of finance) in use. Detailed descriptions and discussion are beyond the scope of this text but would be found in a finance manual.

Interest rate swaps

Suppose there are two companies, A and B. Both have identical amounts of loan finance. Company A is paying fixed rates of interest, but would prefer to be paying variable rates, while Company B is paying variable rates of interest, but would prefer to be paying fixed rates. The reasons could be related to patterns of cash flow from trading, cash flow from investments or beliefs about future directions of interest rates. Whatever the reason, it would seem quite acceptable for them to swap (exchange) so that A pays the variable interest on behalf of B and B pays the fixed interest on behalf of A. This type of arrangement has to be explained carefully because neither company can escape from the legal obligation on the loans taken out initially. The explanation will usually be found in a note to the accounts which gives information on the legal obligation and on the actual impact on the income statement (profit and loss account) of implementing the swap.

Capital instruments of a listed company

The following illustration is based upon the statement of financial position (balance sheet) of a major UK listed company:

Note on borrowings:		Year 2 £m	Year 1 £m
Unsecured borrowings:			
10½% euro-sterling bonds Year 17		100.0	100.0
Loan stocks			
13.625%	Year 16	25.0	25.0
5.675% – 9.3%	Year 3/Year 10	5.9	6.1
Zero coupon bonds Year 3		96.6	87.2
Variable rate multi-option bank facility		15.8	155.2
Bank loans, overdrafts, commercial paper, short- and medium-term notes		257.0	244.8
. . . the nominal value of the zero coupon bonds is £100m and the effective annual rate of interest is 10.85% . . .			

Comment. The euro-sterling bonds and the loan stocks are reported at the amount due for repayment at the end of the loan period. The euro-sterling bonds are loans raised in the eurobond market, repayable in sterling. Those loans which have fixed rates of interest are indicated in the table by a fixed percentage rate. Zero coupon means a zero percentage rate of annual interest payable. That does not mean the company escapes interest payment altogether. The liability on the zero coupon bonds increases by 10.85% each year as indicated in the extract note at the foot of the table. It is presumably due for repayment part-way through Year 3 since the liability shown at the end of Year 2 is quite close to the £100m amount due (called the **nominal value** in the note). The remaining loans are variable rate and so the annual interest charge depends on current rates of interest. Professional investors might want to know more about the nature of the bank facility and also the breakdown of the various components of the figure £257m.

11.7 Summary

- A **non-current liability** is any liability that does not meet the definition of a current liability. Non-current liabilities are also described as **long-term liabilities**.

- Users need information about the **principal sum** repayable and the **interest** payable during the lifetime of a liability. They also need to know the dates on which significant payments will be required (called the **maturity profile of debt**).

- Detailed information about **non-current liabilities** is found in the notes to the financial statements.

- A **provision** is a liability of uncertain timing or amount. The amount of a provision is reported in the liabilities section of a statement of financial position (balance sheet). Changes in provisions are reported in the income statement (profit and loss account).

- **Deferred income** arises where a business receives a government grant or receives cash for goods or services before these are provided. The cash received is reported as an increase in cash and an increase in a liability to represent the obligation to satisfy the conditions of the grant or provide the goods or services. When the conditions are satisfied the liability is reduced and the ownership interest is increased by recording the revenue.

QUESTIONS

The Questions section of each chapter has three types of question. 'Test your understanding' questions to help you review your reading are in the 'A' series of questions. You will find the answers to these by reading and thinking about the material in the book. 'Application' questions to test your ability to apply technical skills are in the 'B' series of questions. Questions requiring you to show skills in problem solving and evaluation are in the 'C' series of questions. A letter [S] indicates that there is a solution at the end of the book.

A Test your understanding

Skills outcomes

A11.1 Explain why a provision may be required. (Section 11.4)

A11.2 Give three examples of situations which may lead to provisions. (Section 11.4)

A11.3 Explain how deferred income is recorded. (Section 11.5)

A11.4 Is it justifiable to report deferred income under the category of liability? (Section 11.5)

A11.5 Explain what is meant by each of the following terms: (Section 11.6)

    (a) loan stock;
    (b) debenture;
    (c) bond;
    (d) maturity date; and
    (e) convertible loan stock.

A11.6 [S] On reviewing the financial statements, the company accountant discovers that a grant of £60,000 towards expenditure of the current year plus two further years has been reported entirely as revenue of the period. What will be the effect on the income statement (profit and loss account) and the statement of financial position (balance sheet) when this error is rectified?

A11.7 [S] On reviewing the financial statements, the company accountant discovers that there has been no provision made for urgent repairs to external doors and window frames, already identified as being of high priority on grounds of health and safety. The amount of £50,000 should be provided. What will be the effect on the income statement (profit and loss account) and the statement of financial position (balance sheet) when this error is rectified?

B   Application

B11.1 [S]
The Washing Machine Repair Company gives a warranty of no-cost rectification of unsatisfactory repairs. It has turnover from repair contracts recorded as:

Year	Amount of turnover
	£
1	80,000
2	90,000

Based on previous experience the manager makes a provision of 10% of turnover each year for warranty costs. In respect of the work done during Years 1 and 2, repairs under warranty are carried out as follows:

Date of repair work	Amount in respect of Year 1 turnover	Amount in respect of Year 2 turnover	Total
	£	£	£
1	4,500		4,500
2	3,200	4,800	8,000
3		5,000	5,000

Required
(a) Show how this information would be recorded in the financial statements of the Washing Machine Repair Company.
(b) Explain how the financial statements would appear if the company made no provision for warranty costs but charged them to income statement (profit and loss account) when incurred.

B11.2 [S]
General Engineering Ltd receives a government grant for £60,000 towards employee training costs to be incurred evenly over the next three years. Explain how this transaction will be reported in the financial statements.

C   Problem solving and evaluation

C11.1
Explain why each of the following is recognised as a provision in the statement of financial position (balance sheet) of a telecommunications company:

(a) On 15 December Year 2, the Group announced a major redundancy programme. Provision has been made at 31 December Year 2 for the associated costs. The provision is expected to be utilised within 12 months.

(b) Because of the redundancy programme, some properties have become vacant. Provision has been made for lease payments that cannot be avoided where subletting is not possible. The provision will be utilised within 15 months.

(c) There is a legal claim against a subsidiary in respect of alleged breach of contract. Provision has been made for this claim. It is expected that the provision will be utilised within 12 months.

C11.2

(Refer also to Chapter 10, section 10.3.2, on Contingent liabilities.)

Explain why each of the following is reported as a contingent liability but not recognised as a provision in the statement of financial position (balance sheet).

(a) Some leasehold properties which the group no longer requires have been sublet to third parties. If the third parties default, the group remains responsible for future rent payments. The maximum liability is £200,000.

(b) Group companies are defendants in the USA in a number of product liability cases related to tobacco products. In a number of these cases, the amounts of compensatory and punitive damages sought are significant.

(c) The Department of Trade and Industry has appointed Inspectors to investigate the company's flotation ten years ago. The directors have been advised that it is possible that circumstances surrounding the flotation may give rise to claims against the company. At this stage it is not possible to quantify either the probability of success of such claims or of the amounts involved.

Activities for study groups

Turn to the annual report of a listed company which you have used for activities in previous chapters. Find every item of information about liabilities. (Start with the financial statements and notes but look also at the operating and financial review, chief executive's review and other non-regulated information about the company.)

As a group, imagine you are the team of fund managers in a fund management company. You are holding a briefing meeting at which each person explains to the others some feature of the companies in which your fund invests. Today's subject is liabilities. Each person should make a short presentation to the rest of the team covering:

(a) The nature and significance of liabilities in the company.

(b) The effect on profit of a 10% error in estimation of any one of the major categories of liability.

(c) The company's comments, if any, on its future obligations.

(d) The risks which might attach to the liabilities of the company.

(e) The liquidity of the company.

(f) The trends in liabilities since last year (or over five years if a comparative table is provided).

(g) The ratio of current assets to current liabilities.

Notes and references

1. IASB (1989), *Framework*, para. 49(b).
2. IASB (2009), IAS 1, para. 69.
3. IASB (2009), IAS 1, para. 69.
4. IASB (2009), IAS 37, *Provisions, Contingent Liabilities and Contingent Assets*, para. 10.
5. IASB (2005), Exposure draft of proposed amendments to IAS 37 *Provisions, Contingent Liabilities and Contingent Assets*, para. 1.
6. IFRS 7 (2009), *Financial Instruments: Disclosures*, para. B12.
7. IASB (2009), IAS 39 *Financial Instruments: Recognition and Measurement*. Definitions section.

Bookkeeping entries for provisions and deferred income

Provisions

In the main text of this chapter there is an example based on the recording of provision for repairs under warranty. The analysis of the transactions and events is set out in Table 11.1. The ledger account will appear as follows:

L3 Provision for warranty repairs

Date	Particulars	Page	Debit £	Credit £	Balance £
Year 5					
Jan. 1	Provision in respect of Year 5	L2		25,000	(25,000)
Jan.–Dec.	Repairs carried out	L1	14,000		(11,000)

LEONA: *At the start of the year (or possibly in practice at the end of each month) the provision is recorded by debiting the profit and loss account (L2) and crediting the provision. When the repairs are carried out there is a credit entry in the cash account (L1) and a debit entry in the provision account. Nothing is recorded as a profit and loss account expense at that time. The overall effect is that the income statement (profit and loss account) carries an expense of £25,000 and the provision account shows a potential liability of £11,000 to cover any further repairs arising from work done during Year 5 (since some of the goods sold will remain under warranty into Year 6).*

Deferred income

In the main text of this chapter there is an example based on the recording of deferred income arising under a grant. The analysis of the transactions and events is set out in Table 11.2. The ledger account will appear as follows:

L3 Deferred income (statement of financial position/balance sheet)

Date	Particulars	Page	Debit £	Credit £	Balance £
Year 1					
Jan. 1	Grant received	L1		30,000	(30,000)
Dec. 31	Transfer to profit and loss account	L2	10,000		(20,000)
Year 2					
Dec. 31	Transfer to profit and loss account	L2	10,000		(10,000)
Year 3					
Dec. 31	Transfer to profit and loss account	L2	10,000		nil

LEONA: *The deferred income account is reported as a liability in the statement of financial position (balance sheet). It is established by a credit entry matched by a debit in the cash account (L1). Each year there is a transfer of one-third to the profit and loss account (L2) so that the revenue is spread evenly over the period.*

S | Test your understanding

S11.1 Prepare bookkeeping records for the information in question B11.1.

S11.2 Prepare bookkeeping records for the information in question B11.2.

Chapter 12

Ownership interest

Revaluation of tangible non-current assets

Significant accounting policies (extract)

c) Tangible assets

In 2008, Portugal Telecom changed the accounting policy regarding the measurement of real estate properties and the ducts infrastructure from the cost model to the revaluation model, since the latter better reflects the economic value of those asset classes (Note 4).

P. 103.

Balance sheet (extract) 2008

Change in shareholders' equity (excluding minority interests)

Balance sheet (extract) 2008

Euro million	31 Dec 2008	31 Dec 2007
Total liabilities	12,513.3	11,040.4
Equity before minority interests	235.6	1,338.2
Minority interests (4)	964.2	743.6
Total shareholders' equity	1,199.8	2,081.8
Total liabilities and shareholders' equity	13,713.1	13,122.2

P. 50.

Change in shareholders' equity (excluding minority interests) 2008

	Euro million
Equity before minority interests (initial balance)	**1,338.2**
Net income	581.5
Currency translation adjustments (1)	(595.4)
Dividends attributed (2)	(533.2)
Acquisition of own stock (3)	(904.6)
Net actuarial gains (losses), net of taxes	(437.2)
Asset revaluation, net of taxes	790.7
Other	(4.3)
Equity before minority interests (final balance)	**235.6**
Change in equity before minority interests	**(1,102.6)**
Change in equity before minority interests (%)	**(82.4%)**

P. 54.

Source: Portuguese Telecom SA (2008) Annual report.

Discussion points

1 What reason did the group give for choosing to measure the revaluation of its property assets?

2 How significant was the magnitude of the revaluation and how was it reported?

Contents

Learning outcomes

After reading this chapter you should be able to:

- Define ownership interest.
- Explain and demonstrate how the ownership interest is presented in company accounts.
- Understand the nature and purpose of the statement of changes in equity in the IASB system and also the UK ASB equivalents.
- Explain the needs of users for information about the ownership interest in a company.
- Read and interpret the information reported by companies in their annual reports, in respect of the ownership interest.
- Explain the accounting treatment of dividends.
- Understand the methods by which a company's shares may be issued when the company has a Stock Exchange listing.
- Show that you understand the impact of transactions and events on ownership interest in company accounts.

Additionally, for those who choose to study the supplement:

- Record end-of-period adjustments as debit and credit adjustments to a trial balance taken from the ledger accounts and produce figures for financial statements.

12.1 Introduction

The final element of the accounting equation has been reached. It was explained in Chapter 2 that the ownership interest is the residual amount found by deducting all liabilities of the entity from all of the entity's assets:

Assets	minus	**Liabilities**	equals	**Ownership interest**

The terminology was also explained in Chapter 2. The words equity and net assets both appear in the press and in commentaries in connection with the ownership interest. **Equity** is a word used to describe the ownership interest in the assets of the business after all liabilities are deducted. This is also referred to as the **net assets**, calculated as the assets minus the liabilities.

The structure which has been adopted for Chapters 8 to 12 is based on a series of questions:

- What are the principles for defining and recognising these items?
- What are the information needs of users in respect of the particular items?
- What information is currently provided by companies to meet these needs?
- Does the information show the desirable qualitative characteristics of financial statements?
- What are the principles for measuring, and processes for recording, these items?

Each of these questions will be addressed in turn.

12.2 Definition and recognition

The definition of **ownership interest** was presented in Chapter 2 as: 'the residual amount found by deducting all of the entity's liabilities from all of the entity's assets'.

Because the ownership interest is the residual item of the equation, it can only increase or decrease if something happens to an asset or to a liability. Recognition conditions are applied to assets and liabilities but there cannot be any additional recognition criteria applied to the ownership interest.

Events which change assets or liabilities include:

1 Making a profit (or loss) through the operations of the business – earning revenue and incurring expenses;
2 A contribution of cash by incoming shareholders purchasing new shares;
3 Holding an asset which increases or decreases in value;
4 Holding a liability which increases or decreases in value.

Each one of these events is important to the users of the financial statements and affects the claims of owners on the assets of the business. Since owners are the user group most interested in the ownership interest, this chapter will focus primarily on the information which is helpful to them. Item (1) of this list, reporting a profit or a loss in the income statement through the operations of the business, has been dealt with in some length in previous chapters. In this chapter we concentrate on item (2), the issue of new shares, and on items (3) and (4), the events which cause increases or decreases in assets and liabilities which are *not* reported in the income statement (profit and loss account). Items (3) and (4) are part of what is called **comprehensive income** (where 'comprehensive' means 'including everything that creates income for the owners').

12.3 Presentation of ownership interest

Chapters 7 to 11 have concentrated primarily on the limited liability company. For any limited liability company the **income statement (profit and loss account)** is the primary financial statement which reports the revenues and expenses of the business that arise through operations.

The change in value of an asset or liability while it is *held* by the company gives more cause for debate. If the asset has increased in value while still being held by the company, then there may be an increase in the valuation for financial reporting purposes. That is not a **realised** gain and so cannot be reported in the income statement (profit and loss account). There is another primary financial statement which companies must use to report **unrealised** gains. For companies using the IASB system in their financial statements, the unrealised gains are reported in a **statement of comprehensive income**. All changes in ownership interest, including contributions and withdrawals by owners, are reported in a **statement of changes in equity**. For companies continuing to follow UK company law and standards the unrealised gains are reported in a **statement of total recognised gains and losses**.

Example of an unrealised gain

A business buys a building at a cost of £10m. One year later similar buildings are selling for £13m. The business does not intend to sell but would like to report the potential increase in the market value of the asset. Because there is no sale, the £3m estimate of the increase in value is unrealised. It is not reported in the income statement (profit and loss account) but is reported in the statement of comprehensive income (statement of total recognised gains and losses).

The presentation of the ownership interest is therefore a potentially complex affair, using more than one financial statement. There is information about the current position of the ownership interest contained in the statement of financial position (balance sheet) and the related notes to the accounts. There is information about changes in the ownership interest in the income statement (profit and loss account) and the statement of comprehensive income (statement of total recognised gains and losses). The approach taken in this chapter is first of all to 'walk through' the early years of operating a limited liability company and the various types of ownership interest which arise.

12.3.1 Issue of shares at the date of incorporation

When the company first comes into existence it issues shares to the owners, who become **equity holders (shareholders)**. The date on which the company comes into existence is called the **date of incorporation**.

Each share has a *named value* which is called its **nominal value**. Sometimes it is referred to as the **par value**. This amount is written on the **share certificate** which is the document given to each owner as evidence of being a shareholder. Exhibit 12.1 shows the share certificate issued by a company which confirms that J. A. Smith is the owner of 100,000 ordinary shares of 25p nominal value each. This means that J. A. Smith has paid £25,000 to the company and that is the limit of this person's liability if the company fails.

All share certificates are recorded in the share register by the company secretary. The share certificate is a piece of paper which may be sold by the existing owner to another person who wishes to become a shareholder. The person who wishes to become a shareholder is often referred to as a **prospective investor**. That is not a legal term but is a useful way of indicating a person who has an interest in finding out more about the company, without having the legal rights of ownership. When the new

Exhibit 12.1
Share certificate issued by a company

Certificate number 24516

Public Company plc

SHARE CERTIFICATE

This is to certify that

J. A. Smith

is the registered owner of 100,000 ordinary shares of 25 pence each.
Given under Seal of the Company the 15th day of August 20XX

Signed *P McDowall*   *J Jones*
Company Secretary   *W Brown*

                                             Directors

---

owner has acquired the shares, the term 'investor' may continue to be used as a description which emphasises that this person now has a financial interest in knowing that the company is performing well.

The issue of 100,000 shares at a price of 25 pence each will collect £25,000 cash for the company. The effect on the accounting equation is that the asset of cash increases by £25,000 and the ownership interest is increased by £25,000.

Assets ↑	–	Liabilities	=	Ownership interest ↑
Increase in cash £25,000				Increase in nominal value of shares £25,000

For a company, the ownership interest created by the issue of new shares at their nominal value is recorded as **share capital**.

Activity 12.1

Look at the financial pages of a newspaper. Find the daily list of share prices. What information does the newspaper provide about shares in each company? Which of these items of information would you expect to find in the annual report of the company? Give reasons for your answer.

12.3.2 Buying and selling shares

The company itself has no concern about the purchase and sale of shares from one owner to another, other than having to record the new owner's name in the share register. The purchase and sale may take place by private arrangement or may take place in an established **stock market** (also called a **stock exchange**) if the company is a public limited company. If the shares are traded in an established stock market they are called listed shares because the daily prices are listed on screens for buyers and sellers to see. If there is high demand for the shares, their price will rise. If there is little demand, the price will fall. The market price on any day will depend on investors' expectations about the future of the company. Those expectations will be influenced by announcements from the company, including financial information but also covering a much wider range of company news. The expectations may also be influenced by information about the industry in which the company operates. One of the main purposes of a well-regulated stock exchange is to ensure that all investors have access to the same information at the same time so that no one has an advantage.

12.3.3 Issue of further shares after incorporation

As time goes by, the company may wish to raise new finance and to issue new shares. This could be intended to buy new non-current (fixed) assets, or even to provide cash so that the company may purchase the shares of another company and create a larger group.

Although the **nominal value** remains the same, the **market value** may be quite different.

Example

Suppose a company has shares of nominal value 25 pence but finds that its shares are selling in the market at 80 pence each. If the company issues 200,000 new shares it will collect £160,000 in cash. That is the important piece of information for the company because it can use the cash to buy new assets and expand the activities of the business. The asset of cash has increased by £160,000 and the ownership interest has increased by £160,000.

The accounting records are required by company law to show separately the nominal value of the shares and any extra amount over the nominal value. The nominal value is 25 pence and the total amount collected per share is 80 pence. So the extra amount collected is 55 pence. This extra amount is called a **premium** (the word means 'something extra'). So the £160,000 increase in the ownership interest is recorded as two separate items, namely the **nominal value** of £50,000 and the **share premium** of £110,000.

12.3.4 Retained earnings

Once the business is in operation it starts to make profits. The income statement (profit and loss account) shows the profit earned in a time period. This profit increases the ownership interest. The accumulation of past profits in the statement of financial position (balance sheet) is called **retained earnings**. The retained earnings represent the ownership interest in the net assets of the business. It is one type of **reserve**. At any point in time someone could ask the owner 'How much would you expect to receive if this business were to close down today?' The owner would look at the statement of financial position (balance sheet) and reply with the total of the **ownership interest**, shown by **equity share capital** plus all **reserves**.

You should be aware that the reserves are given different names in different countries. In some there is a legally defined reserve with a tax-deductible transfer to the reserve from the income statement (profit and loss account). It requires careful reading of the ownership interest section of the statement of financial position (balance sheet). An understanding of the changes in retained profits is helped by reading the **statement of comprehensive income**, explained in section 12.3.5.

12.3.5   Statement of comprehensive income

Companies using IASB standards

Look back to the accounting equation explained in Chapter 3. Section 3.4.1 describes ownership interest as:

Capital at the start of the year
plus/minus
Capital contributed or withdrawn
plus
Profit of the period

That chapter gives the simplest possible definition of 'profit' as 'revenue minus expenses'. A broader definition of 'profit' would be to say 'any changes in assets and liabilities other than those caused by capital contributed or withdrawn'. Chapters 9 and 10 have shown that many changes in inventories, accounts receivable and accounts payable will lead to changes in revenue and expenses, reported in the income statement (profit and loss account). This section and section 12.3.6 of this chapter show that other factors may affect the values of assets and liabilities.

The IASB wants to encourage companies to report all changes in assets and liabilities, whatever the cause, in a **statement of comprehensive income**. The word 'comprehensive' means 'including everything'. However, many companies would like to retain the separate income statement as explained in Chapters 5 and 6. Consequently the IASB allows a two-part approach:

1   A separate income statement
2   A second statement beginning with profit or loss from the income statement and incorporating other components of comprehensive income.

This two-part approach is used by many UK companies which report using IFRS. It is used in this chapter to illustrate the comprehensive income approach. Two examples are provided in this section. The first is the revaluation of non-current assets and the second is the reporting of changes in exchange rates of foreign currency.

Statement of total recognised gains and losses (UK ASB standards)

The statement of total recognised gains and losses (STRGL) was introduced by the UK ASB Standards Board[1] as a result of well-publicised company failures where it was apparent that important information about changes in the ownership interest had not been understood fully by the users of the financial statements. In particular, losses caused by exchange rate fluctuations had been reported in the notes on reserves, apparently without the expert observers pointing to the fact that these losses cancelled out the profits gained from operating activities.

As well as exchange rate gains and losses, the STRGL reports unrealised gains and losses arising on revaluation of non-current (fixed) assets of a period. Its purpose is to show the extent to which shareholders' funds have increased or decreased from all the various gains and losses recognised in the period.

12.3.6   Revaluation of non-current (fixed) assets

Suppose a company buys a hotel costing £560,000. The hotel is run successfully for a period of three years and at the end of that period a professional valuer confirms that

Table 12.3

Office Owner Ltd – income statement and statement of comprehensive income at end of Year 1

Income statement for Year 1	
	£000s
Revenue: rent received	50
Administration costs	(10)
Profit for the year	40
Statement of comprehensive income for Year 1	
Profit for the year	40
Revaluation of asset	15
Total comprehensive income for the year	55

Office Owner Ltd – statement of financial position (balance sheet) at end of Year 1

Office Owner Ltd Statement of financial position (balance sheet) at end of Year 1	
	£000s
Non-current (fixed) asset: Office block (at valuation)	1,015
Current asset: Cash	840
Net assets	1,855
Share capital	1,500
Share premium	300
Revaluation reserve	15
Retained earnings	40
	1,855

Activity 12.3

Suppose you note that a company has revalued its land and buildings as reported in the statement of financial position (balance sheet). What evidence would you expect to see as justification for the amount of the revaluation? What questions might you ask about the basis of revaluation?

12.3.7 Changes in exchange rates of foreign currency

All information in the financial statements of a UK company is shown in pounds (£) sterling. Where exchange rates alter, a company may lose or gain purely because of the exchange rate movement. That loss or gain must be reported.

The accounting process is called translation. Translation from one currency to another is particularly important when the financial statements of companies in a group are added together and so must all be restated in a common currency. The word 'translation' is used because the process is comparable to translating words from one language to another.

There are different methods of reporting depending on the type of transaction or event. Two different stories are considered here. The first is the purchase of an asset located in a foreign country. The second is the purchase, by a group of companies, of the share capital of a company in a foreign country.

Purchase of an asset

Take first of all the example of a UK company which buys a factory in Sweden. The factory is priced at Kr10,000,000. At the date of purchase of the factory the exchange rate is Kr10 = £0.70. The UK company has agreed to pay for the factory on the day of the transfer of legal title.

For accounting purposes the cost of the factory is recorded at the amount paid at the date of purchase. This is calculated as:

$$\frac{0.70}{10} \times \text{Kr}10{,}000{,}000 = £700{,}000$$

The effect of the transaction on the statement of financial position (balance sheet) of the UK company is:

Assets ↑↓	–	Liabilities	=	Ownership interest
Increase in asset of factory £700,000				
Decrease in asset of cash £700,000				

That is the end of the story so far as the UK company is concerned. The exchange rate between the krona and the £ may fluctuate, and this may affect the company's view of the price for which the factory might eventually be sold, but that information will not appear in the financial statements of the UK company until such time as the factory is sold.

Purchase of shares in another company

Suppose now that a UK group of companies has decided to purchase the entire share capital of a Swedish company whose only asset is the same factory. The purchase price is Kr10,000,000. The Swedish company distributes its entire profit as dividend each year so that the only item remaining in its statement of financial position (balance sheet) is the factory at a cost of Kr10,000,000. (This is a very simplistic example but is sufficient to illustrate the exchange rate problem.)

At the date of purchase of the investment, the factory will be recorded in the group statement of financial position (balance sheet) at £700,000.

Assets ↑↓	–	Liabilities	=	Ownership interest
Increase in sterling equivalent of group's asset of factory £700,000				
Decrease in group's asset of cash £700,000				

One year later the exchange rate has altered to Kr10 = £0.68. The factory is the only asset of the subsidiary. In the Swedish accounts it remains at Kr10,000,000 but, translated into £ sterling, this now represents only £680,000:

$$\frac{0.68}{10} \times \text{Kr}10{,}000{,}000 = £680{,}000$$

This represents a potential loss of £20,000 on the translated value of the asset at the start of the year. The loss is unrealised but as a matter of prudence the fall in the translated asset value should be reported. However, there have been strong feelings expressed by companies over many years that the unrealised loss should not affect the reported profit of the period. Consequently the relevant accounting standard[2] allows the effect on the ownership interest to be shown in the **statement of comprehensive income** as a movement in reserves.

Assets ↓	–	Liabilities	=	**Ownership interest** ↓
Reduction in sterling equivalent of assets of subsidiary £20,000				Decrease in reserve £20,000

The reporting of the reduction in the asset value as a decrease in reserves is controversial because less attention is sometimes paid to reserves than is paid to the income statement (profit and loss account). This means that the impact on the ownership interest may pass unnoticed. The IASB is hoping that the use of the statement of comprehensive income will increase the transparency of such information.

This practice of translation is required by the accounting standard on the subject. In group accounting there is considerable complexity to the technical aspects of which exchange rate effects must pass through the income statement (profit and loss account) and which may pass through the reserves. The important message for the reader of the annual reports is to be alert to the possibility of exchange rate effects on the ownership interest being reported in reserves and to look carefully at the statement of comprehensive income.

12.4 Statement of changes in equity

In Chapter 7 it was noted that the IASB specifies four primary financial statements:[3]

1 a statement of financial position (balance sheet)
2 an income statement (showing the profit or loss for the period), as part of a larger statement of comprehensive income
3 a statement of changes in equity for the period, and
4 a statement of cash flows.

The statement of financial position (balance sheet), income statement and statement of cash flows were dealt with in Chapter 7. The statement of comprehensive income has been explained in section 12.3.5 of this chapter. The statement of changes in equity is now explained.

12.4.1 Statement of changes in equity (IASB standards)

The **statement of changes in equity** must show on the face of the statement:

(a) The profit or loss for the period.
(b) Each item of income and expense for the period that is required by accounting standards to be recognised directly in equity.
(c) The effects of changes in accounting policies and corrections of errors.

If these are the only items reported then the statement of changes in equity is called a statement of comprehensive incomes.

An entity must also report, either in the statement of changes in equity or in the notes to the accounts:

(d) Transactions with equity holders (e.g. share capital issued, dividends paid).
(e) The balance of retained earnings at the start and end of the accounting period, and changes during the period.
(f) An explanation of the amounts of changes in each class of equity and each type of reserve.

If items (d), (e) and (f) are included on the face of the statement it is called a **statement of changes in equity**.

The reason for this flexibility of presentation is that different countries have applied different practices in the past. UK companies have been producing a **statement of total recognised gains and losses** for more than ten years while US companies have been presenting a **statement of changes in equity** for some years past. The annual report of Safe and Sure plc shown in Appendix I, presents a statement of total recognised gains and losses with the remaining movements on equity shown in a note to the financial statements.

12.4.2 Reconciliation of movements in shareholders' funds (UK ASB standards)

In addition to the statement of total recognised gains and losses the UK Accounting Standards Board also requires a reconciliation of movements in shareholders' funds. It may also be presented as a primary financial statement,[4] so that it has comparable prominence with other important information, or may be presented as a note to the financial statements. Most companies give this reconciliation the prominence of a primary financial statement.

12.5 Users' needs for information

The owners of a company, and potential investors in a company, are primarily interested in whether the business will make them better off or worse off. They also want to be reassured that the business has taken care of the resources entrusted to it (carrying out the function of **stewardship**). The first source of an increase in the ownership interest is the **profit** generated by the company. Professional investors will use the phrase **quality of earnings** to refer to the different components of profit. They tend to regard profits generated by the main operating activity as being of higher quality than windfall gains such as profits on the sale of non-current (fixed) assets which are not a regular feature of the company's activity.

Owners of a company expect to receive a reward for ownership. One form of reward is to watch the business grow and to know that in the future a sale of shares will give them a satisfactory gain over the period of ownership. That requires a long-term horizon. Some investors prefer to see the reward more frequently in the form of a dividend. They want to know that the ownership interest is adequate to support the dividend and yet leave sufficient assets in the business to generate further profits and dividends.

Creditors of a company know that they rank ahead of the shareholders in the event of the company being wound up, but they want to know that the company is generating sufficient wealth for the owners to provide a cushion against any adverse events.

Therefore creditors will also be concerned with the ownership interest and how it is being maintained or is growing.

Employees, suppliers and customers similarly look for reassurance as to the strength of the business to continue into the future. The ownership interest is a convenient focus which summarises the overall impact of the state of assets and liabilities, although what employees are really interested in is the preservation of the earnings capacity of the business.

12.6 Information provided in the financial statements

In Chapter 7 the statement of financial position (balance sheet) of Safe and Sure plc was presented. The final section of that statement of financial position (balance sheet) presented information on the capital and reserves representing the claim of the shareholders on the assets.

		Year 7 £m	Year 6 £m
Capital and reserves			
Called-up share capital	12	19.6	19.5
Share premium account	13	8.5	5.5
Revaluation reserve	14	4.6	4.6
Retained earnings	15	431.6	340.8
Equity holders' funds		464.3	370.4

In the discussion contained in Chapter 7 it was emphasised that the most important feature of this information is that, in total, it represents the shareholders' legal claim. There is nothing to see, touch, count or hold. If the company were to cease trading at the date of the financial statements, sell all its assets for the statement of financial position (balance sheet) amount and pay off all liabilities, the shareholders would be left with £464.3m to take away. The shareholders have the residual claim, which means that if the assets were to be sold for more than the statement of financial position (balance sheet) amount, the shareholders would share the windfall gain. If the assets were sold for less than the statement of financial position (balance sheet) amount, the shareholders would share the loss.

The total ownership interest is a claim which is described by this company as 'equity holders' funds'. It is equal to the **net assets** of the company. The total claim is subdivided so as to explain how the various parts of the claim have arisen. This section now considers each part of the claim in turn.

12.6.1 Share capital

The information shown by the company at note 12 is as follows:

Note 12 Share capital

	Year 7 £m	Year 6 £m
Ordinary shares of 2 pence each		
Authorised: 1,050,000,000 shares		
(Year 6: 1,000,000,000)	21.0	20.0
Issued and fully paid: 978,147,487 shares	19.6	19.5

Certain senior executives hold options to subscribe for shares in the company at prices ranging from 33.40p to 244.33p under schemes approved by equity holders at various dates. Options on 3,479,507 shares were exercised during Year 7 and 66,970 options lapsed. The number of shares subject to options, the years in which they were purchased and the years in which they will expire are:

Purchase	Expiry	Numbers
	Year 8	13,750
All	Year 9	110,000
Purchased	Year 10	542,500
10 years	Year 11	1,429,000
before	Year 12	2,826,600
expiry	Year 13/14	3,539,942
	Year 15	3,690,950
	Year 16	2,279,270
	Year 17	3,279,363
		17,711,375

Called-up means that the company has called upon the shareholders who first bought the shares to make payment in full. When a new company is brought to the stock market for the first time, investors may be invited to buy the shares by paying an instalment now and the rest later. That was quite common in the 1980s when former nationalised industries, such as electricity and water companies, were being sold to the private sector. The **prospectus**, which is issued to invite the purchase of shares, specifies the dates on which the company would make a call for the rest of the share price due. After all the cash has been received by the company, the shares are described as **fully paid**.

Ordinary shareholders are entitled to vote at meetings, usually in proportion to the number of shares held. That means that the power of the individual shareholder depends on the number of shares held. For most large companies there are relatively small numbers of shareholders who control relatively large proportions of the share capital. A company which is part of a larger group of companies is required to report in the notes to the accounts the name and country of the ultimate parent company. Companies that are listed on the Stock Exchange are required to disclose in the directors' report the name of any shareholder interested in 3% or more of the company's issued share capital.

Before the directors of a company may issue new shares, they must be authorised to do so by the existing shareholders. The existing shareholders need to be aware that their claim will be diluted by the incoming shareholders. (If there are 50 shares owned equally by two persons, each controls 50% of the company. If 25 new shares are issued to a third person, then all three have 33.3% each, which dilutes the voting power of the first two persons.)

One of the controversial aspects of share capital in recent years has been the privilege of share options taken by directors and other employees (usually senior employees of the business but sometimes spreading to the wider employee range). A share option allows the person holding the option to buy shares in the company, at any future date up to a specified limit in time, at an agreed fixed price. The argument in favour of such an arrangement is that it gives senior management an incentive to make the company prosperous because they want the share price to increase above the price they have agreed to pay. The argument against it is that they have no very strong incentive because the worst that can happen to directors and other employees is that they decide not to take up the option when the share price has not performed well. Until 1995 there were also some personal tax advantages in taking options rather than a normal portion of salary, but since then, the tax rules have limited such benefits.

Major companies now disclose, in the directors' report, the options held by each of the directors.

The analyst's view

David and Leona are on the plane flying from London to Aberdeen for a week's holiday in the Cairngorms. David has brought the annual report of Safe and Sure plc as a precaution against inclement weather disturbing their plans for outdoor activities.

12.7 **Dividends**

Shareholders who invest in a company do so because they want the value of their shares to increase over time and return greater wealth when eventually sold. In the meantime the shareholders look for an income to spend each year. That comes to some of them by means of dividends.

Companies are not obliged to pay dividends and may decide not to do so if there is a shortage of cash or it is needed for other purposes. The directors make a recommendation to the shareholders in the annual general meeting. The shareholders may vote against taking the dividend but that happens only very rarely. Final dividend payments usually take place soon after the annual general meeting. Some companies also pay an interim dividend during the accounting year. Major UK companies have in past years ensured that a dividend was paid every year, however small, because it allowed the shares to be regarded as sufficiently 'safe' for investors such as trustees of charitable institutions.

When a company decides it wants to pay a dividend, there are two essential tests. The first is, 'Does the company have the cash resources to pay a dividend?' The second is, 'Has the company made sufficient profits, adding this year to previous years, to justify the dividend as being paid out of wealth created by the business?'

Even where the company has cash in the bank from which to pay the dividend, it must look forward and ensure that there are no other commitments in the near future which will also need cash. The company may decide to borrow short term to finance the dividend. In such a situation the company has to weigh the interest cost of borrowing against the risk of its shares being undervalued because of lack of interest from shareholders. These are all problems of cash management (more often called 'treasury management').

Company law imposes a different viewpoint. It takes the view that a company should not return to shareholders, during the life of the company, a part of the capital contributed by the shareholder body. Accordingly there is a requirement that dividends must be covered by accumulated reserves of past profit in excess of accumulated reserves of past losses. It is not required that the dividend is covered by the profit of the year. A company might choose to smooth things over by keeping the dividend reasonably constant even where profits are fluctuating.

The dividend declared by the company is usually expressed in pence per share. Shareholders receive dividend calculated by multiplying the dividend in pence per share by the number of shares held. For the company there is a reduction in the asset of cash and a reduction in the ownership claim. The management of the company may regard the dividend as an expense of the business but it is more properly regarded as a reduction in the claim which the owners have on the net assets as a whole. The reduction in the ownership interest is reported in the statement of changes in equity because it is a transaction with the owners.

At the end of the accounting period the company will calculate profit and then declare a recommended dividend. The dividend is recommended by the directors to the shareholders. The shareholders, in the annual general meeting, may accept or decline but are not allowed to increase the amount. At the balance sheet date there is no legal liability because the shareholders' meeting has not been held. Therefore there is no information reported in the financial statements. The directors' report, which is required by company law, will contain a statement of the recommended dividend for the year. There will probably also be information in the chairman's statement or on a 'highlights' page.

12.8   Issue of further shares on the Stock Exchange

Once a company has a listing on the Stock Exchange it may decide to issue further shares. There are different methods by which this may be done, depending on the company's motive for the action. This section describes an offer for sale, a capitalisation issue and a rights issue.

12.8.1   Offer for sale

When a company seeks a listing of its shares for the first time, it must offer those shares to the public (using the services of a member firm of the Stock Exchange as a sponsor) and issue a **prospectus** setting out information about itself. Some of the information to be included in the prospectus is required by the Companies Act but this is expanded upon by the **Listing Rules**. The prospectus is a highly informative document, revealing far more about a company than would be found in the annual report. There is a requirement for an accountant's report which includes a three-year history of the financial statements. In particular, there must be a specific statement confirming the adequacy of working capital.

There may also be a forecast of the expected profits for the next accounting period. The reporting accountants will be asked to give an opinion on the forecast. Particularly interesting are the assumptions on which the forecast is based. The reporting accountants will confirm that the amounts in the forecast are consistent with the assumptions but the reader will have to decide how appropriate the assumptions themselves are.

Exhibit 12.2 contains an example of a statement of assumptions taken from a company prospectus.

Exhibit 12.2
Assumptions on which profit forecast is based

> The forecasts have been prepared on a basis consistent with the accounting policies normally accepted by the Group and on the following principal assumptions:
>
> (i)   there will be no changes in taxation or other legislation or government regulations or policies which will have a significant effect on the Group; and
> (ii) the operations of the Group and its suppliers will not be significantly affected by weather conditions, industrial action or civil disturbances.

You may be surprised to learn that the wording in Exhibit 12.2 is extracted from the prospectus of a company retailing high-quality chocolates. You may be further surprised to learn that very similar wording appeared in the prospectus of a company offering dry cleaning services. There is no regulation which says that the statement of assumptions has to be helpful to the user of the annual report.

12.8.2 Capitalisation issue

After the shares have been listed for some time, the market value may have grown to the point where the shares are less marketable because the price of each is too large for convenient trading in small lots. The company may decide to increase the number of shares held by shareholders without making any change to the assets or liabilities of the company. One way of achieving this is to convert reserves into share capital. Take the simplified statement of financial position (balance sheet) in Table 12.4. The company decides to convert £1m of reserves into share capital. It writes to each shareholder saying, 'You will receive one new share for each share already held'. The statement of financial position (balance sheet) now becomes as shown in Table 12.5.

The shareholder now holds twice as many shares by number but is no better or worse off financially because the total value of the company has not changed. The shares will each be worth one-half of the market price of an old share at the moment of issue. This process is sometimes referred to as a bonus issue because the shareholders receive new share certificates, but in reality there is no bonus because no new wealth is created.

Table 12.4
Statement of financial position (balance sheet) of company prior to capitalisation

	£m
Assets	7
Liabilities	(4)
	3
Share capital, in shares of 25 pence each	1
Reserves	2
	3

Table 12.5
Statement of financial position (balance sheet) of company after capitalisation

	£m
Assets	7
Liabilities	(4)
	3
Share capital, in shares of 25 pence each	2
Reserves	1
	3

In terms of the accounting equation the effect on the statement of financial position (balance sheet) is:

Assets	–	Liabilities	=	Ownership interest ↑↓
				Increase in share capital £1m
				Decrease in reserves £1m

12.8.3 Rights issue

Once a company has a market listing it may decide that it needs to raise further finance on the stock market. The first people it would ask are the existing shareholders, who have already shown their commitment to the company by owning shares in it. Furthermore, it is desirable to offer them first chance because if strangers buy the shares the interests of the existing shareholders may be diluted. Suppose the company in Table 12.4 wishes to raise £3m new finance. It will offer existing shareholders the right to pay for, say, 2 million new shares at 150 pence each. There are already 4 million shares of 25p nominal value in issue, so the letter to the shareholders will say: 'The company is offering you the right to buy 1 new share at a price of 150p for every 2 existing shares you hold.' Existing shareholders will be attracted by this offer provided the market price stays above 150 pence for existing shares. They may take up the rights themselves or sell the right to someone else. In either event, the company will receive £3m cash, the company will issue 2 million new shares at 150 pence each and the statement of financial position (balance sheet) will appear as in Table 12.6.

Table 12.6
Statement of financial position (balance sheet) after rights issue

	£m
Assets	7.0
New cash	3.0
	10.0
Liabilities	(4.0)
	6.0
Share capital, in shares of 25 pence each	1.5
Share premium	2.5
Reserves	2.0
	6.0

The issue price of 150 pence is split for accounting purposes into the nominal value of 25 pence and the premium of 125 pence. In terms of the accounting equation the effect of the rights issue on the statement of financial position (balance sheet) is:

Assets ↑	–	Liabilities	=	Ownership interest ↑
Increase in cash £3m				Increase in share capital £0.5m Increase in share premium £2.5m

12.8.4 Buying back shares that have been issued

Companies are permitted to buy back shares that have been issued. The Companies Act sets limits on the proportion of shares that may be bought back from existing shareholders and sets conditions on the availability of retained earnings to support the buy-back. Two possible reasons for buying back shares are (1) to return surplus cash to shareholders and reduce the shareholding base, and (2) to stabilise share prices in the short term where investors want to sell but for some reason there is a temporary lack of demand in the market.

When companies buy back their own shares they may either cancel the shares or hold them as 'treasury shares'. Shares held as 'treasury shares' will be shown as a deduction from share capital in the equity section of the statement of financial position (balance sheet) and the transaction will be reported in the Statement of changes in equity.

Activity 12.4

Look in the financial section of a newspaper for the list of recent issues of new shares. Obtain the address of one company from a trade directory and write politely to ask for a copy of the prospectus. If you are sufficiently fortunate to obtain a copy of a prospectus, look at the accounting information and compare it with the amount and type of information published in the annual report. Why are they not the same?

12.9 Summary

- **Ownership interest** is the residual amount found by deducting all of the entity's liabilities from all of the entity's assets.
- Unrealised gains are reported in a **statement of comprehensive income** in the IASB system. They are reported in a **statement of total recognised gains and losses** in the UK ASB system.
- Each share has a named value when the company is formed. This is called its **nominal value**. It does not change unless the shareholders agree to split shares into smaller units.
- When the shares are sold on a stock market they have a **market value**. The market value of frequently traded shares changes daily with the forces of supply and demand.
- The difference between the nominal value and the market value is called the **share premium**. When the company issues further shares at market price the share premium is recorded separately from the nominal value.
- When non-current assets are revalued, the **unrealised** increase in value is added to the **revaluation reserve**.
- **Dividends** paid to shareholders reduce the ownership interest and are reported in the **statement of comprehensive income**. The effect on the accounting equation is reported when dividends are paid. Dividends proposed to be paid in future are described in the directors' report.
- When a company issues more shares after incorporation it may be through a capitalisation issue, an offer for sale or a rights issue. A **capitalisation issue** gives more shares to equity shareholders. It changes the relationship between share capital and reserves but brings no new resources into the business. An **offer for sale** increases the ownership interest and brings in new cash. A **rights issue** also increases the ownership interest and brings in new cash but it gives the existing shareholders the first choice of maintaining their proportionate interest in the company.

QUESTIONS

The Questions section of each chapter has three types of question. 'Test your understanding' questions to help you review your reading are in the 'A' series of questions. You will find the answers to these by reading and thinking about the material in the book. 'Application' questions to test your ability to apply technical skills are in the 'B' series of questions. Questions requiring you to show skills in problem solving and evaluation are in the 'C' series of questions. A letter [S] indicates that there is a solution at the end of the book.

A Test your understanding

A12.1 Why may it be said that the ownership interest is the residual item in the accounting equation? (Section 12.1)

A12.2 What is the definition of ownership interest? (Section 12.2)

A12.3 What is the effect on the accounting equation where new shares are issued for cash? (Section 12.3.1)

A12.4 Why does the company not record the buying and selling of shares in its statement of financial position (balance sheet)? (Section 12.3.3)

A12.5 What is a share premium? How is it recorded? (Section 12.3.4)

A12.6 How is the revaluation of a non-current (fixed) asset reported? (Section 12.3.5)

A12.7 Why may the revaluation of a non-current (fixed) asset not be reported in the profit and loss account? (Section 12.3.5)

A12.8 Where may the reader of the annual report find out about the effect of movements in foreign exchange rates? (Section 12.3.6)

A12.9 What is the purpose of the statement of total recognised income and expenses? (Section 12.6.4)

A12.10 What is the purpose of the reconciliation of movements in equity? (Section 12.6.5)

A12.11 How do the directors report their recommended dividend for the financial period, to be agreed at the shareholders' meeting? (Section 12.7)

A12.12 What is meant by:

    (a) offer for sale; (section 12.8.1)
    (b) capitalisation issue; and (section 12.8.2)
    (c) rights issue? (section 12.8.3)

    Explain the effect of each of the above on the statement of financial position (balance sheet) of a company.

B   Application

B12.1 [S]
Explain the effect on the accounting equation of each of the following transactions:

(a) At the start of Year 1, Bright Ltd issues 200,000 shares at nominal value 25 pence per share, receiving £50,000 in cash.
(b) At the end of Year 2, Bright Ltd issues a further 100,000 shares to an investor at an agreed price of 75 pence per share, receiving £75,000 in cash.
(c) At the end of Year 3 the directors of Bright Ltd obtain a market value of £90,000 for a company property which originally cost £70,000. They wish to record this in the statement of financial position (balance sheet).

B12.2 [S]
Explain the effect on the accounting equation of the following transactions and decisions regarding dividends:

(a) The company pays a dividend of £20,000 during the accounting period.
(b) The directors recommend a dividend of £30,000 at the end of the accounting year. It will be paid following shareholder approval at the Annual General Meeting, held two months after the accounting year-end.

B12.3 [S]
The following is a summarised statement of financial position (balance sheet) of Nithsdale Ltd.

	£000s
Cash	20
Other assets less liabilities	320
	340
Ordinary shares (400,000 of 25 pence each)	100
Share premium	40
Reserves of retained profit	200
	340

The company is considering three possible changes to its capital structure:

(a) issue for cash 50,000 additional ordinary shares at £1 per share, fully paid; or
(b) make a 1 for 4 capitalisation issue of ordinary shares; or
(c) make a 1 for 5 rights issue at £3 per share.

Show separately the impact of each change on the statement of financial position (balance sheet) of the company.

B12.4 [S]
Fragrance plc has owned a factory building for many years. The building is recorded in the statement of financial position (balance sheet) at £250,000, being historical cost of £300,000 less accumulated depreciation of £50,000. The recent report of a professional valuer indicated that the property is valued at £380,000 on an open market basis for its existing use. Explain the effect this information will have on the reported financial statements.

B12.5 [S]
Suppose the factory building in question B12.4 was valued by the professional expert at £240,000. What effect would this information have on the reported financial statements?

C   Problem solving and evaluation

This question reviews your understanding of Chapters 8–12 and the effect of transactions on ownership interest.

C12.1
Set out below is a summary of the accounting records of Titan Ltd at 31 December Year 1:

	£000s	£000s
Assets		
Land and buildings	200	
Plant and machinery	550	
Investment in shares	150	
Stock	250	
Trade receivables (debtors)	180	
Cash	150	
Liabilities		
Trade payables (creditors)		365
Debenture loan 10% nominal rate of interest		250
Ownership interest		
Share capital		600
Retained earnings at 1 Jan. Year 1		125
Revenue		
Sales		1,815
Cost of goods sold	1,505	
Expenses		
Overhead expenses	145	
Debenture interest paid	25	
Totals	3,155	3,155

The summary of the accounting records includes all transactions which have been entered in the ledger accounts up to 31 December, but investigation reveals further adjustments which relate to the accounting period up to, and including, that date.

The adjustments required relate to the following matters:

(i) No depreciation has been charged for the year in respect of buildings, plant and machinery. The depreciation of the building has been calculated as £2,000 per annum and the depreciation of plant and machinery for the year has been calculated as £55,000.

(ii) The company is aware that electricity consumption during the months of November and December, Year 1, amounted to around £5,000 in total, but no electricity bill has yet been received.

(iii) Overhead expenses include insurance premiums of £36,000 which were paid at the start of December, Year 1, in respect of the 12-month period ahead.

(iv) The stock amount is as shown in the accounting records of items moving into and out of stock during the year. On 31 December a check of the physical stock was made. It was discovered that raw materials recorded as having a value of £3,000 were, in fact, unusable. It was also found that an employee had misappropriated stock worth £5,000.

(v) The company proposes to pay a dividend of £30,000.

(vi) The corporation tax payable in respect of the profits of the year is estimated at £45,000, due for payment on 30 September, Year 2.

Required

(a) Explain how each of the items (i) to (vi) will affect the ownership interest.

(b) Calculate the amount of the ownership interest after taking into account items (i) to (vi).

(*Hint*: first calculate the profit of the year.)

Activities for study groups

Turn to the annual report of a listed company which you have used for activities in earlier chapters. Find every item which relates to the ownership interest (including any discussion in the non-regulated part of the annual report).

As a group, imagine you are shareholders in this company. You are holding a meeting of the shareholders' action group calling for clarity of information about your total interest in the business. Make lists of the good points and weak points in the quality of information available to you and then arrange the weak points in descending order of importance. Then draft an action plan for improved communication with shareholders which you would propose sending to the company.

Notes and references

1. ASB (1992), Financial Reporting Standard (FRS 3), *Reporting Financial Performance*, Accounting Standards Board; and ASB (1999), *Statement of Principles for Financial Reporting*, Chapter 7.
2. IASB (2009), IAS 21, *The Effects of Changes in Foreign Exchange Rates*, International Accounting Standards Board.
3. IASB (2009), IAS 1, *Presentation of Financial Statements*, para. 10.
4. ASB (1992), FRS 3, para. 59.

A spreadsheet for adjustment to a trial balance at the end of the accounting period

End-of-period adjustments and the ownership interest

If you look back to Chapter 6 you will see that it finished with a trial balance and a promise that the trial balance would be used later as the starting point for preparation of financial statements. The moment has now arrived where the trial balance is used as a starting point for making end-of-period adjustments to show the change in the ownership interest during the period.

The accruals concept (or the parallel argument of matching in the income statement [profit and loss account]) requires all items relevant to the period to be included in the financial statements of the period. Most items will be included because they will have been recorded in the ledger and hence in the financial statements. However, there will be some items of information, emerging from enquiry at the end of the period, which have not yet resulted in a transaction but which are undoubtedly based on events relevant to the period.

The enquiry will take a routine form of:

- estimating the depreciation of non-current (fixed) assets where this has not already been recorded;
- examining non-current (fixed) assets for signs of obsolescence beyond the amount allowed for in the depreciation charge;
- counting the inventory (stock) of raw materials, work in progress and finished goods, for comparison with the accounting record;
- evaluating the doubtful debts;
- checking files for any purchase invoices received but not yet recorded;
- checking files for any sales invoices for goods sent out but not yet recorded;
- considering whether any resource has been consumed, or service received, for which a supplier has not yet sent an invoice.

Returning to the trial balance contained in Table 6.15 of Chapter 6, it may be noted that the depreciation for the month has been charged, there are no trade receivables (debtors) and therefore no concerns about doubtful debts, and it would appear from the list of transactions for the month that all sales and purchases have been recorded carefully. Suppose, however, that when M. Carter checks the inventory (stock) of goods at the end of the month it is found that the roof has been leaking and rainwater has damaged goods worth £500. Furthermore, the business uses gas to heat a water boiler and it is estimated that consumption for the month amounts to £80.

These items of information are called *end-of-period adjustments*. Both events could, and would, be recorded in the ledger accounts by the business. If you were presented with this information as a class exercise, or you were the auditor taking the trial balance and adjusting it for this further information, you would use a spreadsheet which set out the trial balance and then provided further columns for the end-of-period adjustments. The spreadsheet for this example is set out in Table 12.7 but before looking at that you should read through the next section which explains the recording of end-of-period adjustments. In this case a one-month period is covered and so the adjustments are referred to as month-end adjustments.

Analysis of the month-end adjustments

Before any entries may be made in the adjustments columns of the spreadsheet, the effect of each adjustment on the accounting equation must be considered so that the debit and credit entries may be identified.

(a) At the end of the month it is found that the roof has been leaking and rainwater has damaged goods worth £500

The loss of inventory (stock) causes the ownership interest to decrease and is recorded as a debit entry in the expense of cost of goods sold. The decrease in the inventory (stock) is recorded as a credit entry in the ledger account.

Dr   Cost of goods sold   £500
Cr   Inventory (stock) of goods   £500

(b) The business uses gas to heat a water boiler and it is estimated that consumption for the month amounts to £80

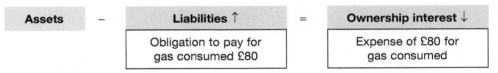

The event of consuming the gas causes the ownership interest to decrease and is recorded as a debit entry in an expense account for gas consumed. The obligation to pay for the gas at a future time is recorded as a credit entry in the ledger account for accruals.

Dr Expense of gas   £80
Cr Accruals   £80

The spreadsheet

Table 12.7 contains, in the left-hand pair of debit and credit columns, the trial balance of Table 6.15 from Chapter 6. The next pair of columns contains the debit and credit entries necessary for the end-of-period adjustments. The third pair of columns shows the resulting amounts on each line of income statement (profit and loss account) items. The final pair of columns shows the resulting amounts on each line of statement of financial position (balance sheet) items. The entire spreadsheet could be thought of as a series of ledger accounts stretched across the page, with one line for each ledger account.

The debit and credit entries identified by the foregoing analysis are shown in the adjustments columns of the spreadsheet with identifying letters in brackets alongside. Where no suitably named line exists, a new line may be inserted. The use of a new line is shown here for accruals and the expense of gas. If the exercise is being carried out using a computer spreadsheet package, the insertion of an extra line is not a problem. For a handwritten exercise it may be necessary to leave spaces at possible insertion points.

Once all adjustments have been entered, each of the adjusted amounts can be carried across to one of the final four columns, depending on whether the item belongs to the income statement (profit and loss account) or the statement of financial position

Table 12.7
Trial balance of M. Carter at the end of May, before month-end adjustments

Ledger account title	Trial balance		Adjustments		Income (profit) statement		Statement of financial position	
	Dr	Cr	Dr	Cr	Expense	Revenue	A	L + OI
	£	£	£	£	£	£	£	£
L3 Buildings	30,000						30,000	
L4 Equipment	5,750						5,750	
L5 Inventory (stock) of goods	8,000			500 (a)			7,500	
L11 R. Welsby	nil							
L1 Cash	6,400						6,400	
Accruals				80 (b)				80
L6 R. Busby		nil						
L2 Ownership interest		49,000						49,000
Subtotal	50,150	49,000					49,650	49,080
Difference: profit of the month								570
L10 Sales		7,000				7,000		
L9 Cost of goods sold	3,500		500 (a)		4,000			
L7 Electricity	100				100			
Gas			80 (b)		80			
L8 Wages	2,000				2,000			
L12 Depreciation	250				250			
Subtotal	5,850	7,000	580	580	6,430	7,000	49,650	49,650
Difference: profit of the month					570			
Total of each column	56,000	56,000	580	580	7,000	7,000	49,650	49,650

(balance sheet). Each pair of columns is added and the difference between the totals in the income statement (profit and loss account) columns should equal the difference between the totals in the statement of financial position (balance sheet) columns. If that is not the case, it means that an error has taken place at some point in the spreadsheet and must be found.

Revised statement of profit

The statement of profit before adjustments is shown in section 6.6.2 of Chapter 6 and the statement of financial position (balance sheet) is in section 6.6.3. From the final four columns of the spreadsheet in Table 12.7, these could now be restated as follows:

M. Carter, Wholesaler
Income statement (profit and loss account) (adjusted)
for the month of May Year XX

	£	£
Revenue (sales)		7,000
Cost of goods sold		(4,000)
Gross profit		3,000
Other expenses		
Wages	(2,000)	
Electricity	(100)	
Gas	(80)	
Depreciation	(250)	
		(2,430)
Net profit		570

Statement of financial position (balance sheet)

M. Carter, Wholesaler
Statement of financial position (balance sheet) (adjusted) at 31 May Year XX

	£
Non-current (fixed) assets	
Buildings	30,000
Equipment	6,000
	36,000
Depreciation	(250)
Depreciated cost of non-current (fixed) assets	35,750
Current assets	
Inventory (stock)	7,500
Cash at bank	6,400
	13,900
Accruals	(80)
Net current assets	13,820
Net assets	49,570
Ownership interest	
Capital at start	50,000
Add profit	570
Less drawings	(1,000)
Total ownership interest	49,570

This completes the study of double-entry bookkeeping in this book. You are now in a position to be able to carry out the following tasks in relation to the business of a sole trader:

- record transactions in ledger accounts
- prepare a trial balance
- make end-of-period adjustments to the trial balance
- prepare an income statement (profit and loss account) and statement of financial position (balance sheet).

S   Test your understanding

S12.1 (a) Using the information provided in question C12.1, prepare a spreadsheet containing a trial balance, adjustment and resulting figures for income statement (profit and loss account) and statement of financial position (balance sheet) items. (Table 12.7 provides a pattern to follow.)

(b) Present the income statement (profit and loss account) for the year and the statement of financial position (balance sheet) at the end of the year in an informative and useful manner.

Part 4

Analysis and issues in reporting

Many users will rely on others to monitor ratios on their behalf. Employees will look to their advisers, perhaps union officials, to monitor performance. Small private investors with limited resources will rely heavily on articles in the financial sections of newspapers. Professional fund managers will look to their own research resources and may also make use of the analysts' reports prepared by the brokers who act for the fund managers in buying and selling shares. Each broker's analyst seeks as much information as possible about a company so that he or she can sell information which is of better quality than that of any other broker's analyst. There is fierce competition to be a highly rated analyst because that brings business to the broking firm and high rewards for the analyst.

In monitoring performance the expert analysts and fund managers will use ratios rather than absolute amounts. A figure of £100m for sales (revenue) means nothing in isolation. The reader who knows that last year's sales (revenue) amounted to £90m sees immediately an increase of 11.1%. The reader who knows that fixed (non-current) assets remained constant at £75m knows that the fixed (non-current) assets this year have earned their value in sales (revenue) 1.33 times (100/75 = 1.33) whereas last year they earned their value in sales (revenue) 1.2 times (90/75 = 1.2). Ratios show changes in relationships of figures which start to create a story and start to generate questions. They do not provide answers.

The fund managers and analysts all have their own systems for calculating ratios and some keep these a carefully guarded secret so that each may hopefully see an important clue before the next person does so. That means there is no standard system of ratio analysis. There are, however, several which are used frequently. A selection of these will be used here as a basic framework for analysis. As you start to read more about company accounts you will find other ratios used but you should discover that those are largely refinements of the structure presented here.

13.2 A note on terminology

Ratio analysis is not a standardised exercise. It is often taught in finance courses and management accounting courses as well as in financial accounting courses. Businesses use ratios to describe their own performance. There is a tendency towards creating ratios that suit the purpose and towards using descriptions that are personal choices of the presenter. This chapter gives commonly used names for ratios (such as 'gross profit percentage') and links these to the terminology of the IASB system of accounting by using additional descriptions in brackets. For example, the title 'gross profit percentage' is used as a name for a ratio and it is defined as follows:

$$\frac{\text{Gross profit}}{\text{Sales (revenue)}} \times 100\%$$

In the denominator of this ratio the word 'sales' describes the activity that creates gross profit; the additional word (revenue) in brackets reminds you that the information will be found in financial statements under 'revenue'. Similarly 'fixed assets (non-current assets)' uses the commonly established words 'fixed assets' with the addition of (non-current assets) in brackets to remind you of where the information will be found in the statement of financial position (balance sheet).

13.3 Systematic approach to ratio analysis

A systematic approach to ratio analysis seeks to establish a broad picture first of all, and then break that broad picture down until there are thumbnail sketches of interesting areas. Four key headings commonly encountered in ratio analysis are:

1 *Investor ratios.* Ratios in this category provide some measure of how the price of a share in the stock market compares to key indicators of the performance of the company.

2 *Analysis of management performance.* Ratios in this category indicate how well the company is being run in terms of using assets to generate sales (revenue) and how effective it is in controlling costs and producing profit based on goods and services sold.

3 *Liquidity and current assets.* The management of cash and current assets and the preservation of an adequate, but not excessive, level of liquidity is an essential feature of business survival especially in difficult economic circumstances.

4 *Gearing (referred to in American texts as 'leverage').* Gearing is a measure of the extent to which there is financial risk indicated in the statement of financial position (balance sheet) and in the income statement (profit and loss account) (see section 13.4 on risk and return). Financial risk means the risk associated with having to pay interest and having an obligation to repay a loan.

In the following sections key ratios for each of these aspects of a systematic analysis are specified by the name of the ratio and the definition in words. Below each definition there is a brief discussion of the meaning and interpretation of the ratio.

13.3.1 Investor ratios

Investors who buy shares in a company want to be able to compare the benefit from the investment with the amount they have paid, or intend to pay, for their shares. There are two measures of benefit to the investors. One is the profit of the period (usually given the name **earnings** when referring to the profit available for equity holders (ordinary shareholders)). The other is the **dividend** which is an amount of cash that is paid to the shareholders. Profit indicates wealth created by the business. That wealth may be accumulated in the business or else paid out in the form of dividend. Four ratios are presented with a comment on each.

Earnings per share	$\dfrac{\text{Profit after tax for ordinary equity holders}}{\text{Number of issued ordinary shares}}$

Comment. **Earnings per share** is the most frequently quoted measure of company performance and progress. The percentage change from year to year should be monitored for the trend. Criticisms are that this strong focus on annual earnings may cause 'short-termism' among investors and among company managers. The IASB and the UK ASB would like to turn the attention of preparers and users of accounts away from reliance on earnings per share as a single performance measure, but the earnings per share remains a strong feature of comments on company results.

Price–earnings ratio	$\dfrac{\text{Share price}}{\text{Earnings per share}}$

Comment. The **price–earnings ratio** (often abbreviated to 'p/e ratio') compares the amount invested in one share with the earnings per share. It may be interpreted as the number of years for which the currently reported profit is represented by the current share price. The p/e ratio reflects the market's confidence in future prospects of the company. The higher the ratio, the longer is the period for which the market believes the current level of earnings may be sustained.

In order to gain some feeling for the relative magnitude of the p/e ratio of any individual company, it should be compared with the average p/e ratio for the industry, given daily in the *Financial Times*. The p/e ratio is quite commonly used as a key item of input information in investment decisions or recommendations.

Dividened per share	$\dfrac{\text{Dividend of the period}}{\text{Number of issued ordinary shares}}$

Comment. The **dividend** per share is one of the key measures announced by the company at the end of the financial year (and sometimes as an interim dividend during the year as well). Shareholders immediately know how much to expect in total dividend, depending on the number of shares held. The figure of dividend per share is the cash amount paid by the company. It may or may not be subject to tax in the hands of the recipient, depending on whether or not the recipient is a taxpayer.

The dividend of the period is equal to any interim dividend paid plus the final recommended dividend (see section 12.7). To find the recommended dividend you will have to look beyond the financial statements. The Directors' Report will contain a note on the recommended dividend which is to be paid to shareholders following their agreement at the annual general meeting. There may also be a description of the recommended dividend in the Chairman's Statement, or a Highlights Statement, or the Operating and Financial Review (OFR).

Dividend cover (payout ratio)	$\dfrac{\text{Earnings per share}}{\text{Dividend per share}}$

Comment. Companies need cash to enable them to pay dividends. For most companies the profits of the business must generate that cash, so the dividend decision could be regarded as a two-stage question. The first part is, 'Have we made sufficient profits?' and the second stage is, 'Has that profit generated cash which is not needed for reinvestment in fixed or current assets?' The **dividend cover** helps in answering the first of these questions. It shows the number of times the dividend has been covered by the profits (earnings) of this year. It could be said that the higher the dividend cover, the 'safer' is the dividend. On the other hand, it could be argued that a high dividend cover means that the company is keeping new wealth to itself, perhaps to be used in buying new assets, rather than dividing it among the shareholders.

The dividend policy of the company is a major decision for the board of directors. Many companies like to keep to a 'target' dividend cover with only minor fluctuations from one year to the next. The evidence from finance research is that company managers have two targets, one being the stability of the dividend cover but the other being a desire to see the dividend per share increase, or at least remain stationary, rather than decrease. Dividends are thought to carry a signal to the market of the strength and stability of the company.

Dividend yield	$\dfrac{\text{Dividend per share}}{\text{Share price}} \times 100\%$

Comment. The **dividend yield** is a very simple ratio comparing dividend per share with the current market price of a share. It indicates the relationship between what the investor can expect to receive from the shares and the amount which is invested in the shares. Many investors need income from investments and the dividend yield is an important factor in their decision to invest in, or remain in, a company. It has to be noted that dividends are not the only benefit from share ownership. Section 13.4 on risk and return presents a formula for return (yield) which takes into account the growth in share price as well as the dividend paid. Investors buy shares in expectation of an increase in the share price. The directors of many companies would take the view that the dividend yield should be adequate to provide an investment income, but it is the wealth arising from retained profits that is used for investment in new assets which in turn generate growth in future profits.

13.3.2 Analysis of management performance

Management of a business is primarily a function requiring **stewardship**, meaning careful use of resources for the benefit of the owners. There are two central questions to test this use of resources:

1 How well did the management make use of the investment in assets to create sales (revenue)?
2 How carefully did the management control costs so as to maximise the profit derived from the sales (revenue)?

Return on shareholders' equity	$\dfrac{\text{Profit after tax for ordinary equity holders}}{\text{Share capital + Reserves}} \times 100\%$

Comment. A key measure of success, from the viewpoint of shareholders, is the success of the company in using the funds provided by shareholders to generate profit. That profit will provide new wealth to cover their **dividend** and to finance future expansion of the business. The **return on shareholders' equity** is therefore a measure of company performance from the shareholders' perspective. It is essential in this calculation to use the profit for ordinary equity holders, which is the profit after interest charges and after tax. The formula uses the phrase **equity** holders which will probably be the wording that you see in the financial statements. It has the same meaning as ordinary shareholders.

Return on capital employed	$\dfrac{\text{Operating profit (before interest and tax)}}{\text{Total assets – Current liabilities}} \times 100\%$

Return on capital employed	$\dfrac{\text{Operating profit (before interest and tax)}}{\text{Ordinary share capital + reserves + long-term loans}} \times 100\%$

Comment. **Return on capital employed** (ROCE) is a broader measure than return on shareholders' equity. ROCE measures the performance of a company as a whole in using all sources of long-term finance. Profit before interest and tax is used in the numerator as a measure of operating results. It is sometime called 'earnings before interest and tax' and is abbreviated to EBIT. Return on capital employed is often seen as a measure of management efficiency. The denominator can be written in two ways, as shown in the alternative formulae. Think about the accounting equation and rearrange it to read:

Total assets – current liabilities = Ordinary share capital plus
reserves plus long-term loans

The ratio is a measure of how well the long-term finance is being used to generate operating profits.

Return on total assets	$\dfrac{\text{Operating profit (before interest and tax)}}{\text{Total assets}} \times 100\%$

Comment. Calculating the **return on total assets** is another variation on measuring how well the assets of the business are used to generate operating profit before deducting interest and tax.

Operating profit as % of sales (revenue)	$\dfrac{\text{Operating profit (before interest and tax)}}{\text{Sales (revenue)}} \times 100\%$

Comment. The ratio of operating profit as a percentage of sales (revenue) is also referred to as the **operating margin**. The aim of many successful business managers is to make the margin as high as possible. The margin reflects the degree of competitiveness in the market, the economic situation, the ability to differentiate products and the ability to control expenses. At the end of this section it is shown that companies are not obliged to seek high **margins**. Some cannot, because of strong competitive factors. Yet they still make a satisfactory return on capital employed by making efficient use of the equipment held as fixed (non-current) assets.

Gross profit percentage	$\dfrac{\text{Gross profit}}{\text{Sales (revenue)}} \times 100\%$

Comment. The gross profit as a percentage of sales (revenue) is also referred to as the **gross margin**. It has been seen in earlier chapters that the gross profit is equal to sales (revenue) minus all cost of sales. That gross profit may be compared with sales (revenue) as shown above. The gross profit percentage concentrates on costs of making goods and services ready for sale. Small changes in this ratio can be highly significant. There tends to be a view that there is a 'normal' value for the industry or for the product that may be used as a benchmark against which to measure a company's performance.

Because it is such a sensitive measure, many companies try to keep secret from their competitors and customers the detailed breakdown of gross profit for each product line or area of activity. Companies do not want to give competitors any clues on how much to undercut prices and do not want to give customers a chance to complain about excessive profits.

Total assets usage	$\dfrac{\text{Sales (revenue)}}{\text{Total assets}} \times 100\%$

Comment. **Total assets usage** indicates how well a company has used its fixed and current assets to generate sales (revenue). Such a ratio is probably most useful as an indication of trends over a period of years. There is no particular value which is too high or too low but a sudden change would prompt the observer to ask questions.

Fixed assets (non-current assets) usage	$\dfrac{\text{Sales (revenue)}}{\text{Fixed assets (non-current assets)}} \times 100\%$

Comment. **Fixed assets usage** is a similar measure of usage, but one which concentrates on the productive capacity as measured by fixed assets, indicates how successful the company is in generating sales (revenue) from fixed assets (non-current assets). The ratio may be interpreted as showing how many £s of sales (revenue) have been generated by each £ of fixed assets.

13.3.3 Liquidity and working capital

Liquidity is a word which refers to the availability of cash in the near future after taking account of immediate financial commitments. Cash in the near future will be available from bank deposits, cash released by sale of stocks and cash collected from customers. Immediate financial commitments are shown in current liabilities. The first ratio of liquidity is therefore a simple comparison of current assets with current liabilities.

Current ratio	Current assets:Current liabilities

Comment. If the current assets amount to £20m and the current liabilities amount to £10m the company is said, in words, to have 'a current ratio of 2 to 1'. Some commentators abbreviate this by saying 'the current ratio is 2'. Mathematically that is incorrect wording but the listener is expected to know that the words 'to 1' have been omitted from the end of the sentence.

The current ratio indicates the extent to which short-term assets are available to meet short-term liabilities. A current ratio of 2:1 is regarded, broadly speaking, as being a reasonable order of magnitude. As with other ratios, there is no 'best' answer for any particular company and it is the trend in this ratio which is more important. If the ratio is worsening over time, and especially if it falls to less than 1:1, the observer would look closely at the cash flow. A company can survive provided it can meet its obligations as they fall due. Some companies therefore operate on a very tight current ratio because they are able to plan the timing of inflows and outflows of cash quite precisely.

Companies which generate cash on a daily basis, such as retail stores, can therefore operate on a lower current ratio. Manufacturing businesses which have to hold substantial stocks would operate on a higher current ratio.

Acid test	Current assets minus inventories (stock):Current liabilities

Comment. In a crisis, where short-term creditors are demanding payment, the possibility of selling stocks (inventories) to raise cash may be unrealistic. The **acid test** takes a closer look at the liquid assets of the current ratio, omitting the stocks (inventories). For many companies this ratio is less than 1:1 because it is unlikely that all creditors will require payment at the same time. As with the current ratio, an understanding of the acid test has to be supported by an understanding of the pattern of cash flows. Analysts in particular will often ask companies about the peak borrowing requirements of the year and the timing of that peak in relation to cash inflows.

Stock holding period (inventories holding period)	$\dfrac{\text{Average inventories (stock) held}}{\text{Cost sales (revenue)}} \times 365$

Comment. The **stock holding period** (inventories holding period) measures the average period during which stocks (inventories) of goods are held before being sold or used in the operations of the business. It is usually expressed in days, which is why the figure of 365 appears in the formula. If months are preferred, then the figure 12 should be substituted for the figure 365. One point of view is that the shorter the period, the better. An opposite point of view is that too short a period may create a greater risk of finding that the business is short of a stock item.

In calculating the stock holding period it is preferable to use the average of the stock (inventories) held at the start of the year and the stock (inventories) held at the end of the year. Some analysts use only the year-end figure if the start-of-year figure is not available. Whatever variation is used, it is important to be consistent from one time period to the next.

Customers (trade debtors collection period)	$\dfrac{\text{Total receivables (trade debtors)}}{\text{Credit sales (revenue)}} \times 365$

Comment. The **customers'** (trade debtors') **collection period** measures the average period of credit allowed to credit customers. An increase in this measure would indicate that a company is building up cash flow problems, although an attempt to decrease the period of credit allowed might deter customers and cause them to seek a competitor who gives a longer period of credit. It is important to be aware of the normal credit period for the industry. Some companies offer discount for prompt payment. Any offer of discount should weigh the cost of the discount against the benefit of earlier receipt of cash from customers. When you are looking for information in the annual report of companies using the IASB system you will probably have to start on the face of the statement of financial position (balance sheet) with the heading 'trade and other receivables' and then read the corresponding Note to the statement of financial position (balance sheet) to find the amount of trade receivables. If you are looking at the statement of financial position (balance sheet) of a company that does not use the IASB system you will have to find the Note to the statement of financial position (balance sheet) that gives detailed information about trade debtors.

Suppliers (trade creditors) payment period	$\dfrac{\text{Trade payables (trade creditors)}}{\text{Credit purchases}} \times 365$

Comment. The **suppliers'** (trade creditors') **payment period** measures the average period of credit taken from suppliers of goods and services. An increase in this measure could indicate that the supplier has allowed a longer period to pay. It could also indicate that the company is taking longer to pay, perhaps because of cash flow problems. If payment is delayed then the company may lose discounts available for prompt payments. A reputation for being a slow payer could make it more difficult to obtain supplies in future. Some large companies have gained a reputation for delaying payment to smaller suppliers. Company law now requires company directors to make a statement of policy in relation to creditor payment.

Companies do not usually report **purchases** directly, so the figure must be calculated as follows:

$$\text{Purchases} = \text{Cost of goods sold} + \text{Closing stock} - \text{Opening stock}$$

Analysts often use **cost of goods sold** rather than calculate purchases, arguing that stock levels are broadly similar at corresponding period-ends.

Working capital cycle	Stock (inventories) holding period PLUS Customers (trade debtors) collection period MINUS Suppliers (trade creditors) payment period

Comment. You saw in Chapter 9 (Figure 9.1) the **working capital cycle** whereby stocks (inventories) are purchased on credit, then sold to customers who eventually pay cash. The cash is used to pay suppliers and the cycle starts again. We can now put some timings into the diagram. The working capital represents the long-term finance needed to cover current assets that are not matched by current liabilities. The longer the total of the stock holding period and customer collection period, compared to the suppliers payment period, the greater the need for working capital to be financed long term.

13.3.4 Gearing

The term **gearing** is used to describe the mix of loan finance and equity finance in a company. It is more properly called **financial gearing** and in American texts is called **leverage**. There are two main approaches to measuring gearing. The first looks at the statement of financial position (balance sheet) and the second looks at the income statement (profit and loss account).

Debt/equity ratio	$\dfrac{\text{Long-term liabilities plus Preference share capital*}}{\text{Equity share capital} + \text{reserves}} \times 100\%$

* Where preference share capital is in existence.

Comment. From the statement of financial position (balance sheet) perspective the **gearing** measure considers the relative proportions of long-term (non-current) loans and equity in the long-term financing of the business. The precise meaning of long-term liabilities will vary from one company to the next. It is intended to cover the loans taken out with the aim of making them a permanent part of the company's financing policy. As they come due for repayment, they are replaced by further long-term finance. The starting point is the loans (but not the provisions) contained in the section headed *non-current liabilities.* However, the accounting rules require separate reporting of loans due for repayment within one year, reported as current liabilities. It is necessary to look in the *current liabilities* for bank loans that are becoming due for repayment. In some companies the bank overdraft is a semi-permanent feature and so is included in this ratio calculation.

Preference share capital is included in the numerator because it has the characteristics of debt finance even although it is not classed as debt in company law. The preference shareholders have the first right to dividend, before the ordinary shareholders receive any dividend. This is why they are called 'preference' shares. The amount of the dividend is usually fixed as a percentage of nominal value of shares. The amount repaid to preference shareholders on maturity is the amount of the share capital only. They do not normally take a share of accumulated profits.

Some companies say 'we have interest-bearing obligations such as bank overdrafts, long-term liabilities and preference shares but we also have cash and cash equivalents that are earning interest. We prefer to deduct the assets from the liabilities to calculate the **net debt**'. An alternative form of gearing ratio is therefore defined by calculating net debt as all interest-bearing liabilities minus cash and cash equivalents.

Debt/equity ratio	$\dfrac{\text{Net debt}}{\text{Equity share capital + reserves}} \times 100$

Different industries have different average levels, depending on the types of assets held and the stability or otherwise of the stream of profits. A low gearing percentage indicates a low exposure to financial risk because it means that there will be little difficulty in paying loan interest and repaying the loans as they fall due. A high gearing percentage indicates a high exposure to financial risk because it means that there are interest charges to be met and a requirement to repay the loans on the due date.

Interest cover	$\dfrac{\text{Operating profit (before interest and tax)}}{\text{Interest}}$

Comment. The importance of being able to meet interest payments on borrowed funds is emphasised by measuring gearing in terms of the income statement (profit and loss account). If the profit generated before interest and tax is sufficient to give high cover for the interest charges, then it is unlikely that the company is over-committing itself in its borrowing. If the interest cover is falling or is low, then there may be increasing cause for concern.

Activity 13.1

Write down the name of each ratio given in this section. Close the book and test your knowledge by writing down the formula for each ratio. Then write one sentence for each ratio which explains its purpose. Be sure that you know each ratio and understand its purpose before you proceed with the rest of the chapter.

13.4 Investors' views on risk and return

Uncertainty about the future means that all investments contain an element of risk. For investors who are averse to risk, there is a fear of income falling below an acceptable level and a fear of losing the capital invested in the company. Given a choice between two investments offering the same expected return, risk-averse investors will choose the least risky investment.

13.4.1 Return

The word **return** has many meanings but for an investor the basic question is, 'What have I gained from owning these shares?' One simple formula which answers that question is:

$$\frac{(Market\ price\ of\ share\ today - Price\ paid\ for\ share) + Dividends\ received}{Price\ paid\ for\ share} \times 100\%$$

Investors in a company which is in a low-risk industry may be willing to accept a low rate of return. Investors in a company which is in a high-risk industry will be seeking a higher rate of return to compensate for the additional risk they take.

Research has shown that share prices react very rapidly to any item of information which is sufficiently important to affect investors' decisions. This phenomenon is sometimes referred to as the **efficient markets hypothesis**, which is a statement that share prices react immediately to make allowance for each new item of information made available. The annual results of a listed company are announced through the Stock Exchange by means of a document called a **preliminary announcement**, issued approximately two months after the accounting year-end. The annual report then goes to the printers and is distributed to shareholders about three months after the related year-end.

When investors evaluate share price by calculating return, they take the most up-to-date price available.

13.4.2 Risk

There are two main types of risk: operating risk and financial risk.

Operating risk exists where there are factors which could cause sales (revenue) to fluctuate or cause costs to increase. Companies are particularly vulnerable to operating risk when they have a relatively high level of fixed operating costs. These fixed costs are incurred independently of the level of activity. If sales (revenue) fall, or the direct costs of sales increase, the fixed costs become a greater burden on profit.

Financial risk exists where the company has loan finance, especially long-term loan finance where the company cannot relinquish its commitment. Loan finance carries an obligation to pay interest charges and these create a problem similar to the fixed costs problem. If the sales (revenue) are strong and the direct costs of sales are well under control, then interest charges will not be a problem. If sales (revenue) fall, or the direct costs of sales rise, then a company may find that it does not have the cash resources to meet the interest payments as they fall due. Repaying the loan could become an even greater worry.

Both operating risk and financial risk are important to the company's shareholders because they have the residual claim on assets after all liabilities are met. If the company's assets are growing then these risks will not pose a problem but if the business becomes slack then the combination of high fixed operating costs and high interest charges could be disastrous. As a rule of thumb, investors look for low financial risk in companies which have high operating risk and, conversely, will tolerate a higher level of financial risk where there is relatively low operating risk.

The terms **operating gearing** and **financial gearing** are frequently used to describe the extent of operating risk and financial risk. (Financial gearing has been explained in the previous section.) In terms of the income statement (profit and loss account) they are defined as follows:

Operating gearing	$\dfrac{\text{Profit before fixed operating costs}}{\text{Fixed operating costs}}$

Financial gearing	$\dfrac{\text{Profit before interest charges}}{\text{Interest charges}}$

In analysis of published accounting information, it is not possible to estimate the operating gearing because detailed information on fixed costs is not provided. Thus the term **gearing** is applied only in measuring financial gearing. Despite the lack of published information, professional investors will be aware of the importance of operating gearing and will try to understand as much as possible about the cost structure of the company and of the industry. The next section illustrates the benefits to shareholders of having gearing present when operating profits are rising and the risks when operating profits are falling.

13.4.3 Impact of gearing when profits are fluctuating

In a situation of fluctuating profits the presence of a fixed charge, such as an interest payment, will cause the profit for ordinary shareholders to fluctuate by a greater percentage. Table 13.1 sets out data to illustrate this fluctuation. Company X has no gearing but company Y has loan finance in its capital structure.

Table 13.1
Data to illustrate the effect of gearing on profits for ordinary shareholders

	X plc £m	Y plc £m
Summary statement of financial position (balance sheet)		
Total assets minus current liabilities	1,000	1,000
Ordinary shares (£1 nominal value per share)	1,000	500
Loan stock (10% per annum)	–	500
	1,000	1,000
Expected level of profit		
Operating profit	100	100
Interest	–	(50)
Net profit for ordinary shareholders (A)	100	50

Table 13.2 uses the data to ask 'what happens to earnings per share if there is an increase or a decrease in operating profit?'

Table 13.2
Fluctuations in profit

(a) Effect of 20% decrease in operating profit		
Operating profit	80	80
Interest		(50)
Net profit for ordinary shareholders (B)	80	30
Percentage decrease of (B) on (A)	20%	40%
(b) Effect of 20% increase in operating profit		
Operating profit	120	120
Interest	–	(50)
Net profit for ordinary shareholders (C)	120	70
Percentage increase of (C) on (A)	20%	40%

The conclusion to be drawn from Table 13.2, panels (a) and (b), is that a 20% increase or decrease in operating profit causes a corresponding 20% increase or decrease in profit for ordinary shareholders in the ungeared company but a 40% increase or decrease in profit for ordinary shareholders in the geared company. It would appear preferable to be a shareholder in a geared company when profits are rising but to be a shareholder in an ungeared company when profits are falling.

13.5 Pyramid of ratios

The various ratios which contribute to the analysis of management performance may be thought of as forming a pyramid, as in Figure 13.1.

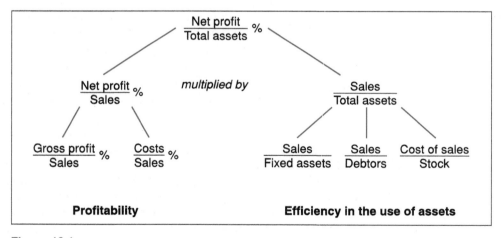

Figure 13.1
Pyramid of ratios for analysis of management performance

At the apex is the **return on capital employed** (measuring capital employed here as total assets). As the pyramid spreads out there are more detailed explanations of how the pyramid is built up. Net profit as a percentage of total assets has two components. One is the net profit as a percentage of sales (revenue) and the other is sales (revenue) as a multiple of total assets. Multiply these two together and you return to the net profit as a percentage of total assets. This relationship indicates that there could be two quite different types of business, both of which may be highly successful. One business trades on low margins, charging prices which look highly competitive, and succeeds by having a high level of sales (revenue) so that the assets are being used very effectively. The other business trades on high margins and sells goods or services less frequently. You could contrast the discount furniture store on the outskirts of town, where the car park is always full and the prices are unbeatable, with the old-world charm of the retail furnisher in the town centre whose prices look high but which attracts customers preferring extra service and attention. Both businesses are able to earn sufficient return on total assets to satisfy the owners.

The pyramid then spreads out into two areas: profitability and efficiency in the use of assets. The relationships here are additive – each component explains a little of the profitability of sales (revenue) or the efficiency in the use of assets. The pyramid is a useful tool of detective work to trace the cause of a change in return on capital employed.

13.6 Use and limitations of ratio analysis

The important feature of ratios is that they indicate trends and deviations from expected patterns. Ratios taken in isolation for a single company or a single period of time are of limited usefulness. The first requirement is to find a benchmark against which to compare ratios calculated for one period only.

13.6.1 Evaluating ratios by comparison

The comparison could be made with any or all of:

- the company's prior expectations of the outcome
- external observers' prior expectations of the outcome
- ratios based on previous years' figures for this company
- ratios calculated from this year's figures for other companies
- ratios calculated from previous years' figures for other companies
- industry averages published by commercial organisations.

The company's prior expectations are set out in a budget which is usually kept confidential. It is therefore unlikely that the user of the financial statements will have access to such a high-quality source of comparison. External observers may also have prior expectations. Professional analysts make forecasts of profits to help them or their clients in making investment decisions. The forecasts may be sent to clients of professional advisers, by way of investment advice bulletins. There are directories which publish such forecasts.

In the absence of information based on expectations, the user of the annual report may have to rely on the past as a possible predictor of the future, or on comparisons with other companies and industry norms. Professional investment advisers will collect data from annual reports and calculate ratios in their preferred manner. Advisory services will process the information and sell the results in the form of directories, online search facilities or CD-ROM with regular updates. One of the most widely used sources of ratio analysis of company accounts is Datastream, available in many colleges and universities and also used commercially. Organisations such as Reuters publish regular analyses of company information but usually charge a commercial fee. Newspapers and weekly journals such as the *Financial Times* and the *Investors Chronicle* are yet another source of information which will include ratios.

It could be argued that companies should themselves publish the norms against which their own particular results may be compared, but most would claim that their business is unique and no comparisons would be entirely valid.

13.6.2 Limitations

No two companies are exactly alike in the nature of their operations. Comparisons must make allowances for differences in the types of business or the relative weighting of different types of business. Many companies operate in more than one industry so that comparison with industry norms has to be treated with care.

Accounting numbers are used in ratio analysis and it has been a theme of the preceding chapters that accounting numbers may be affected by different accounting policies. The most common causes of variation due to accounting policy differences lie in depreciation and stock valuation, both of which are highly subjective.

Ratios are primarily a starting point from which to identify further questions to ask about the present position and future directions of the operations and the financing of a company. They do not provide answers in themselves.

13.7 Worked example of ratio analysis

In the following worked example, information is provided about a company buying and selling television and video equipment. Data are given for the current year in the first pair of columns and there are comparative figures for the previous year in the second pair of columns. Ratios are calculated for the two years as an indication of trends. Tentative comments are provided as to the possible interpretation of the resulting figures.

13.7.1 Financial statements to be analysed

Peter (Television) plc
Income statement (profit and loss account)
for the year ended 31 December Year 2

	Year 2		Year 1	
	£m	£m	£m	£m
Revenue		720		600
Cost of sales		(432)		(348)
Gross profit		288		252
Distribution costs	(72)		(54)	
Administrative expenses	(87)		(81)	
		(159)		(135)
Operating profit		129		117
Interest payable		(24)		(24)
Profit before taxation		105		93
Taxation		(42)		(37)
Profit for the period for ordinary equity holders		63		56

Statement of financial position (balance sheet)
as at 31 December Year 2

	£m	£m	£m	£m
Non-current (fixed) assets:				
Land and buildings		600		615
Plant and equipment		555		503
		1,155		1,118
Current assets:				
Inventories (stock)	115		82	
Trade receivables (debtors)	89		61	
Prepayments	10		9	
Bank	6		46	
	220		198	

Current liabilities				
Trade payables (creditors)	(45)		(30)	
Taxation	(21)		(19)	
Accruals	(29)		(25)	
	(95)		(74)	
Net current assets		125		124
		1,280		1,242
6% debentures		(400)		(400)
		880		842
Ordinary shares of £1 each		500		500
Retained earnings		380		342
Share capital and reserves		880		842

Extract from directors' report

The directors propose a dividend of 6.0 pence per share in respect of Year 2 (Year 1: 5.0 pence), amounting to £30m in total (Year 1: £25m).

Notes to the financial statements: reconcilation of movements in equity

	£m
Share capital and reserves at the end of year 1	842
Less dividend paid in respect of year 1	(25)
Add profit for year 2	63
Share capital and reserves at the end of year 2	880

13.7.2 Share price information

When investors evaluate share price, they take the most up-to-date price available. However, for the exercise of comparing financial ratios it is useful to take the share prices immediately after the preliminary announcement at the end of February or beginning of March, representing the market's opinion when the accounting information has not become too much out of date.

Market price at 1 March Year 2	202 pence
Market price at 1 March Year 3	277 pence

13.7.3 Presenting the ratio calculations

Because there are so many variations on the methods of calculating ratios in accounting, it is extremely important to practise a useful and informative layout. That must include, at a minimum:

- the name of each ratio
- the formula in words
- the workings to show how the formula has been applied
- the value of the ratio
- a narrative comment.

Tables 13.3 to 13.6 present this information in a set of ratio calculations for Peter (Television) plc, each exhibit covering one of the main headings explained earlier. The calculations are given first for the more recent year, Year 2, followed by the comparative figures for Year 1. A commentary is provided for each table.

Activity 13.2

Use the ratios explained in section 13.6 to carry out a full analysis of the Year 2 column of the accounts of Peter (Television) plc. Prepare your analysis before you read Tables 13.3 to 13.6. When you have finished, compare your analysis with the ratios calculated. Where your answers differ, be sure that you understand whether it is due to an arithmetic error or a more fundamental point. Keep a note of your score of the number of items calculated correctly.

Then go back to Year 1 and repeat the exercise. Hopefully your score of correct items will have increased.

Table 13.3
Investor ratios

Ratio	Definition in words	Year 2		Year 1	
		Workings	Result	Workings	Result
Earnings per share	$\dfrac{\text{Profit after tax for ordinary equity holders}}{\text{Number of issued ordinary shares}}$	$\dfrac{63}{500}$	12.6p	$\dfrac{56}{500}$	11.2p
Price earnings ratio	$\dfrac{\text{Share price}}{\text{Earnings per share}}$	$\dfrac{277}{12.6}$	22	$\dfrac{202}{11.2}$	18
Dividend per share	$\dfrac{\text{Dividend of the period}}{\text{Number of issued ordinary shares}}$	$\dfrac{30}{100}$	6.0p	$\dfrac{25}{500}$	5.0p
Dividend cover (payout ratio)	$\dfrac{\text{Earnings per share}}{\text{Dividend per share}}$	$\dfrac{12.6}{6.0}$	2.1 times	$\dfrac{11.2}{5.0}$	2.24 times
Dividend yield	$\dfrac{\text{Dividend per share}}{\text{Share price}} \times 100$	$\dfrac{6.0}{277} \times 100\%$	2.17%	$\dfrac{5.0}{202} \times 100\%$	2.48%

Comment. Earnings per share increased over the period, indicating an improved profit performance for shareholders. The price earnings ratio rose, indicating greater confidence in the stock market about the sustainability of this new level of profit. The dividend cover has fallen marginally, but is still more than twice covered. This marginal decrease in dividend cover is caused by increasing the dividend per share from 5 pence to 6 pence. The dividend yield has fallen, despite the increased dividend per share, because the market price has risen. The fall in yield may not be significant if it reflects a general trend in the market where, possibly, all shares have risen in price over the year. To say anything more about these ratios requires comparative figures for the industry and for the market as a whole. Both types of data would be found in the *Financial Times*.

Table 13.4
Analysis of management performance

Ratio	Definition in words	Year 2		Year 1	
		Workings	Result	Workings	Result
Return on shareholders' equity	$\dfrac{\text{Profit after tax for ordinary equity holders}}{\text{Share capital} + \text{Reserves}} \times 100\%$	$\dfrac{63}{880} \times 100\%$	7.2%	$\dfrac{56}{842} \times 100\%$	6.7%
Return on capital employed	$\dfrac{\text{Operating profit (before interest and tax)}}{(\text{Total assets} - \text{Current liabilities})} \times 100\%$	$\dfrac{129}{1,280} \times 100\%$	10.1%	$\dfrac{117}{1,242} \times 100\%$	9.4%
Operating profit on sales (revenue)	$\dfrac{\text{Operating profit (before interest and tax)}}{\text{Sales (revenue)}} \times 100\%$	$\dfrac{129}{720} \times 100\%$	17.9%	$\dfrac{117}{600} \times 100\%$	19.5%
Gross profit percentage	$\dfrac{\text{Gross profit}}{\text{Sales (revenue)}} \times 100\%$	$\dfrac{288}{720} \times 100\%$	40%	$\dfrac{252}{600} \times 100\%$	42%
Total assets usage	$\dfrac{\text{Sales (revenue)}}{\text{Total assets}} \times 100\%$	$\dfrac{720}{(1,155 + 220)}$	0.52 times	$\dfrac{600}{(1,118 + 198)}$	0.46 times
Fixed assets (non-current assets) usage	$\dfrac{\text{Sales (revenue)}}{\text{Fixed assets (non-current assets)}} \times 100\%$	$\dfrac{720}{1,155}$	0.62 times	$\dfrac{600}{1,118}$	0.54 times

Comment. The return on shareholders' equity and the return on capital employed both show an improvement on the previous year. This is due to an improvement in the use of assets (total assets and fixed assets) which more than offsets a fall in the operating profit as a percentage of sales (revenue). The gross profit percentage fell by a similar amount, which suggests that the price charged for goods and services is not keeping pace with increases in costs. The company should look carefully at either increasing prices or attempting to control costs of goods sold more effectively.

Table 13.5
Liquidity and working capital

Ratio	Definition in words	Year 2		Year 1	
		Workings	Result	Workings	Result
Current ratio	Current assets:Current liabilities	220:95	2.3:1	198:74	2.7:1
Acid test	(Current assets − inventories):Current liabilities	(220 − 115):95	1.11:1	(198 − 82):74	1.11:1
Stock holding period (inventories holding period)	$\dfrac{\text{Average inventories (stock) held}}{\text{Cost of sales}} \times 365$	$\dfrac{(115 + 82)/2}{432} \times 365$	83.2 days	$\dfrac{(*82 + 82)/2}{348} \times 365$	86 days
Customers (trade debtors) collection period	$\dfrac{\text{Trade receivables (trade debtors)}}{\text{Credit sales (revenue)}} \times 365$	$\dfrac{89}{720} \times 365$	45.1 days	$\dfrac{61}{600} \times 365$	37.1 days
Suppliers (trade creditors) payment period	$\dfrac{\text{Trade payables (trade creditors)}}{\text{Credit purchases}} \times 365$	$\dfrac{45}{432 + 115 - 82} \times 365$	35.3 days	$\dfrac{30}{348 + 82 - {}^*82} \times 365$	31.5 days

Note: *Assuming the opening inventories are the same as the closing inventories.

Comment. The current ratio has fallen over the period while the acid test ratio remains constant. The ratios appear relatively high and are probably still within acceptable ranges (although this needs to be confirmed by comparison with industry norms). One cause of the relatively high current ratio at the start and end of the period appears to be in the combination of stock holding period and customers collection period compared to the suppliers payment period. The period of credit taken by customers has increased and this should be investigated as a matter of urgency. There is a marginal decrease in the stock holding period but it remains relatively long, compared to the creditors payment period. The acid test remains similar because there is an increase in the number of customer days for payment and a similar increase in the number of supplier days for payment.

Table 13.6
Gearing (leverage)

Ratio	Definition in words	Year 2		Year 1	
		Workings	Result	Workings	Result
Debt/equity ratio	$\dfrac{\text{Long-term liabilities plus Preference share capital}}{\text{Equity share capital + reserves}} \times 100\%$	$\dfrac{400}{880} \times 100\%$	45.5%	$\dfrac{400}{842} \times 100\%$	47.5%
Interest cover	$\dfrac{\text{Operating profit (before interest and tax)}}{\text{Interest}} \times 100\%$	$\dfrac{129}{24}$	5.38 times	$\dfrac{117}{24}$	4.88 times

Comment. Gearing in the statement of financial position (balance sheet) has remained almost constant and the interest cover has increased marginally. The relative stability of the position indicates that there is probably no cause for concern but the ratios should be compared with those for similar companies in the industry.

13.8 Linking ratios to the statement of cash flows

In Chapter 7 the statement of cash flows of a company was illustrated and discussed. Any ratio analysis which seeks to interpret liquidity, management performance or financial structure should be related to the information provided by the statement of cash flows. Ratios give a measure of position at a particular point in time while the statement of cash flows gives some understanding of the movements in cash and cash-related items.

The operating cash flow will be explained by a note showing the movements in working capital and these may usefully be linked to changes in the rate of movement of stock or the period of credit allowed to customers and taken from suppliers. The ratio will give the change in terms of number of days, while the statement of cash flows will indicate the overall impact on liquid resources.

If the efficiency in the use of fixed assets appears to have fallen, it may be that new assets were acquired during the year which, at the statement of financial position (balance sheet) date, were not fully effective in generating sales. That acquisition will appear in the statement of cash flows. If the gearing has changed, the impact on cash flow will be revealed in the statement of cash flows.

Activity 13.3

Read again the sections of Chapters 3, 4 and 7 on statements of cash flows. What is the purpose of the statement of cash flows? What are the main headings? Which ratios may be used in conjunction with the statement of cash flows to help understand the financial position of the company?

13.8.1 Explanation of a statement of cash flows

The statement of cash flows in Table 13.7 is calculated from the statements of financial position (balance sheets) and income statement (profit and loss account) of Peter (Television) plc (see section 13.6). It is presented using headings similar to those of Safe and Sure in Chapter 7. The headings are taken from the international accounting standard IAS 7.

In Chapters 3, 5 and 6 you saw simple statements of cash flows prepared using the information entered in the cash column of a spreadsheet. Those were examples of what is called the **direct method** of preparing a statement of cash flows because the figures came directly from the cash column of the transaction spreadsheet. The statement of cash flows in Table 13.7 is said to be prepared using the **indirect method** because it takes an indirect route of starting with an accruals-based profit figure and then making adjustments to arrive at the cash figure. Consider each line in turn.

One purpose of the statement of cash flows is to answer the question, 'Why do we have a cash problem despite making an operating profit?' We saw in Table 3.7 of Chapter 3 that profit and cash flow can be different because the cash generated in making a profit is spent in various ways. The statement of cash flows emphasises ways in which cash has come into, or moved out of, the company. So we start with profit before taxation of £129m.

Depreciation is an expense in the income statement (profit and loss account) which represents cost being shared across accounting periods. There is no cash flow and so there should be no deduction for this item. To correct the position, depreciation of £50m is 'added back' as an adjustment to the accounting profit.

Next we consider how changes in working capital have affected cash flow. Looking first at current assets, we find that the inventories (stocks) have increased from £82m to £115m. Allowing inventories (stocks) to increase has reduced the cash available for other purposes. Trade receivables (debtors) have increased from £61 to £89. This

Table 13.7
Statement of Cash flows

Peter (Television) plc
Statement of cash flows
for the year ended 31 December Year 2

Notes: assume depreciation charge for year is £50m.
    No non-current (fixed) assets were sold.

*The words and figures printed in italics are not normally shown in published
statements of cash flows – they are to help you with interpretation.*

	£m	£m
Cash flows from operating activities		
Profit before taxation		129
Adjustment for items not involving a flow of cash:		
Depreciation		50
		179
Increase in inventories (stocks) *(115 – 82)*	33	
Increase in trade receivables (debtors) *(89 – 61)*	28	
Increase in prepayments *(10 – 9)*	1	
Reduction in cash due to increases in current assets	62	
Increase in trade payables (creditors) *(45 – 30)*	(15)	
Increase in accruals *(29 – 25)*	(4)	
Increase in cash due to increases in liabilities	(19)	
Reduction in cash due to working capital changes		(43)
Cash generated from operations		136
Interest paid		(24)
Taxes paid *(42 + 19 – 21)*		(40)
Net cash inflow from operating activities		72
Cash flows from investing activities		
Capital expenditure *(1,155 – 1,118 + 50)*		(87)
		(15)
Cash flows from financing activities		
Equity dividends paid (dividend proposed at end of Year 1)		(25)
Decrease in cash		(40)
Check in statement of financial position (balance sheet)		
Decrease in bank (46 – 6) = 40		

---

means the cash is flowing less fast and so cash is reducing. Prepayments have
increased from £9m to £10m. This is also using up cash. In total the increases in
current assets have used up £62m of the cash generated in making profit.

Looking next at current liabilities, we see that trade payables (creditors) have
increased from £30m to £45m. If payables (creditors) are increasing, it means they are
not being paid. This helps cash flow by not spending it. Accruals have increased by
£4m, again helping cash flow by not making a payment. It is not a good idea to help
cash flow indefinitely by not paying creditors, but where stocks and debtors are
expanding to use up cash flow, it is helpful if current liabilities are expanding in a
similar way to hold back cash flow.

Interest paid is taken from the income statement (profit and loss account) as £24m.
There is no liability for unpaid interest at either the start or end of the period so the
amount in the income statement (profit and loss account) must equal the amount paid.

The taxation payment involves more calculation. Cash has been required to meet
the liability of £19m remaining in the Year 1 statement of financial position (balance
sheet), and also to pay half of the tax expense of Year 2, which is £21m. The calculation is: tax expense of the year as shown in the income statement (profit and loss

account), minus liability at the end of the year in the statement of financial position (balance sheet), plus liability at the start of the year in the statement of financial position (balance sheet).

Capital expenditure is calculated by comparing the book values at the beginning and end of the year and adjusting for changes during the year. We are told there were no sales of fixed assets so any increase must represent an addition. The balance started at £1,118m, fell by £50m for depreciation, increased by the unknown figure for additions, and finished at £1,155m. The missing figure is calculated as £87m.

The dividend paid during Year 2 was the dividend proposed at the end of Year 1. If you look back to section 13.7.1, you will see the dividend paid as an entry in the 'reconciliation of movements on equity'.

Finally the right-hand column of the statement of cash flows is added and produces a figure of £40m which is then checked against the statement of financial position (balance sheet) figures. This shows that cash has fallen from £46m to £6m and so the calculation is confirmed as being correct.

13.8.2 Analyst's commentary

Here is the comment made by one analyst in a briefing note to clients.

Despite making a profit before taxation of £129,000, the cash balances of the company have decreased by £40,000 during the year.

The cash generated by operating profit is calculated by adding back depreciation of £50,000 because this is an accounting expense which does not involve an outflow of cash. The resulting cash flow of £179,000 was eroded by allowing current assets to increase by more than the increase in current liabilities. This suggests that we should ask questions about the rate of usage of inventories (stocks) and the period of credit allowed to credit customers (debtors). Our analysis [see section 13.7] shows that the inventories (stocks) holding period reduced marginally from 86 to 83 days, which is not unexpected in the industry. The period of credit taken from suppliers increased by 4 days but the customers collection period increased by 8 days. Our attention should focus on the control of credit customers to look for any weaknesses of credit control and a potential risk of bad debts.

After paying interest charges and taxation the company was still in cash surplus at £72,000 but swung into cash deficit through capital expenditure of £87,000. Taking in the dividend payment of £25,000 the positive cash flow of £72,000 changed to a negative cash flow of £40,000.

We take the view that in the short run it is reasonable to run down cash balances in this way. The company probably had excessive liquidity at the end of Year 1. However, if there is to be a further major investment in fixed assets we would want to see long-term finance being raised, either through a share issue or through a new long-term loan.

13.8.3 EBITDA

EBITDA stands for earnings before interest, taxation, depreciation and amortisation. It is increasingly used by analysts as an approximate measure of cash flow because it removes the non-cash expenses of depreciation and amortisation from profit. Instead of a price–earnings multiple based on earnings per share, the analyst will relate share price to EBITDA. The reason appears to be a desire to get away from the subjectivity of accruals-based profit and closer to cash flow as something objectively measured.

13.8.4 Free cash flow

'Free cash flow' is a phrase that you may encounter in company reports, particularly in the narrative discussions by the chief executive and the finance director. It is a term that is used differently by different people and so you have to read it in the setting where it is used. A common theme is to say, 'We have calculated our operating cash flow and allowed for investment in working capital and we have deducted the amount of cash invested in capital expenditure.' How much cash does that leave free to pay dividends or to invest in new ideas for expansion?

Following this theme, the calculation of free cash flows generally starts with the net cash flow generated from operations (operating cash flow after tax) and then deducts the capital expenditure of the period. This leaves an amount of 'free' cash (in the sense of 'freely available' for future planning). The free cash is available to pay dividends to shareholders and to pay for further investment to expand the business. Directors have to decide their priorities and allocate the cash accordingly. If the free cash flow is a negative figure then the company will need to borrow to pay dividends or finance expansion.

13.9 Summary

The main areas of ratio analysis explained in this chapter are:

- investor ratios (summarised in Table 13.3)
- analysis of management performance (summarised in Table 13.4)
- liquidity and working capital (summarised in Table 13.5)
- gearing (summarised in Table 13.6).

Section 13.8 explains how the interpretation of ratios may be linked to an understanding of cash flows.

It is essential to treat ratio analysis with great caution and to understand the basis of calculation and the nature of the data used. For that reason the illustrations have been set out in detail using a layout that allows you to demonstrate your knowledge of the formula, your ability to collect data for calculation, and the result of that calculation which can then be interpreted. In this chapter all the information has been made available to you as and when you required it. In Chapter 14 we move on to consider published financial statements where more exploration may be required to find the most useful information.

The general principles explained in this chapter can be applied to the annual report of any profit-seeking business. The precise formulae may require adaptation to suit particular national characteristics. However, international comparison requires great caution. Accounting policies and practices are not yet harmonised entirely. If the underlying data are not comparable then neither are the ratios.

The key is to ask first, 'What value do we expect for this ratio?' Then calculate the ratio and seek an interpretation of the similarity or difference.

QUESTIONS

The Questions section of each chapter has three types of question. 'Test your understanding' questions to help you review your reading are in the 'A' series of questions. You will find the answers to these by reading and thinking about the material in the book. 'Application' questions to test your ability to apply technical skills are in the 'B' series of questions. Questions requiring you to show skills in problem solving and evaluation are in the 'C' series of questions. A letter [S] indicates that there is a solution at the end of the book.

A Test your understanding

A13.1 Which ratios provide information on performance for investors? (Section 13.3.1)

A13.2 Which ratios provide information on management performance? (Section 13.3.2)

A13.3 Which ratios provide information on liquidity and working capital? (Section 13.3.3)

A13.4 Which ratios provide information on gearing? (Section 13.3.4)

A13.5 What is the view of investors on risk and return? (Section 13.4)

A13.6 Why is financial gearing riskier for a company which has fluctuating profits? (Section 13.4.3)

A13.7 Explain the use of the pyramid of ratios in analysis of performance. (Section 13.5)

A13.8 What are the limitations of ratio analysis? (Section 13.6)

B Application

B13.1 [S]

The following financial statements relate to Hope plc:

Income statement (profit and loss account)
for the year ended 30 June Year 4

	£000s	£000s
Revenue		6,200
Cost of sales		(2,750)
Gross profit		3,450
Administration and selling expenses		(2,194)
Operating profit		1,256
Debenture interest		(84)
Profit before taxation		1,172
Taxation		(480)
Profit for equity holder		692

The directors have recommended a dividend of 36.7 pence per share in respect of Year 4, to be paid following approval at the next annual general meeting.

Statement of financial position (balance sheet)
as at 30 June Year 4

	£000s	£000s	£000s
Non-current (fixed assets) net of depreciation			1,750
Current assets:			
Inventory	620		
Trade receivables (debtors)	1,540		
Cash	200	2,360	
less: Current liabilities:			
Trade payables (creditors)	(300)		
Other creditors and accruals	(940)	(1,240)	
Net current assets			1,120
Total assets *less* current liabilities			2,870
Non-current liabilities			
6% debentures			(1,400)
Total net assets			1,470
Share capital and reserves			
Issued share capital:			
900,000 ordinary shares of 50p nominal value			450
Retained earnings			1,020
			1,470

Required
(a) Calculate ratios which measure:
  (i) liquidity and the use of working capital;
  (ii) management performance; and
  (iii) gearing.
(b) Explain how each ratio would help in understanding the financial position and results of the company.
(c) The market price is currently 1,100 pence per share. Calculate ratios which are useful to investors.

B13.2
The following financial statements relate to Charity plc:

Income statement (profit and loss account)
for year ended 30 September Year 4

	£000s	£000s
Revenue		2,480
Cost of sales		(1,100)
Gross profit		1,380
Administration and selling expenses		(678)
Operating profit		702
Debenture interest		(31)
Profit before taxation		671
Taxation		(154)
Profit for equity holders		517

Note: The directors have recommended a dividend of 11.4 pence per share in total in respect of Year 4, to be paid following approval at the next annual general meeting.

Statement of financial position (balance sheet)
as at 30 September Year 4

	£000s	£000s	£000s
Non-current assets, net of depreciation			785
Current assets:			
Inventories (stocks)	341		
Trade receivables (debtors)	801		
Cash	110	1,252	
less: Current liabilities			
Trade payables (creditors)	(90)		
Other payable and accruals	(654)	(744)	
Net current assets			508
Total assets *less* current liabilities			1,293
Non-current liabilities			
7% debentures			(440)
Total net assets			853
Share capital and reserves			
Issued share capital			
(1,360,000 ordinary shares of 25p nominal value)			340
Retained earnings			513
			853

Required
(a) Calculate ratios which measure:
  (i) liquidity and the use of working capital;
  (ii) management performance; and
  (iii) gearing.
(b) Explain how each ratio would help in understanding the financial position and results of the company.
(c) The market price of one share is 800 pence. Calculate ratios which will be of interest to investors.

C   Problem solving and evaluation

C13.1

Carry out a ratio analysis of Safe and Sure plc, using the financial statements set out in Appendix I (at the end of this book) and applying the method of analysis set out in section 13.6. Making a comparison of Year 7 with Year 6, write a short commentary on each ratio separately and then summarise the overall themes emerging from the ratios. Assume a share price of 260 pence is applicable at 31 December Year 7 and a share price of 210 pence is applicable at 31 December Year 6.

Chapter 14

Reporting corporate performance

Stakeholder engagement and performance

Extract from Corporate Responsibility report

These processes [of governance] are supported by stakeholder engagement, which helps to ensure Vodafone is aware of the issues relevant to the business and to provide a clear understanding of expectations of performance. Stakeholder consultations take place with customers, investors, employees, suppliers, the communities where the Group operates and where networks are based, governments, regulators and non-governmental organisations. Established in 2007, the Vodafone Corporate Responsibility Expert Advisory Panel comprises opinion leaders who are experts on CR issues important to Vodafone. The Panel met twice during the 2009 financial year and discussed the results of research on the socio-economic impact of mobile communications in India, climate change, the limits of Vodafone's responsibility and embedding business principles into company culture. In addition, the Group has continued to hold formal stakeholder engagement events, this year focused on climate change and mobile advertising. The Group has also published a CR dialogue on waste.

P. 45.

Key performance indicators

	2009	2008	2007
Vodafone Group excluding operations in India			
Energy use (GWh) (direct and indirect)	3,124	2,996	2,690
Carbon dioxide emissions (millions of tonnes)	1.31	1.37	1.18
Percentage of energy sourced from renewables	19	18	17
Estimate for operations in India			
Energy use (GWh) (direct and indirect)	2,049	–	–
Carbon dioxide emissions (millions of tonnes)	1.90	–	–
Number of phones collected for reuse and recycling (millions)	1.82	1.33	1.03
Network equipment waste generated excluding operations in India (tonnes)	4,860	4,287	9,960
Percentage of network equipment waste sent for reuse or recycling excluding operations in India	97	96	97

P. 47.

Source: Vodafone Group plc, Corporate Responsibility section of the Annual Report 2009.

Discussion points

1 How does the company engage with stakeholders?

2 How would the 'performance' information be viewed by different stakeholders?

Contents

Learning outcomes

After reading this chapter you should be able to:

- Explain the importance of the operating and financial review as a component of the annual report of a company.
- Describe and explain other useful information in the annual report that is relevant to analysis of corporate performance.
- Relate the interpretation of ratios to the information in a statement of cash flows.
- Explain how segmental information is useful to the analysis of corporate performance.

14.1 Introduction

You have learned from Chapter 13 the basic techniques of ratio analysis that may help you to interpret the performance of a company relative to other companies or other periods of time. You have also learned how the ratios may be linked to the statement of cash flows to interpret the factors affecting cash flow. It might be helpful to users of annual reports if companies themselves would carry out some analysis and interpretation of this type. There was a time when it was felt that the role of the company should stop at the presentation of the financial statements. Today, however, there is an expectation that companies will recognise the need to give more information to users, such as an objective discussion. The title of the discussion that is included in the annual report may be the **business review** or it may be the **operating and financial review** (OFR). Companies may choose to provide other guidance such as highlights statements and trends of data. Most large companies report group accounts which, as explained in Chapter 7, are quite complex. Because of this complexity, analysts like to receive segmental information that breaks the total information into key areas of activity of the business. Some companies have sought to avoid disclosing all their activities in group accounts by use of 'off-balance-sheet finance'. Because this omission may distort the view of performance, the standard-setters have tried to restrict the use of off-balance-sheet finance and encourage full reporting of group activities.

Beyond the responsibility for financial performance, the managers of companies have a responsibility and accountability to society in terms of their social and environmental activities. They are expected to demonstrate accountability by reporting on social and environmental activity in the annual report. The managers are also expected to follow best practice in the way they operate their business and in their relations with shareholders. This is described as corporate governance and the compliance with good practice in corporate governance must also be explained in the annual report.

Finally this chapter gives a taste of three areas of debate that extend beyond a first-level course in accounting but which help the student to be aware that studying accounting should include a questioning and thoughtful approach to what is being learned. These three areas of debate are: the meaning of 'true and fair'; the nature of value; and the relevance of the stakeholder model.

14.2 Operating and financial review (OFR) and business review

14.2.1 Development of the OFR and the business review

The operating and financial review (OFR) has been a feature of the annual reports of many UK listed companies since 1993.[1] It was created by the UK ASB as a move towards providing shareholders with information on a company's performance and prospects. The ASB received encouragement from the Cadbury Committee in its 1992 report on the financial aspects of corporate governance. From 1993 to 2005 the provision of an OFR was voluntary. The ASB hoped that giving companies wide discretion would encourage the development of best practice in reporting rather than a slavish adherence to rules which might result in a lacklustre document. Most larger listed companies published an OFR in the annual report.

In 2004 the European Commission issued its Modernisation Directive requiring all member states to incorporate a business review in the legislation governing annual reports. Initially the UK government intended to meet this requirement by making the OFR a legal requirement, because it felt that the OFR could cover all the requirements of the business review and achieve other useful purposes in communicating with shareholders. Very briefly, in 2005, the OFR became mandatory but by the start of 2006 the legislation had been repealed because the government decided that a mandatory OFR would be adding unnecessarily to the regulatory burden facing UK companies (referred to as 'gold plating' the regulation).

From comments made at that time it appeared that the OFR was a somewhat strange target for reducing regulation because users of annual reports found it useful and it was a location for reporting on the activities carried out by companies that harmonised with government policy on social issues. There is also a continuing strong movement towards more narrative discussion in annual reports, as explained later in this chapter.

UK companies are now faced with Company Law requiring a Business Review[2] and the UK ASB providing non-mandatory guidance on the OFR in *Reporting Statement 1 (RS 1): Operating and Financial Review*.[3] The ASB has indicated that following the recommendations of the OFR will cover the requirements of the business review. However, it seems that most companies prefer to use the 'business review' description.

14.2.2 Business review

The Companies Act 2006 explains that the purpose of the business review is to inform members of the company and help them assess how the directors have performed their duty to promote the success of the company. The business review must contain (a) a fair review of the company's business, and (b) a description of the principal risks and uncertainties facing the company.

The fair review is to be a balanced and comprehensive analysis of (a) the development and performance of the company's business during the financial year, and (b) the position of the company's business at the end of that year.

If the company is quoted on a stock exchange it must comply with further requirements that include:

(a) the main trends and factors likely to affect the future development, performance and position of the company's business; and
(b) information about:
  (i) environmental matters, including the impact of the company's business on the environment,
  (ii) the company's employees, and
  (iii) social and community issues
(c) information about persons with whom the company has contractual or other arrangements which are essential to the business of the company.

The review must also, to the extent necessary for an understanding of the development, performance or position of the company's business, include:

(a) analysis using financial key performance indicators, and
(b) where appropriate, analysis using other key performance indicators, including information relating to environmental matters and employee matters.

14.2.3   Key performance indicators (KPIs)

There is no specific guidance in the Companies Act on how to define **key performance indicators** (KPIs) but there is some guidance provided by the UK ASB in its Reporting Statement RS 1 on the *Operating and Financial Review*. KPIs are quantified measures of factors that help to measure the performance of the business effectively. They reflect 'critical success factors' and show how the entity is progressing towards its objectives.

The Reporting Statement RS 1 encourages the entity to provide in its OFR sufficient information to enable members to understand each KPI disclosed in the OFR. These KPIs are expected to become an important help to shareholders in understanding the performance of the entity as seen by the directors. For each KPI the directors should give a definition and explain the calculation. They should explain the purpose of the KPIs and the sources of data used, together with any assumptions made. There should be a commentary on each KPI and future targets, with comparative figures for the previous year. Where there is a change in a KPI there should be an explanation and a calculation giving comparison to previous years.

Examples of KPIs are:

- Return on capital employed (see Chapter 13).
- Market share – the revenue of the entity as a percentage of the industry total (e.g. a market leader demonstrating dominant position).
- Average revenue per customer (e.g. in a pay-per-view television service).
- Sales per square foot of selling space (e.g. a chain of retail stores).
- Employee costs per £ of sales (any labour-intensive business).
- Environmental spillage (e.g. in a business using toxic chemicals).

14.2.4   Directors' and auditors' responsibilities for the business review

The directors of the company are responsible for the preparation of the business review. The auditors read the business review, along with other narrative sections of the annual report, to satisfy themselves that there are no inconsistencies between the information in the narrative report and that in the financial statements. If they find an inconsistency they will discuss it with the directors and attempt to resolve the problem. When the business review was being introduced the government wanted a stronger form of audit that would review the process by which the business review was prepared, but this stronger form of audit was resisted by both auditors and directors. Commentators felt that too strong a burden would be placed on auditors and directors if subsequent events did not correspond to expectations raised by the business review.

14.2.5   Objective and principles of the OFR

Although the business review is the requirement of the Companies Act 2006, the UK ASB has retained its Reporting Statement for the OFR, asserting that a company which applies the OFR will also meet the requirements of the business review.[4]

The stated objective of the OFR is to provide a balanced and comprehensive analysis, consistent with the size and complexity of the business, of:[5]

(a) the development and performance of the business of the entity during the financial year;
(b) the position of the entity at the end of the financial year;
(c) the main trends and factors underlying the development, performance and position of the business of the entity during the financial year; and
(d) the main trends and factors which are likely to affect the entity's future development, performance and position, prepared so as to assist members to assess the strategies adopted by the entity and the potential for those strategies to succeed.

The objective mentions only 'members' of the company, which means the existing shareholders. Earlier drafts of the reporting standard attempted to widen the objective to include intending investors but this was criticised as being too wide-ranging. There is no mention of any other stakeholders. (Look back to Chapter 1 for the potential range of interested parties.)

The ASB sets out seven principles[6] followed by a disclosure framework.

1 The OFR shall set out an analysis of the business through the eyes of the board of directors.
2 The OFR shall focus on matters that are relevant to the interests of members.
3 The OFR shall have a forward-looking orientation, identifying those trends and factors relevant to the members' assessment of the current and future performance of the business and the progress towards the achievement of long-term business objectives.
4 The OFR shall complement as well as supplement the financial statements, in order to enhance the overall corporate disclosure.
5 The OFR shall be comprehensive and understandable.
6 The OFR shall be balanced and neutral, dealing even-handedly with both good and bad aspects.
7 The OFR shall be comparable over time.

What are the significant aspects of these principles? The idea of looking through the eyes of the directors is an important feature. It carries the idea of taking shareholders inside the company to reduce the gap between directors, who manage the company, and shareholders, who own the company. The forward-looking orientation is another important feature because shareholders want to make estimates of the future of their investment. 'Forward-looking' does not mean that the company will be making a forecast. The idea of balancing good and bad aspects is important but in practice it may be difficult to persuade directors to say as much about bad aspects as they do about the good ones. One argument the directors put forward is that if they disclose bad aspects of performance there will be loss of confidence and the bad will become worse.

14.2.6 OFR disclosure framework

The ASB does not set out a format or a template. It does not specify headings that must be included in an OFR. However, the section of the Reporting Standard describing the disclosure framework runs from paragraphs 27 to 76 with headings and bold-lettered paragraphs and liberal sprinkling of the verb 'shall' (meaning 'must'), so it seems likely that companies will tend to use similar headings.

The framework is introduced by a statement that the OFR shall provide information to assist members to assess the strategies adopted by the entity and the potential for those strategies to succeed. Four key elements of the framework are then specified:[7]

(a) The nature of the business, including a description of the market, competitive and regulatory environment in which the entity operates and the entity's objectives and strategies.
(b) The development and performance of the business, both in the financial year under review and in the future.
(c) The resources, principal risks and uncertainties and relationships that may affect the entity's long-term value.
(d) The position of the business including a description of the capital structure, treasury policies and objectives and liquidity of the entity, both in the financial year under review and in the future.

14.2.7   International developments

The International Accounting Standards Board has asked a project team of national standard-setters to develop proposals for a 'management commentary'. The project has been led by the New Zealand Financial Reporting Standards Board and other members of the project team are from standard-setters in Canada, Germany and the UK. From the planning drafts it seems likely that there will be similarities with the principles of the UK ASB's RS 1. In the US there is a requirement for a report called the Management's Discussion and Analysis (MD&A). This is required by the Securities and Exchange Commission (SEC) from all companies listed on one of the US stock exchanges (mainly the New York Stock Exchange or the NASDAQ over-the-counter market). The SEC has detailed regulations setting out the content of the MD&A. If you are studying or researching a US-listed company you may find the company's MD&A in its annual report or you may find it in the company's report to the SEC (called a 'form 10-K'). The company's web page for 'investors' is often the best place to search. Some UK companies have their shares listed on the New York Stock Exchange or NASDAQ. These companies also prepare an MD&A for the SEC but it is within a report called a 'form 20-F'. You will probably find this on the web page for 'investors' if you are studying or researching a UK company that has a listing in both London and New York.

Activity 14.1

Read through the sections on the business review and the OFR again. How much of the information suggested for the business review or the OFR is extracted directly from the financial statements? How much of the information suggested for the business review or the OFR provides additional understanding which is not available from the financial statements?

14.3   Other guidance in analysis

In Figure 7.1, there is a list of 'accompanying information' that may be found in the annual report. The first item listed there is the operating and financial review, explained in section 14.2. The second item is the Chairman's statement, which usually appears at the start of the annual report, as a short narrative lasting no more than a page and often preceded by a 'Highlights' statement of key financial measures. The Chairman sets out key features as an introduction to the detail that follows in later pages. The third item listed there is the Directors' report, which is usually found part-way through the annual report. Its contents are required partly by the Companies Act, partly by the UK Listing Agreement and partly by the Code of Corporate Governance. The fourth item is the historical summaries that allow trends to be seen over several years, with some companies giving five-year trends and others giving ten-year trends. The final item is 'non-accounting and non-financial information'. This covers the rest of the annual report and often provides the most interesting aspects for the reader who wants to understand the company in its entirety.

In this section we will consider the highlights statement and the historical trend analysis.

14.3.1 Highlights statement

Safe and Sure plc presents Highlights of Year 7 as follows:

		Year 7 £m	Increase %	Year 6 £m
Revenue	United Kingdom	323.4	31.1	246.7
	Europe	164.3	7.0	153.5
	North America	104.5	30.5	80.1
	Asia Pacific and Africa	122.4	12.3	109.0
	Total revenue	714.6	21.3	589.3
Profit	United Kingdom	97.4	28.8	69.7
	Europe	45.3	12.4	40.3
	North America	17.0	22.3	13.9
	Asia Pacific and Africa	35.5	17.9	30.1
	Net interest income	2.3		3.0
	Profit before tax	197.5	25.8	157.0
Earnings	Earnings per share	11.74p	20.9	9.71p
Dividends paid (pence per share)		3.02p	20.8	2.50p

The Highlights statement shows what the company regards as important information for investors as the primary users of the annual report. Turnover is a measure of the size of operations, with growth of turnover being an indicator of expansion. Profit is the reward for shareholders, with growth again being an important indicator. Segment figures are provided for both turnover and profit. This company has a target profit growth of 20% per annum and so is emphasising that it has more than met the target. Earnings per share and dividend per share are the key indicators from which investors can calculate yields based on the current market price. There is no regulation of highlights statements and so other companies may give different information. Together with the Chairman's statement, the Highlights present the key messages of the annual report.

14.3.2 Historical summaries and trend analysis

Listed companies usually provide a historical summary of the financial statements of previous years. The historical summary for Safe and Sure may be found in Appendix I. The analyst may use this table to establish trends of:

- year-on-year growth of turnover and operating profit
- growth rates adjusted for annual inflation
- key ratios.

The company does not usually carry out the ratio analysis; this is left to the analysts to calculate and interpret. On relatively rare occasions the company will provide ratios but it is not always clear which formula has been used.

14.3.3 Finance director's review

There are relatively few references to ratios in the annual reports of companies. Some finance directors claim that interpretation of ratios is a very complex matter. They say that if they provide ratio calculations in the annual report, then they will have to provide detailed explanation, which will make the report too lengthy. So in general they leave the ratios for others to calculate and interpret. Sometimes they will comment on a ratio where they know the expert users will ask questions.

In the operating and financial review of Safe and Sure plc the finance director states:

The pleasing return on our tangible net assets (42.4% per annum before tax on average net assets) reflects the high value of the intangible assets of the Safe and Sure brand and of businesses built up over the years. Such value is not reported in the statement of financial position (balance sheet).

Is it possible to check on the finance director's calculation? He has used pre-tax profit which is £177m (£197.5m from continuing and £20.5m from discontinued operations) and the average of the tangible net assets. The respective figures for Year 7 and Year 6 are £464.3m and £370.4m. The average net assets figure is therefore £417.4m. The calculation of the ratio is:

$$\frac{177}{417.4} \times 100\% = 42.4\%$$

which confirms the figure given by the finance director. (It should be noted that confirming ratios reported in annual reports is not always so straightforward, although it ought to be.) We need other evidence before we can agree that 42.4% is a 'pleasing' return.

In the next section, David aims to explain his approach to using ratios to pinpoint target areas for probing by way of questions to the company, while Leona explains how ratios are useful to the auditor.

14.3.4   The analyst and the auditor

DAVID: *We subscribe to the major online database sources of information about companies, so I don't very often sit down to calculate ratios. I'm more interested in the interpretation. There are a few key ratios that I look at for major clues as to strange goings-on and then I scan a more detailed ratio report for unusual changes. We can program in an instruction to set a warning flag against any ratio which has altered by more than a specified range since the previous figures, or over a given period of time.*

What do I look to first? Gross margins on turnover and net margins on turnover, with as much segmental detail as I can find. Segmental information is an area where often we do have to carry out our own analysis using our skills, experience and specialist sources of information. Not many databases break down the company's results by segment. Then I'll check the tax charge as a percentage of the taxable profit. It should be around 30% if the company's accounts have been accepted for tax purposes, but if there are items which the tax authorities don't allow, then the percentage will be different. I'm always interested in what appears in the income statement (profit and loss account) but is not accepted by the tax rules. Depreciation is a notoriously variable figure and is difficult to spot because the accounting rules say that a change in depreciation rate or useful asset life is not a change in policy. Companies have to draw attention to a change in policy and explain the impact. Depreciation escapes that rule. So I calculate the depreciation charge as a percentage of total asset value. If that percentage changes then I start asking questions.

Common-size statements are very useful. That means turning all items in the financial statements to percentages with the total assets represented by 100% in the statement of financial position (balance sheet) and the turnover represented by 100% in the income statement (profit and loss account). It is also useful to have percentage changes from one year to the next. That is all relatively easy when you are using spreadsheets.

Over a period of time I monitor the variability of a ratio for a particular company. I calculate this as:

$$\frac{\text{Maximum value} - \text{Minimum value}}{\text{Mean value of ratio}}$$

Again I am looking for unusual movements outside an expected range.

LEONA: *The auditors don't rely on anyone else's calculations. We carry out our own ratio analysis as part of our analytical review. For commercial, manufacturing and service companies we monitor a standard list of ratios which is:*

- *acid test ratio*
- *current ratio*
- *customers collection period*
- *inventories (stocks) holding period*
- *gearing*
- *interest cover*
- *return on capital employed*
- *return on total assets*
- *gross profit margin.*

We are looking at these with a focus on the particular concerns of the auditor. Possible liquidity crises or working capital shortages could raise a question as to whether the company is a going concern. Customer collection period provides a clue to whether the doubtful debt provision is adequate. Inventories holding period may indicate a need for provision for slow-moving inventories. Gearing and interest cover are further indicators of financial stability or otherwise in relation to the going concern issue. Return on capital employed and on total assets may show inefficient use of assets and perhaps point to assets which have no future benefit. Gross margins may cause us to ask questions about incorrect records of sales or stocks if the margins are different from the norms.

For listed companies we also look at the dividend cover and the Altman Z-score. The Z-score is a model developed for use in predicting insolvency. You need to read a finance textbook to get the details, but basically it is a combined score based on a list of key variables all pointing to potential insolvency problems. We have to be able to say that the business is a going concern, so that kind of information is important to us.

DAVID: *That's OK for the current year. What about trends?*

LEONA: *Yes, trends are an important part of our review. We try to use a predictive approach and estimate the current year's figure from the previous data rather than merely compare this year with last. Taking a predictive approach encourages us to challenge fluctuations and to seek persuasive explanations. We use all the familiar forms of trend analysis – graphical representation, moving averages and simple regression analysis.*

DAVID: *How much reliance do you place on these analytical procedures?*

LEONA: *It can range from conclusive reliance to no reliance at all. It depends very much on the nature of the assertions being tested, the plausibility and predictability of the relationships involved, and the extent to which data is available and reliable.*

DAVID: *Maybe I have underestimated auditors in the past. None of the activities you describe is really apparent from the audit report. Perhaps you undersell your work.*

LEONA: *I probably have to admit that our work stops when we have gained sufficient assurance to write the audit report. We don't give information to the reader – that is not the function of the audit.*

DAVID: *You and I need to spend more time together on this question of analysis in depth. Analysts with insight command top ratings and that's what I'm looking for. And I think the benefit would not all be one-way – I can help you with broader awareness of the strategies used by management in giving the markets the messages they want to convey.*

LEONA: *Sounds fine to me.*

14.4 Segmental information

In Sections 7.7 and 7.8, you read about the group structure used by many companies, and saw the method of construction of consolidated financial statements. Safe and Sure presents consolidated financial statements, which are discussed in section 7.4. The process of consolidation of financial information in group accounts is intended to be an improvement on sending the parent company shareholders a bundle of the separate financial statements of each member of the group. It lets them see, in one set of financial statements, the full picture of the group. On the negative side, the process of aggregation causes a loss of information about the various different activities of the group. In order to balance the benefits of aggregation with the need for detail, accounting provides additional information about the various segments of the group on a year-by-year basis.

14.4.1 Users' needs for information

Consolidated financial statements are a very convenient means of bringing together a large volume of data, but they suffer a major defect in losing much of the rich detail available from seeing each constituent company separately. It is particularly important for users of financial statements to know how the results of various activities compare, where the group of companies is involved in more than one product line and more than one type of market.

Segmental reporting has developed as a means of supplementing the consolidated financial statements by providing more insight into the activities of the group. In particular it reports information about the different types of products and services that an entity produces and the different geographical areas in which it operates.

The accounting standard which deals with segmental reporting[8] requires the entity to disclose information to enable users of its financial statements to evaluate the nature and financial effects of the business activities in which it engages and the economic environments in which it operates[9]. To achieve this objective the managers start by identifying the operating segments from which it earns revenues and incurs expenses. These operating segments will be regularly reviewed by the entity's 'chief operating decision maker'. The information provided about each segment will correspond to that provided to the chief operating decision maker. In this way the standard seeks to help the user of financial statements view the business in the way it is seen by its managers.

The entity must disclose some general information about how the reportable segments have been identified and the types of products and services from which each reportable segment derives its revenues. It must also report a measure of profit or loss and total assets for each reportable segment and a measure of liabilities for each segment if that information is regularly provided to the chief operating officer.

The entity must also disclose specific accounting information as set out in the following list, if these items are reported to the chief operating decision maker:

(a) revenues from external customers
(b) revenues from transactions with other operating segments of the same entity
(c) interest revenue
(d) interest expense
(e) depreciation and amortisation
(f) material items of income and expense
(g) the entity's interest in the profit or loss of associates and joint ventures
(h) income tax expense or income
(i) material non-cash items other than depreciation and amortisation.

The accounting standard containing these requirements took effect from 1 January 2009, so it may take some time to find out whether companies will disclose all the information listed here. Those commentators who were concerned about this standard felt that it gave too much discretion to the company management and could even be damaging to the quality of corporate governance. The IASB supported the standard by referring to research showing that when a similar standard was introduced in the US no detrimental effects were observed.

14.4.2 Information provided in the financial statements

The group statement of financial position (balance sheet) and income statement (profit and loss account) of Safe and Sure plc are presented in full in Chapter 7 and have been explored in more detail in subsequent chapters. Consequently you are already familiar with much of the information about the assets and liabilities of the group.

Parent company

Some companies publish the statement of financial position (balance sheet) of the parent company alongside or near to the group statement of financial position (balance sheet). This is a requirement for groups that continue to report under UK rules, but is not compulsory for group accounts prepared under the IASB system. In most cases the parent company statement of financial position (balance sheet) confirms that the parent is primarily a holding company whose main asset is the investment in its subsidiaries. It owns some of the group's land and buildings and a small portion of the vehicle fleet. Its current assets consist mainly of amounts owed by subsidiaries and dividends due from subsidiaries. Its current liabilities consist mainly of amounts owed to subsidiaries and dividends payable to its own shareholders. The parent company has some long-term liabilities for money borrowed to purchase subsidiaries. Most of the cash used for purchase of new subsidiaries is provided by the new wealth generated by the group as a whole.

Group

Information about the Safe and Sure group is very much more interesting than information about the parent company alone. That is why the preceding chapters have used the group information about Safe and Sure to explain the treatment of assets, liabilities and ownership interest. There are a few particular items of interest in respect of acquisitions of new subsidiaries and the use of the goodwill reserve. There is also some interesting information about the various segments of the business which contribute to the overall picture. This section summarises those particular features of the annual report.

14.4.3 Identifying segments

The IASB system requires the operating segments reported by an entity to be the organisational units for which information is reported regularly to the chief operating decision maker. The chief operating decision maker is likely to be the chief executive, working with the board of directors to use the information for evaluating past performance and making decisions about future allocation of resources. So the intention is that the segment reporting reflects the information that management is using in running the business.

14.4.4 Segmental information in Safe and Sure

As an illustration of the type of segmental information available, the note to the income statement (profit and loss account) of Safe and Sure plc is set out in Note 16 to the financial statements. It is one of the lengthiest notes provided by the company.

Note 16 Operating segments

For the purposes of reporting to the chief operating decision maker, the group is currently organised into two operating divisions, (1) disposal and recycling, (2) security and cleaning. Disposal and recycling includes all aspects of collection and safe disposal of industrial and commercial waste products. Security and cleaning is undertaken by renewable annual contract, predominantly for hospitals, other healthcare premises and local government organisations.

The group's disposal and recycling operation in North America was discontinued with effect from 30 April Year 7.

Business sector analysis

	Disposal and recycling		Security and cleaning		Total	
	Year 7 £m	Year 6 £m	Year 7 £m	Year 6 £m	Year 7 £m	Year 6 £m
REVENUES (all from external customers)						
Continuing	508.9	455.0	205.7	134.3	714.6	589.3
Discontinued	20.0	11.0			20.0	11.0
Total revenues	528.9	466.0	205.7	134.3	734.6	600.3
Operating profit (loss) by service						
Continuing	176.6	139.6	18.6	14.4	195.2	154.0
Discontinued	(20.5)	(10.0)			(20.5)	(10.0)
Total operating profit					174.7	144.0
Interest receivable (net)					2.3	3.0
Profit before tax					177.0	147.0
Taxation					(62.2)	(52.4)
Profit for the period					114.8	94.6

All costs of head office operations are allocated to divisions on an activity costing basis. The company does not allocate interest receivable or taxation paid to reportable segments.

Depreciation and amortisation included in the income statement are as follows:

	Disposal and recycling		Security and cleaning		Total	
	Year 7 £m	Year 6 £m	Year 7 £m	Year 6 £m	Year 7 £m	Year 6 £m
Depreciation	30.2	25.1	3.0	3.9	33.2	29.0
Impairment of goodwill	1.6	–	–	–	1.6	–

The segment assets and liabilities at the end of Years 7 and 6, with capital expenditure for each year are as follows:

	Disposal and recycling		Security and cleaning		Unallocated		Total	
	Year 7 £m	Year 6 £m	Year 7 £m	Year 6 £m	Year 7 £m	Year 6 £m	Year 7 £m	Year 6 £m
Total assets	498.5	370.9	68.7	132.7	120.1	112.3	687.3	615.9
Total liabilities	131.7	147.9	61.3	85.5	30.0	12.1	223.0	245.5
Capital expenditure	50.0	45.0	10.2	2.5	–	–	60.2	47.5

Information about geographical areas

The group's two business segments operate in four main geographical areas, even though they are managed on a worldwide basis. In the following analysis, revenue is based on the country in which the order is received. It would not be materially different if based on the country in which the customer is located. Total assets and capital expenditure are allocated based on where the assets are located.

	Revenues from external customers		Non-current assets	
	Year 7 £m	Year 6 £m	Year 7 £m	Year 6 £m
CONTINUING				
United Kingdom	323.4	246.7	174.2	148.7
Continental Europe	164.3	153.5	90.3	93.0
North America	104.5	80.1	85.9	49.2
Asia Pacific & Africa	122.4	109.0	56.1	75.0
	714.6	589.3	406.5	365.9
DISCONTINUED				
North America	20.0	11.0	–	0.5
Total	734.6	600.3	406.5	366.4

The information contained in Note 16 relates to a service business, so it might be expected that the non-current assets would be relatively low compared to the turnover and operating profit. Professional analysts would be particularly interested in the relationships and trends underlying these figures.

David and Leona have returned from their holiday and are again working on Leona's flat. In the middle of a less than successful attempt to fit a carpet, David pauses for coffee and explains how he looked at the segmental information presented by the company.

DAVID: *The first thing I did here was to feed all these tables of segmental information into our spreadsheet package. I asked for two printouts initially. The first calculated the sales (revenue) as a multiple of net assets and the operating profit as a percentage of sales, using continuing activities in each case because the assets remaining at the end of the period do not include the assets of the discontinued activity. [The results are shown in Table 14.1, panel (a).] The second printout shows the sales to non-current assets for each geographical area. [The results are shown in Table 14.1, panel (b).] From this the relative strengths and weaknesses within the organisation begin to emerge. The percentage changes (Table 14.2) also show some interesting differences. I need to ask why the total assets for security and cleaning have reduced so much when there was no disposal in this segment. Perhaps the assets were transferred into disposal and recycling to replace those that were discontinued.*

Table 14.1
Analysis

(a) Analysis of business segment revenues and operating profit (based on continuing activities)

	Revenues as a multiple of total assets		Operating profit as a % of sales	
	Year 7	Year 6	Year 7 %	Year 6 %
Segment				
Disposal and recycling	1.02	1.23	34.7	30.7
Security and cleaning	2.99	1.01	9.0	10.7

(b) Analysis of geographical segment sales compared to non-current assets

	Sales as a multiple of non-current assets	
	Year 7	Year 6
Geographical analysis		
United Kingdom	1.86	1.66
Continental Europe	1.82	1.65
North America	1.22	1.63
Asia Pacific and Africa	1.76	1.61

Table 14.2
Percentage changes on previous year

	Disposal and recycling Year 7 % on Year 6	Security and cleaning Year 7 % on Year 6	Total Year 7 % on Year 6
Sales (revenue)	+11.8	+53.0	+21.3
Operating profit	+26.5	+29.2	+25.0
Total assets	+34.4	negative	+11.6

Then I turned to the front of the annual report. The importance of segmental information becomes apparent as soon as you start to read the chairman's statement and it continues through the business reviews, presented on a segmental basis with some helpful illustrations to reinforce the message. The chief executive's review continues the segmental theme strongly and gives further information to augment the basic tables which I have already analysed. That attention to detail in their reports is a reflection of the thorough questioning which these people receive from the fund managers and analysts who follow the company closely. I know one analyst who would put Sherlock Holmes in the shade. She collects the accounts of each individual UK company in the group, and as many overseas subsidiary companies as she can get hold of. She puts them all together like a jigsaw and then starts to ask intensive questions based on what she has and what she can deduce about the missing pieces. Seasoned finance directors wilt visibly under her interrogation!

LEONA: *Segmental reporting is an area where you and your analyst friends probably put more pressures on the companies than we can as auditors. That's a good example of market forces at work, but it does assume that the information you prise out of the company is made available more widely. Companies make use of the business review or the operating and financial review to answer the questions which they know the investors ask on a regular basis.*

14.5 Off-balance-sheet finance

One major problem for UK accounting emerged in the 1980s in a period of business expansion. To finance expansion, companies were borrowing and therefore increasing their gearing ratios. Some companies looked for ways of avoiding disclosing in the statement of financial position (balance sheet) the full extent of the commitment on borrowed funds. Omitting the item from the statement of financial position (balance sheet) could not remove the commercial obligation but it could reduce the questions arising from those who would read the financial statements.

The accounting question is: How do you remove, or fail to include, a liability so that no one will notice? The answer, as with all accounting questions, starts in the accounting equation. To keep the equation in balance, any removal of a liability must be matched by removal of an asset of equal amount.

Many ingenious schemes emerged, but one of the least complex is the sale and leaseback of land and buildings.

14.5.1 Sale and leaseback of property

Consider the following scenario. A company has the following statement of financial position (balance sheet):

	£m
Land and buildings	20
Other assets, *less* current liabilities	15
	35
Less long-term loan	(20)
Net assets	15
Share capital	15

The company sells the land and buildings for £20m and repays the loan. The statement of financial position (balance sheet) now appears to contain no gearing:

	£m
Other assets, *less* current liabilities	15
Share capital	15

However, enquiry behind the scenes reveals a complex arrangement. The land and buildings were sold to a consortium of finance companies, but on the same day a lease was signed that allowed the company to continue occupying the property at a rental payment which would vary according to current rates of interest and would be calculated as a percentage of the £20m cash received. In five years' time the company would have the option to repurchase the land and buildings at £20m and the consortium of finance companies would have the option to force the company to repurchase at £20m. These options would mean that if the price rose over the next five years the company would wish to buy at £20m. If the price fell over the next five years the consortium would insist on repurchase.

Now ask yourself, where do the benefits and risks of this contract lie? The benefits of a rise in value and the risks of a decrease in value remain with the company, as they would if the company had remained the owner. The company will pay a rental which looks very much like an interest payment on a loan of £20m. If the company fails to meet its obligations, then the consortium will claim the asset. The commercial effect of this transaction is that of a loan based on the security of the asset of land and buildings.

14.5.2 UK response

In the absence of a standard to back up the argument, auditors felt unable to argue against the directors of companies who moved assets and liabilities off the statement of financial position (balance sheet). After some years of consultation and discussion with interested parties, the UK ASB decided that such transactions did not change the commercial substance of the transaction and it is the commercial substance which matters. A standard was introduced to require a transaction of this type to be reported on the statement of financial position (balance sheet)[10] in the form of an asset and matching liability. Not all countries shared this view because it involved making a judgement on the balance of risks and rewards. Making judgements leaves the company and the auditors open to challenge and so it could be argued that specific rules are preferable to general principles. In particular the US had a more rules-based approach to defining recognition on and off the statement of financial position (balance sheet).

14.5.3 Special purpose entities

The problems associated with off-balance-sheet finance received a high public profile at the end of 2001, running into 2002, with the failure of a large US company called Enron. Because of the size of the company and the political impact of its failure, hearings were called by the US Congress at which witnesses gave evidence on accounting practices, among other matters. One of the accounting issues discussed was the question of 'off-balance-sheet finance'. The Chief Accountant of the Securities and Exchange Commission described to the House of Representatives how money could be borrowed at advantageous rates of interest using a 'special purpose entity' which was not consolidated with the rest of the group accounts. Provided the assets of the special purpose entity retained sufficient value, the lender would be content with the arrangement. If the assets fell in value then the lender would look to the parent company for reimbursement. Shareholders in the parent would be unaware of the extent of such borrowing until the lenders demanded repayment. At the time of the failure of Enron the US standard-setting body (the Financial Accounting Standards Board) was still in the process of providing guidance on consolidation of such special purpose entities. The International Accounting Standards Board had no standard that directly addressed such entities.

Subsequently the US regulators and the IASB strengthened their rules relating to special purpose entities, to bring these entities into group financial statements.

Activity 14.2	Off-balance-sheet finance is one example of information which would never come to the attention of the users of financial statements but for the concern of some auditors. Make a list of other types of information which may be evident to the auditors but which are unlikely to be conveyed to the readers. Consider this list in the light of the requirement that financial statements must show a true and fair view. To what extent is the reader of financial statements reliant on the directors and the auditors?

14.6 Corporate social responsibility

Corporate social responsibility means that entities report to stakeholders on the ways in which social and environmental concerns are integrated with their business operations.

Definition	**Corporate social responsibility** means that companies integrate social and environmental concerns in their business operations and in their interactions with stakeholders.

Companies disclose in their annual reports more information than is represented only in financial statements. Depending on social attitudes or pressures, companies may voluntarily disclose additional information intended to confirm the company's sense of social responsibility. In some instances, the provisions of law eventually catch up with the values of society and disclosures become mandatory. Section 14.2.5 explains that in the UK the OFR Regulation requires the OFR to include information about environmental matters and social and community issues.

Investors are increasingly asking questions about the corporate social responsibility of the companies in which they invest. Many investors want to be reassured that the businesses in which they have a stake adopt ethical business practices towards employees, the community and the environment. You will see increasing numbers of what are described as 'ethical investment funds' which make careful enquiry before buying shares. Some ethical investors feel that they are best placed to influence a company if they become shareholders; others feel that they should not become shareholders until the company has a sound policy.

14.6.1 Types of disclosure

Examples of social disclosure on mandatory topics include: information about pensions for employees, employees' share option schemes, policy regarding employment of disabled persons, donations to charity and consultation with employees. Social disclosure on a voluntary basis includes: information about employee matters, health and safety, community work, energy and the environment.

In terms of relative volume, the amount of information disclosed about employee-related matters exceeds other types of social and environmental disclosures, but the area where there is the fastest growth in interest is that of environmental issues. Many leading companies now have an 'environment' section in the annual report and some go even further in producing a separate environmental report.

Below are extracts from the 'environment' section of the report of the directors of Safe and Sure plc, the company used for illustration throughout this text.

> *Safe and Sure is committed to the provision of services and products which improve the quality of life, both for our customers and the community, using working practices designed to protect the environment.*
>
> *Heightened awareness of environmental issues and increased legislation provide a focal point for developing greener techniques and solutions to problems, both in our more traditional businesses and also in offering opportunities to develop new businesses.*
>
> *Antibacterial deep cleaning of premises, in particular high-risk areas such as washrooms, drains and food production and preparation areas, has been developed to meet increased legislation and concern as to health and food safety.*
>
> *It is the responsibility of the company and all its employees to ensure that all services and products are procured, produced, packaged and delivered, and waste materials ultimately disposed of, in ways which are appropriate from an environmental viewpoint. It is the responsibility of our employees to carry out their work in a manner that will not cause damage to the environment.*

14.6.2 Need for measurement

Social and environmental disclosures in annual reports have so far centred on narrative description in the directors' report or in the non-statutory part of the document. There is little evidence of impact on the accounting numbers but that may be the next step. Environmental obligations create liabilities. An oil rig in the North Sea will eventually have to be removed. The liability may be regarded as existing now because the event creating the obligation was the original act of positioning the rig in the oil field. But what will eventual removal cost? Will the rig be dismantled to a few hundred feet below the surface, out of the way of fishing nets? Will it be dismantled down to the sea bed with the debris left behind? Will the rig be towed away for dismantling elsewhere? Until these questions can be answered, the liability cannot be measured as a money amount and therefore cannot be recognised in the statement of financial position (balance sheet). Most oil companies make a provision each year towards the ultimate cost of removal of the rig and they accumulate the provision in the statement of financial position (balance sheet). They do not, in general, report the full liability at the outset.

14.6.3 The Global Reporting Initiative

The Global Reporting Initiative (GRI) is a venture that was started through a link between the United Nations Environmental Programme and a US body called the Coalition for Environmentally Responsible Economies. It has developed into a global institution that sets out a disclosure framework, called the GRI Guidelines, for sustainability reporting. Companies are increasingly referring to the GRI Guidelines in designing parts of their annual report. The recommendations include reporting on vision and strategy, the profile of the organisation, the governance structure and management system and performance indicators. These indicators should cover economic, environmental and social performance. This combination is sometimes referred to in the press as 'the triple bottom line'. The reason for this description is that for many years the earnings for equity holders has been described as 'the bottom line' (of the income statement): extending to three performance measures leads to a triple bottom line.

14.6.4 The Kyoto Protocol

International agreements on supporting sustainable development have consequences for accounting. One example is seen in the Kyoto Protocol, an agreement resulting from a conference held in Kyoto, Japan in 1997 as an amendment to the United Nations Framework Convention on Climate Change. The Kyoto Protocol set out measures for dealing with problems of climate change by reducing greenhouse gas emissions. Some countries were more reluctant than others to ratify the agreement (confirm that they will make it operational) although gradually more countries have agreed. All member states of the EU have ratified the Protocol but by 2005 the US government was still not committed. A further meeting held in Copenhagen in 2009 resulted in limited US agreement but left some confusion about details.

The Kyoto agreement requires action to be taken to reduce carbon-based emissions (particularly carbon dioxide) over a defined timescale. Countries are given limits of emissions of greenhouse gases. The countries then set limits on companies in specified industries.

One interesting feature of the Kyoto agreement is that companies are given 'allowances to emit'. The allowance, in the form of a licence, is capable of being transferred from one company to another. The entity that buys a licence to emit acquires an asset. This in turn creates new assets and liabilities for individual companies. The liabilities are easier to see: companies which do not reduce emissions will face penalties. However, there are also opportunities to take actions that prevent emissions and extract value from the new carbon market. If these actions meet the definition and recognition criteria, they are regarded as assets. The European Union Greenhouse Gas Emissions Trading Scheme began in January 2005. It establishes a market in carbon dioxide gas emissions for companies in specified industry sectors. Information on emissions trading is seen in annual reports published from 2005 onwards.

There is no international accounting standard dealing directly with accounting for the environment and sustainable development but there are interested groups working on the accounting issues in various countries.

Activity 14.3 *Write down the accounting equation: Assets minus Liabilities equals Ownership interest. Suppose you are the accountant for an oil company and you have been asked to record the full liability for dismantling an oil rig in 20 years' time. How would you make the accounting equation balance?*

14.7 Corporate governance

The term **corporate governance** is used to describe the way in which companies are directed and controlled. In Chapter 1 the idea of stewards and their agents was put forward briefly as a model of the relationship between shareholders and the directors of a company. It could be argued that these two groups could be left together to work out their fate, but a series of well-publicised corporate failures and financial scandals of the 1980s raised concern that such a system does not always work and the public interest may suffer as a result.

There has therefore been considerable interest in intervening to improve the quality of corporate governance. The issue has been high on the agenda in several of the

English-speaking countries and the ideas have strong international interest although perhaps translated into different words and phrases.

14.7.1 The Combined Code

In the UK, the government has taken some action through legislation but has largely followed the traditional route of encouraging the self-regulatory approach. One of the most important aspects of this self-regulatory approach was the 1992 report of what is usually referred to as the Cadbury Committee.[11]

The Cadbury Committee was set up by the Financial Reporting Council, the London Stock Exchange and the accountancy profession. It was asked to report on a range of issues concerned with the way directors run their companies and auditors monitor those companies, considering also the links between directors, auditors and shareholders. The recommendations of the Cadbury Committee were wide-ranging but included proposed improvements in financial reporting such as:

- more detail in the interim reports
- clearer information about directors' remuneration
- effective use of the operating and financial review
- the effectiveness of the internal control procedures used by the business
- reassurance that the business is a going concern
- a statement of the responsibilities of directors.

Although the report was issued in 1992 it took some time for further working parties to agree on the manner of reporting on internal controls and the going concern confirmation. By the end of 1995 these were in place and 1996 saw the start of a review of the first three years of implementing the Cadbury Report.

The review was chaired by Sir Ronald Hampel, so that the report which eventually appeared in 1998 was called 'The Hampel Report'.[12] It took as its starting point the view that good corporate governance was not merely a matter of complying with a number of hard and fast rules. There was seen to be a need for broad principles. It was important to take account of the diversity of circumstances and experience among companies, and within the same company over time. On this basis Hampel suggested that the true safeguard for good corporate governance lay in the application of informed and independent judgement by experienced and qualified individuals – executive and non-executive directors, shareholders and auditors. Relatively little was said about financial reporting, beyond the assertion that the board of directors should present a balanced and understandable assessment of the company's position and prospects.[13]

Following the Hampel Report, the Stock Exchange issued a Combined Code for listed companies containing recommendations on directors; directors' remuneration; relations with shareholders; and accountability and audit. The accountability section emphasised the responsibilities of directors in respect of financial reporting. They should present a balanced and understandable assessment of the company's position and prospects. In particular they should explain their responsibilities and they should also report that the business is a going concern.

The Combined Code was subsequently taken into the responsibility of the Financial Reporting Council. The FRC revised the Code in 2003, 2006 and 2008. The work is carried out by the FRC's Committee on Corporate Governance.

14.7.2 Directors' remuneration

There is a continuing interest in the subject of directors' remuneration, partly because it provides opportunities for newspaper headlines. Typically the interest of financial journalists focuses on the salary of the highest paid director and the amount that person is gaining through share option schemes. These schemes allow directors to obtain each year the option to buy shares at an agreed price. If the share price rises subsequently the directors exercise the option, buy the share at the agreed price and may sell immediately at a profit. Some companies offer such options to some or all of their employees by way of encouraging loyalty to the company and supplementing cash salaries.

In response to well-publicised concerns about the need to disclose and control the level of directors' remuneration, a study group chaired by Sir Richard Greenbury (1995) produced a code of best practice on disclosure and remuneration policy.[14] These recommendations are now incorporated partly in the Companies Act 2006 and partly in the Combined Code on Corporate Governance. A typical annual report of a listed company contains several pages on the remuneration policy and the payments to directors.

Activity 14.4	*Obtain the annual report of a listed company. Turn to the report on corporate governance. What does the company say about corporate governance and about compliance with the Combined Code? What do the auditors say about the report on corporate governance? What is disclosed about the remuneration committee? What information is given elsewhere in the annual report, relating to directors' remuneration?*

14.8 Developing issues: 'present fairly' and 'true and fair view'

The IASB system of accounting requires financial statements to *present fairly* the financial position, financial performance and cash flows of an entity.[15] In virtually all circumstances a fair presentation is achieved by compliance with the applicable IFRSs.[16] Entities cannot use notes or explanatory material to compensate for inappropriate accounting policies – the choice of policies must in itself achieve a fair presentation.[17] In the extremely rare circumstances where management considers that compliance with a requirement of an IFRS would conflict with the objective of a fair presentation, the entity will depart from the requirement and explain the reasons and consequences.[18]

The Companies Act 2006 requires that financial statements of companies should show *a true and fair view*.[19] In most situations a company will achieve a true and fair view by following the requirements of company law and UK accounting standards. In the rare circumstances where management considers that compliance with a requirement of law and standards would conflict with the true and fair view, the entity will depart from that requirement and explain the reasons and consequences.

14.8.1 Equivalence of meaning

The question arises as to whether 'present fairly' and 'a true and fair view' have different meanings. The Financial Reporting Council (FRC)[20] has obtained legal opinion that 'present fairly' and 'true and fair view' are not different requirements. They are different ways of expressing the same concept. The FRC has also pointed out that the IASB Framework equates 'true and fair view' and 'fair presentation' in asserting that the application of the principal qualitative characteristics and of appropriate accounting standards normally results in financial statements that convey what is generally understood as a true and fair view or a fair presentation of information.[21]

The remainder of this section discusses the meaning of 'true and fair view' because it has a longer history of debate and development in the UK. The phrase 'true and fair' was taken into European Directives when the UK joined as a member state but it has never found an exact equivalent in the underlying meaning. For example the French wording 'image fidèle' is closer to 'a faithful picture'.

The UK has traditionally taken the position that it may be necessary for individual companies to take action which contravenes legal rules, in the interest of presenting 'a true and fair view'. In other countries, including the US, the position taken is generally that the law prevails and any questions about fair presentation should be analysed within the legal framework. The US wording is 'faithful representation'.

14.8.2 Meaning of a true and fair view

The UK Companies Act provides no definition of the meaning of 'a true and fair view'. Consequently from time to time those who set accounting standards have sought the opinion of expert legal advisers. The lawyers have put forward the view that the requirement for a true and fair view is a dynamic concept which changes its nature as the general values of society change. Although the words stay the same, the meaning of the words changes because the opinions of society in general change.

What does that mean in practice? The lawyers have provided an example.[22] The Bill of Rights 1688 prohibited 'cruel and unusual punishments'. The dictionary definition of 'cruel' has changed little since that time but a judge today would characterise as 'cruel' some punishments which a judge of 1688 would not have regarded as cruel. The meaning of the word remains the same but the facts to which it is applied have changed. Based on reasoning of that type, the lawyers have argued that the words 'true and fair' may carry the same dictionary meaning from one time to another but the accounting principles and practice contributing to a true and fair view will change as circumstances change.

One very important issue is the question of whether society, and the public interest, would expect the application of accounting standards to be necessary as evidence of intent to apply a true and fair view. Legal advice provided to the ASB analysed the role of an accounting standard:

> *What is the purpose of an accounting standard? The initial purpose is to identify proper accounting practice for the benefit of preparers and auditors of accounts. However, because accounts commonly comply with accounting standards, the effect of the issue of standards has also been to create a common understanding between users and preparers of accounts as to how particular items should be treated in accounts and accordingly an expectation that, save where good reason exists, accounts will comply with applicable accounting standards.[23]*

Accounting standards have, over a period of years, become regarded as an authoritative source of accounting practice. The legal opinion given to the ASB is that accounting standards provide very strong evidence of the proper practice which should be adopted. The 'true and fair view' is seen as a dynamic concept:

> *Thus what is required to show a true and fair view is subject to continuous rebirth and in determining whether the true and fair requirement is satisfied the Court will not in my view seek to find synonyms for the words 'true and fair' but will seek to apply the concepts which those words imply.[24]*

14.8.3 Who is responsible for the true and fair view?

Under company law, it is the directors who are responsible for ensuring that the accounts are prepared in such a way as to show a true and fair view. The auditors state whether, in their opinion, the accounts show a true and fair view. If you turn back to Chapter 4 you will see an example of the statement of directors' responsibilities which now appears in many company reports and also a copy of the auditors' report. Both contain the phrase 'a true and fair view' and emphasise the different types of responsibility held by directors and auditors.

14.8.4 How specific is the 'true and fair' concept?

You should have gained an understanding, from various chapters of this book, that there is more than one accounting treatment for many transactions and events. It is a great puzzle to many people that companies could produce different accounting statements for one particular period of time, each of which would show a true and fair view. The answer lies in one very small word. The requirement of law is for 'a true and fair view' but not for 'the true and fair view'. Thus the directors do not have to find 'the very best true and fair view', which may surprise some users of financial statements. It also becomes very difficult for auditors to enter into dispute with directors where there are two acceptable alternatives, either of which could result in a true and fair view. To be successful in contradicting the directors, the auditors need to show that a particular practice does *not* show a true and fair view. If they can successfully argue that opinion then the company has the choice of revising the proposed treatment or facing a *qualified* audit opinion. Here is an example of a qualified audit opinion where the auditor and directors were in disagreement:

> **Qualified audit opinion**
> *We found that the company has made no provision for doubtful debts, despite circumstances which indicate that such a provision is necessary.*
> *In our opinion the accounts do not give a true and fair view . . .*

It is therefore essential, in reading the annual report, to read the auditors' report at an early stage in order to be aware of any problems with the financial statements. It is also essential to realise that the meaning of 'true and fair' is highly subjective and changes over a period of time.

Activity 14.5	Looking back through Chapters 8 to 12, identify matters of accounting practice where more than one accounting policy is permitted. If you were an auditor, how would you decide whether one or other of the permitted choices gave a true and fair view?

14.9 Measurement of value

Throughout the majority of this financial accounting text the value of assets and liabilities has been measured at historical cost. That means the price paid, or the liability agreed, when the transaction was first undertaken. In times when prices are changing, that information about the cost at the date of the transaction will become less relevant to the needs of users (although it may be seen as a reliable measure). The IASB Framework says relatively little about measurement,[25] perhaps because of the difficulties of obtaining international agreement. Consequently this section refers to the UK ASB's *Statement of Principles* where the ideas have been developed further.

14.9.1 Stages of recognition and measurement

At the moment when the transaction takes place, the historical cost is also the current value, where current value is regarded as the value of the item at the accounting date. In the *Statement of Principles* this is identified as the point of initial recognition. If an asset or a liability is involved, then there will be various points at which it may be appropriate to remeasure the amount at which the asset or liability is recorded. This is referred to as subsequent remeasurement. Finally there may come a point at which the asset or liability should be removed from the financial statements. This is referred to as derecognition.[26]

The conditions to be applied in deciding on initial **recognition** have been explained in Chapter 2. **Derecognition** reverses the conditions so that an asset or a liability should cease to be recognised if there is no longer sufficient evidence that the entity has access to future economic benefits or an obligation to transfer economic benefits.[27]

14.9.2 Limitations of historical cost accounting

Throughout this text you have studied historical cost accounting where the acquisition of assets is recorded at the amount paid at the time of acquisition. The academic literature is bursting at the seams with criticisms of historical cost accounting, but the practice has proved hard to change. There were brief practical attempts in the UK to apply a different approach for a period from the mid-1970s to the mid-1980s but the rate of inflation then became less of a problem and interest waned.

Critics of historical cost accounting have said that in the statement of financial position (balance sheet) there is the addition of items bought at different times and with £s of different purchasing power. That is not a satisfactory procedure. In the income statement (profit and loss account) the costs are matched against revenue without regard for the fact that goods were bought and expenses paid for at an earlier point in time. Sales are therefore matched against outdated costs. The tax system takes the accounting profit as its starting point and therefore the tax payable is dictated by outdated accounting figures.

Supporters of historical cost accounting point to its reliability and objectivity because the monetary amount of the transaction is known. Verifiability is straightforward because documentation exists. The preference for historical cost values remains strong; if companies do decide to revalue fixed assets then both the IASB and UK ASB require them to keep the current values up to date in each year's statement of financial position (balance sheet).[28]

14.9.3 Subsequent remeasurement

Subsequent remeasurement poses more problems and is one of the more controversial aspects of the *Statement of Principles*. It is suggested that there should be a change in the amount at which an asset or liability is recorded if there is sufficient evidence that: (a) the amount has changed and (b) the new amount can be measured with sufficient reliability.[29] In times of inflation (when prices generally are increasing), the idea of remeasurement becomes particularly important. Even when inflation is not a major problem, there may be one particular asset whose value increases through scarcity of supply or decreases through lack of demand.

That leads into an extremely controversial question: 'How do you measure value?' Chapter 6 of the *Statement of Principles* outlines some approaches to value. Methods of valuation are also listed in the *IASB Framework*.[30]

14.9.4 Entry price and exit price

Taking fixed assets and stocks as the main examples to begin with, it could be said that there are two different categories of measures of value. There is a price which the organisation will have to pay to acquire the asset and there is a price at which the organisation will be able to sell the asset to someone else. If you have ever tried buying and selling second-hand goods you will know that the buying price and the selling price are often quite different. The student who tries to sell an outdated personal computer through an advertisement on the college noticeboard knows that any enquirer will try to push the price downwards. The student attempting to enquire about a similar item of equipment knows that the seller will try to keep the price high. Somehow the price for which you are able to sell your second-hand posses-sions invariably appears to be lower than the price someone else is asking for their unwanted belongings.

The price paid by a business to acquire an asset is called in accounting the **entry price** and the price at which the business would be able to sell the asset is called the **exit price**. Academic authors will argue long and hard on both sides of the case and if you pursue the study of accounting further you will meet that academic debate. In the real world a decision has to be made. In the UK, that decision was made by the standard-setting body at the beginning of the 1980s, when SSAP 16 required companies to use the entry price approach and to measure the value of fixed assets and stocks at the cost of replacement at the date of the financial statements.[31] That approach was used to provide additional information in annual reports of the UK for the first half of the 1980s, but gradually the enthusiasm of companies waned and by the late 1980s they had reverted to their traditional practice of using primarily historical cost for most aspects of measurement.

14.9.5 Current values

In a current value system, changes in value are recorded as they occur. This idea, if accepted, puts quite a large hole in the concept of **realisation**, which is at the heart of traditional accounting practice. It has been the practice to record changes in ownership interest only when the change in an asset or liability is realised, in the form either of cash or of other assets the ultimate realisation of which can be assessed with reason-able certainty.[32] That practice finds continuing support in the Companies Act 2006 which states that the income statement (profit and loss account) reported under the Act may report only those profits which are realised (although this requirement does not apply to companies reporting under full IFRS).

Chapter 12 has explained how the Statement of changes in equity in the IASB system and the Statement of total recognised gains and losses in the UK ASB system both provide the location for reporting changes in assets and liabilities which are not. There is therefore a place in which to report changes in current value, but the question of how to measure value is still unanswered.

The argument favoured by the UK ASB, as indicated in the *Statement of Principles*, is the one which leads to a measurement system based on **value to the business**. Those who support this idea start by asking: What is the worst that can happen to a person, or business, which owns a fixed asset or item of trading stock? The answer is that they may be deprived of the item, perhaps by theft, fire, obsolescence or similar cause. The next question is: What would the owners need in order to be returned to the position they enjoyed previously? The answer, in most cases, is that they need to be provided with the cost of replacement of a similar item so that they may continue with the activity of the business. In a few rare cases, where the owners may have decided to sell rather than continue using the asset, the selling price is the measure of deprival.

From this analysis it is argued that the value to the business of a fixed asset or an item of stock is usually the **replacement cost** at the accounting date. The replacement cost is that of a similar item in a similar state. Such a replacement cost might be found in a catalogue of prices of used equipment or it could be estimated by starting with the cost of a new item and applying an appropriate proportion of depreciation.

14.9.6 Fair value

The IASB standards have moved towards a fair value approach to valuation rather than a deprival value approach. Several of the standards in the IASB system permit or require the use of **fair value**.

Definition	**Fair value** is the amount for which an asset could be exchanged, or a liability settled, between knowledgeable, willing parties in an arm's length transaction.

In this definition, a fair value does not require an active market to exist, although the presence of an active market may make it easier to decide on a fair value. If an active market does not exist then the IASB standards give guidance which depends on the nature of the asset or liability. For property, plant and equipment[33] the suggestion is to use depreciated replacement cost where market-based evidence is not available. For biological assets a range of suggestions is given such as market price of similar assets or discounted present values of future cash flows.[34]

The IASB's view of fair value, which is closer to the **exit value** approach, is also favoured by the Financial Accounting Standards Board (FASB) in the USA. There is a continuing discussion as to the definition of 'fair value' to be used if the IASB and FASB converge their respective standards.

14.9.7 Current practice

In annual reports of UK companies there is a general adherence to historical cost but some companies show evidence of using revaluation, which is permitted by the UK ASB as well as by the IASB system.

The International Accounting Standard IAS 16 permits entities to choose either the cost model or the revaluation model. Under the cost model, property, plant and equipment are carried at cost less accumulated depreciation. Under the revaluation model an item of property, plant and equipment may be carried at a revalued amount. The revalued amount is fair value less accumulated depreciation. Revaluations must be made regularly so that the carrying amount remains close to fair value at the date of the financial statements.

Activity 14.6	*Look at the items you possess. These might include a house or a flat or a car, but equally well they could be a bicycle and some modest items of furniture. Whatever their nature, write down on a piece of paper a figure in £s which answers the question: What is the value of these possessions? Now think about how you arrived at that figure. Did you use the original cost because that was the amount you paid to acquire them? Did you use replacement cost because that is the amount you would have to pay to replace them? Did you use selling price because that is the amount you could collect in cash for conversion to other uses? Did you have some other method? What was the reason for the method you chose? Would you obtain the same answer using all the methods listed for this activity? Which answer is the most relevant for your information needs? Which is the most reliable? Is there any conflict here between relevance and reliability? Would other students answer these questions as you have done?*

14.10 Developing issues: how valid is the stakeholder model?

This book takes as its starting point the IASB's *Framework*, and has constantly returned to that *Framework* for explanation or discussion of the accounting practices explained in various chapters. The *Framework* is, in its turn, built on a model which sees the objective of accounting as serving the needs of a wide range of users. Those users are sometimes referred to as **stakeholders** and the *Framework* is regarded as an example of a stakeholder model of the process of regulating accounting.

There are, however, those who would argue that the stakeholder model is the wrong place to start and therefore the significant problems of accounting will not be solved using a statement of principles of this type. At the basic level of understanding existing accounting practice, which is the limit of this book, the validity of one model versus another may not be a critical issue, but you should be aware that there are views that more complex accounting problems may not be solved using a stakeholder approach (although the ASB might not subscribe to such views).

Those who argue against the 'user needs' approach suggest that accounting regulation is a much more complex process of social interaction. Standard-setters producing accounting rules in a self-regulatory environment need to be sure of a consensus of opinion supporting the proposed rules. They will therefore seek out a range of opinions and will undoubtedly be subjected to lobbying (letters of comment and personal contact) by persons or organisations seeking to put forward a particular viewpoint. Indeed, part of the UK standard-setting process involves issuing an exposure draft for comment before a financial reporting standard is issued, although there is no way of knowing what lobbying occurs behind the scenes.

The process of standard-setting may therefore be regarded as one of negotiating and balancing various interests. There has been research after the event, both in the UK and in other countries, which has shown that the standard-setting bodies were influenced by one or more powerful forces. One particularly clear example may be seen in the development of an accounting standard to tighten up practices in reporting expenditure on research and development.[35] There is a significant amount of academic literature on factors influencing the process of setting accounting standards.

Those who have identified these 'political' pressures would suggest that the accounting standard-setting process should openly admit that there are influential factors such as: the relative balance of power among those who prepare and those who use accounting information; relative dependency of some on others; the balance of individual liberty against collective need; and the ideology observed in particular systems of social relations. (Ideology means that a group in society may hold strong beliefs which make it genuinely unable to appreciate different positions taken by others.)

Thus claims that the standard-setting process is neutral in its impact on the economy or on society may be unrealistic. This book does not seek to impose any particular view on its readers. It has used the *Framework* as a consistent basis for explaining current practice, but it leaves to the reader the task of taking forward the knowledge of external financial reporting and the understanding of what influences the future development of external financial reporting.

14.11 Summary

- The **operating and financial review** (OFR) provides a balanced and comprehensive analysis of the business, its year-end position, the trends in performance during the year and factors likely to affect future position and performance. It is good practice for quoted UK companies.

- A **highlights statement** in the annual report shows what the company regards as important information for investors as the primary users of the annual report. A table of five-year trends is also useful in evaluating the position and performance of the business.

- **Segmental reporting** has developed as a means of supplementing the consolidated financial statements by providing more insight into the activities of the group. In particular it reports information about the different types of products and services that an entity produces and the different geographical areas in which it operates.

- **Off-balance-sheet finance** describes the situation where an asset and a liability are omitted from the financial statements of an entity. The UK ASB takes the view that such transactions should remain on the entity's statement of financial position (balance sheet) if the risks and rewards remain with the entity. The IASB has specific rules to deal with special purpose vehicles, which are one form of off-balance-sheet finance.

- **Corporate social responsibility** means that companies integrate social and environmental concerns in their business operations and in their interactions with stakeholders. Many companies include social and environmental disclosures in their annual reports. The Global Reporting Initiative provides a framework for such disclosures.

- Carbon trading, arising from the Kyoto Protocol, provides a new form of asset in the licence to emit carbon dioxide and a new form of liability in the obligation to reduce emissions.

- The term **corporate governance** is used to describe the way in which companies are directed and controlled. Listed companies in the UK are required to follow the Combined Code of Corporate Governance. In the annual report the directors must either confirm compliance with the Code or explain reasons for non-compliance.

- Directors' remuneration is one aspect of corporate governance that receives a great deal of attention. There are rules and guidance on the disclosure of remuneration (pay) policy and the amount due to each director. The information is usually contained in the report of the Remuneration Committee.

- The IASB system of accounting requires financial statements to **present fairly** the financial position, financial performance and cash flows of an entity. The Companies Act 2006 requires that financial statements of companies should show a **true and fair view**. The Financial Reporting Council has given an opinion that the two phrases are broadly equivalent.

- There is a continuing debate on the methods of measuring assets and liabilities. **Reliability** points towards historical cost accounting but **relevance** points towards current values.

- **Entry price** values are values that measure the cost of buying, acquiring or replacing an asset or liability. **Exit price** values represent the sale, disposal or other form of realisation of an asset.

- **Fair value** is the amount for which an asset could be exchanged, or a liability settled, between knowledgeable, willing parties in an arm's length transaction.

- Finally, it should be noted that this entire book on financial accounting has been built on a **stakeholder** model of user needs which itself is the basis of the IASB's *Framework*. That idea meets general acceptance in the accounting profession from those who set accounting standards, but you need to be aware that further study of the academic literature will encourage you to question the user needs model.

Further reading

Gray, R. and others (1998), *Valuation of Assets and Liabilities: Environmental Law and the Impact of the Environmental Agenda on Business*, The Institute of Chartered Accountants of Scotland.

Parker, R. H. and Nobes, C. W. (1994), *An International View of True and Fair Accounting*, Routledge.

Testimony Concerning Recent Events Relating to Enron Corporation, by Robert K. Herdman, Chief Accountant, US Securities and Exchange Commission, before the Subcommittee on Capital Markets, Insurance and Government Sponsored Enterprises and the Sub-committee on Oversight and Investigation, Committee on Financial Services, US House of Representatives. www.sec.gov/news/testimony/121201tsrkh.htm.

The development of the Operating and Financial Review can be traced on the website of the Department of Trade and Industry (DTI), UK Company Law Review, www.dti.gov.uk.

QUESTIONS

The Questions section of each chapter has three types of question. 'Test your understanding' questions to help you review your reading are in the 'A' series of questions. You will find the answers to these by reading and thinking about the material in the book. 'Application' questions to test your ability to apply technical skills are in the 'B' series of questions. Questions requiring you to show skills in problem solving and evaluation are in the 'C' series of questions. A letter [S] indicates that there is a solution at the end of the book.

A   Test your understanding

A14.1   What is the objective of the operating and financial review? (Section 14.2.1)

A14.2   Why is there no prescribed format for the OFR? (Section 14.2.2)

A14.3   What are the main principles set by the ASB for the OFR? (Section 14.2.2)

A14.4   What are the main elements of the disclosure framework for the OFR? (Section 14.2.3)

A14.5   What are key performance indicators (KPIs)? (Section 14.2.4)

A14.6   What are the particular requirements of the OFR Regulation that must be reported in an OFR? (Section 14.2.5)

A14.7   What are the responsibilities of the directors and auditors in relation to the OFR? (Section 14.2.6)

A14.8   What is the purpose of a highlights statement? (Section 14.3.1)

A14.9   How does a five-year summary of historical results help investors? (Section 14.3.2)

A14.10 How does segmental information help the users of financial statements? (Section 14.4.1)

A14.11 Which items are reported on a segmental basis? (Section 14.4.1)

A14.12 How are segments identified? (Section 14.4.3)

A14.13 Why is off-balance-sheet finance a problem in accounting? (Section 14.5)

A14.14 What principles are recommended by the UK ASB for determining whether assets and liabilities should be reported on the statement of financial position (balance sheet)? (Section 14.5.2)

A14.15 What is a special purpose entity? (Section 14.5.3)

A14.16 What is corporate social responsibility? (Section 14.6)

A14.17 What is the Global Reporting Initiative? (Section 14.6.3)

A14.18 What accounting issues arise in relation to carbon trading? (Section 14.6.4)

A14.19 What is meant by corporate governance? (Section 14.7)

A14.20 What is the Combined Code? (Section 14.7.1)

A14.21 How does financial reporting help to improve corporate governance? (Section 14.7)

A14.22 Why has it been found impossible to write a definitive guide on the meaning of 'a true and fair view'? (Section 14.8)

A14.23 What are the limitations of historical cost accounting? (Section 14.9.2)

A14.24 Why is it desirable to remeasure assets and liabilities subsequent to acquisition? (Section 14.9.3)

A14.25 Explain what is meant by entry price and exit price. (Section 14.9.4)

A14.26 Explain what is meant by fair value. (Section 14.9.6)

A14.27 Should accounting standards focus primarily on the needs of users? (Section 14.10)

B Application

B14.1

Suggest, with reasons, three KPIs for each of the following types of business, and explain why it is unlikely that two businesses will choose identical KPIs.

(a) a private hospital
(b) a car repair garage
(c) a clothing manufacturer.

C Problem solving and evaluation

C14.1 [S]

Carry out a trend analysis on Safe and Sure plc, using the historical summary set out in Appendix I. Write a short report on the key features emerging from the trends.

Activities for study groups

Case 14.1

Turn to the annual report of a listed company which you have used for activities throughout the previous chapters. Split the group to take two different roles: one half of the group should take the role of the finance director and the other half should take the role of the broker's analyst writing a report on the company.

Look through the annual report for any ratio calculations performed by the company and check these from the data in the financial statements, so far as you are able. Prepare your own calculations of ratios for analysis of all aspects of performance. Find the current share price from a current newspaper.

Once the data preparation is complete, the finance director subgroup should prepare a short report to a meeting with the analysts. The analysts should then respond with questions arising from the ratio analysis. The finance directors should seek to present answers to the questions using the annual report. Finally write a short report (250 words) on problems encountered in calculating and interpreting financial ratios.

Case 14.2

Turn to the annual report of a listed company which you have used for activities in previous chapters. Is this a group? How do you know? Where is the list of subsidiary companies?

If you do not have a group report, obtain another annual report which is for a group of companies (nearly all large listed companies operate in group form). As a group, imagine that you are a team of analysts seeking to break down the component segments of the group for analytical purposes. How much information can you find about the segments? What are the problems of defining segments in this group? If you can obtain the annual report for the previous year, compare the definitions of segments. Are they consistent from one year to the next?

Based on your analysis, prepare a short essay (250 words): 'The usefulness of segmental information in the analysis of group performance'.

Case 14.3

Divide the group into sections to take on four different roles: a private shareholder in a company; a financial journalist; a finance director of a company; and a broker's analyst providing an advisory service to clients.

In each section develop your opinion on the subject Taking the user needs perspective will solve all the problems of accounting.

Arrange a meeting to present all four opinions and then discuss the extent to which the International Accounting Standards Board will be able to obtain the co-operation of all parties in solving accounting problems.

Notes and references

1. ASB (1993, revised 2003), Statement, *Operating and Financial Review*, Accounting Standards Board.
2. Companies Act 2006, section 417; http://www.opsi.gov.uk/ACTS/acts2006/pdf/ukpga_20060046_en.pdf.
3. ASB (2006), *Reporting Statement 1: Operating and Financial Review*, issued January, 2006.
4. ASB (2006), RS 1 paras 75–7.
5. ASB (2006), RS 1 para. 1.
6. ASB (2006), RS 1 paras 4, 6, 8, 13, 16, 22 and 24.
7. ASB (2006), RS 1 para. 27.
8. IASB (2009), IFRS 8 *Operating Segments*, International Accounting Standards Board.
9. IASB (2009), IFRS 8 para. 1.
10. ASB (1994), Financial Reporting Standard (FRS 5), *Reporting the Substance of Transactions*, Accounting Standards Board.
11. The Committee on the Financial Aspects of Corporate Governance (1992) *The Financial Aspects of Corporate Governance* (The Cadbury Report), December. The Committee Chairman was Sir Adrian Cadbury.
12. *The Committee on Corporate Governance Final Report* (1998), Gee Publishing Ltd. (The Committee chairman was Sir Ronnie Hampel.)
13. Hampel Report, Principle DI.
14. *Report of a Study Group on Directors' Remuneration* (1995) (The Greenbury Report), Gee Publishing Ltd.
15. IASB (2009), IAS 1 *Presentation of financial statements*, para. 15.
16. IASB (2009), IAS 1 para. 15.
17. IASB (2009), IAS 1 para. 18.
18. IASB (2009), IAS 1 paras 19 and 20.
19. Companies Act 2006, section 393.
20. FRC (2008), The True and Fair Requirement Revisited. Opinion by Mr. Martin Moore, QC. April 2008. Financial Reporting Council website, www.frc.org.uk.
21. IASB *Framework*, para. 46.
22. Hoffman, L. and Arden, M. H. (1983), 'Legal opinion on "true and fair"', *Accountancy*, November, pp. 154–6.
23. ASB (1993), *Foreword to Accounting Standards*, appendix, 'Accounting Standards Board: the true and fair requirement', para. 4. Opinion prepared by Mary Arden, barrister of Erskine Chambers, Lincoln's Inn, London.
24. *Ibid.*, para. 14.
25. IASB *Framework*, paras 99–101.
26. ASB (1999), *Statement of Principles for Financial Reporting*, Chapter 5, 'Recognition in financial statements', paras 5.22–5.25.
27. *Ibid.*, para. 5.23, also explained in various IFRS such as IFRS 9 *Financial Instruments*
28. IASB (2009), IAS 16 *Property, Plant and Equipment*, para 31; ASB (1999), Financial Reporting Standard (FRS 15), *Measurement of Tangible Fixed Assets*, Accounting Standards Board, paras 43–52.
29. *Ibid.*, para. 6.19.
30. IASB *Framework*, para. 100.
31. ASC (1980), Statement of Standard Accounting Practice (SSAP 16), *Current Cost Accounting*, Accounting Standards Committee (issued March 1980 and withdrawn July 1988).

32. ASB (2000), Financial Reporting Standard (FRS 18), *Accounting Policies*, para. 28, Accounting Standards Board.
33. IASB (2009), IAS 16 *Property, Plant and Equipment*, para. 33.
34. IASB (2009), IAS 41 *Agriculture*, paras 13–25.
35. Hope, T. and Gray, R. (1982), 'Power and policy making: the development of an R&D standard', *Journal of Business Finance and Accounting*, **9** (4), pp. 531–58.

Chapter 15

Reporting cash flows

Descriptions of cash flow

Chairman's statement (extract)

Operating cash flow was £43.0 million (2008: £30 million), representing 93% of adjusted operating profit, despite an increase in stock and debtors commensurate with the growth of the business. Net debt for the year was reduced to £15.4 million (2008: £21.8 million) as operating cash flow was more than sufficient to fund acquisitions (including further investment in DB Power Electronics), capital expenditure, dividend payments, tax and interest.

. . . .

Net debt for the year was reduced to £15.4 million (2008: £21.8 million) as operating cash flow was more than sufficient to fund acquisitions (including further investment in DB Power Electronics), capital expenditure, dividend payments, tax and interest.

(Chairman's statement p. 4)

Financial review (extract)

Adjusted operating cash flow was again strong, nevertheless the strong growth in the business resulted in some investment in working capital. Good credit control was exercised (year-end debtor days were 76 [77 in 2008] and the level of overdue debtors remained constant at 15 days). This once again underpins the quality of the customer base and the related earnings. Management of the supply chain has been tightened further with inventory turns improving, although terms with key suppliers have been held or shortened in some cases to ensure quality and speed of delivery. Management remains committed to turning profits into cash to enable reinvestment in the businesses.

Financial review p. 20.

Adjusted operating profit

The reported basic earnings £26.617m was increased by a gain of £2.341m described as 'amortisation of acquired intangibles' to an adjusted profit of £28.958m.

Note 9, p. 67.

Source: Chloride plc Annual report 2009; http://www.chloridepower.com/upload/Financial%20reports/AR%202009.pdf.

Discussion points

1 How does the discussion explain the company's view on the cash invested in working capital?

2 Why might the company want to use cash flow to reduce net debt?

Contents

Learning outcomes

After reading this chapter you should be able to:

● Explain why statements of cash flows are regarded as providing useful information.

● Explain the meaning of cash and cash equivalents.

● Explain the direct and the indirect forms of presentation of a statement of cash flows.

● Prepare a statement of cash flows using the direct and the indirect method.

15.1 Introduction

The statement of cash flows is one of the primary financial statements. It provides information that can not be seen in the balance sheet and income statement (profit and loss account) alone. Users of financial statements want to know about changes in financial position. This involves providing information about an entity's ability to generate cash flows and the entity's use of those cash flows.

Chapter 3 gives a very simple introduction to the statement of cash flows. In particular it shows why cash flow and profit differ because of the different timings of cash flow and profits. Chapter 9 indicates the working capital cycle through which inventories are acquired from suppliers on credit and sold to customers on credit. The cash eventually received from customers is used to pay suppliers and the cycle starts again. Chapter 13 illustrates a statement of cash flows prepared from the balance sheets and income statement of the illustrative company used in that chapter. The case study of Safe and Sure plc runs throughout several chapters with outline discussion of the statement of cash flows in Chapter 4.

This chapter provides a more thorough explanation of a statement of cash flows as presented in the IASB system. It explains in sections 15.2 and 15.3 the nature of the two choices – the 'direct' and the 'indirect' methods. Section 15.4 explains the nature and purpose of each line item of a statement of cash flows prepared using the indirect system. Section 15.5 explains the nature and purpose of each line item of a statement of cash flows prepared using the direct system. Section 15.6 presents a worked example for those who wish to practise preparation of a statement of cash flows based on the IASB system.[1]

15.2 Cash and cash equivalents

The IASB system[2] presents a statement of cash flows that explains changes in **cash** and **cash equivalents**.

Definitions   **Cash** comprises cash on hand and demand deposits.

Cash equivalents are short-term, highly liquid investments that are readily convertible to known amounts of cash and which are subject to an insignificant risk of changes in value.[3]

Cash is relatively easy to understand – it is cash that is immediately available. Cash equivalents are investments that are held to meet short-term commitments. To qualify as a cash equivalent the investment must be readily convertible to a known amount of cash and there must be an insignificant risk of changes in value. An investment qualifies as a cash equivalent only when it has a short maturity of, say, three months or less from the date of acquisition.[4]

Bank borrowings are generally considered to be financing activities. However, bank overdrafts that are repayable on demand are part of the cash management of a business. The bank balance fluctuates from a positive balance to an overdrawn balance at different times of the year.[5]

15.3 The direct method and the indirect method

There are two approaches to presenting the cash flows arising from operations. The direct method presents cash inflows from customers and cash outflows to suppliers and employees, taken from the entity's accounting records of cash receipts and payments. The indirect method starts with the operating profit and makes a series of adjustments to convert profit to cash. The data in Table 15.1 and Table 15.2 is used to illustrate each method.

Table 15.1
Income statement (profit and loss account), Year 2

	£
Revenue	100
Cost of sales: materials	(40)
Wages	(20)
Depreciation	(10)
Operating profit	30

Table 15.2
Statements of financial position (balance sheets), end of Years 1 and 2

		Year 2		Year 1
		£		£
Non-current assets		90		100
Current assets				
Inventory (stock) of materials	55		40	
Trade receivables (debtors)	12		15	
Cash	35		10	
	102		65	
Current liabilities				
Trade payables (creditors)	(11)		(14)	
Current assets net of current liabilities		91		51
Non-current liabilities				
Long-term loans		(100)		(100)
Net assets		81		51
Ownership interest		81		51

15.3.1 Direct method

The direct method reports the cash inflows from customers and cash outflows to suppliers, employees and other aspects of operations. This information is contained in the cash book or in the cash receipts and cash payments records used as input to the bookkeeping records in the general ledger. The direct method calculation is presented in Table 15.3. It is followed by a comment on each line in the calculation.

Table 15.3
Direct method

Operating cash flow, Year 1	
	£
Cash received from customers	103
Cash paid to suppliers	(58)
Wages paid	(20)
Operating cash flow	25

General comment. In the direct method the cash flows are taken from the cash records. The cash records have to be analysed into categories suitable for the statement of cash flows. In Chapters 5 and 6 you have seen spreadsheets in which the cash record is the 'cash at bank' column. That column was used as the basis for the simple statement of cash flows on the direct method illustrated in those chapters (see sections 5.5.1 and 6.6.1). This chapter does not provide the detail of the cash records of receipts and payments but the following comments explain how the cash figures can be confirmed from the information in the balance sheet and the income statement (profit and loss account).

Cash received from customers. The cash inflows from customers may be confirmed by starting with the revenue earned in the period. Some of the revenue has been earned from selling to customers on credit. The amounts receivable from customers (debtors) at the start of the period will have been collected in cash during the period. The amounts shown as receivable from customers (debtors) at the end of the period are the revenue not yet collected in cash. This analysis is presented in the following calculation:

	£m
Revenue of the period	100
Add receivables at the start of the period	15
Less receivables at the end of the period	(12)
Cash received from customers	103

Cash paid to suppliers. The cash outflows to suppliers may be confirmed by starting with the materials purchased in the period. Some of the purchases have been obtained from suppliers on credit. The amounts payable to suppliers (creditors) at the start of the period will have been paid in cash during the period. The amounts shown as payable to suppliers (creditors) at the end of the period are the payments not yet made.

The next question is – how to confirm the figure for purchases?

The purchases of materials are needed to supply the goods sold and to provide an inventory at the end of the period. If there is an inventory (stock) at the start of the period this reduces the need to make purchases. This analysis is presented in the following calculation:

	£m
Cost of materials sold in the period	40
Add inventory at the end of the period	55
Less inventory at the start of the period	(40)
Purchases of materials	55

Then the payment to suppliers is calculated.

	£m
Purchases of the period	55
Add payables at the start of the period	14
Less payables at the end of the period	(11)
Cash paid to suppliers	58

Wages paid. Usually the wages are paid as soon as the work is done so the amount shown for wages in the income statement (profit and loss account) is the same as the cash payment. To confirm the wages payment, if any amount of wages remains unpaid at the start or end of the period then the wages cost must be adjusted for these unpaid amounts in a manner similar to the calculation of cash paid to suppliers.

15.3.2 Indirect method

The indirect method starts with the operating profit and makes adjustments to arrive at cash flow from operations. The indirect method calculation is presented in Table 15.4. It is followed by an explanation of each line in the calculation.

Table 15.4
Indirect method

Operating cash flow, Year 1	
	£
Operating profit	30
Add back depreciation	10
	40
(Increase) in inventory	(15)
Decrease in receivables	3
(Decrease) in payables	(3)
Operating cash flow	25

Operating profit. This figure is taken from the income statement in Table 15.1.

Add back depreciation. **Depreciation** is an accounting expense that does not involve any flow of cash. It is an **allocation** of the cost of the non-current (fixed) asset. So if we are looking for the cash generated by making profits, this depreciation needs to be excluded. It was deducted as an expense to calculate profit, so now it is added back to exclude it.

(Increase) in inventory. When a business acquires inventory it uses up cash. The cash is recovered when the inventory is sold. The greater the build-up of inventory, the greater the amount of cash that the business is waiting to recover. So an increase in inventory uses cash. A decrease in inventory releases cash and so is a source of cash.

Decrease in receivables. When a business sells goods or services to customers on credit it has to wait to collect the cash. The greater the increase in receivables (debtors) the greater is the amount of cash that the business is waiting to collect. So an increase in receivables has the effect of decreasing cash flow. A decrease in receivables releases cash and so is a source of cash.

(Decrease) in payables. When a business buys goods or services from suppliers on credit it delays payment of the cash. The greater the increase in payables (creditors) the greater is the amount of cash payment that the business is delaying. So an increase in payables has the effect of increasing cash flow by postponing payments. A decrease in payables means that suppliers are being paid sooner and so is equivalent to a use of cash.

Change in cash in the balance sheet. Finally it is important to check that the cash flow matches the change in cash in the balance sheet. Looking at the balance sheets in Table 15.2 you will see that the cash has increased from £10m to £35m which equals the positive cash flow of £25m calculated by both the direct and the indirect method.

15.3.3 Which to choose – direct or indirect?

When students are asked at this point whether they prefer the direct or the indirect method they usually choose the direct method because it looks less cumbersome. In practice almost all companies choose the indirect method because it can be prepared from the opening and closing balance sheets and the income statement (profit and loss account). Some supporters also argue that it is useful to highlight the effect of working capital on cash flows.

The direct method needs more work to identify all the operating flows from the cash records. Bookkeeping records, as illustrated in the supplements to previous chapters in this book, are based on ledger accounts which include non-cash items. The sales ledger account, for example, combines cash sales and credit sales. All expense accounts combine expenses paid in cash and expenses obtained on credit. In practice the direct method creates additional work in analysing the accounting records, because there are many aspects to operating cash flow. Supporters of cash flow reporting advocate the direct method because it gives a clearer picture of cash flows. It also provides information on details of cash flows that is not available under the indirect method.

The standard-setters recognise that there are valid arguments for and against each method and so continue to permit both. The IASB 'encourages' entities to report cash flow from operating activities using the direct method,[6] but this encouragement appears to have been ineffective in many cases.

15.4 Preparing a statement of cash flows: the indirect method

Most companies prepare their statement of cash flows using the **indirect method**. This means they start with the reported operating profit and then make adjustments to work back to the cash amounts that are incorporated in profit and in working capital. This section explains the indirect method. A format for a statement of cash flows is presented in Table 15.5. Line numbers have been added at the left-hand side. Each line is explained in the section following Table 15.5.

Table 15.5
Format for statement of cash flows, indirect method

Line		£m	£m
1	**Cash flows from operating activities**		
2	Profit before taxation		xx
3	Adjustment for items not involving a flow of cash:		
4	Depreciation, amortisation, gain or loss on disposal of non-current assets etc.		xx
5	*Adjusted profit*		xx
6	(Increase)/decrease in inventories	xx	
7	(Increase)/decrease in trade receivables	xx	
8	(Increase)/decrease in prepayments	xx	
9	Increase/*(decrease)* in cash due to (increases)/decreases in current assets	xx	
10	Increase/(decrease) in trade payables	xx	
11	Increase/(decrease) in accruals	xx	
12	Increase/(decrease) in cash due to increases/(decreases) in liabilities	xx	
13	Increase/(decrease) in cash due to working capital changes		xx
14	Cash generated from operations		xx
15	Interest paid		(xx)
16	Taxes paid		(xx)
17	*Net cash inflow from operating activities*		xx
18	**Cash flows from investing activities**		
19	Purchase of non-current assets	xx	
20	Proceeds from sale of non-current assets	xx	
21	Interest received	xx	
22	Dividends received	xx	
23	*Net cash used in investing activities*		xx
24	**Cash flows from financing activities**		
25	Proceeds from issue of share capital	xx	
26	Proceeds from long-term borrowing	xx	
27	Dividends paid	xx	
28	*Net cash used in financing activities*		xx
29	Increase/(decrease) in cash and cash equivalents		xx
30	**Cash and cash equivalents at the start of the period**		xx
31	**Cash and cash equivalents at the end of the period**		xx

Line 1 Cash flows from operating activities

This line indicates the start of the first major section of the statement of cash flows, showing how cash flows are generated from the operations of the business.

Line 2 Profit before taxation

The indirect method always starts with the operating profit *before* deducting interest and taxation, taken from the income statement (profit and loss account). This is because interest is seen as a separate payment to reward lenders and taxation is seen as a separate outflow of cash to government which needs to be emphasised. If the operating profit includes any investment income or interest received this must also be removed because it is reported in the separate section for investing activities (see lines 21 and 22). So the following checklist should be used to ensure the correct starting point:

	£m
Operating profit before taxes	xx
Is there any interest expense included in this figure? If so add it back to arrive at:	<u>xx</u>
Operating profit before deducting interest payable and taxes	xx
Is there any interest received/receivable or any dividends received in this figure? If so deduct it to arrive at:	(<u>xx</u>)
Operating profit before deducting interest payable and taxes and before including interest receivable and dividends received.	<u><u>xx</u></u>

Line 3 Adjustment for items not involving a flow of cash

The finance director now looks at the profit figure and asks, 'Are there any items in here that do not involve a flow of cash? If so we want to remove these so that we can get closer to cash.' Most income statements (profit and loss accounts) contain depreciation and amortisation, which have no effect on cash. Other items to look out for are changes in provisions, unrealised gains and losses on foreign currency translation.

Line 4 Adding back depreciation, amortisation, gain or loss on disposal etc

So the depreciation and amortisation are 'added back' to remove them from the profit figure. This usually causes some problems for readers of a statement of cash flows. If it worries you, just ask yourself – how did the depreciation get in there in the first place? The answer is that it was deducted as an expense, so if we add it back we exclude the expense. Other items that could come under this heading of 'not involving a flow of cash' are changes in provisions charged through income statement and gains or losses calculated on disposal of a non-current (fixed) asset. The following table summarises the action to be taken in the statement of cash flows:

Item in calculation	*Reason*
Add back any **expenses** that do not involve a flow of cash (e.g. depreciation, amortisation, loss on disposal of non-current assets).	These expenses reduced the profit but they do not involve any flow of cash and so must be excluded by adding back.
Deduct any **revenue** that does not involve a flow of cash (e.g. gain on disposal of non-current assets).	These revenues increased the profit but they do not involve any flow of cash and so must be excluded by deducting.

Line 5 Adjusted profit

In some presentations of the statement of cash flows this line is not shown separately, but it is a useful subtotal to remind yourself that you have now removed all non-cash items and you are ready to think about how working capital changes affect cash flow from operations.

Line 6 (Increase)/decrease in inventories (stocks)

When a business buys inventories of raw materials or produces work in progress and finished goods, it uses up cash. The cash is only recovered when the inventories are sold. While the inventories are increasing the cash invested in them is increasing and there is a negative impact on cash flow.

The following table summarises the action to be taken in the statement of cash flows:

Item in calculation	Reason
Deduct increase in inventories	Allowing inventories to increase takes up more cash in paying for them, or prevents cash being obtained through sale.
Add decrease in inventories	Allowing inventories to decrease reduces the cash needed to pay for them, or allows cash to be obtained through sale.

Line 7 (Increase)/decrease in trade receivables (debtors)

When a business sells goods and services on credit to customers, these customers are given some time to pay. They become debtors of the business until they pay cash. Selling goods and services on credit encourages customers to buy from the business but it delays the flow of cash to the business. The longer the period of credit taken by customers, the longer the delay. The danger of allowing the period of credit to increase is that the customer may become increasingly reluctant to pay. Chapter 13 explains how to estimate the average period of credit taken by credit customers.

The following table summarises the action to be taken in the statement of cash flows:

Item in calculation	Reason
Deduct increase in receivables	Allowing amounts of receivables to increase means that cash is not being collected from credit customers.
Add decrease in receivables	Allowing amounts of receivables to decrease means that cash is being collected faster from credit customers.

Line 8 (Increase)/decrease in prepayments

When a business makes payments for expenses in advance of enjoying the benefit of the payment, there is an outflow of cash. Examples are rent in advance or insurance premiums in advance (see Chapter 9 for the accounting treatment of prepayments). If the business is making more prepayments, there is a greater outflow of cash. If the business reduces its prepayments the cash flow position improves.

The following table summarises the action to be taken in the statement of cash flows:

Item in calculation	Reason
Deduct increase in prepayments	If prepayments increase then more cash is being used to make payments in advance.
Add decrease in prepayments	If prepayments decrease then less cash is being used to make payments in advance.

Line 9 Increase/(decrease) in cash due to (increases)/decreases in current assets

This line adds all the increases in current assets and deducts all the decreases in current assets. If the current assets have increased in total then the cash flow has decreased. If the current assets have decreased in total then the cash flow has increased. It is good practice to delete the alternative words here that do not apply to the particular circumstances of the company. Some published statements of cash flows leave all the words in the statement but this can be very confusing to readers.

Line 10 Increase/(decrease) in trade payables (creditors)

When a business buys goods or services on credit, the supplier often allows a period of credit. This helps the cash flow of the business in the gap between buying inputs and selling outputs of goods or services. The longer the period of credit taken from the supplier, the better the effect on cash flow. The danger of delaying payment beyond an agreed date is that the supplier may refuse to supply more goods or services and may even begin legal action for recovery of amounts owing. Chapter 13 explains how to calculate the average period of credit taken from suppliers.

The following table summarises the action to be taken in the statement of cash flows:

Item in calculation	Reason
Deduct decrease in payables	Allowing amounts of payables to decrease means that more cash is being paid to suppliers and other creditors.
Add increase in payables	Allowing amounts of payables to increase means that less cash is being paid to suppliers and other creditors.

Line 11 Increase/(decrease) in accruals

Accruals is the general description for unpaid expenses. If a business delays paying expenses there is a benefit for cash flow. If the accruals increase then there is a greater benefit for cash flow. The danger of delaying payment beyond an agreed date is that the supplier may refuse to supply more goods or services and may even begin legal action for recovery of amounts owing.

The following table summarises the action to be taken in the statement of cash flows:

Item in calculation	Reason
Deduct decrease in accruals	Allowing amounts of unpaid expenses (accruals) to decrease means that more cash is being paid to settle these obligations.
Add increase in accruals	Allowing amounts of unpaid expenses (accruals) to increase means that less cash is being paid to settle these obligations.

Line 12 Increase/(decrease) in cash due to increases/(decreases) in liabilities

This line adds all the increases in current liabilities and deducts all the decreases in current liabilities. If the current liabilities have increased in total then the cash flow has benefited – less cash has been paid to settle current liabilities. If the current liabilities have decreased in total then the cash flow has suffered – more cash has been paid to settle liabilities. It is good practice to delete the alternative words here that do not apply to the particular circumstances of the company. Some published statements of cash flows leave all the words in the statement but this can be very confusing to readers.

Line 13 Increase/(decrease) in cash due to working capital changes

This line shows the result of comparing the change in current assets with the change in current liabilities. There are several combinations of increases and decreases in current assets and liabilities so the easiest way to think about the outcome is to ask 'what has happened to working capital (current assets less current liabilities) overall?'

If the working capital has *increased*, then cash flow has *decreased*.
If the working capital has *decreased*, then cash flow has *increased*.

Line 14 Cash generated from operations

This is a subtotal combining the cash flow effect of the adjusted profit and the cash flow effect of the changes in working capital.

Line 15 Interest paid

Interest must be paid on loans. If it is not paid on time the lender will take action to demand payment of the interest and might even demand immediate repayment of the loan in full, depending on the conditions of the loan agreement. The interest expense in the income statement represents the interest cost of the accounting period but if the payment dates fall outside the accounting period there may be an accrual of unpaid interest in the balance sheet. A calculation is required to arrive at the amount of cash paid during the accounting period.

Item in calculation	Reason
Interest expense in income statement	We are starting with the expense in the income statement, to adjust it to a cash figure.
minus liability at end of period	This is the part of the expense that has not yet been paid in cash.
plus liability at start of period	During this period the liability at the start of the period has been paid.
equals cash paid to lenders	

Line 16 Taxes paid

There is a corporation tax expense in the income statement (profit and loss account). The due dates for payment depend on the size of the company, as explained in Chapter 10. Any unpaid taxation at the start or end of the period will appear as a liability in the balance sheet. A calculation is required to arrive at the amount of tax paid in the accounting period.

Item in calculation	Reason
Taxation expense in income statement	We are starting with the expense in the income statement, to adjust it to a cash figure.
minus liability at end of period	This is the part of the expense that has not yet been paid in cash.
plus liability at start of period	During this period the liability at the start of the period has been paid.
equals cash paid to tax authorities	

Line 17 Net cash inflow from operating activities

This is a subtotal that indicates the end of the first major section of the statement of cash flows.

Line 18 Cash flows from investing activities

This line starts the second major section of the statement of cash flows showing how cash has been used for making new investment in non-current assets and also released from sales of existing investment in non-current assets.

Line 19 Purchase of non-current assets

In many cases the amount spent on non-current assets will be known from the accounting records. However, if you are preparing a statement of cash flows using only the balance sheet and income statement plus some notes, you may find that you need to calculate the amount spent on non-current assets. The following table summarises the calculation of changes in non-current assets which includes the cash payment. It assumes that all assets of one type are recorded together as one category (e.g. vehicles, plant and machinery). The following table summarises the calculation of changes in non-current assets which includes the cash payment for additions to non-current assets.

Item in calculation	Reason
Original cost of non-current assets in a specified category at start of period	Begin with the amount of the assets at the start of the period.
plus cash paid for additions	**Cash is spent during the period on additions to the assets.**
minus disposals at original cost	Assets are removed – see later calculation of gain or loss on disposal.
equals Non-current assets at end of period	The result is the amount of the assets at the end of the period.

Line 20 Proceeds from sale of non-current assets

This line reports the cash received from sale or disposal of non-current assets. It is important to use the cash received from the disposal of the asset and not the gain or loss on disposal recorded in the income statement (profit and loss account). Look back to Chapter 8 and you will see that the gain or loss on disposal arises only when the cash received is different from the book value. If the depreciation had been calculated with perfect foresight then the net book value would be equal to the cash received and there would be no gain or loss. A gain or loss on disposal is the result of estimating depreciation at the start of the asset's life when the proceeds on disposal have to be estimated.

The following table summarises the calculation relating to the sale or disposal of non-current assets which includes the cash received.

Item in calculation	Comment
Original cost of non-current asset at start of period	This item of information is shown as 'disposal' in the 'cost' section of the schedule of non-current assets.
minus accumulated depreciation of non-current asset at start of period	This item of information is shown as 'disposal' in the 'accumulated depreciation' section of the schedule of non-current assets.
***minus* cash received on disposal**	**This is the amount of cash received for the asset sold.**
equals gain or loss on disposal	The gain or loss on disposal is reported in the income statement.

Line 21 Interest received

Interest received is a reward for investment and so it is regarded as part of the cash flows relating to investing activities. Look back to the calculations in the workings for line 2 and you will see the item:

> Is there any interest received/receivable or any dividends received in this figure? If so deduct it.

The interest receivable is removed in calculating operating profit at line 2 so that interest received can be inserted at line 21. The following table summarises the action to be taken in the statement of cash flows:

Item in calculation	Reason
Interest receivable in the income statement	We are starting with the revenue reported in the income statement, to adjust it to a cash figure.
minus asset at end of period	This is the part of the revenue that has not yet been received in cash.
plus asset at start of period	During this period the asset at the start of the period has been received.
equals interest received in cash	

Line 22 Dividends received

The dividends received relate to equity investments held by the company. The calculation is very similar to that for interest received.

Item in calculation	Reason
Dividend receivable in the income statement	We are starting with the revenue reported in the income statement, to adjust it to a cash figure.
minus asset at end of period	This is the part of the revenue that has not yet been received in cash.
plus asset at start of period	During this period the asset at the start of the period has been received.
equals dividend received in cash	

Line 23 Net cash used in investing activities

This subtotal indicates the end of the second major section of the statement of cash flows. It will usually be a negative figure showing that the business is expanding through more investment in non-current assets. Less commonly, a business may be selling off existing investments to raise cash for future plans. Having the separate subtotal draws attention to the magnitude and direction of investing activities.

Line 24 Cash flows from financing activities

This line starts the third and final major section of the statement of cash flows showing how cash has been raised from financing activities. This usually means issuing new share capital and raising or repaying long-term loans.

Line 25 Proceeds from issue of share capital

Chapter 12 explains the process of issuing share capital, both when the business starts and when it looks for more finance some time later. In many cases the shares are issued at market price, which is higher than nominal value. The difference is called a share premium. The total cash raised is measured in terms of the market price but company law requires separate reporting of the change in nominal value and the changes in the share premium. The calculation required is as follows:

Item in calculation	Reason
Increase in nominal value of share capital *Increase* in share *plus* premium reserve *equals* cash received from issue of shares	The amount of cash raised by issuing shares at market price is the nominal value plus the share premium.

Line 26 Proceeds from long-term borrowings

The proceeds from long-term borrowings can be seen from the change in the balance sheet figures for long-term borrowings, after allowing for any long-term borrowings that have changed category to short term in the accounting period.

Item in calculation	Reason
Long-term borrowing in balance sheet at the start of the period	We are starting with amount reported in the balance sheet at the start of the accounting period.
minus long-term reclassified as short-term during the period	This is the part of loan that is reclassified but remains in the balance sheet.
plus new loans taken up in cash	Cash received.
minus loans repaid	Cash paid out.
equals long-term borrowing in balance sheet at the end of the period	The amount reported in the balance sheet at the end of the accounting period.

Line 27 Dividends paid

The dividend paid during the period may be a combination of the dividend paid in respect of the previous year's profit plus an interim dividend for the current year. Chapter 12 explains in more detail the accounting procedures for reporting dividends. The amount of dividend paid will appear in the statement of changes in equity.

Line 28 Net cash used in financing activities

This subtotal indicates the end of the third section of the statement of cash flows.

Line 29 Increase/(decrease) in cash and cash equivalents

This line is the arithmetic total of the three separate sections as reported in lines 17 + 23 + 28.

Lines 30 and 31 Cash and cash equivalents at the start and end of the period

This is the moment of truth where you find out whether you have made errors on the way through the statement of cash flows. Lines 30 and 31 are taken from the balance sheet. If your statement of cash flows is correct then line 29 plus line 30 will equal line 31. The following table is used to record the information extracted from the balance sheet.

	Start of period	End of period
Cash on hand and balances with banks	xx	xx
Short-term investments	xx	xx
Cash and cash equivalents	xx	xx

15.5 Preparing a statement of cash flows: the direct method

Line 1 Cash flows from operating activities

This line indicates the start of the first major section of the statement of cash flows, showing how cash flows are generated from the operations of the business.

Line 2 Cash receipts from customers

This line reports the total cash received from customers in the period. Some customers may have paid immediate cash for goods and services. Others may have taken credit and paid later.

Line 3 Cash paid to suppliers

This line reports the total cash paid to suppliers in the period. The business may have paid immediate cash for some goods and services. In other cases the suppliers may have allowed a period of credit to be paid later.

Line 4 Cash paid to employees

This line reports the total cash paid to employees in the period. Usually the employees are paid promptly each week or each month and so the cash payments are closely related to the wages expense.

Lines 14 to 31 have the same meaning as described for these lines in Section 15.4.

The alternative *direct method* is shown in Table 15.6 and explained as follows.

Table 15.6
Format for statement of cash flows, direct method

Line		£m	£m
1	**Cash flows from operating activities**		
2	Cash receipts from customers		xx
3	Cash paid to suppliers		xx
4	Cash paid to employees		xx
5–13	*(Lines not used)*		
14	Cash generated from operations		xx
15	Interest paid		(xx)
16	Taxes paid		(xx)
17	*Net cash inflow from operating activities*		xx
18	**Cash flows from investing activities**		
19	Purchase of non-current assets	xx	
20	Proceeds from sale of non-current assets	xx	
21	Interest received	xx	
22	Dividends received	xx	
23	*Net cash used in investing activities*		xx
24	**Cash flows from financing activities**		
25	Proceeds from issue of share capital	xx	
26	Proceeds from long-term borrowing	xx	
27	Dividends paid	xx	
28	*Net cash used in financing activities*		xx
29	Increase/(decrease) in cash and cash equivalents		xx
30	**Cash and cash equivalents at the start of the period**		xx
31	**Cash and cash equivalents at the end of the period**		xx

15.6 Interpretation of cash flow information

The cash flow information is useful in itself in showing trends in the company's cash resources. Some businesses operate on cycles lasting several years where the cash position moves from negative to positive. The industry position is often a useful starting point for understanding company cash flows. If the industry is cyclical and all companies in the sector have negative cash flow then we might expect any company in the sector to show the same trends. Equally, any company in the sector should be showing signs of improvement as the cycle moves upwards.

For the indirect method, which reports the cash flow effects of working capital, it may be useful to link the increases or decreases in working capital items to the number of days in the working capital cycle. The calculation of the working capital cycle appears in Chapter 13. For example, if there is an increase in cash invested in inventory there are two possible causes: one is a lengthening of the stock holding period and the other is an increase in sales volume causing more inventory to be held. The stock holding period helps to narrow down the possible cause. If the trade receivables increase there are two possible causes. One is that customers are taking longer to pay and the other is that credit sales are increasing. The period of credit given to customers helps to narrow down the cause here.

The amount of cash invested in capital expenditure is an important sign of the continuing development of the business. Ratios are used by analysts in comparing capital expenditure to depreciation and comparing capital expenditure to the existing asset base.

15.7 Illustration

The following information is used to illustrate the indirect method and then compare the direct method of preparing and presenting a statement of cash flows.

Income statement Year 2

	£m
Revenue	246
Cost of sales	(110)
Gross profit	136
Investment income – interest received	4
Gain on disposal of equipment	5
Depreciation	(30)
Administrative and selling expenses	(10)
Operating profit before interest	105
Interest expense	(15)
Profit after deducting interest	90
Taxation	(30)
Profit after tax	60

Statements of financial position (balance sheets) at 31 December

	Year 2		Year 1	
	£m	£m	£m	£m
Non-current assets				
Property, plant and equipment at cost		150		100
Accumulated depreciation 40 + 30 − 10		(60)		(40)
		90		60
Investments		100		100
Current assets				
Inventory (stock)	20		15	
Trade receivables (debtors)	18		16	
Cash and cash equivalents	32		5	
	70		36	
Current liabilities				
Trade payables (creditors)	(14)		(13)	
Interest payable	(6)		(7)	
Taxes payable	(8)		(7)	
	(28)		(27)	
		42		9
Non-current liabilities				
Long-term loans		(20)		(15)
Net assets		212		154
Capital and reserves				
Share capital		140		130
Share premium		20		18
Retained earnings		52		6
		212		154

Further information

1 The dividend paid during Year 2 was £14m. The retained earnings increased by £60m profit of the period and decreased by the amount of the dividend £14m.
2 During Year 2 the company acquired property, plant and equipment costing £80m.
3 During Year 2 the company sold property, plant and equipment that had an original cost of £30m and accumulated depreciation of £10m. The proceeds of sale were £25m.

15.7.1 Indirect method

A statement of cash flows using the indirect method is presented in Table 15.7.

Table 15.7
Statement of cash flows using the indirect method

Notes		£m	£m
	Cash flows from operating activities		
1	Profit before taxation		101
	Adjustment for items not involving a flow of cash:		
2	Depreciation	30	
3	Gain on disposal of equipment	(5)	
			25
	Adjusted profit		126
4	(Increase) in inventories	(5)	
5	(Increase) in trade receivables	(2)	
6	Increase in trade payables	1	
	Increase/(decrease) in cash due to working capital changes		(6)
	Cash generated from operations		120
7	Interest paid		(16)
8	Taxes paid		(29)
	Net cash inflow from operating activities		75
	Cash flows from investing activities		
9	Purchase of non-current assets	(80)	
10	Proceeds from sale of non-current assets	25	
11	Interest received	4	
	Net cash used in investing activities		(51)
	Cash flows from financing activities		
12	Proceeds from issue of share capital	12	
13	Proceeds from long-term borrowing	5	
14	Dividends paid	(14)	
	Net cash used in financing activities		3
	Increase/(decrease) in cash and cash equivalents		27
15	**Cash and cash equivalents at the start of the period**		5
15	**Cash and cash equivalents at the end of the period**		32

Working note 1

	£m
Operating profit before taxes	90
Is there any interest expense included in this figure? If so add it back to arrive at:	15
Operating profit before deducting interest payable and taxes	105
Is there any interest received/receivable or any dividends received in this figure? If so deduct it to arrive at:	(4)
Operating profit before deducting interest payable and taxes and before including interest receivable and dividends received.	101

Working note 2

The depreciation is seen in the income statement (profit and loss account). It is added back to exclude the effect of a non-cash item.

Working note 3

The gain on disposal is seen in the income statement (profit and loss account). It is added back to exclude the effect of a non-cash item.

Working note 4

There is an increase in inventory seen by comparing the balance sheets at the end of year 1 and year 2. This decreases the cash flow.

Working note 5

There is an increase in trade receivables (debtors) seen by comparing the balance sheets at the end of year 1 and year 2. This decreases the cash flow.

Working note 6

There is an increase in trade payables (creditors) seen by comparing the balance sheets at the end of year 1 and year 2. This has a positive effect on the cash flow by increasing the amount unpaid.

Working note 7

Interest paid is calculated from the profit and loss account expense £15m plus the unpaid interest at the start of the year £7m minus the unpaid interest at the end of the year, £6m.

Working note 8

Taxes paid are calculated from the profit and loss account charge £30m plus the unpaid liability at the start of the year £7m minus the unpaid liability at the end of the year £8m.

Working note 9

The purchase cost of non-current assets is given in the further information. It can be checked by taking the cost at the start of the year £100m, adding £80m and deducting the £30m cost of the disposal to leave £150m as shown in the balance sheet at the end of the year.

Working note 10

The proceeds of sale £25m are given in the further information. This can be checked by taking the net book value of the asset sold (£30m – £10m = £20m) and adding the gain on disposal, the £5m shown in the income statement.

Working note 11

The interest received is taken from the income statement. There is no interest receivable shown in the balance sheet so the profit and loss account figure must be the same as the cash figure.

Working note 12

The proceeds from the share issue are the total of the increase in share capital £10m plus the increase in share premium £2m.

Working note 13

The proceeds from long-term borrowings are the increase in long-term loans calculated by comparing the opening and closing balance sheets.

Working note 14

The dividend paid is given in the further information. It can be checked by taking the retained earnings at the start of the period, £6m, add the profit of the period, £60m, and deduct dividend £14m to arrive at the retained earnings at the end of the period, £52m.

Working note 15

The cash and cash equivalents at the start and end of the period are taken from the balance sheet.

15.7.2 Direct method

A statement of cash flows presented by the direct method is presented in Table 15.8.

Table 15.8
Statement of cash flows using the direct method

Notes		£m	£m
	Cash flows from operating activities		
1	Cash receipts from customers		244
2	Cash paid to suppliers and employees		(114)
3	Cash paid for administrative and selling expenses		(10)
	Cash generated from operations		120
4	Interest paid		(16)
5	Taxes paid		(29)
	Net cash inflow from operating activities		75
	Cash flows from investing activities		
6	Purchase of non-current assets	(80)	
7	Proceeds from sale of non-current assets	25	
8	Interest received	4	
	Net cash used in investing activities		(51)
	Cash flows from financing activities		
9	Proceeds from issue of share capital	12	
10	Proceeds from long-term borrowing	5	
11	Dividends paid	(14)	
	Net cash used in financing activities		3
	Increase/(decrease) in cash and cash equivalents		27
12	**Cash and cash equivalents at the start of the period**		5
12	**Cash and cash equivalents at the end of the period**		32

In practice the cash receipts from customers and cash payments to suppliers and employees are taken from the records of cash received and paid, which requires analysis of the cash records. In this relatively straightforward situation the figures may be confirmed from the information in the balance sheet and income statement (profit and loss account).

Working note 1

The cash receipts from customers may be confirmed from revenue £246m, plus receivables at the start of the period £16m, minus receivables at the end of the period £18m, equals £244m.

Working note 2

There are two stages to the confirmation of cash paid to suppliers. First the purchases are calculated from cost of sales £110m plus inventory at the end £20m minus inventory at the start £15m = £115m. Next the payment to suppliers is confirmed from purchases: £115m plus liability at the start £13m minus liability at the end £14m equals £114m. It is assumed that the wages are all paid when the work is done so there is no accrual.

Working note 3

The administrative and selling expenses are seen in the income statement. There is no accrual indicated in the balance sheet and so the cash figure equals the expense figure.

Working notes 4 to 12

See working notes 7 to 15 for the indirect method.

15.7.3 Comment on statement of cash flows

The cash flow from operating activities amounted to £75m. The purchase of non-current (fixed) assets cost £80m but this was offset by £25m proceeds of sale of non-current assets no longer required and was also helped by the £4m interest received from investments. The net outflow from investments was £51m. This left £24m of cash flow available to increase cash resources but £14m was required for dividend payments. The remaining £10m was added to the proceeds of a share issue, £12m and an increase in long-term loans, £5m, giving an overall cash inflow of £27m.

15.8 Summary

- The statement of cash flows provides information about changes in financial position that adds to the understanding of the business obtainable from the balance sheet and income statement (profit and loss account).
- It explains changes in cash and cash equivalents arising from operating activities, investing activities and financing activities.
- **Cash** comprises cash on hand and demand deposits.
- **Cash equivalents** are short-term, highly liquid investments that are readily convertible to known amounts of cash and which are subject to an insignificant risk of changes in value.
- The **indirect method** and the **direct method** are alternative approaches to calculating the cash flow arising from operating activities.
- The **indirect method** starts with the profit from operations, eliminates non-cash expenses such as depreciation, and adds on or deducts the effects of changes in working capital to arrive at the cash flow arising from operating activities.
- The **direct method** takes each item of operating cash flow separately from the cash records to arrive at the cash flow arising from operating activities.
- The cash flow is useful in analysis when combined with ratio analysis that shows relationships of liquidity, working capital management, rates of investment in non-current assets and financial gearing.

Further reading

The following standard is too detailed for a first-level course, but the definitions section may be helpful and the Appendices give illustrations of statements of cash flows.

IASB (2004), IAS 7, *Statement of Cash Flows*, International Accounting Standards Board.

QUESTIONS

The Questions section of each chapter has three types of question. 'Test your understanding' questions to help you review your reading are in the 'A' series of questions. You will find the answers to these by reading and thinking about the material in the book. 'Application' questions to test your ability to apply technical skills are in the 'B' series of questions. Questions requiring you to show skills in problem solving and evaluation are in the 'C' series of questions. A letter [S] indicates that there is a solution at the end of the book.

A   Test your understanding

A15.1   What is the definition of 'cash'? (Section 15.2)

A15.2   What is the definition of 'cash equivalent'? (Section 15.2)

A15.3   What is meant by the 'direct method' of calculating operating cash flow? (Section 15.3.1)

A15.4   What is meant by the 'indirect method' of calculating operating cash flow? (Section 15.3.2)

A15.5   Why is depreciation 'added back' to operating profit in the indirect method of calculating operating cash flow? (Section 15.3.2)

A15.6   What is the effect on cash flow of an increase in inventory levels? (Section 15.3.2)

A15.7   What is the effect on cash flow of an increase in trade receivables (debtors)? (Section 15.3.2)

A15.8   What is the effect on cash flow of an increase in trade payables (creditors)? (Section 15.3.2)

A15.9   What are the relative benefits of the direct method compared to the indirect method? (Section 15.3.3)

A15.10 What are the three main sections of a statement of cash flows? (Section 15.4)

A15.11 What kinds of items in a profit and loss account do not involve a flow of cash? (Section 15.4)

A15.12 What happens to cash flow when working capital increases? (Section 15.4)

A15.13 How is taxation paid calculated from the taxation payable and the taxation liability at the start and end of the period? (Section 15.4)

A15.14 How is the cash paid for additions to fixed assets if we know the opening and closing balances and there are no disposals? (Section 15.4)

A15.15 Explain how the proceeds of sale of a non-current asset differ from the net book value. (Section 15.4)

A15.16 Explain how the cash proceeds of a share issue are calculated from knowledge of the share capital and the share premium reserve. (Section 15.4)

A15.17 Explain how cash received from customers is calculated if we know the sales of the period and the receivables (debtors) at the start and end of the period. (Section 15.5)

A15.18 Explain how the purchases of goods or materials is calculated if we know the cost of goods sold and the inventory (stock) at the start and end of the period. (Section 15.5)

A15.19 Explain how the cash paid to suppliers is calculated if we know the purchases and the payables (creditors) at the start and end of the period. (Section 15.5)

B   Application

B15.1 [S]
Sales on credit during Year 2 amount to £120m. The trade receivables (debtors) at the start of Year 2 were £8. The trade receivables (debtors) at the end of Year 2 were £10. What is the amount of cash received from customers during Year 2?

B15.2 [S]
Purchases on credit during Year 3 amount to £20m. The trade payables (creditors) at the start of Year 3 were £6m. The trade payables (creditors) at the end of Year 3 were £4m. What is the amount of cash paid to suppliers during Year 3?

B15.3 [S]

The equipment at cost account at the start of Year 2 records a total of £34m. The equipment at cost account at the end of Year 2 records a total of £37m. An asset of original cost £5m was sold during the period. What was the amount spent on acquisition of equipment?

B15.4

A vehicle costing £20m and having accumulated depreciation of £12m was sold for £5m. How will this information be reported in the statement of cash flows?

B15.5

The share capital account increased by £40m during Year 4. The share premium reserve increased by £20m. What amount of cash was raised by the issue of shares?

B15.6

The corporation tax charge in the income statement (profit and loss account) for Year 2 was £30m. The tax liability in the balance sheet at the start of Year 2 was £6m. The tax liability in the balance sheet at the end of Year 2 was £10m. What was the amount of cash paid in taxation during Year 2?

B15.7

D Ltd has an operating profit of £12m, which includes a depreciation charge of £1m. During the year the trading stock has increased by £4m, trade debtors have increased by £3m and trade creditors have increased by £5m. Prepare a statement of cash flow from operations.

B15.8

E Ltd has an operating profit of £16m, which includes a depreciation charge of £2m. During the year the trading stock has increased by £1m, trade debtors have decreased by £3m and trade creditors have decreased by £2m. Prepare a statement of cash flow from operations.

C   Problem solving and evaluation

C15.1 [S]

The directors of Fruit Sales plc produced the following income statement (profit and loss account) for Year 2 and balance sheet at the end of Year 2.

Income statement for year 2

	£m
Revenue	320
Cost of sales	(143)
Gross profit	177
Investment income – interest received	5
Gain on disposal of equipment	7
Depreciation	(39)
Administrative and selling expenses	(13)
Operating profit before interest	137
Interest expense	(20)
Profit after deducting interest	117
Taxation	(35)
Profit after tax	82

Statements of financial position (balance sheets) at 31 December

	Year 2		Year 1	
	£m	£m	£m	£m
Non-current assets				
Vehicles at cost		195		130
Accumulated depreciation		(79)		(52)
		116		78
Investments		100		80
Current assets				
Inventory (stock)	26		20	
Trade receivables (debtors)	23		21	
Cash and cash equivalents	43		6	
	92		47	
Current liabilities				
Trade payables (creditors)	(18)		(13)	
Interest payable	(8)		(7)	
Taxes payable	(10)		(7)	
	(36)		(27)	
		56		20
Non-current liabilities				
Long-term loans		(26)		(18)
Net assets		246		160
Capital and reserves				
Share capital		152		120
Share premium		26		23
Retained earnings		68		17
		246		160

Further information

1 The dividend paid during Year 2 was £31m. The retained earnings increased by £82m profit of the period and decreased by the amount of the dividend £31m.
2 During Year 2 the company acquired vehicles costing £90m.
3 During Year 2 the company sold vehicles that had an original cost of £25m and accumulated depreciation of £12m. The proceeds of sale were £20m.
4 Cost of sales consists entirely of purchases of fruit on credit from suppliers. Wages are included in administrative and selling expenses and are paid when incurred.

Required

1 Prepare a statement of cash flows using (a) the direct method and (b) the indirect method of calculating operating cash flow.
2 Write a comment on the cash flow of the period.

C15.2

Consider the following:

	£m
Revenue	320
Cost of sales	(143)
Gross profit	177
Investment income – interest received	5
Loss on disposal of equipment	(8)
Depreciation	(39)
Administrative and selling expenses	(13)
Operating profit before interest	122
Interest expense	(6)
Profit after deducting interest	116
Taxation	(39)
Profit after tax	77

Statements of financial position (balance sheets) at 31 December

	Year 2		Year 1	
	£m	£m	£m	£m
Property, plant and equipment at cost		225		150
Accumulated depreciation		(90)		(60)
		135		90
Investment		70		100
Inventory (stock)	30		22	
Trade receivables (debtors)	27		24	
Cash and cash equivalents	48		8	
	105		54	
Trade payables (creditors)	(21)		(20)	
Interest payable	(9)		(11)	
Taxes payable	(12)		(9)	
	(42)		(40)	
		63		14
Long-term loans		(20)		(15)
Net assets		248		189
Share capital		144		140
Share premium		26		23
Retained earnings		78		26
		248		189

Further information
1 The dividend paid during Year 2 was £25m. The retained earnings increased by £77m profit of the period and decreased by the amount of the dividend, £25m.
2 During Year 2 the company acquired property, plant and equipment costing £94m.
3 During Year 2 the company sold for scrap property, plant and equipment that had an original cost of £19m and accumulated depreciation of £9m. The proceeds of disposal were £2m.
4 Investments were sold during the year for cash proceeds of £30m. There were no purchases of investments.

Required
1 Prepare a statement of cash flows using (a) the direct method and (b) the indirect method of calculating operating cash flow.
2 Write a comment on the cash flow of the period.

Notes and references

1. Statements of cash flows in published financial statements are often prepared for a group as a whole. The details of group statements of cash flows are too complex for a first-level text, but in general appearance they are similar to those for individual companies.
2. IASB (2009), IAS 7 *Statement of Cash Flows*.
3. IAS 7 para. 6.
4. IAS 7 para. 7.
5. IAS 7 para. 8.
6. IAS 7 para. 19.

Financial accounting terms defined

The definition of one word or phrase may depend on understanding another word or phrase defined elsewhere in the reference list. Words in **bold** indicate that such a definition is available.

account payable An amount due for payment to a supplier of goods or services, also described as a **trade creditor**.

account receivable an amount due from a customer, also described as a **trade debtor**.

accountancy firm A business partnership (or possibly a limited company) in which the partners are qualified accountants. The firm undertakes work for clients in respect of audit, accounts preparation, tax and similar activities.

accountancy profession The collective body of persons qualified in accounting, and working in accounting-related areas. Usually they are members of a professional body, membership of which is attained by passing examinations.

accounting The process of identifying, measuring and communicating financial information about an entity to permit informed judgements and decisions by users of the information.

accounting equation The relationship between assets, liabilities and ownership interest.

accounting period Time period for which financial statements are prepared (e.g. month, quarter, year).

accounting policies Accounting methods which have been judged by business enterprises to be most appropriate to their circumstances and adopted by them for the purpose of preparing their financial statements.

accounting standards Definitive statements of best practice issued by a body having suitable authority.

Accounting Standards Board The authority in the UK which issues definitive statements of best accounting practice.

accruals basis The effects of transactions and other events are recognised when they occur (and not as cash or its equivalent is received or paid) and they are recorded in the accounting records and reported in the financial statements of the periods to which they relate (see also **matching**).

accumulated depreciation Total **depreciation** of a **non-current (fixed) asset**, deducted from original cost to give **net book value**.

acid test The ratio of liquid assets to current liabilities.

acquiree Company that becomes controlled by another.

acquirer Company that obtains control of another.

acquisition An acquisition takes place where one company – the **acquirer** – acquires control of another – the **acquiree** – usually through purchase of shares.

acquisition method Production of **consolidated financial statements** for an **acquisition**.

administrative expenses Costs of managing and running a business.

agency A relationship between a principal and an agent. In the case of a limited liability company, the shareholder is the principal and the director is the agent.

agency theory A theoretical model, developed by academics, to explain how the relationship between a principal and an agent may have economic consequences.

aggregate depreciation See **accumulated depreciation**.

allocate To assign a whole item of cost, or of revenue, to a simple cost centre, account or time period.

allocated, allocation See **allocate**.

amortisation Process similar to **depreciation**, usually applied to intangible fixed assets.

annual report A document produced each year by limited liability companies containing the accounting information required by law. Larger companies also provide information and pictures of the activities of the company.

articles of association Document setting out the relative rights of shareholders in a limited liability company.

articulation The term 'articulation' is used to refer to the impact of transactions on the balance sheet and profit and loss account through application of the accounting equation.

assets Rights or other access to future economic benefits controlled by an entity as a result of past transactions or events.

associated company One company exercises significant influence over another, falling short of complete control.

audit An audit is the independent examination of, and expression of opinion on, financial statements of an entity.

audit manager An employee of an accountancy firm, usually holding an accountancy qualification, given a significant level of responsibility in carrying out an audit assignment and responsible to the partner in charge of the audit.

bad debt It is known that a credit customer (**debtor**) is unable to pay the amount due.

balance sheet A statement of the financial position of an entity showing assets, liabilities and ownership interest. Under the **IASB system** the preferred title is **statement of financial position**.

bank facility An arrangement with a bank to borrow money as required up to an agreed limit.

bond The name sometimes given to loan finance (more commonly in the USA).

broker (stockbroker) Member of a stock exchange who arranges purchase and sale of shares and may also provide an information service giving buy/sell/hold recommendations.

broker's report Bulletin written by a stockbroking firm for circulation to its clients, providing analysis and guidance on companies as potential investments.

business combination A transaction in which one company acquires control of another.

business cycle Period (usually 12 months) during which the peaks and troughs of activity of a business form a pattern which is repeated on a regular basis.

business entity A business which exists independently of its owners.

business review A report by the directors giving a fair review of the company's business to inform members of the company and help them assess how the directors have performed their duty to promote the success of the company.

called up (share capital) The company has called upon the shareholders who first bought the shares, to make their payment in full.

capital An amount of finance provided to enable a business to acquire assets and sustain its operations.

capital expenditure Spending on **non-current** (**fixed**) assets of a business.

capitalisation issue Issue of shares to existing shareholders in proportion to shares already held. Raises no new finance but changes the mix of share capital and reserves.

cash Cash on hand (such as money held in a cash box or a safe) and deposits in a bank that may be withdrawn on demand.

cash equivalents Short-term, highly liquid investments that are readily convertible to known amounts of cash and which are subject to an insignificant risk of changes in value.

cash flow projections Statements of cash expected to flow into the business and cash expected to flow out over a particular period.

chairman The person who chairs the meetings of the board of directors of a company (preferably not the chief executive).

charge In relation to interest or taxes, describes the reduction in ownership interest reported in the income statement (profit and loss account) due to the cost of interest and tax payable.

chief executive The director in charge of the day-to-day running of a company.

close season Period during which those who are 'insiders' to a listed company should not buy or sell shares.

commercial paper A method of borrowing money from commercial institutions such as banks.

Companies Act The Companies Act 1985 as modified by the Companies Act 1989. Legislation to control the activities of limited liability companies.

comparability Qualitative characteristic expected in financial statements, comparable within company and between companies.

completeness Qualitative characteristic expected in financial statements.

conceptual framework A statement of principles providing generally accepted guidance for the development of new reporting practices and for challenging and evaluating the existing practices.

conservatism See **prudence**. Sometimes used with a stronger meaning of understating assets and overstating liabilities.

consistency The measurement and display of similar transactions and other events is carried out in a consistent way throughout an entity within each accounting period and from one period to the next, and also in a consistent way by different entities.

consolidated financial statements Present financial information about the group as a single reporting entity.

consolidation Consolidation is a process that aggregates the total assets, liabilities and results of the parent and its subsidiaries (the group) in the **consolidated financial statements**.

contingent liabilities Obligations that are not recognised in the balance sheet because they depend upon some future event happening.

control The power to govern the financial and operating policies of an entity so as to obtain benefits from its activities.

convertible loan Loan finance for a business that is later converted into **share capital**.

corporate governance The system by which companies are directed and controlled. Boards of directors are responsible for the governance of their companies.

corporate recovery department Part of an accountancy firm which specialises in assisting companies to recover from financial problems.

corporate social responsibility Companies integrate social and environmental concerns in their business operations and in their interactions with stakeholders.

corporation tax Tax payable by companies, based on the taxable profits of the period.

cost of a non-current asset is the cost of making it ready for use, cost of finished goods is cost of bringing them to the present condition and location.

cost of goods sold Materials, labour and other costs directly related to the goods or services provided.

cost of sales See **cost of goods sold**.

coupon Rate of interest payable on a loan.

credit (bookkeeping system) Entries in the credit column of a ledger account represent increases in liabilities, increases in ownership interest, revenue, or decreases in assets.

credit (terms of business) The supplier agrees to allow the customer to make payment some time after the delivery of the goods or services. Typical trade credit periods range from 30 to 60 days but each agreement is different.

credit note A document sent to a customer of a business cancelling the customer's debt to the business, usually because the customer has returned defective goods or has received inadequate service.

credit purchase A business **entity** takes delivery of goods or services and is allowed to make payment at a later date.

credit sale A business **entity** sells goods or services and allows the customer to make payment at a later date.

creditor A person or organisation to whom money is owed by the entity.

critical event The point in the business cycle at which **revenue** may be recognised.

current asset An asset that is expected to be converted into cash within the trading cycle.

current liability A liability which satisfies any of the following criteria: (a) it is expected to be settled in the entity's normal operating cycle; (b) it is held primarily for the purpose of being traded; (c) it is due to be settled within 12 months after the balance sheet date.

current value A method of valuing assets and liabilities which takes account of changing prices, as an alternative to historical cost.

customers' collection period Average number of days credit taken by customers.

cut-off procedures Procedures applied to the accounting records at the end of an accounting period to ensure that all transactions for the period are recorded and any transactions not relevant to the period are excluded.

debenture A written acknowledgement of a debt – a name used for loan financing taken up by a company.

debtor A person or organisation that owes money to the entity.

deep discount bond A loan issued at a relatively low price compared to its nominal value.

default Failure to meet obligations as they fall due for payment.

deferred asset An asset whose benefit is delayed beyond the period expected for a current asset, but which does not meet the definition of a fixed asset.

deferred income Revenue, such as a government grant, is received in advance of performing the related activity. The deferred income is held in the balance sheet as a type of liability until performance is achieved and is then released to the income statement.

deferred taxation The obligation to pay tax is deferred (postponed) under tax law beyond the normal date of payment.

depreciable amount Cost of a **non-current (fixed) asset** minus **residual value**.

depreciation The systematic allocation of the **depreciable amount** of an asset over its useful life. The depreciable amount is cost less **residual value**.

derecognition The act of removing an item from the financial statements because the item no longer satisfies the conditions for **recognition**.

difference on consolidation Difference between **fair value** of the payment for a **subsidiary** and the **fair value** of **net assets** acquired, more commonly called **goodwill**.

direct method (of operating cash flow) Presents cash inflows and cash outflows.

Directive A document issued by the European Union requiring all member states to adapt their national law to be consistent with the Directive.

director(s) Person(s) appointed by shareholders of a limited liability company to manage the affairs of the company.

disclosed, disclosure An item which is reported in the notes to the accounts is said to be disclosed but not **recognised**.

discount received A supplier of goods or services allows a business to deduct an amount called a discount, for prompt payment of an invoiced amount. The discount is often expressed a percentage of the invoiced amount.

dividend Amount paid to a shareholder, usually in the form of cash, as a reward for investment in the company. The amount of dividend paid is proportionate to the number of shares held.

dividend cover Earnings per share divided by dividend per share.

dividend yield Dividend per share divided by current market price.

doubtful debts Amounts due from credit customers where there is concern that the customer may be unable to pay.

drawings Cash taken for personal use, in **sole trader** or **partnership** business, treated as a reduction of **ownership interest**.

earnings for ordinary shareholders Profit after deducting interest charges and taxation and after deducting preference dividends (but before deducting extraordinary items).

earnings per share calculated as **earnings for ordinary shareholders** divided by the number of shares which have been issued by the company.

effective interest rate The rate that exactly discounts estimated future cash payments or receipts through the expected life of the financial instrument.

efficient markets hypothesis Share prices in a stock market react immediately to the announcement of new information.

endorsed International financial reporting standards approved for use in member states of the European Union through a formal process of **endorsement**.

endorsement See **endorsed**.

enterprise A business activity or a commercial project.

entity, entities Something that exists independently, such as a business which exists independently of the owner.

entry price The value of entering into acquisition of an asset or liability, usually **replacement cost**.

equities analyst A person who investigates and writes reports on ordinary share investments in companies (usually for the benefit of investors in shares).

equity A description applied to the **ordinary share** capital of an entity.

equity accounting Reports in the **balance sheet** the parent or group's share of the investment in the **share capital** and **reserves** of an **associated company**.

equity holders Those who own ordinary shares in the **entity**.

equity interest See **ownership interest**.

equity portfolio A collection of **equity shares**.

equity shares/share capital Shares in a company which participate in sharing dividends and in sharing any surplus on winding up, after all liabilities have been met.

eurobond market A market in which bonds are issued in the capital market of one country to a non-resident borrower from another country.

exit price See **exit value**.

exit value A method of valuing assets and liabilities based on selling prices, as an alternative to **historical cost**.

expense An expense is caused by a transaction or event arising during the ordinary activities of the business which causes a decrease in the ownership interest.

external reporting Reporting financial information to those users with a valid claim to receive it, but who are not allowed access to the day-to-day records of the business.

external users (of financial statements) Users of financial statements who have a valid interest but are not permitted access to the day-to-day records of the company.

fair value The amount at which an asset or liability could be exchanged in an arm's-length transaction between a willing buyer and a willing seller.

faithful presentation Qualitive characteristic, information represents what it purports to represent.

financial accounting A term usually applied to *external reporting* by a business where that reporting is presented in financial terms.

financial adaptability The ability of the company to respond to unexpected needs or opportunities.

financial gearing Ratio of loan finance to equity capital and reserves.

financial information Information which may be reported in money terms.

Financial Reporting Standard Title of an accounting standard issued by the UK *Accounting Standards Board* as a definitive statement of best practice (issued from 1990 onwards – predecessor documents are Statements of Standard Accounting Practice, many of which remain valid).

financial risk Exists where a company has loan finance, especially long-term loan finance where the company cannot relinquish its commitment. The risk relates to being unable to meet payments of interest or repayment of capital as they fall due.

financial statements Documents presenting accounting information which is expected to have a useful purpose.

financial viability The ability to survive on an ongoing basis.

financing activities Activities that result in changes in the size and composition of the contributed equity and borrowings of the entity.

fixed asset An asset that is held by an enterprise for use in the production or supply of goods or services, for rental to others, or for administrative purposes on a continuing basis in the reporting entity's activities.

fixed assets See **non-current assets**.

fixed assets usage Revenue divided by **net book value** of **fixed assets**.

fixed capital Finance provided to support the acquisition of fixed assets.

fixed cost One which is not affected by changes in the level of output over a defined period of time.

floating charge Security taken by lender which floats over all the assets and crystallises over particular assets if the security is required.

forecast estimate of future performance and position based on stated assumptions and usually including a quantified amount.

format A list of items which may appear in a financial statement, setting out the order in which they are to appear.

forward exchange contract An agreement to buy foreign currency at a fixed future date and at an agreed price.

fully paid Shares on which the amount of share capital has been paid in full to the company.

fund manager A person who manages a collection (portfolio) of investments, usually for an insurance company, a pension fund business or a professional fund management business which invests money on behalf of clients.

gearing (financial) The ratio of debt capital to ownership claim.

general purpose financial statements Documents containing accounting information which would be expected to be of interest to a wide range of user groups. For a limited liability company there would be: a balance sheet, a profit and loss account, a statement of recognised gains and losses and a cash flow statement.

going concern basis The assumption that the business will continue operating into the foreseeable future.

goodwill Goodwill on **acquisition** is the difference between the **fair** value of the amount paid for an investment in a **subsidiary** and the **fair value** of the **net assets** acquired.

gross Before making deductions.

gross margin Sales minus cost of sales before deducting administration and selling expenses (another name for **gross profit**). Usually applied when discussing a particular line of activity.

gross margin ratio Gross profit as a percentage of sales.

gross profit Sales minus cost of sales before deducting administration and selling expenses (see also **gross margin**).

group Economic **entity** formed by **parent** and one or more **subsidiaries**.

highlights statement A page at the start of the annual report setting out key measures of performance during the reporting period.

historical cost Method of valuing assets and liabilities based on their original cost without adjustment for changing prices.

HM Revenue and Customs (HMRC) The UK government's tax-gathering organisation (previously called the Inland Revenue).

IAS International Accounting Standard, issued by the IASB's predecessor body.

IASB International Accounting Standards Board, an independent body that sets accounting standards accepted as a basis for accounting in many countries, including all Member States of the European Union.

IASB system The accounting standards and guidance issued by the **IASB**.

IFRS International Financial Reporting Standard, issued by the **IASB**.

impairment A reduction in the carrying value of an **asset**, beyond the expected **depreciation**, which must be reflected by reducing the amount recorded in the **balance sheet**.

impairment review Testing assets for evidence of any **impairment**.

impairment test Test that the business can expect to recover the carrying value of the intangible asset, through either using it or selling.

improvement A change in, or addition to, a **non-current (fixed) asset** that extends its useful life or increases the expected future benefit. Contrast with repair which restores the existing useful life or existing expected future benefit.

income statement Financial statement presenting revenues, expenses, and profit. Also called **profit and loss account**.

incorporation, date of. The date on which a company comes into existence.

indirect method (of operating cash flow) Calculates operating cash flow by adjusting operating profit for non-cash items and for changes in working capital.

insider information Information gained by someone inside, or close to, a listed company which could confer a financial advantage if used to buy or sell shares. It is illegal for a person who is in possession of inside information to buy or sell shares on the basis of that information.

institutional investor An organisation whose business includes regular investment in shares of companies, examples being an insurance company, a pension fund, a charity, an investment trust, a unit trust, a merchant bank.

intangible Without shape or form, cannot be touched.

interest (on loans) The percentage return on **capital** required by the lender (usually expressed as a percentage per annum).

interim reports Financial statements issued in the period between annual reports, usually half-yearly or quarterly.

internal reporting Reporting financial information to those users inside a business, at various levels of management, at a level of detail appropriate to the recipient.

inventory Stocks of goods held for manufacture or for resale.

investing activities The acquisition and disposal of long-term assets and other investments not included in cash equivalents.

investors Persons or organisations which have provided money to a business in exchange for a share of ownership.

invoices When a sale is made on credit terms the invoice is the document sent to the customer showing the quantities sold and the amount due to be paid.

joint and several liability (in a partnership) The partnership liabilities are shared jointly but each person is responsible for the whole of the partnership.

key performance indicators Quantified measures of factors that help to measure the performance of the business effectively.

leasing Acquiring the use of an **asset** through a rental agreement.

legal form Representing a transaction to reflect its legal status, which might not be the same as its economic form.

leverage Alternative term for **gearing**, commonly used in the USA.

liabilities Obligations of an entity to transfer economic benefits as a result of past transactions or events.

limited liability A phrase used to indicate that those having liability in respect of some amount due may be able to invoke some agreed limit on that liability.

limited liability company Company where the liability of the owners is limited to the amount of capital they have agreed to contribute.

liquidity The extent to which a business has access to cash or items which can readily be exchanged for cash.

listed company A company whose shares are listed by the Stock Exchange as being available for buying and selling under the rules and safeguards of the Exchange.

listing requirements Rules imposed by the Stock Exchange on companies whose shares are listed for buying and selling.

Listing Rules Issued by the UK Listing Authority of the Financial Services Authority to regulate companies listed on the UK Stock Exchange. Includes rules on accounting information in annual reports.

loan covenants Agreement made by the company with a lender of long-term finance, protecting the loan by imposing conditions on the company, usually to restrict further borrowing.

loan notes A method of borrowing from commercial institutions such as banks.

loan stock Loan finance traded on a stock exchange.

long-term finance, long-term liabilities Money lent to a business for a fixed period, giving that business a commitment to pay interest for the period specified and to repay the loan at the end of the period Also called **non-current liabilities** information in the financial statements should show the commercial substance of the situation.

management Collective term for those persons responsible for the day-to-day running of a business.

management accounting Reporting accounting information within a business, for management use only.

market value (of a share) The price for which a share could be transferred between a willing buyer and a willing seller.

marking to market Valuing a marketable **asset** at its current market price.

margin Profit, seen as the 'margin' between revenue and expense.

matching Expenses are matched against revenues in the period they are incurred (see also **accruals basis**).

material See **materiality**.

materiality Information is **material** if its omission or misstatement could influence the economic decisions of users taken on the basis of the financial statements.

maturity The date on which a liability is due for repayment.

maturity profile of debt The timing of loan repayments by a company in the future.

memorandum (for a company) Document setting out main objects of the company and its powers to act.

merger Two organisations agree to work together in a situation where neither can be regarded as having acquired the other.

minority interest The **ownership interest** in a company held by persons other than the **parent company** and its **subsidiary** undertakings. Also called a **non-controlling interest**.

net After making deductions.

net assets Assets minus **liabilities** (equals **ownership interest**).

net book value Cost of **non-current** (**fixed**) **asset** minus **accumulated depreciation**.

net debt Borrowings minus cash balances.

net profit Sales minus cost of sales minus all administrative and selling costs.

net realisable value The proceeds of selling an item, less the costs of selling.

neutral Qualitative characteristic of freedom from bias.

nominal value (of a share) The amount stated on the face of a share certificate as the named value of the share when issued.

non-controlling interest See **minority interest**.

non-current assets Any asset that does not meet the definition of a current asset. Also described as **fixed assets**.

non-current liabilities Any liability that does not meet the definition of a **current liability**. Also described as **long-term liabilities**.

notes to the accounts Information in financial statements that gives more detail about items in the **financial statements**.

off-balance-sheet finance An arrangement to keep matching assets and liabilities away from the entity's balance sheet.

offer for sale A company makes a general offer of its shares to the public.

operating activities The principal revenue-producing activities of the entity and other activities that are not investing or financing activities.

operating and financial review Section of the annual report of many companies which explains the main features of the financial statements.

operating gearing The ratio of fixed operating costs to variable operating costs.

operating margin Operating profit as a percentage of sales.

operating risk Exists where there are factors, such as a high level of fixed operating costs, which would cause profits to fluctuate through changes in operating conditions.

ordinary shares Shares in a company which entitle the holder to a share of the dividend declared and a share in net assets on closing down the business.

ownership interest The residual amount found by deducting all of the entity's liabilities from all of the entity's assets. (Also called **equity interest**.)

par value See **nominal value**.

parent company Company which controls one or more subsidiaries in a group.

partnership Two or more persons in business together with the aim of making a profit.

partnership deed A document setting out the agreement of the partners on how the partnership is to be conducted (including the arrangements for sharing profits and losses).

partnership law Legislation which governs the conduct of a partnership and which should be used where no partnership deed has been written.

portfolio (of investment) A collection of investments.

portfolio of shares A collection of shares held by an investor.

preference shares Shares in a company which give the holder a preference (although not an automatic right) to receive a dividend before any ordinary share dividend is declared.

preliminary announcement The first announcement by a listed company of its profit for the most recent accounting period. Precedes the publication of the full annual report. The announcement is made to the entire stock market so that all investors receive information at the same time.

premium An amount paid in addition, or extra.

prepaid expense An expense paid in advance of the benefit being received, e.g. rentals paid in advance.

prepayment An amount paid for in advance for an benefit to the business, such as insurance premiums or rent in advance. Initially recognised as an asset, then transferred to expense in the period when the benefit is enjoyed. (Also called a **prepaid expense**.)

present fairly A condition of the **IASB system**, equivalent to **true and fair view** in the **UK ASB system**.

price–earnings ratio Market price of a share divided by earnings per share.

price-sensitive information Information which, if known to the market, would affect the price of a share.

primary financial statements The balance sheet, profit and loss account, statement of total recognised gains and losses and cash flow statement.

principal (sum) The agreed amount of a loan, on which interest will be charged during the period of the loan.

private limited company (Ltd) A company which has **limited liability** but is not permitted to offer its shares to the public.

production overhead costs Costs of production that are spread across all output, rather than being identified with specific goods or services.

profit Calculated as revenue minus expenses.

profit and loss account Financial statement presenting revenues, expenses, and profit. Also called **income statement**.

prospective investor An investor who is considering whether to invest in a company.

prospectus Financial statements and supporting detailed descriptions published when a company is offering shares for sale to the public.

provision A liability of uncertain timing or amount.

provision for doubtful debts An estimate of the risk of not collecting full payment from credit customers, reported as a deduction from **trade receivables (debtors)** in the **balance sheet**.

prudence A degree of caution in the exercise of the judgements needed in making the estimates required under conditions of uncertainty, such that gains and assets are not overstated and losses and liabilities are not understated.

public limited company (plc) A company which has **limited liability** and offers its shares to the public.

purchase method Method of producing consolidated financial statements (see **acquisition method**).

purchases Total of goods and services bought in a period.

qualified audit opinion An audit opinion to the effect that: the accounts do *not* show a true and fair view; or the accounts show a true and fair view *except for* particular matters.

quality of earnings Opinion of investors on reliability of earnings (profit) as a basis for their forecasts.

quoted company Defined in section 262 of the Companies Act 1985 as a company that has been included in the official list in accordance with the provisions of Part VI of the Financial Services and Markets Act 2000, or is officially listed in an EEA state, or is admitted to dealing on either the New York Stock Exchange or the exchange known as Nasdaq.

realised profit, realisation A profit arising from revenue which has been earned by the entity and for which there is a reasonable prospect of cash being collected in the near future.

recognised An item is recognised when it is included by means of words and amount within the main financial statements of an entity.

recognition See **recognised**.

Registrar of Companies An official authorised by the government to maintain a record of all annual reports and other documents issued by a company.

relevance Qualitative characteristic of influencing the economic decisions of users.

reliability Qualitative characteristic of being free from material error and bias, representing faithfully.

replacement cost A measure of **current value** which estimates the cost of replacing an asset or liability at the date of the balance sheet. Justified by reference to **value to the business**.

reserves The claim which owners have on the *assets* of a company because the company has created new wealth for them over the period since it began.

residual value The estimated amount that an entity would currently obtain from disposal of the asset, after deducting the estimated cost of disposal, if the asset were already of the age and in the condition expected at the end of its useful life.

retained earnings Accumulated past profits, not distributed in dividends, available to finance investment in assets.

retained profit Profit of the period remaining after **dividend** has been deducted.

return The yield or reward from an investment.

return on capital employed Operating profit before deducting interest and taxation, divided by share capital plus reserves plus long-term loans.

return on shareholders' equity Profit for shareholders divided by share capital plus reserves.

return on total assets Operating profit before deducting interest and taxation, divided by total assets.

return (in relation to investment) The reward earned for investing money in a business. Return may appear in the form of regular cash payments (dividends) to the investor, or in a growth in the value of the amount invested.

revaluation reserve The claim which owners have on the **assets** of the business because the balance sheet records a market value for an asset that is greater than its historical cost.

revenue Created by a transaction or event arising during the ordinary activities of the business which causes an increase in the ownership interest.

rights issue A company gives its existing shareholders the right to buy more shares in proportion to those already held.

risk (in relation to investment) Factors that may cause the profit or cash flows of the business to fluctuate.

sales See **revenue, turnover**.

sales invoice Document sent to customers recording a sale on credit and requesting payment.

secured loan Loan where the lender has taken a special claim on particular assets or revenues of the company.

segmental reporting Reporting revenue, profit, cash flow assets, liabilities for each geographical and business segment within a business, identifying segments by the way the organisation is managed.

share capital Name given to the total amount of cash which the shareholders have contributed to the company.

share certificate A document providing evidence of share ownership.

share premium The claim which owners have on the assets of a company because shares have been purchased from the company at a price greater than the nominal value.

shareholders Owners of a **limited liability company**.

shareholders' funds Name given to total of **share capital** and **reserves** in a company balance sheet.

shares The amount of share capital held by any shareholder is measured in terms of a number of shares in the total capital of the company.

short-term finance Money lent to a business for a short period of time, usually repayable on demand and also repayable at the choice of the business if surplus to requirements.

sole trader An individual owning and operating a business alone.

specific purpose financial statements Documents containing accounting information which is prepared for a particular purpose and is not normally available to a wider audience.

stakeholders A general term devised to indicate all those who might have a legitimate interest in receiving financial information about a business because they have a 'stake' in it.

statement of cash flows Provides information about changes in financial position.

statement of changes in equity A financial statement reporting all items causing changes to the ownership interest during the financial period, under the **IASB system**.

statement of comprehensive income Provides information on all gains and losses causing a change in **ownership interest** during a period, other than contributions and withdrawals made by the owners.

statement of financial position Provides information on assets, liabilities and equity at a specified reporting date. It is the preferred title under the **IASB system** for the document that is also called a **balance sheet**.

statement of principles A document issued by the Accounting Standards Board in the United Kingdom setting out key principles to be applied in the process of setting accounting standards.

statement of recognised income and expense A financial statement reporting **realised** and **unrealised** income and expense as part of a **statement of changes in equity** under the **IASB system**.

statement of total recognised gains and losses A financial statement reporting changes in equity under the UK ASB system.

stepped bond Loan finance that starts with a relatively low rate of interest which then increases in steps.

stewardship Taking care of resources owned by another person and using those resources to the benefit of that person.

stock A word with two different meanings. It may be used to describe an **inventory** of goods held for resale or for use in business. It may also be used to describe **shares** in the ownership of a company. The meaning will usually be obvious from the way in which the word is used.

stock exchange (also called **stock market**). An organisation which has the authority to set rules for persons buying and selling shares. The term 'stock' is used loosely with a meaning similar to that of 'shares'.

stock holding period Average number of days for which inventory (stock) is held before use or sale.

stock market See **stock exchange**.

subsidiary company Company in a group which is controlled by another (the parent company). (*See* Chapter 7 for full definition.) Sometimes called subsidiary undertaking.

substance (economic) Information in the financial statements should show the economic or commercial substance of the situation.

subtotal Totals of similar items grouped together within a financial statement.

suppliers' payment period Average number of days credit taken from suppliers.

tangible fixed assets A **fixed asset** (also called a **non-current asset**) which has a physical existence.

timeliness Qualitative characteristic that potentially conflicts with **relevance**.

total assets usage Sales divided by total assets.

trade creditors Persons who supply goods or services to a business in the normal course of trade and allow a period of credit before payment must be made.

trade debtors Persons who buy goods or services from a business in the normal course of trade and are allowed a period of credit before payment is due.

trade payables Amounts due to suppliers (**trade creditors**), also called **accounts payable**.

trade receivables Amounts due from customers (**trade debtors**), also called **accounts receivable**.

treasury shares Shares which a company has repurchased from its own shareholders and is holding with the intention of reselling the shares in the future.

true and fair view Requirement of UK company law for UK companies not using **IASB system**.

turnover The sales of a business or other form of revenue from operations of the business.

UK ASB system The accounting standards and company law applicable to corporate reporting by UK companies that do not report under the IASB system.

understandability Qualitative characteristic of financial statements, understandable by users.

unlisted (company) Limited liability company whose shares are not **listed** on any stock exchange.

unrealised Gains and losses representing changes in values of assets and liabilities that are not **realised** through sale or use.

unsecured creditors Those who have no claim against particular assets when a company is wound up, but must take their turn for any share of what remains.

unsecured loan Loan in respect of which the lender has taken no special claim against any assets.

value to the business An idea used in deciding on a measure of **current value**.

variance The difference between a planned, budgeted or standard cost and the actual cost incurred. An adverse variance arises when the actual cost is greater than the standard cost. A favourable variance arises when the actual cost is less than the standard cost.

working capital Finance provided to support the short-term assets of the business (stocks and debtors) to the extent that these are not financed by short-term creditors. It is calculated as current assets minus current liabilities.

working capital cycle Total of stock holding period plus customers collection period minus suppliers payment period.

work in progress Cost of partly completed goods or services, intended for completion and recorded as an asset.

written down value See **net book value**.

Information extracted from annual report of Safe and Sure Group plc, used throughout Financial Accounting

Safe and Sure Group plc
Consolidated statement of financial position (balance sheet)
at 31 December

	Notes	Year 7 £m	Year 6 £m
Non-current assets			
Property, plant and equipment	1	137.5	121.9
Intangible assets	2	260.3	237.6
Investments	3	2.8	2.0
Taxation recoverable	4	5.9	4.9
		406.5	366.4
Current assets			
Inventories (stocks)	5	26.6	24.3
Amounts receivable (debtors)	6	146.9	134.7
Six-month deposits		2.0	–
Cash and cash equivalents		105.3	90.5
		280.8	249.5
Current liabilities			
Amounts payable (creditors)	7	(159.8)	(157.5)
Bank overdraft	8	(40.1)	(62.6)
		(199.9)	(220.1)
Net current assets		80.9	29.4
Total assets less current liabilities		487.4	395.8
Non-current liabilities			
Amounts payable (creditors)	9	(2.7)	(2.6)
Bank and other borrowings	10	(0.2)	(0.6)
Provisions	11	(20.2)	(22.2)
Net assets		464.3	370.4
Capital and reserves			
Called-up share capital	12	19.6	19.5
Share premium account	13	8.5	5.5
Revaluation reserve	14	4.6	4.6
Retained earnings	15	431.6	340.8
Equity holders' funds		464.3	370.4

Safe and Sure Group plc
Consolidated income statement (profit and loss account)
for the year ended 31 December Year 7

	Notes	Year 7 £m	Year 6 £m
Continuing operations			
Revenue	16	714.6	589.3
Cost of sales	16	(491.0)	(406.3)
Gross profit		223.6	183.0
Distribution costs		(2.2)	(2.5)
Administrative expenses	17	(26.2)	(26.5)
Profit from operations		195.2	154.0
Interest receivable (net)	18	2.3	3.0
Profit before tax	19	197.5	157.0
Tax	20	(62.2)	(52.4)
Profit for the period from continuing operations		135.3	104.6
Discontinued operations			
Loss for the period from discontinued operations	21	(20.5)	(10.0)
Profit for the period attributable to equity holders		114.8	94.6
Earnings per share	22	11.74	9.71

Safe and Sure plc
Consolidated statement of comprehensive income
for the year ended 31 December Year 7

	Year 7 £m	Year 6 £m
Profit for the period	114.8	94.6
Exchange rate adjustments	5.5	(6.0)
Total comprehensive income for the year	120.3	88.6

Safe and Sure plc
Statement of changes in equity for the year ended
31 December Year 7

	Share capital	Share premium	Revaluation reserve	Retained earnings (including exchange rate adjustments)	Total
	£m	£m	£m	£m	£m
Balance at 1 Jan Year 6	19.4	3.6	4.6	276.6	304.2
Share capital issued	0.1	1.9			2.0
Total comprehensive income				88.6	88.6
Less dividend				(24.4)	(24.4)
Balance at 1 Jan Year 7	19.5	5.5	4.6	340.8	370.4
Share capital issued	0.1	3.0			3.1
Total comprehensive income				120.3	120.3
Less dividend				(29.5)	(29.5)
Balance at 31 Dec Year 7	19.6	8.5	4.6	431.6	464.3

Safe and Sure Group plc
Consolidated statement of cash flows for the years ended 31 December

	Notes	Year 7 £m	Year 6 £m
Cash flows from operating activities			
Cash generated from operations	23	196.7	163.5
Interest paid		(3.1)	(2.4)
UK corporation tax paid		(20.1)	(18.3)
Overseas tax paid		(30.5)	(26.5)
Net cash from operating activities		**143.0**	**116.3**
Cash flows from investing activities			
Purchase of property, plant and equipment		(60.0)	(47.5)
Sale of property, plant and equipment		12.0	10.1
Purchase of companies and businesses	25	(27.7)	(90.1)
Sale of a company		3.1	–
Movement in short-term deposits		(30.7)	36.3
Interest received		5.0	5.9
Net cash used in investing activities		**(98.3)**	**(85.3)**
Cash flows from financing activities			
Issue of ordinary share capital		3.1	2.0
Dividends paid to equity holders		(29.5)	(24.4)
Net loan movement (excluding overdraft)		16.2	(24.0)
Net cash used in financing activities		**(10.2)**	**(46.4)**
Net increase/(decrease) in cash and cash equivalents*		**34.5**	**(15.4)**
Cash and cash equivalents at the beginning of the year		27.9	45.3
Exchange adjustments		2.8	(2.0)
Cash and cash equivalents at the end of the year	28	65.2	27.9

* Cash on demand and deposits of maturity less than 3 months, net of overdrafts

Accounting policies (extracts)

Intangible non-current (fixed) assets

Purchased goodwill is calculated as the difference between the fair value of the consideration paid for an acquired entity and the aggregate of the fair values of that entity's identifiable assets and liabilities. An impairment review has been undertaken at the balance sheet date.

Freehold and leasehold property

Freehold and leasehold land and buildings are stated either at cost or at their revalued amounts less depreciation. Full revaluations are made at five-year intervals with interim valuations in the intervening years, the most recent being in Year 0.

Provision for depreciation of freehold land and buildings is made at the annual rate of 1% of cost or the revalued amounts. Leasehold land and buildings are amortised in equal annual instalments over the periods of the leases subject to a minimum annual provision of 1% of cost or the revalued amounts. When properties are sold the difference between sales proceeds and net book value is dealt with in the income statement (profit and loss account).

Other tangible non-current (fixed) assets

Other tangible non-current assets are stated at cost less depreciation. Provision for depreciation is made mainly in equal annual instalments over the estimated useful lives of the assets as follows:

4 to 5 years   vehicles
5 to 10 years   plant, machinery and equipment

Inventories (stocks and work in progress)

Inventories (stocks and work in progress) are stated at the lower of cost and net realisable value, using the first in first out principle. Cost includes all direct expenditure and related overheads incurred in bringing the inventories to their present condition and location.

Deferred tax

The provision for deferred tax recognises a future liability arising from past transactions and events. Tax legislation allows the company to defer settlement of the liability for several years.

Warranties

Some service work is carried out under warranty. The cost of claims under warranty is charged against the profit and loss account of the year in which the claims are settled.

Deferred consideration

For acquisitions involving deferred consideration, estimated deferred payments are accrued in the balance sheet. Interest due to vendors on deferred payments is charged to the profit and loss account as it accrues.

Notes to accounts

Note 1 Property, plant and equipment

	Land and buildings £m	Plant and equipment £m	Vehicles £m	Total £m
Cost or valuation				
At 1 January Year 7	28.3	96.4	104.8	229.5
Additions at cost	3.9	18.5	37.8	60.2
On acquisitions	0.3	1.0	0.7	2.0
Disposals	(0.6)	(3.1)	(24.7)	(28.4)
At 31 December Year 7	31.9	112.8	118.6	263.3
Aggregate depreciation				
At 1 January Year 7	2.2	58.8	46.6	107.6
Depreciation for the year	0.5	13.5	19.2	33.2
On acquisitions	0.1	0.7	0.6	1.4
Disposals	(0.2)	(2.8)	(13.4)	(16.4)
At 31 December Year 7	2.6	70.2	53.0	125.8
Net book value at 31 December Year 7	29.3	42.6	65.6	137.5
Net book value at 31 December Year 6	26.1	37.6	58.2	121.9

Analysis of land and buildings at cost or valuation

	Year 7 £m	Year 6 £m
At cost	10.4	7.1
At valuation	21.5	21.2
	31.9	28.3

The majority of the group's freehold and long-term leasehold properties were revalued during Year 5 by independent valuers. Valuations were made on the basis of the market value for existing use. The book values of the properties were adjusted to the revaluations and the resultant net surplus was credited to the revaluation reserve.

Analysis of net book value of land and buildings

	Year 7 £m	Year 6 £m
Freehold	24.5	21.0
Leasehold:		
Over 50 years unexpired	2.1	2.4
Under 50 years unexpired	2.7	2.7
	29.3	26.1

If the revalued assets were stated on the historical cost basis the amounts would be:

	Year 7 £m	Year 6 £m
Land and buildings at cost	15.7	14.5
Aggregate depreciation	(2.2)	(1.9)
	13.5	12.6

Note 2 Intangible non-current assets

	Year 7 £m	Year 6 £m
Goodwill at 1 January	237.6	139.1
Additions in year	24.3	98.5
Reduction in year	(1.6)	–
Goodwill at 31 December	260.3	237.6

The reduction of £1.6m results from the annual impairment review.

Note 3

Relates to investments in subsidiary companies and is not reproduced here.

Note 4

Explains the nature of taxation recoverable after more than 12 months from the balance sheet date. The detail is not reproduced here.

Note 5 Inventories (stocks)

	Year 7 £m	Year 6 £m
Raw materials	6.2	5.4
Work in progress	1.9	1.0
Finished products	18.5	17.9
	26.6	24.3

Note 6 Amounts receivable (debtors)

	Year 7 £m	Year 6 £m
Trade receivables (trade debtors)	128.1	117.0
Other receivables (debtors)	10.9	9.8
Prepayments and accrued income	7.9	7.9
	146.9	134.7

Note 7 Current liabilities: amounts payable

	Year 7 £m	Year 6 £m
Deferred consideration on acquisition	1.1	4.3
Trade payables (trade creditors)	23.6	20.4
Corporation tax	31.5	26.5
Other tax and social security payable	24.5	21.2
Other payables (creditors)	30.7	23.8
Accruals and deferred income	48.4	61.3
	159.8	157.5

Note 8 Bank borrowings: current liabilities

	Year 7 £m	Year 6 £m
Bank overdrafts due on demand:	40.1	62.6

Interest on overdrafts is payable at normal commercial rates appropriate to the country where the borrowing is made.

Note 9 Non-current liabilities: payables (creditors)

	Year 7 £m	Year 6 £m
Deferred consideration on acquisition	0.6	–
Other payables (creditors)	2.1	2.6
	2.7	2.6

Note 10 Non-current liabilities: bank and other borrowings

	Year 7 £m	Year 6 £m
Secured loans	–	0.3
Unsecured loans	0.2	0.3
	0.2	0.6
Loans are repayable by instalments:		
Between one and two years	0.1	0.2
Between two and five years	0.1	0.4
	0.2	0.6

Interest on long-term loans, which are denominated in a number of currencies, is payable at normal commercial rates appropriate to the country in which the borrowing is made. The last repayment falls due in Year 11.

Note 11 Provisions

	Year 7 £m	Year 6 £m
Provisions for treating contaminated site:		
At 1 January	14.2	*14.5*
Utilised in the year	(2.2)	*(0.3)*
At 31 December	12.0	*14.2*
Provisions for restructuring costs:		
At 1 January	4.2	*–*
Created in year	1.0	*4.3*
Utilised in year	(1.0)	*(0.1)*
At 31 December	4.2	*4.2*
Provision for deferred tax:		
At 1 January	3.8	*2.7*
Transfer to profit and loss account	0.5	*1.2*
Other movements	(0.3)	*(0.1)*
At 31 December	4.0	*3.8*
Total provision	20.2	*22.2*

Note 12 Share capital

	Year 7 £m	Year 6 £m
Ordinary shares of 2 pence each		
Authorised: 1,050,000,000 shares		
(Year 6: 1,000,000,000)	21.0	*20.0*
Issued and fully paid: 978,147,487 shares	19.6	*19.5*

Certain senior executives hold options to subscribe for shares in the company at prices ranging from 33.40p to 244.33p under schemes approved by equity holders at various dates. Options on 3,479,507 shares were exercised during Year 7 and 66,970 options lapsed. The number of shares subject to options, the years in which they were purchased and the years in which they will expire are:

Purchase	Expiry	Numbers
	Year 8	13,750
All	Year 9	110,000
purchased	Year 10	542,500
10 years	Year 11	1,429,000
before	Year 12	2,826,600
expiry	Year 13/14	3,539,942
	Year 15	3,690,950
	Year 16	2,279,270
	Year 17	3,279,363
		17,711,375

Note 13 Share premium account

	Year 7 £m	Year 6 £m
At 1 January	5.5	*3.6*
Premium on shares issued during the year under the share option schemes	3.0	*1.9*
At 31 December	8.5	*5.5*

Note 14 Revaluation reserve

	Year 7 £m	Year 6 £m
At 1 January	4.6	4.6
At 31 December	4.6	4.6

Note 15 Retained earnings

	Year 7 £m	Year 6 £m
At 1 January	340.8	276.6
Exchange adjustments	5.5	(6.0)
Profit for the year	114.8	94.6
Dividend paid	(29.5)	(24.4)
At 31 December	431.6	340.8

Note 16 Operating segments

For the purposes of reporting to the chief operating decision maker, the group is currently organised into two operating divisions, (1) disposal and recycling, (2) security and cleaning. Disposal and recycling includes all aspects of collection and safe disposal of industrial and commercial waste products. Security and cleaning is undertaken by renewable annual contract, predominantly for hospitals, other healthcare premises and local government organisations.

The group's disposal and recycling operation in North America was discontinued with effect from 30 April Year 7.

Business sector analysis

	Disposal and recycling		Security and cleaning		Total	
	Year 7 £m	Year 6 £m	Year 7 £m	Year 6 £m	Year 7 £m	Year 6 £m
REVENUES (all from external customers)						
Continuing	508.9	455.0	205.7	134.3	714.6	589.3
Discontinued	20.0	11.0			20.0	11.0
Total revenues	528.9	466.0	205.7	134.3	734.6	600.3
Operating profit (loss) by service						
Continuing	176.6	139.6	18.6	14.4	195.2	154.0
Discontinued	(20.5)	(10.0)			(20.5)	(10.0)
Total operating profit					174.7	144.0
Interest receivable (net)					2.3	3.0
Profit before tax					177.0	147.0
Taxation					(62.2)	(52.4)
Profit for the period					114.8	94.6

All costs of head office operations are allocated to divisions on an activity costing basis. The company does not allocate interest receivable or taxation paid to reportable segments.

Depreciation and amortisation included in the income statement are as follows:

	Disposal and recycling		Security and cleaning		Total	
	Year 7 £m	Year 6 £m	Year 7 £m	Year 6 £m	Year 7 £m	Year 6 £m
Depreciation	30.2	25.1	3.0	3.9	33.2	29.0
Impairment of goodwill	1.6	–	–	–	1.6	–

The segment assets and liabilities at the end of Years 7 and 6 are as follows:

	Disposal and recycling		Security and cleaning		Unallocated		Total	
	Year 7 £m	Year 6 £m	Year 7 £m	Year 6 £m	Year 7 £m	Year 6 £m	Year 7 £m	Year 6 £m
Total assets	498.5	370.9	68.7	132.7	120.1	112.3	687.3	615.9
Total liabilities	131.7	147.9	61.3	85.5	30.0	12.1	223.0	245.5

Information about geographical areas

The group's two business segments operate in four main geographical areas, even though they are managed on a worldwide basis. In the following analysis. revenue is based on the country in which the order is received. It would not be materially different if based on the country in which the customer is located. Total assets and capital expenditure are allocated based on where the assets are located.

	Revenues from external customers		Non-current assets	
	Year 7 £m	Year 6 £m	Year 7 £m	Year 6 £m
CONTINUING				
United Kingdom	323.4	246.7	174.2	148.7
Continental Europe	164.3	153.5	90.3	93.0
North America	104.5	80.1	85.9	49.2
Asia Pacific & Africa	122.4	109.0	56.1	75.0
	714.6	589.3	406.5	365.9
DISCONTINUED				
North America	20.0	11.0	–	0.5
Total	734.6	600.3	406.5	366.4

Notes 17–20

Contain supporting details for the profit and loss account and are not reproduced here.

Note 21 Discontinued operations

On 31 March Year 7, the Group entered into a sale agreement to dispose of Carers Inc., its recycling business in North America. The purpose of the disposal was to prevent further loss-making activity. The disposal was completed on 30 April Year 7, on which date control of Carers Inc. passed to the acquirer.

The results of the discontinued operations which have been included in the consolidated income statement, were as follows:

	Year 7 £m	Year 6 £m
Revenue	20.0	11.0
Expenses	(40.5)	(21.0)
Loss attributable to discontinued operations	(20.5)	(10.0)

Note 22

Contains supporting details for earnings per share and is not reproduced here.

Note 23 Cash flow from operating activities

Reconciliation of operating profit to net cash flow from operating activities

	Year 7 £m	Year 6 £m
Profit before tax from continuing operations	195.2	154.0
Loss from discontinued operations	(20.5)	(10.0)
Profit from operations	174.7	144.0
Depreciation charge	33.2	30.1
Increase in inventories (stocks)*	(1.9)	(1.1)
Increase in trade receivables (debtors)*	(7.4)	(5.3)
Decrease in trade payables (creditors)*	(0.4)	(3.6)
Net cash inflow from continuing activities	198.2	164.1
Cash outflow in respect of discontinued item	(1.5)	(0.6)
Net cash inflow from operating activities	196.7	163.5

*Note: It is not possible to reconcile these figures with the balance sheet information because of the effect of acquisitions during the year.

Note 24 Information on acquisitions (extract)

The group purchased 20 companies and businesses during the year for a total consideration of £25m. The adjustments required to the balance sheet figures of companies and businesses acquired, in order to present the net assets at fair value, are shown below:

	£m
Net assets of subsidiaries acquired, as shown in their balance sheets	4.1
Adjustments made by directors of Safe and Sure plc	(3.4)
Fair value of net assets acquired (a)	0.7
Cash paid for subsidiaries (b)	25.0
Goodwill (b − a)	24.3

From the dates of acquisition to 31 December Year 7, the acquisitions contributed £13.5m to revenue, £2.7m to profit before interest and £2.2m to profit after interest.

If the acquisitions had been completed on the first day of the financial year, they would have contributed £30m to group revenues for the year and £5m to group profit attributable to equity holders of the parent.

Notes 25–27

Contain supporting detail for the cash flow statement and are not reproduced here.

Note 28 Cash and cash equivalents

Reconciliation of cash flow for the year to the balance sheet items

	Year 7 £m	Year 6 £m
Balance sheet items		
Cash and cash equivalents	105.3	90.5
Bank overdraft	(40.1)	(62.6)
Net	65.2	27.9

Notes 29–32

Contain various other items of information required by company law and are not reproduced here.

Note 33 Contingent liabilities

The company has guaranteed bank and other borrowings of subsidiaries amounting to £3.0m (Year 6: £15.2m). The group has commitments, amounting to approximately £41.9m (Year 6: £28.5m), under forward exchange contracts entered into in the ordinary course of business.

Certain subsidiaries have given warranties for service work. These are explained in the statement on accounting policies. There are contingent liabilities in respect of litigation. None of the actions is expected to give rise to any material loss.

Note 34

Contains commitments for capital expenditure and is not reproduced here.

Five-year summary

(Continuing and discontinued operations combined)

	Year 3	Year 4	Year 5	Year 6	Year 7
	£m	£m	£m	£m	£m
Group revenue	309.1	389.0	474.1	600.3	734.6
Group profit before tax	74.4	90.4	114.5	147.0	177.0
Tax	(27.2)	(33.9)	(44.3)	(52.4)	(62.2)
Group profit after tax	47.2	56.5	70.2	94.6	114.8
Earnings per share	4.88p	6.23p	8.02p	9.71p	11.74p
Dividends per share	1.32p	1.69p	2.17p	2.50p	3.02p
	£m	£m	£m	£m	£m
Share capital	19.4	19.4	19.4	19.5	19.6
Reserves	160.8	195.3	284.8	350.9	444.7
Total equity	180.2	214.7	304.2	370.4	464.3

Operating and financial review (extract)

The Directors' Report explains that the requirement to prepare a business review is satisfied by the production of the operating and financial review, extracts of which are presented here.

CHIEF EXECUTIVE'S REVIEW OF OPERATIONS

Group results

Group revenue from continuing operations in Year 7 increased by 21.3% to £714.6m, while continuing profits before tax increased by 25.8% to £197.5m. Earnings per share increased by 20.9% to 11.74 pence. These results show the benefits of our geographic diversification across the major economies of the world. We have achieved excellent growth in the UK, together with continued good growth in North America. Growth in Europe continued to be constrained by depressed economies, while excellent results in Australia were held back by disappointing growth in South East Asia. Segmental results are set out in detail in Note 16 to the financial statements.

In Disposal and Recycling, revenue improved by 13.4% and profits improved by 20.4%. Revenue in Security and Cleaning improved by 53.2% and profits improved by 29.2%.

Organisation

We continue to be organised into four geographic regions, each headed by a regional managing director. Group services are provided for finance, legal, research and development, corporate affairs, business development and management development. These costs are allocated to divisions on the basis of activity costing.

Strategy

Our ultimate objective is to achieve for our equity holders a high rate of growth in earnings and dividends per share each year. Our strategies are to provide customers with the highest standards of service and to maintain quality of service as we enter new fields. We also operate a prudent financial policy of managing our businesses to generate a strong operating cash flow.

Disposal and recycling

Disposal and recycling includes all aspects of collection and safe disposal of industrial and commercial waste products. During Year 7 all our operational landfill sites gained certification to the international environment management standard. Organic waste deposited in landfill sites degrades naturally and gives off a gas rich in methane which has to be controlled for environmental reasons. However, landfill sites can also be a cheap, clean and highly efficient source of renewable energy. Through strategic long-term contracts we are generating 64MW of electricity each year from landfill waste to energy schemes. New waste transfer and recycling centres in Germany and France were added to the Group's network during Year 7.

Security and cleaning

Security and cleaning is undertaken by renewable annual contract, predominantly for hospitals, other healthcare premises and local government organisations. During Year 7 we acquired a security company in the UK and some smaller operations in Switzerland and Spain. Improved margins in contract cleaning reflected continued demands for improved hygiene standards and our introduction of new techniques to meet this need.

FINANCE DIRECTOR'S REVIEW OF THE POSITION OF THE BUSINESS

Profits

Operating profits, including the effect of discontinued operations, rose to £174.7m in Year 7, up from £144.0m in Year 6. Interest income fell £0.7m to £2.3m in Year 7, as a result of the cash spent on acquisitions towards the end of Year 6. At constant average Year 6 exchange rates, the Year 7 profit before tax, including the effect of discontinued operations, would have been £0.6m higher at £177.6m, an increase of 20.8% over the reported Year 6 figures.

Cash flow

The Group's businesses are structured to utilise as little fixed and working capital as is consistent with the profit and earnings growth objective in order to produce a high cash flow. The impact of working capital on cash flow was held to an increase in Year 7 of £9.7m (Year 6: £10.0m).

A net cash flow of £196.7m was generated from operating activities. That was boosted by other amounts of cash from interest received. After paying interest and tax, the Group had £143.0m remaining. Fixed assets required £48.0m after allowing for the proceeds of selling some of our vehicle fleet in the routine replacement programme. That left £95m from which £24.6m was required to pay for acquisitions. The remaining £70.4m covered dividends of £29.5m leaving £40.9m. We received £5m interest on investments and raised £3.1m in ordinary share capital to give a net inflow of liquid funds in the year of £49.0m. Out of that amount, short-term deposits have increased by £14.5m, leaving an increase in cash of £34.5m.

Foreign currency

We borrowed £35.2m of foreign currency bank borrowings to fund overseas acquisitions. The main borrowings were £26.8m in US dollars and £8.4m in yen (to fund our Japanese associate investment). The borrowings are mainly from banks on a short-term basis with a maturity of up to one year. We have fixed the interest rate on $20m of the US dollar loans through to November Year 8 at an overall cost of 4.5%.

All material foreign currency transactions are matched back into the currency of the Group company undertaking the transaction. It is not the Group's current practice to hedge the translation of overseas profits or assets back into sterling, although overseas acquisitions may be financed by foreign currency borrowings.

Capital expenditure

The major items of capital expenditure are vehicles, equipment used on customers' premises and office equipment, particularly computers. Disposals during the year were mainly of vehicles being replaced on a rolling programme.

Taxation

The overall Group taxation charge comprises tax at 30% on UK profits and an average rate of 38% on overseas profits, reflecting the underlying rates in the various countries in which the Group operates.

Future development and performance

Once again, in Year 7 Safe and Sure met its declared objective of increasing its pre-tax profits and earnings per share by at least 20% per annum. The board expects a return to much better growth in Europe and a substantially improved performance in the USA to underpin good Group growth for the year.

Directors' report (extract)

The directors recommend a final dividend of 3.54 pence per ordinary share to be paid to shareholders on the register on 31 March Year 8. The proposed dividend for Year 6 of 3.02 pence per share was paid on 31 March Year 7. There is no interim dividend in either year 6 or year 7.

Appendix II

Solutions to numerical and technical questions in Financial Accounting

Note that solutions are provided only for numerical and technical material since other matters are covered either in the book or in the further reading indicated.

Chapter 1 has no solutions given in this Appendix because there are no numerical questions.

Chapter 2

Application   **B2.1**

Classify each of the items in the following list as: asset; liability; neither an asset nor a liability:

Cash at bank	Asset
Loan from the bank	Liability
Letter from the bank promising an overdraft facility at any time in the next three months	Neither
Trade debtor (a customer who has promised to pay later)	Asset
Trade debtor (a customer who has promised to pay later but has apparently disappeared without leaving a forwarding address)	Neither
Supplier of goods who has not yet received payment from the business	Liability
Inventory (stock) of finished goods (fashion clothing stored ahead of the spring sales)	Asset
Inventory (stock) of finished goods (fashion clothing left over after the spring sales)	Neither, unless value remains
Investment in shares of another company where the share price is rising	Asset
Investment in shares of another company where the share price is falling	Asset while there is still some benefit expected
Lender of five-year loan to the business	Liability
Customer to whom the business has offered a 12-month warranty to repair goods free of charge	Liability
A motor vehicle owned by the business	Asset
A motor vehicle rented by the business for one year	Neither
An office building owned by the business	Asset
An office building rented by the business on a 99-year lease, with 60 years' lease period remaining	Asset, but may not be shown

B2.2

Yes to all, except the rented building where risks and benefits are mainly for the owners, not the users.

B2.3

A letter from the owner of the business, guarantee the bank overdraft of the business.	Transaction is between owner and bank, not addressed to the bank manager, promising to with business
A list of the customers of the business.	Has benefit for the future but no event, also not measurable with reliability.
An order received from a customer.	Future benefit expected but insufficient evidence that it will be obtained.
The benefit of employing a development engineer with a high level of 'know-how' specifically relevant to the business.	Future benefit exists but not measurable with sufficient reliability.
Money spent on an advertising campaign to boost sales.	Future benefit exists but not measurable with sufficient reliability.
Structural repairs to a building.	Repairs put right the problems of the past – do not create future benefits.

Chapter 3

Application **B3.1**

Sunshine Wholesale Traders
Statement of financial position (balance sheet) at 30 June Year 2

	£	£
Non-current (fixed) assets		
Fleet of delivery vehicles		35,880
Furniture and fittings		18,800
Total fixed assets		54,680
Current assets		
Receivables (debtors)	34,000	
Bank deposit	19,000	
Total current assets	53,000	
Current liabilities		
Trade payables (trade creditors)	(8,300)	
Current assets less current liabilities		44,700
Net assets		99,380
Ownership interest at the start of the year		56,000
Profit of the year		43,380
Ownership interest at end of year		99,380

Note that ownership interest at the start of the year is entered as the missing item.

Sunshine Wholesale Traders
Income statement (profit and loss account) for the year ended 30 June Year 2

	£	£
Revenues		
Sales		294,500
Expenses		
Cost of goods sold		(188,520)
Gross profit		105,980
Wages and salaries	(46,000)	
Transport costs	(14,200)	
Administration costs	(1,300)	
Depreciation	(1,100)	
Total expenses		(62,600)
Net profit of the year		43,380

B3.2

Statement of financial position (balance sheet) at . . .

	£	£
Non-current (fixed) assets		
Land and buildings		95,000
Vehicles		8,000
Total fixed assets		103,000
Current assets		
Inventory (stock) of goods for resale	35,000	
Cash at bank	9,000	
Total current assets	44,000	
Liabilities due within one year		
Trade payables (trade creditors)	(43,000)	
Wages due	(2,000)	
	(45,000)	
Current liabilities less current assets		(1,000)
		102,000
Liabilities due after one year		(20,000)
		82,000
Ownership interest		82,000

(a) Decrease liability to employees £2,000, decrease asset of cash £2,000.
(b) Decrease ownership interest by £8,750, decrease asset of inventory (stock) by £8,750.
(c) Increase asset of inventory (stock) £5,000, increase liability of trade creditors £5,000.

Test your understanding

S3.1

(a) Debit liability to employees £2,000, credit asset of cash £2,000.
(b) Debit ownership interest £8,750, credit asset of inventory (stock) £8,750.
(c) Debit asset of inventory (stock) £5,000, credit liability of trade creditors £5,000.

Chapter 4

Application

B4.1
This requires a narrative answer based on sections 4.5.1, 4.5.3 and 4.5.5.

B4.2
This requires a narrative answer based on section 4.3. The more difficult aspect of this question is explaining how each convention affects current accounting practice. One example of each would be:

● *Going concern*: In historical cost accounting the fixed assets of an enterprise are recorded in the statement of financial position (balance sheet) at the historical cost, after deducting depreciation, rather than at estimated selling price, because the enterprise is a going concern and it is expected that the fixed assets will be held for long-term use.

- *Accruals*: The expense of electricity consumed during a period includes all units of electricity used, irrespective of whether an invoice has been paid.
- *Consistency*: It would be inconsistent, in a statement of financial position (balance sheet), to measure inventory (trading stock) at selling price at one point of time and at cost at another point of time.
- *Prudence*: It is prudent to measure inventory (stock of goods) at cost, rather than at selling price, because to value at selling price would anticipate a sale which may not take place.

B4.3

This is an essay which shows the student's understanding of the issues in the chapter and the ability to think about them in the context of a variety of users' needs. It requires the student to link the information in Chapter 4 with the ideas set out in section 1.5.

Chapter 5

A5.1

	Transaction	Asset	Liability	Ownership interest
(a)	Owner puts cash into the business	Increase†		Increase
(b)	Buy a vehicle for cash	Increase and decrease†		
(c)	Receive a bill for electricity consumed		Increase	Decrease*
(d)	Purchase stationery for office use, paying cash	Increase and decrease†		
(e)	Pay the electricity bill in cash	Decrease†	Decrease	
(f)	Pay rental for a computer, used for customer records	Decrease†		Decrease*
(g)	Buy spare parts for cash, to use in repairs	Increase and decrease†		
(h)	Buy spare parts on credit terms	Increase	Increase	
(i)	Pay garage service bills for van, using cash	Decrease†		Decrease*
(j)	Fill van with petrol, using credit account at local garage, to be paid at the start of next month		Increase	Decrease*
(k)	Carry out repairs for cash	Increase†		Increase*
(l)	Carry out repairs on credit terms	Increase		Increase*
(m)	Pay wages to an employee	Decrease†		Decrease*
(n)	Owner takes cash for personal use	Decrease†		Decrease

A5.2

Symbol * shows items which will have an effect on an income statement (profit and loss account).

A5.3

Symbol † shows items which will have an effect on a statement of cash flows.

A5.4

All items other than those asterisked will have a direct effect on a statement of financial position (balance sheet). The asterisked items will collectively change the accumulated profit which will increase the ownership interest reported in the statement of financial position (balance sheet).

A5.5

Transactions analysed to show the two aspects of the transaction:

	£		
Apr. 1	60,000	Increase asset of cash	Increase ownership interest
Apr. 1	800	Decrease asset of cash	Decrease ownership interest (expense)
Apr. 2	35,000	Increase asset of equipment	Decrease asset of cash
Apr. 3	5,000	Increase asset of supplies	Increase liability to trade creditor
Apr. 4	1,200	Increase asset of cash	Increase ownership interest (revenue)
Apr. 15	700	Decrease asset of cash	Decrease ownership interest (expense)
Apr. 20	500	Decrease asset of cash	Decrease ownership interest (voluntary)
Apr. 21	2,400	Increase asset of cash	Increase ownership interest (revenue)
Apr. 29	700	Decrease asset of cash	Decrease ownership interest (expense)
Apr. 29	1,900	Increase asset of debtor	Increase ownership interest (revenue)
Apr. 30	80	Decrease asset of cash	Decrease ownership interest (expense)
Apr. 30	*1,500	Decrease asset of supplies	Decrease ownership interest (expense)

*Inventory (stock) acquired £5,000, less amount remaining £3,500 = £1,500 asset used in period.

Application B5.1

		Cash and bank	Other assets	Liabilities	Capital contributed or withdrawn	Revenue	Expenses
		£	£	£	£	£	£
April 1	Jane Gate commenced her dental practice on April 1 by depositing £60,000 in a business bank account.	60,000			60,000		
April 1	Rent for a surgery was paid, £800, for the month of April.	(800)					800
April 2	Dental equipment was purchased for £35,000, paying in cash.	(35,000)	35,000				
April 3	Dental supplies were purchased for £5,000, taking 30 days' credit from a supplier.		5,000	5,000			
April 4	Fees of £1,200 were collected in cash from patients and paid into the bank account.	1,200				1,200	
April 15	Dental assistant was paid wages for two weeks, £700.	(700)					700
April 20	Jane Gate withdrew £500 cash for personal use.	(500)			(500)		
April 21	Fees of £2,400 were collected in cash from patients and paid into the bank.	2,400				2,400	
April 29	Dental assistant was paid wages for two weeks, £700.	(700)					700
April 29	Invoices were sent to patients who are allowed 20 days' credit, for work done during April amounting to £1,900.		1,900			1,900	
April 30	Telephone bill for April was paid, £80.	(80)					80
April 30	Dental supplies unused were counted and found to be worth £3,500, measured at cost price (i.e. inventory [stock] decreased by £1,500).		(1,500)				1,500
	Totals	25,820	40,400	5,000	59,500	5,500	3,780

Accounting equation:

Cash	plus	other assets	less	liabilities		
25,820	+	40,400	−	5,000	=	61,220
Capital contributed or withdrawn	plus	revenue	less	expenses		
59,500	+	5,500	−	3,780	=	61,220

B5.2

Dental Practice of Jane Gate
Statement of cash flows for the month of April Year XX

	£
Operating activities	
Inflow from fees	3,600
Outflow: rent paid	(800)
wages	(1,400)
telephone	(80)
Net inflow from operations	1,320
Investing activities	
Payment for equipment	(35,000)
Net outflow for investing activities	(35,000)
Financing activities	
Capital contributed by owner	60,000
Capital withdrawn as drawings	(500)
Net inflow from financing activities	59,500
Increase in cash at bank over period	25,820

Dental Practice of Jane Gate
Income statement (profit and loss account) for the month of April Year XX

	£	£
Fees charged		5,500
Dental supplies used	1,500	
Wages	1,400	
Rent	800	
Telephone	80	
		3,780
Profit		1,720

Dental Practice of Jane Gate
Statement of financial position (balance sheet) at 30 April Year XX

	£
Non-current (fixed) assets	
Dental equipment at cost	35,000
Current assets	
Dental supplies	3,500
Receivables (debtors)	1,900
Cash at bank	25,820
	31,220
Current liabilities	
Trade payables (trade creditors)	(5,000)
Current assets less current liabilities	26,220
Net assets	61,220
Capital at start	60,000
Add profit	1,720
Less drawings	(500)
Total ownership interest	61,220

Chapter 6

A6.1

(a) Profit is only reported when there is a sale. The number of items sold is 60. Each one gives a profit of £5 so the total profit is £300.

(b) When the 200 items are purchased there is an increase of £4,000 in the asset of inventory (stock) of spare parts and a decrease of £4,000 in the asset of cash. When the 60 items are sold for £1,500 there is an increase in the asset of cash and an increase in the ownership interest reported as revenue. The 60 items cost £1,200 to purchase and so at the date of sale there is a reduction in the asset of inventory (stock) amounting to £1,200 and a decrease in the ownership interest due to the expense of cost of goods sold £1,200.

A6.2

(a) Transactions summarised by spreadsheet

	Cash	Inventory (stock)	Revenue	Expense
	£	£	£	£
Purchase 200 items @ £20 each	(4,000)	4,000		
Sell 60 items @ £25	1,500		1,500	
Cost of goods sold 60 @ £20		(1,200)		1,200
Totals	(2,500)	2,800	1,500	1,200

(b) Inventory (stock) increases by £2,800 while cash decreases by £2,500, overall increase in assets amounting to £300. Ownership interest increases by £300 when expenses of £1,200 are set against revenue of £1,500.

A6.3

(a) Calculation of profit on sale:

	£
Sale of 50 trays for £8 each	400
Cost of 50 trays at £5.50 each	275
Profit on sale	125

(b) Analysis of transactions using the accounting equation

	£		
June 1	300	Increase asset of inventory (stock) of raw materials.	Decrease asset of cash.
June 3	210	Decrease asset of inventory (stock) of raw materials.	Increase asset of work in progress.
June 5	175	Decrease asset of cash.	Increase asset of work in progress.
June 6	385	Increase asset of finished goods.	Decrease asset of work in progress.
June 11	275	Decrease ownership interest: expense of cost of goods sold.	Decrease asset of finished goods.
June 14	400	Increase asset of cash.	Increase ownership interest: revenue.

A6.4

Date	Amount		
	£		
Apr. 1	60,000	Increase asset of cash.	Increase ownership interest.
Apr. 2	20,000	Increase asset of buildings.	Decrease asset of cash.
Apr. 4	12,000	Increase asset of equipment.	Decrease asset of cash.
Apr. 6	8,500	Increase asset of inventory (stock).	Decrease asset of cash.
Apr. 7	7,000	Increase asset of inventory (stock).	Increase liability to supplier.
Apr. 11	7,000	Decrease liability to supplier.	Decrease asset of cash.
Apr. 14	400	Decrease ownership claim (expense).	Decrease asset of cash.
Apr. 17	5,500	Decrease ownership claim (expense).	Decrease asset of inventory (stock).
Apr. 17	6,000	Increase asset of cash.	Increase ownership claim (revenue).
Apr. 17	4,200	Increase asset of debtor.	Increase ownership claim (revenue).
Apr. 24	4,200	Increase asset of cash.	Decrease asset of debtor.
Apr. 28	2,700	Decrease ownership claim (voluntary withdrawal).	Decrease asset of cash.
Apr. 30	2,800	Decrease ownership claim (expense).	Decrease asset of cash.
Apr. 30	550	Decrease ownership claim (expense of depreciation).	Decrease asset of equipment.

Application B6.1 (a)

		Cash at bank	Fixed assets and debtors	Inventory (stock) of goods	Trade creditor	Capital contributed or withdrawn	Revenue	Expenses
		£	£	£	£	£	£	£
Apr. 1	The owner pays cash into a bank account for the business.	60,000				60,000		
Apr. 2	The business acquires buildings for cash.	(20,000)	20,000					
Apr. 4	The business acquires equipment for cash.	(12,000)	12,000					
Apr. 6	The business purchases an inventory (stock) of goods for cash.	(8,500)		8,500				
Apr. 7	The business purchases goods on credit from R. Green and receives an invoice.			7,000	7,000			
Apr. 11	The business pays R. Green in cash for the goods it acquired on credit.	(7,000)			(7,000)			
Apr. 14	The business pays a gas bill in cash.	(400)						400
Apr. 17	Some of the goods purchased for resale (items costing £5,500) are removed from the store because sales have been agreed with customers for this date.			(5,500)				5,500
Apr. 17	The business sells goods for cash.	6,000					6,000	
Apr. 17	The business sells goods on credit to P. Weatherall and sends an invoice.		4,200				4,200	
Apr. 24	P. Weatherall pays in cash for the goods obtained on credit.	4,200	(4,200)					
Apr. 28	The owner draws cash from the business for personal use.	(2,700)				(2,700)		
Apr. 30	The business pays wages to employees, in cash.	(2,800)						2,800
Apr. 30	The business discovers that its equipment has fallen in value over the month.		(550)					550
	Totals	16,800	31,450	10,000	nil	57,300	10,200	9,250

(b) Accounting equation:

Assets	–	Liabilities	=	Ownership interest
16,800 + 31,450 + 10,000		nil	=	57,300 + 10,200 – 9,250
58,250				58,250

B6.2

Peter Gold, furniture supplier
Statement of cash flows for the month of April Year XX

	£
Operating activities	
Cash from customers	10,200
Outflow: payment for goods	(8,500)
payment to supplier (R. Green)	(7,000)
Wages	(2,800)
Gas	(400)
Net outflow from operations	(8,500)
Investing activities	
Payment for buildings	(20,000)
Payment for equipment	(12,000)
Net outflow for investing activities	(32,000)
Financing activities	
Capital contributed by owner	60,000
Capital withdrawn as drawings	(2,700)
Net inflow from financing activities	57,300
Increase in cash at bank over period	16,800

Peter Gold, furniture supplier
Income statement (profit and loss account) for the month of April Year XX

	£	£
Revenue		10,200
Cost of goods sold		(5,500)
Gross profit		4,700
Other expenses		
Wages	(2,800)	
Gas	(400)	
Depreciation	(550)	
		(3,750)
Net profit		950

Peter Gold, furniture supplier
Statement of financial position (balance sheet) at 30 April Year XX

	£
Non-current (fixed) assets	
Buildings	20,000
Equipment	12,000
	32,000
Depreciation	(550)
Depreciated cost of fixed assets	31,450
Current assets	
Inventory (stocks)	10,000
Cash at bank	16,800
	26,800
Net assets	58,250
Capital at start	60,000
Add profit	950
Less drawings	(2,700)
Total ownership interest	58,250

Chapter 7

Application **B7.1 to B7.4**

The questions at the end of Chapter 7 provide opportunities for writing about accounting information. An outline for an answer could be developed from the chapter and it could be illustrated by using annual reports obtained from companies or their websites.

To write a short essay for question B7.1 or question B7.3 the IASB *Framework* would be very helpful.

Problem solving and evaluation Question C7.1 requires you to show that you have thought about all the material in the first seven chapters of the book. A reader of your essay might expect to find some or all of the following questions addressed:

(a) This is a listed company and so shares are bought and sold through the stock market. Does your answer show that you have thought about this active market process?

(b) In giving advice on principles have you made use of the IASB *Framework*?

(c) Have you given examples of the kind of information which would be relevant to the *Framework*? Furthermore, have you carried out some research on company annual reports so that you can provide first-hand examples or illustrations?

Chapter 8

Test your understanding **A8.14**

Judgement on value, amount and future economic benefit.

Application **B8.1**

(a) The amount of £8,000 has been reported as an asset. Since this is a repair it must be removed from the assets. Removing an asset causes a decrease in the ownership interest through an additional expense of £8,000 in the income statement (profit and loss account).

Problem solving and evaluation **C8.1 The Biscuit Manufacturing Company**

(a) Depreciation calculated on a straight-line basis: $\dfrac{22,000 - 2,000}{4} = £5,000$ per annum

		Assets			Ownership interest	
	Transaction or event	Machine at cost	Accumulated depreciation of van	Cash	Capital contributed or withdrawn	Profit = revenue minus expenses
Year 1		£	£	£	£	£
1 Jan.	Owner contributes cash			22,000	22,000	
1 Jan.	Purchase biscuit machine	22,000		(22,000)		
All year	Collected cash from customers			40,000		40,000
All year	Paid for wages, other costs			(17,000)		(17,000)
31 Dec.	Calculate annual depreciation		(5,000)			(5,000)
	Totals	22,000	(5,000)	23,000	22,000	18,000

		Assets			Ownership interest		
	Transaction or event	Machine at cost	Accumulated depreciation of machine	Cash	Ownership interest at start of year	Capital contributed or withdrawn	Profit = revenue minus expenses
Year 2		£	£	£	£	£	£
1 Jan.	Amounts brought forward at start of year	22,000	(5,000)	23,000	40,000		
All year	Collected cash from customers			40,000			40,000
All year	Paid for wages, fuel, etc.			(17,000)			(17,000)
31 Dec.	Calculate annual depreciation		(5,000)				(5,000)
	Totals	22,000	(10,000)	46,000	40,000		18,000

		Assets			Ownership interest		
	Transaction or event	Machine at cost	Accumulated depreciation of machine	Cash	Ownership interest at start of year	Capital contributed or withdrawn	Profit = revenue minus expenses
Year 3		£	£	£	£	£	£
1 Jan.	Amounts brought forward at start of year	22,000	(10,000)	46,000	58,000		
All year	Collected cash from customers			40,000			40,000
All year	Paid for wages, fuel, etc.			(17,000)			(17,000)
31 Dec.	Calculate annual depreciation		(5,000)				(5,000)
	Totals	22,000	(15,000)	69,000	58,000		18,000

		Assets			Ownership interest		
	Transaction or event	Machine at cost	Accumulated depreciation of machine	Cash	Ownership interest at start of year	Capital contributed or withdrawn	Profit = revenue minus expenses
Year 4		£	£	£	£	£	£
1 Jan.	Amounts brought forward at start of year	22,000	(15,000)	69,000	76,000		
All year	Collected cash from customers			40,000			40,000
All year	Paid for wages, fuel, etc.			(17,000)			(17,000)
31 Dec.	Calculate annual depreciation		(5,000)				(5,000)
	Totals	22,000	(20,000)	92,000	76,000		18,000

(b)

Biscuit Manufacturing Company
Statement of financial position (balance sheet) at 31 December Year 3

	£
Non-current (fixed) assets	
Machine at cost	22,000
Accumulated depreciation	(15,000)
Net book value	7,000
Current assets	
Cash	69,000
Total assets	76,000
Ownership interest	
Ownership interest at the start of the year	58,000
Profit of the year	18,000
	76,000

Biscuit Manufacturing Company
Income statement (profit and loss account) for the year ended
31 December Year 3

	£	£
Revenue		
Sale of biscuits		40,000
Expenses		
Wages, ingredients and running costs	(17,000)	
Depreciation	(5,000)	
		(22,000)
Net profit		18,000

C8.2

(a)

	Transaction or event	Assets			Ownership interest		
		Machine at cost	Accumulated depreciation of machine	Cash	Ownership interest at start of year	Capital contributed or withdrawn	Profit = revenue minus expenses
Year 4		£	£	£	£	£	£
1 Jan.	Amounts brought forward at start of year	22,000	(15,000)	69,000	76,000		
All year	Collected cash from customers			40,000			40,000
All year	Paid for wages, fuel, etc.			(17,000)			(17,000)
31 Dec.	Calculate annual depreciation		(5,000)				(5,000)
31 Dec.	Machine disposal	(22,000)	20,000	3,000			1,000
	Totals	nil	nil	95,000	76,000		19,000

Note that at the end of Year 4 the net book value is £2,000 (cost £22,000 less accumulated depreciation £20,000). The cash received £3,000 is therefore £1,000 more than expected. The amount of £1,000 is recorded as an increase in the ownership interest.

(b)

Biscuit Manufacturing Company
Statement of financial position (balance sheet) at 31 December Year 4

	£
Non-current (fixed) assets	
Machine at cost	nil
Current assets	
Cash	95,000
Total assets	95,000
Ownership interest	
Ownership interest at the start of the year	76,000
Profit of the year	19,000
	95,000

Biscuit Manufacturing Company
Income statement (profit and loss account) for the year ended
31 December Year 4

	£	£
Revenue		
Sale of biscuits		40,000
Expenses		
Wages, ingredients and running costs	(17,000)	
Depreciation less gain on disposal	(4,000)	
		(21,000)
Net profit		19,000

(c) There is apparently a gain on disposal because the cash collected is greater than the net book value of the asset. In reality, all that has happened is that the estimate of depreciation over the asset life is, with the benefit of hindsight, a marginally incorrect estimate. Perfect foresight at the outset would have used £3,000 as a residual value, rather than £2,000, in calculating the annual depreciation charge. However, it is known that accounting involves estimates so it would be inappropriate in most cases to attempt to rewrite the income statements (profit and loss accounts) of the past. Accordingly all of the 'gain' is reported in Year 4, as a deduction from annual depreciation.

C8.3 Souvenir Company

(a) Straight-line depreciation

Machine cost £16,000, estimated residual value £1,000, so depreciate the difference, £15,000, over five-year life to give annual depreciation of £3,000.

End of Year	Depreciation of the year (b)	Total depreciation (c)	Net book value of the asset (£16,000 – (c))
	£	£	£
1	3,000	3,000	13,000
2	3,000	6,000	10,000
3	3,000	9,000	7,000
4	3,000	12,000	4,000
5	3,000	15,000	1,000

(b) Guess a rate which is at least twice the percentage applied on a straight-line basis (i.e. in this case guess $20\% \times 2 = 40\%$).

Calculation of reducing balance depreciation (as in Table 8.2):

Year	Net book value at start of year (a)	Annual depreciation (b) = 40% of (a)	Net book value at end of year (a – b)
	£	£	£
1	16,000	6,400	9,600
2	9,600	3,840	5,760
3	5,760	2,304	3,456
4	3,456	1,382	2,074
5	2,074	830	1,244

(The residual value at the end of Year 5 should ideally be £1,000, so a first estimate which arrives at £1,244 is quite reasonable.)

(c) The net book value at the end of Year 5 is £1,000 and therefore disposal at £2,500 gives an apparent gain of £1,500 which is best described as caused by over-depreciation of earlier years. The effect on the accounting equation is that the asset of machine decreases by £1,000 while the asset of cash increases by £2,500 so that overall the ownership interest increases by £1,500.

(d) The net book value at the end of Year 5 is £1,000 and therefore disposal at nil scrap value gives an apparent loss of £1,000 which is best described as caused by underdepreciation of earlier years. The effect on the accounting equation is that the asset of machine decreases by £1,000 with no increase in any other asset so that overall the ownership interest decreases by £1,000.

Chapter 9

Test your understanding

A9.10

Use lower of cost and net realisable value on each category separately:

Description	Basis	Stock value £
Engine	Cost	6,500
Chassis	Net realisable value	1,600
Frame	Net realisable value	4,600

A9.11

The recorded inventory (stock) will increase by £18,000 and the ownership interest will increase by £18,000 (reported as a reduction in the cost of goods sold).

A9.12

The asset of debtor (trade receivable) will be reduced by £154,000 and the ownership interest will decrease by £154,000 (reported as an expense of cost of bad debts).

Application

B9.1

(a) The FIFO approach to the issue of units for sale, where:
  (i) the calculation is carried out at the date of sale; and
  (ii) the calculation is carried out at the end of the month without regard for the date of sale.

Date	Number of units purchased	Unit cost	Number of units sold	Cost of goods sold (i) £	Cost of goods sold (ii) £	Inventory (stock) (i)	Inventory (stock) (ii)
Jan. 5	100	£1.00					
Jan. 10			50	50			
Jan. 15	200	£1.10					
Jan. 17			150	50 110			
Jan. 24	300	£1.15					
Jan. 30			200	110 115	100 220 115		
	600		400	435	435	230	230

	£
Sales 400 × £2	800
Cost of goods sold	435
Profit	365

Inventory (stock) = 200 × £1.15 = £230

(b) The LIFO approach to the issue of units for sale, where:
   (i) the calculation is carried out at the date of sale; and
   (ii) the calculation is carried out at the end of the month without regard for the date of sale; and

Date	Number of units purchased	Unit cost	Number of units sold	Cost of goods sold (i) £	Cost of goods sold (ii) £	Inventory (stock) (i)	Inventory (stock) (ii)
Jan. 5	100	£1.00					
Jan. 10			50	50		50	
Jan. 15	200	£1.10					
Jan. 17			150	165		55	
Jan. 24	300	£1.15					
Jan. 30			200	230	345	115	100
					110		110
	600		400	345	455	220	210

either (i):

	£
Sales 400 × £2	800
Cost of goods sold	345
Profit	455

Inventory (stock) = (50 × £1.00) + (50 × £1.10) + (100 × £1.15)
= 50 + 55 + 115 = 220

or (ii):

	£
Sales 400 × £2	800
Cost of goods sold	455
Profit	345

Inventory (stock) = (100 × £1) + (100 × £1.10)
= 100 + 110 = £210

Note that in all cases the Cost of goods sold plus the unsold Inventory (stock) = £665.

(c) The average-cost approach to the issue of units for sale, making the calculation at the end of the month without regard for the date of sale.

Date	Number of units purchased	Unit cost	£
Jan. 5	100	£1.00	100
Jan. 10			
Jan. 15	200	£1.10	220
Jan. 17			
Jan. 24	300	£1.15	345
Jan. 30			
	600		665

Average cost = £665/500 = £1.108

	£
Sales 400 × £2	800
Cost of goods sold 400 × £1.108	443
Profit	357

Inventory (stock) 200 × £1.108 = £222

B9.2

Group of items	Basis	Inventory (stock) value £
A	Cost	1,000
B	Net realisable value	800
C	Net realisable value	1,900
D	Cost	3,000
Total inventory (stock)		6,700

Chapter 10

A10.9

The liability to the supplier will increase and the ownership interest will decrease (recorded as an increase in the cost of goods sold).

A10.10

The recorded asset of cash will decrease and the recorded liability to the supplier will decrease.

A10.11

First the original incorrect entry must be reversed. When the entry was made, it was treated as an increase in the ownership interest and an increase in the asset of debtor. This error must be reversed by decreasing the ownership interest and decreasing the asset of debtor.

Then the correct entry must be made which is a decrease in the ownership interest and an increase in a liability to the landlord.

B10.1

The aim of the calculation is to show the cost of telephone used during the year.

	£
Cash paid	3,500
Less rental in advance for July, one-third of £660	(220)
Add calls for May and June, two-thirds of £900	600
Expense of the period	3,880

The rental paid in advance will be shown as a prepayment of £220 in the statement of financial position (balance sheet) and the calls made during May and June will be shown as an accrual of £600 in the statement of financial position (balance sheet).

B10.2

		Asset	Liability	Ownership interest profit of the period
Date	Transactions with security company	Cash	Security company	Security expense
Year 1		£	£	£
Mar. 31	Invoice received £800		800	(800)
Apr. 5	Security company paid £800	(800)	(800)	
June 30	Invoice received £800		800	(800)
July 5	Security company paid £800	(800)	(800)	
Sept. 30	Invoice received £800		800	(800)
Oct. 5	Security company paid £800	(800)	(800)	
Dec. 31	Invoice received £800		800	(800)
	Totals	(2,400)	800	(3,200)

B10.3

The tax charge reduces the ownership interest and is shown as an expense of £8,000 in the income statement (profit and loss account). The accounting equation remains in balance because there is a matching liability of £8,000 recorded. However, the liability is split as £6,000 current liability and £2,000 deferred liability to reflect different patterns of payment of the overall liability.

Problem solving and evaluation C10.1

The year-end is 31 December Year 1.

Item	Description	Amount £		
1	Invoice dated 23 December for goods received 21 December.	260	Increase asset of inventory (stock).	Increase liability to supplier.
2	Invoice dated 23 December for goods to be delivered on 3 January Year 2.	310	Nothing recorded – this will be an asset and a liability of the following year.	
3	Foreman's note of electricity consumption for month of December – no invoice yet received from electricity supply company.	100	Decrease ownership interest (expense of electricity).	Increase liability to electricity supplier.
4	Letter from employee claiming overtime payment for work on 1 December and note from personnel office denying entitlement to payment.	58	Nothing recorded in the financial statements because it is not yet clear that there is an obligation (might be a contingent liability note).	
5	Telephone bill dated 26 December showing calls for October to December.	290	Decrease ownership interest (expense of telephone calls).	Increase liability to phone company.
6	Telephone bill dated 26 December showing rent due in advance for period January to March Year 2.	90	Nothing recorded – this will be an expense of the following year.	
7	Note of payment due to cleaners for final week of December (to be paid on 3 January under usual pattern of payment one week in arrears).	48	Usually nothing recorded if payment in arrears is normal, since the corresponding payment from January Year 1 will be included in the year's expense.	
8	Invoice from supplier for promotional calendars received 1 December (only one-third have yet been sent to customers).	300	Decrease ownership interest £300 (expense of calendars).	Increase liability to calendar supplier £300.
			Increase inventory (stock) of calendars by £200.	Reduce expense by £200.
9	Letter dated 21 December Year 1 to customer promising a cheque to reimburse damage caused by faulty product – cheque to be sent on 4 January Year 2.	280	Decrease ownership interest (expense of damage).	Increase liability to customer.
10	Letter dated 23 December promising donation to local charity – amount not yet paid.	60	Decrease ownership interest (expense of donation).	Increase liability to charity.

Chapter 11

Test your understanding A11.6

Reduce revenue by £40,000 (two-thirds of £60,000) and increase statement of financial position (balance sheet) deferred income by £40,000. Effect on income statement (profit and loss account) is to reduce reported profit. Reason is application of the matching concept. The £40,000 deferred income will be transferred to income statement (profit and loss account) over the next two years.

A11.7

Increase expense of provision for repairs by £50,000 (reporting as an expense in the income statement (profit and loss account)) and create a liability under the 'provisions' heading. Effect on income statement (profit and loss account) is to reduce reported profit.

Application **B11.1**

The income statement (profit and loss account) would show an expense of £8,000 provision in Year 1 and an expense of £9,000 provision in Year 2. The actual amount of expenditure as shown in the question would be set against the provision in the statement of financial position (balance sheet).

Date of repair	Profit and loss expense	Statement of financial position (balance sheet) provision in total before expense charged	Actual expense matched against provision	Provision remaining in statement of financial position (balance sheet)
Year	£	£	£	£
1	8,000	8,000	4,500	3,500
2	9,000	12,500	8,000	4,500
3	*500	4,500	*4,500	nil

* The actual cost in Year 3 is £5,000 but there is only £4,500 provision remaining, so the extra £500 must be charged to income statement (profit and loss account) as an unexpected expense.

Note that the total amount charged to income statement (profit and loss account) is £17,500 and the total amount paid out for repair work is also £17,500. The accounting entries in the income statement (profit and loss account) are an attempt to spread the expense on the basis of matching with revenue, but the total must be the same over the three-year period, whatever matching approach is taken.

Date of repair	Profit and loss expense using provision approach	Profit and loss expense using actual repair amount paid
	£	£
1	8,000	4,500
2	9,000	8,000
3	*500	5,000
Total	17,500	17,500

B11.2

The grant will initially be recorded as an increase in the asset of cash and an increase in the statement of financial position (balance sheet) liability item headed 'deferred income'. The deferred income is transferred from the liability to revenue over three years (so that the ownership interest increases evenly over the three-year period).

Chapter 12

Application **B12.1**

(a) Increase the asset of cash by £50,000. Increase the ownership interest by the nominal value of shares, £50,000.
(b) Increase the asset of cash by £75,000. Increase the ownership interest by (i) nominal value of shares £25,000 and (ii) share premium £50,000.
(c) Increase asset of property by £20,000. Increase ownership interest by revaluation reserve £20,000.

B12.2

(a) Decrease asset of cash by £20,000. Decrease ownership interest by £20,000 as a reduction in the owners' claim on the business.
(b) Record a note in the directors' report. There is no liability at the date of the financial statements.

B12.3 Nithsdale Ltd

	£000s	(a) £000s	(b) £000s	(c) £000s
Cash	20	70.0	20	260
Other assets less liabilities	320	320.0	320	320
	340	390.0	340	580
Ordinary shares (400,000 of 25 pence each)	100	112.5	125	120
Share premium	40	77.5	40	260
Reserves of retained profit	200	200.0	175	200
	340	390.0	340	580

B12.4

If the directors decide that they wish to incorporate the revaluation in the statement of financial position (balance sheet), then the asset will be reported at £380,000. The difference between the previous recorded book value £250,000 and the new value £380,000 is £130,000. This is an increase in the ownership interest and will be reported as a revaluation reserve as part of the total ownership interest.

B12.5

In this case the value has decreased by £10,000. This is a reduction in the value of the asset and a decrease in the ownership claim. On grounds of prudence the loss should be reported in the income statement (profit and loss account) immediately and the recorded book value of the asset should be reduced.

Chapter 13

Application **B13.1**
(a) Hope plc
(i) Liquidity

		Hope plc	
Ratio	Definition in words	Workings	Result
Current ratio	Current assets:Current liabilities	2,360:1,240	1.90:1
Acid test	(Current assets – Inventory (stock)): Current liabilities	(2,360 – 620):1,240	1.40:1
Inventory (stock) holding period*	$\frac{\text{Average inventory held}}{\text{Cost of sales}} \times 365$	$\frac{620}{2,750} \times 365$	82.3 days
Customers collection period	$\frac{\text{Trade receivables (debtors)}}{\text{Credit sales}} \times 365$	$\frac{1,540}{6,200} \times 365$	90.7 days
Suppliers payment period†	$\frac{\text{Trade payables (creditors)}}{\text{Credit purchases}} \times 365$	$\frac{300}{2,750} \times 365$	39.8 days

* Assuming the opening inventory (stock) is the same as the closing inventory (stock).
† Assuming purchases = cost of goods sold

(a) 50,000 × 25p = £12,500; 50,000 × £0.75 = £37,500.
(b) Transfer £25,000 from reserves to share capital.
(c) 80,000 × £3 = £240,000; 80,000 × 25p = £20,000; 80,000 × £2.75 = £220,000.

(ii) Analysis of management performance

Ratio	Definition in words	Hope plc Workings	Result
Return on shareholders' equity	$\dfrac{\text{Profit after tax}}{\text{Share capital} + \text{Reserves}} \times 100\%$	$\dfrac{692}{1,470} \times 100$	47.1%
Return on capital employed	$\dfrac{\text{Profit before interest and tax}}{\text{Total assets} - \text{Current liabilities}} \times 100\%$	$\dfrac{1,256}{2,870} \times 100$	43.8%
Net profit on sales	$\dfrac{\text{Profit before interest and taxes}}{\text{Sales}} \times 100$	$\dfrac{1,256}{6,200} \times 100$	20.3%
Gross profit percentage	$\dfrac{\text{Gross profit}}{\text{Sales}} \times 100$	$\dfrac{3,450}{6,200} \times 100\%$	55.6%
Total assets usage	$\dfrac{\text{Sales}}{\text{Total assets}}$	$\dfrac{6,200}{1,750 + 2,360}$	1.5 times
Fixed assets usage	$\dfrac{\text{Sales}}{\text{Non-current (fixed) assets}}$	$\dfrac{6,200}{1,750}$	3.5 times

(iii) Gearing (leverage)

Ratio	Definition in words	Hope plc Workings	Result
Debt/equity ratio	$\dfrac{\text{Debt} + \text{Preference share capital}}{\text{Ordinary share capital reserves}} + 100\%$	$\dfrac{1,400}{1,470} + 100$	95.2%
Interest cover	$\dfrac{\text{Profit before interest and tax}}{\text{Interest}}$	$\dfrac{1,256}{84}$	15.0 times

(c) Investor ratios

Ratio	Definition in words	Hope plc Workings	Result
Earnings per share	$\dfrac{\text{Profit after for ordinary shareholders}}{\text{Number of ordinary shares}}$	$\dfrac{692}{900}$	76.9 pence
Price/earnings ratio	$\dfrac{\text{Share price}}{\text{Earnings per share}}$	$\dfrac{1,100}{76.9}$	14
Dividend cover (payout ratio)	$\dfrac{\text{Earning per share}}{\text{Dividend per share}}$	$\dfrac{76.9}{36.7}$	2.1 times
Dividend yield	$\dfrac{\text{Dividend per share}}{\text{Share price}} \times 100\%$	$\dfrac{36.7}{1,100} \times 100\%$	3.34%

Chapter 14

Problem solving and evaluation

C14.1 Trend analysis: Safe and Sure

	Year 3	Year 4	Year 5	Year 6	Year 7
Group revenue	309.1	389.0	474.1	600.3	734.6
Group profit before tax	74.4	90.4	114.5	147.0	177.0
Tax	(27.2)	(33.9)	(44.3)	(52.4)	(62.2)
Group profit after tax	47.2	56.5	70.2	94.6	114.8
Earnings per share	4.88	6.23	8.02	9.71	11.74
Dividends per share	1.32	1.69	2.17	2.50	3.02
Share capital	19.4	19.4	19.4	19.5	19.6
Reserves	160.8	195.3	265.4	350.9	444.7
Total equity	180.2	214.7	284.8	370.4	464.3
Ratios					
Pre-tax profit to sales	24.1%	23.2%	24.2%	24.5%	24.1%
Tax charge as % of pre-tax profit	36.6%	37.5%	38.7%	35.6%	35.1%
Dividend cover	3.70	3.70	3.70	3.88	3.89
Growth in revenue	n/a	25.9%	21.9%	26.6%	22.4%
Growth in eps	n/a	27.7%	28.7%	21.1%	20.9%
Growth in dividend per share	n/a	28.0%	28.4%	15.2%	20.8%
Return on shareholders' equity	26.2%	26.3%	24.7%	25.5%	25.3%

Commentary. The company has exceeded its annual earnings growth target of 20% in each year for which calculations can be made. The dividend cover is relatively high, indicating a policy of retaining new wealth to finance expansion. In Year 6 the dividend cover increased because the dividend growth decreased. In Year 7 the cover remains higher and the dividend growth improved. With the expansion the company has maintained its rate of return on shareholders' equity. The company is likely to be attractive to investors if future prospects are similar to the historical trend.

Chapter 15

Application

B15.1

£120m + £8m − £10m = £118m

B15.2

£20m + £6m − £4m = £22m

B15.3

£34m − £5m + ? = £37m Missing number is £8m acquisition.

Problem solving and evaluation

C15.1

Fruit Sales plc – indirect method

Notes		£m	£m
	Cash flows from operating activities		
1	Profit before taxation		132
	Adjustment for items not involving a flow of cash:		
	Depreciation	39	
	Gain on disposal of equipment	(7)	
			32
	Adjusted profit		164
	(Increase) in inventories	(6)	
	(Increase) in trade receivables	(2)	
	Increase in trade payables	5	
	Increase/(decrease) in cash due to working capital changes		(3)
	Cash generated from operations		161
2	Interest paid		(19)
3	Taxes paid		(32)
	Net cash inflow from operating activities		110
	Cash flows from investing activities		
4	Purchase of vehicles	(90)	
5	Proceeds from sale of vehicles	20	
6	Investments acquired	(20)	
	Interest received	5	
	Net cash used in investing activities		(85)
	Cash flows from financing activities		
7	Proceeds from issue of share capital	35	
8	Proceeds from long-term borrowing	8	
	Dividends paid	(31)	
	Net cash raised from financing activities		12
	Increase/(decrease) in cash and cash equivalents		37
9	**Cash and cash equivalents at the start of the period**		6
9	**Cash and cash equivalents at the end of the period**		43

Working note 1

	£m
Operating profit before taxes	117
Is there any interest expense included in this figure? If so add it back to arrive at:	20
Operating profit before deducting interest payable and taxes	137
Is there any interest received/receivable or any dividends received in this figure? If so deduct it to arrive at:	(5)
Operating profit before deducting interest payable and taxes and before including interest receivable and dividends received.	132

Working note 2

Interest paid = expense £20m plus liability at the start £7m minus liability at the end £8m.

Working note 3

Taxes paid = tax charge of the period £35m plus liability at the start £7m minus liability at the end £10m.

Working note 4

The vehicles at cost start with a balance of £130m. Additions are £90m and disposals cost £25m originally, leaving a balance of £195m.

Vehicles at cost – ledger account

	Debit	Credit	Balance
	£m	£m	£m
Balance at start	130		130
Additions	90		220
Disposals		25	195

Working note 5

The accumulated depreciation starts with a balance of £52m. This increases by the expense of the period £39m and decreases by the accumulated depreciation of the vehicles sold £12m, leaving a balance of £79m. The net book value of the vehicles sold was £13m (£25m – £12m). Deduct this from the proceeds of sale £20m to calculate the gain on disposal of £7m shown in the income statement.

Vehicles accumulated depreciation – ledger account

	Debit	Credit	Balance
	£m	£m	£m
Balance at start		52	(52)
Depreciation expense for the period		39	(91)
Accumulated depreciation on vehicles sold	12		(79)

Vehicles disposal – ledger account

	Debit	Credit	Balance
	£m	£m	£m
Asset at cost	25		25
Accumulated depreciation		12	13
Proceeds of sale		20	(7)
Transfer to income statement, gain on disposal	7		nil

Working note 6

The statement of financial position (balance sheet) investments increase by £20m. Assume no sales.

Working note 7

Increase in share capital £32m plus increase in share premium £3m.

Working note 8

Increase in borrowings £8m. Assume no repayments.

Fruit sales plc – direct method

Notes		£m	£m
	Cash flows from operating activities		
1	Cash receipts from customers		318
2	Cash paid to suppliers and employees		(144)
	Cash paid for administrative and selling expenses		(13)
	Cash generated from operations		161
	Interest paid		(19)
	Taxes paid		(32)
	Net cash inflow from operating activities		110
	Cash flows from investing activities		
	Purchase of vehicles	(90)	
	Proceeds from sale of vehicles	20	
	Investments acquired	(20)	
	Interest received	5	
	Net cash used in investing activities		(85)
	Cash flows from financing activities		
	Proceeds from issue of share capital	35	
	Proceeds from long-term borrowing	8	
	Dividends paid	(31)	
	Net cash used in financing activities		12
	Increase/(decrease) in cash and cash equivalents		37
	Cash and cash equivalents at the start of the period		6
	Cash and cash equivalents at the end of the period		43

Working note 1

Revenue in income statement £320m plus receivables at start of period £21m minus receivables at the end of the period £23m.

Accounts receivable – ledger account

	Debit	Credit	Balance
	£m	£m	£m
Balance at start	21		21
Revenue – sales	320		341
Cash received		318	23

Working note 2

Purchases = cost of goods sold £143m plus inventory at the end £26m less inventory at the start £20m = £149m.

Purchases – ledger account

	Debit	Credit	Balance
	£m	£m	£m
Balance of inventory at start	20		(20)
Purchases of supplies	149		(169)
Cash paid		144	26

Payment to suppliers = £149m plus payables at the start £13m less payables at the end £18m.

Accounts payable – suppliers

	Debit	Credit	Balance
	£m	£m	£m
Balance of payables at start		13	(13)
Purchases		149	(162)
Cash paid	144		(18)

Index

MOONWALK

Published in 2010 by Evans Publishing Ltd,
 2A Portman Mansions,
Chiltern St, London WIU 6NR

© Evans Brothers Limited 2010

Editor: Su Swallow
Designer: D.R. Ink

Picture credits:
7: iStock, Carolina K. Smith/iStock. 9: Popperfoto/Getty Images. 13: Duncan P Walker/iStock, iStock. 17: iStock.
19: Bettmann/CORBIS. 21: Neil A. Armstrong/NASA/Time Life Pictures/Getty Images. 23: iStock.

British Library Cataloguing in Publication Data

 Callery, Sean.
 Moonwalk. -- (Take 2)
 1. Moon--Exploration--Juvenile literature.
 I. Title II. Series
 629.4'54-dc22

ISBN-13: 9780237542061

Printed in China.